THE BOOK OF
DAYS

THE BOOK OF
DAYS

❖ *Elizabeth & Gerald Donaldson* ❖

A Jonathan-James Book

A&W Publishers, Inc.
New York

First published in the United States of America in 1979 by
A & W Publishers, Inc.
95 Madison Avenue
New York, New York 10016

By arrangement with
Jonathan-James Books
5 Sultan Street
Toronto, Canada
M5S 1L6

Library of Congress Catalog Card Number: 79-64840

ISBN: 0-89479-055-2

Printed in the United States of America

Design: Don Fernley
Editor: Lydia Burton

Elizabeth and Gerald Donaldson would like to thank the
following people for their help in producing this book:

Clare Bassett	Jenny Gubb
Cecily Burwash	Indra Seja
Alicia Freundlich	Mitchell Temkin
Shelley Gaffe	Lesley Zideman

THE BOOK OF
DAYS

Intended for daily use and diversion, THE BOOK OF
DAYS is devised in the honorable tradition of
appropriating each day in the year for the memory of
remarkable persons or events.

THE BOOK OF DAYS chronicles the origin of some of
these three hundred and sixty-five occurrences with
interesting accounts of the individuals and circumstances
commemorated, together with certain curious and fugitive
pieces. Space is provided so that readers may record their
own remarkable days.

I tell of festivals, and fairs, and plays,
Of merriment, and mirth, and bonfire blaze;
I tell of Christmas mummings, new year's day,
Of twelfth-night king and queen, and children's play;
I tell of Valentines, and true-love's knots,
Of omens, cunning-men, and drawing lots—
I tell of brooks, of blossoms, birds and bowers,
Of April, May, of June, and July-flowers;
I tell of May-poles, hock-carts, wassails, wakes,
Of bridegrooms, brides, and of their bridal cakes;
I tell of groves, of twilights, and I sing
The court of Mab, and of the fairie-king.
  Robert Herrick (1591-1674)

JANUARY

Then came old January, wrapped well
In many weeds to keep the cold away;
Yet did he quake and quiver like to quell,
And blowe his nayles to warm them if he may;
For they were numbed with holding all the day
An hatchet keene, with which he felled wood,
And from the trees did lop the needlesse spray;
Upon an huge great Earth-pot Steane he stood,
From whose wide mouth there flowed forth the Romane
   flood.
   Edmund Spenser (1552-1599)

JANUARY

History

It is very appropriate that this should be the first month of the year, as far as the northern hemisphere is concerned because it follows the winter solstice, embracing annual vegetation as well as the first movements of spring in its frozen arms. Yet the earliest calendars—Jewish, Egyptian, and Greek—did not place the commencement of the year at this point. It began only with the formation of the Roman calendar, usually attributed to the second Roman king, Numa Pompilius (whose reign is set down as terminating in 672 B.C.). Numa, it is said, decreed that the year should commence now and added two new months to the ten into which the year had previously been divided. He called the first Januarius, in honour of Janus, the deity supposed to preside over doors (Lat. *jauna,* a door), who might very naturally be presumed also to have something to do with the opening of the year.

   The beginning of the year was popularly regarded as the 1st of January, although the ancient Jewish year, which opened with the 25th of March, continued long to have a legal position in Christian countries. In England, it was not till 1752 that the 1st of January became the initial day of the legal, as well as of the popular year. Before that time, it was customary to set down dates between the 1st of January and the 24th of March inclusive, thus: January 30, 1648-9: meaning that popularly the year was 1649, but legally 1648. In Scotland, the amalgamation of the legal and popular date for the new year was made by decree of James VI, in privy council, in the year 1600. It was effected in France in 1564; in Holland, Protestant Germany, and Russia in 1700; and in Sweden in 1753.

Proverb

The blackest month of all the year
Is the month of Janiveer.

Birthstone

The garnet, which signifies truth and constancy, is the birthstone for those born in January.

1

Births

Lorenzo de Medici (Florentine ruler) 1449; Paul Revere (revolutionary rider) 1735; J. Edgar Hoover, (FBI head) 1895; Barry Goldwater (U.S. senator) 1909.

Deaths

Louis XII (French king) 1515; Thomas Hobson (carrier) 1631; Maurice Chevalier (French entertainer) 1972.

New Marriage, 1900

At one minute after midnight in 1900, William Witt and Anna Wassilove became the first American couple to be married in the 20th century. They repeated their vows before the Reverend Rufus Johnson in Liedenkranz Hall in Jersey City.

Ball Kicking

At the end of the first Rose Bowl Game in Pasadena, California the scoreboard read University of Michigan 49, Stanford 0 (1902).

Cow Tickling

Farmyards were the scene of New Year's Day celebrations in parts of medieval England wherein a baked flat cake was placed on one horn of the leading cow in a herd while everyone sang:

Here's health to thee, Brownie, and to thy white horn
God send thy master a good crop of corn
Thee eat thy cake and I'll drink my beer
God send thy master a Happy New Year.

Brownie was then tickled until she tossed the cake to the ground. If the cake fell in front of her it bode well for the coming year. When it fell behind, the reverse could be expected.

Yankee Doodling

Captain Matthews, member of the Assembly of Upper Canada, called for hats off for "Yankee Doddle" as if it were a National Anthem, an act which caused him to be sent to England for trial (1826).

Apple Gifting

In many British counties it was customary to give gifts of apples or oranges variously stuck with cloves or nutmeg, or rolled in meal or oats, topped with a sprig of mistletoe, and perhaps mounted on a tripod of twigs. This *Callenig* or *Apple Gift* was carried about by carolers or used to decorate the house to bring good luck.

New Proverb

Thomas Hobson was the first person in England who let horses for hire. He insisted that they be let out in rotation without allowing his customers to choose among the steeds in his Cambridge stables. "This or none" became the proverb *Hobson's Choice:* the necessity of taking what one can get.

New Era

"I do order and declare that all persons held within said designated states . . . are, and henceforward shall be, free." Thus, in 1863, President Lincoln's Proclamation of Emanication abolished slavery in Arkansas, Texas, Alabama, Mississippi, Florida, Georgia, the Carolinas, and parts of Louisiana and Virginia.

New Year's Revelry

Beginning in 1198, Parisians celebrated *The Festival of Fools* when every kind of absurdity and indecency was committed in order to ridicule nunnery and priestcraft.

New Year's Gift

As a New Year's Gift in 1545, Hugh Latimer, a bishop and one of the leaders of the English Reformation, presented the oft-married Henry VIII with a New Testament opened at Chapter 13 of Hebrews with Verse 4 conspicuously marked: "Marriage is honourable in all, and the bed undefiled: but whoremongers and adulterers God will judge." (Latimer was later burnt at the stake at Oxford.)

Births

James Wolfe (general) 1727; Dana Andrews (actor) 1909; Isaac Asimov (author) 1920.

Deaths

Ovid (poet) 18; St Macarius (patron of pastry cooks) 394; General Tom Thumb (dwarf) 1879.

Adages by Ovid

The Roman poet Ovid died on this day in the year 18 at the age of sixty-one. At the age of fifty he was banished from Rome by Emperor Augustus in consequence of a scandalous amour with a female member of the imperial family. From his forced abode at Tomi on the Black Sea he reflected on his life and times in epic poems. Legacies from these works include: To be loved, be loveable; While fortune smiles you will have a host of friends, but they'll desert you when the storm descends; How little you know about the age you live in if you fancy that honey is sweeter than cash in hand; I bar the doors in time of peace, lest peace depart.

First U.S. Flag

George Washington, commander-in-chief of the Continental Army, designed a flag that was run up on the flag staff at his headquarters in Cambridge, Massachusetts in 1776. It had thirteen stripes of red and white representing the thirteen colonies with the British Union Jack in the corner now occupied by the stars.

Dollar Day

In 1965 Joe Namath became the richest rookie in U.S. football history when he signed a contract with the New York Jets that provided him with $100,000 annual salary for the next three years, $100,000 in bonuses, and a $5,000 guaranteed annual pension at the end of his career.

A Gnat Martyr

The Roman saint of this day, St Macarius, was a notable example of those early Christians who, for the sake of heavenly meditation, forsook the world and retired to live in savage wildernesses. Originally a confectionery in Alexandria, he withdrw in 325 to a remote area bordering on Libya. One day he inadvertently killed a gnat that had bitten him. In a penitent and self-mortifying humour he immediately hastened to the marshes of Scete, which abounded with great flies whose stings were a torment even to wild boars. He exposed himself to these ravaging insects for six months, at the end of which time his body was a mass of putrid sores, and he could only be recognized by his voice.

A Military Martyr

General James Wolfe was born on this day in 1727 in Westerham, Kent. His death, thirty-two years later, was a kind of military martyrdom. He had failed in several attempts as leader of the British forces against the French at Québec. Dreading a court martial, he resolved by a bold and original stroke to do or die in a final battle. He massed his army on the Plains of Abraham behind the fortress of Québec. The French came out to fight and were beaten . . . but a stray shot brought down the young hero at the very moment of victory. His body was brought to England and interred at Greenwich.

Lucky Day

Macedonians practised an ancient ritual on the 2nd of January to protect themselves against witches and demons. Someone would draw water from the well without speaking and splash the courtyard and steps of the house. Then all members of the family would drink silently from the bucket and sprinkle water over themselves. Any work begun on this day in Japan, Shigoto Hajimi (Beginning of Work Day), will be successful.

Unlucky Day

Ancient Saxon astronomers decreed today to be extremely unlucky. It was vitally important that the veins be kept full and no blood be let. If anyone drank today they would die within fifteen days. Should they eat any goose they would surely die within forty days and if a child were born today it would die a wicked death. It was perilous to take any sickness, to be hurt, to be wedded, or to work today.

3
JANUARY

Friends

There are three faithful friends: an old wife, an old dog, and ready money.

Poor Richard's Almanac, 1789

Wit against Bores

Douglas Jerrold, the conversational chief of his day, was famed for his wit. He was particularly effective in dealing with bores. One such tiresome gentleman tried to engage him in conversation as the wit was passing along Regent Street in London at his usual quick pace. "Well Jerrold, my dear boy, what is going on?" The wit snapped out, "I am" and proceeded to do so at an even higher rate of speed. Tired of endless dinners and diners, he once declared, "If an earthquake were to engulf England tomorrow, the English would manage to meet and dine somewhere among the rubbish just to celebrate the event."

Births

Isaiah (the prophet) 700 B.C.; Cicero (Roman emperor) 106 B.C.; Douglas Jerrold (wit) 1803; J.R. Tolkein (author) 1892.

Deaths

Josiah Wedgwood (potter) 1795; William Joyce (hanged in Britain for treason) 1946.

Religion

In 964 the Roman citizens attacked the Vatican. Martin Luther was excommunicated in 1521. B.T. Onderdonk, bishop of the Protestant Episcopal Diocese of New York, was suspended from the ministry on the charge of immorality and impurity in 1845.

Education

Two hundred students were expelled from Moscow University and several other places of learning were closed because of disturbances (1888).

Politics

In 1777 the Americans under Washington won the Battle of Princeton (New Jersey) over the British. In Italy the Milanese gave up smoking for this day in 1848 to testify their hatred of Austria. Batista was overthrown by Castro in 1959, and the U.S. severed diplomatic relations with the Cuba in 1961.

American Milestones

The California town of Yerba Buena was renamed San Francisco in 1847. Construction work began on Brooklyn Bridge in 1870. Waxed paper drinking straws were patented in 1888.

A Wilde Declaration

Oscar Wilde arrived at the port of New York in 1882 on his first visit to America. "Have you anything to declare?" queried the customs inspector. "Nothing but my genius," replied Oscar.

The First Actresses

In that singular chronicle of gossip, his diary, Samuel Pepys made an entry for this day in 1661, after he had been to the theatre. He saw the *Beggar's Bush,* which was well performed and "the first time that ever I saw women come upon the stage." Prior to that time it was customary for effeminate young men to act the female parts.

Migratory Bogs

On this bitter winter night in 1853, when rain had softened the ground and loosened such soil as was deficient in cohesiveness, the whole mass of an Irish bog of peat moss shifted from its place in a wild region called Enagh Monmore. The mass was nearly a mile in circumference, and several feet deep. On it moved, urged apparently by the force of gravity, over sloping ground, and continuing its strange march for twenty-four hours, when a change in the contour of the ground brought it to a halt. Its extent of movement averaged about a quarter of a mile.

Births

Jacob Grimm (fairy tales) 1785; Louis Braille (blind alphabet) 1809; Sir Isaac Pitman (shorthand inventor) 1813; Augustus John (painter) 1879.

Deaths

Mademoiselle Rachel (tragedienne) 1858; Cornelius Vanderbilt (millionaire) 1877; Albert Camus (novelist) 1960; T.S. Eliot (poet) 1965.

Enemies

In Turkey the Montenegrins (now citizens of Yugoslavia) made incursions into the territory of Sosina, only to meet up with the deadly Bashi-Bazouks. These mercenaries of the Turkish irregular army were notorious for lawlessness, plundering, and brutality—most of which they inflicted on the Montenegrins on this day in 1862.

Flowers

The monks of the Middle Ages compiled a catalogue of flowers for each day of the year, and dedicated that flower to a particular saint, on account of its flowering about the time of the saint's festival. Today's flower is the common hazel (*Corylus avellana*) dedicated to St Titus.

Dress

On this day in the year 536 two monks returned from the Indies to Constantinople, bringing with them the means of teaching the manufacture of silk. In 1700 Western European dress was declared the rule in Russia.

Liars

"I am charmed with many points of the Turkish law ... particularly the punishment of convicted liars: they are burnt in the forehead with a hot iron, when they are proved the authors of any notorious falsehood."
Lady Montagu in a letter from Turkey, 1716

Humiliation

A day of humiliation was observed throughout the United States by appointment of President Buchanan because of the threatened secession of several of the states (1861).

Wars

In 48 B.C. Julius Caesar chased Gnaues Pompeius Magnsus (Pompey), a rebel Roman general and consul who opposed him, into Greece. In 871 the marauding Danes defeated the English at Reading. In 1847 the U.S. government bought 1,000 Colt pistols.

Tragedy

When Rachel, the reigning tragedy queen of France died in 1858, she was thirty-eight years old. An exhausting professional tour in America is believed to have had much to do with bringing the great tragedienne to a premature grave. Her style of acting was more calculated to excite terror than to melt with pity. Her greatest triumph came in 1848 when she sang the "Marseillaise," an event which left the audience overwrought with emotion, and for which her lover M. Ledru Rollin of the provisional government paid her openly with a grant of public money.

Tennis

Today in 1664 Samuel Pepys went "to the tennis-court and there saw the king (Charles II) play at tennis. But to see how the king's play was extolled, without any cause at all, was a loathsome sight; though sometimes, indeed, he did play very well, and deserved to be commended; but such open flattery is beastly."

Disaster

The northern coast of Wales, between the towns of Rhyl and Abergele, was thrown into excitement on the 4th of January 1847, by the loss of one gallant lifeboat, and the success of another. A schooner, the *Temperance of Belfast,* was in distress in a raging sea. The Rhyl lifeboat pushed off in a wild surf to aid the sufferers but all the crew, thirteen in number, were overwhelmed by the sea, and found a watery grave. The *Temperance,* however, was not neglected; another lifeboat set out, and braving all dangers, brought the crew of the schooner safely to land.

5
JANUARY

Births

Zebulon Pike (Pike's Peak) 1778; Sir John Burke (*Burke's Peerage*) 1814; Konrad Adenauer (German statesman) 1876.

A First Lady

Nellie Taylor Ross of Wyoming became the first woman governor in the U.S. in 1925.

An American Failure

On January 5 in 1778 the first naval contact mines were set afloat by David Bushnell to destroy the British fleet in the Delaware River at Philadelphia, but none of them exploded. "The Ballad of the Kegs" described the effect of this attempt on the British leader, Sir William Howe:

Sir William, he, as snug as a flea
Lay all this time a-snoring;
Nor dreamed of harm, as he lay warm
In bed with Mrs. Loring.

Deaths

St Simeon Stylites (pillar saint) 459; Edward the Confessor (English king) 1066; Theodore Roosevelt (26th U.S. president) 1919; Calvin Coolidge (30th U.S. president) 1933; Amy Johnson (aviatrix) 1941.

Edward the Confessor

Son of Ethelred the Unready, Edward reigned as king of England from 1042 until his death on this day in 1066. His death and burial are commemorated on the celebrated Bayeux Tapestry. He was canonised in 1161 and served as patron-saint of England until replaced by St George in the thirteenth century.

A French Failure

On this day in 1757 Robert Francis Damiens attempted to stab the worthless French king, Louis XV, but was foiled by the thickness of the royal robes. Shortly thereafter the failed assassin was publicly drawn and quartered by a team of horses.

Plunder

Benedict Arnold and the British troops plundered and burned Richmond, Virginia in 1781.

Astonishing Mortifications

The Roman saint for this day is St Simeon Stylites, so named from the Greek word *stylos* (pillar). This gentleman astonished the whole of the Roman empire with his mortifications. At first he confined himself within a circle of stones on a mountain top, but deeming this mode of penance not sufficiently severe, he then fixed his residence on top of a pillar nine feet high. The pillar was successively raised until it reached the somewhat incredible height of sixty feet, measuring but three feet in diameter at the top. The saint's clothing consisted of the skins of beasts and an iron collar around his neck. He exhorted the assembled multitude twice a day and spent the rest of his time in assuming various postures of devotion. He lived thusly for thirty-six years.

Wage Demands

In 1914 police had to restrain hordes of over-enthusiastic applicants for jobs at the Ford plant in Detroit. The reason: Henry Ford had just doubled assembly-line workers' salaries to $5.00 for an eight-hour day.

Napoleon Abominated

"All this devlish political business is going from bad to worse and [Napoleon] that infernal creature who is the curse of all the human race becomes every day more and more abominable."
  Alexander I, czar of Russia, in a letter to his sister Catherine, 1812

Apple Howling

Today is the Eve of Epiphany, the last day of the Feast of Nativity, which continued for twelve days after Christmas. Originally a festival of great solemnity, it gradually deteriorated into one of hell-raising of various types in rural England of the 17th century. One of the unrestrained celebrations was *Apple Howling*. The revellers would meet in the orchards of the southwest, surround a favourite tree, and do any or all of the following: drink a toast of hot cider, sing, beat the tree with sticks, set off firearms and shoot the tree, and make as much noise as possible.

6
JANUARY

Births

Joan of Arc (martyr) 1412; Alexander Scriabin (composer) 1872; Carl Sandburg (poet) 1878; Kahlil Gibran (prophet) 1883.

Deaths

Catherine of Aragon (ex-wife of Henry VIII) 1536; Fanny Burney (novelist) 1840;

Marriages

King Henry VIII to his fourth wife, Ann of Cleves, in 1540; George Washington to the widow, Martha D. Curtis, in 1759.

King of the Bean

One of today's celebrations in medieval France involved a cake baked in elaborate shapes. All in attendance were given slices of cake, one of which contained a bean. The one who found the bean in his portion became "King of the Bean" and acted as monarch of the festivities, with everyone doing his bidding. Mary, queen of Scots

brought the custom to England, adding a pea to the bean—the recipient of which would become "Queen of the Bean," to share the throne with the "King." In 1676 a diarist named Henry Teonge mentions further additions to the cake: "We had a great cake made, in which was put a bean for the King, a pease for the Queen, a clove for the Knave, a forked stick for the Cuckold, a rag for the Slut."

Upper-Class Revelry

Today's diversions for the English nobility included the blowing up of pasteboard castles; letting claret flow like blood from a stag's head made of paste; bombarding the castle from a pasteboard ship with cannon, in the midst of which the company pelted each other with egg shells filled with rose water. Large pies were made, filled with live frogs, which hopped and flew in their faces when the celebrants tried to eat it. Meanwhile, out in the wheat fields, the ancient ritual of *Blaze Night* was observed, wherein the farmhands ran through the fields with lighted torches to scare off witches and other enemies of the crops.

Sherlock's Day

The birthday of the fictional detective in the works of Sir Arthur Conan Doyle is celebrated today each year by the *Baker Street Irregulars,* a society of Holmes enthusiasts.

A Privilege of Position

"The inkpot used by the Secretaries of State should be of crystal and silver, not glass and brass. It must be replaced immediately!" Thus spake George Nathaniel Curzon on his appointment as Foreign Secretary for Britain and Viceroy of India in 1919.

Epiphany Hijinks

Also known as Twelfth-Day, the *Feast of The Epiphany* was celebrated on this, the twelfth day after Christmas, in most European countries. In old Bohemia the carnival season began on Twelfth-Night with a mad procession of fantastic animals. Parades featured monsters with assorted grotesqueries that frightened children, threatened maidens, and harassed the countryside. Norway "swept out" Christmas and processions of "star boys" went about the town passionately singing and performing biblical dramas. In Russia devout peasants chopped holes in the frozen Volga and threw themselves into the frigid waters to cure disease and immunise themselves for the rest of the year.

Births

Gregory XIII (pope) 1502; Millard Fillmore (13th U.S. president) 1800; François Poulenc (composer) 1899; Charles Addams (cartoonist) 1912.

Deaths

Alessandro de Medici (assassinated) 1537; Robert Boyle (inventor of air pump) 1691; Adolph Zukor (film producer) 1873; André Maginot (French war minister) 1932.

Quick Turnover

In 1558 the French port of Calais was recovered from the French by the British who had ceded it to them on the previous day.

St Distaff's Day

So named for the staff on which wool or flax was wound for spinning, this day in England marked the return of women to their spinning after resting during the Christmas festival season. (Spinning was deemed a suitable pastime for ladies because it "stoppeth a gap and saveth a woman from being idle.") The occasion was marked by the spinners drenching with pails of water those men who amused themselves by setting fire to the wool or flax. Robert Herrick captured the spirit of the day in a poem:

Partly work and partly play
Ye must on St. Distaff's Day.
From the plow soone free the teame,
Then come home and fother them.
If the Maides a-spinning goe,
Burn the flax and fire the tow.
Bring the pailes of water then,
Let the maides bewash the men.
Give St. Distaff all the right,
Then bid Christmas sport good night;
And next morrow, every one.
to his owne vocation.

Sermon to the Jews

It was customary in Rome during the seventeenth century that on each January 7th a sermon be preached to a compulsory congregation of Jews in the hope of their conversion. Mr John Evelyn, an English traveller to the Holy City, reported on the sermon of 1645: "They are constrained to sit until the hour is done, but it is with so much malice in their countenances, spitting, humming, coughing, and motion, that it is almost impossible they should hear a word from the preacher. A conversion is very rare."

Enforced Absinthe Abstinance

Thousands of French imbibers went into mourning in 1915 when a decree prohibited the sale of absinthe in France.

Finished Symphony

George Gershwin, then aged twenty-six, completed the score for "Rhapsody in Blue" in 1924.

Hot Air Transit

The first aerial crossing of the English Channel took place in 1785 when M. Blanchard and Dr Jeffries used an air balloon as a means of conveyance.

Election Results

The first national election in the United States of America was held in 1789. The winner on the presidential ballot was Mr George Washington.

Rice against Disaster

In certain parts of Japan this is a festival day on which a rice gruel cooked with seven kinds of herbs is eaten as a charm against bad luck, disease, and other misfortunes.

A Typing Error

The first typewriter patent was issued to Mr Mill, an Englishman, on this day in 1714. Unfortunately his device proved to be totally impractical and was never manufactured. (It took Mr Philo Remington to make a success of the idea, which he placed on the U.S. market in 1874.)

Births

Wilkie Collins (novelist) 1824; Frank Doubleday (publisher) 1862; Peter Arno (cartoonist) 1904; Elvis Presley (singer) 1935.

Deaths

Ste Gedula (saint) 712; Marco Polo (explorer) 1324; Galileo Galilei (astronomer) 1642; Chou En-Lai (Chinese premier) 1976.

Chastity Power

In 664, Sainte Gedula, patroness of Brussels, made a vow of perpetual virginity. From then until her death on this day in 712 she was said to possess the miraculous power of praying an accidentally extinguished candle a-light again.

St Nathalan's Day

There are two legends concerning the Scottish saint of this day, the first being the most likely to account for his sainthood:
1   During a scarcity he fed the starving and gave away his seed corn. In the spring, having no seed, he sowed his lands with the finest sand which miraculously produced rich crops for the following harvest.
2   St Nathalan, having given away his seed corn to the starving, used fine sand to sow his fields in the spring. The crop flourished but a storm swept all away. In his anger Nathalan blasphemed and then in his repentence placed an iron chain round his ankle and threw away the key, vowing to remain thus manacled until after a pilgrimage to Rome. On his arrival at Rome he is rumoured to have purchased a fish from a young boy and the key to his chains lay therein.

Messages from Washington

On January 8, 1780, George Washington wrote from his winter quarters in Morristown: "For a fortnight past, the troops, both officers and men, have been almost perishing with want." It was necessary to requisition both food and cattle from the county of New Jersey to stop the army from starving. Ten years later to the day, Washington delivered the first State of the Union message.

And the Earth is Flat

Galileo Galilei, the Italian pioneer of modern astronomy and telescopy, the discoverer of the irregular surface of the moon, of four of the satellites of Jupiter, of the rings of Saturn, of sunspots, and of the crescent shape of Venus, died in obscurity on this day in 1642. Twice brought before the Inquisition in Rome, he was forced to disavow as heresy the doctrine, which his discoveries supported, that the sun, not the earth, is at the centre of the solar system, and to promise to never teach it again.

Sic Transit Gloria

A newspaper of January 8, 1821, mentioned an extraordinary feat by Mr Huddy, the postmaster of Lismore, in the ninety-seventh year of his age. He travelled, for a wager, from that town in Scotland to Fermoy in a Dunvargon oyster-tub (drawn by a pig, a badger, two cats, a goose, and a hedgehog) with a large red nightcap on his head, a pig-driver's whip in one hand, and in the other a common cow's-horn, which he blew to encourage his team and to give notice of this new mode of postal delivery.

The Battle of New Orleans

The last battle in the War of 1812 was fought on January 8, 1814, after the peace treaty had been signed. News of the treaty had not yet been received in America. The British tried to take the American position at New Orleans and were driven back with a loss of 2,000 men. The day is also known as Jackson Day, or Old Hickory's Day, in honour of Andrew Jackson who commanded the victorious American troops.

Invitation to a Witch Burning

On January 8, 1650, a letter was sent to the Berwickshire (Scotland) Naturalists' Club from Mr William Turnbull who: "desyres some of our number to attend the judgeing and burning some witches within his parische, Wednesday and Thursday, in his necessitate absence."

9
JANUARY

Births

Carrie Lane Chapman (U.S. suffragette) 1859; Simone de Beauvoir (novelist) 1904; Richard Nixon (37th U.S. president) 1913; Joan Baez (singer) 1941.

Deaths

St Marciana (virgin martyr) 309; St Fillan (Scottish saint) 650; Caroline Herschel (astronomer) 1848; Napoleon III (emperor of France) 1873; Katherine Mansfield (novelist) 1923.

A Virgin Sacrifice

On this day in the year 309 St Marciana, a virgin saint in Italy, placed on her head the laurel of martyrdom. She was later torn to pieces by a wild bull and a leopard in the ampitheatre of Caesarea.

Mississippi Missing

In 1861 Mississippi seceded from the United States.

An Astronomical Lady

Caroline Lucretia Herschel, sister to and co-worker with the more famous William Herschel, was an excellent astronomer in her own right. A discoverer of seven comets, in 1789 she published the long valued *Catalogue of the Stars,* and after William's death in 1822, a *Catalogue of Nebulae and Star-Clusters* observed by him. She was awarded the Astronomical Society's gold medal in 1828 for her achievements. She continued her scientific labours until her death, in Hanover, in her ninety-seventh year.

No Cure for Cholera

In 1849 a cholera epidemic made frightful ravages in New Orleans decimating large numbers of the population. The place presented the appearance of a deserted city.

A Cure for Lunacy

St Fillan is a Scottish saint who died on this day in Strathfillan, in Perthshire, in the 7th century. The ruins of a chapel and a pool there still bear his name, and his Quigrich or abbot's staff is the property of the Society of Antiquaries of Scotland. A dipping in the pool on January 9 is supposed to be a cure for lunacy. The dipped person must retrieve three stones from the pool bottom, walk three times around each of three cairns on the bank, and throw one stone onto each cairn. They must then be left tied and supine in the proper corner of St Fillan's chapel for the rest of the night. If in the morning they are found loose, the cure is deemed perfect.

A Disaster at Church

At Locarno in Switzerland in 1863 the dome of the Church of La Madonna del Sasso crashed through the roof of the building, entombing in its ruins fifty-three women who were worshipping there at the time.

Balloonist Goes Broke

At 10 a.m. in Philadelphia, the first balloon ascent in America was undertaken by the Frenchman Francois Blanchard. He took off from the yard of the old Walnut Street Prison and landed forty-five minutes later at Cooper's Ferry, New Jersey. M. Blanchard tried to charge the high price of $5 a head for entrance to the prison yard to watch the lift off, but a poor response forced him to lower the price to $2. Some 200 people responded, but the receipts didn't cover his expenses (1793).

Destination New York

Peter Miniut set sail from Amsterdam in 1626 on a voyage to Manhattan, which he later bought from the Indians.

A Cure for Scrofula

Since the time of Edward the Confessor it has been believed by many that the laying on of the true king's hands is a cure for the King's Evil, otherwise known as scrofula—a tubercular condition. The efficacy of the royal touch was taken by some to be hereditary and a certain sign of genuine succession. Demand for the "Touch" was sometimes very great, and on January 9, 1683, Charles II, in council at Whitehall, issued orders for the future regulation of the ceremony of Touching for the King's Evil, so that the public could be accommodated and contagion avoided. The King's Evil is supposedly also curable by the breath of a seventh son of a seventh son.

Penny Postage

On January 10, 1840, in Britain, pre-paid postage by means of stamped labels first came into use. The cost of any letter below a certain weight was a single penny, and the system became known as the Penny Post. It had been devised by Sir Rowland Hill to replace a cumbersome and expensive system that charged according to the number of enclosures in the letter and distance travelled.

A Steamboat Success

The first steamboat, *The New Orleans,* arrived at that city having paddled down the Mississippi from Pittsburgh (1812).

Buffalo Bill

The famous Buffalo Bill Cody died on this day in Denver, Colorado in 1917. He was born William Frederick Cody in Iowa in 1845. He got the name "Buffalo Bill" when, as a young twenty-year-old cavalry colonel in charge of provisioning gangs of railway men, he killed 4,280 buffalo in eighteen months.

Births

Ethan Allen (poet) 1739; Francis X. Bushman (actor) 1883; Robinson Jeffers (poet) 1887; Ray Bolger (performer) 1904.

Deaths:

St William Bourges (saint) 1209; William Laud, archbishop of Canterbury (beheaded for treason) 1645; William F. Cody (Buffalo Bill) 1917; Dashiell Hammett (author) 1961; Coco Chanel (fashion designer) 1971.

St William Expires

St William Bourges stretched himself out on a bed of ashes laid in the form of a cross and died of voluntary mortification (1209).

Peculiar People

An inquest was held in London on the body of a member of the Peculiar People sect. No attempt had been made to obtain medical aid for the deceased woman since that would have been contrary to the principles of the sect. In case of illness, they considered it right to allow the illness to take its course and when the coroner said that he would send such cases to be tried as manslaughter, an elder of the sect argued that nowhere in the Bible was it said that man should make use of medical aid and knowledge (1888).

Money to Burn

On January 10, 1838 at 10:30 a.m., the Royal Exchange in London began to burn. Owing to the intense frost there was much difficulty in procuring water, and the flames were not got under control till the fire had in a measure exhausted itself, at noon the following day. The flames reached the new tower about 1 o'clock and the bells, eight in number, which had been chiming during the destruction, fell one after the other.

High Flying

On January 10, 1910 the first international air meet was held in Los Angeles. The U.S. Curtis bi-planes demonstrated their power in competition with two Farman bi-planes and two Bleriot monoplanes. To highlight the show, pilot Paulhan broke the world altitude record by flying at 4,165 feet.

London Fog

Such was the accumulation of smoke in the atmosphere about London in 1812 that darkness descended on the city for several hours at the height of the day. Shops and offices were lighted as at night, but the streets were not, and great care had to be taken by travellers to avoid accidents or losing their way. Whenever light penetrated the cloud it showed a deep bronze colour, and the effect could be seen from forty miles away.

For Medicinal Purposes Only

On this day in 1872 a manifesto in regard to the use of alcohol for medical purposes was circulated among the leading members of the medical profession in Britain. Those signing it expressed an opinion that no medical practitioner should prescribe it without a sense of grave responsibility for all its effects.

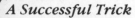

A Successful Trick

Amelia Earhart, the first woman to fly solo across the Pacific, left Wheeler Field in Honolulu and arrived in Oakland, California 18 1/4 hours later (1935).

A Failed Trick

Prior to leaping into the Thames, Samuel Scott, the American diver and escape artist, accidently hung himself when performing his rope trick on Waterloo Bridge in London (1841).

Today's Fortune

According to occultists the number 11 is very ominous. It signifies dangers, trials, and tribulations and can mean treachery from others. Anyone who believes in numerology will have great difficulties contending with this day.

A Hair Shirt

St Theodosius, the saint of this day, wore a hair shirt, ate coarse pulse and wild herbs, never tasted bread for thirty years, founded a monastery for an unlimited number of monks, and dug one grave large enough to hold the whole community. When he received strangers, and had not food enough, he prayed for its miraculous increase and had it multiplied accordingly. He prophesied even while dying on this day in 529, aged 104. After his death a count wore his hair shirt and won a victory in battle because of it.

A Giant Disinterred

A human-like skeleton was found in 1613 entombed eighteen feet below the surface of a spot later called the Giant's Field in France. It measured twenty-five and one-half feet long and ten feet wide at the shoulders.

A Roadster for $395

At the National Automobile Show in New York eighty car manufacturers showed more than 700 vehicles. The "sedan," a new type of luxury car, was unveiled for the first time and a roadster could be purchased for $395 (1913).

Another Failed Trick

Ellen Bright, the Lion Queen, was killed in London by a tiger in the menagerie of her uncle. The brute was beaten off by one of the keepers, and the unfortunate girl removed from the stage. The coroner's jury expressed a strong opinion against the practice of entering the dens of wild animals (1850).

Births

Francesco Parmigiano (painter) 1503; Alexander Hamilton (U.S. politician) 1757; St John A. Macdonald (first Canadian prime minister) 1815.

Deaths

St Theodosius (saint) 529; Samuel Scott (failed escape artist) 1841; Francis Scott Key ("Star Spangled Banner") 1843; Thomas Hardy (British author) 1928.

English Lotteries

Though lotteries were known in Italy at an earlier date, the first in England was drawn on the 11th of January, 1569, at the west door of St Paul's Cathedral. It consisted of 40,000 lots at ten shillings each, and included a great number of good prizes of ready money and certain sorts of merchandise. Lotteries were then used almost continuously as a source of revenue by English governments until 1826.

False Pregnancy

During the trial of Christina Edmunds at the Old Bailey in London, there was an unexpected announcement that the prisoner claimed to be with child. Shouts of "Let the Sheriff impanel a jury of matrons forthwith," such being the law from ancient times. A dozen well-to-do and respectably dressed women were captured and directed to enter the jury box. After an hour's suspense, the verdict was spoken by the forewoman in a single word "Not." The trial continued with the lady being convicted and sentenced (1872).

Anti-Mole Precautions

It if should happen to be mild on this day, the mole—Talpa Europaeus—begins to work and to throw up those noted hillocks which if not levelled by the bush farrow but left to get hard, are such an obstruction to the scythe in mowing in the solstitial season.
Gardening Advice from the *Catholic Annal,* 1830

Cheese Prices

As a war rationing measure the French government, in a circular to prefects, fixed the price of Gruyere cheese (1917).

12
JANUARY

Births

Edmund Burke (statesman) 1729; John Singer Sargent (artist) 1856; Jack London (novelist) 1876; Herman Goering (Nazi) 1893.

An Apocalypse Prediction

There was considerable excitement in Birmingham, England on this date in consequence of a prophecy that "the world was about to come to an end." The credence the prophecy obtained was strengthened by five days of the thickest fog ever experienced in that locality (1888).

The Bad Luck of Leyden

On the 12th of January, 1807, in the populous Dutch city of Leyden, a vessel loaded with gunpowder exploded at its mooring in the Rapenburg canal, in front of the house of one Professor Rau. The blast leveled 200 buildings, including the town hall, left 151 dead immediately in the ruins and many more thereafter, wounded 2,000 persons, and was heard fifty miles away. The anchor of the destroyed ship was found in a field outside of the town.

Troubles were not new to Leyden: It suffered under seige in 1573, under the plague in 1624, and again in 1635 when 15,000 of its inhabitants were lost. A convent fire in 1415 killed almost all the nuns; and a powder explosion in 1481 destroyed the town council chambers and left most of the magistrates dead. Curiously, in Dutch, the word *Leyden* is pronounced the same as *Lijden:* the latter means "to suffer."

La Salle's Last Journey

The explorer La Salle, who discovered the Ohio River, had set out in 1866 to settle the Mississippi Valley in the name of France. But the mission aborted and he set out on this day from Matagorda Bay, on the coast of what is now Texas, to walk back to his possessions in Canada. He was killed by some of his men enroute.

A Fine for Witch Wives

On January 12, 1644, Archibald and Thomas Wanderson were ordered to pay "ane (one) hundred merks for defraying of the chairges despursit upon their wives," who were executed for witchcraft in Scotland.

Deaths

Toung Chi (Chinese emperor) 1875; Sir Isaac Pitman (shorthand inventor) 1897.

Weather Predictions

Ancient weather prognosticators for this day decreed that:
if the sun shines it foreshows much wind but betokens a good year;
if it should rain or snow the weather following will be indifferent;
if the day is misty it predicts great dearth;
if it thunders and storms many people will die in the year.

A Festival for Slaves

Roman slaves from 576 B.C. onwards celebrated *The Compitalia* on this day which allowed them to forget their condition and become their own masters for a day.

A Cure for Heartburn

The Heart-Burn is an uneasy Sensation of Heat in the Stomach, occasioned by Indigestion, which is the Mother of Gout, Rheumatism, Gravel and Stone . . . To prevent it, Eat no Fat, especially what is burnt or oily; and neither eat or drink any thing sour or acid . . . To cure it, Dissolve a Thimble-full of Salt of Wormwood in a Glass of Water, and drink it.

    Poor Richard's Almanac, 1756

Births

Fortunately, few persons of significance have been born on this day.

Deaths

Ste Veronica (saint of Milan) 1497; Charles Fox (founder of Quakers) 1691; James Joyce (novelist) 1941.

A Bad Day to be Born

Numerology dictates that January 13 is a bad day to enter the world. Persons doing so are likely to suffer from melancholia, mental disorders, anemia, and pains in the head, back, bladder, and kidneys. These troubles are best treated by electric shocks, mental suggestion, and hypnotism. Particular care should be taken to avoid drugs, highly seasoned dishes, and red meat.

War Measures

The German General Staff introduced the idea of ruthless submarine warfare in 1919. The War Office of Great Britain abolished the lance as a weapon of battle in 1928.

The Vicious British

"The English have always been a wicked race, but since their King William they have become worse and fallen into very vicious ways. It has been noticed that islanders are always more treacherous and wicked than the inhabitants of the terra firma."

The Duchess of Orleans in a letter to her step-sister Louisa, 1718

Weather Bothers

In 1881, after a period of deceptive mildness in Europe, winter set in with a vengeance, and coldness of extreme severity occurred in France, Germany, and Spain. All communications between London and the counties of England ceased.

The New Year

On January 13, 1752, an Act for the *Change of Style* came into effect which provided that the new year in England would start as of the first of January instead of on March 25.

A Virgin Coronated

Queen Elizabeth, the Virgin Queen, was crowned on this day in 1559.

The Old Yew

Today's flower, according to medieval floral directories, is from the yew tree (*Taxus bacata*), which has a life span of up to 1,000 years. It was used to line graves in Europe and often planted in churchyards to ward off storms fetched up by evil witches.

Veronica's Origins

Ste Veronica of Milan was a poor peasant girl who by her exemplary piety became prioress of the nunnery of Ste Martha, and who was canonised by Pope Leo x. More interesting than Veronica's life is the origin of her name. It is stated that Christ, at his passion, had his face wiped by a devout female attendant, and that the cloth became miraculously imprinted with His image; it became a *Vera Iconica,* or true portrait, of his features. The handkerchief has been kept for many centuries at St Peter's in Rome. From the term *Vera Iconica* came the name Veronica.

A Lucky Cabin Boy

A severe storm was experienced round the entire English Channel. Among the many shipwrecks reported, the most calamitous, so far as the loss of life was concerned, was the East Indiaman *Conqueror,* which was driven ashore off Lionel, on the French coast. Out of seventy-eight persons on board, only one—a cabin boy—was saved (1843).

Old Glory Grows

On this day in 1794 two stars and two stripes, for Kentucky and Vermont, were added to the American flag.

The Pope Ad Libs

On the Octave of the Epiphany, which marks the baptism of Christ, when celebrated preacher Padre Ventura failed to arrive at the church of Santa Andrea della Valle at Rome for his expected ceremony, Pope Pius IX took the pulpit and preached a sermon extempore. It was said to have been a good, plain, simple sermon, easily intelligible to all. This was the first time in 300 years that any pope had preached a sermon (1847).

14
JANUARY

Births
Albert Schweitzer
(missionary/philosopher) 1875.

Deaths
Edmund Halley (astronomer) 1742;
George Berkely (philosopher/
bishop) 1753; Lewis Carroll (*Alice in
Wonderland*) 1898.

The Labour Party
The Labour Party in England was
founded and christened on this day
in 1893.

A Pen in the Head
An inquest was held at the London Hospital on Moses
Raphael, aged 32 who had suffered from severe pains in
the head. The doctors found a penholder and nib
measuring 3" protruding from the top of the right orbital
plate. The man's wife had never heard him allude to the
accident which, it was supposed, must have happened
during his schooldays (1888).

Frozen Lands
"On this day, in 1205, began a frost which continued until
the two and twentieth day of March, so that the ground
could not be tilled." Thus ran the report in Stowe's
Chronicle. Thereafter this day came to be regarded as the
coldest of the year in England, though this was the case
only until 1820 when the temperature fell to ten degrees
below zero Farenheit.
In 1734 thermometers in Yeneseisk, Siberia registered
120 degrees below zero Farenheit. Smoke was unable to
rise in the frigid air and birds dropped frozen to the
ground.

A Python's Problems
The pythoness in the Zoological Gardens in London today
laid about 100 eggs, the whole of which were addled in
the cold occasioned by the absence of the creature when
casting its skin. She then abstained from food for the long
period of 32 weeks (1862).

Pasteur's Penicillin
Four children bitten on this day by a
mad dog in Newark, New Jersey were
sent to Paris for treatment under
Louis Pasteur. His penicillin was
effective and they returned in good
health (1886).

America In Debt
Alexander Hamilton made his first
report on the state of public credit
and foreign and domestic debt. He
estimated foreign debt at $11,710,000
(mainly French) and domestic debt at
$27,383 (1790).

Mallard Day
In All Souls College in Oxford, today is *Mallard Day,*
marked with merrymaking to commemorate the finding
of an overgrown mallard duck in the drain when digging
the foundations for the college in 1437. Boisterous
students chant this verse:

Griffin, Bustard, Turkey, Capon,
Let to her hungry mortals gape on;
And on the bones their stomach fall hard,
But let All Souls' men have their MALLARD.
Oh! by the blood of King Edward,
Oh! by the blood of King Edward,
It was a wopping, wopping MALLARD.

The Feast of the Ass
Today was the traditional date of the *Feast of the Ass,* a
religious burlesque consisting of theatrical
representations of the flight of the Holy Family into Egypt.
This and similar festivals were instituted by the Patriarch
Theophylact of Constantinople, and designed to wean
people's minds from pagan revelry with Christian
spectacles. In time the Feast of the Ass degenerated into a
mock service in which the congregation brayed and
hee-hawed their responses instead of speaking them.

Part of Niagara—Falls
In 1887 a hugh portion of Upper
Table Rock on the Canadian side of
Niagara Falls thundered down with a
mighty crash.

A Star Day
The Greeks considered this to be a
star day and the most propitious of
the year for the birth of women,
because it naturally provided the
three virtues of beauty, patience, and
kindness to create a little knot that
binds the world.

15
JANUARY

Births

Molière (dramatist) 1622; Talma (actor) 1763; Gene Krupa (drummer) 1909; Martin Luther King, Jr (civil rights leader) 1929.

Deaths

St Paul (the first hermit) 342; Mathew Brady (pioneer photographer) 1896; Fanny Farmer (cook/writer) 1915.

Today's Number

The number 15 is peculiarly associated with good talkers and eloquence, and with those gifted in music and art. People born on this day are likely to have a dramatic personality combined with a voluptuous temperament and strong personal magnetism. It is a useful number to be associated with as it facilitates the obtaining of money, gifts, and favours from others.

Napoleon on Acting

The great French tragedian, Talma, who was born on this day, was a close friend of Napoleon, who much admired his artistry. When Napoleon was setting out on his expedition to Egypt, his actor friend offered to accompany him. But Bonaparte refused: "Talma," he said, "You must not commit such an act of folly. You have a brilliant course before you; leave fighting to those who are unable to do anything better."

An Overdone Steak

A test to determine the heat resistance of asbestos was conducted in Paris on this day in 1827. Monsieur Chabert, a volunteer clad in an asbestos suit, entered a large oven bearing a raw steak in his hand. When he emerged twelve minutes later M. Chabert, though rather warm and bothered, was otherwise quite well. The steak was pronounced to be overdone.

Hedera helix (Ivy)

Ivy, the plant accorded to the fifteenth of January, is dedicated to St Paul on account of its long life and its propensity for attaching itself to old churches. It is said that an alcoholic may be cured by taking a drink from a cup of ivy wood.

Island Events

In 1639 Governor Kieft purchased part of Long Island from the Indians on behalf of New Netherlands (later New York). In 1778 Captain Cook discovered Hawaii.

Adult's Day

Many families and organizations in Japan observe Seijin-No-Hi (Adult's Day) on this day to mark the coming of age of young men and women.

Historic Francis Tavern Day

This event is held to pay tribute to the oldest building in modern New York City, the DeLancey Mansion, purchased in 1762 by Samuel Francis, an inn-keeper.

A Crowd on Ice

When ice-bound, the Serpentine in Hyde Park, London, was the most popular place in the city for skaters. According to one estimate, on January 15, 1826 there were no less than 100,000 persons, both skaters and gazers, gathered on its surface between Kensington Gardens and Knightsbridge.

The First Hermit

St Paul, the first hermit, is said by St Anthony to have fled at the age of twenty-two years from the persecution of Decius to a cavern near which grew a palm tree that supplied him with fruit for food and leaves for clothing until he was forty-three years of age—after which he was fed daily by a raven until he died (aged 113), in the ninetieth year of his solitude.

The Czartoryski-de Nemours Nuptials

Celebrated in the parish church of Chantilly, France in 1872, the marriage of the Princess Margaret of Orleans, eldest daughter of the Duc de Nemours, with Prince Ladislas Czartoryski, son of the famous Polish leader in the great insurrection against Russia.

16
JANUARY

Births
Ethel Merman (actress) 1908.

Deaths
St Marcellus (pope and martyr) 310;
Edmund Spenser (poet) 1599;
Edward Gibbon (historian) 1794.
(Illustration)

Northern Lights
This day in 1781 became known as *Dies Electricia* because of the great prevalence of brilliant illumination caused by the Aurora Borealis in the skies of Europe.

The Decline and Fall of Gibbon
Edward Gibbon, famous author of *The Decline and Fall of the Roman Empire,* as a consequence of his sedentary habits, became very corpulent late in his life. Though he died a bachelor on this day in 1794, there is a story representing him as falling in love with a young lady of great beauty and merit, and one day throwing himself at her feet to declare his passion, but then being unable to raise himself again without her aid because of his enormous bulk.

The Orient Express
The first railway train connecting Turkey with Europe steamed into the station at Stamboul (1872).

A Bottled Hoax
Ex-butcher Antonio De Angelis, accused of perpetrating the greatest swindle in United States' history, was arrested and held on bail of $46,500,000 (also a record). He was convicted of making a profit of $175 million on sales of a specially blended salad oil that consisted mainly of sea water(1964).

The Kid
A film released for distribution entitled *The Kid* featured Charlie Chaplin and the child star Jackie Coogan (1920).

A Terrible Coronation
The first Russian czar, Ivan the Terrible, was crowned in 1547.

The Bottle Hoax
A person advertised that he would this evening at the Haymarket Theatre in London play on a common walking cane the music of every instrument now used, to surprising perfection; that he would, on the stage, get into a tavern quart bottle, without equivocation, and while there sing several songs and suffer any spectator to handle the bottle. Tickets ranged in price from two shillings to seven shillings and six pence. On the given evening the theatre was jammed but the conjurer failed to show up. The theatre-owner offered to return the money but the crowd went wild and tore the theatre to shreds (1749).

Biblical Prohibition
The British Parliament passed an act prohibiting any "woman, or artificer's prentices, journeymen, serving men of the degree of yeomen, or under husbandmen or labourers, to read the New Testament in English" (1543).

Warm and Cold Events
Columbus set sail from Haiti to return home in 1493; English pirates captured the island of Tobago in 1666; Captain Cook discovered the Sandwich Islands in 1778; the Shackleton expedition reached the magnetic South Pole in 1909; President Nasser declared Egypt an independent republic in 1956.

Down-under Dictum
George Barrington was a transported London pickpocket, who became an Australian historian. He delivered the prologue at the ceremonial opening of the first theatre in Sydney in 1796 with these words:

True patriots we; for be it understood
We left our country for our country's
   good

17
JANUARY

Births

Benjamin Franklin (statesman) 1706; Anton Chekhov (writer) 1860; Al Capone (criminal) 1899; Cassius Clay (boxer) 1942.

Deaths

St Anthony (saint) 356; Chang and Eng (Siamese twins) 1874; Rutherford B. Hayes (19th U.S. president) 1893; Patrice Lumumba (Congolese president) 1961.

U.S. Business

In a speech to newspaper editors, Calvin Coolidge, 30th president of the USA said: "The business of America is business."

A Tribute to Ben

A statue of Benjamin Franklin, a gift from the printers of the city, was unveiled in New York on this 165th anniversary of the philosopher's birth. Mr Horace Greeley said on the occasion, "I love and revere him as a journeyman printer who was frugal and didn't drink: a parvenu who rose from want to competence, from obscurity to fame without losing his head; a statesman who did not crucify mankind with long-winded speeches or documents, a diplomatist who did not intrigue, a philosopher who never lied, and an office holder who didn't steal" (1872).

A Bargain

On this day in 1917 the U.S. bought the Virgin Islands from Denmark for the sum of $25,000,000.

Aquatomic Power

The world's first atomic powered submarine, *The Nautilus,* was launched on this day in 1955 by the United States Navy.

A Divorced Woman

Lady Stanley, wife of the governor-general of Canada, refused to receive a divorcee who had become the wife of an American minister, at a state dinner in Ottawa (1890).

The Feast of St Anthony

St Anthony, among the most famous Christian saints, was revered for his lifelong battle against Satan's temptations. He is the patron saint of butchers, brushmakers, and domestic animals. On this day in California, Switzerland, Mexico, and Spain, domestic animals are decorated with flowers and bells and are blessed at the church door.

St Anthony Outdone

St Anthony once heard a voice from heaven telling him that he was not as perfect as a certain Alexandrian cobbler. The saint hastened to the city, found the cobbler, and asked him to relate the story of his life. "Sir," said the cobbler, awed by a visit from such a reverend person, "as for me, good works have I none, for my life is but simple and slender; I am but a poor cobbler. In the morning when I rise, I pray for the whole city wherein I dwell, especially for all such neighbours and poor friends as I have; after I set me at my labour, where I spend my whole day in getting my living; and I keep me from all falsehood, for I hate nothing so much as I do deceitfulness; wherefore, when I make to any man a promise, I keep to it, and perform it truly. And thus I spend my time poorly with my wife and children, whom I teach and instruct, as far as my wit will serve me, to fear and dread God. And this is the sum of my simple life."

Chang and Eng

These famous Siamese twins died in North Carolina in 1874, aged sixty-three. Their bodies were joined by a band of flesh stretching from one end of the breast bone to the same place on the opposite twin. They were married to two sisters and had offspring; but owing to domestic quarrels, two houses were found necessary—each twin living with his wife a week at a time alternately.

The Shrewsbury Duel

On January 17, 1667, George Villiers, duke of Buckingham and Francis Talbot, earl of Shrewsbury accompanied by seconds and thirds, fought a duel that was "all about my Lady Shrewsbury, at that time, and for a great while before, a mistress of the Duke of Buckingham." Shrewsbury challenged Buckingham and in the duel was: "run through the body from his right breast through the shoulder; and Sir John Talbot all along and up one of his arms; and one of the seconds killed upon the place, and the rest all in a little measure wounded" according to Samuel Pepys. Shrewsbury later died of his wounds; the lady remarried someone else altogether.

18
JANUARY

Births

Peter Mark Roget (Thesaurus author) 1779; Daniel Webster (U.S. statesman) 1782; Konstantin Stanislavski (actor) 1863; A.A. Milne (*Winnie The Pooh*) 1882; Archie Leach (Cary Grant) 1904.

Deaths

Ste Prisca (virgin and martyr) 50; Archangelo Corelli (composer) 1713; Diving Mouse (Indian princess) 1835; Rudyard Kipling (author) 1936.

The Death of a Perfectionist

The violinist and composer, Archangelo Corelli, died on this day in Naples in 1713, apparently from a state of melancholy and chagrin induced by the successes of Neapolitan artists inferior to himself. As well as for his art and sensitivity, Corelli was known for his fastidiousness in the rehearsal hall, where he would immediately stop the music if the bows of his performers were not perfectly synchronous.

The Death of Diving Mouse

In 1835 a party of North American Indians of the Michigan tribe, their chief Muk Conee (Little Boar) among them, was due to be presented to King William in London on this day. But when the day came, Muk Conee's wife, Diving Mouse, aged only twenty-six, sickened. Preferring her fate to any white man's medicine, and allowing that she be baptised only so that her funeral might be more ceremonious, she died that same day. She was buried in a churchyard in Waterloo Road, wearing her native garments amid elaborate English funeral trappings. Shaw Whash (Big Sword) pronounced the oration in her native tongue.

A Chair Festival

This is the annual date of the Festival of St Peter's Chair held in Rome in honour of the founding of the papacy. The ceremony takes place in the Church of St Peter where the chair, on which the saint is said to have pontificated, is enshrined.

Panama Seized

In 1671 Henry Morgan and his buccaneers attacked and captured Panama on behalf of the British Government, who received his successes with approval (he was knighted in 1673) but preferred not to hear about the indescribable brutality and debauchery that marked his operations.

Livingstone Presumed

Intelligence was received that the Livingstone Search Expedition in Africa had returned satisfied that the great traveller was not killed, as his bearers had reported, but that they had deserted him when setting out from Marenga. The searchers obtained traces of him further on and were on the whole satisfied that he was still alive, and would probably return by the Nile (1868).

A Jazz Festival

It was jazz versus the classics in a concert held in the New York Metropolitan Opera House which featured Louis Armstrong, Lionel Hampton, Roy Eldridge, Big Sid Catlett, Oscar Pettiford, Barney Bigard, Jack Teagarden, Dave Tough, Benny Goodman, and Artie Shaw. Jazz won (1944).

The Horrors of Ste Prisca

The thirteen-year-old Sainte Prisca was decapitated on this day in 50 A.D. in Rome after four days of horrible torture for refusing to deny Christ. An eagle hovered over her body, beating back the scavenging dogs until nightfall when she was retrieved for Christian burial.

Today's Cures

Persons born on this day, who might be ailing can choose from onions, garlic, leeks, horse-radish, rhubarb, mustard seed, wormwood, spear-wort, white nellebore, ginger, pepper, broom rape, madder, hops, danewort, and nettles as cures. These are the most favourable remedial herbs prescribed by numerologists who have studied the number 18.

19
JANUARY

Births

James Watt (inventor) 1736; Robert E. Lee (general) 1807; Edgar Allan Poe (poet) 1809; Paul Cezanne (artist) 1839.

Deaths

William Congreve (poet) 1729; Dr Thomas Dooley (medical missionary) 1961.

Today's Flower

The flower of this day, dedicated to St Martha, is popularly known as white dead nettle, and properly known as *Camium alblum*. It is a hairy herb with leaves so closely resembling those of the stinging nettles that many persons are afraid to handle them. A common but not inelegant weed, it is a great favourite with bees and is encouraged to grow near hives by knowledgeable beekeepers who desire its flavour to be incorporated into the honey.

Today's Number

The number 19 is regarded as fortunate and extremely favourable, promising happiness, esteem, honour, and success in one's plans for the future.

Ben's Bomb

When Ben Jonson's last comedy, *New Inn,* was presented in London "it was driven from the stage and pursued with brutal hostility by his ungenerous and unrelenting enemies" (1630).

Hot Air Myth

According to popular history James Watt, who was born on this day in 1736, is supposed to have conceived of his steam engine while watching the lid of a boiling kettle being lifted by the escaping vapours. But the facts are less picturesque. In his position as instrument maker in a university, Watt was required to effect repairs on an early, crude variation of the steam engine that had been contrived by a man named Newcomen. It was Watt's improvement of this early model that gave a new source of power to the world.

A Poem By Poe

Edgar Allan Poe, the American poet most famous for "The Raven," paid the price of genius in happiness and health. He lived only forty years from his birth on this day in 1809, and was unlucky in love. A legacy of this latter state remains:

And neither the angels in heaven above,
Nor the demons down under the sea,
Can ever dissever my soul from the soul
Of the beautiful—Annabel Lee!

Missing Jewels

The jewel case of the Russian ambassador was stolen at Paddington Station under circumstances precisely similar to the theft of the countess of Dudley's jewels. His Excellency was at the station and while the train was being prepared, the dressing case was stolen from the pile of luggage (1875).

Sour Grapes

On this day in 1911 the winegrowers of France staged a revolt in protest against the fraud and deception of illegally selling white wine as Champagne. They sacked the Perrier cellars at Epernay, destroying thousands of bottles of perfectly good wine.

Congreve the Conceited

Congreve was once visited at Bath by the French writer Voltaire, who had a great admiration of him as a writer. "Congreve spoke of his works," says Voltaire, "as of trifles that were beneath him, and hinted to me . . . that I should visit him on no other footing than upon that of a gentleman who led a life of plainess and simplicity. I answered that, had he been so unfortunate to be a mere gentleman, I should never have come to see him; and I was very much disgusted at so unreasonable a piece of vanity."

20
JANUARY

Births

Misha Elman (violinist) 1891; Harold L. Gray (*Little Orphan Annie*) 1894; Patricia Neal (actress) 1926.

Deaths

Charles II (emperor) 1745; David Garrick (actor) 1779; John Howard (prison reformer) 1790; R.D. Blackmoor (*Lorna Doone*) 1900; John Ruskin (philosopher) 1900; George V (king of England) 1936.

NYC Frozen

On January 20, 1852, the East River in New York was so frozen over that for several hours, thousands of people crossed the ice from Brooklyn to New York.

Grandmother's Day

Today in Bulgaria, young girls and boys are traditionally ducked in water to ensure their good health. The festival is known as *Baba Den* which translates from Bulgarian into Grandmother's Day.

Basketball Day

As a boy in Canada, James Naismith played a game with stones called *Duck on the Rock*. He later parlayed this singular pastime into the game of basketball, the first game of which was played on this day in 1892 at Springfield, Massachucetts.

U.S. and G.B. O.K.

On this day in 1783 at Versailles in France, the United States and Great Britain signed the Declaration of Suspension of Hostilities.

The First Parliament

The first English Parliament, called by Simon de Montfort, earl of Leicester in the reign King Henry III, met in the hall at Westminster on January 20, 1265. Though councils of great landholders had been held earlier, this was the first in which the Commons were represented, there being present two knights for each county and two citizens for each borough. Ever since, the Commons have had their share in matters of state.

Mixed Blessings

Two of the saints for this day had quite different fates. St Fabian was chosen for the office of pope in consequence of a dove settling on him while the people and clergy were electing a successor to the pontifical chair. St Sebastian was sentenced to be shot to death with arrows, but when these failed to kill him he was beaten to death with cudgels.

An Historic Speech

"My fellow Americans, ask not what your country can do for you; ask what you can do for your country. My fellow citizens of the world, ask not what America will do for you, but what together we can do for the freedom of man."
  President John F. Kennedy's inaugural address, 1961

The Talkies Outdoors

On January 20, 1929, *In Old Arizona*, the first full-length talking picture filmed outdoors was released by Fox. Nine-tenths of the movie was shot on location in Utah, the Mohave desert, and the San Fernando Mission, California.

Husband Divining

On this, the eve of St Agnes' Day, it was thought possible for a girl to divine knowledge of her future husband. She would take a row of pins and stick them into her sleeve one after another saying a paternoster . . . or she might take her right leg stocking and knit her left leg garter around it, saying:

I knit this knot, this knot I knit,
to know the thing I know not yet,
That I may see
The man that shall my husband be.

In bed that night, her future husband would come in a dream and salute her with a kiss.

A Blasphemer Nabbed

On January 20, 1891, Professor Charles A. Briggs of Union Theological Seminary, New York City delivered an address on "The Authority of the Scriptures," which caused him to be tried and convicted of heresy.

21
JANUARY

Births

Henry VII (English king) 1456; "Stonewall" Jackson (U.S. Civil War hero) 1824; Jack Nicklaus (golfer) 1940.

Deaths

Ste Agnes (virgin martyr) 304; Louis XVI (French king) 1793; Vladmir Ilyich Lenin (revolutionary) 1924; Cecil B. DeMille (movie producer) 1959.

Media Events

On this day in 1930 the first Buck Rogers comic strip was published in the United States while the first BBC broadcast to the world was aired from London.

Astrology

The sun now enters the constellation of Aquarius (the water-carrier) which bodes ill or well according to the signs of the Zodiac:

Manners & Actions, when well dignified
Then he is profound in Imagination, in his Acts severe, in his words reserved, in speaking and giving very spare, in labour patient, in arguing or disputing grave, in obtaining the goods of this life studious and solicitous, in all manners of actions austere.
When ill
Then he is envious, covetous, jealous and mistrustful, timorus, sordid, outwardly dissembling, sluggish, suspitious, stubborne, a contemner of women, a close lyar, malicious, murmuring, never contented, ever repining.

From *Christian Astrology,* 1647

The Loud Death of Louis XVI

On the 21st of January, 1793, a victim of the wrath of the French Revolution, in a square before the Palace of the Tuileries, Louis XVI of France died under the knife of the guillotine. It is said that upon the scaffold he beseeched: "I die innocent of the crimes inputed to me," and "I pardon the authors of my death, and I pray heaven that the blood you are about to shed may never be visited upon France." His voice could be heard as far away as the Pont-Tournant.

Women's Rights

In 1891 a large demonstration was held in Brussels by suffragettes in support of women's rights and a demand for a revised Belgian constitution. In 1908 a law was passed in New York City making it illegal for women to smoke in public.

More Women's Rights

There's nothing like to keep you warm
As loving wife laid in your arms;
Who'll say, good husband, turn unto me,
For all the world I'd not forego thee,
Refuse not then such gentle proffer,
Which she so kindly doth thee offer,
Nor in thy duty be not scant,
But give her that which she doth want.
Poor Robin's Almanac, 1683

A Woman Wronged

"Sir: In the *Daily Mail* report of the inquest on the sad death of the lady who was drowned in the Hampstead Heath pond, one of the witnesses gave as a reason why he did not enter the water that he was hot. May I point out that it is quite a mistake to think you should not enter the water when warm; as a matter of fact, the opposite is the truth."

Alfred Rowley
Honorary Secretary of
the Serpentine Swimming Club
A letter to the editor in the *Daily Mail* of London, 1907

The Strange Marriage of St Agnes

St Agnes, patroness of purity, virginity, and girl scouts, was martyred by beheading in the thirteenth year of her age, in 304 A.D. It is related that a priest in a church dedicated to the saint desired to marry, and was given license to do so by the pope if he would first pay his addresses to the image of Agnes in his own church. But when he did so, the image put out her finger. The priest encircled it with an emerald ring given him by the pope; then the image withdrew the finger together with the ring, which was held fast. After that the priest was content to remain a bachelor.

22 JANUARY

Births

Francis Bacon (philosopher) 1561; Lord Byron (poet) 1788; August Strindberg (playwright) 1849; Yehudi Menuhin (violinist) 1916.

Deaths

St Vincent (patron of vintners) 304; Victoria (English queen) 1901; Anna Pavlova (ballerina) 1931; Lyndon B. Johnson (36th U.S. president) 1973.

An Erotic Festival

Licentious citizens of Ephesus, one of the principle Ionian cities on the coast of Asia Minor in the Roman times, indulged in *The Catagogia*—an erotic and bacchanalian festival celebrated on this day about the 1st century A.D.

Wine and the Weather

There was an old remark in Latin, "Vincenti festi, si sol radiet, memo esto," which enjoins us to "remember" if the sun should shine on the Festival of St Vincent. Its meaning was for many years unclear until a scrap of old French poetry was discovered stating that sun on St Vincent's day indicated that that year's wine would be more plentiful than water. This can be taken either as good news for imbibers of wine, or an indication to vintners that the year would be a dry one, and therefore good for the vintage. Weather predictions are also possible on this day, which is sometimes called Sunbeam Day.

The Fortunes of England

On this day in 1690 the Indians of the Five Nations Council in Onondaga renewed their declaration of loyalty to England. Forty-five years earlier the Scots had invaded England in the war between the High Church Royalists and the Covenanters who advocated Puritanism.

Health Tip

Now Phaeton's rays afford but little heat,
And men are apter for to quake than sweat,
To cheer thy head, then, to warm thy blood,
A glass of sack I count is wondrous good.
Poor Robin's Almanac, 1684

A Diary Entry

In 1924 Ramsay Macdonald formed the first Labour Government in England. "Today twenty-three years ago dear Grandmama (Queen Victoria) died. I wonder what she would have thought of a Labour Government."
From the diary of George V, king of England

Great, but Mean

Francis Bacon, who was born on this day in 1561, is best known as the developer of the inductive reasoning school of philosophy. He has also been called the father of the English Renaissance and the alter ego of Shakespeare. But his bribe-taking during his term as a judge caused the poet Alexander Pope to describe him as "The wisest, greatest, meanest of mankind."

Births

John Hancock (U.S. statesman) 1737;
Edouard Manet (artist) 1832;
Humphrey Bogart (actor) 1899.

Deaths

St Eusebius (saint) 400; William Pitt
(British statesman) 1806; Sir
Alexander Korda (film producer)
1956.

A Fixed Day

On January 23, 1845, the United
States Congress fixed the presidential
elections on one day—the first
Tuesday after the first Monday in
November. Since 1792 elections had
been ordered "within 34 days
preceding the first Wednesday in
December."

A Saintly Secret

St Eusebius, a fourth-century Assyrian
abbot, ate only once every four days,
but would not let any of his monks
go for more than two without
nourishment. Insiders revealed that,
though the intervals were longer on
Eusebius' part, his proportions were
more generous.

Westminster Hall Illegalities

January 23 is the traditional date of the opening of the
Hilary law term in England. It was an ancient custom on
the first day of the term for the judges to breakfast with
the lord chancellor in Lincoln's Inn-hall, and then
proceed with him, in their respective carriages, to
Westminster Hall. Another ancient custom in the hall,
though one not so innocent, was the practice of
professional "witnesses" swearing on oath to any
evidence required, for a fee. Persons willing to sell
themselves as witnesses advertised the fact by wearing a
straw in their shoe.

A Dog's Death

An enquiry into the death of "Master McGrath," a famous
greyhound racing dog, resulted in the discovery that the
heart weighed 9 1/2 ounces, this being rather more than
the average weight of a man's heart. Master MGrath's
running weight was 54 pounds from which it appears that
the celebrated canine possessed three times the heart
force of a man. It was believed that this was the real cause
of its extraordinary running powers (London, 1872).

Random Occurrences

Lichenstein came into being in 1719.

Louisiana became a royal province of France in 1732.

Elizabeth Blackwell became the first American women to
take a M.D. degree in 1849.

The duke of Edinburgh and the grand duchess Marie
Alexandrovna were wed in St Petersburg in 1879.

The U.S. Navy bathysphere made a record descent to the
bottom of the Mariana Trench in the Pacific in 1960.

A Great Wonder in Heaven

A pamphlet describing the following remarkable
occurrence was published on this day in 1647: Weekend
travellers and shepherds in the area near Keniton in
Northamptonshire, England witnessed in the air the
apparition of a battle that had taken place two months
before between the forces of the king and of Parliament.
The ghostly manifestation lasted until three a.m. and was
complete down to the sounds of drums, the clashing of
arms, and the groans of the dying. For some nights
afterwards the sky was filled with the tumult of battle. The
final appearance was witnessed by emissaries from the
king. By that time the most experienced of the witnesses
were able to recognise individual combatants who had
been present at the actual battle.

24
JANUARY

Births
Frederick II (the Great) 1712; Edith Wharton (novelist) 1862; Maria Tallchief (ballerina) 1925.

Deaths
St Timothy (martyr) 97; Lord Randolph Churchill (statesman) 1895; Sir Winston Churchill (statesman) 1965.

A Deadly Dance
St Timothy met his demise when he tried to disband an idolatrous group of revellers who were dancing in his temple. The frenzied mob turned upon him and struck him down with stones and clubs on this day in 97 A.D.

Proverb
Old Janus wills thee keep thy Body warm
With kitchin physic thy diseases charm,
Sweet wine is good, but exercise is best
For him that in old age would live at rest.
Fly Almanac, January 1679

Better Weather
On January 24 in 1684, the weather was cold but bright in London and a Frost Fair took place on the frozen Thames. The diaryist John Evelyn was in attendance: "all sortes of trades and shopes furnish'd and full of commodities . . . and sleds, a bull baiting, horse and coach rases, puppet plays and interludes, cookes, Eipling, so that it seemed to be a bachannaliar triumph or carnival on the water."

California Gold
This was the day in 1848 when the gleam of gold in a tributary of the Sacramento River near Coloma, California caught the eye of James W. Wheeler. In a short period of time the ensuing Gold Rush deposited more than 200,000 would-be strike-it-richers on the spot.

FIN

A Cat Sacrifice
It used to be the custom on the feast of John the Baptist at Aix-en-Provence on January 24 to put a number of cats into a basket and throw them, still alive, onto a huge fire kindled in the public square by the bishop and the clergy. Hymns were sung and a procession was made by the people and priests in honour of the sacrifice.

Deadly Weather
A violent storm in Scotland left a grim toll of death washed up on the shores of the Solway Firth. Observers recorded the bodies of: one woman, two men, three horses, nine black cattle, forty-five dogs, 180 rabbits, and 1,840 sheep (1794).

Frederick's Turbulent Youth
Though he came to be one of the greatest generals of all time, Frederick II the king of Prussia was lucky to survive his early years which began today in 1712. His sternly militaristic father, Frederick William I, disapproved of his son's tastes for music and literature. To stem these enthusiasms, the savage old king had a young lady who accompanied the prince's flute playing on the pianoforte publicly flogged in the streets of Potsdam. Fearing for her son, the queen arranged for his escape, with two friends, to the court of his uncle, George II of England. The prince and one of the two friends were caught by the king and thrown into dungeons. Frederick William wanted to have his son killed on the scaffold, but was prevented from doing so by the intervention of Charles VI of Austria. To satisfy himself, he instead had the friend executed and the prince imprisoned for life in a fortress at Custrin. Once again the queen intervened and the prince went on to become Frederick II.

25
JANUARY

Births

Robert Boyle (chemist) 1627; Robert Burns (poet) 1759; W. Somerset Maugham (writer) 1874.

Deaths

Louis Hebert (Canada's first farmer) 1627; Dorothy Wordsworth (William's sister) 1855; J. Carroll Naish (actor) 1973.

Marriages

Princess Margaret, eldest daughter of Henry VII of England to James IV of Scotland (1502); Henry VIII, king of England to his second wife (of six) Anne Boleyn (1533); King Frederick III of Germany and Prussia to Victoria, Princess Royal of England (1858).

Robert Burns Day

Today features great outpourings of sentiment as Burns Clubs all over the world celebrate "the immortal memory of Robert Burns." The traditional Burns Dinner is centred around the infamous "Haggis," a dish composed of minced heart and liver of sheep, with suet and oatmeal, seasoned and sewn into the stomach of the animal and boiled for three hours.

The evening ends with the passionate singing of Burns' "Auld Lang Syne" accompanied by a profusion of toasts that make extensive use of Scotland's national beverage.

Proverb

March in Janiveer,
January in March, I fear.

The Birth of Burns

Upon a stormy winter night
Scotland's bright star first rose in
   sight;
Beaming upon as wild a sky
as ever to prophetic eye
Proclaimed, that nature had on hand
Some work to glorify the land.
Within a lonely cot of clay,
that night her great creation lay.

Coila—the nymph who round his
   brow
Twined the red-berried holly
   bough—
Her swift-winged heralds sent abroad,
To summon to that bleak abode
All who on Genius still attend,
For good or evil to the end.

They came obedient to her call;
The immortal infant knew them all.
   From the poem by Thomas Miller, circa
   1830

St Paul and the Weather

In both the Roman and the Anglican churches, January 25 is celebrated as the feast day of St Paul, in honour of the apostle's conversion to Christianity. Throughout western Europe it was believed that the fortune of the coming year could be foretold on St Paul's day by the weather.

If St. Paul's day be fair and clear,
It does betide a happy year;
But if it chance to snow or rain,
Then will be dear all kind of grain'
If clouds or miste do dark the sky,
Great store of birds and beasts shall
   die;
And if the winds do flie aloft,
Then war shall vexe the kingdom oft.

Long Bows Unstrung

On this day in 1904 the English Parliament met to pass statutes and liveries in an effort to curb warfare among the more unruly of the upper classes. One of the statutes read in part: "It is enacted that no man shall shoot a long bow without the King's license, except he be a Lord."

A Youthful Bride

With the wedding of Princess Margaret to James IV, the father of the bride hoped to bring about the union of the two kingdoms. Margaret was described on her wedding day as beautiful, modest, educated, and graceful. She was thirteen years old.

Proverb

Under water dearth,
Under snow bread.

Births

J.B. Bernadotte (Swedish king) 1764; Douglas MacArthur (general) 1880; Paul Newman (actor) 1925.

Deaths

St Polycarp (bishop) 166; St Conon (Scottish saint) 648; Dr Edward Jenner (inventor of smallpox vaccine) 1823.

The Difficulty of Sainthood

At the age of 86, in Smyrna, St Polycarp was told to blaspheme Christ. He refused and was tied to the stake to be burnt. The flames formed a vault around him but did not burn him. A soldier was ordered to thrust his spear through the old man's side. So much blood gushed forth that the flames were quenched. But he did eventually die on this day in the year 166, thereby achieving sainthood.

St Conon and the Devil

St Conon, was for some years, bishop of the Southern Isles in Scotland. His name continued to be remembered with veneration in the Highlands for many years after his death in 648. One of his legacies is his retort to the great spiritual enemy of the Scots. "Claw for claw," as Conon said to Satan, "and the devil take the shortest nails."

Australian Day

This is Foundation Day in Australia to mark the landing on that continent of Captain Arthur Phillips in 1788 which began the settlement of the country. (In 1865 on this day, it was formally announced that England could no longer send convicts to Australia.)

British Blast

In the biggest ever blast to date, a charge was sunk in the base of the cliffs at Dover, and into this was placed the enormous quantity of 18,500 lbs of gun powder. The charge was fired by the voltaic battery, when not less than one million tons of chalk was dislodged by the shock, and settled gently down into the sea below (1843).

American Success

The Flying Fish was the first successful hydroplane. Its designer, Glen Curtiss, piloted the first flight at San Diego, California, on January 26, 1911.

A Keel Laid

On January 26, 1676 the keel was laid of *The Groffin,* the first vessel to be built in North American waters. The ship was built by the explorer La Salle near Niagara Falls.

French Lottery

The Grand Prize in the Paris Exhibition Lottery of 125,000 francs, was won by a poor currier named Aubriot, a native of Toul (1879).

Swiss Weather

The Lake of Zurich, for the first time in this century and the twenty-fourth time since 1233, was completely frozen over. Yesterday a kind of fair was held and half the population of the city were on the ice (1880).

27
JANUARY

Births

W.A. Mozart (composer) 1756; Lewis Carroll (*Alice In Wonderland*) 1832; Wilhelm II (kaiser) 1859; Jerome Kern (composer) 1885.

Deaths

St John Chrysostom (archbishop) 407; Robert Burton (author) 1039; John James Audubon (naturalist) 1851; Guiseppe Verdi (composer) 1901.

Proverbs

Lustful he was, at forty needs must wed,
Old January will have many in bed.

January commits the fault and May bears the blame.

A January spring is worth naething

If Janiveer's calends be summerly gay
'Twill be winterly weather 'til the calends of May

Golden Mouthed, 407

This is the feast day of St John Chrysostom who died on this day in 407, in the Eastern Orthodox church. In his own time he was called simply John of Constantinople, but was given the name Chrysostom (which means golden mouthed) by later writers on account of his eloquence.

Today's Number

According to numerologists, the number 27 is a good one. It is a promise of authority, power, and command. It indicates that reward will come from the productive intellect; that the creative faculties have sown good seeds that will reap a harvest. Persons with this "compound" number at their back should carry out their own ideas and plans. It is a fortunate number if it appears in any connection with future events.

A Precise Death, 1039

Robert Burton, author of *Anatomy of Melancholy*, died on or very near the time that he had predicted for himself from his horoscope. Because of his concern for exactness, it was rumoured among his students after his death that rather than admit to an error in his calculations, he had taken his own life to ensure his dying at the proper time.

A Guilty Witch, 1591

On January 27, 1591 the trial of Agnes Sampsoune was held in Nether Keythe, Scotland, for conspiring King James VI's death with witchcraft, scorcery, and incantations at a Halloween gathering. Agnes Sampsoune confessed that an accomplice Geillis Duncan played the song "Gyllatripes" on the Jew's harp at the great gathering on Halloween, while the others danced. Agnes was strangled and burnt at the stake on Castle Hill, Edinburgh.

Television Begins, 1926

The earliest public demonstration of television was given by John Logie Baird of Scotland, using a development of the mechanical scanning system suggested by Paul Nipkov in 1884.

An Apollo Tragedy, 1967

During a pre-flight simulation exercise of the Apollo mission to the moon, fire broke out in the sealed capsule. Astronauts Gus Grissom, Edward White, and Roger Chaffee were killed.

One Vietnamese War Ends, 1973

Formal peace accords were signed in Paris by North and South Vietnam, the United States, and the National Liberation Front.

28
JANUARY

Births

Henry Morton Stanley (finder of Livingstone) 1841; Arthur Rubenstein (pianist) 1887.

Today's Word

Most words in the English Language evolve over many centuries, but one of them began on this day in 1754. In 1722 a fairy tale called "The Travels and Adventures of Three Princes of Sarendip" was translated into English. In the story, the heroes from Sarendip—the old name for Ceylon (now Sri Lanka)—constantly made discoveries by accident. The English writer Horace Walpole was delighted with the tale. And in a letter, written on January 28, 1754 he coined the word serendipity to describe the princes' curious capability.

Proverb

Jack Frost in Janiveer
Nips the nose of the nascent year

Deaths

Charlemagne (French king) 814; Henry VIII (English king) 1547; Sir Francis Drake (navigator) 1596; Peter I (czar of Russia) 1725; Stella (muse) 1728.

Double Daisy

Today's flower is the *Bellis perennus plenis* or the double daisy. The daisy had both lucky and unlucky associations. To step on the first daisy of the year was a lucky omen; if however a child were to touch it, this was felt to be very unlucky. Should the plant be pulled up by the roots this meant that the growth of the children of the family would be severely stunted.

A Madman in the Streets

On January 28, 1807 London's Pall Mall became the first street in the world to be illuminated with gaslight. The idea of lighting the London streets with gas belonged to a German named Winser. At first Winser was considered a quack and an idiot—Sir Walter Scott wrote that there was a madman proposing to light London with—what do you think?—why, with smoke! But in a few years gaslight had spread to all the towns and cities of Europe.

Coffee Commotion

Housewives in America raged at the sky-high costs of Brazilian coffee—$1.35 a pound. The price increase marked the end of another era in the continuing saga of a restaurant cup of coffee—prices were raised to 15 cents per cup instead of the usual 10 cents (1954).

Epitaphs for the Deceased of this Day

Charlemagne, Charles the Great, king of the Franks, crowned by the pope as emperor of the West in the year 800 is remembered today in France on St Charlemagne's Day. At colleges and universities there is much speech-making in his honour at a champagne breakfast.

The oft-married Henry VIII, who died today having reigned for thirty-seven years and nine months, was succeeded on the throne by his son Edward VI, aged nine years.

Of Sir Francis Drake, who died on his ship off the coast of Panama, the historian Fuller remarked: "he lived by the sea, died on it and was buried in it."

When Peter I visited England with an entourage of twenty persons, they had the following breakfast at an inn in Godalming: half a sheep, a quarter of a lamb, ten pullets, twelve chickens, three quarts of brandy, six quarts of mulled wine, seven dozen eggs, with salad in proportion. At dinner on the same day they had: one sheep of 56 lbs, three-quarters of a lamb, a shoulder and loin of veal broiled, eight pullets, eight rabbits, two-and-a-half dozen bottles of sack, a dozen bottles of claret.

Stella was an Irish girl who inspired the author Jonathan Swift; he often refers to her in his letters and poems: "Never was any of her sex born with better gifts of the mind, or more improved than by reading and conversation. Her advice was always the best, and with the greatest freedom, mixed with the greatest decency. Never was so happy a conjunction of civility, freedom, easiness, and sincerity" (Swift).

29
JANUARY

Births

Emmanuel de Swedenborg (Swedish mystic) 1688; Thomas Paine (American writer) 1757; Frederick Delius (English composer) 1862.

French First

Alexis Maneyrol, a French aviator, established a world record for duration for a glider flight, at Vauville, France. The flight lasted eight hours and four minutes (1923).

Deaths

Aurelian (Roman emperor) 275; St Francis (French saint) 1662; Edward Lear (nonsense poet) 1888.

His Own Epitaph

He reads but he cannot speak
  Spanish,
He cannot abide ginger beer:
Ere the days of his pilgrimage vanish,
How pleasant to know Mr. Lear!
  Edward Lear

The First Victoria Cross

Queen Victoria announced the establishment of the order of the Victoria Cross as a reward for individual acts of bravery (1856).

America First

On January 29, 1795 a New Naturalisation Act in the U.S. extended residency requirements from two to five years and required the renouncing of allegiance to a former sovereign and any title of nobility.

The First Beggar's Opera

On January 29, 1728 there took place in London, at the Drury Lane Theatre, the first ever performance of John Gay's *Beggar's Opera,* which ever since has been a stock play in the traditional theatre. The idea of a play with malefactors among its characters arose in a remark by Jonathan Swift to the author: "What an odd sort of pretty thing a Newgate (prison) pastoral might make," said the author of *Gullivers Travels.* Gay set to work on the idea immediately, and was made rich by its success.

His Last Will and Testament

St Francis, the saint who watches over writers and journalists, was asked about his funeral affairs just before he died on this day in 1662 in Switzerland: "My body be given to the Theatre of Anatomy to be dissected; for it will be a comfort to me if I can be of any advantage, when dead, having been of none, whilst alive."

A Conflagration Conjured

One evening in 1759 the mystic de Swedenborg was at dinner with friends in Gottenburg. All at once he became agitated, left the party, then returned and announced that a huge, fast-spreading fire had broken out in Stockholm (about 300 miles distant). He said that the home of a good friend of his had already been destroyed and that his own was threatened. After about two hours of worry Swedenborg suddenly breathed a sigh of relief; the fire was out, he said, and his house was saved. The following Tuesday a royal messenger arrived from Stockholm with the melancholy news of the fire, and confirmed exactly the spiritualist's description of it.

The First Hall of Fame

The Baseball Hall of Fame was established on this day in 1936 in Cooperstown, New York. The first five players elected to it were Ty Cobb, Walter Johnson, Christy Mathewson, Honus Wagner, and Babe Ruth.

Births

Franklin D. Roosevelt (32nd U.S. president) 1882; Carol Channing (actress) 1923; Vanessa Redgrave (actress, activist) 1937.

Deaths

King Charles I, king of England (beheaded) 1649; Peter II, czar of Russia (of smallpox on his wedding day) 1730; Mahatma Gandhi, prime minister of India (assassinated) 1948.

The Beheading of Charles

On January 30, 1649, at a time of civil strife in England between forces loyal to the king and those loyal to Parliament, Charles I was beheaded by his foes upon a scaffold raised in front of the Banqueting House, Whitehall. Charles was as well known for his personal piety, especially in his latter days, as for his tyranny in office, and the justice of his execution was an item of controversy for many, many years after.

Loyalty to Charles

On January 30, 1649, after the execution of Charles I, Virginia announced its allegiance to his family, the House of Stuart. As a result, during that year 330 loyalists took refuge in Virginia.

The Revenge of Charles

Eighty-four years after his death, those still sentimentally loyal to Charles found considerable satisfaction in the malady that afflicted London during the last week of January. From January 23, 1733, which was the anniversary of the day on which Charles was sentenced, to the thirtieth, the anniversary of his death, almost no person in London escaped suffering from severe headache and fever. During that week more than 1,500 people died in London and Westminster. Loyalists took this plague as a sign of the guilt of Charles' executioners.

St Charles' Day

On this day each year the *Society of St Charles the Martyr* holds a memorial service at the scaffold site in the courtyard of the Royal United Services Museum in London.

Woman's Peerage Day

On January 30, 1958, a bill was passed in the House of Lords in London establishing lifetime peerages for men and women, the first time in six-and-a-half centuries that women were admitted in the House of Lords.

A Dark Day

Adolph Hitler was appointed chancellor of Germany by President von Hindenberg (1933).

An Historic Day

In the United States the first jazz record was cut on this day in 1917, and the *William Tell* overture on wireless sets across the nation heralded the first broadcast of "The Lone Ranger" in 1933.

An Escape Day

Sir Lewis Dyves, on trial in London, escaped from Whitehall by leaping down a "loo" into the Thames, then making his way to safety in Scotland disguised as a woman (1790).

A Celebration Against Charles

As late as 1735 young, noble opponents of Charles I gathered on this day in a meeting of The Calve's-Head Club to symbolically express their satisfaction with his execution. One of the company, representing the executioner, was masked. After numerous toasts drunk to the pious memory of Oliver Cromwell, and damning to the race of the Stuarts, a calf's head, representing the unfortunate Charles, was tossed into a roaring bonfire.

31
JANUARY

Births

Ben Jonson (dramatist) 1574; Franz Schubert (composer) 1797; Anna Pavlova (ballerina) 1885; Tallulah Bankhead (actress) 1903.

Deaths

The inhabitants of Glencoe, Scotland (massacred) 1692; 250 people in Amsterdam (drowned in canals because of thick fog) 1790.

Dicing for Maid's Money

In this custom perpetuated in Guildford, England, two maidservants are required to cast lots for the interest from a trust. The practice stems from a will left by John How who died in 1674. He left instructions for two maidservants to toss dice for the interest on £400, which he had banked for that purpose.

Botched Bonfires

In 1803-4 Britain was under threat of invasion from France, and national spirit was pitched high. On the evening of January 31, 1804, an alarm beacon at Hume Castle in Berwickshire was accidently lit. In response many other beacons were lit, and by morning all the volunteers of the southern Scottish counties were in arms and ready to fight. Later, to save face, it was decided that the false alarm served as an indication of Scottish loyalty and of Britain's defensive readiness.

The First Train Hijacking

A group of tramps, riding the rails in Ohio on an Erie-Western Railroad freight, seized the train from its crew. Their possession was short-lived and after the smoke had cleared, six of the hijackers were captured, seven escaped, and one brakeman was injured (1892).

The First Glider/Dirigible Drop

At an altitude of 3,000 feet, Lt Commander Herbert Wiley in Command of the dirigible *Los Angeles,* cast loose a glider piloted by Lt Ralph Barnaby in a U.S. Navy aerial manoeuvre (1930).

The First Elective Franchise Act

This act provided that there should be no denial of elective franchise to any United States citizen on account of race, colour, or previous condition of servitude (1867).

First Minstrel Show

The Virginia Minstrels led by Daniel Emmet played a benefit performance at the Chatham Theatre in New York City. They wore white trousers, striped calico shirts, long blue calico swallow-tail coats, and sang songs like "Happy Uncle Tom" accompanying themselves on violin, banjo, tambourine, and bones (1843).

EBRUARY

Then came old February, sitting
In an old wagon, for he could not ride,
Drawn of two fishes for the season fitting,
Which through the flood before did softly slide
And swim away; yet had he by his side
His plough and harness fit to till the ground,
And tools to prune the trees, before the pride
Of hasting pride did make them burgeon wide.
  Edmund Spenser

FEBRUARY

History

February was one of the two months (January being the other) introduced into the Roman calendar by Numa Pompilius, when he extended the year to twelve periods. Its name arose from the practice of religious expiation and purification that took place among the Romans at the beginning of this month (*Februare,* to expiate, to purify). It has been on the whole an ill-used month, perhaps in consequence of its noted want (in the northern hemisphere) of what is pleasant and agreeable to the human senses. Numa let fall upon it the doom — unavoidable for some one of the months—of having (three out of four times) a day less than even those months that were to consist of thirty days. Thus, he arranged that it should have only twenty-nine days, excepting in leap years when, by the intercalation of a day between the 23rd and 24th, it was to have thirty. No great occasion here for complaint. But when Augustus chose to add a thirty-first day to August (that the month named for him might not lack in the dignity enjoyed by six other months of the year), he took it from February, which could least spare it, thus reducing the month to twenty-eight days in all ordinary years. In our own arrangement of the calendar, it being necessary to drop a day out of each century except those of which the ordinal number could be divided by four, it again fell to the lot of February to be the sufferer. It was deprived of its 29th day for all such years, and so it befell in the years 1800 and 1900, and will in 2100, 2200, etc.

Birthstone

The February birthstone is the amethyst, which once denoted sincerity and had the power of preventing drunkenness in those who wore it.

Health

Of cold beware with Venison and Fish,
Do not in any case maintain thy Dish,
'Tis very good to Purge, to Bath and Bleed,
If learned Physician's say thy standit in need.
  Fly Almanac, February, 1679

1
FEBRUARY

Births

Madam Clara Butts (prima donna) 1873; Louis St Laurent (Canadian prime minister) 1882; Clark Gable (actor) 1901.

Deaths

St Ignatius (martyr) 107; St Brigid (patronness of Ireland) 523; Mary Shelley (author of *Frankenstein*)1851.

A Dismembered Saint

St Ignatius was submitted to martyrdom in the reign of Trajan for declaring that he carried the crucified Christ about him. He was dismembered on this day in 107 by wild beasts in the amphitheatre in Rome.

A Reappearing Saint

Though she is the patronness of Ireland, St Bride or St Brigid chose Scotland to visit annually. In Glenelg, near Scalasiag farm, a mound can be found that is linked to serpent cults. The Celtic goddess Bride was known as the "serpent queen" because snakes were her sacred animal and on this, her saint's day, she is said to emerge from the mound.

A Collapse

On this day in 1694 the Tower of Limerick in Ireland fell suddenly, in which were 218 barrels of powder, which by striking on the stones, took fire and blew up. The explosion greatly shattered the town, killing about 100 persons.

An Erection

In West Orange, New Jersey, Thomas A. Edison finished erecting the world's first moving-picture studio at a total cost of $637.37 (1893).

Ralph the Rover Sunk

The beacon on the lighthouse on Bell Rock was first lit on this day in 1811. This ocean hazard, located twenty-four miles east of Dundee, Scotland, was formerly known as Inch Cape Rock, or Scape Rock on the oldest charts. It became Bell Rock when an abbot of Aberbrothock, as a warning to mariners, erected a wave-rocked bell on its surface. A notorious pirate by the name of "Ralph the Rover" cut the bell from its framework just to plague the abbot. He received his just reward when his ship was wrecked on the spot shortly after.

February Firsts

1327: Edward III was crowned king of England at the age of fifteen.

1682: East Jersey was sold to William Penn and associates.

1790: The Supreme Court of the United States met for the first time.

1793: France declared war against England and Holland.

1893: Two men from St Louis crossed the Colorado Desert on bicycles.

1917: Germany began unrestricted submarine warfare.

1957: The first turbo-prop airliner entered scheduled service in Britain.

1958: Egypt merged with Syria to form the United Arab Republic.

1958: The European Nuclear Energy Agency was formed.

Eavesdropping

The king of the Belgians, from his palace at Brussels, carried on a long conversation by telephone with M. Grevy at the Elysée in Paris and in the evening, the queen of the Belgians listened by telephone to an entire act of Gounod's *Faust,* performed at the Paris Opera (1887).

Freedom Gained

National Freedom Day is celebrated in the United States every February 1 to mark the 1865 signing of the thirteenth amendment to the Constitution, which abolished slavery. Presidential proclamation in 1949 established that the day would be observed in perpetuity.

2
FEBRUARY

Births

Christopher Marlowe (poet) 1564; Geoffery O'Hara (composer of "K-K-K-Katy") 1882; James Joyce (author) 1882.

Deaths

Giovanni Palestrina (composer) 1594; Buddy Holly (singer) 1959; Boris Karloff (actor) 1969; Bertrand Russell (philosopher) 1970.

Groundhog Day

Depending on the part of the world, the animal involved might be a badger, hedgehog, bear, or groundhog. The theory is that if the creature comes out of its winter quarters on this day and sees its shadow there will be six more weeks of winter, but if the day is cloudy it will return to the den for a short sleep, as the winter weather will soon give way to balmy spring.

Chasing Crows

It was at Candlemas that the lasses of olden times chased the crows. In the grey dawn of the morning a maid would steal forth and with fluttering heart give chase to the first crow she chanced to see and watch with anxiety the direction in which it flew, for there dwelt her husband to come. But should the crow go by way of the churchyard, it meant the unfortunate miss would die an old maid.

Cleopatra's Needle

Cleopatra's Needle was brought up the Thames River from the East India Docks and moved opposite the houses of Parliament near the Lambeth shore. Crowds assembled on the banks of the river and cheered the vessel as it passed, while salutes were fired from Nelson Dock and the Continental Wharf. The Needle's journey from Egypt had cost £15,000 and the lives of six seamen (1888).

Vassar's Will

The prosperous brewer Mathew Vassar left money in his will to be used to found a college for women in New York State (1861).

Today's Weather

If Candlemas Day be fair and bright,
Winter will have another flight;
But if it be dark with clouds and rain,
Winter is gone, and will not come again.

Today's Flower

Already now the Snowdrop dares appear,
The first pale blossom of the unripened year,
As Flora's breath by some transforming year;
Had changed an icicle into a flower,
Its name and hue the scentless plant retains,
And winter lingers in its icy veins.

The snowdrop (*Galanthus nivalis*) is a symbol of hope or consolation. It was said to have been transformed by an angel from a snowflake to give some solace to Adam and Eve following their expulsion from the Garden of Eden.

Stabbing Enemies

Lazare Carnot, organiser of the French revolutionary armies, issued his Order of the Day for February 2, 1794: "always to manoeuvre in a body and on the attack; to maintain strict but not pettifogging discipline, to keep the troops constantly at the ready; to employ the utmost vigilance on sentry go; to use the bayonet on every possible occasion; and to follow up the enemy remorselessly until he is utterly destroyed."

Candlemas Day

Candlemas is a very ancient Christian festival held in celebration of the purification of the Virgin Mary (Luke, 2:22) and of the presentation of the baby Jesus to the Lord in the temple at Jerusalem, all according to the Mosaic law (Leviticus, 12:6,7). It is called Candlemas because before mass is said on this day, the church blesses the candles for the whole year, and makes a procession with hallowed or blessed candles in the hands of the faithful. The candle bearing is understood to refer to the words of Simeon, pronounced in the temple, when he took the infant Jesus in his arms and declared him "a light to lighten the gentiles" (Luke, 2:32).

American Elephant Buying

For the entertainment of each "sucker born every minute," the renowned circus empressario, P.T. Barnum, bought his world-famous elephant Jumbo (1882).

Births

Felix Mendelssohn (composer) 1809; Gertrude Stein (author) 1874; Charles Lindberg (aviator) 1902.

Deaths

St Blaize (martyr) 316; Johann Gutenberg (printer) 1468; Richard Nash (Beau Nash) 1762; Woodrow Wilson (28th U.S. president) 1924.

A Stubborn Refusal

On February 3, 1893, Mrs Abigail Ashbrook of Willingboro, New Jersey, refused to pay taxes because she was not allowed to vote.

British Theatrical Crushing

Sixteen persons were crushed to death in attempting to obtain admission into the Little Theatre in the Haymarket in which the Drury Lane Company was performing (1794).

Japanese Bean Throwing

To mark the last day of winter by the lunar calendar, the custom of Setsubun as a sign of good fortune has been observed for centuries in Japan. It stems from an old legend wherein brave warriors threw soy beans into the eyes of wicked demons to drive them away. Nowadays the demon is winter and some Japanese spend this day joyfully throwing beans at each other.

A Throat Clearing

St Blaize, Bishop of Sebaste, executed today in 316, was famed, among other things, for his miraculous ability to cure a sore throat with prayer, and for having, again with prayer, cured a boy who had a fish-bone lodged in his throat. Aetius, an ancient Greek physician, gives the following recipe for a stoppage in the throat: "Hold the diseased party by the throat and pronounce these words: Blaize, the martyr and servant of Jesus Christ, commands thee to pass up or down!"

Irish Police Beating

An inspector of police named Martin was beaten to death in Donegal by an excited crowd which resented his attempt to arrest Father McFadden between the chapel and his residence. The head of the murdered man was literally beaten in; a number of arrests were made and the priest surrendered himself and was taken to goal. The Grand Jury awarded the widow of the inspector £4,000 as compensation for the loss of her husband (1809).

A Gambling Lesson

Richard "Beau" Nash, though justifiably famed as an adroit gambler, did not think highly of his own pursuit, and went to great lengths to dissuade a wealthy young earl from following his example. He engaged his lordship one evening to a serious amount; and having first won all his ready money, then the title-deeds of his estates, and finally the very watch in his pocket and the rings on his fingers, Nash read him a lecture on the flagrant impropiety of trying to make money by gambling, when poverty could only be pleaded in justification of such conduct. He then returned all his winnings, at the same time exacting from the earl a promise that he would never play again.

A Messy February Thaw

Muttering, the winds at eve, with blunted point
Blow hollow blusreing from the south. Subdued
   the frost resolces into a trickling thaw.
Spotted the mountains shine, loose sleet descends
   and floods the country round. The rivers swell
Of bonds impatient. Sudden from the hills
   O'er rocks and woods, in broad brown cataracts
   A thousand snow fed torrents rush at once
and where they rush, the wide resounding plain
is left one slimy waste.
   Anonymous, 18th century

Births

George Lillo (obscure dramatist) 1693; Tadeus Kosiusko (obscure politician) 1746; Harrison Ainsworth (forgotten author) 1805.

Deaths

Lucius Septimus Severus (little-known emperor) 211; Giambattista Porta (inventor of the camera obscura) 1615

Cloudy Politics, 1508

On February 4, 1508, the Proclamation of Trent was issued by Maximilian I, who assumed the title of emperor without being crowned. Pope Julius II subsequently confirmed the title and the German king became head of the Holy Roman Empire. The City of Venice refused to give Maximilian free passage to Rome, for which he attacked the city. (Venice was secretly being aided by Louis XII of France.)

700,000 Spider Webs, 1877

The empress of Brazil presented Queen Elizabeth with a dress the like of which had never been seen. It was woven of spider webs, quite unparalleled, a work of art as regards quality and beauty. In 1710 it had been discovered that to make a piece of silk for a dress would require the webs of 700,000 spiders. (Spaniards had already tried to use spider's threads to make gloves and stockings but they were so troublesome and yielded so little profit that in spite of the fabulous prices paid, they were obliged to abandon trade.)

In a Royal Bedroom, 1685

"Charles II took delight to have a number of little spaniels follow him, and lie in his bedchamber, where often times he suffered the bitches to puppy and give suck, which rendered it very offensive."
 A diary entry of John Evelyn, February 4, 1685

A Snow-Drift Survivor, 1799

On a snowy, windy 4th of February 1799, Elizabeth Woodcock, of Impington, aged forty-two, while travelling home from Cambridge early in the evening, lost control of her horse, Tinker, when he was startled. She lost a shoe and exhausted herself in trying to keep the beast from stumbling into a snow-covered ditch, and, unable to go on, she sat down on the ground and let go the bridle. By eight that evening, which she could tell from the ringing of nearby churchbells, Elizabeth was buried under six feet of drifted snow. She managed to shove a thin branch through the snow above her with a handkerchief tied to it. It was eight days before the handkerchief was noticed. She had survived on snow and a single pinch of snuff, but her toes had to be amputated.

Beautification of Canal Street, 1930

Work was completed on this day on Canal Street in New Orleans, which was paved in the fashion of the old-world mosaics.

Lesser Known Events

1667: The first Ball in Canada was given by Chartier de Lotbiniere in Québec.

1716: The Old Pretender, James Francis Edward Stuart (son of the British King James II) and his officers left Montrase for France.

1757: Clive of India (Sir Robert Clive) drove the Nabob of Bengal from India.

1877: Two large amphorae containing 500 pounds of old Roman coins were found in Verona.

1890: The Providence Ladies Cycling Club was organised at Rhode Island.

1889: An order of the British lord chamberlain authorised, under certain circumstances, high-necked dresses in the queen's drawing rooms.

1924: French air forces made the first ever flight to the remote desert city of Timbuktu in the Sahara.

1952: The United Nations Disarmament Committee held its first meeting on this day.

Births

Sir Robert Peel (English Bobbies) 1788; Adlai Stevenson (politician) 1900; Belle Starr (horse thief) 1919.

Deaths

Ste Agatha (virgin martyr) 251; 123 British Soldiers (in the Black Hole of Calcutta) 1757.

The Peaceful End of Agatha

Ste Agatha was a beautiful young woman who spurned the advances of Quintianus. He accused her of being a Christian and ordered the torturers to cut off her breasts and flog her. During the night two angels came and revived her to wholeness. Quintianus was much angered and ordered her to be beaten by rods and then burned. An earthquake interrupted the beating and Quintianus stopped the punishment. Agatha died peacefully the next day—February 5, 251 A.D.

The Beginning of Bobbies

Born on February 5, 1788, was Robert Peel, British M.P. and reformer whose concern with public safety and criminal reforms led him to establish the first police force in London. The British Police came to be known as "Bobbies" after him.

The Fortunes of America

1631:   The ship Lyon arrived from Bristol with provisions to end the long famine of the Massachusetts Bay Company.

Royal Excesses

In his diary John Evelyn recorded an evening spent in the palace with King Charles II, destined to die tomorrow: "the inexpressible luxury and profaneness, gaming and all dissolutness, and total forgetfulness of God . . . the king sitting and toying with his concubines Portsmouth, Cleveland, Mazarine & Co., a French boy singing love-songs in that glorious gallery, whilst about twenty of the great courtiers were gaming around a large table, a bank of at least £2,000 in gold; upon which two gentlemen who were with me made strange reflections."

Primula acaulis

Today's flower, dedicated to the unfortunate Ste Agatha, is commonly known as the primrose, which has a faint but characteristic fragrance. It flowers from December to May, depending on the weather.

Primrose Properties

The leaves of the primrose were sometimes made into a soporific wine and in the Alps they were used as a cough medicine. If a primrose was seen blooming in the winter, or if a single primrose was brought into the house, it augured death. If less than thirteen primroses were founded in the first posy of spring, that number would predict the number of chicks each hen would lay in the year.

Sent to Siberia

The Russian explorers, Vitus Bering, Martin Spanberg, and Alexei Chirikov today left St Petersburg. They proceeded across Siberia to Okhotsk, reached Kamchatka by boat in July, and crossed the peninsula in sledges during the winter to the Bering Sea (1725).

Widespread Disasters

Ancient almanacs refer to this day as one of dire calamity in which certain Greek ladies called "The Furies" make their rounds. The Furies were at work in several locations on February 5:

Nearly 3,000 inhabitants of Scylla in Italy, ran to the beach to escape the falling houses caused by a severe earthquake. A tidal wave swept them into eternity (1783).

A false alarm of fire in the Opera House at Cincinnati, Ohio caused a panic among the audience. In the ensuing stampede eleven persons were trampled and thirty injured (1876).

The twenty-first person to do so, leapt over the rails of the Clifton Suspension Bridge in Bristol, England. He landed in the rock-strewn gorge 300 feet below (1886).

6
FEBRUARY

Births

Anne (English queen) 1665; Christian Heinecker (precocious child) 1721.

Deaths

St Dorothy (virgin martyr) 304; Clements (Catholic pope) 740; Charles II (English king) 1685.

America and France Versus England

The French nation recognised the independence of the thirteen American States by signing a treaty of defensive alliance with the colonies. The English ambassador was immediately withdrawn from Paris and acts of war commenced.

A Royal Birth

Queen Anne is dead is often said
With tones of varying scorn
But how few carry in their head
The date that she was born.

Police Brutality

On February 6, 1629, a complaint was made to the Scottish Privy Council by John Trinche about the assault of jailers who had confined his mother, the late Marion Hardie, in the pit of Eyemouth. In the complaint he said the jailers tied his mother's arms and so threw her about that both arms were mutilated and disjointed; they tied her waist so tight she dropped to the floor where they kicked her, drove a spear through her left foot causing great loss of blood. She died from this maltreatment before standing trial.

A Royal Crowning

Queen Elizabeth II was crowned in London on this day in 1952. This event is marked annually by a royal salute fired by the Troops of the Royal Horse Artillery.

A Precocious Child

Christian Heinecker was born in Lubeck, Germany, February 6, 1721. At the age of ten months he could speak and repeat every word which was said to him; when twelve months old, he knew by heart the principal events narrated in the Pentateuch; in his second he learned the greater part of the history of the Bible, both of the Old and New Testaments; in his third year he could reply to most questions on universal history and geography, and in the same year he learned to speak Latin and French; in his fourth year he employed himself in the study of religion and the history of the church, and he was able not only to repeat what he read, but also to reason upon it, and express his own judgment. When the king of Denmark wished to see this wonderful child he was taken to Copenhagen, examined before the court, and proclaimed to be a wonder. On his return home he learned to write. But shortly after he fell ill, and died on the 27th of June 1725, without, it is said, showing very much uneasiness at all at his coming death.

A Royal Death

On this day in 1685 as Charles II lay on his deathbed he asked his attendants to pull aside the curtains that he might, for a final time, look upon the day. He apologised to those who stood round him all night. He had been, he said, a most unconscionable time dying, but he hoped they would excuse it. His last words addressed to his brother James: "Let not poor Nelly starve," referring to his actress-mistress Nell Gwyn. She was said to have been born in an alley near Drury Lane, and her ghost now wanders through the Gargoyle Club leaving a strong aroma of gardenias wherever she goes.

Births

Thomas More (statesman) 1478; Charles Dickens (author) 1812; James Murray (lexographer) 1837; Sinclair Lewis (novelist) 1885.

Deaths

Romuald (saint) 1037; Abraham Le Grove (murderer) 1690; Aaran Hill (poet) 1750; Anne Radcliffe (novelist) 1823.

Shocked, Humiliated, Scandalised

St Romuald had been (at his father's orders) present at a duel in which his father killed his adversary. He retired shocked and humiliated to the Benedictine monastery of Classis, to do penance for the crime of being accessory to murder. He was soon so scandalised by the licentious lives led by his brethren that he gave up the world and retired to a desert where he passed away on this day in 1037.

Horrid Murder, 1698

Abraham Le Grove, was executed and hanged in irons below Rings End in London for a horrid murder he committed on a Dutch skipper, whose body he cut into pieces and cast into the river. Most of the pieces were found.

Gothic Madness

Anne Radcliffe, who died on this day in 1823, was the originator of the Gothic Romance. Of her works *The Romance of the Forest, Mysteries of Udolpho,* and *The Italian,* Sir Walter Scott said: "The scenes were inartificially connected, and the characters hastily sketched, without any attempt at individual distinction; being cast in the mould of ardent lovers, tyrannical parents, with domestic ruffians, guards and others, who had wept or stormed through the chapters of romance, without much alteration in their family habits or features." In spite of Scott's criticism, the public loved her work, but perhaps because of it, she suddenly stopped writing and disappeared from public view. Another theory to explain her silence was that as a consequence of brooding over the terrors that she had depicted, Mrs Radcliff's reason had been overturned and she was the melancholy inmate of a private madhouse.

Daring Escape, 1778

On February 7, 1778, Daniel Boone and about thirty other men engaged in making salt at Blue Licks, Kentucky, were captured by the Indians and all except Boone were delivered to the English commander in York. Boone was taken to Chilicote where he made a daring escape and walked 160 miles through the forest to freedom.

Screaming Teenagers, 1964

More than 3,000 screaming American Beatle fans thronged to New York's Kennedy Airport to await the arrival of their British rock and roll idols. Hundreds of police were needed to protect the four boys from Liverpool from the assembled multitude.

Advice on Handling Rogues

Tender-handed stroke a nettle;
And it stings you for your pains;
Grasp it like a man of mettle,
And it soft as silk remains.

'Tis the same with common natures,
Use them kindly, they rebel;
But be rough as nutmeg-graters,
And the rogues obey your will.
    Aaran Hill, who died on this day in 1750

Wanton Destruction, 1845

On February 7, 1845, Mr William Lloyd walked into the British Museum and wantonly dashed to pieces the famous Portland Vase, which had been dug up in Rome over 300 years earlier. For his vandalism Lloyd was sentenced merely to pay a fine, which was paid anonymously by another gentleman. The 2,000 pieces of the shattered vase were expertly reassembled by a Mr Doubleday, who did such an excellent job that the fractures were not noticeable.

8
FEBRUARY

Births

Dame Edith Evans (actress) 1888; Lana Turner (actress) 1920; James Dean (actor) 1931.

Deaths

Mary, queen of Scots (beheaded) 1587; Paulus Herstorter of Austria (aged 189) 1690; Lord Mayo (assassinated) 1870.

A Queen Beheaded

On this day at Fotheringay Castle in Northamptonshire, after almost nineteen years of cruel captivity in England, Mary, queen of Scots, charged with plotting the murder of her cousin, Queen Elizabeth of England was beheaded (1587).

A Queen Assaulted

At about half past five as Her Majesty, Queen Victoria was entering Buckingham Palace, a lad suddenly presented himself at the side of the carriage holding a paper in one hand and a pistol in the other. He apparently mistook Lady Churchill for the queen and tried to attract her attention. A personal attendant caught him and took him into police custody. The paper in his hand was found to be a petition written on parchment paper for the release of Fenian prisoners (1872).

A President Dazzled

On seeing the premiere performance of the film *Birth of a Nation* by D.W. Griffith, President Woodrow Wilson was dazzled and overwhelmed. Of the romanticized three-hour epic about the American south during reconstruction, the Virginia-born president was moved to say: "It is like history written in lightning, and all too true" (1915).

A Girl's Speechlessness

Considerable curiosity was excited at a village near Leigh in England when a fasting girl, who had not spoken for about four-and-one-half years, suddenly recovered her powers of speech. Ellen Smith, then eleven years old was taken ill and confined to bed where she ceased taking food and in a few months gradually lost her voice. From then on she had remained speechless partaking of no solid foods and only occasionally having her lips moistened with wine or brandy. Throughout these years her breathing was all but imperceptible although on regaining her speech she claimed never to have lost consciousness of what went on around her (1876).

A Bridge's Timeliness

For nearly 100 years, an old wooden bridge had spanned the Kangaroo Valley in New South Wales, Australia. Six days ago it had been replaced by a modern suspension bridge. On this day a mighty flood washed away the old wooden bridge (1898).

A Poet's Ponderousness

"As often as fever and ague attend the best contributions from the worst air, so does that malignant air of calumny soonest attack the sound and elevated in mind, as storms of wind the tallest and most fruitful trees; whilst the low and weak for bowing and moving to and fro are secured from the violence of the tempest."

  William Wycherly, in a letter to a fellow poet, Alexander Pope (1707)

The Queen Speaks

Queen Elizabeth II announced that henceforth all of her descendants, excepting those enjoying the title "Royal Highness" were to bear the name of Mountbatten-Windsor (1960).

The Earth Trembles

Considerable commotion was caused and shock experienced from an English earthquake. The tremors, which made church bells ring, dogs howl, and fish jump out of water, caused "earthquake gowns" to be created. These warm garments, to wear while sitting out of doors at night while waiting for the threat of earthquakes, became very popular among English women (1750).

Births

Daniel Bernoulli (mathematician) 1700; William Henry Harrison (9th U.S. president) 1773; Gypsy Rose Lee (stripper) 1914.

Deaths

St Apollonia (tooth martyr) 249; Daumier (French caricaturist) 1879; Adolphe Sax (instrument maker) 1894.

For Comet Watchers

The next visit by Halley's Comet will take place on this day in 1986.

Pancake Day

Shrove Tuesday or Pancake Day, a moveable feast to mark the last day before Lent, often occurs on this day. Originally it was a day for the confession of sins and seeking forgiveness for them but the baking and consuming of pancakes came to be the day's principal event. A medieval historian wrote: "It is customary to present the first pancake to the greatest slut or lie-a-bed in the party, which commonly falls to the dog's share at last, for no-one will own it their due."

Our Lady of the Toothache

During a persecution of Christians in Alexandria, St Apollonia was seized, and all her teeth were beaten out and threats made that she would be cast into the fire if she did not utter certain impious words; whereupon, of her own accord, she leaped into the flames on this day in 249 A.D. Because of this Apollonia has become the patron saint of persons afflicted with toothache and those who would treat them — dentists.

Today's Burnings

Others to meet the same fate as St Apollinia on this day were Mr Sawtre, a Collard heretic in 1401 and Bishop Hooper in 1555, both of whom were burnt at the stake in England for their unpopular religious views. Places as well as people succumbed to flames today, including Schenectady, New York, which was put to torch by the French and Indians in 1690.

The Price of Admission

Each of the separate states in America were asked to provide 35,211 men by drafts or otherwise before April, and to bring the continental treasury $1,250,000 every month to April in 1781 (1780).

The Price of Vagabonding

The English Parliament passed an act to establish workhouses for the poor and to punish vagabonds (1590).

Rabble Catering

On February 9, 1898, a copy of a letter written by the Spanish minister to the U.S., Dupuy de Lome, in which he referred to President McKinley as "weak and catering to the rabble" was published in the newspapers. The ensuing hullabaloo caused the minister to cable his resignation to Spain.

Hats Off to a Math Man

Daniel was the most celebrated of eight Bernoullis who are eminent in the history of mathematics. He spent the greatest part of his life in Basle, Switzerland, where he was held in such esteem that it was part of the education of every child to learn to take off the hat to him.

Churchill to Roosevelt

"We shall not fail or falter; we shall not weaken or tire. Neither the sudden shock of battle nor the long-drawn trials of vigilance and exertion will wear us down. Give us the tools and we will finish the job."

A radio broadcast by Winston Churchill in 1941, addressed specifically to President Roosevelt

A Crime Against Nature

"In these vernal seasons of the year when the air is calm and pleasant, it were an injury and sullenness against nature, not to go out and see her riches, and partake in her rejoicing with heaven and earth".

The advice in the *Fly Almanac* for this day in 1679

The Devil on the Loose

The morning of February 9, 1855, after a night of snow and frost, brought to light a strange sight for people in the coastal towns of Cornwall in England. A trail, running almost 100 miles, of single-track, cloven hooves wandered around the countryside. It was said to be the trail of the Devil himself. It walked over roofs, through walls, over gates and haystacks, under a gooseberry bush and even through a six-inch pipe. It made an impression of frozen ice as though a hot iron had been used—or fiery hooves.

10
FEBRUARY

Births

Charles Lamb (essayist) 1775; Boris Pasternek (*Dr. Zhivago*) 1890; Harold MacMillan (British statesman) 1897.

Today's Weddings

Queen Victoria of England to Albert of Saxe-Coburg-Gotha in 1840; P.T. Barnum's General Tom Thumb (two feet, five inches high) to Mercy Lavinia Warren Bump (of similar size) in 1863.

Today's Riot, 1354

On the St Scholastica's Day in 1354 a dire conflict took place between the students of the University of Oxford and the citizens of the town. The townspeople called to their aid the country folk from round about and, thus reinforced, overpowered the scholars and killed or wounded several of their number. As a consequence the citizens were debarred the rights and consolations of the church: their privileges were greatly narrowed; and they were heavily fined by way of an annual penance forever which decreed that, on each anniversary of St Scholastica, the mayor and sixty-two citizens attend at St Mary's Church, where the Litany should be read at the altar, and an oblation of one penny be made by each man.

Deaths

St Scholastica (virgin martyr) 543; Isaac Vossius (hair-fetishist) 1689; John Goode (lunatic) 1883.

Today's Sacking, 1676

Lancaster, Massachusetts was sacked, burned, and pillaged by Indians who killed all the men and took all the women and children as captives, including Mrs Joseph Rawlandson, wife of the minister, who was later ransomed for £20 (1676).

Today's State, 1665

Governor Berkely and Carteret signed the "Concessions and Agreements" of the lords proprietors of New Jersey—the first constitution of the colony, which also made Carteret governor (1665).

Today's Firsts

Philadelphia was first lighted by gas (1835).
Singing Telegrams were introduced by the New York Postal Telegraph Company (1933).

A Plea on This Day, 1776

"Without men, without arms, without ammunition, there is little to be done."
> George Washington writing at Charlestown (1776)

Today's Comet, 1680

On February 10, 1680 the Great Comet disappeared from view. It had terrorized New England settlers while permitting Isaac Newton to ascertain the parbolic form of the trajectory of the comet.

Today's Hair Fetishist, 1689

Isaac Vossius, an eccentric Dutch scholar, died on this day in 1689. He took an odd delight in having his hair combed in a rhythmical manner and wrote about it: "Many people take delight in the rubbing of their limbs and the combing of their hair; but these exercises would delight much more, if the servants of the baths, and of the bathers, were so skilful in this art, that they would express any measure with their fingers. I have fallen into the hands of men of this sort, who could initiate any measure of songs in combing the hair . . . from whence there arose in me no small delight."

Today's Lunatic, 1883

John Goode, formerly a captain in the 10th Royal Hussars, grievously afflicted with the notion of being the soverign power in Britain, died today in 1883, at the Broadmoor Lunatic Asylum.

11
FEBRUARY

Births

Princess Elizabeth (queen of Henry VII) 1466; Lydia Child (American novelist) 1802; Thomas Edison (American inventor) 1847.

Deaths

Caedom (first English poet) 680; Elizabeth (queen of Henry VII) 1554; René Descartes (French philosopher) 1650.

National Inventor's Day

Held on the anniversary of the birth of Thomas Edison, who took out over 1,000 patents—among them the incadescent lamp and the phonograph—this day features programs and displays by inventors all over North America.

White-Shirt Day

To pay tribute to the end of 1937 sit-down strikes at plants in Flint, Michigan, blue-collar workers traditionally wear white shirts as a symbol of the dignity of labour.

Wigs and Wooden Legs

By 1765 gentlemen in England were wearing their own hair in society rather than wigs. This drastic change in style was a source of tremendous distress to the peruquiers (wig-makers) of London, and on February 11 they petitioned King George III to provide them with relief by patronising their products. The king replied, though graciously, in the negative. The public was quick to see the ludicrous side of the petition, and some wag hurried into print a fictitious petition from the town's body carpenters asking His Majesty and all his servants to please be seen in public wearing wooden legs.

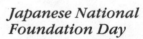

Japanese National Foundation Day

The founding of the nation of Japan by the emperor in 660 B.C. is commemorated in a day of celebration in that country.

The Garsparilla Carnival

Since 1904 this day in Tampa, Florida, has been set aside as a festival to recreate the times when pirates such as Garsparilla and his buccaneers ruled the high seas.

Today's Fortunes

Persons born on this day, particularly in their twentieth, twenty-fifth, twenty-ninth, forty-third, forty-seventh, fifty-second, and sixty-fifth years, must take care to guard against ill health. This can be done by eating the principal herbs accorded them by numerologists: lettuce, cabbage, turnips, cucumbers, melons, chicory, rapeseed, colevort, moonwort, linseed, water plantain, and ash of willow.

The Feast of our Lady's Miraculous Apparitions

This event is held at the grotto of Lourdes in France where Bernadette Soubirious claimed to see visions of the Virgin Mary. After years of skepticism, when she suffered several examinations and abuse, she became St Bernadette in 1933.

Other Apparitions

On this day in 1753, Sir Francis Drake climbed a high tree on top of a hill to become the first white man to see the Pacific Ocean. In 1914 a French pilot flew over Mont Blanc in the Alps, to a height of 16,000 feet, from where he could see much of Europe.

12
FEBRUARY

Births

Abraham Lincoln (16th U.S. president) 1809; Charles Darwin (British naturalist) 1809; John L. Lewis (U.S. labour leader) 1880.

The Creek Tribe's Objections

A treaty with the Creek Indians was signed by their chief on this day in 1825. It provided that the Creek cede all their territory in Georgia and Alabama in return for a tract of land between the Arkansas and Canadian Rivers. The Indians rejected the treaty, killed MacIntosh, their chief who signed it, and sent delegates to Washington to protest it.

Thomas Flyer's Chequered Flag

The New York to Paris Automobile Race was flagged off on February 12, 1908. Six entrants, three from France, one each from Germany, Italy, and America travelled a route through Alaska, Siberia, and Russia; 12,116 miles later, the American Thomas Flyer drove across the finish line in Paris in first place.

Deaths

Catherine Howard (5th wife of Henry VIII, beheaded) 1542; Lady Jane Grey (hanged) 1554; Ethan Allen (American patriot) 1799; Lily Langtry (mistress of King Edward VIII) 1929.

George Gershwin's "Rhapsody in Blue"

Today in 1924 Paul Whiteman conducted a program of symphonic jazz in New York. The featured performer was George Gershwin who, for the first time, played his "Rhapsody in Blue" for the public.

Sir John Falstaff's Dead Herrings

On this day in 1429 the renowned British rogue, Sir John Falstaff successfully repelled the advances of the French cavalry at Orleans. His major line of defence was formed by an encirclement of 400 wagons of Yarmouth herrings that he was delivering to the British troops.

Robinson Crusoe's Rescue

Alexander Selkirk was a Scottish sailor who requested to be put ashore on the uninhabited island of Juan Fernandez where he remained alone for five years. The original model for Daniel Defoe's "Robinson Crusoe" was rescued on this day in 1709.

Rufus McIntyre's Imprisonment

On February 12, 1839, Rufus McIntyre, the land agent for Maine set out to break up lumber camps being established by Canadians, was arrested at a camp near the Little Madawaska River by Canadians from New Brunswick, and sent to jail in Fredericton.

Queen for a Few Days

Lady Jane Grey was the Queen of England for nine days. Her reign ended abruptly when she was hanged on this day in 1554. Not surprisingly she has a ghost—a white shape—which is believed to appear February 12th in the Tower of London. It was last sighted in 1957.

ALBERT LEVERING

13
FEBRUARY

Births
Charles Maurice de Talleyrand-Perigord (diplomat) 1754; Randolph Churchill (Winston's father) 1849; Fiodor Chaliapin (opera singer) 1873.

Deaths
Benvenuto Cellini (sculptor) 1576; Richard Wagner (composer) 1883; Dame Christabel Pankhurst (suffragette) 1958.

Liquor Traffic Snarled
"What the temperance men demand is, not the regulation of the liquor traffic, but its destruction."
New York Tribune, February 13, 1852

How to Prepare for Valentine's Day
" . . . the night before, I got five bay leaves, and pinned four of them to the four corners of my pillow, and the fifth to the middle; and then if I dreamt of my sweetheart, Betty said, we should be married before the year was out. But to make it more sure, I boiled an egg hard, and took out the yolk and filled it with salt; and when I went to bed, ate it, shell and all, without speaking or drinking after it. We also wrote our lovers' names upon bits of paper, and rolled them up in clay, and put them into water; and the first that rose up was to be our Valentine."
Written by an anonymous Miss in *The Connoisseur,* 1754

The Witches Confess
On February 13, 1621, at Inverkiething, Scotland, Bessie Harlow, Bessie Chalmers, Beatrice Mudie, Christiane Hamyltoun, Margaret Kent, and Marioun Chatto were tried on suspicion of witchcraft. The first five confessed under examination by a minister and magistrate to their "devilish practices and giving themselves over soul and body to the devil," but said that Marioun Chatto "was the principal person in all their conventions and meetings with the devil."

Good Morrow, Valentine
"The Streets swarm with carriers, and baskets laden with treasures; bang, bang, bang, go the knockers, and away rushes the banger, depositing first upon the doorstep some packages from the basket of stores labelled only 'St. Valentine's Love', or 'Good Morrow, Valentine' . . . "

"Another custom was to give as gifts monstrous packages composed entirely of wrappings, at the centre of which was a final envelope containing the message: "Happy is he who expects nothing, and he will not be disappointed.""
Madders Rambles in an Old City (Norwich, England) 18th century

Liberty Deprived
The bank in the town of Liberty, Missouri, reluctantly took its place in history as the first-ever bank to be robbed by the notorious James-Younger gang (1866).

Proverb
When the cat lies in the sun in February,
She will creep behind the stove in March.

14
FEBRUARY

Births

Benny Kubelsky (Jack Benny) 1894; Thelma Ritter (actress) 1905; Mel Allen (sportscaster) 1913.

Deaths

St Valentine (beheaded) 278; King Richard II (murdered) 1400; Captain Cook (dismembered) 1779; seven Chicago hoodlums (machine-gunned) 1929; James Rogers (bled to death) 1748.

A Pagan Festival

The St Valentine's tradition originated in the Roman feast *Lupercalia*, in honour of Pan and Juno (later this was known as Februata). In this pagan festival the names of young women were put into a box from which they were drawn by the men as chance directed.

Bulgarian Bacchanalia

Many Bulgarians spend this day in undisciplined revelry while celebrating Trifon Zarezan (Viticulturist's Day), a centuries-old observance in praise of the cult of Dionysius, god of wine and merriment.

St Valentine's Day Firsts

1803: Moses Coats, a mechanic, invented the apple parer.
1879: "La Marseillaise" officially became the French national anthem.
1918: The movie *Tarzan of the Apes* was released for the first time.
1939: The German battleship the *Bismarck* was launched.

A Warning to Maidens

This is the leaping month, Maiden beware,
And of your maiden-head have a special care;
Better with Valentine to chuse a mate;
Than trade before, and to repent too late.
Poor Robin's Almanac, 1683

A Load of Embarrassment

The Chicago post office once rejected 25,000 coarse and vulgar St Valentine's cards as being unfit to go through the mails. English newspapers used to give annual reports on how many hundreds of

thousands of silly cards had overburdened the post office. Charles Lamb noted that on this day: "The weary and all forspent postman sinks beneath a load of embarrassment not his own."

A Vulgar Custom

"The vulgar custom of sending Valentines on this day had its origin in an endeavour of several zealous persons of the clerical order to put an end to the superstitious practice of boys drawing by lots the names of girls, in honour of Juno Februata, celebrated on the 15th of February in ancient Rome. Instead of this custom they permitted the names of saints to be drawn. These got the name of Valentines, but being afterwards much abused and converted into love letters, the ceremony degenerated again into a pagan and foolish custom."
Catholic Annal, 1830

Passion in the Air

A popular St Valentine's belief in olden times dictated that the first person of the opposite sex that an unmarried person saw this day was destined to be their future mate. It was also felt that birds began their spring sexual activities today:

The raven plumes his jetty wing
To please his croaking paramour
The lark's responsive love-tales sing
And tell their passions as they roar.

Death of a Prodigious Bulk

James Rogers died today in 1748 at the age of 31 in England. He was a person of such prodigious bulk, that though five people could be in his coffin, covered with the lid—his friends were obliged to have eighty-four pounds of fat taken from him before the lid could be fixed over him. A little before his death, he discharged from his stomach over twenty-one quarts of blood.

15 FEBRUARY

Births

Galileo Galilei (astronomer) 1564;
Susan B. Anthony (suffragette) 1820;
Cesar Romero (actor) 1907.

Deaths

John Handley (invented sextant)
1744; General Lew Wallace (wrote
Ben Hur) 1905; Nat King Cole
(singer) 1965.

Nude Mark, 60 B.C.

At a Roman festival in honour of Pan,
the emperer-to-be and Cleopatra's
lover-to-be, Mark Antony, ran naked
through the Forum.

Doctor in the House, 1319

St Swithin's monastery in Winchester,
England, granted one Thomas
Shaftesbury two dishes daily from the
kitchen, robes, and a competent
chamber for the term of his life in
exchange for his obligement to serve
the monastery in the art of medicine.

New Cleaner, 1870

Sand-blasting was unveiled in
Philadelphia. This method of cutting
hard substances by the erosive action
of a jet of driven sand was invented
by Mr B.C. Tilgham.

Women in Law, 1879

For the first time in history lady
lawyers were authorised to practise
law before the United States Supreme
Court.

Yale's Treasure, 1926

The original Gutenberg Bible, from
15th-century Germany, was sold in
New York for $106,000 and presented
to Yale University.

Canada's Flag, 1965

To the accompaniment of a
twenty-one gun salute, Canada's new
red and white Maple Leaf Flag was
unfurled for the first time on
Parliament Hill in Ottawa.

Correspondence, 1493

In a letter sent to Luis de Sant Angel,
Christopher Columbus included
extracts from his journal which told
of his discovery of new and far-off
lands.

Weird Will, 1717

The will of William Granville left a
prize of forty shillings to go each year
to five poor boys under sixteen years
of age. To collect their reward they
must recite the Lord's Prayer with
their hands on Granville's gravestone.

Proverbs

The Welshman would rather see his
  dam on her bier,
Than see a fair Februeer.

A'the months o' the year
Curse a fair Februeer.

If February fills the dykes:
March winds blow the organ pipes.

Yale's Treasure, 1926

The original Gutenberg Bible, from 15th-century
Germany, was sold in New York for $106,000 and
presented to Yale University.

Canada's Flag, 1965

To the accompaniment of a twenty-one gun salute,
Canada's new red and white Maple Leaf Flag was unfurled
for the first time on Parliament Hill in Ottawa.

Pence Sense, 1971

After 1200 years of using pounds, shillings, and pence
based on twelve pennies to a shilling, Britain adopted the
decimal currency system.

Shadrack, 1851

On this day Shadrack was arrested in Boston and
imprisoned as a fugitive slave. With the help of some
friends he escaped this night and via the "Underground
Railroad" eventually found refuge in Canada.

New Cleaner, 1970

Sand-blasting was unveiled in Philadelphia. This method
of cutting hard substances by the erosive action of a jet of
driven sand was invented by Mr B.C. Tilgham.

Women in Law, 1879

For the first time in history lady lawyers were authorised
to practise law before the United States Supreme Court.

16
FEBRUARY

Births

No one of note seems to have entered the world on this day!

Deaths

Richard Mead (English doctor) 1754; Giovan Batista Casti (Italian poet) 1803; Lindley Murray (U.S. grammarian) 1826; Elisha Kent Kane (U.S. explorer) 1857.

Politics, 1783

A "Dissertation of the Political Union and Constitution of the 13 United States of North America" was published by P. Webster—the first proposal of a new federal system of government.

Anatomy, 1852

The Homeopathic College in Cleveland, Ohio, was attacked today by a mob in consequence of the robbing of graves for anatomical subjects.

Economy, 1900

On February 16, 1900, the Gold Standard Bill was passed by Congress providing for gold reserves of $150 million for redemption of legal tender notes, the redemption not to fall below $100 million—after which the sale of bonds was to be required to replenish the gold stock.

Poetry, 1803

Giovan Batista Casti was an Italian poet in the courts of the grand duke of Tuscany and the emperor of Germany. He is best known for the publication of his *Tre Giuli,* a book of 200 droll sonnets descriptive of the troubles that the author was pleased to represent himself as having as a consequence of his borrowing three giuli which he was never able to repay. A giuli is a miniscule amount. Through 2,800 poetic lines the creditor, Chrysophilus, hounds him mercilessly, up to 100 times a day.

Medicine, 1754

Dr Richard Mead, who died on this day in 1754, was a distinguished physician under whose auspices innoculation for smallpox was first introduced in England. The experiment was successfully tried on seven condemned criminals in London in 1721. Mead once fought a duel under the gate of Gresham College with a certain Dr Woodward. Woodward's foot slipped, and he fell. "Take your life!" exclaimed Mead. "Anything but your physic," replied Woodward. The quarrel arose from a difference of opinion on medical subjects.

Education, 1838

The State of Kentucky passed a law that permitted women, under certain conditions, to attend school.

17
FEBRUARY

Births

Horace de Saussure (Swiss mountaineer) 1740; Thomas Malthus (English economist) 1766; Dr Rene Theophile Laennec (French inventor of stethoscope) 1781.

Today's Flower

The flower for the seventeenth day of February is the saffron crocus (*Crocus sativus*), which often appears even while snow is on the ground.

Welcome, wild harbinger of spring!
To this small nook of earth;
Feeling and fancy fondly cling
Round thoughts which owe their
   birth
To thee and to the humble spot
Where chance has fixed thy lowly
   plot.
   Bernard Barton, circa 1775

Deaths

Michaelangelo Buonarotti (Italian artist) 1563; Molière (French writer) 1673; Geronimo (Indian chief) 1909; Sir Wilfred Laurier (Canadian prime minister) 1919.

On the Walls of the Armoury

Modern Art was officially introduced to Americans at an exhibition hung in the sixty-ninth Regiment Armory in New York. Works by such contemporary French painters as Picasso, Matisse, Braque, and Duchamp baffled and annoyed visitors whose hue and cry of derision seemed enough to shake the paintings from the walls (1913).

In the Can at Eastport

On February 17, 1876, the first sardines were canned at Eastport in Maine by Mr Julius Wolff of the Wolff and Reesing Cannery.

On the Sistine Chapel Ceiling

After he had finished the decoration of the ceiling of the Sistine Chapel, Michaelangelo was asked by Pope Julius II, who loved splendour, and from whom the artist had accepted the commission for the work, to ornament the figures with gold leaf. The painter refused saying, "In those days gold was not worn, and the characters that I have painted were neither rich, nor desirous of riches; they were holy men [for] whom gold was an object of contempt."

On the Stage in Paris

Jean Baptiste Poquelin Molière passed away today in Paris in 1673. Styled by Voltaire as "the best comic poet that ever lived in any nation," he died in his fifty-third year whilst acting in the character of a sick man in *Le Malade Imaginaire,* one of his own plays.

In the Czar's Basement

Another attempt on the life of the czar was made at 8:00 this evening. A mine was exploded in the basement of the Winter Palace at St Petersburg. None of the Imperial family was hurt but others were injured. Had there not been a delay in the eating hour, the Imperial family would have been assembled in the dining room where the floor was badly damaged by the explosion (1880).

On Top of Mont Blanc

Horace Benedict de Saussure, born this day in Geneva in the year 1740, was the first to climb Mont Blanc, which he accomplished in 1787 after several attempts.

18
FEBRUARY

Births

Queen Mary I (Bloody Mary) 1516; Niccolo Paganini (violinist/composer) 1784; Andrei Segovia (guitar virtuoso) 1893; Jack Palance (film villain) 1919.

Deaths

St Simon (Christ's cousin) 116; George (duke of Clarence) 1478; Martin Luther (Protestant reformer) 1546; Miss Charlotte Cushmen (American actress) 1876.

Death by Crucifixion

St Simon (bishop of Jerusalem) was nephew to Joseph and Mary and therefore cousin germain to Christ. The unfortunate bishop suffered martyrdom when 120 years old, by crucifixion on this day in the year 116.

A Television Spectacular

Lucille Ball and Desi Arnaz were given an $8 million contract, the highest single TV contract yet, to continue their show, "I Love Lucy," through 1955 (1953).

Death by Wine

Among the historic traditions of the Tower of London is the story that George, duke of Clarence (brother of Edward IV), who met his death on February 18, 1478, was by order of his own brother, Richard, duke of Gloucester, drowned in a butt of Malmsey wine in the Tower (Malmsey being a strong, sweet wine from Greece or Spain). It is said that, being condemned to die, the duke himself selected this strange way of quitting life because of his partiality for the drink. Rumour has it that he went out smiling.

Island Unrest

On February 18, 1892, the Princess Kaiulani of Hawaii issued an appeal to the American people regarding her rights as crown princess of the Hawaiian Islands. This was followed by an appeal of native Hawaiians to the American government for redress, not annexation. In it they said their country was overrun by foreigners who, by bringing coolies from the Orient, were propagating leprosy in every village.

Underground Events

The Cave of the Winds at Niagara Falls was practically dry for the first time in fifty years (1896). The seven-mile long Moffat Tunnel, dug at a cost of $12,000,000 was formally opened in Colorado (1927).

A Celestial Event

Astronomer Clyde W. Tombaugh, at the Lovell Observatory in Flagstaff, Arizona, discovered the planet Pluto (1930).

Colonial Progress

Jean de Ribaut sailed from Dieppe with a load of colonists for the promised land of Florida (1562). *Pilgrim's Progress* by John Bunyan was published to great acclaim (1678). The explorer La Salle made the first settlement in what was to become the State of Texas (1685). The *Pennsylvania Gazette* published an advertisement proposing to insure houses in Philadelphia against fire (1752).

Births

Nicholas Copernicus (astronomer) 1473; Henry Frederick (Prince of Wales) 1594; Sven Hedin (explorer) 1865.

Deaths

Isobel Cockie (burnt witch) 1596; Lucilio Vanini (burnt atheist) 1553; André Gide (novelist) 1951.

The Prediction Fulfilled, 1888

Mount Vernon, Illinois, was destroyed by a tornado which swept a path 500 yards wide and several miles long within which everything was devastated. The ruins afterwards caught fire and loss of life and damage to property were great.

Today's Health Rules

Rise early and take exercise in plenty,
But always take it with your stomach empty.
After your meals sit still and rest awhile,
And with your pipe a careless hour beguile.
To rise at light or five, breakfast at nine,
Lounge til eleven, and at five to dine,
To drink and smoke till seven, the time for tea,
And then to dance or walk two hours away
Till ten o'clock—good hour to go to nest,
Till the next cock shall wake you from your rest.
Catholic Annal, 1830

The Price of Obscurity, 1848

On this day in 1848, Thomas Edison received a patent for his invention of the phonograph. For his labours, Edison's assistant Mr John Kreusi, who made the machine from the inventor's drawings, was paid the sum of $18.00.

Bad Weather Predicted

The sun enters the zodiacal constellation of Pisces at about this time of the month. The sign of Pisces, two fishes, is said to symbolize the fishery of the Nile, which usually opened at this season of the year. According to an ancient fable, the sign represents Venus and Cupid who, to avoid Typhon, a dreadful giant with a hundred heads, transformed themselves into fish. The Romans believed that the entrance of the sun into Pisces was attended by bad weather, and gales of uncertainty to the mariner.

A Reward for Meritorious Service, 1814

On February 19, 1814, Joseph Gardiner Swift was made a Brigadier-General for "meritorious service in defence of New York." He had been Westpoint's first graduate.

The Cost of Burning a Witch, 1596

On February 19, 1596, Isobel Cockie of Scotland was convicted of "twelff poynts of witchcraft" and of being "ane commoun witche." She was strangled, then burned at the stake. The bill for her expenses was presented for account as follows:

Item, for tuentie leads of peattis to burn thame	10 sh
Item, for an boill of coillis	24 sh
Item, for four tar barrellis	24 sh 8 d
Item, for a stake and dressing of it	16 sh
Item, for four fadome of Towis	4 sh
Item, for carying the peattis, coillis and barrellis to the hill	13 sh 4 d
Item, for Jon Justice for their execution	13 sh 4 d

20
FEBRUARY

Births

Voltaire (French philosopher) 1694; David Garrick (British actor) 1717; Honoré Daumier (French artist) 1808; Sidney Poitier (American actor) 1927.

Deaths

James I (Scottish king, stabbed) 1437; La Voisin (French sorceress, beheaded) 1680; ten American Indians (scalped) 1725.

Scalping

On February 20, 1725, a party of volunteer Indian hunters came across a band of ten sleeping Indians. The white men killed them all and scalped them, collecting the $100 per scalp bounty offered by the Boston treasury.

Voting

The British House of Lords was voted to be "useless and dangerous" (1648).

The Anti-Duelling Law was voted into the United States Constitution (1839).

Cardinal Pecci was voted the new pope in Rome and assumed the name of Leo XIII (1878).

North and South Dakota, Washington, and Montana were voted into the American Union bringing the total to forty-two states (1889).

Planting

Many old almanacs suggest that this is a good day to plant beans, weather permitting:

Sew Peans and Beans in the wane of the moon
Who soweth them sooner, he soweth them soon.

The bean is linked with ghosts and death in folklore. The souls of the dead were supposed to live in bean fields and anyone who dared sleep in a bean field was dicing with a likely case of insanity. In areas rife with witches, a man was advised to carry a bean in his mouth to spit at the first witch he bumped into.

Elevating

On February 10, 1872 Cyrus Baldwin received the patent for a vertical-geared hydraulic electric elevator. It was installed in a hotel in New York.

Orbiting

John Glenn became the first American astronaut to orbit the earth. His vehicle was the *Mercury* space capsule, *Friendship 7* (1962).

Opening

The Metropolitan Museum of Art in New York City was opened on this day in 1877.

Chequing

The first Family Allowance cheques were mailed in Canada (1945).

Today's Horoscope

Fortunes under the sign of Pisces (the fishes, February 20 to March 20) are variable according to *Christian Astrology* by William Lilly published in 1647:

Manners & Actions when well placed Then he is Magnanimous, Faithfull, Bashfull, Aspiring in an honourable way at high matters, in all his actions a Lover of faire Dealing, desiring to benefit all men, doing Glorious things, Honourable and Religious, of sweet and affable Conversation, wonderfully indulgent to his Wife and Children, reverencing Aged men, a great Reliever of the Poore, full of Charity and Godlinesse, Liberal, hating all Sordid actions, Just, Wise, Prudent, Thankfull, Vertuous; so that when you find 4 of the Significator of any man in a Question, or Lord of his Ascendant in a Nativity, and well dignified, you may judge him qualified as abovesaid.

When ill
When 4 is unfortunate, then he wastes his Patrimony, suffers every one to cozen him, is Hypocritically Religious, Tenacious, and stiffe in maintaining false Tenents in Religion; he is Ignorant, Careless, nothing Delightfull in the love of his Friends; of a grosse, dull Capacity, Schismaticall, abasing himselfe in all Companies, crooching and stooping where no necessity is.

Births

Cardinal Newman (theologian/author) 1801; Sacha Guitry (actor) 1885; W.H. Auden (poet) 1907.

Deaths

Julius II (pope) 1513; Benedict de Spinoza (philosopher) 1677; Nathaniel P. Gordon (slave trader) 1862; Malcolm Little (Malcolm X) 1965.

A Bearded Pope

During the ten years of his papacy, Pope Julius II waged continual war—first against the Venetians and then against the French. It is said that when Michaelangelo was employed making a statue of the pope he asked, "Holy Father, shall I place a book in your hand?" Julius replied, "No, a sword rather, I know better how to handle it." Julius II was the first pope to let his beard grow, in order to inspire greater respect among the faithful.

A Punished Slave Trader

On this day in 1862 Nathaniel P. Gordon, convicted of engaging in the slave trade, was hanged—the first execution for this offence for forty years in the United States.

A Day of Rest

On February 21, 1887, in Oregon, a law was enacted recognising *Labour Day* as an official holiday. Oregon was the first state in the U.S. to do so. The observance of Labour Day had started with a Knights of Labour parade in New York City, February 21, 1882.

A Puffing Locomotive

The first self-propelled railway locomotive, built by Mr Richard Trevithick, was demonstrated on this day in 1804. It steamed along ten miles of track, carrying a ten-ton load (partly composed of seventy passengers) in Mid-Glamorgan, Wales.

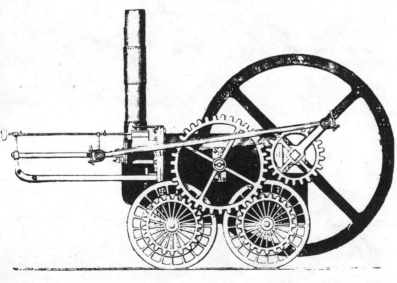

Sewing and Reading

On this day in 1842 John Greenough received a U.S. patent for his invention of the sewing machine and in 1925 the first issue of a magazine entitled *The New Yorker* made its appearance.

Omens and Predictions

When struck by a thunderbolt it is unnecessary to consult the *Books of Dates* as to the precise meaning of the omen.
E.B. Smith (1868-1942)

Oh, every year hath its winter,
And every year hath its rain—
But a day is always coming
When the birds go north again.
Ella Higginson (1862-1940)

You can only predict things after they've happened.
Eugene Ionesco

A Marrying Priest

Robert Elliott, a priest in Gretna Green, wrote to the *Times* of London stating that he had married 4,444 persons in twenty-eight years. The largest number in any one year was 198 and the smallest forty-two (1843).

A Thin Telephone Directory

The New Haven Connecticut Telephone Company issued a telephone directory, the first of its type in the world, listing the names of fifty subscribers (1878).

Proverb

If February calends be summerly gay, 'Twill be winterly weather in the calends of May.

Births

George Washington (1st American president) 1732; Frederic Chopin (Polish composer) 1810; Edna St Vincent Millay (British poet) 1892; Edward Kennedy (American politician) 1932.

Deaths

St Margaret (today's saint) 1297; Amerigo Vespucci (for whom America is named) 1512; John Jacob Astor (American millionaire) 1890.

Scared into Sainthood

St Margaret of Cortuna was a native of Alviano in Tuscany. The harshness of a stepmother and her own indulged propension to vice cast her headlong into the greatest disorders. The sight of a man half putrified, who had been her lover, struck her with so great a fear of divine judgments, that she became a perfect penitent until her death on this day in 1297.

A Flower for the Lady

Today's flower is herb Margaret (*Bellis percanis*) in honour of today's saint.

There is a double flow'ret, white and red,
That our lasses call Herb Margaret,
In honovre of Cortona's penitent,
Whose contrite sowle with red
  remorse was rent,
While on her penitence kinde
  Heaven did throwe
The white of puritie, surpassing
  snowe;
So white and red in this fair flowre
  entwine,
Which maids are wont to scatter at
  her shrine
  Catholic Annal, 1830

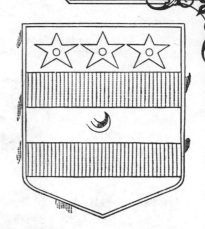

The Stars and Stripes Source

In Brington Church in Northampton there is a sepulchral stone at the grave of George Washington's uncle that bears on a brass shield a representation of the Washington family crest. It is composed of alternating red and white stripes surmounted by three five-pointed stars. It is believed that the stars and stripes which figure in the American flag were taken from the crest in Washington's honour.

Wicked Witch Whipped

On February 22, 1599, Mr Andrew Duncan reported in the St Andrew's Register, Soctland and that he had apprehended Geillis Gray, suspected of witchcraft. The laird of Lothaker took her from him back to his manor and "thair tortorit and whipped hir, whairby now she is become impotent and cannot labour for hir living."

Popcorn Proffered Proudly

On February 22, 1630, popcorn was introduced to the colonists by the Indians at the first Thanksgiving dinner in America. It was the proud contribution of Quadequina, brother of Massasoit and it was proffered "popped" in a big deerskin bag.

First "Five-and-Ten"

Frank Winfield Woolworth open his first five-cent store in Utica, New York on this day in 1879. It was a disaster, with sales often totalling less than $2.50 a day. He later moved his location to Lancaster, Pennsylvania, where sales improved.

Trees Tortured with Torches

It was once the curious custom in rural France for farmers to take lighted torches to all the orchards at night and with them beat every tree severely while very loudly promising to put the trees to death if they were not fruitful in the coming season. Fortunately for the trees this ceremony, *Branch Sunday,* occurred only when February 22 fell on a Sunday.

23
FEBRUARY

Births

Samuel Pepys (diarist) 1632; George Frederick Handel (composer) 1685; Sally Victor (hat designer) 1905.

Deaths

Josuah Reynolds (artist) 1792; John Keats (poet) 1821; Dame Nellie Melba (singer/peach melba) 1931.

Pepys, 1632

Samuel Pepys was secretary of the British Admiralty for six years. But the reason his birthday is remembered today was not his record of public service, but his diary—which he wrote in shorthand and kept faithfully for nine years and five months until his eyesight failed. Each entry finished with "And so to bed" and the last entry of all read: "And so I betake myself to that course, which is almost as much as to see myself go into my grave; for which, and all the discomforts that will accompany my being blind, the good God prepare me."

Rosenthal, 1945

On this day on the Pacific Island of Iwo Jima in 1945, an Associated Press photographer, Joe Rosenthal, took the most famous picture of World War II. His camera captured the dramatic moment when six members of the Fifth Division of U.S. Marines raised the American flag atop Mount Suribachi.

Stone, 1902

On February 23, 1902 Miss Ellen Stone, American missionary captured by Turkish brigands in 1901, was released on payment of a ransom of $72,500 raised by subscription in the United States.

Handel, 1685

The great composer George Frederick Handel owed not just his fame, but his very life, to music. In 1703, at Hamburg, he was arguing with Mattheson, another musician, who violently assaulted him. A duel followed, and the young Handel might have been killed but for a thick musical score buttoned under his coat, upon which his antagonist's sword broke. After 1710 Handel lived his whole life in England although he had promised to return to Hanover. Thus, when in 1714 George I of Hanover became the British king, Handel was afraid to present himself in court. He arranged with a friend that he should meet the king, as if by accident, during an excursion on the Thames, with a nearby band playing *The Water Music,* which he had written for the occasion. His Majesty succumbed to the stratagem and was reconciled with the composer.

Keats, 1821

On February 23, 1821, John Keats, the poet, died at the very beginning of his career. Virulent and unmerited attacks upon his literary ability by an unprincipled and malignant reviewer injured his rising reputation, overwhelmed his spirit, and he sank into consumption. In that state he fled to Italy, caught cold on the voyage, and died in Rome at the age of twenty-five.

Bowdlerised, 1818

Thomas Bowdler, a Scottish doctor who died in Edinburgh on this day in 1825, was the editor of the *Family Shakespeare,* which he published in 1818. In his preface he called it an edition "in which those words and expressions are omitted which cannot with propriety be read aloud in a family." Mr Bowdler has been immortalised with the word *bowdlerise* meaning "to expurgate."

Births

Robert Lord Clive (of India) 1726; Wilhelm Karl Grimm (fairy tales) 1786; Winslow Homer (artist) 1836.

Deaths

Henry Cavendish (amateur chemist) 1810; Thomas Bowdler (bowdleriser) 1825; Henri Desire Landru (Bluebeard) 1922.

Botany Travestied, 1830

The early monkish calendars awarded the somewhat obscure flower *Osmanda regalis* to February 24. It was also known as osman roy as indicated in this poem from a work entitled *Botany Travestied* (1830):

Auld Botany Ben was want to jog
Thro' rotten slough and quagmire bog,
Or brimfull dykes and marshes dank,
Where Jack a Lanterns play and prank,
To seek a cryptogamious store
Of moss, of carix and fungus hoare,
Of ferns and brakes, and such like sights,
As tempt out scientific wights
On winter's day, but most his joy
Was finding what's called Osman Roy.

Today's Number

A 2 and a 4 together, forming the compound number of today's date, bodes well for those who are closely associated with it, whether by birth or circumstance. In numerology it is a fortunate number that promises the assistance of important and learned persons should one be making plans. It also denotes gain through love and the opposite sex.

Bluebearded, 1922

Henri Desire Landru, alias Bluebeard, had a list of 250 "sweethearts" from which he began to select victims for his bizarre philosophy of "win a woman, get her money, rub her out." His technique was to lure women to his secluded villa after they had become his "fiancée," hack them up, then burn them piece by piece in his cookstove. By the time his scheme was discovered he had only 240 to go. Bluebeard was executed on this day in Versailles in the year 1922.

Porpoise Puddynge

During the fourteenth century gourmets paid epicurean prices for choice morsels of whale and porpoise. These animals, being then considered as fish, were held as allowable food during Lent. Says one chronicler of February 24, 1866 "It is lamentable to think how much sin they thus occasioned among our forefathers, before they were discovered to be mammalian." There is still a manuscript in the British Museum that contains a recipe for "puddynge of porpoise."

25
FEBRUARY

Births

August Renoir (painter) 1841; Enrico Caruso (opera singer) 1873; John Foster Dulles (statesman) 1888; George Harrison (Beatle) 1943.

Deaths

Earl of Essex (beheaded) 1601; Count Wallenstein (assassinated) 1634; Sir Christopher Wren (architect) 1723.

A Sharp Spear

Among his many famous extravagencies, Count Wallenstein, a Bohemian general of the Catholic forces during the Thirty Years War, had a mania for quiet. While his army devoted itself to pleasure, the deepest silence reigned about the count. He could not endure the rumbling of carts, loud conversations, or even simple sounds. One of his chamberlains was hanged for waking him without orders, and an officer put to death because his spurs had clanked when he came to visit. Wallenstein's 1,000 servants glided around his household like phantoms and a dozen sentries perpetually moved around his tent or palace to maintain incessant tranquility. Chains were stretched across the streets in order to guard him against any sound when he passed. On the 25th February 1634, under suspicion for treason, he was impaled on the point of a spear and died in proud silence.

Titled Events on this Day

1570: The Pope excommunicated Queen Elizabeth I of England and called her an usurper.

1601: The earl of Essex, a one-time favourite of Queen Elizabeth I was beheaded at Her Majesty's request.

1673: Lord Arlington and Lord Culpepper were given the colony of Virginia for thirty-one years at a rental of forty shillings a year.

1964: Cassius Marcellus Clay knocked out Charles (Sonny) Liston for the Heavyweight Championship of the World.

A Financial Event

On February 25, 1791, an Act incorporated the Bank of the United States as a national bank chartered for twenty years with capital of $10,000,000.

A Non-Event

On February 25, 1744, with England under threat of invasion from France, the English Channel Fleet, under Sir John Norris, came within a league of the Brest Squadron of sixteen French ships off the coast of Sussex. In anticipation of a ferocious naval battle thousands of people lined the coast. But at seven in the evening the wind changed and the French fleet escaped.

A Pedestrian Event

On this day in 1838, at Notting Hill, London, a pedestrian named Earle performed the task of walking twenty miles backward, and the same number forward, in eight hours.

A Big Candle for a Big Voice

The great opera tenor, Enrico Cruso, was born on February 25, 1873 in Naples, Italy. By 1924, he was so important to his country, and especially to Neapolitans, that Naples dedicated the world's largest candle to his memory in that year. The candle, eighteen feet high and seven feet in circumference, is lit every year on his birthday, and is expected to last 1,800 years.

26
FEBRUARY

Births

Victor Hugo (novelist) 1802; William Cody (Buffalo Bill) 1846; Jackie Gleeson (comedian) 1916.

Deaths

St Victor (mysterious saint) 7th century; Dr William Kitchener (eccentric writer) 1827; a bystander (suspected spy) 1871.

Lesser Periwinkle

The flower of this day is known botanically as *Vinca minor* and popularly as the lesser periwinkle.

A Mysterious Saint

St Victor was born of noble parentage in the diocese of Troyes in Champagne. He lived the recluse life of an anchoret in such a strict manner that he was emphatically said to live without a body and was therefore seldom seen, especially after his death on this day sometime during the 7th century.

A Suspected Spy, 1871

A person, thought to be a public spy, whilst watching the National Guards defiling in front of the Column of July, was seized by a mob of infuriated Republicans and, after being subjected for hours to a series of outrages, was bound hand and foot and thrown into the Seine (Paris).

The Disuse of Ardent Spirit, 1833

On February 26, 1833, the Congressional Temperance Society of America was formed "by example and kind moral influence to discountenance the use of ardent spirit and the traffic in it throughout the community."

An Eccentric Writer, 1827

Dr William Kitchener, who died on February 26, 1827 in London, wrote books such as *The Pleasures of Making a Will* and *Cook's Oracle* (which contained a chapter on "How to Roast a Pound of Butter"), but spent much of his time dining. Persons invited to his public dinners were faced with a sign over the hearth which read "Come at seven, go at eleven."

A Long Distance Call, 1927

A conversation between parties in San Francisco and London established a new long distance record of 7,287 miles.

A Sailboat Underground, 1870

New York's first subway line opened for the first time today with only one car and a fare set at 23 cents. It was powered by a rotary blower which propelled it like "a sailboat before the wind."

A Singular Mass, 1732

Mass was celebrated today in the newly built Roman Catholic church in Philadelphia— the only such church allowed in any Anglo-American colony prior to the Revolution.

27
FEBRUARY

Births

Henry Wadsworth Longfellow (poet) 1807; John Steinbeck (novelist) 1902; Elizabeth Taylor (actress) 1932; Ralph Nader (crusader) 1934.

Deaths

St Thalilaeus (the weeping saint) 5th century; John Evelyn (diarist) 1706; G.H. Putnam (publisher) 1930; Ivan Pavlov (psychologist) 1936.

A Weeping Saint in a Cage

One of the saints for February 27 is St. Thalilaeus who died in his wooden cage on this day sometime in the 7th century in Syria. Prior to taking up residence in this strange abode he had lived alone on a mountain for sixty years, during which time he wept almost without intermission as a penance for his sins.

A Body in a Haunted House

The most haunted house in England was reputedly Borley Rectory. It burnt to the ground today in 1939. Locals claimed they saw the figure of a cowled nun, as well as other strange looking apparitions. The nun was seen walking around the upper rooms of the house, even though the floors were in ruins. In 1943, a young woman's body, supposedly that of the murdered nun, was found buried three feet below the cellar floor.

A Nazi Pyromaniac on the Loose

This was the day in which the Reichstag, the home of the German Legislative Assembly in Berlin, was badly damaged by fire. Though the Nazis had secretly engineered the blaze, their leader Adolph Hitler denounced it as a communist plot and suspended civil liberties and freedom of the press (1933).

A Russian Ambassador at Sea

On February 27, 1558, Ivan, the czar of Russia, formally opened commercial relations with England. The new ambassador set off in ships laden with gifts but ran into bad weather and the ships were wrecked. The ambassador himself barely made it to the shore of England. The goods were all lost.

A Polar Bear in a Cage

Captain Atkins captured a polar bear in Greenland and shipped it to London where it aroused much curiosity being the first of its species to appear there (1734).

A Problem at the Leaning Tower

Italian engineers pronounced the Leaning Tower at Pisa to be in danger of over-doing it and toppling its 14,000 tons onto the populace below. In order to straighten it the necessary eleven feet to make it perpendicular again, Pisa asked the Italian government to spend several million lira (1964).

28
FEBRUARY

Births

Michael de Montaigne (essayist) 1533; Vladislav Nijinsky (dancer) 1890; Stephen Spender (poet) 1909.

Deaths

St Romanus, 460; St Lupicinus, 479; St Proterius, 557 (saints who achieved martyrdom via violent deaths of various means).

The Bible Goes Public, 1759

For the first time the pope gave his permission for the Bible to be translated into all languages of the Catholic states.

The Sweating System, 1888

In the House of Lords, Lord Dunraven moved for a Select Committee to enquire into the "sweating system." He based his remarks upon a report of the Board of Trade on the conditions of those engaged in workshops and at their own homes in the East End of London and declared that no slaves were as unhappy as these free citizens of a free country. The remuneration given them was so small that they could only just exist, their hours of work dangerously excessive and the rooms of work overcrowded to the total disregard of sanitary rules.

Finnish Festival, 1835

Kalevala Day is a national holiday in Finland to remember the Finnish epic poem *Kalevala,* and Dr Elias Lonnrot who transcribed more than 22,000 verses from the memories of his countrymen. The first edition of this collection was published on February 28, 1835.

Dead Drunk for Twopence, 1736

On this day in 1736 a proposal was submitted to the British House of Commons "for laying such a duty on distilled spirituous liquors as might prevent the ill consequences of the poorer sort drinking them to excess." Appended to the proposal to express its urgency was a copy of a liquor retailers sign: *Drunk for a penny, dead drunk for twopence, clean straw for nothing.*

Luxemburgher's Burgsonndeg

Today in Luxembourg the Burgosonndeg festival—an ancient custom to mark the end of winter—is celebrated with assorted revelries illuminated by huge bonfires that burn all night to greet the sun.

American Accident, 1844

On February 28, 1844, the gun of the American warship "Princeton" exploded accidentally during a pleasure cruise, killing the secretary of state and the secretary of navy and wounding 12 crew members.

Common Sleeping, 1643

On February 28, 1643 in Massachusetts, Roger Scott was tried in court for "common sleeping at the public exercise on the Lord's Day and for striking him that waked him." He was severely whipped.

Deerfield Done In, 1704

At the end of this day in Massachusetts, the town of Deerfield was no more. A marauding band of French and Indians killed forty people and took 100 more as prisoners.

29
FEBRUARY

Births

Gioacchino Rossini (composer) 1792.

Deaths

John Whitgift (archbishop) 1604; John Landseer (engraver) 1852; E.F. Benson (author) 1940.

A Dark Day

According to the prognostications of numerologists it is fortunate that February 29 occurs infrequently on the calendar. The number 29 indicates uncertainties, treachery, and deception of others; it foreshadows trials, tributions, and unexpected dangers, unreliable friends, and grief and deception caused by members of the opposite sex.

Sleighing Through Albany, 1795

All day long a procession of 500 sleighs passed through Albany, New York. They were loaded with settlers on their way to the far west.

Look Before You Leap

As the ancients say wisely,
Have a care o'th'main chance,
And look before you ere you leap;
For as you sow, ye are like to reap.
   Samuel Butler (1600-1680)

Leap Year

In spite of the warnings of numerology, Leap Year has long been associated with the tradition of having spinsters propose to bachelors rather than await proposals of marriage from them. In old Scotland, Parliament even went so far as to pass a law forbidding any man to turn down a girl who proposed to him on Leap Year. If he did decline the proposal, he was fined a hefty sum.

Proverb

February rain is the husbandman's gain.

ARCH

Sturdy March, with brows full sternly bent,
And armed strongly, rode upon a ram,
The same which over Hellespontus swam,
Yet in his hand a spade he also bent
And in a bag all sorts of weeds, y same
Which on the earth he strewed as he went,
And filled her womb with fruitful hope of nourishment.
   Edmund Spenser

MARCH

History

We derive the present name of this month from the Romans, among whom at an early period it was the first month of the year. It continued to be so in several countries down to a comparatively late time; the legal year began in England on the 25th of March until the change of style in 1752. For commencing the year with this month there is a sufficient reason in the fact that March is the first month in which a decided renewal of nature's growth takes place. And for the Romans to dedicate their first month to Mars, the god of war, and to call it *Martius,* seems equally natural considering the importance they attached to war and the use they made of it.

   "This is supposed by divines and philosophers to be the time of man's creation; and it carries a good reason, especially considering that man is said to be made of the dust of the earth: now we see that in January and February there is no dust upon the earth, but dirt; and therefore the sage astrologers judge that He borowed his ingredients from March."
   The Rogue's Calendar, 1662

Welcome

Slayer of the winter, art thou here again?
   O welcome, thou that bring'st the summer night!
The bitter wind makes not the victory vain.
   Nor will we mock thee for thy faint blue sky.
   William Morris (1834-1896)

Birthstone

This month's birthstone is the bloodstone, which once brought (and perhaps might still bring) courage and presence of mind to it possessor.

1
MARCH

Births

Dinah Shore (entertainer) 1917;
Harry Belafonte (entertainer) 1920.

Deaths

St David (patron of Wales) 544;
Francois Rabelais (writer) 1553;
Manuel Johnson (astronomer) 1859.

Reeking Leeks in Wales

March 1 is the festival of St David, the patron saint of Wales, and it used to be customary among Welshmen to celebrate the day by fixing leeks to their hats. During a great battle against the Saxons, St David caused the Britons under King Cadwallader to distinguish themselves from their enemies with leeks worn on their hats, and the victory they achieved that day is recalled by the same emblem.

Why on St David's Day, do Welshmen seek
To beautify their hat with verdant leek
Of nauseous smell? For *Honour* 'tis heard say,
"Dulce et decorum est pro patria"—
Right, Sir, to die or fight it is, I think,
But how is't *Dulce,* when you for it stink?
Diverting Post, 1705

Vestal Virgins in Heaven

Ancient mythological sources report that, upon this day, the vestal virgins (few in number) annually renewed the sacred fire from the solar rays. Should any of them suffer it to be extinguished, they were promptly whipped. The punishment of any virgin who violated her vow of chastity was of the highest severity—no less than being buried alive while her paramour was beaten to death.

U.S. Counterfeiter in England

Great excitement was created in London on this day in 1873 by the discovery that bills to an enormous amount—90,000 to 100,000 notes in various denominations—had been forged and presented to the Bank of England. The perpetrator of the fraud was thought to be an American named Warren.

Witchcraft in America

On March 1, 1698, Elspeth McEwan, a recently arrived immigrant in New England, was charged with witchcraft by means of which she could draw milk from her neighbour's cow; she could also interfere with the poultry to increase or diminish the supply of eggs. When the minister's horse was sent to fetch her, it trembled with fear when she mounted and sweated drops of blood. She was so tortured that she prayed to be put to death. Her prayer was granted.

Chalanda Marz in Switzerland

This festival heralds the coming of spring in Engadine, Switzerland. Young people dress in herdsman's clothing with wide belts from which are suspended many cow-bells which are used to "ring out the winter."

Cotton Capers in Memphis

The *Cotton Carnival* was first held in Memphis, Tennessee on March 1, 1931 and is now an annual 5-day event, beginning the first Tuesday in March with parades and dances showing what life was like in the Old South.

TO the right noble/right excellent & vertuous prince George duc of Clarence Erle of warwyk and of salisburye/grete chamberlayn of Englonde & leutenant of Irelonde oldest broder of kynge Edward by the grace of god kynge of Englande and of fraunce / your most humble seruant william Caxton amonge other of your seruantes sendes vnto yow pees. helthe . joye and victorye vpon your Enempes /

The First Book in English

Today in 1469 William Caxton began to translate *Receuil of the Histories of Troy* from the French. Soon after he completed the work he set up a printing office and the book came off the press—the first ever printed in English.

Whuppity Scoorie in Scotland

In Lanark, Scotland, today is the festival of Whuppity Scoorie. The custom began when the prisoners of a nearby jail were first whipped and then taken for their annual bath in the Clyde. In Scottish vernacular this is "whupped and scoored" or Whuppity Scoorie. The bells of Lanark church, quiet from October 31, sound again on March 1 and small boys run around the church three times hitting one another with paper balls.

Births

Sam Houston (U.S. soldier/statesman) 1793; Benito Juarez (Mexican president) 1806; Bedrich Smetana (Czech composer) 1824.

Deaths

St Chad (saint of medicinal springs) 673; John Wesley (founder of Methodism) 1791; Horace Walpole (writer) 1797.

Health

St Chad was a bishop of Lichfield in England in the seventh century. Upon his canonisation he became the patron saint of medicinal springs. On the east side of the town is St Chad's Well, described as "A spring of pure water, with a stone in the bottom of it, on which St Chad was wont, naked, to stand in the water and pray." The waters of the well are particularly known for their benefits for sore eyes. There was also a St Chad's Well in London, off Gray's Inn Road near King's Cross; its waters were famous as a laxative.

Science, 1889

On March, 2, 1889, the first American electrocution experiment was performed on several dogs, four calves, and a horse. The deaths were instant and apparently painless.

Travel, 1870

Mr Plimsoll's Railway Travelling Bill, compelling British railway companies to supply foot warmers in second- and third-class carriages in cold weather, was rejected on the proposal for a second reading by 108 to 76 votes.

Balloons, 1784

Blanchard, the aeronaut, made his first ascent from Paris, in a hydrogen balloon. He had added wings and a rudder but both proved useless.

Flight, 1949

After 23,452 miles in the air, the U.S. Air Force B-50 Superfortress *Lucky Lady II* landed at Fort Worth, Texas to complete the first non-stop round-the-world flight.

Hygiene

Bath oft, bleed not, unless occasion
  urge
Nor yet thy body too untimely purge.
More health is gotten by observing
  Diet
Than pleasures taken by vain
  excesses and Riot.
  The Fly Almanac, March 2, 1679

Literacy, 1897

As one of his last acts in office, the American President Cleveland today vetoed a bill that would have required all immigrants to take literacy tests.

Royalty, 1881

Queen Victoria was fired at when entering her carriage at Windsor Station. No one was injured but the criminal, Roderick McLean, was tried for the offence of high treason.

Discrimination, 1492

King Ferdinand v banished 800,000 Jews from Spain.

Time, 1923

A new weekly news magazine, *Time,* was first published by Briton Hadden and Henry R. Luce.

Texas, 1836

A group of fifty-nine citizens of Mexico founded the Republic of Texas.

Railways, 1863

The U.S. Congress authorised a track width of 4'8-1/2" as the standard for the Union Pacific Rail Road. This gauge became the accepted width for most of the world's railroads.

Impeachment, 1876

On March 2, 1876 U.S. Congress passed a resolution to impeach Secretary Belknap for selling official places in the Navy Department. He resigned a few hours later.

Privateering, 1585

Sir Francis Drake sailed for the West Indies as a privateer, attacking Vigo and St Domingo en route.

Births

Edmund Waller (poet) 1605; Alexander Graham Bell (telephone inventor) 1847; Jean Harlow (actress) 1911.

Deaths

St Winwaloc (saint of March 3) 529; Robert Hooke (philosopher) 1703; Robert Adam (architect) 1792; Copley Fielding (painter) 1855.

Waging War with Camels

On March 3, 1855, the United States Congress approved an appropriation of $30,000 to be placed at the disposal of the secretary of war for the importation of camels from the Orient, to be tested in Texas for military purposes.

A Saint and a Goose

St Winwaloc, an Abbot in Amorica, died today in 529. A bishop Patrick cites this miracle from the Latin *Acts of the Saints*. "A sister of St Winwaloc had her eye plucked out by a goose as she was playing. St Winwaloc was taught by an angel a sign whereby to know the goose from the rest, and having cut it open, found the eye in its entrails, preserved by the power of God unhurt, and shining like a gem; which he took and put in its proper place, and recovered his sister; and was so kind also to the goose as to send it away alive, after it had been cut up, to the rest of the flock."

A Poet and a Lady

Go lovely Rose
Tell her that wastes her time and me.
That now she knows,
When I resemble her to thee,
How sweet and fair she seems to be.

When he was young the English poet Edmund Waller was the suitor of Lady Dorothea Sidney, whom he described as haughty and scornful. Nevertheless, he immortalised her in verse, calling her there by the name of Sacharissa. Many years later Sacharissa and the poet met once more. She asked him when he would write some fine verses about her. Waller ungallantly replied: "Madam, when you are as young again."

Bigger Girls and Floral Temptations

A meditative maiden walking in a garden of early spring flowers, exclaimed: "As these blooms brave the winds of March in the cold prime of the year, but fade before the summer sun, so the flowers of virtue, which open in the infancy of our days and can resist the storms of youthful rage, fade nevertheless under the heat of noontide passions and the cupidity of the meridan of life."

From *Florilegium,* 1830

The Salary Grab Act

On March 3, 1873, the U.S. president's salary was raised from $25,000 to $50,000 per year. At the same time the salaries of senators also went up from $5,000 to $7,500 per annum, and because the act was retroactive, it gave House members about to retire a bonus of $5,000—which gave the law its name. The Act was repealed in 1874 except for the president's salary and salaries of justices of the Supreme Court.

Little Girls and Dolls

Today in Japan is Hina Matsuri *(Doll's Festival)* an annual event to honour little girls and their dolls. Since the flower that symbolizes all the attributes of little girls is the Peach Blossom, the festival is sometimes called Peach Blossom Day. Little girls are hostesses to their friends, and their dolls are all on display as a sign of honour by their families.

Births

Knute Rockne (football player) 1888; Charles Goren (bridge player) 1901.

Deaths

Saladin (sultan of Egypt) 1193; Sergei Prokofiev (composer) 1953.

Famous First Words, 1865

"With malice toward none; with charity for all; with firmness in the right, as God gives us to see the right."
President Lincoln's Inaugural Address, 1865

Famous Last Words, 1861

"Without firing a gun, without drawing a sword, should the North make war on us . . . no cotton will be furnished for three years . . . England would topple headlong, and carry the whole civilized world with her . . . No power on Earth dares to make war on cotton. Cotton is king."
Speech in U.S. Senate by J.H. Hammond of South Carolina, 1861

Famous First Words, 1933

"This nation asks for action, and action now . . . We must act, and act quickly . . . The only thing we have to fear is fear itself."
President Roosevelt's Inaugural Address, 1933

Veneration for a Luminary

The ancient Egyptians made sacrifices to the sun on the fourth day of every month. So great was their veneration for this luminary that they burnt incense of appeasement three times on every day: resin at the sun's morning appearance, myrrh at high noon, and a special mixture called Kupli as the sun sank beneath the western horizon.

A Holy Experiment, 1681

William Penn, an English Quaker, obtained from King Charles II, in payment of a £16,000 debt owed his father, a charter for Pennsylvania (named by the king). The charter was for the establishment of his "holy experiment," a colony where religious and political freedom could flourish.

U.S. Pirates Halted, 1891

The International Copyright Act, halting the piracy of British, Belgian, French, Swiss books by American publishers, was passed by the United States Congress.

A Grave Burial, 1841

A gravedigger was buried in St Bride's Churchyard, England, by the falling in of the grave in which he was working.

Canadian Silver Bought, 1890

Canadian silver mines were bought by a syndicate of English and American interests for $10,000,000.

Trouble at Sea, 1873

A Royal Commission was established to inquire into the condition of, and certain practices connected with the commercial marine of the U.K. There was a great concern as on average, 2,754 lives were lost per annum at sea.

Lady at Labour, 1933

Miss Francis Perkins took up her post as secretary of labour, in President F.D. Roosevelt's Cabinet. She became the first woman cabinet minister in the U.S.

5
MARCH

The Florida Scalp Act

A resolution of the Florida Legislature was passed requesting their delegate in Congress to press for a law authorising rewards for Indian scalps and every Indian taken alive (1842).

The Green Hellebore

Today's flower should be admired but not eaten. Botanically, green hellebore is known as *Helleborus viridis,* which is derived from the Greek *helein:* to take away, and *bora:* food. If consumed, this plant will immediately and violently take away whatever food is in the stomach by means of vomitting.

Births

Hector Villa-Lobos (composer) 1887; Rex Harrison (actor) 1908.

Deaths

Dr Thomas Arne (composer of "Rule Britannia") 1778; Joseph Stalin (Russian premier) 1953.

The Texas Mother-in-Law Celebration

The first Mother-in-Law Day was celebrated at Amarillo, Texas on this day in 1934. The guest of honour was Mrs W.F. Donald, the mother-in-law of Gene Howe, a local newspaper editor, who conceived the idea for the celebration.

Rouge on her Cheeks

"I saw the lady you inquired after, when I was last in London, and a prodigious fine one she is; she has a strong suspicion of rouge on her cheeks, a cage of foreign birds and a piping bullfinch at her elbow; two little dogs on a cushion in the lap, and a cockatoo on her shoulder."
  Thomas Gray, in a letter written on March 5, 1766

The Gallant Pedestrian

Edward Payson Weston, an American pedestrian, commenced the task of walking 500 miles in six consecutive days starting at five minutes after midnight on Sunday, March 5, 1876. At the end of the first twenty-four hours he had covered nearly ninety-six miles. This speed gradually decreased until on Saturday there still remained another eighty-six miles to cover, a task obviously impossible in the eleven hours left. Nonetheless, he gallantly struggled on and at twelve minutes to noon was stepping briskly along his 450th mile when a pistol shot was fired and he withdrew from his impossible effort.

The Boston Massacre

In Boston, there was resentment against the British troops sent to maintain order and to enforce the Townshend Acts (passed to collect custom duties on certain imported goods). On this day, the troops, constantly tormented by irresponsible gangs, finally fired into the rioting crowd and killed five men. This became known as the *Boston Massacre.* The funeral of the victims was the occasion for a great patriotic demonstration. The British captain, Thomas Preston, and his men were tried for murder, with Robert Treat Paine as prosecutor, John Adams and Josiah Quincy as lawyers for the defence. Preston and six of his men were acquitted; two others were found guilty of manslaughter, punished, and discharged from the army (1770).

6
MARCH

Births

Michelangelo Buonarotti (Italian artist) 1475; Cyrano de Bergerac (French novelist) 1619; Elizabeth Barret Browning (British poet) 1806; Ring Lardner (American writer) 1885.

At the Alamo, 1836

On March 6, 1836, Mexican forces, commanded by Santa Anna, captured Fort Alamo, a mission compound in jsan Antonio, Texas, which they had held under siege since February 23. They massacred the whole garrison of eighty-seven people including Davey Crockett.

In the Heavens, 1716

On this day in 1716 a very brilliant and spectacular Aurora Borealis display lit the skies of Europe. It was visible from the west coast of Holland to the interior of Russia.

In the Arts, 1887

On March 6, 1887, the customs authorities in Toronto, Canada, siezed and destroyed 100 copies of Emile Zola's novels because they were said to be of an immoral character and obscene.

In the Night, 1854

A block of marble, sent from Rome by Pope Pius IX and intended for use in the Washington Monument, was destroyed by persons unknown in the middle of the night.

Today's Illnesses

Persons born on March 6 are inclined to suffer from problems in the throat, nose, and upper lungs. Women born under this number often have breast problems and in childbirth are prone to "milk fever."

Deaths

Davey Crockett (U.S. frontiersman) 1836; John Philip Sousa (U.S. composer) 1932; Oliver Wendell Holmes (U.S. jurist/author) 1935.

For the Record, 1938

On this day in 1938 Thomas Garson of Chicago, Illinois, ate twenty-two hamburgers and two quarts of ice cream in twenty-five minutes. He collected a wager of $40.00

Today's Flower

Named after Narcissus, the Greek youth in mythology who was changed into a flower, the *Narcissus pseudo narcissus simplex* or Lent lily has a single bloom notched and curled at its edges. If the flower is white it is said to symbolize purity, but when yellow it represents falsehood.

Today's Foods

Beneficial herbs for this day, accorded by numerology include beans, parsnips, spinach, manvers, mints, melons, motherwort, pomegranites, apples, peaches, apricots, figs, walnuts, the juice of the maiden-hair fern, daffodils, wild thyme, musk, violets, vervaine, and rose leaves.

7
MARCH

Births
John Herschel (astronomer) 1792; Thomas Masaryk (philosopher) 1850; Maurice Ravel (composer) 1875.

Deaths
St Perpetua (martyr) 203; Molly Mogg (barmaid) 1766; Monsieur Blanchard (balloonist) 1809.

Molly Mogg, 1776
On 7th March in 1766, Mrs Molly Mogg, of the Rose Tavern at Wokingham in England, died peacefully in her sleep. Forty years earlier her remarkable beauty had inspired the poet John Gay:

The schoolboy delights in a play-day,
The schoolmaster's joy is to flog;
The milkmaids delight is in May Day,
But mine is in sweet Molly Mogg.
. . .
When she smiles on each guest like her liquor,
Then jealousy sets me a-gog'
To be sure, she's a bit for the vicar,
And so I shall lose Molly Mogg.

St Perpetua, 203
St Perpetua related a strange vision she had of a narrow ladder reaching to Heaven beset with spikes on either side, and having a dragon at the bottom on whose head she had to tread to mount the first step. When she did finally reach Heaven it was with the assistance of a more earthly creature. She was martyred on this day in 203 A.D., being torn to pieces by a wild cow before a crowd of thousands in the amphitheatre of Rome.

Mary Ann Cotton, 1873
Today in 1873 at Durham in England, Mary Ann Cotton, charged with wholesale poisoning, was tried, found guilty, and sentenced to death. It was suspected that she had caused the deaths of no fewer than eighteen people, among them, husbands, children, stepchildren, and lodgers.

Ignoramus at Cambridge, 1617
On his return to England on this night in 1617, King James IV of Scotland was invited to attend a command performance of the play *Ignoramus* at Cambridge.

Alexander Graham Bell, 1876
On March 7, 1876, Mr Alexander Graham Bell was issued a patent for his talking device, which he called the telephone.

Pennsylvania Tax Rebellion, 1799
John Fries led a disgruntled group of citizens to Philadelphia, Pennsylvania, in a rebellion to protest the collection of direct tax on this day in 1799.

Births

Oliver Wendell Holmes (jurist/author) 1841; Otto Hahn (nuclear physicist) 1879.

Deaths

William of Orange (king of England) 1702; Karl Johann Bernadotte (king of Sweden) 1844; Hector Berlioz (composer) 1869.

Cape Cod's Pearls, 1616

Edward Braunde sailed from Dartmouth, England, for Cape Cod to look for pearls.

London's Shakes, 1750

A violent earthquake, which shook the river Thames, was felt in London.

Tar and Feathers, 1775

A citizen of Billericay in England was tarred and feathered, the first person to be treated in such a way.

California's Russians, 1806

Nikolai Resanov, chamberlain of the czar of Russia, sailed to California with food and supplies for starving Russian settlers there.

America's Technology, 1854

Commodore Perry at a conference with the Japanese at Yokohama, made a presentation of American gifts, which represented the arts of western civilisation. The gifts included a fully equipped miniature railroad, a telegraph line, and a steamboat.

Japan's Isolation, 1854

The conference attended by Commodore Perry concluded with the signing of a treaty with Japan, ending Japan's isolation policy and opening two ports for trade with the U.S.

Hero's Valour, 1834

Two young boys, playing alongside the Thames in London, accidently fell in. Both sank and their lives were in great danger. It happened that at that moment an actor, Mr Ryan was passing with a Newfoundland dog named Hero. A bystander threw two pebbles into the pool to show where the boys had gone down, the dog plunged in, and shortly pulled the friends, unharmed, back to the surface then to the shore. As a result of this success ten Newfoundland dogs were brought to Paris and appointed as savers of human life in the river Seine. They were first trained in pulling stuffed figures of men and women and children from the water, and, in time, acquired "such a skill and facility as to prove quite serviceable."

Russia's Revolution, 1917

The Russian Revolution began in St Petersburg.

Vietnam's Independence, 1949

Independence of Vietnam within the French Union was proclaimed.

Proverbs

Winter still ling'ring on the verge of spring
Returns reluctant, and from time to time
Looks back, while at his keen and chilling breath
Fair Flora sickens

A bushel of March dust is worth a king's ransom.

A dry March and a wet May
Fills barns and bays with corn and hay.

A March wind is salt which reasoneth all pulse.

As it rains in March so it rains in June.

March comes in with an adder's head and goes out with a peacock's tail.

March winds and April showers
Bring forth May flowers.

New Developments

1865:   Construction began on the Amsterdam-North Sea Canal.
1911:   New York City police introduced a new prosecutor's tool: latent-fingerprint evidence, to prove Caesar "Charley Crispi" Cella's presence during a burglary. He was convicted.

Births

Amerigo Vespucci (explorer) 1454; Alan Ladd (actor) 1913; Mickey Spillane (writer) 1918; Yuri Gagarin (first astronaut) 1934.

Deaths

Earl of Kent (beheaded) 1329; St Frances (widow) 1440; five Scottish witches (burnt) 1659.

Wedded Bliss

St Frances of Rome, who died on this day in 1440, was married for forty years. During all of that time she never once had an argument with her husband.

Burnt Witches

"Thair wer fyve wemen witches, brint (burnt) in the Castelhill for witchcraft, all of thame confessed thair covenanting with Satan, some of thame renunced their baptisme, and all of thame oftymes danced with the Devill."
  From the diary of Mr Nicholl, March 9, 1659

Baron Bliss

Today is *Baron Bliss Day,* a public holiday in Belize, formerly the British Honduras. It is held in honour of Baron Bliss, a mysterious Englishman who left his entire fortune to the city of Belize.

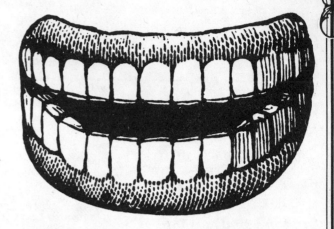

False Teeth

On 9th March in the year 1822, in New York City, Mr C.M. Howard was granted a patent for his invention of artificial teeth.

March Wedding

Miss Marie Rose Josephine Tascher de la Pagene of the island of Martinique united in marriage with Mr Napoleon Bonaparte of Corsica on this day in 1796—to have and to hold until 1809 when they were divorced "for reasons of state."

Today's Gardening Tips

Stake and binde up your weakest plants and Flowers against the Windes before they come too fiercely, and in a moment prostrate a whole year's labour. Now do the farewell-frosts and Easterly-winds prejudice your choicest tulips, and spot them; therefore cover such with mats or canvas to prevent freckles. Dress up and string your strawberry-beds, and uncover your asparagus, spreading and loosening the Mould about them. Also may you now transplant Asparagus roots to make new beds.
  By this time your Bees sit; keep them close Night and Morning if the weather prove ill.
  From the *Kalendrium Hortense* by John Evelyn, 1666

A Wild March-Morning

And in the wild March-morning I
   heard the angels call;
It was when the moon was setting,
   and the dark was over all;
The trees began to whisper, and the
   wind began to roll,
And in the wild March-morning I
   heard them call my soul.
Alfred Lord Tennyson (1809-1892)

10
MARCH

Births

Arthur Honneger (composer) 1892; Henry Watson Fowler (English usage expert) 1858.

Deaths

The forty martyrs (of St Sebaste) 320; Benjamin West (painter) 1820; Charles Worth (dress designer) 1895.

Beheadings

Heliogabalus (emperor) 222; Thomas Seymour (lord) 1549.

Dante's Inferno, 1302

On this day in 1302 the poet Dante was threatened with burning should he ever return to Florence, his birthplace.

The Thundering Legion of Marcus Aurelius

The forty martyrs, all members of the above group, who died on this day in 322, were noted for their ability to bring about miraculous rain by their prayers.

A Manifestation of Aurora Borealis

". . . a shining cloud in the air, in shape resembling a sword, the point reaching to the north: it was as high as the moon, the rest of the sky being very serene. It began at about eleven at night and vanished not till above one, being seen by all the south of England."
From the diary of John Evelyn, 10 March, 1643

Battles

The Salvation Army sent a pioneer party to the United States (1880).

Suffragettes rioted in London with injuries to both sides (1914).

The battle of Neuve-Chapelle began in World War I (1915).

The British aircraft carrier *Hermes* was sunk by the Germans (1942).

Treason, 1949

"Axis Sally" was convicted of treason for Nazi propoganda broadcasts.

Elementary My Dear Watson, 1876

Today in 1876 marked the first complete, intelligible sentence transmitted over Alexander Graham Bell's device. The inventor spoke to his assistant: "Mr Watson, come here, I want you."

Russian Relief, 1892

On March 10, 1892 residents of McLean County, Illinois made up a train of twenty-eight cars loaded with shelled corn for the famine sufferers in Russia. It was part of a larger relief effort mounted across the USA.

Capital Occurrences

The capital of New York State was moved from New York to Albany (1797). The first paper money of the U.S. government, available in $5, $10, $20, $100, $500, and $1,000 was issued on this day in 1892.

Benjamin West, 1820

The American artist Benjamin West died today in 1820. Early on in his son's life, Benjamin West's father was shocked one day by the sickly appearance of his favourite pet cat. The animal was losing the fur from his tail and looked seriously diseased. What he did not know wat that young Ben, in his youthful enthusiasm for painting, and unable to get camel hair brushes in Pennsylvania at the time, had been shaving the cat to manufacture his own brushes. After he was found out West's parents supported his choice of career more than they had earlier, but whether from sympathy for the boy or the cat is not clear.

Births

Torquato Tasso (poet) 1544; Sir Malcolm Campbell (record racer) 1885; Vannever Bush (computer inventor) 1890.

Deaths

St Constantine (martyr) 6th century; two witches of Belvoir (burnt) 1618; John Chapman (Johnny Appleseed) 1845; Sir Alexander Fleming (bacteriologist) 1955.

Marriages

The union of Romeo Montevecchio was solemnised with Juliet Cappelletto at Cittadella in Italy (1302).

Napolean Bonaparte wed Marie Louise, daughter of Emperor Francis II of Austria (1810).

President James Madison's sister-in-law married a Supreme Court justice in the first wedding at the White House (1811).

The Trials of Sainthood

St Constantine was once a noble king of Cornwall in England. After his conversion he turned to a simple, priestly life which ended this day during a mission among the heathens of Scotland, who cut off his right arm and left him to bleed to death.

Anne Baker   Joane Willmott   Ellen Greene

Hancock in a Chariot

"John Hancock of Boston appears in public with all the state and pageantry of an Oriental prince; he rides in an elegant chariot . . . attended by four servants dressed in superb livery, mounted on fine horses richly caparisoned; and escorted by 50 horsemen with drawn sabers, the one half of which precedes and the other follow his carriage."

The Pennsylvania Ledger, March 11, 1778

Germany in the Saddle

"Gentlemen, let us work speedily! Let us put Germany, so to speak, in the saddle. You will see, well enough, that she can ride."

From a speech by Bismark to the German Assembly, March 11, 1867

Stocking-Frame Smashing

On March 11, 1811, frustrated with unemployment and falling wages, a band of distressed framework knitters in Nottinghamshire, England broke into a factory and destroyed sixty-three stocking frames. The protesters were known as Luddites. The name was said to have been derived from a youth named Ludlam who one day took a hammer and smashed the machine he was working at.

Cornish Heath

Today's flower, the Cornish heath *(Erica vagans),* is found in several parts of the world but grows in profusion in Cornwall where it covers thousands of acres on the Goonhilley Downs.

The Trials of Witchcraft

On this day in 1618, the Flower sisters, Margaret and Philippa, were burnt at the stake for witchcraft in Lincoln, England. Earlier, their mother Joan Flower, had asked for bread at her trial saying "May this choke me if I am guilty." She died on the spot in the courtroom. The Flower ladies had been found guilty of casting spells on the family of their employer, the earl of Rutland, by stealing locks of hair and pieces of clothing from them. They confessed to killing the two sons of the earl and making his wife sterile. The Flowers had been advised and assisted in their labours by Anne Baker, Joanne Willmott, and Ellen Greene, all of whom were later put to death. Collectively the infamous group came to be known as the Witches of Belvoir, the district in which they practised their craft.

Births

Godfrey Bidloo (Dutch anatomist) 1649; Bishop Berkely (English philosopher) 1684.

Deaths

St Gregory the Great (Roman pope) 604; Caesar Borgia (Italian soldier) 1507; Sun Yat Sen (Chinese leader) 1925.

Baseball in Britain

Two teams of American baseball players appeared in London at Kennington, Oval. The game, which was reported to be somewhat similar to rounders, excited but a mild interest. Several other matches were given in public before the players returned to America (1889).

Saintly Celibacy

St Gregory helped earn his sainthood by fasting with such vigour that his health was seriously impaired and he became an invalid for most of his life. In spite of this, or perhaps because of it, he was responsible for introducing celibacy into the clergy. For his efforts he had the Gregorian Chant named after him.

A Chat on the Radio

President Franklin D. Roosevelt, broadcasted his first "Fireside Chat" on American radio, after being in office for only six days (1933).

Calamity in Hungary

The Hungarian town of Szegedin was submerged by the cojoined waters of the Theiss and Maros rivers breaking through ingeniously constructed lines of defence raised against the calamity that had threatened for over a week past; 6,000 houses were destroyed and 2,000 lives lost (1879).

Disaster in Canada

The railway suspension bridge crossing the Desjardins Canal between Toronto and Hamilton gave way under a train which had gone off the rails, and the carriages, filled with passengers, were precipitated into the abyss beneath. Of ninety-seven passengers only twenty were saved (1857).

Robbery in New York

Three boy burglars aged ten, twelve, and thirteen—the youngest ever to engage in this lawlessness—were apprehended, arrested, and arraigned in New York City (1893).

Girl Scouts in America

A group of local girls were organised into a troop by Mrs Juliette Gordonhow of Savannah, Georgia. She called them the Girl Scouts of America (1912).

Hair Today, Gone Tomorrow

On March 12, 1825 a British court was besieged by a throng of poor hairless women, all with a similar story to tell. Each had been called on by a barber by the name of Thomas Rushton, who politely asked to look at her hair. He professed to be in raptures with its beauty and offered one guinea for it. As the woman was poor, she accepted. Then, before she knew what was happening, he had cropped it to the length of pig bristle and ran off without paying her a penny. He had pulled the ruse on many women in the same neighbourhood and then fled. He continued to do this all day until apprehended and brought to trial.

13
MARCH

Births

Joseph Priestley (discovered oxygen) 1733; Percival Poet (discovered Pluto) 1855; Hugh Walpole (author of *Rogue Herries*) 1884.

Deaths

Jean de la Fontaine (poet) 1695; Nicholas Boileau (poet) 1711; Sophia Lee (novelist) 1824; Regina Maria Roche (novelist) 1845.

More Celestial Events

An eclipse of the moon was recorded in Rome by Josephus today in the year 4 B.C.

Halley's Comet reached its perihelion (nearest to the sun)—just as he predicted in 1682—on this day in 1758.

Today's Witch

Amy Duny was brought to trial on charges of bewitching children. One piece of evidence brought against her was given by a Mrs Durant whose child had apparently taken to having fits after Amy entered the household as a childminder. On the advice of a white witch, Mrs Durant wrapped her infant up in a blanket which she had placed up the chimney. A toad is said to have come out of the child and it exploded when thrown in the fire. Amy was then found to have severe burns about her body. She was found guilty on this day in 1664 in London. (She was hanged three days later, protesting her innocence.)

English Events

In 1783 a bill was defeated in the House of Lords by a vote of 74 to 49. It was entitled *Marriage with a Deceased Wife's Sister Bill*.

From this day onward in 1886 British soldiers of all ranks and in all regiments were allowed to wear beards.

Star Wars

On March 13 in 1781 William Herschel, the German astronomer working under the patronage of George III in England, discovered a new planet beyond the orbit of Jupiter. It was the first since ancient days to be added to the list, and controversy raged over what to call the new body. Herschel demanded that it be called *Georgium Sidus,* after his patron. His colleagues insisted it be named *Herschel* after its discoverer. In the end it was called *Uranus,* at the suggestion of continental astronomers who wanted to keep to the old mythological system of names.

American Events

Harvard University, the oldest university in the USA was named for clergyman John Harvard (1639).

Jews were now permitted to worship in their own houses in New Amsterdam (New York), but not publicly in synagogues (1656).

The province of Maine was purchased by Mr John Usher for £1,250 (1677).

The New York Lantern published the first newspaper cartoon of "Uncle Sam" (1852). (The original Uncle Sam character was Samuel Wilson who marked "U.S.—Uncle Sam" on all shipments of provisions he sent to U.S. troops.)

14
MARCH

Births

Johann Strauss (composer) 1804; Charles Charlesworth (old child) 1829; Albert Einstein (physicist) 1879; Michael Caine (actor) 1933.

Deaths

Simon Morin (burned) 1663; Admiral Byng (shot) 1757; Theophilos Klopstock (poet) 1803; Karl Marx (philosopher) 1883.

Thirteen O'Clock, 1861

On the morning of the 14th of March 1861, the great bell of Westminster in London repeatedly marked the hour with thirteen chimes. The event was taken as a token of ill for the royal family, and less than twenty-four hours later the duchess of Kent died.

A Conviction, 1964

Jack L. Ruby was convicted in Dallas, Texas of the "murder with malice" of Lee Harvey Oswald, alleged assassin of John F. Kennedy.

A Premature Death

Charles Charlesworth was born today in 1829 in Staffordshire, England. At age four he began growing whiskers and body hair, and within the next three years his veins and tendons stood out in relief from his skin, like those of a man of 70. His hair turned white, his skin wrinkled like a prune's, and his posture became stooped. At age seven, young Charles passed out and died. According to the coroner, the cause of death was old age.

War News

1915: The German battleship *Dresden* was sunk.
1917: The Germans began to retreat behind the Hindenberg Line.
1938: Austria submitted to Hitler's Nazis and he marched into Vienna triumphantly.
1945: A huge bomb, "Ten-Ton Tess," was dropped on Germany.

A Lynching, 1891

On March 14, 1891, eleven Italians, members of a secret society known as the Mafia and accused of the murder of the police chief of New Orleans (but acquitted) were taken from the prison and lynched by an angry mob of New Orleans citizens. Three of the dead were Italian citizens whose lynching provoked international repercussions.

An Execution, 1757

Admiral Byng of the British Navy was executed today in 1757 for neglect of duty resulting in England's loss of Minorca: ". . . we approached Portsmouth. A multitude of people covered the shore looking attentively at a stout gentleman who was on his knees with his eyes bandaged, on the quarter deck of one of the vessels of the fleet. Four soldiers, placed in front of him put each three balls in his head, in the most peaceable manner, and all the assembly dispersed quite satisfied."
From *Candide,* by Voltaire (1694-1778)

Social Advice

Visits should be short like a winter's day,

Lest you're too troublesome, hasten away.

Poor Richard's Almanac, 1733

15
MARCH

Births

John Barbeyrac (French jurist/writer) 1674; Andrew Jackson (7th U.S. president) 1767.

Deaths

Julius Caesar (murdered) 44 B.C.; Attilla (the Hun) 459; Theodore Mayerne (physician) 1655; Cardinal Mezzofanti (linguist) 1949.

The Ides of March

Today was the Ides of March on the Roman calendar, named from an Etruscan word which meant "to divide" because the day divided the lunar month into two equal parts. When Julius Caesar was murdered on the steps of the Senate House on this day in 44 B.C., March 15 came to be considered an ill omen.

The Scourge of God, 459

Today in 459 A.D., Attilla, the Hun, known by the Romans as "the scourge of God" from his ravaging of the Roman Empire, was profaning divine things at a wedding when he suddenly developed a nose bleed and bled to death.

Hitler's Prophetic Speech, 1936

"I go the way that Providence dictates with the assurance of a sleepwalker."
Given in Munich on March 15, 1936

An Eminent Gamester, 1674

Jean Barbeyrac, born today in 1674, was an eminent jurist and professor of his time, a publisher of many works of jurisprudence, who would not be remembered if he was not compelled by fate to live with a gambling mother-in-law and sit for hours by the side of a pack of card-playing and garrulous old women. From this experience he gained the material for his most famous work, a four-volume treatise on gaming, entitled *Traite de Jeu*.

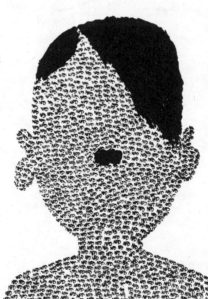

London Wine, 1655

Sir Theodore Mayerne, a French physician, who died today in 1655, was a celebrated gourmet. "Good wine," he used to say, "is slow poison: I have drunk it all my lifetime and it has not killed me yet; but bad wine is sudden death." (He died from having drunk bad wine at a tavern in London.)

Charles Dickens' Last Reading, 1870

Charles Dickens was in great demand as a reader, both in the United States and England. He kept his engagements in the last year of his life in spite of physical weakness. His last reading was in St James Hall, London, on this date in 1870. Soon after this appearance he was received in private audience by Queen Victoria who presented to him her *Leaves from a Journal of Our Life in the Highlands* with the inscription, "From one of the humblest authors to one of the greatest."

My Fair Lady's First Performance, 1956

The longest-running musical in the history of Broadway theatre, *My Fair Lady* was first performed in New York today in 1956 with Julie Andrews and Rex Harrison as the stars. (By the end of its 6-1/2-year run, 3,750,000 people had paid $20 million to see it.)

A Shakespearian Epitaph, 1618

Richard Burbage who died today in 1618 was a close friend and partner of Shakespeare. His name stands next to that of Shakespeare in the licenses for acting granted to the company at the Globe Theatre by James I in 1603. He was buried in the church of St Leonard's in Shoreditch, and the only inscription put over his grave were the simple and expressive words: *Exit Burbage.*

Births

James Madison (4th U.S. president) 1751; George Ohm (physicist) 1787; Elsie Janis (actress) 1889.

Deaths

Tiberius Claudius Nero (Roman emperor) 37; Richard Burbage (actor) 1618; Nathaniel Bowditch (astronomer) 1838; Gaston Calmette (shot) 1914.

An Academy Opening, 1802

An act of Congres established West Point Military Academy in West Point, New York.

A Slow Day, 1830

The New York Stock Exchange experienced its slowest-ever day when just thirty-one shares were traded.

A First Visit, 1621

On March 16, 1621, Samoset, Indian chief from the Island of Monhegan, was the first chief to pay a visit to the new Colony of Plymouth.

A Long Sitting, 1660

Today in 1660, the British Long Parliament of the Puritans was finally dissolved. It had been sitting since 1640.

An Editorial Objection, 1914

On March 16, 1914, Madame Caillaux, wife of the French Finance Minister, shot and fatally wounded Gaston Calmette, editor of *Le Figaro,* because of his attacks in the paper on her husband.

A Name Change, 1641

A general court declared Rhode Island a democracy and adopted a new constitution granting freedom of religion to all citizens and changed the name of the island from Aquedneck to Rhode Island.

A Peculiar Number

The number 16 has a most peculiar occult symbolism. It is pictured by a tower struck by lightning from which a man is falling with a crown on his head. It is also called "the shattered citadel." It gives warning of some strange fatality awaiting one, and danger of accidents and defeat of one's plans. In matters of the future it is a warning sign that should be carefully noted and plans made in advance in the endeavour to avert its fatalistic tendency.

An Acting Debut, 1918

An unknown actress, Tallulah Bankhead, made her debut in a play entitled *The Squab Farm* in a New York Theatre.

A Treaty Violation, 1935

Adolf Hitler, ignoring the Treaty of Versailles, re-established military training in Germany.

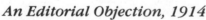

Births

Frank Buck (animal collector) 1882; Bobby Jones (golfer) 1902; Nat King Cole (singer) 1919; Rudolph Nureyev (dancer) 1938.

Deaths

St Patrick (Irish saint) 464.

St Patrick

The most famous legend about St Patrick, the patron saint of Ireland, is that he miraculously drove snakes and all venomous beasts from the island by banging a drum, and did this so well that to touch Irish soil is supposed to be instant death for any such creature. Even Irish wood has a virtue against poison, it is said, "so that it is reported of King's College, Cambridge, that being built of Irish wood, no spider doth ever come near it."

His Mission

Patrick was sent back to Ireland by Pope Celestine to preach the gospel to the heathens. He found that the pagan Irish had great difficulty comprehending the doctrine of the Trinity, until he gave them a concrete example by holding up a shamrock to show the three leaves combining to make a single plant. The Irish understood at once, and the shamrock became the symbol of the land. Irishmen wear it in their hats on the saint's day.

His Death

When he was dying on this day in 464, he urged his friends not to lament, but rather to celebrate his comfortable exit. To this end his last request was that each of them take a small drop of something to drink to ease their pain. Out of reverence for the saint, and in compliance with his last words is supposed to have come the Irish prediliction for whiskey.

Boxing Events

Bob Fitzsimmons knocked out "Gentleman" Jim Corbett for the heavyweight boxing title, in 14 rounds at Carson City, Nevada. Fitzsimmons weighed only 167 pounds (1897).

Canada's Tommy Burns fought in Dublin for the heavyweight championship of the world. He knocked out Jem Roche in a record time of one minute, 28 seconds (1906).

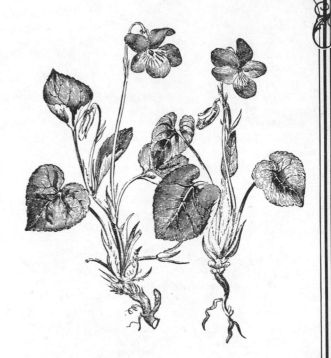

Flower of the Day

The flower for March 17 is the sweet violet *(Viola odorata).* "As violets are perceived by their fragrant smell before they are seen, so are those who have a fair reputation, shedding around them the sweet odour of virtue while they themselves are concealed."
Florilegium, 1830

In the Air

John Montgomery was given the title "The Father of Gliding" because he was the first man to fly in a glider. On March 17, 1884, he put his 130-pound frame behind the joystick of a 30-pound glider and travelled about 600 feet across a California valley.

Beneath the Sea

John P. Holland's underwater device, said to be the first practical submarine in marine history, was submerged off Staten Island, New York, remaining under water for almost an hour and three-quarters (1898).

18
MARCH

Births

Grover Cleveland (24th U.S. president) 1837; Nikolai Rimsky-Korsakov (composer) 1844; Rudolph Diesel (engineer) 1858.

Inoculation Resisted, 1718

On this day in 1718 Lady Mary Wortley Montagu inoculated her infant son with a smallpox virus—the first time that inoculation against disease had been used. She learned of the practice while travelling in Turkey, and brought it back to England as a patriotic gesture to a country ravaged by the disease that she herself had suffered from. Though her son's inoculation was entirely successful, the practice of inoculation was firmly resisted by both the clergy and the medical establishment for many years, during which the lady had to put up with much abuse.

Peace, 1962

France and Algeria made a peace agreement after more than seven years of war, costing 250,000 lives and $20,000,000,000.

Charlie's Luck, 1964

A $29-per-week London public utility clerk, Charlie Cooper (46 and a bachelor) won the equivalent of $630,375.20 after betting 70c in an English soccer pool.

Space Walk, 1965

Lieutenant Colonel Alexei Leonov of Russia eased out of an opening in his space capsule and walked in space for twenty minutes, secured by a long lifeline.

Alarms, 1944

Approximately 2,500 women trampled guards and floorwalkers in their panic for 1,500 alarm clocks announced for sale in a Chicago department store. They had been unobtainable since the war started.

Deaths

St Edward (martyr) 978; Czar Ivan (the Terrible) 1584; John Luther Jones (Casey Jones) 1900.

Stabbed Into Sainthood

St Edward, king of England, was treacherously stabbed in the back, on this day in 978, on the orders of his wicked stepmother. His body was buried in unhallowed ground but the grave was marked by a heavenly pillar of light and became a place of miraculous cures and healing.

Crashed Into Imortality, 1900

John Luther Jones, veteran engineer of the Chicago and New Orleans Limited Railway, stayed at his post despite the certainty of a wreck, in an effort to slow down his hurtling, brakeless express and protect as many lives as possible. He died in the crash, today in 1900, but lives on in the folk ballad, "Casey Jones."

Caruso's Foresight, 1902

Enrico Caruso recorded ten operatic arias for the Gramophone Company in a Milan, Italy, hotel room converted into a makeshift studio. He was the first great artist to recognise the phonograph as a viable medium for musicians. His fee was $500.

Banned Butter, 1923

Butter had inflated so much in price in Berlin, that the government decreed that it no longer be served in restaurants. Germans who dined out brought their own butter with them.

First Shavers, 1931

The first electric shavers went on sale in the United States.

Big Bargain, 1954

Howard Hughes paid $23,489,478 for RKO Pictures Corporation.

19
MARCH

Births

Tobias George Smollett (Scottish novelist) 1721; David Livingstone (Scottish explorer) 1813; William Jennings Bryan (American lawyer) 1860.

Deaths

St Joseph (Mary's husband) 1st century A.D.; Rene Robert Cavelier, Sieur de La Salle (French explorer) 1687; Brighton Billy (boxer) 1838.

Valencia, Spain

This is the last day of the week of *Saint Joseph's Fiesta* in Valencia, Spain. The climax of the festival is the burning of quaint effigies and humorous, ironic caricatures at the street corners and intersections. The effigies are sometimes three or four stories high and are filled with explosives. Rockets burst, people dance, bands play, and the effigies burn with deafening explosions.

Athens, Greece

Claudius Ptolemaeus (Ptolemy), the Greek astronomer, recorded the first-ever eclipse of the moon which had taken place today in 721 B.C.

Capistrano, USA

If all goes according to plan, this is the day that the swallows should return to San Juan Capistrano Mission, California.

Rome, Italy

On March 19 began the Roman festival, *Minervalia,* in honour of the virgin goddess Minerva, or, as she was known to the Greeks, Athena (Athens is named after her). She was born, fully grown and armed, from the head of Zeus, and trusted to carry his shield and his thunderbolt. She was the goddess of the city, of handicrafts and agriculture, and the inventor of the bridle to tame horses. The olive was her tree, and the owl her bird.

New York, USA

The first bank robbery in the U.S. took place at the City Bank of New York. A vault was opened with duplicate keys and robbed of $245,000. Edward Smith was later convicted and sentenced to five years at Sing Sing (1831).

Bergemoletto, Italy

On March 19, 1755, three women were buried by snow in the ruins of a stable in the village of Bergemoletto, near Piedmont, and survived until their rescue thirty-seven days later.

Lhasa, Tibet

The Dalai Lama, Tibet's spiritual ruler, fled from his country following a revolt by natives against communist Chinese troops (1959).

Barkway, England

Owen Swift killed Brighton Billy in a prize-fight at Barkway, Hertfordshire today in 1838, this being his third victim. At the inquest a verdict of manslaughter was returned.

Massachusetts, USA

On March 19, 1628 the Massachusetts colony was founded by six Englishmen:
> "They purchased a bit of land extending from ocean to ocean and from three miles north of the Merrimac River to three miles south of the Charles River and Massachusetts Bay."

London, England

King Henry VII confiscated the annates (the year's church revenue to be paid to the Vatican) in an effort to force Pope Clement VII to grant him a divorce from Catherine of Aragon (1532).

Births

Publius Ovidius Naso (Ovid) 43 B.C.; Heinrich Ibsen (dramatist) 1828; Ray Goulding (comedian) 1922.

Deaths

Henry IV (king of England) 1413; Sir Isaac Newton (philosopher) 1727.

An Accurate Prophecy, 1413

A fortune teller had told Henry IV that he would die in Jerusalem. While on a journey he fell so ill that he could not go on, and lay for a long while, unconscious, in the home of the abbot of Westminster. When he came to he asked at once where he was, and if the room had any special name. It had: Jerusalem. The king then said, "Loving be to the Father of Heaven, for I know I shall die in this chamber, according to the prophecy of me before said that I should die in Jerusalem." So he made himself ready, and died shortly thereafter on this day in 1413.

A Genius' Death, 1727

Sir Isaac Newton, who gave the first rational account of the laws regulating the motion of the planets and the principle of gravitation, died on March 20, 1727. Alexander Pope created an epitaph for him:

Nature and all her works lay blind in the night
God said: Let Newton be, and all was light.

Isaac Newton

A Calendar Alteration, 1751

The calendar in Britain was altered by act of Parliament today in 1751, so that as of September, 1752, the number of days would be moved ahead by eleven days and the new year would start on January 1.

A Sight for Sore Eyes, 1667

"In favor of my eyes I stayed at home reading the ridiculous *History of My Lord Newcastle,* wrote by his wife; which shows her to be a mad, conceited, ridiculous woman and he an ass to suffer her to write what she does about him."

From the diary of Samuel Pepys, March 20, 1667

The Spring Equinox

On, or about this day of every year, spring begins in the northern hemisphere as the sun passes north over the equator, and the sun enters the constellation of Aries. According to many old calendars this signifies the advent of the new year, because it is the season in which new life arises from the ruinous winter of the old. Aries, or the ram, was derived as a sign of the Zodiac from the golden fleece in the legend of Jason and the Argonauts by the Greeks; but it appears with even greater antiquity on Egyptian monuments, where it symbolizes the beginning of the lambing season.

A Best Seller, 1857

On March 20, 1857, *Uncle Tom's Cabin*, by Mrs Harriet Beecher Stowe, "depicting the possibilities of horror and tragedy rooted in the Institution of slavery" was published. The first printing of 5,000 copies sold out in one week. Sixteen months later one million copies had been sold. The novel provoked a wave of hatred against slavery, as well as the publication of thirty books in defence of slavery.

Births

Robert the Bruce (Scottish king) 1274; Johann Sebastian Bach (composer) 1685.

Deaths

St Benedict (abbot) 543; Thomas Cranmer (archbishop of Canterbury) 1556; Pocahantas (Indian princess) 1617.

Obedience, Charity, and Poverty

Benedict was so shocked by the licentiousness of his school mates that he vowed to live a life of solitude. But as a hermit his fame spread far and wide and he was frequently sought out for his wisdom. As abbot of Monte Casino he drew up the rules which became the foundation of the Benedictine Order. Their credo is based on these main rules: obedience, charity, and voluntary poverty.

Learning, Piety, and Courage

Thomas Cranmer, archbishop of Canterbury was burnt at Oxford for heresy, today in 1556. His learning and his piety earned him universal respect and the courage of his martyrdom made him the hero of the Protestant party.

Pocahantas

At the age of twenty-two, Mrs John Rolfe—formerly Pocahantas—died in London on this day in 1617. At home in Virginia, this daughter of the Indian Chief Powhattan, had saved Captain John Smith from death at the hands of her father who had imprisoned him. She was seized as a hostage in 1612, then married the colonist, Mr Rolfe, who took her to England.

Love Conquers All

On March 21, 1891, the long-standing Hatfield-McCoy vendetta of West Virginia was declared ended. A son and a daughter, one from each faction, announced their engagement to be married.

A Hissing, Detonating Meteor

"A hissing, detonating meteor passed over Italy, two hours after sunset, on this day in 1676. Its apparent diameter was greater than that of the moon: its real diameter about three-quarters of a mile; and the velocity was calculated at one hundred and sixty miles in a minute of time."
   From an 18th-century almanac

Astrological Predictions

According to *Christian Astrology* of 1647, the fortunes of those born under the sign of Aries the ram (March 21 to April 20) are as follows:

Manners when well dignified
In feats of Warre and Courage invincible, scorning any should exceed him, subject to no Reason, Bold Confident immoveable, Contentious, challenging all Honour to themselves, Valiant, lovers of Warre and things pertaining thereunto, hazarding himselfe to all Perils, willingly will obey no body, or submit to any; a large Reporter of his owne Acts, one that slights all things in comparison of Victory, and yet of prudent behaviour in his owne affairs.

When ill placed
Then he is a Pratler without modesty or honesty, a lover of Slaughter and Quarrels, Murder, Theevery, a promoter of Sedition, Frayes and Commotions, an Highway-Theefe, as wavering as the Wind, a Traytor, of turbulent Spirit, Perjured, Obscene, Rash, Inhumane, neither fearing God or caring for man, Unthankful, Trecherous, Oppressors, Ravenous, Cheaters, Furious, Violent.

Births

Anthony Van Dyck (Flemish painter) 1599; Robert Andrews Millican (American physicist) 1868.

Deaths

Jacques de Molay (templar) 1312; Jean Baptist Lully (French composer) 1687; Johann Wolfgang Van Goethe (German philosopher) 1832.

Goethe Goes Graciously

The great German literary genius, Johann Wolfgang von Goethe, was so precocious that he knew all of German, French, Italian, Latin, and Greek before he was eight years old. As he lay dying in Weimar on March 22, 1832, his final words were "Let the light enter."

A Prophetic Pyre Prediction

On March 22, 1312, covetous of their wealth and power, King Philip of France, and Pope Clement IV, moved to suppress the Order of the Knights Templars, soldiers of the crusades since 1118. The grand master of the order, Jacques de Molay, was tortured by them and readied for burning. As he mounted the pyre he said: "None of us have betrayed either our God or our country; we die innocent; the decree which condemns us is an unjust one, but there is in heaven an august tribunal where the oppressed never implore in vain: to that tribunal I cite thee, O Roman Pontiff: within forty days thou shalt be there: and thee, O Philip, my master and my king; in vain do I pardon thee, thy life is condemned; within the year I await thee before God's throne." Both king and pope were dead within their appointed times.

Toe-Tapping To Te Deum

During a rehearsal of his own *Te Deum* the early French composer Jean Baptiste Lully became so excited that he struck himself violently on the toe with the cane with which he was beating time. The toe became seriously inflamed, and the doctor recommended amputation. Lully delayed, and the inflammation spread to his foot; he delayed some more, and it spread even further. The composer died on March 22, 1687, during an attempted operation to amputate his inflamed leg.

March Massacre

On March 22, 1621 Jamestown, Virginia and other settlements were saved from general massacre by the warning given by a "converted red man" who revealed the plot the previous evening. Exactly a year later they were not so lucky: 347 white settlers out of a population of 1,240 were killed in the first massacre in America by Indians.

States Starts Stamps

The Stamp Act of March 22, 1765, required revenue stamps to be put on all commercial and legal documents, pamphlets, newspapers, playing cards, and dice in the United States.

States Sinks Steamer

On March 22, 1929, the Canadian steamer *I'm Alone* with a cargo of liquor was fired upon and sunk by the U.S. Coast Guard ten miles off the Louisiana coast. Captain J.T. Randell and crew were taken prisoner to New Orleans.

States Starts Stopping Slavery

An act was passed on this day in 1794 prohibiting American citizens from engaging in the slave trade in foreign countries on pain of forfeiture of their vessels and a fine of $82,000.

Raleigh Runs Riot

Sir Walter Raleigh arrived today in 1595 on the island of Trinidad where he pillaged and burned the town of San Joseph in revenge for some Trinidadians having betrayed and shot eight sailors the previous year.

Births

Pierre Laplace (French physicist) 1749; Joan Crawford (American actress) 1904; Werner Von Braun (German scientist) 1912.

Deaths

St Ethelwold (hermit) 699; Peter the Cruel (king of Castille) 1369; John D. Lee (Mormon bishop) 1877.

King John Versus the Pope

On March 23, 1208, Pope Innocent III laid all of England under interdict because of a conflict with King John over the appointment of an archbishop of Canterbury. All the churches were closed and all religious services except baptism, confession, and the administration of the viaticum on the point of death, were discontinued. John retaliated by seizing church property and swearing to banish all the English clergy after tearing out their eyes and splitting their noses. The interdict lasted for over six years.

John D. Lee Versus the Settlers

John D. Lee, a Mormon bishop, was shot today in 1877 for complicity in the massacre of 120 emigrants on their way to California.

St Ethelwold Versus the Sea

Ethelwold lived as a hermit on the sea shore until his death today in 699. During a raging storm he quelled the savage seas and skies with his prayers, to enable a party of monks to reach the shore safely in their boats.

Peter the Cruel Versus Illiteracy

The cruelties for which Peter, king of Castille (who died on this day in 1369) is remembered are mostly fictitious. What is less well known is that he was the very first European king who could write.

A Great White Father Speaks

"My white children in Alabama have extended their law over your country. If you remain in it, you must be subject of that law. If you remove across the Mississippi, you will be subject to your own laws and the care of your father, The President."

President Jackson's message to the Creek Indians on March 23, 1829

King George II Starts a Custom

A London audience heard Handel's *Messiah* for the first time. As the "Hallelujah Chorus" was sung, King George II started a precedent by rising to his feet (1743).

A Lady Unlocked

On March 23, 1837, doctors in Edinburgh operated on a woman to remove from her a brass padlock that she had swallowed a month before.

Tennessee Damns Darwin

On March 23, 1925, Tennessee enacted a law forbidding the teaching of evolution in any school or college supported by public funds. Georgia and Mississipi soon followed suit.

Patrick Henry's Immortal Words

Patrick Henry, the American revolutionary leader, gave a speech today in 1775, in the Virginia House of Delegates, wherein he uttered the famous words: "I know not what course others may take; but as for me, give me liberty, or give me death!"

Nellie Melba's Toast

On this day in 1901 Helen Porter Mitchell—the Australian soprano singer better known professionally as Dame Nellie Melba—explained how she prepared her toast by cutting paper-thin slices of bread and baking them until crisp and dry.

24
MARCH

Births

Edgerton Ryerson (Canadian educator) 1803; Thomas Dewey (American politician) 1902; Steve McQueen (American actor) 1930.

Deaths

St Simon (child martyr) 1475; Elizabeth I (queen of England) 1603; Henry Wadsworth Longfellow (American poet) 1881.

The Flower of the Day

For March 24th, the ancient monks appointed the golden saxifrage (*Chrysosplenium oppositifolium*) as the flower of the day.

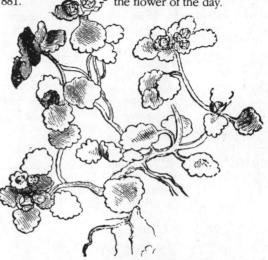

The Beginning of Bombs, 1580

The first bombs ever used were thrown upon the town of Watchendonck in Guelderland, Germany, on March 24, 1580. Their invention is commonly attributed to Galen, bishop of Munster.

Filibuster, 1840

The opposition in the American House of Representatives, determined to defeat a ministerial bill regulating the issue of treasury notes, protracted the sitting through the whole of this day and night and up to 5 p.m. on the 25th. Members were kept awake by the prodding of officers for the purpose of giving their votes.

Time Marches On, 1603

On March 24, 1603, Queen Elizabeth I of England died at the age of seventy at Richmond, Surrey, in the forty-fifth year of her reign. She once asked her Chief Justice Papham: "Now, Mr Speaker, what hath passed in the Commons House?" He replied: "If it please your Majesty, seven weeks."

A Cure for Distemper, 1656

On this day in 1656, the niece of Blaise Pascal (the French man of letters) was miraculously cured of inveterate distemper by a touch of one of the thorns in the Holy Crown.

Lady Chatterly Liberated, 1960

The U.S. Court of Appeals today ruled that the novel *Lady Chatterley's Lover* by D.H. Lawrence was not an obscene book and could therefore be sent through the mail.

A Summit Reached, 1965

Senator Robert F. Kennedy reached the summit of Mount Kennedy in the Yukon Territory, the first person ever to scale the highest unclimbed mountain in North America. (The Canadian government had named the 13,000 foot mountain in honour of the late president of the U.S.) At the summit, the senator planted a black-bordered flag and a copy of his brother's 1961 inaugural address.

Births

Arturo Toscanini (conductor) 1867; Béla Bartók (composer) 1881; Pierre Boulez (composer) 1926.

Deaths

Thomas Moore (Irish poet) 1852.

Lady Day Prophecy

An old English couplet said:

When my Lord falls in my Lady's lap, England beware of some mishap

meaning that when Easter, which is a moveable feast, falls on Lady Day, the country is in for some calamity.

Celebration in Greece

On March 25, 1828 the Greek flag was first raised against the Ottoman Empire. The occasion is commemorated annually in Greece and Cyprus with parades and dancing.

A Protest March in Ohio

On March 26, 1894 Jacob Coxey of Massillon, Ohio, led a group of seventy-five unemployed—"The Commonwealth Army"—for a march on Washington to proclaim the wants of poor people. He gathered recruits from each town as he passed through.

Lady Isabella Tichborne's Bequest

As she lay gravely ill, Lady Isabella Tichborne asked her husband to give her some land so that she might bequeath the poor of Tichborne a yearly gift of flour. Her husband cruelly told her she could have as much as she could crawl around carrying a blazing torch. She was able to encircle twenty-three acres and cursed the Tichbornes should they ever stop the dole. In 1796, they did, but suffered such great disasters that it was re-introduced and continues to this day on March 25 in Tichborne, Hampshire, England.

Birds in Belgium

The Belgians believed that, on the day of the Annunciation, the Lord bade all to quiet contemplation, even birds and animals. The cuckoo was the only bird to disobey and its raucous cry echoed through the country. He was punished to eternal wandering—never with a nest of his own.

Lady Day

March 25 is the festival of the Annunciation of the immaculate conception by the archangel Gabriel. In France the day is called *Notre Dame de Mars,* and in England, *Lady Day,* an abridgment of Day of Our Blessed Lady. An English country gentleman once sent a letter to a lady of rank in London, inscribed with the following address: To, the 25th of March, Foley-Place, London. The postman duly delivered the letter to the house of a Lady named Day.

Waffles in Sweden

Today is *Waffle Day* in Sweden when waffles are traditionally consumed by the populace.

Pancakes in America

The first public demonstration of pancake-making astonished New Yorkers, gazing at the scene through a department store window (1882).

Ladies and the Maestro

The great orchestral conductor, Arturo Toscanini who was born on this day in 1867 once said: "I kissed my first woman and smoked my first cigarette on the same day; I have never had time for tobacco since."

Births

Robert Frost (poet) 1874; Tennessee Williams (playwright) 1914.

Deaths

Ludwig van Beethoven (composer) 1827; Sarah Bernhardt (acress) 1923.

Economics, 1925

In Rome, 100,000,000 lira went up in smoke on this day in 1925. The public bonfire, attended by Signor Stefani, minister of finance, was the opening event in the Italian government's campaign to reduce the circulation of paper money.

Culture, 1937

"Popeye," the comic strip character created by Elzie Crisler Segar, was immortalised by residents of Crystal City, Texas, who dedicated a statue of the spinach fanatic during a local Spinach Festival.

Medicine, 1906

"Witchcraft and superstition die hard in Devonshire. There has lately been an epidemic of measles at Chittlehampton, and in the hope of curing their children parents have dragged the little sufferers through three parishes in one day, which proceeding is said to effect a certain cure."
    Daily Mail, March 26, 1906

Ecology, 1699

"After an extraordinary storm, there came up the Thames a whale which was 56 feet long. Such, and a larger of the Serpent kind, was killed there forty years ago. *That* year died Cromwell."
    From the diary of John Evelyn, March 26, 1699

Athletics, 1949

The University boat race between Oxford and Cambridge was won by the latter by a quarter length.

Numerology

The number 26 is full of the gravest warnings for the future. It foreshadows disasters brought about by association with others and financial ruin by bad speculations, partnerships, unions, and bad advice. People born on this day are often greatly misunderstood in their lives, and therefore often feel extremely lonely. By nature they are very intense and have a great sense of individuality but tend towards fanaticism which often makes bitter enemies.

Politics

1776: The Constitution was adopted in South Carolina.
1788: The slave trade was prohibited in Massachusetts.
1790: The Naturalisation Act required U. S. citizens to have a two-year residency.
1825: The Republic of Mexico was proclaimed at Monterey.
1925: Field Marshal Hindenburg was elected president of Germany.
1971: Citizens of Bangladesh celebrated the Proclamation of Independence.

27
MARCH

Births

William Konrad von Rontgen (physicist) 1845; Edward Steichan (photographer) 1879; Rostopovich (composer) 1927.

Deaths

Walt Whitman (poet) 1892; John Bright (orator) 1889; Roberrt Falcon Scott (explorer) 1912.

John Bright

John Bright, an English politician renowned for his oratory who died on March 27, 1889, left the following memorable words:

"The knowledge of ancient languages is mainly a luxury." (A letter in the *Pall Mall Gazette,* 1886).

"My opinion is that the Northern States will manage somehow to muddle through." (Said during the American Civil War.)

"England is the mother of Parliaments." (A speech at Birmingham in 1865.)

"Force is not a remedy." (Speech on the Irish troubles, 1880.)

Robert Falcon Scott

"Scott of the Antarctic" perished with his men on this day in 1912 in a blizzard, on the way back from their trip to the South Pole. The following are entries from his last journal:

"Make the boy interested in natural history if you can; it is better than games." (Last journal message to his wife.)

"He [Oates] said: "I am just going outside, and may be some time." He went out into the blizzard and we have not seen him since. We knew that poor Oates was walking to his death, but though we tried to dissuade him, we knew that was the act of a brave man and an English gentleman. We all hope to meet the end with a similar spirit, and assuredly the end is not far." (March 16, 1912.)

"Had we lived, I should have had a tale to tell of the hardihood, endurance, and courage of my companions which would have fired the heart of every Englishman. These rough notes and our dead bodies must tell the tale." (Last journal message to the public.)

"For God's sake look after our people." (Last journal entry, March 25, 1912.)

Walt Whitman

Walt Whitman, the American poet who died on this day in 1892, wrote poems on moral, social, and political questions in an unconventional form between rhythmical prose and verse.

A-foot and light-hearted I take to the open road,
Healthy, free, the world before me.

I think I could turn and live with the animals, they are so
    placid and self-contained,
I stand and look at them long and long.
They do not sweat and whine about their condition,
They do not lie awake in the dark and weep for their sins,
They do not make me sick discussing their duty to God,
Not one is dissatisfied, not one is demented in the mania
    of running things,
Not one kneels to another, nor to his kind that lived
    thousands of years ago,
Not one is respectable or unhappy over the whole earth.

Come lovely and soothing death,
Undulate round the world, serenely arriving, arriving,
In the day, in the night, to all, to each,
Sooner or later, delicate death.

Births

Paul Whiteman (band leader) 1891;
Rudolph Serkin (composer) 1903.

Deaths

Henry Garner (Jesuit) 1606; Sergei
Rachmaninoff (composer) 1943; W.C.
Handy (composer) 1958.

Today's Illnesses

Persons born on this day have a
tendency to suffer from heart
problems such as palpitation,
irregular circulation, and high blood
pressure in later years. They are also
prone to eye troubles and would be
well advised to have their sight
checked frequently.

A Gunpowder Plotter, 1606

After confessing his part in the Gunpowder Plot, Henry
Garner, a Jesuit, was executed in London near St Pauls on
this day in 1606.

Gunpowder Comes to Europe, 1380

Though discovered very early by the Chinese, and known
to have been used by the Arabs in a battle near Mecca in
690, gunpowder was first used in Europe on March 28,
1380 by the Venetians in a battle against the Genoese.

Gunpowder in Use

1854:   The Crimean War began with Russia versus
Turkey, France, and Britain.
1918:   Massed German troops attacked Vimy Ridge in
France.
1939:   The city of Madrid fell in Spain and General
Franco triumphed.
1942:   The St Nazaire docks in France were raided by the
British.

The Jenkins' Ear Debate, 1738

At a debate in the British Parliament on March 28, 1738
some members urged a war with Spain in retaliation for
the Spaniards pillaging Captain Jenkins' ship in 1731,
setting it adrift, and cutting off Jenkins' ear.

The Weather

A hill five hundred feet in height was carried four miles
from its site by the dreadful Calabrian earthquake in
southern Italy on this day in 1783.

A severe hurricane ravaged the island of Mauritius today
in 1874, devasting sugar-cane crops, wreaking havoc on
shipping in the harbour of Port Louis, and forcing
everyone to lie flat on the ground to escape being blown
away.

Expeditions, 1611

Ernest van de Wall sailed from Holland in search of the
Northwest Passage. The result of his expedition was the
founding of the Compagnie van Niew Nederland,
forerunner of the Dutch West India Company.

On the same day, Adrian Block and Hendrick
Christiaensen sailed to Manhattan Island to trade with the
Indians.

Washing Machines, 1797

Nathaniel Briggs of New Hampshire received a patent for
a washing machine, describing his invention as an
"improvement for washing clothes."

Radio Ban, 1944

"Singing commercials" were banned by radio station
WQXR in New York City.

29
MARCH

Births

Menes (Egyptian king) 3400 B.C., Raphael (painter) 1483; John Tyler (10th U.S. president) 1790.

Deaths

Raymond Lully (alchemist) 1315; Thomas Parkyns (eccentric) 1741; Thomas Coram (hospital founder) 1751.

The Alchemy of Love

The most famous alchemist of his day, Raymond Lully, was stoned to death by the natives of Mauritania on March 29, 1315. Lully became an alchemist when the woman he loved refused him her hand in marriage because she had a cancerous breast. He resolved to study alchemy and learn a cure for his beloved. Eventually he had the good fortune to cure and marry her.

Rat Labour, 1875

The *Telegraphic Journal* in London states that a mode had been found of utilising the labour of rats. An inspector who had been sent to relay some worn-out underground cables and who had been foolish enough to pull out the old wires without thinking how to get the new ones in, hit upon the idea of placing a rat to which a piece of string had been tied, in the tube and sending a ferret after him. The contrivance worked admirably, but on being repeated the rat faced about and fought the ferret. However, by twitching the string the electrician succeeded in parting the combatants and the rat performed for the second time the task required of it.

Babies in Baskets

Captain Thomas Coram, founder of the London Foundling Hospital, died on this day in 1751. In compliance with an Act of Parliament, a basket was hung outside the hospital in which the foundling infants were put, and a bell to be rung to notify the hospital's officers. In this way, in 1741, the first year of its operation, the hospital received 3,296 basketfuls.

Further Justice, 1621

On March 29, 1621 Christiane Couper, of Culros, Scotland, had already confessed to "the useing of charmes," but since several "famous personis" had spoken against her, she was ordered "for the glorie of God and the punishment of so heavenous and foull a cryme, further justice be done upon her." She was burned.

Niagara Falls Stops, 1848

On this day in 1848 the mighty roar of Niagara Falls stopped. A heavy wind on Lake Erie had caused an ice-jam to block the Niagara River near Buffalo, New York. The phenomenon lasted for thirty hours until the ice broke up and the Falls recommenced.

Wrestling with the Law

Sir Thomas Parkyns, barrister, of Bunny Park, Nottinghamshire, who died on 29th March, 1741, was equally at home in the wrestling ring or on the magisterial bench; and it was said that he could throw an antagonist, combat a paradox, quote the classics, and lay down the law at quarter sessions, with any man in England. He hired as servants only wrestlers who could best him, because, he said, a good wrestler could not be a drunkard.

Births

Sir Henry Wotton (ambassador) 1568; Francisco Jose de Goya (painter) 1746; Vincent Van Gogh (painter) 1853; Warren Beatty (actor) 1937.

Deaths

Phocion (Athenian general) 317 B.C.; Somner (archbishop of Canterbury) 1669; Beau Brummel (man of fashion) 1840.

The Sicilian Vespers

On Easter Monday, 30th March 1282, a Sicilian woman of Palermo was sexually assaulted by a French soldier while she was on her way to evening prayers. The people of Palermo attacked the French in the town and massacred the whole garrison of 8,000, sparing neither age nor sex. The rebellion quickly spread and within days tens of thousands of French had been killed and the island recovered from the hands of the occupiers. The revolt is known as the Sicilian Vespers because those were the prayers the young woman of Palermo was on her way to attend.

Today in History

1741: Dr. Samuel Johnson was "touched" by Queen Anne to cure the "King's Evil."

1858: Hyman L. Lipman of Philadelphia patented a pencil equipped with a rubber eraser.

1880: President Hayes opened the Metropolitan Museum of Art in New York City.

1920: G. C. Bergdoll, a millionaire draft-dodger from Philadelphia, in captivity since January 7, was sentenced to five years' imprisonment.

1923: Cunard lines *Laconia,* the first passenger liner to sail around the world, returned to New York after 130 days cruising.

1942: A directive from Washington decreed that men's suits be manufactured without trouser cuffs, pleats, and patch pockets for the duration of the war.

Ambassador Wotton

How happy is he born and taught
That serveth not another's will:
Whose armour is his lowest thought
And simple truth his utmost skill.

Thus wrote Sir Henry Wotton, born on this day in 1568, and for twenty years English ambassador to Venice. He also coined the famous definition of an ambassador: An honest man sent to lie abroad for the good of his country.

Today in Flowers

Today's flower, *Cardamine hirsuta,* alias hairy bitter cress, alias rough cardamine is actually a weed and a violent one at that. When ripe its seed pods curl up then burst, elastically scattering seeds for a considerable distance.

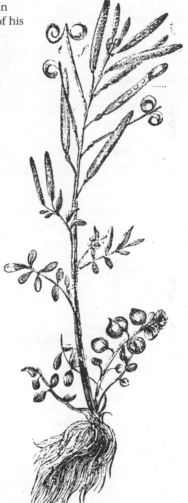

31
MARCH

Births

David, youngest son of Jesse and the slayer of the Philistine giant Goliath (Samuel, XVII). On the death of Saul he became king of Judah, and later king of all Israel (1086 B.C.).

René Descartes, the celebrated French mathematician, physicist, and philosopher known as "the father of modern philosophy." In 1637 he authored *Le Discours de la Méthode* in which he expounded a quasi-mechanical conception of the universe, which he reduced to space, matter, and motion, operating under mathematical laws (1596).

Franz Joseph Haydn, Austrian-born composer of many symphonies, concertos, and cantatas. He has often been described as "the Father of modern instrumental music" (1732).

Edward Fitzgerald (born Edward Purcell but his father changed the family name to Fitzgerald), an English scholar best known for his poetic translation of the *Rubaiyat of Omar Khayyam* (1809).

Robert Wilhem von Bunsen, the German chemist credited with the invention of the bunsen (gas) burner which produces a very hot, non-luminous flame by the mixture of air with the stream of gas before it is lighted (1811).

Andrew Lang, Scottish scholar, journalist, and poet who collected fairy tales as a hobby and was the author of prose translations of Homer (1844).

Henry Morgan (American comedian) 1915; Sidney Chaplin (American actor) 1926; John Fowles (novelist) 1926; Herb Alpert (American musician) 1935; Richard Chamberlain (American actor) 1935.

Deaths

John Donne, dean of St Paul's, famous as a preacher and as a metaphysical poet, author of satires, epistles, and elegies (1631).

John Constable, English landscape painter who specialised in pastoral rural scenes with vast skies overhead (1837).

Charlotte Bronte, eldest of the three novelist daughters of a Yorkshire clergyman of Irish descent. She is best known for *Jane Eyre* and *Villette* (1855).

Ebenezer Butterick, originator of the tissue-paper dress pattern for home dressmakers (1903).

Otto Ringling, circus owner and pioneer of the "Big Top" circus productions in America (1911).

John Pierpont Morgan, American banker who amassed a huge fortune (1913).

Knute Rockne, American football immortal, killed in a plane crash (1931).

Clarence Darrow, American lawyer (1938).

Events

The Eiffel Tower was officially opened in Paris, in spite of indignant protests from 100 leading writers, composers, and artists that it outraged French taste and overwhelmed French architecture (1889).

An Act of the American Congress authorised the Mount Rushmore National Memorial, carved on the face of the mountain in the Black Hills, South Dakota. Presidents Washington, Jefferson, Lincoln, and Theodore Roosevelt were to be sculpted by Gutzon Borgium (1925).

PRIL

Next came fresh April, full of lustyhed,
And wanton as a kid whose horne new buds;
Upon a bull he rode, the same which led
Europa floating through th'Argolick fluds:
His horns were gilden all with golden studs,
And garnished with garlands goodly dight,
Of all the fairest flowers and freshest buds,
Which th'earth brings forth; and wet he seemed in sight
With waves through which he waded for his love's delight.
   Edmund Spenser

APRIL

History

In the ancient Alban calendar in which the year had ten months, April stood first, and had thirty-six days. In the calendar of Romulus it was the second month and had thirty days. Numa's twelve-month calendar assigned it the fourth place, with twenty-nine days, and so it remained till the calendar reformation by Julius Caesar, when it recovered its former thirty days, which it continues to enjoy.

It is commonly supposed that the name was derived from the Latin *aperio,* "I open," as marking the time when the buds of the trees and the flowers open. If this were the case it would make April unique among the months, for the names of none of the rest, as designated in Latin, have any reference to natural conditions or circumstances. It seems more likely that April was considered by the Romans to be Venus' month, obviously because of the reproductive powers of nature now in motion in several of her departments. The first day was specially set aside as *Festum Veneris et Fortunae Virilis.* The probability is, therefore, that *Aprilis* was *Aphrilis,* founded on *Aphrodite,* the Greek name for Venus, the goddess of love.

The Anglo-Saxons called the month, *Oster Monath,* because it was the month during which the east wind prevailed. The term Easter may have come from the same origin.

Birthstone

The diamond, symbol of innocence and light, is the April birthstone. But the diamond is also the hardest of all precious stones.

Rebirth

Make me over, Mother April,
When the sap begins to stir!
When they flowery hand delivers
All the mountain-prisoned rivers,
And thy great heart beats and quivers,
To revive the days that were.
   Richard Hovey (1864-1900)

Births

William Harvey (discovered blood circulation) 1578; Otto Edward Leopold Bismark (German statesman) 1815; Sergei Rachmaninoff (composer) 1873.

Deaths

Sultan Timur (Tamerlane) 1405; Robert III (Scottish king) 1406; Sigmund I (Polish king) 1548.

April Fool's Day

'Twas on the morn when April doth appear,
And wets the Primrose with her maiden tear;
'Twas on the morn when laughing Folly rules,
And calls her sons around and dubs them Fools,
Bids them to be bold, some untryed path explore,
And do such deeds as Fools ne'er did before.
   Triumphs of Folly, London 1777

Auld Fool's Day

The beginnings of April Fool's Day are lost in history. Some hold that it started with Auld Fool's Day, which used to fall on January 1 in the Catholic calendar. Others say that it originated in the Hindu festival known as *Huli,* which falls on the last day of March, and during which it is customary to play practical jokes and send people on useless errands.

Poisson d'Avril

In France today is known as Poisson d'Avril, named after the mackerel, a silly fish that is easily caught in vast multitudes at this time of year. When Napoleon married Maria Louisa, archduchess of Austria on April 1, 1810, the Paris newspapers labelled him "un poisson d'avril."

April Gawk

In Scotland the person who falls for an April fool trick is called an April Gawk. A gawk is a cuckoo that simpletons were sent to look for.

On the first day of April
Hunt the gawk another mile.

Foolish Males

Among ancient Romans today was marked in their calendar as consecrated to fools. A festival was held in honour of the goddess Fornax who taught the Romans the mystery of baking bread. On the day of the celebration, little tablets were suspended 'round the forum directing the city guards to the temple they were to go to, and the joke or trick consisted in calling those persons fools who could not read the labels and whose ignorance prevented them from going to the place of entertainment till it was too late to share in the festivity.

Foolish Females

The Roman courts were closed on April first, and the women performed ablutions under myrtle trees, crowned themselves with the leaves, and offered sacrifices to Venus. The custom originated in a mythological story that as Venus was drying her wetted hair by a riverside, she was abashed by the lusty gaze of some satyrs:

But soon with myrtles she her beauties veiled,
From whence this annual custom was entailed.
  Ovid

Foolish Folk

While April morn her Folly's throne exalts:
While Dob calls Nell, and laughs because she halts;
While Nell meets Tom, and says his tail is loose,
Then laughs in turn, and calls poor Thomas goose.

April Fool's Crimes

A judge commented in a *New York Herald* article that various crimes could be assigned to ethnic groups. Murders, riots, and violent assaults were the work of Irishmen. Daring burglaries and highway robberies he assigned to Englishmen. Petty thefts and larcenies were attributed to Germans. Skilful forgeries and obtaining goods under false pretences were designated as strictly American offences (April 1, 1855).

An April Fool Vehicle

On April 1, 1898 Robert Allison paid $1,000 to Alexander Winton for a motorised device called a Winton. Its one-cylinder engine propelled it at ten miles per hour and was cooled by a block of ice. This was the first car sold in the United States.

Births

Charlemagne (king of the Franks) 742; Casanova (lover and scoundrel) 1752; Hans Christian Andersen (writer) 1805; Emile Zola (writer) 1840.

A Saint Expires

From his earliest years St Francis of Paula made patience, charity, and humility the bases of his conduct. At the age of nineteen St Francis became founder of an eminent religious order. He performed several miracles during his life, including raising a young man from the dead. He died of a fever on April 2 in the year 1508, being 99 years old.

Deaths

Arthur (Prince of Wales) 1502; St Francis of Paula (saint) 1508; Thomas Carte (historian) 1754.

Today's Luck

Persons born on this day can look to certain colours to bring luck. They should wear all shades of green from the darkest to the lightest. Cream and white are lucky to a somewhat lesser extent, but all dark colours, especially dark red, purple, and black are to be avoided at all costs. Any pale green stone, as well as pearls and moonstones will assure reasonable fortune, but for absolute certainty of good luck a piece of jade must be carried next to the skin at all times.

A Writer Flees

On his birthday today in 1840, Emile Zola, the French naturalistic novelist, escaped to England having been charged with defamation of several eminent persons in his writings concerning the Esterhazy Court Martial.

The Undeserving and Worthless Rich

"Wealth daily bestows his greatest Kindnesses on the undeserving and worthless . . . for the glorious cause of Lucre, I will do anything, be anything, but the horse-leech of private oppression, or the vulture of public robbery!"

Robert Burns, April 2, 1789

First Congress, 1718

The first meeting of the American Congress was held.

Design Sense, 1792

The U.S. Mint was authorised to produce copper coins in one-cent and half-cent pieces. There were four designs: the "chain" cent, the "wreathed" cent, the "flowing hair" cent, and the "liberty cap" cent.

Punjab Annexed, 1849

India annexed the neighbouring state of Punjab.

The Indian Connection, 1870

The railway between Calcutta and Bombay opened for through traffic.

Ten-Cent Movie, 1902

America's first moving picture cinema opened in Los Angeles. The Electric Theatre, domiciled in a tent under the management of Thomas L. Tally, charged ten cents for admission to a one-hour show.

In America, 1917

President Woodrow Wilson declared the "world safe for democracy."
President Woodrow Wilson called for a declaration of war on Germany.

In England, 1918

An evening curfew marked the rationing of gas and electric lights in England as a war conservation measure.

In France, 1925

The French finance minister, M. Clemental, was forced to resign after it was discovered that the Bank of France had issued several milliards over the legally permitted number of bank notes.

Births

Washington Irving (writer) 1783; Doris Day (actress) 1924; Marlon Brando (actor) 1924.

Deaths

Agape, Chiona, and Irene (three sister saints) 304; John Tyrwitt (learned divine) 1828; Miss Finch (glutton) 1888.

Saintly Sisters Singed

Though their parents were heathens, these three sisters who lived in Thessalonica suffered martyrdom because of their devoutedness. Contrary to the orders of the Emperor Diocleasian the girls had hidden many volumes of the Holy Scriptures in their rooms. These were discovered, the sisters denounced and burnt alive on April 3, 304.

John Tyrwitt's Wine Fit

Here lies John Tyrwitt
A learned divine;
He died in a fit
Through drinking port wine
Died 3rd April, 1828, aged 59
    An epitaph found in Malta

Miss Finch's Hot Cross Bun Binge

On April 3, 1888, Miss Finch of Kilburn in Scotland passed away from the results of eating twelve hot cross buns in celebration of Easter.

Emperor Augustus' Will

Today in the year 13, Augustus, emperor of Rome from 27 B.C., signed his will written upon two skins of parchment, although he had another year to live.

Absolute Power Corrupts Absolutely

On this day, 1887, J.E.E. Dalberg Acton, the British historian, made the well known statement: "Power tends to corrupt, and absolute power corrupts absolutely. Great men are almost always bad men, even when they exercise influence and not authority."

A Lunatic Loose at St Paul's

At St Paul's Cathedral in London, during the celebration of the Holy Communion, a well-dressed young man swept off the table onto the floor the chalice, patin, and other vessels used in the service. He was at once taken into custody and removed. Even though he pleaded to be a lunatic who had escaped from an asylum, he was sentenced to a month's hard labour (1885).

The Pony Express Rides

On April 3, 1860, the first two Pony Express riders set out, one moving east from San Francisco, the other west from St Joseph, on the Missouri River. The mail followed a pre-established route along which fresh horses and riders were available at 153 stations. The mail was expected to cover the 1,900-mile-long route in about seven-and-a-half days, or at about twelve miles per hour. Eighty riders and 500 horses were eventually involved in the routine.

Count Greppo Rides

A certain Count Greppo, having made a wager of 10,000 francs that he would drive four horses from Rome to Naples, without changing, in twenty-four hours, started tonight in 1850. At Gaeta, one of the horses began to limp and at 9 p.m. when 10 kilometres from Naples, fell down exhausted.

A Wantonly Destructive Suffragette

Today in 1913 the militant leader of the English suffragettes was sent to jail for three years for instigating destruction of property in the pursuit of women's rights.

Births

Robert Sherwood (playwright) 1896;
Tony Perkins (actor) 1932.

Deaths

St Ambrose (oratorical saint) 397; St
Isidore (studious saint) 606; William
Henry Harrison (9th U.S. president)
1841.

The Dripping-Spring Saint

St Isidore found his studies hard as a
boy and ran away from school. But
his attention was caught by a steadily
dripping spring that had worn a deep
hollow in a rock. He returned to
school and persevered with his
studies, finally becoming a great
scholar. He died today in 606.

Throgmortons Bewitched

Today in 1593 three members of the
Samuels family of Warboys in
England were condemned for
bewitching the children of Mr
Throgmorton. As a result of their
crime a lecture on witchcraft was to
be preached annually by a Doctor of
Divinity of Queen's College,
Cambridge.

Today's Flower

The *Fritillaria Imperialus*—red
crown imperial—is dedicated to
today's saints Ambrose and Isidore.

The Perils of Pauline

Today in 1914, one of the earliest
movie "thrillers," *The Perils of
Pauline,* opened to rave reviews in
New York City.

Promenade Pyrotechnics

A fierce blaze completely destroyed
the pier—the Promenade Des
Anglais—in Nice, France, on the eve
of its opening.

Quakers Called Names

On April 4, 1627, many people of the
Quaker sect in the U.S. were
arraigned before the courts as
recusants—persons who refused to
attend the Church of England
services.

Messenger Called Liar

In 1689 a messenger arrived in
Boston, announcing the invasion of
England by William III. He was
denounced as a liar and thrown into
prison. He was released two weeks
later when the truth was known in
the colonies.

The Queen, Drake, and the Pelican

Today in 1581 Queen Elizabeth dined at Deptford on
board the *Pelican,* the ship in which Drake had
circumnavigated the globe and, after dinner, conferred on
him the honour of knighthood. This celebrated vessel was
then broken up and a chair made out of the relics was
presented to the University of Oxford. It now stands in the
Bodleian Library.

The When-in-Rome Saint

St Ambrose died on April 4, 397. While in his cradle a
swarm of bees settled on his lips and thereby foretold the
future powers of oratory, for which he was remarkable.
To him has been attributed the precept:

"When you are at Rome
Do as they do at Rome."

Births

Elihu Yale (godfather of the university) 1649; Algernon Swinburne (poet) 1837; Booker T. Washington (author) 1856; Spencer Tracy (actor) 1900.

Deaths

St Vincent Ferrer (passionate saint) 1419; John Stow (historian) 1605; Robert Raikes (originator of Sunday Schools) 1811; Charles Chillicot (large man) 1815.

Pulpit Passions

Today's saint, St Vincent Ferrer, was born in Valencia, Spain and made rapid progress on the path of perfection. He was noted for performing several miraculous cures and for his passionate sermons from the pulpit, after which persons often fainted away.

Chubby Charles

On April 5, 1815 died Charles Chillicot of Tintagel, Cornwall, England. He stood six-foot four, measured six-foot nine around the waist, and weighed 460 pounds. He smoked three pounds of tobacco weekly, and his stocking would hold six gallons of wheat.

Christ's Comeback?

Though the precise date of the first Easter has never been fixed, certain scholars believe that April 5, in the year 33, was the day on which Christ rose from the dead.

Taiwan Tombs

Today in Taiwan is *Tomb Sweeping Day,* an annual holiday observed to clean tombs and hold rituals honouring the dead.

Monumental Miracle

John Stow, the great chronicler of Elizabethan London, was much ignored and reviled in his own lifetime, and when he did gain some recognition it was just enough for him, at the age of eighty, to successfully petition King James I for permission to beg for his living. It is fitting, then, that when the Great Fire of 1666 destroyed so much of London—which afterwards could only be known from his works—the fire miraculously left untouched a monument set up for him by his wife after his death on April 5, 1605.

Taunton Trial

Today in 1845 Sarah Freeman was sentenced to be executed at Taunton, in Somerset, England for the series of crimes known as the Shapwick murders, involving the destruction by arsenic of her husband, her illegitimate son, her mother, and her brother.

Captivating Caroline

George IV is quoted as saying on April 5, 1795, after first meeting Caroline of Brunswick: "Harris, I am not well, pray get me a glass of brandy." They were married three days later.

Beauty Betrothed

In 1614, Pocahontas, the beautiful Indian princess was wed in Virginia to the English colonist John Rolfe.

Willard Wins

Jess Willard knocked out Jack Johnson for the heavyweight championship of the world today in 1914.

Charlie Chaplin

On this day in 1916, Charlie Chaplin became the highest priced film star in the world after signing a contract worth $675,000 for one year's work.

Hackett Hailed

On April 5, 1827, the first American actor to play abroad, James Henry Hackett, was hailed and acclaimed at a performance in London.

Proverb

April showers
Make May flowers.

6

APRIL

Births

Houdini (escape artist) 1874; Anthony Fokker (airplane designer) 1890; Lowell Thomas (author) 1892.

Deaths

King Richard I (the Lionheart) 1199; Laura de Noves (Petrarch's Laura) 1348; Igor Stravinsky (composer) 1971.

A Frozen Moment

Numb with cold, Robert Edwin Peary and his group of explorers reached the North Pole on April 6, 1909, having left New York in the ship *Roosevelt* in July of the previous year. He thus became the discoverer of the North Pole along with his companions—a black called Henson, and four Eskimos.

A Dastardly Development

News was received in Washington today in 1868 of the murderous outrages perpetrated in Georgia by a newly organised band of desperadoes known as the Ku Klux Klan.

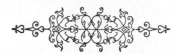

A Heart-Stopping Feat

Richard I died today in 1199 from complications arising from a cross-bow wound. Earlier in his career Modard, the king of Almayn, had imprisoned Richard and condemned him to death for the killing of his son and the seduction of his daughter. Modard starved a lion for three days to make it more vicious, and then put it into Richard's cell. The young English king grabbed the lion, thrust his arm down his throat, and pulled out its heart, killing it on the spot. He took the heart up into the hall where Modard and his courtiers were dining, dipped it in salt, and then ate it raw. Ever since he has been called Richard the Lionheart.

A Heart-Rending Tragedy

"The sainted Laura, illustrious for her virtues, and for a long time celebrated in my verses, was first seen of me in my youth on the 6th of April, 1327, in the church of St. Clara, at Avignon, at the first hour of the day; and in the same city, in the same month of April, on the same sixth day, and at the same hour, in the year 1348, this light disappeared from our day . . ." So wrote the Italian poet Petrarch when Laura de Noves, the object of his love and poetic veneration for nineteen years passed away of the plague after twenty years of unhappy marriage to another man.

Musical Moments

1870:   Wagner's *Tannhauser* was performed for the first time at the Royal Italian Opera.

1871:   Bach's *Passion Music* was heard for the first time in Westminster Abbey.

1886:   Franz Liszt gave his first public performance in London.

A Deadly Riot

Today in Salonica in 1876 the *Musselman Riot* took place. The American consul attempted to carry off a young Bulgarian girl in his carriage to prevent her Musselman protectors from converting her, a Christian, to the Mohammedan faith. An excited crowd surrounded the carriage at the mosque to regain the girl. The French and German consuls arrived on the scene to assist the American and were immediately murdered.

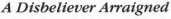

Births

St Francis Xavier (Spanish Jesuit) 1506; William Wordsworth (poet) 1770.

Deaths

St Herman Joseph (confessor) 1226; Richard Richards (of gangrene) 1656; Dick Turpin (highwayman) 1739; John Mardeunle (debaucher) 1749; D'Arcy McGee (Canadian statesman) 1868.

Anemone Nemerosa

Today's flower is also known as the wood anemony.

Hyde Park Demonstrations

1876:   A demonstration in favour of opening London's museums and picture galleries was well attended.

1907:   Three thousand chanting women turned out for a woman's suffrage demonstration.

A Monk, a Virgin, and Shoes

As a child, Herman Joseph, the monk and confessor who was rewarded with sainthood on his death today in 1226, was especially devoted to the Virgin Mary. One day the young Herman confided in her that his family was very poor and this was why he entered the church without shoes. She pointed to a stone and beneath it he found money to buy food and shoes for himself and his family.

A Toe, a Leg, a Life

On a gravestone in the churchyard at Banbury in England the following words are inscribed:

To the memory of Richard Richards who by gangrene lost first a Toe, afterwards a Leg, and lastly his Life on the 7th April, 1656.
Ah cruell Death, to make 3 meals of one,
To taste and taste till all was gone.
But know, then Tyrant, when the trumpet shall call,
He'll find his feet and stand when thou shall fall.

A Disbeliever Arraigned

On April 7, 1657, Henry Dunster, ex-president of Cambridge College, was arraigned before the U.S. Court for refusing to have his infant child baptised.

Master, Misses, Debauching

John Mardeunle, master of the Charter-School of Waterford in England, was executed at that city today in 1749 for debauching some of the young girls committed to his care for education.

Proverb

If the first three days of April be foggy,
Rain in June will make the lanes boggy.

The Reclamation of Fallen Women

At a meeting of the Supporters of the Midnight Meeting Movement for the Reclamation of Fallen Women, held at Freemasons' Hall, it was stated that there were 50,000 unfortunates in London alone, and about 40,000 in the rest of England. Of these 40,000 died annually by disease, starvation, and suicide, while the average term of their career did not exceed seven years (1863).

The Price of a Wife

On April 7, 1832, in Carlisle England, one Joseph Thomson sold his wife by auction to one Henry Mears for twenty shillings and a Newfoundland dog. Both Joseph and his wife, Mary Anne Thomson, willingly agreed to the sale, it being widely believed at the time that such a sale legally nullified the marriage vows.

Irish Revenge

D'Arcy McGee, a prominent statesman in the New Dominions, was shot on the steps of his residence in Ottawa, Canada by an Irish assassin. The victim in this case was said to have incurred bitter dislike by the zeal he had shown in the prosecution of disloyal Irishmen in Canada (1868).

8
APRIL

Births
Mary Pickford (actress) 1893; Ilka Chase (actress/author) 1905; Sonja Henie (ice skater) 1913.

Deaths
St Dionysius (saint of Corinth) 180; Lorenzo de Medici (Florentine ruler) 1492; El Greco (Spanish painter) 1614; Frank Woolworth (U.S. merchant) 1919.

Elephant Subdued
During the battle of Thassus between Caesar and Scipio on this day in the year 46, a veteran of the Fifth Legion was snatched up by the trunk of an elephant, which whirled him about in the air. But the soldier, losing none of his presence of mind, began to hack at the proboscis with his sword. At length the beast was compelled to relinquish its prey; it retired with a marvellous noise, joining its companions in the herd.

Livingstone Well
Letters were received today in London from Dr Livingstone in Africa, dated from a district greatly beyond where he was said to have been murdered, and announcing that the traveller was in good health (1868).

Florida Found
Ponce de Leon, searching in vain for the fountain of youth, landed on the coast of Florida near the present site of St Augustine, on this day in 1513. Probably because the discovery occurred at the time of the Easter feast (*Pascua Florida*), Ponce de Leon named the land he claimed for Spain, La Florida.

Wholesome Tea
Today's flower, ground ivy (*Nepeta glechoma*), is dedicated to St Dionysius who died today in the year 180. Since he was the god of wine and fertility in Greek mythology, it is appropriate that his flower has beverage capabilities. In olden times, ground ivy tea was celebrated as a wholesome spring febrifuge.

Fateful Eight
Numerologists have difficulty explaining the number 8. It represents two separate worlds: the material and the spiritual. Being composed of two equal numbers, 4 and 4, it is like two circles just touching together. From the earliest times it has been associated with the symbol of irrevocable Fate in connection with the lives of individuals or nations. In astrology it is represented by the planet Saturn which is also known as the planet of fate. Persons born on this day or nations contemplating any action can do little but accept their fate.

Woman Best
What is better than gold? Jasper.
What is better than Jasper? Wisdom.
What is better than wisdom? Woman.
And what is better than a good woman? Nothing.
   Geoffrey Chaucer, from the *Anniversary Calendar,* April 8, 18th century

9
APRIL

In Ancient Rome

April 9th marked the beginning of the *Cerealia* festivals in Rome held in honour of the return of the six vegetative months.

Births

Charles Baudelaire (poet) 1821; Efram Zimbalist (violinist) 1889; Hugh Hefner (playboy) 1926.

Deaths

St Mary of Egypt (penitent) 421; Simon Lovat (English lord) 1747; Frank Lloyd Wright (architect) 1959.

Mary's Burial, 421

St Mary of Egypt left her father and mother when she was twelve years of age. She went without their consent to Alexandria where she lived an immoral life until the age of twenty-nine. She was then miraculously converted and went beyond the Jordan River where she lived alone in constant prayer. Zosimus, a religious man, is said to have found her corpse today in 421, stretched out by the bank of the Jordan, and with the help of a lion dug her grave and buried her.

Simon's Beheading, 1747

Simon, Lord Lovat, today in 1747, became the last person beheaded in England and the last British peer to be executed for high treason. He is best remembered for his cowardice and genius for duplicity.

A Federal Victory, 1865

On this day in 1865 General Robert E. Lee surrendered the army of Northern Virginia to General Ulysses S. Grant, head of the Union Army in the American Civil War.

A New Bill, 1918

On April 9, 1918 a new Military Service Bill was introduced in the English House of Commons raising the age of eligibility for the army to fifty years.

A Vulgar Error, 1830

"A vulgar error prevails that small birds are destructive in gardens, but we have ascertained by accurate observation, and it has been confirmed by the experience of others, that every sort of bird does more good than harm by the innumerable insects they destroy, and they ought not therefore to be molested in flower and fruit gardens."
Catholic Annal, April 9, 1830

A Word Hunt, 1890

A letter appeared today in 1890 in the *London Times* asking for suggestions for a verb to express progression by electric power such a word being "urgently required for immediate use." There was a strong response and numerous different words were recommended, in many cases pedantic and ridiculous. Among those suggested were to mote, to vril, to electriate, to volt, to bijle, to lect, to edison, to electrofer, and to propelect. The word "motor" was later decided upon but this choice didn't seem to be largely adopted by the public.

A Swiss Victory, 1388

The *Glarus Festival* is celebrated in Switzerland today to mark the Swiss victory over the Austrians April 9, 1388. On that day a pilgrimage to Nafels makes its way past eleven memorial stones signifying the eleven successful attacks on that city by the Austrians.

10
APRIL

Births

James v (English king) 1512; John Pringle (English medical writer) 1707; William Hazlitt (English writer) 1778; Matthew Perry (American statesman) 1794; William Booth (British founder of the Salvation Army) 1829; Joseph Pulitzer (U.S. journalist/philanthropist) 1847; George Arliss (American film star) 1868; Omar Sharif (Egyptian actor) 1932.

Deaths

St Bademus (Persian saint) 376; Louis II (French king) 879; St Mechtildes (Bavarian saint) 1300; William of Pembroke (English earl) 1630; William Cheselden (English anatomist) 1752; John Byron (English admiral) 1786; Alexander Nasmyth (Scottish painter) 1840; three Irishmen (hanged) 1854.

An Organ Plays

King Pepin of France had an organ installed in the church of St Corneille at Conpiègne on April 10, 787—the first recorded instance of this musical instrument.

A Paper Begins

Horace Greeley published the first issue of the *New York Tribune* today in 1841. He was to edit it for over thirty years, the single greatest journalistic influence in the United States.

Animals Appreciated

On April 10, 1866, the American Society for the Prevention of Cruelty to Animals was incorporated.

Arbor Day

On April 10, 1872, Governor Morton of Nebraska suggested declaring a holiday and planting trees. The idea was soon adopted by other states.

Golfers' Day

The annual U.S. Professional Golf Association tournament began today in 1916.

Saints Die

Bademus, today's saint, was a rich and noble citizen in Persia. He founded a monastery and was later apprehended with seven of his monks and lay four months in a dungeon. St Bademus was put to death, April 10, 376 by Narsan, an unhappy prince, who then renounced his faith at the sight of the torments.

St Mechtildes, an abbess in Bavaria, died today in the year 1300. She entered a convent at the age of seven and lived a life of virtue and extreme austerity, abstaining entirely from many things, among them wine and meat.

An Earl Dies

William, Earl of Pembroke, who died on April 10, 1630 left the following verse for posterity:

What voice is this, I prithee mark,
With so much music in it?
Too sweet me thinks to be a lark,
Too loud to be a linnet.

Three Happy Irishmen

Today in 1854, at Monaghan in Ireland, three men were executed for murder. The scene near the scaffold was striking and unusual. After partaking of a good breakfast, they walked together in the prison yard, all seemingly exhilarated. One of them, Coomey, said he had never felt so happy. Quin said he would not accept a reprieve if it arrived. They felt sure of meeting their saviour and once on the scaffold Quin said: "Hell cannot now scare us"; and addressing the hangman, "he's doing the best job ever done for us."

Proverb

When April blows his horn
It's good for both hay and corn.

Births

Christopher Smart (poet) 1722; David Hamilton (architect) 1768; Marshal Lannes (French duke) 1769.

Deaths

St Leo the Great (pope) 461; St Guthlac (bandit/saint) 714; Stanislaus Poniatowski (last Polish king) 1789.

In the Swamp

St Guthlac, who died today in 714, was a bandit in his youth. After his conversion to Christianity, he lived for the rest of his life as a hermit on a remote island in a vast swamp in the English fens, dressed only in animal skins. His one daily meal consisted of bread and water.

A Dandy Flower

Taraxicumdens lionis, the dandelion, is the flower for April 11. The dandelion's name is thought to originate from the fact that Leo Major is the constellation now conspicuous in the heavens. The fact that the flower is dedicated to St Leo, who died today in 461, is just a coincidence.

Roman Trial, 52

All the unwashed of Rome crowded into the forum for the trial of Milo for the murder of Claudius.

Lost Wars, 1471

Henry VI was deposed as king of England because he lost the Wars of the Roses.

Beginnings and Endings, 1713

The island of Gibralter became British, and the peace Treaty of Utrecht terminated the War of the Spanish Succession.

Napoleon Departed, 1814

Napoleon Bonaparte abdicated the government of France and left for Elba.

Unusual Sale, 1817

A man sold his wife (with a rope around her neck) at Dartmoor in England, to her first lover for two guineas.

American Strife, 1861

The American Civil War began.

Lincoln Speaks, 1865

President Lincoln gave his last public speech.

China Trembles, 1871

An earthquake in China, extending over an area of 400 miles, killed 2,298 people.

New Americans, 1882

A German report showed that 193,687 German subjects had emigrated, chiefly to the U.S.

Short Order, 1918

England began compulsory food rationing across the country.

Abdication, 1931

Alfonso XIII, king of Spain abdicated.

Landing, 1940

British troops landed in Norway.

Occupation, 1941

German forces occupied Belgrade, Yugoslavia.

Advance, 1944

The Soviet army advanced into the Crimea.

Capture, 1945

Essen, Germany was captured by allied troops.

Jerusalem Trial, 1961

The trial of Adolph Eichman began in Jerusalem.

12
APRIL

Births

Edward Bird (painter) 1772; Henry Clay (American statesman) 1777; Lily Pons (opera singer) 1904.

Deaths

Seneca (Roman philosopher) 65; St Sabas (martyr) 372; Richard Smith (saddler) 1727; George Cheyne (fat doctor) 1742; F.D. Roosevelt (32nd U.S. president) 1945.

Sabas' Suffering

St Sabas the Goth became a martyr when he refused to eat meat that had been sacrificed to idols. He was dragged naked over thorns and then drowned in the river Mussouo on April 12, 372.

Weight's Wit

Dr George Cheyne, died today in London in 1742. Earlier in his life he fell prey to epicurean indulgence and eventually weighed in at 448 pounds. A self-imposed diet of milk and vegetables helped him reduce to a more normal weight. His battle with the scales had prompted a colleague to write:

Suppose we own that milk is good,
And say the same of grass;
The one for babes is only food,
The other for an ass.

To which Cheyne replied:
Were you to milk and straw confined,
Thrice happy might you be;
Perhaps you might regain your mind,
And from your wit get free.

Sage's Suicide

Seneca, the mild Roman philosopher, was both tutor and minister to Nero, arch-tyrant, famous fiddler, and emperor of Rome. In his official position Seneca tried to restrain the excesses of the emperor, but to no avail. He finally drew Nero's tyrannous whim upon himself, and upon the first pretext he was ordered to do away with himself. On April 12, 65, with philosophical calm, before an audience of his wife and friends, Seneca opened his veins and took a draught of poison. To hasten his death he was put in a warm bath. But these measures did not satisfy Nero's soldiers, who finally suffocated him in an oven.

Syphilis Suspicions

On April 12, 1938 anyone applying for a marriage licence in the state of New York would henceforth have to undergo a test for syphilis.

Lincoln Reburied

The remains of ex-president Lincoln were removed from a secret grave in which they had been deposited at Springfield, Illinois and re-buried with that of his wife in the same cemetary (1887).

Saddler's Sticking

In 1727 a twenty-year-old British saddler, Richard Smith, was run through by a recruiting sergeant he had been teasing. Every April 12th, the date of his death, his tombstone is said to sweat blood.

Aircraft Arrival

On April 12, 1928 the *Bremen,* a single-wing aircraft with pilots Hunefeld, Koehl, and Fitzmaurice became the first plane to cross the Atlantic east to west. After being in the air for thirty-four hours it crashed on Greenery Island off the coast of Labrador.

Corn Quit-Rent

On April 12, 1678, Massachusetts Governor Winslow made peace with the Indians by guaranteeing them that each English family would pay them a pack of corn annually as quit-rent.

Space Success

Cosmonaut Yuriy Alekseyevich Gagarin made the first manned space flight in the Russian space vehicle *Vostok.* He completed a single orbit of the earth in just under ninety minutes today (1961).

13
APRIL

Births

Jean Pierre Crousaz (Swiss philosopher) in Lausanne 1663; Thomas Jefferson (3rd U.S. president) in Virginia, 1743; Philip Louis (French duke) in St Cloud, 1747.

Deaths

St Hermengild (martyr) in Spain 586; George Frederick Handel (German composer) in London 1759; Lady Morgan Sydney (miscellaneous writer) in London 1859.

Conviction Kills

Hermengild, the eldest son of Levigild (a Goth king of Spain), was educated in the Arian heresy, but converted by his wife. Levigild, knowing of his son's new beliefs used every means possible to re-convert him, but finding it impossible, kept him in prison for some time, and had him put to death on April 13, 586.

Statue of Liberty

In ancient Rome this day was celebrated as the feast of the goddess Liberty. Unlike the modern Liberty, variously represented with her torch, book, blindfold, and scales of justice, the ancient Liberty was depicted as a woman holding a rod in one hand and a cap in the other. The rod was used by magistrates in setting free slaves, and the cap was worn by slaves about to be set free. Sometimes Liberty was represented with a cat at her feet.

Falling Wine

On April 13, 1859, David Ritchie, secretary to the Committee of the Treasury at the Bank of England, was killed in King William Street by a cask of wine falling on him from the top of a loaded wagon.

Two Seas Connected

The railway connecting Tiflis and Baku opened for traffic, thus bringing the Caspian Sea into direct communication with the Black Sea ports of Batoum and Poti (1883).

Van Cliburn Succeeds

Twenty-three-year-old Van Cliburn of Kilgore, Texas, won the Tchaikovsky International Piano Contest in the Soviet Union on April 13, 1958.

Charles Collapses

"On Friday night, April 13, the sword, buckler and straps fell from the equestrian statue of King Charles the First at Charing Cross. The Appendages of bronze were picked up by a man of the name of Moxon, in whose possession they remain until that gentleman receives instructions relative to their reinstatement."

A London newspaper of 1810

Conversion of Seamen

On April 13, 1819 a charter was issued for the Society of Promoting the Gospel Among Seamen in the Port of New York.

Women's Rights

1888: The British House of Lords threw out a Women's Suffrage Bill introduced by Lord Denman.
1920: U.S. President Wilson appointed Helen Hamilton Gardiner the first woman Civil Service Commissioner.

14
APRIL

Births

Christian Huyghens (Dutch mathematician) 1629; Sir John Gielgud (British actor) 1904.

Deaths

St Lidwina (virgin) 1433; Abraham Lincoln (16th U.S. president) 1865.

A Dutch Accident, 1433

St Lidwina was born at Squidam, Holland. She made a vow of perpetual virginity at twelve years of age. She fell and hurt herself while skating on the canals, and died a martyr to a dreadful internal complaint on this day in 1433.

Parisian Disaster, 1360

"It is to be noted that the 14th of April, and the morrow after Easter Day, 1360, King Edward III with his host lay before the city of Paris; which day was full dark of mist and hail, and so bitter cold, that many men died on their horsebacks with the cold; wherefore unto this day it hath been called the *Black Monday*."

From *Stow's Chronicle* of the 14th century

London Quacks Suppressed, 1684

In London, on April 14, 1684, an order was issued suppressing all mountebanks, (itinerant quacks or impudent charlatans) rope-dancers, and ballad-singers who had not taken a licence from the Master of Revels. The Master of Revels was at this time the celebrated player Killigrew, who was thus allowed, by favour of the king, to tax all makers of fun excepting those of his own order. His function seems to have been of an oppressive character strangely at odds with his festive title.

An American Calamity, 1865

"An unlooked for and terrible calamity befell the American nation this day in the assassination of President Lincoln under circumstances which place it among the most dramatic and exciting occurrences of modern times. At half past ten in his private box at Lord's Theatre, Washington, the assassin shot Mr. Lincoln through the back of the head. He then leaped from the box on to the stage, brandishing a dagger and exclaiming 'Sic semper tyrannis,' and escaped in the rear of the theatre. He, John Wilkes Booth, was found and shot dead when refusing arrest on the 26th of this month. The body of Booth was reported to have been cut into pieces and sunk in the Potomac."

From *Irvings Annals of Our Time,* 1881

Channel Showdown, 1293

By mutual agreement, the French and English fleets met with the whole of their respective forces in a showdown battle in the middle of the channel today in 1293. The victor, Edward I, carried off more than 250 ships of his opponent, Philip the Fair.

Hungarian Comeback, 1880

A convict named Takacs, aged 23, was hanged today in 1880, at Rabb, near Budapest, for the murder of two women. After the execution, the body —having been cut down and life being declared extinct—was made the subject of galvanic experiments. The body speedily showed signs of life and after a few hours Takacs recovered complete consciousness. Soon afterwards however, he became delirious and attacked his keepers. He died the following day.

A Surprise Ending, 1722

Miss Elizabeth Russel of Streatham, England, was buried on April 14, 1772, at the venerable age of 104 years. Much to the surprise of all the neighbours, who had never seen her in anything but skirts, it was discovered upon her death that the elderly Miss Russel was a man.

Births

Leonardo da Vinci (genius) 1452;
Henry James (novelist) 1843.

Deaths

St Peter Gonzales (confessor) 1246;
William Oldys (antiquarian) 1761.

Pregnant Cows

In ancient Rome today was called *Fordicidia,* when
pregnant cows were offered as religious sacrifices to the
goddess Tellus.

Sunken Cambridge

The Oxford and Cambridge boat race on the Thames river
to Putney was won by Oxford today in 1859 when the
Cambridge boat was sunk by a passing steamer.

Titanic Struggle

The largest steamer afloat, the *Titanic,* struck an iceberg
on her maiden voyage. After two-and-three-quarter hours
of desperate struggle with the sea, she finally sank. Lost
were 1513 of the 2224 passengers aboard (1912).

Threatened Czar

In Moscow eighty workmen employed in the cathedral in
the preparations for the czar's coronation were arrested
when a mine was discovered under his edifice. The
prefect of police received an anonymous letter and a
basket of eggs, several of which were found to be charged
with dynamite. A little note said "we have plenty more for
the Czar's coronation" (1882).

Straggling Birds

Ancient calendars and almanacs refer to April 15 as
Swallow Day in England when the first members of this
species are expected to straggle in for the spring and
summer season.

The Swallow, for a moment seen,
Skim'd this morn the village green;
Again at eve, when thrushes sing,
I saw her glide on rapid wing
O'er yonder pond's smooth surface, when
I welcom'd her back again.
   Anon. circa 18th century

Green Stitchwort

Today's flower, known formally as
Stellaria holostea, is better known as
great stitchwort and is dedicated to
the steadfastly chaste St Peter
Gonzales.

Fiery Chastity

While he was a Franciscan friar,
Peter's enemies tried to trap him into
an indiscretion with a woman of ill
repute. But he saw through the plot
and confounded them all by throwing
himself into a blazing fire. He was
unharmed and his enemies were
penitent, but he did finally die today
in 1246.

Beery Verse

William Oldys was a quaint and
simple-minded soul who gave his life
to searching among dusty old
volumes of literature. When his throat
became dry from this pursuit he was
wont to moisten it in London pubs.
He died on this day in 1761 but left
behind the following verse inspired
by a fly drinking from his cup of ale.

Busy, curious, thirsty fly!
Drink with me, and drink as I!
Freely welcome to my cup,
Couldst thou sip and sip it up;
Make the most of life you may:
Life is short and wears away.

16
APRIL

Births

Anatole France (author) 1844; Wilbur Wright (airplane inventor) 1867; Charles Chaplin (actor) 1889.

Deaths

St Magnus (martyr) 1110; Aphra Behn (poetess) 1689; Francisco Goya (artist) 1828; Madame Tussaud (wax sculptress) 1850.

Under the Axe, 1110

St Magnus of Orkney, patron saint of fishmongers, died bravely on this day in 1110 beneath the executioner's axe saying: "Stand *before* me and strike at me with all thy might for it becometh not a prince to be beheaded as a thief."

On a Marble Slab, 1689

In her day Aphra Behn was celebrated throughout Europe as a writer, poetess, and wit. A plain black marble slab covering her grave in Westminster Abbey bears this inscription:

MRS. APHRA BEHN DIED APRIL THE 16TH, 1689
Here lies a proof that wit can never be
Defence enough against mortality.
Great poetess, O thy stupendous lays
The world admires, and the Muses praise.

Defeats

1746: England defeated Scotland and "Bonnie Prince Charlie" at Culloden.
1846: Lecompte attempted to assassinate Louis-Philippe of France.
1940: The Cleveland Indians beat the Chicago White Sox 1 to 0 on Bob Feller's no-hitter.

Openings

1787: *The Contrast* by Robert Tyler became the first professional U.S. play to be presented on the stage.
1889: Sara Bernhardt opened in *Lena,* the first English play to be done in Paris.
1912: *The Daily Herald,* the first Labour newspaper, was published in London.

Sales

1813: The first mass production factory in America began to turn out 20,000 pistols.
1834: John Marck patented self-lighting cigars in the U.S.

Sympathetic Actions

1862: Slavery in the District of Columbia was abolished by the U.S. Congress.
1871: Thousands gathered in Hyde Park to express sympathy for Parisian communists.

Hard Times

1917: Lenin returned to Russia after ten years in exile.
1917: In Berlin 200,000 workers went on strike for less bread rationing.

Bookselling

1926: The *Book of the Month Club* began in the United States.

Rising Waters

1966: The last piece of the Abu Simbel temple was saved from the Aswan Dam waters.

Panda Present

1972: The Chinese gift to President Nixon of two giant pandas arrived in the U.S.

Births

J.P. Morgan (financier) 1837; Nikita Khrushchev (politician) 1894; Thornton Wilder (writer) 1897; William Holden (actor) 1918.

Deaths

Benjamin Franklin (publicist/writer/ scientist/politician/inventor/ philosopher/statesman) 1790.

Disaster, 1421

A tremendous flood in Holland destroyed seventy-two villages and swept away 100,000 persons.

The Water American

Benjamin Franklin, whose death took place on this day in 1790, was known as the *Water American* by his fellow workers at a printing house in London. "I drank only water, while the other workmen, nearly fifty in number, were great drinkers of beer. We had an alehouse boy, who always attended in the house to supply the workmen. My companion at the press drank every day a pint before breakfast, a pint at breakfast with his bread and cheese, a pint between breakfast and dinner, a pint at dinner, a pint in the afternoon about six o'clock, and another when he had done his day's work. . . . and thus these poor devils kept themselves always under."

Sports, 1860

A boxing match between Tom Sayers of England and "Benica Boy" Heenan of the United States took place today at Farnborough in England. The contest was generally regarded as a kind of international trial of "pluck." In a few minutes over two hours, thirty-seven rounds were fought—the last five amid great confusion, police and others breaking in upon the ring—and the men were hurried away, Heenan all but blind, and Sayers with his powerful right arm useless. The split-decision of the judges gave rise to much controversy that was far from settled by the presentation of a belt to each of the champions. ·

Exploration, 1492

The Spanish sovereigns, Ferdinand and Isabella, signed a grant to Columbus giving him the title Admiral and Viceroy over all the islands and lands he might discover during his expedition, with a benefit of a tithe of any profits to be made from the venture.

Religion, 1725

On April 17, 1725, John Rudge bequeathed to the parish of Trysull in Staffordshire, England, twenty shillings a year so that a poor man might be employed to go around the church during the sermon and keep people awake. He was also to be used to shoo dogs from the building.

Drama, 1880

The *Adventuière* was revived at the Théâtre Français in Paris, with Miss Sarah Bernhardt in the part of Clorinde. Her success with the public was unmistakable, but her performance did not please some of the critics, who expressed themselves on the subject with more vigour than politeness. Thereupon the lady lost her temper and revenged herself by sending in her resignation. She was ordered to pay damages of 100,000 francs for breech of contract.

Fashion, 1885

The *Sphenophogones,* a Paris Club composed of men who wore pointed or Vandyck beards, held their annual dinner today in 1885. The members comprised amongst others of less note, Gérome and Detaille the painters, Léo Delibes, the musician, Charles Garnier, the architect of the Opera, and others.

Labour, 1944

The man/woman power shortage became so acute in Seattle, Washington that a restaurant owner placed the following advertisement "Woman wanted to wash dishes. Will marry if necessary."

Politics, 1961

The United States government-supported Bay of Pigs invasion was crushed by Cuban forces on this day.

Aviation, 1964

Mrs Jerrie Mock became the first woman to fly solo around the world landing today at the Columbus, Ohio, airport in 1964 after logging some 23,000 miles in twenty-nine days.

18
APRIL

Births

Leopold Stokowski (conductor) 1882; Frederika of Greece (Queen Mother) 1917.

A Sold Throne

At the Hôtel Drouot in Paris today in 1885, amongst the lots offered for sale by auction, was the throne of Louis XIV, accompanied by a certificate of genuiness showing that at the accession of Louis XV it formed a part of the garde-meuble of the crown. It was sold for 6,500 francs after very slight competition.

Our Lady of the Law Suits

St Aya, who passed away on this day sometime in the 7th century, is the patron saint of those engaged in law suits. Early in her life she gave away all her possessions to the Chapter of Cannonesses at Mons in France. Shortly after her death her heirs claimed what she had given to the Chapter. To decide the dispute the claimants gathered around her tomb. From it issued St Aya's voice saying the property belonged to the cannonesses.

"The British are Coming!"

On the night of April 18, 1775, the leading silversmith of New England, Paul Revere, rode through the Massachusetts countryside to warn the populace of the approaching British troops. His midnight ride is generally regarded as the beginning of the American Revolution.

The First Transatlantic Letter Arrives

On April 18, 1494, the Municipal Council of Seville, Spain, received what is believed to be the First Transatlantic Letter. It was written by Dr Diego Chanca from Isabella, San Domingo in the West Indies where he was living, having accompanied Columbus on his second voyage. He had been the physician to the king and queen of Spain. The letter is now in the Seville Library.

Deaths

St Aya (patroness of law suits) 7th century; Mad Lucas (hermit) 1874; Ernie Pyle (journalist) 1945.

The San Francisco Earthquake

Just before dawn on this day in 1906 the San Andreas Fault in California settled violently causing a severe earthquake to devastate San Francisco. Buildings collapsed, fires roared unchecked through the city, four square miles of buildings were destroyed, and nearly 700 people were killed.

Proverb

Plant your 'taters when you will
They won't come up before April.

Roman Fox Burning

On this day, among the early Romans, it was the practice to tie lighted bunches of straw to the tails of foxes and then set them free to run in pain and terror.

Whylome fox was catched within his hole,
A Fox that often had their poultry stole,
On Renard's back, and fast to either side,
Of hay and straw they little bundles tied;
Then did thereon some lighted matches lay,
And let the burning creature scour away.
  Ovid

Mad Lucas

"Mad Lucas," a hermit who lived at Redcoats Green in England, died today in 1874 of apoplexy at the age of sixty. On the death of his mother twenty-five years earlier he barricaded himself in his large house during which time he lived in sackcloth and ashes never wearing any clothes and ignoring the use of soap and water. He was an educated gentleman and quite willing to receive visitors. Charlies Dickens once paid him a visit and immortalised his idiosyncracies in his "Tom Tiddler's Ground."

19
APRIL

Deaths

St Alphege (archbishop) 1012; Duke Antonio Fernando (Italian ruler) 1729; Lord Byron (poet) 1824; Charles Darwin (naturalist) 1882; Pierre Curie (scientist) 1906.

St Alphege, 1012

The archbishop of Canterbury, St Alphege, who died violently today in 1012, was captured and imprisoned and his cathedral burned by marauding Danes. During his imprisonment he ministered to his captors who fell sick of the plague. Later they demanded a ransom for his release. When it was not paid the Danes drove a rotten stake through his heart and left him to die. Shortly thereafter the stake blossomed forth with green leaves.

Today's Aphrodisiac and Antiseptic

The flower accorded to April 19 by medieval monks is Ursine garlic or *Allium ursinum*. When bruised the whole plant emits an overpowering stench of garlic. In olden times the juice of garlic was believed to be the best of all aphrodisiacs and during the time of plagues, robbers drank it to immunise themselves prior to stealing from the dead bodies of plague victims.

Duke Antonio Fernando, 1729

During his lifetime Duke Antonio Fernando, ruler of Guastalla in Italy, never took a drink because a soothsayer had warned that alcohol would kill him. On this day, in 1729 the duke rubbed his aching muscles with alcohol after a hunting trip, caught fire, and burned to death.

Lord Byron, 1824

Lord George Gordon Byron died of malaria on April 19, 1824 in Greece. Earlier in his life he had married in England but left for Europe a year later after his wife had separated from him, taking their one-month-old daughter with her. In some of his poetry Byron pined for the daughter Ada whom he never saw again:

Is thy face like thy mother's, my fair child?
Ada! sole daughter of my house and heart!
When last I saw thy young blue eyes they smiled,
And then we parted . . .
. . . To hold thee lightly on a gentle knee,
And print on thy soft cheek a parent's kiss—
This, it would seem was not reserved for me
  From the third book of *Childe Harold,* 1816

The First Protestants, 1529

On this day in 1529 a few of the electors and princes of Germany, joined by the inhabitants of Strasburg, Nuremburg, Ulm, and nine other cities, published a protestation against a decree of the Diet (the assembly of the states of the German Empire) and petitioned the emperor to have it revoked. Hence the name of Protestants was first given to reformers of religion in Germany.

War Commences, 1775

The first shots of the civil war between Great Britain and her colonies were fired today in skirmishes at Lexington and Concord.

A Cuckoo Calls

The 20th of April is traditionally the day on which the cuckoo is first heard in Europe. A strange belief about the bird is that whatever one is doing when the cuckoo is first heard in the spring is what one will do most frequently all the year. In the north of Europe it is widely believed that if one asked the cuckoo how much longer one had to live, it would sound its note as many times as there were years remaining.

A Lustful God

Today the sun enters the constellation of Taurus, the Bull. Among the Greeks Taurus was considered to be the bull in the guise of which Jupiter, king of the gods, seduced and carried away Europa, daughter of Agenor.

A Flower Miracle

St Agnes, who died today in 1317, was made an abbess at the age of fifteen. At her installation holy manna fell on the altar and afterwards, as she prayed, roses and lilies with wondrous perfume fell all around her.

Births

Adolph Hitler (German leader) 1889; Joan Miro (Spanish artist) 1893; Harold Lloyd (American comedian) 1894; Lionel Hampton (American musician) 1913.

Deaths

St Agnes (Italian saint) 1317; Edouard Manet (French artist) 1883; Christian x (Danish king) 1947.

A Disappointing Opera

April 20, 1767 had been the scheduled date for the performance of America's first comic opera *The Disappointment,* a satire about treasure hunting that was popular at the time. At the last minute the opera was cancelled for fear of offending.

A Fall from Grace

Today in 1840 Prince Albert was thrown from his horse in the Home Park, but was injured so slightly as to be able to mount again immediately, and proceed to a stag hunt at Ascot.

A Child Stars

On April 20, 1934 the film *Stand up and Cheer* was previewed in New York City, thus launching the career of its child star, Miss Shirley Temple.

A Failed Ruse

On April 20, 1916 a German vessel, disguised as a neutral merchant ship, attempted to land arms on the coast of Ireland but was discovered and detained by the British.

Proverb

Till April's dead
Change not a thread.

A Fool's Bauble

Today in 1653 Oliver Cromwell strode into the British House of Commons clad in plain black clothes and grey worsted stockings. He began the process of dissolving the Parliament by pointing to the sacred mace of the house speaker and saying "take away that fool's bauble."

Angler's Epitaph

A tombstone to a renowned fisherman in Ripon, Yorkshire, England, bears the following inscription:

Here lies poor but honest
Bryan Tunstall
He was a most expert Angler
Until Death, envious of his merits,
Threw out his line, hook'd him,
And landed him here—
21st day of April, 1790

Births

Prince George (consort of Queen Anne) 1653; Charlotte Bronte (novelist) 1816; Elizabeth II (queen) 1926.

Proverb

When that Aprilis blows her horn,
It is both good for hay and corn.
A dry time is for sowing best,
Before the garden's richly dresst
In all the pomp of vernal flowers;
Then come the hasty April showers,
Which freshen each enamelled way,
The painted carpet of the lovely May.

Deaths

Alexander (the Great) 323 B.C.; Diogenes (philosopher) 323 B.C.; Bryan Tunstall (angler) 1790.

Cynic's Search

Diogenes of Sinope, the Cynic, was an early Greek philosopher who (among other things) believed that all virtue resided in action, and therefore had to demonstrate his philosophy with acts rather than in discourse. This he did at various times by living in a tub, embracing statues in the dead of winter, and looking for an honest man in broad daylight with a lantern. His lantern of life was snuffed out on this day in 323 B.C.

Bull Beliefs

According to medieval almanacs persons born under the sign of Taurus, the bull (April 21 to May 20) exhibit the following qualities.

Manners and quality when well placed
Shee signifies a quiet man, not given to Law, Quarrel or Wrangling; not Vitious, Pleasant, Neat and Spruce, Loving Mirth in his actions, cleanly in Apparel, rather Drinking much than Gluttonous, prone to Venery, oft entangled in Love-matters, Zealous in their affections, Musicall, delighting in Baths, and all honest merry Meetings, or Maskes and Stage-playes, easie of Beliefe, and not given to Labour, or take any Pains, a Company keeper, Cheerful, nothing Mistrustful, a right vertuous Man or Woman, oft had in some Jealousie, yet no cause for it.

When ill
Then he is Riotous, Expensive, wholly given to loosnesse and Lewd companies of Women, nothing regarding his reputation, coveting unlawful Beds, Incestuous, an Adulterer, Fantastical, a meer Skip-jack, of no Faith, no Repute, no Credit; spending his Meanes in Ale Houses, Taverns, and amongst Scandalous, Loose people; a meer Lazy companion, nothing careful of the things of this Life, or any thing Religious; a meer Atheist and natural man.

Roman Rejoicing

Today in 753 B.C. Romulus began to lay the foundations for the city of Rome on the banks of the Tiber. April 21st then became known as "Dies Natalis Urbis Romae"—the birthday of Rome. Citizens celebrated the event with speeches, music, plays, and by running through fires of straw, which served to pardon them for any sacrilege.

Births

Henry Fielding (novelist) 1707;
Immanuel Kant (philosopher) 1724;
V.I. Lenin (revolutionary) 1870.

Deaths

Henry VII (English king) 1509;
Antoine de Jussien (botanist) 1758;
Thomas Bailey (poet) 1839.

A Dark Moment in 1715

The greatest eclipse of the sun that had been seen in 500 years occurred today in 1715. At 9:00 a.m. the darkness was so great for about three minutes that the stars appeared and the birds and other animals seemed to be in great consternation.

A Lighter Moment in 1348

An embarrasing moment took place on this evening in the year 1348 at a royal ball in England. The countess of Salisbury was dancing rather vigorously with King Edward III when one of her garters became dislodged from its moorings beneath her dress and eventually fell to the floor. The gallant king immediately retrieved it and fastened it to his own leg. Thus began the Order of the Garter, the highest order of English knighthood.

A Dangerous Day in Numerology

The number 22 is symbolized by a Good Man, blinded by the folly of others, with a knapsack full of errors on his back. This is a warning of delusion, illusion, and false judgment to be heeded by anyone to whom the number 22 is of significance.

In God We Trust in 1864

Today in the United States in 1864 a suggestion of Rev. M.R. Watkinson was incorporated onto U.S. coins when the motto "In God We Trust" was authorised by Congress.

Sniff-The-Breeze-Day in Egypt

On April 22, Egyptians living near the Nile traditionally observed Shem-el-Nissin or Sniff-The-Breeze-Day by picnicking near the river and inhaling breaths of the departing spring air.

An Improper Suggestion in 1692

On April 22, 1692, Edward Bishop, having by flogging supposedly cured someone accused of witchcraft in Massachusetts, proposed that others be cured the same way. He was sent to prison for his suggestion.

Contrary Clergy in 1892

Today in 1892 the archbishop of Avignon and the bishops of Nimes, Montpellier, Valence, and Viviers were arrested because they opposed the state in their talks from the pulpit to Roman Catholic congregations.

Electric Shock in 1830

"The nights are still very cold, and the clear northerly and easterly winds that so often prevail are occasionally exchanged for rapid showers of rain and hail, with western gales. The great power of this last sort of weather over vegetation is very remarkable. The highly electrified showers of spring seem to produce the most rapid germination, and it is probable that the advance of vegetable life is principally owing to electrical causes."
Catholic Annal, 1830

23
APRIL

The Gentle Shakespeare

Be absolute for death; either death or
   life
Shall therefore be sweeter. Reason
   thus with life:
If I do lose thee, I do lose a thing
That none but fools would keep: a
   breath thou art
Servile to all the skyey influences.

The author of these words, William Shakespeare (in *Measure For Measure*), lost his own breath for life on this day in 1616. Some sources believe that his death came on the same day as his birth, fifty-two years earlier. It is ironic that Shakespeare, possibly the greatest writer of all time, should have had such a quiet and obscure life that barely enough is known about him to fill a respectable biography. In his own time he was known as the gentle Shakespeare. It seems that he just spent more time working and less time posturing than his contemporaries. It is traditional on this day for people to place flowers on his grave at Stratford-on-Avon. By the end of the day the grave is covered with bouquets of daffodils, primroses, and wallflowers.

St George and the Dragon

The legendary St George is famed for having saved the town of Sylene in Libya from the man-slaying breath of a dragon who had demanded the town's children to satisfy his appetite. St George wounded the dragon and led him back to town leashed on the girdle of the king's daughter, where he promised to slay the beast if only the people of Sylene would accept baptism. The king was the first to do so, and 15,000 others followed. The reign of the beast was over. So it is that St George is commonly represented on horseback, tilting against a dragon.

St George and the Axe

Having embraced the profession of a soldier, St George was made a colonel in the army. He complained to the Emperor Dioclesian himself of his severity and bloody edicts and was immediately cast into prison, and soon after was beheaded, thereby receiving the crown of martyrdom on this day in 303.

George of Albania

In Albania on this day it was traditional to have a picnic by flowing springs in honour of the Albanian national hero George Castriota. It was customary for each person to weigh themselves while holding a sweet smelling herb and a stone to auger well for the future.

Don Quixote's Author

It is fitting that Cervantes, the creator of Don Quixote, that tilter at windmills and arch-parody of the chivalric knight, should have died on the feast of St George, the tilter at dragons and the arch-paragon of the chivalric knight.

Today's Flower

The *Hyacinthus non-scriptus,* also known as the wild hyacinth, named after a species of lily into which the youth Hyacinthus was fabled to have been changed by Apollo.

St George of England

St George is the patron saint of England. In 1344 the feast of St George was made memorable by the creation of the noble order of St George, or the Blue Garter. The institution was inaugurated by a grand joust in which forty of England's best and bravest knights challenged the best the continent had to offer. As late as the nineteenth century it was still customary for gentlemen to wear blue on April 23.

24
APRIL

Today and Ghosts

This being the eve of St Mark, it used to be customary for superstitious people in England to watch in the porch of the church all night, in the hope of seeing the ghosts of those who would be buried in the churchyard during the following year.

'Tis now, replied the village belle,
St Mark's mysterious eve,
And all that old traditions tell
I tremblingly believe;
How, when the midnight signal tolls,
Along the churchyard green,
A mournful train of sentenced souls
In winding sheets are seen.
The ghosts of all whom death shall
  doom
Within the coming year,
In pale procession walk the gloom,
Amid the silence drear.
  Anonymous (medieval)

Today and Politics

1184: After ten years of siege, the Greeks sacked the fabled city of Troy, thus ending the Trojan War.
1877: In the morning Prussia declared war and by evening 50,000 troops had marched into Rumanian territory.
1898: Spain declared war against the United States, thus beginning the Spanish-American War.
1914: The Ulster volunteers managed to get a large shipment of rifles and ammunition landed in Ireland.
1916: The Sinn Fein or Easter Rebellion for independence from Britain began today in Ireland.
1932: The Nazi party won Prussia, Bavaria, Wurttemberg, and Hamburg in the elections.
1941: The allied forces withdrew from Greece, giving it over to German occupation.
1945: Delegates of forty-six nations met in San Francisco to discuss organising a permanent United Nations.
1949: Communist troops continued their advances and occupied the City of Nanking.

Births

William de Kooning (artist) 1904; Robert Penn Warren (author) 1905; Shirley MacLaine (actress) 1934.

Deaths

Daniel Defoe (author) 1731; Willa Cather (author) 1947; Albert Einstein (physicist) 1955.

Proverb

A cold April
The barn will fill.

Today's Flower

The juice of the blackthorn *(Prunus spinosa)* was once used to fortify spurious port wine.

Today and the Printed Word

1704: The brothers John and Duncan Campbell printed the *News-Letter* in Boston, producing America's first continuous newspaper.
1792: Claude Joseph Rouget de Lisle wrote and composed "La Marseillaise," later to become the French national anthem.
1800: The Library of Congress—the national library of the United States—was established in Washington.
1900: The first issue of *The Daily Express* newspaper was published in London.

25
APRIL

Births

Edward II (English king) 1284; Oliver Cromwell (English statesman) 1599; Ella Fitzgerald (American singer) 1918.

Deaths

St Mark (Israeli secretary) 68; Torquato Tasso (Italian poet) 1595; William Cowper (English poet) 1800.

A Biblical Secretary

St Mark, who died today in the year 68, was the secretary to Peter, the disciple of Jesus. He collected and wrote down many of the oral teachings of the apostles that appear in the Bible under his name.

A Fast Pardon

On April 25, 1357, King Edward III pardoned one Cecilia (who had been locked up in Nottingham jail for the murder of her husband John de Rygeway) on account of her having fasted and remained mute for forty days.

An Engine Puffs

Mr Samuel Browne of London, England sat behind the controls of his four-horsepower carriage as it puffed up Shooters Hill in Kent, thus proving the capabilities of the first true internally combusted engine.

Preventing Blasts and Mildew

Today in ancient Rome sacrificial rites were paid to the goddess Robigo in the ceremony of the *Robigalia* which averted the influence of unseasonable blasts and creeping mildew from the corn crops.

Preventing Fog, Hail, Storms, and Fire

In Hungary this was the day when people went into the wheat fields for the "Blessing of the Wheat." Each person returned with a stalk of the grain and was blessed "so fog shall not strangle, hail shall not destroy, storm shall not trample, fire shall not consume the only hope of the people."

An End to Duelling

Amended articles against duelling issued from the British War Office declared that it is suitable to the character of honourable men to apologise and offer redress for wrong or insult committed, and equally so for the party aggrieved to accept, frankly and cordially, explanation and apologies for the same (1844).

An End to Idlers

On April 25, 1868 the California Labor Exchange was brought into being in a state that was overstocked with idlers seeking employment without being able to obtain it. In a period of seven months, no less than 13,000 persons, representing 153 different occupations, were found jobs.

A Dreadful Conflagration

On this day in 1536 there occurred on Mount Etna in Sicily a dreadful conflagration when the volcano erupted demolishing the church of St Leon and consuming many therein, including the famous physician Piazzi.

A Whip-poor-will Calls

"On or about the 25th of April, if the season be not uncommonly cold, the whip-poor-will is heard in Pennsylvania, in the evening as the dusk of twilight commences; or in the morning as soon as dawn is broke."
The Anniversary Calendar, Natal Book and Universal Mirror, 1832

26
APRIL

Births

Marcus Aurelius (Roman emperor) 121; John James Audubon (American naturalist) 1785; Alfred Krupp (German industrialist) 1812.

Baptism, 1564

John Shakespeare and his wife, Mary Arden, had their third child and first son baptised William Shakespeare in the parish church at Stratford-On-Avon.

Shooting, Leaping, and Pitching, 1569

On April 26, 1569, Queen Elizabeth issued a licence allowing Sunday sports in the County of Middlesex. Games allowed were "the shooting with the standard, the shooting with the broad arrow, the shooting at twelve score prick, the shooting at the Turk, the leaping for men, the running for men, the wrestling, the throwing of the sledge, and the pitching of the bar, with all such other games as have at any time heretofore or now been licensed, used, or played."

Colonising, 1607

John White, with 150 men and three vessels, arrived from Portsmouth, England to settle a colony in Virginia at Cape Henry.

Terrorizing, 1715

On April 26, 1715 the Yamani Indian tribe began terrorizing the white settlers and imperilling the town of Charleston, South Carolina.

Feelings, Ambitions, and Humiliations

Persons born on the 26th often appear cold and undemonstrative (though secretly they are warm-hearted towards the oppressed in all classes) and tend to hide their feelings and allow others to think what they please. When ambitious, people born today are likely to aim high in public life or for government responsibilities involving great sacrifice on their part. Unfortunately numerology predicts that those born under this number will often have to face the greatest sorrows, losses, and humiliations.

Deaths

St Basil (Roman saint) 322; Ferdinand Magellan (Portuguese navigator) 1521; Artemus Ward (American humorist) 1834.

Beheading, 322

On April 26, 322, Basil became a saint when he was cruelly tortured and his head struck off for having sheltered a beautiful Christian maiden named Glaphiga from the lust of the Emperor Lucinius.

Submerging, 1880

Mr Fleuss, the inventor of a submarine diving dress, remained two hours under water at the Westminster Aquarium in London without any communication by tubes or otherwise with the upper air. According to his own statement, he was able to remain under water for five hours without inconvenience and enjoy perfect freedom of movement.

Fasting, 1890

An Italian named Succi concluded a forty-day fast at the Royal Aquarium, London. After some food had been taken, his general condition was declared feeble with a pulse of 66.

Paying, 1920

Today in 1920 the allied premiers asked the German nation to start making reparation payments for the cost of World War I.

Uniting, 1964

Zanzibar and Tanganyika united to form a single sovereign republic to be called Tanzania.

Births

Edward Gibbon (historian) 1737; Mary Wollstonecraft (writer) 1759; Ulysses S. Grant (18th U.S. president) 1822.

Deaths

St Zita (virgin) 1272; James Bruce (explorer) 1794; Ralph Waldo Emerson (writer) 1882.

St Zita's Extreme Unction

St Zita was a pious and devoted maidservant who served the same family all her life. She lived always in the closest communication with the unseen world and fasted a whole year on bread and water. When she died after extreme unction on this day in 1272 a bright star hung over the place where she lay.

James Bruce's Last Steps

On April 27, 1794, James Bruce, famous African traveller of his time and searcher for the sources of the Nile through then uncharted Abyssinia, Nubia, and Ethiopia, died at the age of sixty-four, after falling down the steps of his own home.

Ralph Waldo Emerson's Death

Emerson began his career as a Unitarian parson in Boston, but retired after three years at the pulpit to devote his life to literature and learning. One of America's most distinguished philosophers, he passed away today in 1882 at Concord, Massachusetts from the effects of a cold caught while attending the funeral of the poet Longfellow.

Edward Gibbon's Resolution

"1737—April 27th I was born at Putney in Surrey". These words opened the *Journal of my Life* by Edward Gibbon (who later wrote *The History of the Decline and Fall of the Roman Empire*). In a later entry in his *Journal* he wrote that he proposed "to keep an exact journal of my actions and my studies: both to assist my memory and to accustom me to set a due value upon my time."

Babe Ruth's Ovation

On April 27, 1947, 58,339 baseball fans gathered in Yankee Stadium gave a thunderous standing ovation to the "Sultan of Swat," who was seriously ill.

William Foxley's Big Sleep

April 27, 1546, "being Tuesday in Easter week, William Foxley, pot-maker for the Mint in the Tower of London, fell asleep, and so continued sleeping, and could not be wakened with pinching, cramping, or otherwise burning whatsoever, till the first day of term, which was fourteen days and fifteen nights. The cause of his thus sleeping could not be known, although the same were diligently searched after by the King's physicians and other learned men: yea, and the King himself examined the said William Foxley, who was in all point found at his waking to be as if he had slept but one night; and he lived more than forty years after in the Tower."

Stow's Chronicle, 1546

John Milton's Contract

Today in 1667 Milton signed a contract dispensing of the copyright of his *Paradise Lost* to Samuel Simmons, a London publisher, for the sum of five pounds and five pounds more when 1,300 copies of the first edition were sold.

28
APRIL

Births

James Monroe (5th U.S. president) 1758; John Jacob Niles (folksinger) 1892.

Deaths

St Vitalis (martyr) 62; Benito Mussolini (Italian dictator) 1945.

Discovered in 1770

Captain James Cook, seaman and explorer, wrote in his journal today in 1770 of his discovery of Botany Bay: "At daylight in the morning we discovered a bay, which appeared to be tolerably well sheltered from all winds, into which I resolved to go with the ship."

Shot and Hanged in 1945

Today in 1945 Benito Mussolini was captured by Italian partisans, court-martialed, and shot with his mistress, Clara Petacci. Their bodies were then taken to Milan, hanged in a public square, and buried in an unmarked grave.

Married in 1748

John Flaherty, parish clerk of Duncormuck, in the county of Wexford in England, aged seventy-five, married Mrs Anne White of Bannow, in the ninetieth year of her age.

The Cuckoo-pint

Today's flower is the *Arum maculation* or the cuckoo-pint.

Cursed in 1795

Captain James Pye Molloy, of the ship *Caesar,* had acted dishonourably to a woman to whom he was betrothed, and she laid this curse upon him. "Captain Molloy, you are a bad man. I wish you the greatest curse that can befall a British officer. When the day of battle comes may your false heart fail you." Though previously in his career Molloy had proved himself a brave sailor, on the 28th of April, 1795, he was tried for cowardice in a sea battle, found guilty, and relieved of his command.

A Travelling Goat, 1772

On April 28, 1772, there died at Mile End, England a goat that had twice circumnavigated the globe; first, in the discovery ship *Dolphin,* under Captain Wallis; and secondly in the renowned *Endeavour* under Captain Cook. The lords of the Admiralty had just previous to her death signed a warrant admitting her to the privileges of an in-pensioner of Greenwich Hospital, a boon she did not live to enjoy.

Mutiny on the Bounty, 1789

The British naval vessel, *Bounty,* commanded by Captain William Bligh, was en route to transport breadfruit trees from the Society Islands to the West Indies. On April 28, 1789, the crew led by Fletcher Christian mutinied and put Bligh and eighteen others in a small open boat which was set adrift.

The First Parachute Jump, 1919

Today in 1919 at Dayton, Ohio, Mr Irwin leaped from a plane, carrying on his back a parachute designed by the U.S. Army Air Corps, pulled the rip cord, and floated safely to earth.

Stretched and Buried Alive in 62

St Vitalis was stretched on a rack and, after other torments, was buried alive in a place called the Palmtree in Ravenna, Italy in the year 62. In his last words he glorified God and pledged the persecution of Nero.

Revelries in Rome

Today, according to the Roman calendar, was the festival of Flora, the goddess of flowers and gardens. Among the Greeks she was known as Chloris. She was originally a common courtesan who left to the Romans the immense riches that she had acquired in her trade, in remembrance of which a yearly festival was instituted in her honour. The *Floralia* revelries, held annually in her honour in Rome, were very licentious, consisting in part of spectacles of public prostitution.

Births

William Randolph Hearst (publisher) 1863; Jeremy Thorpe (politician) 1929.

Deaths

John Cleveland (poet) 1659; Michael Ruyter (admiral) 1676; James Montgomery (poet) 1854.

Rioting in Wales

During the Chartist riot at Llanidloes, Wales, the Trewythen Arms Inn was ransacked, and the inmates expelled. The mob was armed with guns, pistols, and pikes, and seemed to be, for a while, in entire possession of the town (1839).

Explosions in New York

Two infernal machines containing half a pound of explosive powder each, were discovered in the post office mails at New York. One exploded prematurely in the mail bag while in transmission. Both were addressed to separate individuals. The general opinion was that the attempts were due to socialists (1882).

Zippers in Hoboken

On April 29, 1913, Mr Gideon Sandback of Hoboken, New Jersey received a patent for a device he claimed would greatly aid the fastening of clothing. He called it a zipper.

Railway News

1857: A locomotive of the B & O Railroad made the trial trip on the Washington-Baltimore line powered by electricity. It averaged nineteen miles per hour on the run.

1878: In consequence of an announcement by the North British Railway Co. that they intended to increase the men's working time from fifty-one to fifty-four hours per week, 2,000 workers went out on strike.

1880: A murder of a nature very disquieting to elderly gentlemen who are in the habit of sleeping in railway carriages was committed tonight in the express train between Marseille and Lyon. M. Palangeon, a railway conductor, was asleep when he was unpleasantly restored to consciousness by a stab in the side. He was then shot in the thigh but managed to keep his assailant at bay until the next station and help. The assassin was arrested and hanged himself in his cell. M Palangeon later died from his wounds.

Telephones in Boston

"A Telephone, Complete—$3.00—guaranteed to work 1 mile.

One guaranteed to work 5 miles—$5.00."
  An advertisement in a Boston newspaper, 1878

Births

Mary II (English queen) 1662; Juliana (Dutch queen) 1909.

Deaths

St Catherine (virgin) 1380; Sarah Hale (author of *Mary Had a Little Lamb*) 1879.

Scottish Women and Snails

In Scotland during the middle ages young women took this day as the one that would reveal the identity of their future husbands. A snail was placed under a bowl overnight and the husband's name would be written out by its trail by morning.

Warding off Witches

In Czechoslovakia on this night it was thought wise to scatter sand or grass on one's doorstep. Witches were out to do people ill, but they could not enter a house before counting the grains of sand or the blades of grass.

A Dedicated Spinster Saint

For five years Catherine defied her father's wishes that she should marry. She cut off her hair and wore a veil to make herself unattractive. When she was seventeen her father relented and allowed her to enter a religious order. The accomplishment of her mind and body made her the darling and delight of all who knew her. For three years she spoke to no one but to God and her confessor. She died today in 1380 in Sienna, Italy.

A Philosopher's Wife

"Ah my dearest wife Terentia, let me see you again as soon as possible, that I may have the satisfaction of breathing out my last departing sigh in your arms."
From the diary of the Roman philosopher Cicero, April 30, 58 B.C.

Impoverished Women Pensioned

On April 30, 1877 a pension of £75 was granted to the great, great granddaughters of the author of *Robinson Crusoe,* Daniel Defoe. They were over fifty years of age and living in extreme poverty.

Princess Victoria Weds

Today in 1884 at Darmstadt in Germany, Princess Victoria, eldest daughter of the grand duke of Hesse and the great granddaughter of the queen of England, married Prince Louis of Battenburg.

Gentlemen at War

On April 30, 1745, the allied armies of England, Holland, and Austria engaged a superior French army in the battle of Fountenoy. Captain Lord Charles Hay of the English guards advanced from the ranks with his hat off; at the same moment Lieutenant Count D'Auteroche of the French guards advanced, uncovered, to meet him. Lord Charles bowed: "Gentlemen of the French guards," he said, "Fire!" The count bowed to Lord Charles. "No my lord," he answered, "We never fire first." They again bowed; each resumed his place in his own ranks; and after these testimonies of "high consideration," the bloody conflict commenced with a slaughter of 12,000 men on each side.

MAY

Then came fair May, the fayrest mayd on ground,
Deckt all with dainties of her season's pride,
And throwing flowres out of her lap around:
Upon two brethren's shoulders she did ride,
The twinnes of Leda; which on either side
Supported her, like to their soveraine queen.
Lord! how all creatures laughed, when her they spide,
And leapt and daunc't as they had ravisht beene!
And Cupide self about her fluttered all in greene.
  Edmund Spenser

MAY

History

May was the second month in the old Alban calendar, the third in that of Romulus, and the fifth in the one instituted by Numa Pompilius—a position it has held from then until the present. It consisted of twenty-two days in the Alban, and of thirty-one in Romulus' calendar; Numa deprived it of one day, which Julius Caesar then restored, and it has remained with thirty-one since. The month is probably named in honour of *Maia,* the mother by Jupiter of the god Hermes, or Mercury. Another explanation of the name is that it was assigned in honour of the *Maiores,* the original senate in the Roman constitution. Among the Anglo-Saxons the month was called *Tri-Milchi,* the cows being supposed to be able to give milk three times daily when feeding on the new, spring grass.

Birthstone

The emerald is the birthstone of May. Found mainly in South America, Siberia, and India, it promises success in love to those who wear it.

Love's Month

This is love's month; but yet men have a care for women, for they are like fiddles that have four strings to them; modesty, faith, vows and maidenheads. Now, if any one of these four strings crack or break, there is little delight in such marriage music.
  Poor Robins Almanac, 1683

1
MAY

Births

Kate Smith (singer) 1909; Glenn Ford (actor) 1917; Jack Parr (TV personality) 1918.

Deaths

John Dryden (poet) 1700; David Livingstone (explorer) 1873; Anton Dvořák (composer) 1904.

The May Pole

"Oxen drawe home this Maie poole, which is covered all over with flowers and herbes, bounde rounde aboute with strings, from the top to the bottome, and sometyme painted with variable colours, with two or three hundred men, women, and children followying it, with great devotion. And then fall they to banquet and feast, to leape and daunce aboute it, as the Heathen people did at the dedication of their Idolles."

Stubbes, an ancient chronicler

May Dew

"My wife away to Woolwich in order to get a little air, and to gather May dew which Mrs. Turner hath taught her is the only thing in the world to wash her face in." Samuel Pepys was referring to the custom of ladies to bathe their faces in the morning dew of May 1. The precious liquid made them beautiful and gave them more luck for the next year.

Chimney Sweep's Day

Long after most other May Day customs passed out of use, May first in London continued to be celebrated as a holiday by the chimney sweeps. They used to dance and parade through the city streets wearing elaborate costumes and bearing the tools of their trade aloft.

May Day

The origin of European May Day celebrations lies in the Roman feast of flowers, the sometimes decadent *Floralia,* which began on April 28, but ran for several days. More recent celebrations were also feasts of flowers. Early in the morning of May 1 the young men and women used to go into the new flowering forests to gather blooms with which they decorated their houses, the may pole, and themselves. The day was full of dancing, feasting, and singing.

May Day Objections

The Puritans were strongly opposed to the frolickings of May Day, one of the objections being that young men "doe use commonly to runne into woodes in the night time, amongst maidens, to set bowes, in so muche, as I have hearde of tenne maidens whiche went to set May, and nine of them came home with childe."

May Day's End

May Day was celebrated with great enthusiasm in Padstow, England, as the Oss appeared and ran after young girls. Oss was a man dressed up in a huge black cape and horrific mask and he danced and leapt all day long until at midnight he died and everyone sang goodbye.

O'Donohugh's Ghost

Each year early in the morning of May first the ghost of O'Donohugh, an ancient Irish chieftain, is supposed to gallop his charger across the waters of the lake of Killarney, the lands about which he ruled in his time. O'Donohugh is said to have died by walking out upon the waters of the lake until he disappeared. If his ghost is seen by very many people, it portends a good harvest.

First Advertisement

"At Oyster Bay on Long Island in the province of New York, there is a good Fulling Mill to be Let or Sold, as also a plantation having on it a large new Brick house, and another good house by it for a Kitchen and Workhouse etc."

The first U.S. advertisement as it appeared in the Boston *News-Letter,* 1704

2
MAY

Births

Catherine the Great (Russian empress) 1729; Bing Crosby (singer/actor) 1904.

Scottish Witches Burnt

In parts of Scotland today saw the kindling of massive bonfires. People tossed up the blazing fire and ran around holding flaming portions high on the top of pitchforks. Children danced through the smoke shouting, "Fire! blaze an' burn the witches; fire! fire! burn the witches."

Today's Birthday Fortunes

Number 2 persons are gentle, imaginative, artistic, and romantic by nature but not particularly forceful in carrying out their ideas. Their qualities tend to be more on a mental rather than physical plane. This is a fortunate day for them to carry out their plans, but they have to guard against unsettled and restless feelings (today in particular but throughout their lives). People born today are also inclined to be oversensitive and prone to melancholy.

Deaths

Leonardo da Vinci (artist/inventor) 1520; J. Edgar Hoover (FBI director) 1972.

Scottish Queen Escapes

Mary, queen of Scots, aided by gallant George Douglas, escaped this night from Lochleven Castle in Kinrosshire, Scotland, thus delaying her long imprisonment and beheading that were ultimately to follow.

British Bridge Collapses

The suspension bridge in Yarmouth, England collapsed today in 1845, under pressure of a crowd congregated to see a professional clown drawn down the river in a tub by four geese. Daring efforts were made by spectators of every rank to bring sufferers ashore, but the calamity was so unlooked for and overwhelming in its magnitude that on reckoning the loss, the fearful toll amounted to seventy-nine.

Man-Eater Killed

A man-eating leopard suspected of killing and devouring 125 people was finally put to death today in 1926 in Radraprayag, India.

Italian Composer Comes Home

The remains of Rossini, which had been removed from the cemetery of Père-la-Chaise, at Paris, reached Florence and were received with great honour in anticipation of their reinterment in Santa Croce (1887).

Von Hindenburg's Resurrection

On May 2, 1919, Field Marshal von Hindenburg announced his resignation at the conclusion of peace arrangements. Six years later he was elected president of Germany.

Airline Inauguration

America's first passenger airplane service began today in 1919 when pilot Robert Hewitt took off from New York City with passengers Mrs Hoagland and Miss Hodges, bound for Atlantic City, New Jersey.

Coarse Fishing Begins

Medieval British almanacs claim that May 2 was the beginning of the fishing season for the chubb, pike, gudgeon, eel, dace, bleak, and finnock.

3
MAY

Births

Niccolo Machiavalli (Italian philosopher) 1469; Golda Meir (Israeli leader) 1898.

The Dismal Day

Scottish Highlanders called May 3 "the dismal day," believing that this is the day the fallen angels were sent from Paradise and so it was important not to do anything evil on this day.

Deaths

James Sharp (Scottish archbishop) 1679; Thomas Hood (British poet) 1845; Sir John Bright (British electrician) 1888.

Presbyterian Fury, 1679

Today in 1679, the Presbyterians of Scotland became so furious that they murdered Dr Sharp, the archbishop of St Andrew's, in his coach.

Holy Cross Day, 326

St Helena, mother of Constantine the Great, journeyed to Palestine in 329, to visit holy sites. She felt a need to find the exact cross upon which Christ was crucified and so had buildings torn down and dug up to great depths in search. Three crosses were found and to identify the correct one an ailing woman was touched with each. The touch of one cured her on this day in 326 thereby marking it as the original Holy Cross.

A Singular Interment, 1881

A singular interment took place today at Sheffield Cemetry, the first of its kind in England. The remains were those of an old lady who had been deaf and dumb for years. The mourners were all deaf and dumb and the service was completely conducted with deaf and dumb signs. Hitherto the service in similar cases had been conducted orally and then interpreted.

Disaster at Sea, 1855

On May 3, 1855, the wreck of the emigrant ship *John* occurred on the Manacle Rocks off Falmouth, England with the loss of 190 lives. All the life boats on board were either unseaworthy or improperly stowed so as to be unavailable for immediate service. Ninety survivors were taken from the wreck by rescue vessels. It was remarked at the time as a significant circumstance that this number included the whole of the officers and crew.

Fire in San Francisco, 1851

Today in 1851 San Francisco was almost entirely destroyed by fire, it being the seventh time the city had been thus scourged during the four years of its existence.

A Successful Swim, 1810

Today in 1810 Lord Byron, the British poet, swam across the Dardanelles—the body of water linking the Aegean Sea with the Sea of Marmara. The total distance of his swim, including the distance he was carried by the currents, was over four miles.

A Successful Operation, 1650

"At the Hospital of La Charité in Paris I saw the operation of cutting for gallstones. A child of eight or nine years old, underwent the operation with most extraordinary patience."
　　From the diary of John Evelyn, May 3, 1650

Births

Thomas Huxley (philosopher) 1825;
Audrey Hepburn (actress) 1929;
Roberta Peters (opera singer) 1930.

Deaths

Isaac Barrow (mathematician) 1677;
Tippoo Sahib (Indian sultan) 1799;
Horace Twiss (writer) 1849.

Floralia Finale

This was the last day of the Roman
Floralia festival held in honour of
Flora, goddess of fruit and flowers.
The lowest classes of women, giving
way to their depravity, danced naked
in the streets, and set the example for
every other species of lascivious
abasement.

Proverb

The haddocks are good
When dipped in May flood.

The Limits of Courtesy

Isaac Barrow, who died on this day in
1677, was an eminent British
mathematician best remembered for
an exchange of courtesies at court
with Lord Rochester. When the two
met Rochester said to Barrow,
"Doctor, I am yours to my shoe tie,"
and the other replied, "My lord, I am
yours to the ground." Rochester went
on "Doctor, I am yours to the
centre," to which Barrow replied,
"My Lord, I am yours to the
antipodes." Not to be outdone
Rochester ventured, "Doctor, I am
yours to the lowest pit of hell," upon
which Barrow turned from him
saying, "There, my Lord, I leave you."

Hoary Shrubby Stock

Today's flower, the *Mathiola incana*,
is also known as the hoary shrubby
stock as well as the stock gilly flower.

Greek Blast

The first sod of the new canal dividing the Isthmus of
Corinth was turned by the king of Greece and the rock
where Nero began cutting the Isthmus was blown to
pieces by dynamite discharged by the queen today in
1882.

The Cost of New York

On May 4, 1626 Governor Peter Minuit arrived with four
shiploads of settlers and 300 cattle and bought the island
of Manhattan — all 20,000 acres — from the Indians for
$24.00 worth of scarlet cloth and brass buttons.

A 200-Foot Painting

The nineteen-year-old artist-writer Robert Ker Porter of
London was so inspired by the taking of Seringapatam by
the British on May 4, 1799, that within six weeks he had
completed a panoramic painting of the storming of the
Indian fortress that covered a canvas over 200 feet long.

Public Enemy Number One

Today in 1932 Al Capone, labelled by the U.S. Justice
Department as "Public Enemy Number One" was jailed in
Atlanta Penitentiary for income-tax evasion.

Lady Art Critics

On May 4, 1914 militant suffragettes slashed a portrait of
Henry James displayed at a Royal Academy Exhibition in
London.

Lady Doctors and Patients

On May 4, 1855 the Women's Hospital of New York City
opened. It was the first U.S. hospital founded by women
for women. Dr Marion Sims was resident surgeon.

Oscars Begin

The Academy of Motion Picture Arts and Sciences, the
dispenser of the Hollywood "Oscars," was formed today
in 1927.

5
MAY

Births

Soren Kierkegaard (philosopher) 1813; Karl Marx (philosopher) 1818.

Deaths

Napoleon Bonaparte (emperor) 1821; Bret Harte (author) 1902.

A Poetic Will

The poetic will of John Hedges was approved on May 5, 1737 in London:

This fifth of May,
Being airy and gay,
To hip not inclined,
But of vigorous mind,
And my body in health,
I'll dispose of my wealth;
And of all I'm to have
On this side of the grave
To some one or other,
I think to my brother.
But because I foresaw
That my brothers-in-law,
If I did not take a care,
Would come in for a share,
Which I no ways intended
Till their manners were mended—
And of that there's no sign—
I do therefore enjoin,
And strictly command,
As witness my hand,
That naught I have got
Be brought to hotch-pot;
And I give and devise,
Much as in me lies,
To the son of my mother,
My own dear brother,
To have and to hold
All my silver and gold
As the affectionate pledges
Of his brother.

Today's Riots

1849:   Riotous proceedings at Fen Ditton, Cambridgeshire, arose out of an attempt to inflict penance upon a person charged with slandering the rector's wife.

1885:   Extensive strikes of colliers occurred at Joliet, Illinois and in Chicago coal fields. At the Lemare mines, 1,000 strikers assembled to attack the troops which, 400 strong and provided with cannon, had been sent against them. Two of the colliers were killed and nine wounded in the ensuing rioting.

1886:   In Chicago socialist and anti-socialist factions squared off in fierce rioting that killed several of them and also some policemen.

1927:   German police armed with truncheons waded into parading Fascists, cracking skulls left and right and effectively dissolving the Fascist group for the moment.

Today's Fire

A fearful conflagration began today in Hamburg, Germany in 1842. An eye witness reported from the scene: "It burst forth at 12 o'clock on Wednesday night, and has so gained up to this time, aided by high winds, in the midst of misdirected efforts to extinguish it or arrest its progress, that it rages now with increased violence over a space so wide, that I believe it will yet require the sacrifice of nearly one half the remainder of the town." (The blaze lasted five days and levelled much of the city.)

Today's Arrest

John T. Scopes, a biology teacher in the Dayton, Tennessee public school system, was arrested today in 1925 for teaching the theory of evolution, which violated a state statute.

Today's Hanging

The earl of Ferrer was hanged for murder today in 1760, the last English nobleman to die a felon.

Proverb

Change not a clout (i.e. don't put away winter clothes)
Till May be out.

Births

Robespierre (French politician) 1758; Phoebe Ann Coffin (American minister) 1829; Sigmund Freud (Austrian psychologist) 1856; Rudolph Alfonzo Raffaele Pierre Filibert Guglielmi de Valentina d'Antonguolla (Rudolph Valentino) 1895; Orson Welles (American actor) 1915; Willie Mays (American baseball player) 1931.

Anne Boleyn's Last Letter

In her last letter (prior to her beheading for unfaithfulness) to Henry VIII written from her prison in the Tower of London on this day 1536, Anne Boleyn wrote: "Never had a prince a more dutiful wife than you have in Anne Boleyn; with which name and place I could willingly have contented myself; if God and your Grace's pleasure had so been pleased."

Margaret Davidson's Temptations

"Margaret Davidson, spouse of James, is to be rebuked in sackcloth, if she fall into the three sins, or any of them, of cursing, drunkenness, or Sabbath breaking."
   From the Session records of Dumries, Scotland, May 6, 1652

Zeppelin Zapped, 1937

The *Hindenburg,* a German zeppelin, exploded and burned at Lakehurst, New Jersey.

Author Honoured, 1957

John Fitzgerald Kennedy, a thirty-nine year old U.S. Senator, was awarded a Pulitzer Prize for his book, *Profiles in Courage.*

Globeflower

Today's flower is known popularly as the globeflower and botanically as *Trollius europus.*

Proverbs

Mist in May, and heat in June,
Make the harvest right soon.

A cold May is kindly
And fills the Barn finely.

A Sword Mightier than a Pen

Today in 1858 an editor of the French newspaper *Figaro* landed himself in a duel for writing about an undesirable officer who had not attended a ball: "he who tears ladies' laces with his spurs, that plague of the drawing-room—was not there." The editor wounded the officer-challenger but while standing around congratulating himself was challenged by another officer who ran him through. While recovering from his wounds the editor discovered that his second adversary was a fencing master in the army.

New News, 1835

The *New York Herald Tribune* began publication.

New Cold, 1851

Dr John Forrie of New Orleans patented a "mechanical refridgerating machine" that cooled by compressing air in a cylinder in a chamber immersed in cooling water.

Theatre Blaze, 1872

Nibbo's Theatre in New York City was destroyed by fire.

Sioux Surrenders, 1877

Crazy Horse, chief of the Oglala Sioux Indians, surrendered, after he and his followers had spent a winter of near starvation.

Chinese Checked, 1882

An act restricting immigration of Chinese labourers into the U.S. for a period of ten years was passed by Congress. It also denied them naturalisation.

7
MAY

Births

Robert Browning (poet) 1812;
Johannes Brahms (composer) 1833;
Peter Tchaikovsky (composer) 1840;
Gary Cooper (actor) 1901; Ann Baxter
(actress) 1923; Johnny Unitas
(football player) 1933.

Deaths

Socrates (philosopher) 399 B.C.

Heavenly Apparition, 351

Today in the year 351 a miraculous
meteor, encircled by a large rainbow
to form a vast luminous cross,
appeared over Jerusalem.

Cricket Devastation, 1888

News was received in Paris on May 7,
1888 of a fearful devastation caused
by crickets in Algeria. The light of the
sun was shut out by their swarms; all
traces of vegetation were destroyed;
and a railway train was stopped,
being unable to plough its way
through the heaps of dead insects.

A Beautiful Day

The scenery of a May morning is particularly beautiful; a
serene sky, a refreshing fragrance arising from the face of
the earth, and the melody of the birds, all combine to
render it inexpressibly delightful, to exhilarate the spirits,
and call forth a song.

How fresh the breeze that wafts the rich perfume,
And swells the melody of waking birds!
The hum of Bees beneath the verdant grove
And Milkmaid's song, and low of distant herds!
    Catholic Annal, 1830

English Extermination, 1763

On May 7, 1763, Pontiac, chief of the Ottawas instigated a
conspiracy "to surprise every English post between the
Alleghenies and the Mississippi by a confederacy of all the
tribes, and thus exterminate the English in the West." An
Indian maiden at Detroit exposed the scheme which the
garrison there was able to defeat.

Germany on May 7th

1875: One of the greatest sea disasters ever took place
    this night near the entrance to the British Channel. The
    German steamship *Schiller,* which ran from New York
    to Hamburg, was totally wrecked and more than 300
    lives were lost—as well as the whole cargo.

1915: A German U-boat torpedoed the Cunard liner
    Lusitania off the coast of Ireland. The huge liner sank
    below the waves in less than twenty minutes taking
    1,200 passengers to the bottom.

1919: A draft treaty of peace was presented to the
    German delegation at the post World War I peace
    conference. They protested the terms and presented
    counter-proposals without success.

1928: A German opera was performed in the original in
    Paris for the first time since 1914.

1943: German troops were driven back into the desert
    from the North African cities of Bizertas and Tunis.

1945: At 2:41 a.m., Germany formally surrendered to
    Allied Commander General Eisenhower at his
    headquarters in Rheims, France.

Births

Harry S. Truman (33rd U.S. president) 1884; Thomas B. Costain (author) 1895; Roberto Rossellini (film maker) 1906.

Deaths

Captain Barclay Allardice (walker) 1854; John Stuart Mill (philosopher) 1873; Gustave Flaubert (novelist) 1880.

Opium is Okay

On May 8 in 1911, England signed a treaty with China to use opium as the main trading commodity with the Chinese.

Stork Day in Denmark

On May 8 storks traditionally start arriving at Ribe, Denmark to repair their nests on housetops in preparation for spring mating.

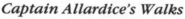

Madame Bovary's Immorality

M. Gustave Flaubert, the French novelist, died today in 1880 at Rouen at the age of fifty-eight. His first distinct success was the novel *Madame Bovary*, the sales of which were greatly enhanced by a prolonged government prosecution that maintained the novel was immoral.

Ferdinand and Isabella's Expansion

The Spanish monarchs Ferdinand and Isabella today in 1493 drew up a decree ordering that a "line be marked, passing from the Azores to the Cape de Verd Islands, from the north to the south, from pole to pole; so that all which is beyond the aforesaid line to the west is ours, and belongs to us."

Furry Day in Helston

Helston in Cornwall, England gets its name from a large granite stone placed at the mouth of Hell. The Devil is said to have tried to steal the stone but was intercepted by St Michael. Furry Day celebrates this story annually on May 8. Current festivities have been modified somewhat from the earlier times when those of every rank in the vicinity of the place joined in tumultuous dissipations, dancing through the streets in every wanton attitude, and drawing by force into the general vortex all who attempted to evade the riotous excesses. Were any youth discovered inattentive to the summons issued for universal indulgence he was seized, conveyed sitting on a pole to the river, and plunged headlong into the stream.

Mississippi River Found

On May 8 in 1541, Hernando de Soto and a group of Spanish explorers discovered the Mississippi River at a point near the present city of Memphis, Tennessee.

Captain Allardice's Walks

Captain Barclay Allardice, who died on May 8, 1854, was one of the greatest British walkers of all time. At the age of twenty-two, he walked 300 miles in five days. His greatest feat was to have walked 1,000 miles in 1,000 consecutive hours, one mile within each hour, between the first of June and the twelfth of July. Over £100,000 was staked on the issue, and Barclay did not fail his backers.

Sarah Henley's Jump

Today in 1885 a young girl named Sarah Henley, having quarrelled with her lover, jumped off the Clifton Suspension bridge in Bristol, England. The tide being low, she fell upon the soft mud where she would have suffocated but for prompt assistance. Although she had fallen 230 feet, she was conscious and uninjured. During her short stay in hospital she received one offer of marriage and two engagements from showmen.

9
MAY

Births

John Brown (abolitionist) 1800; Henry J. Kaiser (industrialist) 1887; Pancho Gonzalez (tennis player) 1928.

Deaths

Frederic Schiller (poet) 1805; Joseph Louis Gay-Lussac (chemist) 1850.

John Brown's Body

John Brown, the American anti-slavery leader was born today in 1800. In 1859 he led a successful attack on the Federal Arsenal at Harper's Ferry in Virginia, for which he was hanged and immortalised in song — "John Brown's Body lies A-Mouldering in the Grave, but his Soul Goes Marching on."

Ben Franklin's Cartoon

On May 9, 1754, Benjamin Franklin published the first American cartoon in his *Pennsylvania Gazette*. It was titled "Join or Die" and showed a snake cut up in pieces, each piece representing a state.

Captain Blood's Crown-Jewel Caper

On May 9, 1671, Colonel Thomas Blood, a life-long rogue and enemy of the monarchy, made an extraordinary attempt to steal the crown, orb, and sceptre of the king from London Tower. The attempt was nearly successful, but was aborted by Talbot Edwards, the keeper of the items, and his son. When he was brought before the king to explain his crimes, Blood so threatened and flattered the king that he was punished for his attempt with the reward of an estate in Ireland. It seemed that the king simply hoped that the man would go away. For their own troubles, Edwards and son were each awarded £200, which they subsequently had trouble collecting.

The Macready-Forrest Hostilities

Today in 1849 there was rioting in New York theatres, caused by a rumoured jealousy between English tragedian Macready, on a visit to the states, and a native actor named Forrest. Macready was driven from the stage on May 7, but returned tonight to find his friends forcibly removing the disaffected from the theatre. Riots ensued in the streets and three or four were killed. Macready embarked for England at the earliest opportunity.

Anna Jarvis' Suggestion

Miss Anna Jarvis of Philadelphia suggested that one day a year be set aside to honour America's mothers. President Wilson agreed and today in 1914 issued a proclamation that the second Sunday of May be set aside as a "public expression of our love and reverence for the mothers of the country."

10
MAY

Births

Fred Astaire (actor/dancer) 1899; David O. Selznick (film producer) 1902.

Extorting, 1853

An attempt was made today in 1853 to extort money from Mr Gladstone (later to become British prime minister) by charging him with improper conduct towards a female in the Haymarket in London. Gladstone had been accosted by one of the unfortunates of the locality and while listening to her story, a man calling himself Wilson approached and threatened to expose him in the *Morning Herald*. The man was apprehended, tried, and sentenced to twelve months' imprisonment.

Deaths

Botticelli (artist) 1510; Mrs Honeywood (grandmother) 1620; Henry Stanley (explorer) 1904.

Expiring, 1904

James Gordon Bennett of the *New York Herald* financed an expedition to find David Livingstone, the Scottish missionary lost in darkest Africa. He was found and greeted with the well-known words "Doctor Livingstone, I presume" by Henry Morton Stanley who died on this day in 1904.

Grandmothering, 1620

Mrs Mary Honeywood, of Charing in Kent, England, who died on this day in 1620, aged 93, had sixteen children, 114 grandchildren, 228 great grandchildren, and nine great-great-grandchildren at the time of her death.

Plagiarising, 1888

A case of importance to literature was decided in London on May 10, 1888. Seebohm, a dramatist, had prepared a stage version of *Little Lord Fauntleroy,* a story by Mrs Hodgson Burnett, who proceeded to bring an action against him which was decided in her favour. The court didn't dispute Seebohm's right to dramatise the novel, but held that since several passages were extracted almost verbatim, he had infringed the law.

Stargazing, 1930

On May 10, 1930 the first planetarium in the U.S. was opened in Chicago. The planetarium showing an elaborate model of the stars man could see, and was contained in a domed building that was a $1,000,000 gift from Max Adler.

Prognosticating

For those born today the number 10 in numerology is symbolized as the wheel of fortune. It is a number of faith, honour, and self-confidence. According to their desires people influenced by the number 10 will go down in history as being either good or evil, because their desires are quite likely to be carried out.

Railroading, 1869

The first transcontinental railway in America was completed today in 1869 when Governor Stanford of California drove a golden spike into the last railway tie at Promontory Point, Utah.

11
MAY

Births

Irving Berlin (composer) 1888; Margaret Rutherford (actress) 1892; Salvador Dali (artist) 1904.

Deaths

David I (Scottish king) 1153; Tom Cribb (boxer) 1848; Madame Récamier (beauty) 1849.

A Mysterious Beauty

Jeanne Françoise Julia Adelaide Bernard, Madame Récamier, was beautiful, had a mysterious charm of placid and kind demeanour, a sweet natural manner and a dignified obsequiousness, all of which combined to make many famous men of her time fall hopelessly in love with her. A list of some of her more distinguished admirers includes Napoleon Bonaparte, Bernadotte, king of Sweden, the king of Wurtemberg, the hereditary grand-duke of Mecklenberg-Strelitz, the prince of Bavaria, the Prince of Wales, the dukes of Beaujolais and Montpensier, and Prince Augustus of Prussia. Others who were not crowned heads but dallied with her: Wellington, Metternich, Duke Mathieu de Montmorency, Benjamin Constant, Canova, Ballanche, and Chateaubriand. She died on May 11, 1849.

Three Mysterious Ships

On May 11, 1553, three ships, the *Edward Bonadventure,* the *Bona Esperanza,* and the *Bona Confidentia,* all financed by *The Mystery Company and Fellowship of the Merchant Adventures for the Discovery of Unknown Lands,* set sail from England to search for the northwest passage to China. But the fates of the ships belied their optimistic names. They at once met with a storm in the North Sea and were driven upon the coast of Scandinavia. Two were marooned and eventually locked in the ice for the winter, where all their sailors were frozen to death. The third waited vainly at an appointed meeting place. The marooned ships had new sailors brought over from England in the spring and set off again with the third vessel. None of the three was ever seen again.

The Mysterious Powers of the Hawthorn

In olden times, today's flower the hawthorn *(Crategus oxycantha)* had properties other than the edible haw berries which it bears. Its wood was used to make may poles, as it symbolized the returning summer. It was also auspicious to have some laid on house rafters by a non-family member as it kept off spooks. Hung outside the cowshed, it assured plenty of milk. It also inspired men and birds to make utterances:

Every shepherd tell his tale
Under the Hawthorn in the dale

In every hedge the Hawthorn blooms
And the wild Woodlark chants his
   early song.

Fire Insurance in America

On May 11, 1752 there was a meeting of the Board of Directors of the Philadelphia Contributionship for the Insurance of Houses from Loss of Fire. Board members included James Hamilton, lieutenant governor of the province, and Benjamin Franklin. They ordered a seal for the company "being four hands united." The seals, made of lead and mounted on wood, were put in all insured houses. Their first policy was issued to John Smith, the company's treasurer, who wrote his own policy whereby it cost him one pound to insure a house worth £1,000.

12
MAY

Births

Dolly Madison (U.S. first lady) 1768; Edward Lear (poet) 1812; Florence Nightingale (nurse) 1820; Yogi Berra (baseball player) 1925.

Deaths

Sylvester II (pope) 1003; Christopher Smart (poet) 1771; Amy Lowell (poet) 1925.

Marriage

On May 12, 1621 Edward Winslow and Susanna White became the first couple to wed in the new colony of Plymouth.

A Nonsensical Poet

How pleasant to know Mr. Lear!
Who has written such volumes of
    Stuff!
Some think him ill-tempered and
    queer,
But a few think him pleasant enough!
    From *Nonsense Songs,* by Edward Lear
    who was born today in 1812

Lady with a Lamp

The efforts of Florence Nightingale, born today in 1820, to ease the sufferings of the wounded soldiers in the Crimea inspired Henry Wadsworth Longfellow to write *Santa Filomena:*

. . . Lo! in that house of misery
A lady with a lamp I see
Pass through the glimmering doom,
And flit from room to room.

And slow, as in a dream of bliss,
The speechless sufferer turns to kiss
Her shadow, as it falls
Upon the darkening walls . . .

Plowing for Breeches

"Merry doings at the Heart Inn today being Whit Monday; plowing for a Pair of Breeches; running for a Shift, and Raffling for a Gown etc."
    From the diary of Parson Woodfode, May 12, 1788

Screwing up Doors

Today in 1880 undergraduates of University College, Oxford, were chastised in a body, in consequence of an affront offered by some of their number to Mr Charasse, Senior Doctor to the University. It appeared that, after a supper held last night, some of the undergraduates revived the good old standard university piece of facetiousness, and screwed up Mr Charasse's door.

A Head Crowned

After his brother Edward VIII had abdicated the throne in preference to private life with Mrs Wallace Simpson, George VI was crowned king of England today in 1937.

Sluggards Arise!

The month of May was long considered to be a trying time for persons with chronic ailments. It used to be common to say of them, "If he can climb over *May-hill* he'll do." In his *Perenniel Calendar,* for May 12, Dr Forster said, "As a rule of health for May, we may advise early rising in particular, as being essentially conducive to that blessing. Everything now invites the sluggard to leave his bed and go abroad."

364 Heads Removed

The last person guillotined in a French prison was the Tunisian child murderer Ali Benyanes, in Marseilles on May 12, 1973. It was the seventy-four-year-old executioner's 364th successful execution.

13
MAY

Births

Maria Theresa (Austrian empress) 1717; Arthur Sullivan (British composer) 1842; Daphne Du Maurier (British novelist) 1907.

Deaths

Karl Baedeker (German publisher) 1859; Juan Gris (Spanish artist) 1927; Fridj of Nansen (Norwegian explorer) 1930.

Marriage, 1515

Mary, sister of King Henry VIII and widow of King Louis XII of France, to Charles, duke of Suffolk — against her brother's wishes.

Americans, 1607

On May 13, 1607, 105 colonists arrived at Jamestown, Virginia in the ships *Sarah Constant, Godspeed,* and *Discovery.* "Only 12 are labourers, 10 or 12 are mechanics, while 48 are gentlemen, and there are no women."

Common Comfray

The flower for May 13 is the *Symphetum officinale* or common comfray.

Burial, 1775

The *Leicester and Nottingham Journal* on this day reported the case of a young man, sorely troubled with rheumatism, who allowed himself to be buried naked in the ground, with only his face showing, for two hours at a stretch. He said he already felt much better for the treatment, and was prepared to repeat it for a further three hours on the morrow.

Bibles, 1881

The revised edition of the New Testament went on sale on May 13, 1881 in the U.S. and caused great activity in the book trade. The sheets had arrived by steamer from the English publishers to their agents in New York and Philadelphia. The sale began at daybreak and 800,000 copies were ordered on the first day.

Churchill, 1940

Churchill gave a speech in the House of Commons today, 1940, where he uttered his famous words: "I have nothing to offer but blood, toil, tears and sweat."

Sheep Shearing

"Who shears his sheep before St Servatius' day (a saint who died today in 384) loves more his wool than his sheep."
   An old proverb

Scottish Sacrificing

Until the eighteenth century, there used to be celebrated in Scotland the pagan festival of *Beltein* each May 13. A town in Perthshire was called Tillee Beltein (the high place of the fire of *Baal*). There, on the top of the hill, near two old Druid temples of standing stones, a great fire was built for the celebration. Lots were drawn to choose the one to be sacrificed to *Baal.* Symbolic of the sacrifice, the chosen one then had to leap three times through the flames.

Births

Marguerite de Valois (queen of Navarre) 1553; Gabriel Daniel Fahrenheit (thermometer inventor) 1686.

Deaths

Henry IV (French king) 1610; Louis XIII (French king) 1643.

Fending off Lunacy

The seeds of today's flower the common peony (*Paeonia officinalis*) were once woven into necklaces and worn to fend off lunacy, epilepsy, and nightmares. The roots of the plant eased a child when teething.

A Strange Ram

Today in 1752 was shown before the Royal Society in London, a ram full grown, having a horn growing under his throat, of the shape of an elephant's tooth, about two feet long, and thirty pounds weight.

Condensed Milk Begins

On May 14, 1853 Mrs Gail Borden applied for a U.S. patent for her process for making condensed milk. There were some doubts about the value of such a product but her process was eventually marketed by a firm known as the Borden Company.

Cow-pox versus Smallpox

On May 14, 1796 Edward Jenner of England proved that human beings could be safely inoculated against smallpox with a vaccine made from the blood of cattle infected with the cow-pox. But there were disbelievers, including many in the medical profession.

Said one Dr Smyth: "Among the numerous shocking cases of cow-pox which I have heard is a child at Peckham, who, after being inoculated with cow-pox, had his former natural disposition absolutely changed to the brutal; so that *it* ran upon all fours, bellowing like a cow, and butting with *its* head like a bull."

A satirical poet was moved to write:

There, nibbling at thistles, stand Jem, Joe and Mary;
On their foreheads, oh horrible! crumpled horns bud:
Here, Tom with a tail, and poor William all hairy,
Reclined in a corner, are chewing their cud.

Proverb

Come it early or come it late,
In May comes the cow-quake.

Beating the Band

The custom of perambulating the parishes or beating the bands on May 14 began in the year 550. A procession walked to each parochial landmark in England, chanting such words as: "Cursed be he which translateth the bands and doles of his neighbours."

The Stabbing Speaker

Today in 1838, the speaker of the Arkansas House of Assembly was tried for killing a member with a bowie knife on the floor of the House while in session. The jury found him guilty of excusable homicide.

The Rush to America

Today in 1880 the extraordinary tide of immigration into New York reached such numbers that problems developed. To so great an extent had the overcrowding of Atlantic steamers been carried, that the law offices of the United States were actively stirring themselves to put a stop to it. Warrants were issued for the arrest of captains of fourteen steamers.

15
MAY

Births

Frank Baum (creator of *The Wonderful Wizard of Oz*) 1856; Pierre Curie (scientist) 1859; James Mason (actor) 1909; Richard Avedon (photographer) 1923.

Deaths

St Dympna (virgin martyr) 7th century; Alban Butler (author of *Lives of the Saints*) 1773; Donald F. Duncan (inventor of the yo-yo) 1971.

The Patron Saint of the Insane

Geel is a town in Belgium well known for its system of billeting mental patients with families in the community. The patroness of the insane, St Dympna, is said to have fled here from Ireland, in an effort to escape her incestuous father. She was killed today in the 7th century when he caught her; this day in Geel is dedicated to her canonisation.

Proverb

Married in May
Rue the day.

A Master Cattle Thief

The Romans celebrated this day as the anniversary of the birth of Mercury (Hermes to the Greeks), the son of Zeus and Maia. He was the messenger of Zeus, and with his winged sandals and cap could travel with the speed of thought. He also bore a magic wand, the famous Caduceus. He was renowned for his cunning, and was sometimes known as the Master Thief for having stolen Apollo's cattle before he was a day old.

Papaver Cambricum

Today's flower, also known as the Welsh poppy is dedicated to the virgin martyr, St Dympna.

A Raging Storm in Vienna

Today in 1885 one of the most terrible storms ever witnessed raged over Vienna destroying shrubs, trees, and even houses. In the outskirts of the city the cold was so intense that the persons who had been thrown down and injured were found frozen to death.

Milestones

On May 15, 1764 at 5 a.m. two men started at Front and Market streets in Philadelphia and, together with the surveyor-general, began to plant milestones every mile for twenty-nine miles. These stones were donated by the directors of an insurance company, paid out of "fines" imposed for missing or arriving late at board meetings.

More Milestones

1602: Cape Cod was discovered by Batholomew Gosnold of England.
1796: Napoleon and his army entered Milan, Italy.
1858: The Royal Opera House, Covent Garden, opened in London.
1862: The U.S. Department of Agriculture was established.
1883: Geronimo's Mexican camp was captured by the U.S. army.
1905: Las Vegas, Nevada, was founded.
1921: Irish Republican arsonists lit fires all over London.
1940: The first nylon stockings were sold in America.

16
MAY

Births

Honoré de Balzac (novelist) 1799; Henry Fonda (actor) 1905; Liberace (pianist) 1919.

Deaths

St Brendan (explorer) 578; the duke of Baubleshire (eccentric) 1796; Emily Dickinson (poet) 1886.

Frogs and Bogs

The poet Emily Dickenson, who died on May 16, 1886 left an observation on frogs for posterity.

How dreary to be somebody!
How public, like a frog
To tell your name the livelong day
To an admiring bog!

The Duke of Baubleshire

Until his death on May 16, 1796, the self-appointed duke of Baubleshire, who was a labourer until his mind began to slip and he assumed his new role, wandered the streets of Durham, England, with a star of coloured paper on his breast, a cockade in his hat, and brass curtain rings on his fingers, instructing all those who would stop and listen in the business and matters of his imaginary dukedom.

Bootleg Taxation

Despite the fact that the manufacture and sale of alcoholic beverages was unlawful, the U.S. Supreme Court ruled that "bootleggers" must file income-tax forms (1927).

The Legend of St Brendan

In the 6th century the Irish saint who died today in 587, Brendan, set out into the Atlantic with two monks in a skin boat to search for a fabled island that was supposed to contain the paradise of Adam and Eve. Seven years later they came to a beautiful land where a man met them with the words: "Be ye now joyful, for this is the land ye have sought. So lade your ship with fruit and depart hastily, for ye may no longer abide here. Ye shall return to your own country, and soon after die. And this river that ye see here parteth the world asunder, for on that side of the water no man may come that is in this life." It is now considered by some authorities that Brendan's paradise was North America which he reached many hundreds of years before anyone else.

Sea-Lion Offspring

At the Brighton Aquarium in England, the female sea lion gave birth to a fine young one. This was the first instance on record of a sea lion breeding in captivity (1876).

Big Bridge

A scheme for constructing a gigantic bridge across the English Channel was described in a Paris journal. Its height would have to be sufficient to allow all vessels to pass beneath it, and the cost was estimated at £32,000,000 (1888).

Love's Triumph

Female dancers, the first to appear on a Parisian stage, kicked up their heels at the theatre of the Palais Royale, in a court opera called *Le Triomphe de L'Amour* (1681).

Ill-Fated Marriage

The Dauphin (Louis XVI) of France was wed to one Marie Antoinette, archduchess of Vienna. A remarkable tempest that accompanied the ceremony was said by the superstitious to be an omen of their future misfortunes (1770).

Proverb

A hot May makes a fat churchyard.

17

MAY

Births

John Penn (American statesman) 1741; Alphonso XIII (Spanish king) 1886; Stewart Alsop (columnist) 1914.

Deaths

Heloise (lover) 1163; Catherine I (Russian empress) 1727; Samuel Jessup (English hypochondriac) 1817; Prince Talleyrand (French statesman) 1838.

Heloise and Abelard

Heloise and Abelard were the tragic twelfth-century lovers who were exiled from their passions to monastic life. At the time of their affair Heloise was a young girl, and Abelard, her tutor, was twice her age. She survived him by twenty-one years. When she finally died on May 17, 1163, she was buried in the same tomb as he was. Legend says that when the grave was opened for her burial, Abelard held out his hand to receive her.

Catherine and Peter

Today in 1727, there died in St Petersburg in Russia, in her thirty-eighth year, the extraordinary Catherine I. She was the illegitimate offspring of an obscure country girl in Livonia. Her being taken prisoner at Marienburgh when it was captured by the Russians was the occasion of her becoming the favourite and at length the consort of Peter the Great. She was then elevated to the throne and declared empress of Russia.

Samuel Jessup, Pill-Popper

On May 17, 1817 Mr Samuel Jessup died at Heckington, England. The year before he had been taken to court by an apothecary for the payment of a bill. The court learned that in twenty-one years, Mr Jessup consumed 226,934 pills and over 40,000 bottles of various elixirs. In the last five years of his life he swallowed 51,590 of those pills or seventy-eight pills per day.

Prince Talleyrand's Bon-Mot

Charles Maurice de Talleyrand, who died today in 1838, was famous for his *bon-mots,* one of the most famous of which was that language was given to man not so that he could express his thoughts, but so that he could hide them.

Elizabeth Taylor's Strange Secret

A woman named Elizabeth Taylor, who was taken before the magistrates on a charge of being drunk and disorderly, told an incredible story of her adventures. She appeared in the dock of a London court today in 1885 dressed in male attire, which she had begun to wear thirteen years before while employed as a sailor. She had made several trips from South Wales to the American Coast and was known by the names of Happy Ned and Navvy Ned. She had been married, her husband dying twenty-one years previously.

Horse Tales

1817: A respectable English farmer of Kirton Lindsey, for a wager of a few pounds, undertook to ride a pony up two flights of stairs into a chamber of the George Inn, and down again, which he actually performed before an astonished company.

1875: The first Kentucky Derby horse race was held at Churchill Downs, Louisville, Kentucky.

1880: The Prix de Diane, or French Oaks, 1 mile 2-1/2 furlongs, for three-year-old fillies at Chantilly was won cleverly by the favourite, M. Lefevre's Versigny, beating Violette, La Flandrie, and nine others.

18
MAY

Births

Bertrand Russell (philosopher) 1872; Perry Como (singer) 1913; Margot Fonteyn (ballerina) 1919.

Deaths

William Stuart (father) 1685; Charles Perrault *(Mother Goose)* 1703; Nathaniel Hawthorne (writer) 1864.

A Tombstone Tale

Here lies the body of
William Stuart of Patrington.
Buried 18th May 1685. Aged 97 years.
He had children by his first wife, 28;
by his second, 17; and father to 45;
Grandfather to 86, great grandfather to 97;
great great grandfather to 23.
In all 251 descendants.
 On a gravestone in Patrington, Yorkshire, England

Mother Goose's Father

After a long and studious scholarly life, Charles Perrault was father to a son in his old age. Putting aside his studies Perrault spent his time composing fables for the enjoyment of his child. They were published under his son's name, at Paris, in 1697, with the title *Tales of Mother Goose* on the cover. The stories such as "Bluebeard," "Tom Thumb," and "Cinderella" have achieved such legendary fame that their author is often forgotten. Perrault died on May 18, 1703.

Lamentable Abominations

"Whit Monday took place today in 1812. Most of the ancient superstitious pastimes are now discontinued near the city; but it is to be lamented that one of these abominations is yet retained in Lancashire. In that country it is a common frolic for one person to hold a stick over the head of another, and a third slyly to strike it, so as to cause a smart blow to the unsuspecting object of their jocularity."
 Clavis Calendaria, 1812

Dishorning Discontinued

Today in 1889 judgment was given in the queen's bench division in London declaring the practice of dishorning —that is sawing off the horns of cattle close to the skull—to be cruel and illegal. Dishorning had been considered necessary as it added considerably to the value of the animals.

Mt. St. Helens
volcano
erupts

Acre Assaulted

Today in 1291 the Israeli city of Acre (captured by the Christians in 1191) fell after a siege of thirty-three days. The double wall was penetrated by the Moslem Mamelukes from Turkey who then stormed the city. In the ensuing assault 60,000 Christians were slaughtered or made slaves.

Aerial Achievement

On May 18, 1930 the *Graf Zeppelin* under the command of Captain Eckener and a crew of forty-two left Germany with twenty-two passengers. After a stop in Spain they landed safely in Pernambuco, Brazil sixty-two hours later. It then went on to Lakehurst, New Jersey and returned to Friedrichshafen, Germany in June —having covered 18,000 miles and spending 301 hours in the air.

Mouse Ear

Today's flower is botanically known as *Hieraciuna pilosella* which comes from the Greek word *hierax* (hawk), but the popular name refers to its resemblance to a mouse's ear.

19
MAY

Births

Johan Theophilus Fichte (German philosopher) 1762; Ho Chi Minh (North Vietnamese president) 1890.

Deaths

St Dunstan (English saint) 988; Anne Boleyn (English queen) 1536; James Boswell (English writer) 1795.

Proverb

They who bathe in May
Will soon be laid in clay.

Frogs Enter Contest

In 1928, fifty-one frogs today entered the "Frog Jumping Jubilee" staged at Angel's Camp, Calaveras County, California each year to commemorate Mark Twain's story "The Celebrated Jumping Frog of Calaveras County."

Monk's Hood Flower

The *Aconitum napellus* (monk's hood), today's flower, is dedicated to St Dunstan, the devil burner.

Lawyers Seek Pardons

The *Pardon of St Ives*, a religious celebration, takes place today in France. Because St Ives is the patron saint of lawyers, the occasion attracts people of that profession from several countries.

Settlers Get Land

On May 19, 1862 the *Homestead Bill* was passed by the U.S. Congress granting 160-acre lots of land to settlers who had resided on their lands for three years.

The Devil's Nose Burned

St Dunstan, as the story goes,
Once pulled the Devil by the nose
With red-hot tongs, which made him
  roar,
That he was heard three miles or
  more.

The doggeral refers to St Dunstan, an archbishop of Canterbury, who died today in 988. Dunstan was also a goldsmith, and one night while hard at work at his forge he was annoyed by the sudden appearance of the Devil who had come round to tempt the man so famous for his piety. The saint promptly applied his red hot tongs to Satan's nose and set him wailing.

Anne Boleyn's Head Removed

Anne Boleyn was beheaded today in 1536 at the Tower of London on the orders of her husband, King Henry VIII, who sentenced her to death for adultery and treason on the birth of a stillborn son. At midnight on the anniversary of her execution four headless horses and a headless coachman drive the ghost of Anne, severed head in her lap, up to Blickling Hall in a phantom coach.

Boswell's Ego

James Boswell died on May 19, 1795 at fifty-five years of age. His *Life of Dr Johnson*, with whom he lived in habits of the closest intimacy, was received by the world with the utmost avidity. With some learning and much conversational talent, Mr Boswell did have one failing— it was the grossest egotism both in his speech and writings: too often he himself was the "hero of each petty tale."

Births

Albrecht Dürer (painter) 1471; William Fargo (of Wells Fargo) 1818; James Stewart (actor) 1908.

Deaths

Christopher Columbus (explorer) 1506; Marquis de Lafayette (U.S. revolutionary hero) 1834.

To Have and to Hold

The day after he beheaded his second wife Anne Boleyn, Henry VIII, the king of England took the hand of Jane Seymour in marriage.

Last Will and Testament

On May 20, 1736, in compliance with an injunction in his will, the body of Samuel Baldwin, Esq., was buried without ceremony at sea off Lymington, England. His motive for his extraordinary mode of interment was to prevent his wife from dancing over his grave, which she had threatened to do if she survived him.

Broken Ribs and Injured Organs

Today in 1885, a professional swimmer named Odlum succeeded, in spite of great efforts by the authorities to prevent him, in jumping off Brooklyn Bridge into the water below, a drop of about 130 feet. For a second or two, he preserved a straight balance, but before touching the water his back bent, and falling on it, he broke every rib in his body, besides inflicting injuries to all other organs of his frame.

Justice is Served

1880:   In France today, two young Basques were tried by the Court of Assizes for burning to death a miserable old drunken gipsy fortune teller who had acquired the reputation of a witch, mainly it would seem, from the extraordinary antics she indulged in while in a state of delirium-tremens. They were sentenced to two years' imprisonment.

1886:   The first conviction for bribery ever obtained in the state of New York occurred today when Alderman Sharpe of New York was convicted of accepting a bribe for voting the Broadway Railway franchise. He was sentenced to nine years and ten months' imprisonment.

The Air is Conquered

1929:   Charles Lindberg flew *The Spirit of St Louis* from New York to Paris, winning $25,000 for completing the first solo non-stop flight across the Atlantic ocean.

1932:   Amelia Earhart Putnam became the first woman in aviation history to fly the Atlantic alone when she took off from Newfoundland for Ireland.

1939:   The first regular transatlantic passenger service began as Pan American Airways' *Yankee Clipper* took off from Port Washington, New York for Europe.

In Poverty and Neglect

There passed away today in 1506, in Valladolid in the province of Leon, Spain in conditions of the most extreme poverty and neglect, Mr Christopher Columbus, who some years earlier had known better circumstances.

21
MAY

Births

Plato (philosopher) 427 B.C.; Alexander Pope (poet) 1688; Harold Robbins (novelist) 1912.

An Earthshaking Event

"There was a great earthquake in England, at nine of the clock, fearing the hearts of many; but in Kent it was most vehement, where it sunk some churches and threw them down to the earth."

Stow's Chronicles, May 21, 1382

Astrology

Anyone Born between today and June 21 lives under the sign of Gemini (the Twins) and can look forward to the following mixed fortunes according to *Christian Astrology* of 1647:

Manners when well placed
Being well dignified, he represents a man of subtill and politick braine, intellect, and cogitation; an excellent disputant or Logician, arguing with learning and discretion, and using much eloquence in his speech, a searcher into all kinds of Mysteries and Learning, sharp and witty, learning almost any thing without a Teacher; ambitious of being exquisite in every Science, desirous naturally of travell and seeing foraign parts: a man of an unwearied fancie, curious in the search of any occult knowledge; able by his owne Genius to produce wonders; given to Divination and the more secret knowledge; if he turne Merchant no man exceeds him in any way of Trade or invention of new ways whereby to obtain wealth.

Manners, when ill placed
A troublesom wit, a kinde of Phrenetick man, his tongue and Pen against every man, wholly bent to foole his estate and time in prating and trying nine conclusions to no purpose; a great lyar, boaster, pratler, busybody, false, a tale-carrier, given to wicket Arts, as Necromancy, and such like ungodly knowledges; easie of beleefe, an asse or very ideot, constant in no place or opinion, cheating and theeving every where; a newes-monger, pretending all manner of knowledge, but guilty of no true or solid learning; a trifler; a meere frantick fellow; if he prove a Divine, then a meer verball fellow, frothy, of no judgement, easily perverted, constant in nothing but idle words and bragging.

Deaths

Henry VI, king of England (murdered) 1471; James Graham, the marquis of Montrose (hanged) 1650.

The Purple Star of Jerusalem

Today's plant, known botanically as *Tragopogon porrifolius,* has the distinction of closing its flower at high noon for which it is sometimes called Jack-Go-To-Bed-At-Noon.

Heavenly Adventures

Today in the heavens, the sun enters Gemini, the constellation of the twins, Castor and Pollux. Castor and Pollux were sons of Zeus by Leda, who he ravished in the form of a swan. The two loved each other very much, and when Castor was stabbed and killed by Idas in a dispute over cattle, Pollux wished he could die also. Zeus took pity on him and allowed him to be with his brother again, one day in Hades and the next on Olympus, forever.

A Beautiful Eruption

Today in 1858, an eruption of great grandeur commenced from Mount Vesuvius. It continued for a considerable time, and the magnificence of the spectacle brought crowds of visitors to Naples. No fewer than seven new craters opened in the side of the mountain when the lava issued in a broad stream, and fell in wonderful cascades down the side.

22
MAY

Births

Richard Wagner (composer) 1813; Arthur Conan Doyle (creator of Sherlock Holmes) 1859; Sir Laurence Olivier (actor) 1907.

Deaths

Alexander VII (pope) 1667; Ferdinand II Bomba (Sicilian king) 1859; Victor Hugo (author) 1885.

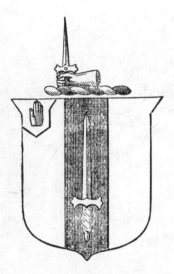

Bloody Red Irish Hands

On May 22, 1611 to raise money for the amelioration of Ulster, King James I of England created the first 200 baronets—the lowest of the hereditary ranks—at 1,000 pounds a piece. The first baronets were allowed to place in their coats of arms the open red hand, formerly borne but forfeited by the O'Neils, the famous *Lamh derg Eirin,* or Red Hand of Ulster. The red hand is commonly thought to signify some bloody deed or murder in the history of the line.

Uncivilised Scottish Celebrations

Today was once a great sports day in Scotland, many of the games seeming rather uncivilised. The Carter's Race involved tying a goose by its feet from a crossbeam, leaving it to the mercy of men on horseback who would try to prove their dexterity by being the first to pull off its head. Once this game finished, an equally amusing one took its place. A cat was placed in a soot-filled barrel which was hung from the beam. The men beat and lunged at the barrel with poles and the first to smash a hole, thus freeing the frenzied, soot-covered cat, won the day.

Ghostly Battles and Songs

Today is the anniversary of the Battle of St Albans, England in 1455. On this day it is said that any house on the site of the battle reverberates with the noises of clashing armour as the fight takes place. At St Albans Abbey ghosts of monks sing the ancient matins.

Cane-Bashing Politics

Senator Charles Sumner of Massachusetts had yesterday made derogatory remarks about Senator Butler of South Carolina, who was absent. Today in 1856, Preston S. Brooks, the nephew of Butler went into the Senate Chamber and said to Sumner that he had "published a libel on my State and uttered a slander on my relative, who is aged and absent, and I have come to punish you." He then beat Sumner with a cane until it was broken and his victim was lying bleeding on the floor. Brooks was arrested and fined $400. Senator Sumner was incapacitated for four years as a result of the assault.

A Biblical Discovery

The German Academy stated today in 1877 that the director of the Ducal Archives at Zerbst (Anhalt) had discovered the second part of Martin Luther's Old Testament translation in the reformer's own handwriting. It dated back as far as 1523 and on 216 quarto pages gave a translation of nearly the whole Bible text from Joshua to Esther.

A Sale of Musical Instruments

On May 22, 1786 John Jacob Astor took out an advertisement in U.S. newspapers saying he'd "just imported from London, an elegant assortment of Musical Instruments, such as piano fortes, spinnets, flutes, clarinets, hautboys, the best Roman violin strings"—all for sale—"on very low terms for cash."

Births

Elias Ashmole (antiquary) 1617;
Douglas Fairbanks (actor) 1883.

Deaths

Kit Carson (frontiersman) 1868;
Bonnie, of Bonnie and Clyde
(criminal) 1934.

Divorce Day

Thomas Cramner, archbishop of
Canterbury, pronounced sentence of
divorce at the court held in the priory
of Dunstable, between King Henry
VIII and Catherine of Aragon.

Bifocals Day

On May 23, 1785, Benjamin Franklin
wrote about his new invention, the
bifocal eye-glasses: "I have only to
move my eyes up and down as I want
to see distinctly far or near."

Hot Penny Scramble

Today is also known as Mayoring Day, in Rye, Sussex,
England. The mayor of Rye traditionally tosses hot
pennies to the children of Rye. The custom dates back to
the days when Rye had its own mint and the pennies were
still hot from the moulds.

Vulcan's Day

This day in ancient Rome was dedicated to Vulcan, the hot
and cold divinity, when the sacred trumpets were once
again purified.

Blowing up Glasgow

On May 23, 1914 several militant suffragettes were
apprehended as they attempted to blow up certain
Glasgow landmarks, mainly the water viaduct, to gain
attention for their cause.

Abie's Irish Rose

In 1922 a new comedy by Anne Nichols opened at the
Fulton Theatre in New York. The play *Abie's Irish Rose* has
been in continuous performance around America ever
since.

Lucky Day

This is the anniversary of the battle of Ramilles, in the
Netherlands, where the duke of Marlborough gained a
victory over the French in 1706. During that battle a
young ensign named Gardiner received a shot in the
mouth from a musket ball which, without touching his
tongue or any of his teeth, passed back through his neck
and came out next to his spine. Gardiner recovered and
went on to become a colonel.

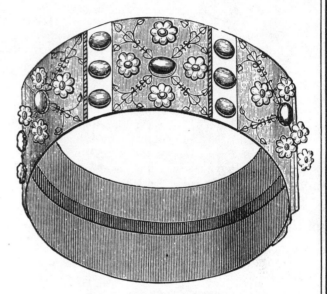

Iron Crown of Italy

The Iron Crown of Italy, with which Napoleon crowned
himself king of Italy on May 23, 1805, is actually a broad
circle of gold set with rubies, emeralds, and sapphires on
a ground of blue and gold enamel. But around the inside
of the crown, in a band three-eighths of an inch thick and
one-tenth of an inch deep runs a ring of iron that was
supposed to have been hammered out of one of the nails
used at the crucifixion and brought back from Jerusalem
by the Empress Helena, mother of Constantine.

24
MAY

Births

Carl Linnaeus (naturalist) 1707; Princess Alexandrina Victoria (Queen Victoria) 1819.

Deaths

Nicolas Copernicus (astronomer) 1543; Jonathan Wild (politician) 1725; Chief (the last U.S. cavalry horse) 1968.

A Stable for Motor Vehicles

The opening of America's first public garage took place on May 24, 1899 in Boston. The Back Bay Cycle and Motor Company advertised their garage as a "stable for the renting, sale, storage and repair of motor vehicles."

A Good Day for Love

The number 24 is endowed with favourable characteristics where love and the opposite sex are concerned. Activities in that area undertaken today are likely to be rewarding.

A Natural Man Born

Carl Linne (later latinised to Linnaeus) was born today in Sweden in the year 1707. As he was wont to say—he walked out of his cradle into a garden and devoted his life to observing and writing about nature. He also said "If a tree dies plant another in its place" and over his bedchamber were inscribed the words: "Live innocently; God is here."

A Tutor of Thieves Hanged

"Jonathan Wild, a most exquisite tutor of thieves, practised and taught for a long series of years; at length his philosophy failing, by a glut of vast success, he turned his hand to politics at a certain instalment, which attempt cost him a journey to the other world up Holborn-Hill, London. He was hanged there May 24, 1725."
   Howlett's *Victorian Golden Almanac,* 1852

An Imposter Crowned

Today in 1485, Albert Simnel, posing as King Edward VI of England, was crowned at Dublin. Later King Henry VI, who had had the real Edward put to death, pardoned Simnel and made him royal falconer.

"What Hath God Wrought?"

Samuel Morse tapped out this message today in 1844, on wires between Washington and Baltimore, thus inaugurating America's telegraph industry.

The Brooklyn Bridge

Today in 1883, the Brooklyn Bridge over the East River, connecting New York and Brooklyn was opened with great ceremony in the presence of many federal and state officials. It was the longest suspension bridge in the world having a total length of 5,989 feet.

Births

Marshall Tito (Yugoslav leader) 1892; Ralph Waldo Emerson (poet) 1803.

Deaths

St Urban (wine saint) 230; St Adhelm (bishop of Salisbury) 709.

Fast Fists Flatten Sonny

The fastest knockout in a heavyweight title bout to date took place in Lewiston, Maine, when Cassius Clay defeated Sonny Liston in one minute and fifty-six seconds today in 1965.

Proverb

May rain kills lice.

The Claims of Women

Lady Amberly lectured today in 1870 at Stroud in England on the claims of women: "that equal privileges with boys should be afforded them for attaining the higher education; that all professions should be open to them; that a widow should be recognised by law as the only natural guardian of her children; that the franchise be extended to women; that married women no longer be debarred from separate ownership of property; and that the same wages should be given for the same work."

Today's Flower

The common arens or *Geum urbanum* is the flower appointed by medieval monks to represent May 25.

Filth and Mire on the Saint

St Urban, the pope and martyr who died today in 230, was important to vintners and wine lovers. On St Urbans Day in old Germany, vintners would set up a table in the market, cover it with fine napery, green leaves, and sweet flowers and place upon it the image of the holy bishop. If the day was clear and fair, they crowned the image with wine, if it was rugged and rained, they cast filth, mire, and puddle water upon it, feeling that the day foretold a good or bad vintage.

A Saint's Coathanger

Sometime prior to his expiration on this day in the year 709, St Adhelm, while saying mass at the church of John the Lateran in Rome, took off his vestment and hung it on a sunbeam when he found no servant at hand to take it from him.

Beneath the Laird's Kilt

On 25 May, 1427, Alexander, laird of the Isles in Scotland, performed a curious penance of submission to King James of England, clad only in his shirt and drawers at Holyrood Church.

Flitting Day

In Scotland, May 25 used to be called Flitting Day, because it was the date on which most leases expired. Annually, as the day approached, tenants would have to decide if they would "sit or flit"—that is, sit for another year in the same house, or flit to a new. The Scots were great movers about, and Flitting Day usually witnessed a great bustle of transported households.

The Price of Philosophy

From a communication published in *Leipsic Buchandlung Eeitung* today in 1885 by Herr Bohlan of Weimar, it appeared that the philosopher Goethe, during his lifetime between 1795 and 1832, received from his publisher 233,969 florins.

Fire Insurance for Sale

On May 25, 1721, John Copson of Philadelphia inserted an advertisement in *The American Weekly Mercury* offering insurance on "vessels, goods and merchandise" in case of fire, thus marking him the first insurance agent in the U.S.

26
MAY

Births

Shute Barrington (bishop) 1734; Victoria Mary of Teck (Queen Mary) 1867; Al Jolson (singer) 1886.

Deaths

Samuel Pepys (diarist) 1703; Isaac Babbitt (inventor) 1862.

Today's Colours

The lucky colours for people born on this day, or for anyone who wishes to take advantage of numerological predictions are dark grey, black, dark blue, and purple. People should wear clothes of those hues. To dress in light colours is to look awkward.

A One-Hit Game

Harvey "The Kitten" Haddix pitched twelve perfect innings, but one hit in the thirteenth inning let Milwaukee defeat Pittsburgh, 2-0 (1959).

Extraordinary Cricket

An extraordinary score was run up by the Cambridge University Cricket Twelve in their match with the Gentlemen of England, the total reaching 593. Of this the Honourable Ivo Bligh contributed 90, Mr H. Whitfield, 116, and Mr R.S. Jones, 127. The Gentlemen made 232 in their single innings, and the match was drawn (1880).

Today's Jewellery

The lucky stones for the 26th are the amethyst, the dark-toned sapphire, the black pearl, and the black diamond. If possible they should be worn next to the skin.

Today's Herbs

The principle herbs accorded to this day are spinach, winter green, angelica, wild carrot, marshmallow, plantain, sage, pileworth, ragwort, shepherd's purse, Solomon's seal, vervain, elder flowers, gravel root, mandrake root, and celery.

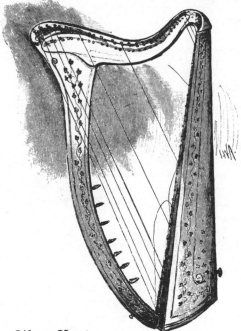

A Fenian Bomber Hanged

The last public execution in England took place outside Newgate Prison, London at 8 a.m. when Michael Barrett was hanged for his part in the Fenian bombing on December 13, 1867 when twelve people were killed outside the Clerkenwell House of Detention, London (1868).

An Illustrious Resting Place

The French government, having decided to secularise the church of St Genevieve, otherwise known as the Panthéon, signed a decree constituting it the burying place of illustrious citizens, subject in each case to parliamentary consent to interrment therein (1885).

America Gets a House

The Betsy Ross Memorial Association gave The American Flag House, Betsy Ross' home, to the City of Philadelphia (1941).

A Funeral Ship Found

The funeral ship of the Egyptian Pharaoh Cheops was discovered in a limestone chamber near the Great Pyramid of Giza in Egypt (1954).

The Silver Harp

An *Eisteddfod* of the Welsh bards and minstrels was held at Cayroes, in Flintshire, by Queen Elizabeth's Commission. The great prize of the silver harp was won by Simon ap Williams ap Sion (1568).

27
MAY

Births

Amelia Bloomer (feminist) 1818; Julia Ward Howe (activist) 1819; Henry Kissinger (statesman) 1923.

Deaths

St Bede (confessor) 735; John Calvin (theologian) 1564; Pandit Jawaharlal Nehru (1st prime minister of India) 1967.

A Small Marriage

General Mite, twenty-two inches high and Miss Millie Edwards, nineteen and one-half inches high, known as the American midgets, were married at the St James' Hall, Manchester, England, today in 1884.

Buttercups

Today's flowers, buttercups (*Ranunculis acris*), have a watery, acrid, and semi-poisonous juice but a pleasant visage.

Amen, Venerable Bede

St Bede, also known as the Venerable Bede, Father of the Church, died today in 735. He is the first English author who used the modern mode of date, *Anno Domini*. When blind he preached to a heap of stones, thinking himself in a church, and the stones were so much affected by his eloquence and piety, that they answered "Amen, venerable Bede, Amen."

John Calvin

John Calvin, the celebrated church reformer, died on 27 May, 1564, at Geneva in Switzerland. Although a man of many talents and extensive learning, his extreme rigour and defence of the burning of heretics brought him many enemies. His labours were unceasing and excessive. He preached every day, gave three lessons in divinity each week, and allowed himself one frugal meal per day. Emaciated to a skeleton on his deathbed he took God to witness that he had preached the Gospel purely and exhorted all to walk worthy of the divine goodness.

Amelia Jenks Bloomer

Mrs Bloomer, born today in 1818, was an American advocate of "rational dress" for women. The costume she introduced—loose trousers gathered tightly about the ankles and worn beneath skirts— became very popular and were called "bloomers."

Julia Ward Howe

Julia Ward Howe, an American leader in anti-slavery and women's suffrage movements and author of the lyrics of the "Battle Hymn of the Republic," was born today in 1819.

The Hares and Rabbits Bill

In the British House of Commons today in 1880, the home secretary introduced a bill for the better protection of occupiers of land against injury from ground-game, a measure which went under the name of the Hares and Rabbits Bill.

28
MAY

Births

Solomon (Israeli king) 970 B.C.; Joseph Guillotin (inventor) 1783.

Deaths

Noah Webster (dictionary writer) 1843; duke of Windsor (formerly King Edward VIII) 1972.

A Deer Hunter's Dues

On the 28th of May, 1320, Henry Burgwash became bishop of Lincoln, England, and took up residence in a manorial house at Fingest. Henry was fond of both venison and the hunt. The poor people nearby learned to hate the prelate on account of seeing their beef and mutton turned into venison when he ran out of deer. After Burgwash died in 1340, his ghost appeared one night dressed as a forester, all in green, with a bow and quiver, and a bugle hanging at its side, and reported that on account of the injustice done during his life, he was now condemned to be a game warden for ever.

Whale Hunter's Boon

"Giant Blasting Powder" was patented today in 1868, and a company incorporated under the name of the Giant Powder Company in San Francisco. The whalers who used the Giant Powder instead of common powder in their bomb lances obtained 300 to 400 barrels of whale oil where they formerly got 100.

Joan of Arc Speaks, 1431

"If I said that God did not send me, I should condemn myself, truly God did send me . . . all this I have done, I did for fear of the fire and my retraction was against the truth . . . I prefer to do penance once, by dying rather than suffer long punishment in prison."
    Joan of Arc at her trial, May 28, 1431

Edmund Burke Speaks, 1794

Edmund Burke, British political philosopher, said in a speech today: "There's but one law for all, namely that law which governs all law, the law of our Creator, the law of humanity, justice, equity—the law of nature and of nations."

Captain Boyton Swims, 1875

Captain Boyton started from the Cape Grisnez in his life-saving dress at 3 a.m. to cross the English Channel today in 1875. He walked ashore at Faro Bay, Kent, little the worse at 2 a.m. the following morning, having on this occasion successfully battled with the waves for twenty-three hours, supported only by three meals of strong green tea and beef sandwiches.

Severe Storms Sink Ships, 1860

So calamitous were the storms of the early summer that on this day alone 143 wrecks took place off the English coast, thirty-six of the ships being completely beaten to pieces.

Hair and Breeches Removed

"An interlude is performed at the Black Bear Inn, Cambridge at which one Dominus Pepper was seen with an improper habit, having deformed long locks of unseemly sight, and indecent great breeches of Persian origin, ridiculously large. The said Pepper was commanded to appear presently and have his hair and new fangled breeches removed."
    The Anniversary Calendar, Natal Book, and Universal Mirror, 1832

29 MAY

Births

Charles II (English king) 1630; Patrick Henry (U.S. hero: "Give me liberty or give me death") 1736; John Fitzgerald Kennedy (35th U.S. president) 1917.

Deaths

Josephine (wife of Napoleon) 1814; William Gilbert (of Gilbert and Sullivan) 1911; John Barrymore (actor) 1942.

Royal Oak Day

After the defeat of his army by Cromwell at Worcester in 1651, Charles took refuge at Boscobel House, in a forest in Shropshire. One night while Charles was at Boscobel House, to escape the searches of Cromwell's soldiers, the deposed monarch hid himself up a thick old oak where he remained for twenty-four hours. Thereafter the tree was called the Royal Oak, and on Restoration Day it was a long-time custom for royalists to wear oak leaves in their hats.

> The twenty-ninth day of May
> Is Royal Oak day;
> If you cannot give us a holiday,
> We'll all run away.
> Old school rhyme

Restoration Day

In Britain, May 29 is celebrated as Restoration Day, being the anniversary of the day on which Charles II re-entered London and restored the monarchy after the fall of Cromwell's government. That day in 1660 was also Charles' thirtieth birthday.

A Bugger Done, 1953

Edmond P. Hillary, a thirty-four year old New Zealand bee-keeper, and Tensing Norkay, forty-two, a tribesman from Nepal, today in 1953 became the first to reach the top of Mount Everest, the world's highest mountain, at more than 29,000 feet above sea level. On arrival at the summit Mr Norkay's first words were "We've done the bugger!"

The Rites of Spring

Igor Stravinsky's ballet with choreography by Nijinsky premiered today in Paris in 1913 to mixed reviews. The audience, divided into opponents and defenders of the production, shouted, whistled, booed, and stomped. An outraged gentleman smashed the top hat of an over-enthusiastic neighbour with his cane. A woman slapped the man next to her because he was hissing, and her escort rose to exchange cards for a duel. Stravinsky was so outraged by the audience's reception of his music that he left in the middle of the performance.

A Half-Clad Lunatic, 1840

Today in 1840, great confusion and many narrow escapes took place in Kensington Gardens, London caused by the sudden appearance of a half-clad lunatic, on horseback, while the crowd of nobility in their carriages were listening to the band of the First Life Guards.

Theatrical Flop, 1880

At the Vaudeville Theatre, London, today in 1880, a new comedy called *Jacks & Jills* was produced with unfortunate results. The audience, which was quiet during the first act, lost their interest in the second, and their tempers in the third. It was to be regretted that Mr James Albery, the author, on presenting himself after the curtain should have irritated the public by attributing the problem to an organised opposition and was cat-called off the stage.

A Curtain Raised, 1453

Constantinople was taken on May 29, 1453 by Mahomet II, emperor of the Turks, after an existence of ten centuries from its commencement under Constantine the Great. Thus ended the Greek Empire. The capture of this city was one of the greatest events in the history of modern Europe—establishing the Turks in Europe, bringing about the revival of literature after a long period of darkness, and opening to Europe the intellectual richness of the Greeks.

30
MAY

Births

Peter the Great (Russian czar) 1672.

Deaths

Arthur (English king) 542; Joan of Arc
(French martyr) 1431?; Voltaire
(French writer) 1778.

The Mystery of Joan of Arc

Many historians believe that today in
1431, Joan of Arc charged with
sorcery and heresy, was burned at the
stake in Rouen. But certain others
maintain that documentary evidence
to be found in the City of Mentz
proves that she visited there in 1436.
Records there also show the marriage
contract between the Chevalier de
Armoise and Jeanne d'Arc of Orleans
in the same year.

Brooklyn Bridge Bothers

Today in 1883 there was a panic
amongst a crowd on the new
Brooklyn Bridge at New York in
consequence of a cry being raised
that the structure was giving way. In
the rush that followed, several
persons were killed and a large
number injured.

The Illegitimate Origins of Arthur

Later in his life King Arthur and his Knights of the Round
Table achieved considerable fame, but lesser known is the
story of his birth. According to legend, at the time when
the Saxons were ravaging Briton but had not yet made
themselves masters of it, the Britons were ruled by a wise
and valiant king named Uther Pendragon. Among the
most distinguished of Uther's nobles was Gorlois, Duke of
Cornwall, whose wife Igerna was a woman of incredible
beauty. The king fell in love with Igerna the very first time
he saw her, so that Gorlois took her away from the court
and home to Cornwall without asking for leave. Angered,
Uther led an army into Cornwall to punish his vassal.
Gorlois had shut his wife up in the impenetrable castle of
Tintagel, but with the help of his magician, Merlin, Uther
assumed the form of Gorlois, entered Tintagel and slept
with the beautiful Igerna. The consequence was the birth
of a child who was destined to be founder of the Round
Table and the Hercules of the Britons. That child was the
far-famed King Arthur, who died on May 30, 542, after
many conquests, and from wounds received in battle
against his nephew, Modred, who had tried to usurp his
empire. He was buried at the Isle of Avalon
(Glastonbury).

The Achievements of Voltaire

On May 30, 1778, in Paris, at the age of eighty-four there
died François Marie Arouet, who called himself Voltaire.
He had made a revolution, served two terms in the
Bastille, became a friend of Frederick the Great, wrote
Candide, fought all his life against what he believed to be
tyranny, and was a man of letters who stands in the first
rank among the famous for his brilliancy of imagination,
his versatility of talents, and the extent of his knowledge.

The Frenchman first in literary fame
(Mention him if you please—Voltaire?—the same)
With spirit, genius, eloquence supplied
Liv'd long, wrote much, laugh'd heartily and died
The Scripture was his jest-book whence he drew
Bon-mots to gall the Christian and the Jew.
  William Cowper (1731-1800)

Andrew Jackson's Duels

On May 30, 1806, Andrew Jackson shot and killed Charles
Dickinson in a duel. It was one of several in which the
future president of the United States was said to have
been involved.

31
MAY

Births

Ludwig von Tiek (poet) 1773; Walt Whitman (poet) 1819; Prince Rainier (of Monaco) 1923; Joe Namath (football player) 1943.

Lady Godiva's Ride

The Godiva Procession, celebrating Lady Godiva's ride, was first held on May 31, 1678. Lady Godiva, who died in 1067, was the benefactor of several monastries, especially that of Coventry, which her husband founded at her instigation. He agreed to remit the heavy taxation on the people of Coventry if she would ride naked through the town on a white horse. The story of Peeping Tom, the only man who peeked through the closed shutters, did not enter the legend until the mid-18th century.

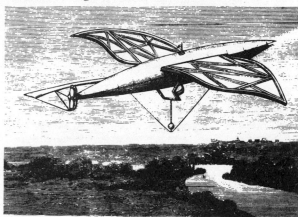

A Steerable Balloon

A new steerable balloon, the invention of Herr Baumgarten and Dr Waelfert, was tried at Charlottenburg near Berlin. It was of huge size, having a capacity of about 473 cubic yards and ellipsoid in form. It differed from all other aerostats in that although inflated with hydrogen, it had no ascensional force (1882).

An Arctic Misadventure

Though they became the first American expedition to reach the Arctic circle today in 1853, Elisha Kane and his crew in their boat *Advance* got stuck in the ice, requiring them to remain there twenty-one months. When disease broke out, the crew trekked 1,000 miles to the nearest Eskimo village for help.

Deaths

Franz Joseph Haydn (composer) 1809; Adolph Eichmann (Nazi) 1962.

Robbery on the Orient Express

The Orient Express, conveying passengers from Constantinople to Paris, was thrown off the line between Constantinople and Adrianople, several rails being taken up by a band of brigands. The men immediately boarded the train and proceeded to strip the passengers of their valuables and to ransack their baggage. They made off—carrying with them four German tourists (whom they supposed to be the wealthiest) to the mountains. The prisoners were liberated for a large ransom. The brigands were thought to be in league with the railway officials (1891).

Washington Pow-Wow

The Indian chiefs Red Cloud and Spotted Tail arrived at Washington and were entertained by President Grant, preparatory to a "palaver" regarding the grievances said to have been suffered by the Sioux tribe at the hands of their enemies, the Cheyennes (1870).

A Lecture on Bloomers

Various American female lecturers delivered addresses in London on a new costume known as the "Bloomer," with a view to recommending its adoption in England (1851).

JUNE

After her came jolly June, arrayed
All in green leaves, as he a player were;
Yet in his time he wrought as well as played,
That by his plough-irons mote right well appear.
Upon a crab he rode, that him did bear,
With crooked crawling steps, an uncouth pace,
And backward rode, as bargemen wont to fare,
Bending their force contrary to their face;
Like that ungracious crew which feigns demurest grace.
  Edmund Spenser

JUNE

History

In the old Latin or Alban calendar June had twenty-six
days. Under Romulus it had thirty, and then twenty-nine in
the system of Numa. Finally, in the Julian calendar, June
settled down to the thirty days it still retains. The name of
the month is said to come from the Latin word *Junonius,*
which means "sacred to the goddess Juno! the wife and
sister of Jupiter, the king of the gods on Olympus." Ovid,
in his *Fasti,* gives us this interpretation. Others think the
name may have come from the Latin *Junioribus,* the word
for the junior branch of the original Roman legislature.
The Saxons called this month *Weyd Monath;* "weyd"
meant meadow, and June was the month that the animals
took to the meadows.

Weddings

June is considered to be the month most propitious for
weddings suggesting that it is indeed named after Juno,
for as well as being the queen of the gods in the Roman
pantheon, she was the protector of marriages and of
married women. Thus the Romans considered June the
best month of the year in which to get married, especially
if it could be arranged so that the wedding day was the
day of the full moon, or the conjunction of the sun and
the moon.

This is the best month to enter marriage state,
To try the love each bears unto his mate;
For if that they do now lay close together,
No doubt they'll do the same in colder weather.
  Poor Robin's Almanac, 1683

Birthstones

For June the agate or sometimes the pearl were the
accepted birthstones. The latter stood for purity, and also
for tears. The agate gave health and long life, healed
fevers, drew out the venom of insect and reptile bites if
laid against the bitten place, and strengthened the sight.

1

JUNE

Births

Brigham Young (Mormon leader) 1801; John Masefield (poet) 1878; Marilyn Monroe (actress) 1925.

Quakers Quashed

On June 1, 1660 Mary Dyer, an American Quaker in New England, was executed because she had returned from banishment. Quakers were described as "A motley tribe—half fanatic, half insane, and without definite purposes" and the penalty for attending a Quaker meeting was set at 10 shillings and for speaking at a Quaker meeting, £10.

Deaths

St Wistan (martyr) 849; Christopher Marlowe (dramatist) 1593; James Buchanan (15th U.S. president) 1868.

United States Inundated

Stock taking today in 1889 after heavy rainstorms and flood in Pennsylvania, New Jersey, and Maryland, and districts further to the south in the U.S. showed the loss of about 6,000 lives and the destruction of an immense amount of property.

Hair Today, Gone Tomorrow

St Wistan was a Saxon prince who objected to his mother's remarriage to his godfather, Britfardus. For his concern and interference he was murdered in 849 in a lonely wood by having his head slit open by his godfather. Hair grew from the ground where the blood had spilled and a shaft of light appeared over the grave. Britfardus went mad. Each year on the date of the murder, June 1, 849, there is an hour when hair springs up again for twenty-four hours.

Excitement in California

"The whole of this part of California is in the highest state of excitement relative to the Placera or gold regions recently discovered on the branches of the Sacramento River. Three-fourths of the houses in San Francisco are vacated. Even lawyers have closed their books and taken passage with spade and wooden dish to make fortunes by washing out gold from the sands of the Sacramento."
A letter from San Francisco, 1848

Don't Give up the Ship

Today in 1813 Captain James Lawrence, commander of the U.S.S. *Chesapeake,* was ordered to proceed northward to intercept British supply ships coming to Canada. He engaged the British frigate *Shannon,* which had been blockading Boston. As he was carried from the deck mortally wounded, he shouted the famous words, "Don't give up the ship!"

A Peek at Hell

St Patrick, when he was trying to convert the Irish by telling them of all the torments of hell, miraculously caused the earth to open so that the unbelievers could see the demons in the flaming entrance to purgatory. He left the cave opened, and built a gate about it so that all that desired to see purgatory could make a pilgrimage to do so. The Cave of St Patrick's Purgatory is located on a small island in Lough Derg amid the hiss of Donegal. June 1st is the annual date of the pilgrimage to the cave.

Our Lady of the Liver and Hinges

In the Roman calendar the first of June was dedicated to the goddess Carna, or Cardinea, who presided over the vital parts of man, especially the liver and heart. She was also in charge of hinges; the Romans ate a cake made of beans, barley, and bacon in her honour.

Carna, the goddess of the hinge demands
The first of June; upon her power depends
To open what is shut, what's shut unbar . . .
Ovid

2
JUNE

Births

Marquis de Sade (writer) 1740; Thomas Hardy (novelist) 1840; Hedda Hopper (columnist) 1890.

Deaths

St Pothinus (martyr) 177; Madelaine de Scuderi (writer) 1701; Lou Gehrig (baseball player) 1941.

Marriages

King Henry V of England to Catherine of France (1420); Grover Cleveland to Frances Folsom (1886; the first U.S. president to be married while in office).

Saintly Sufferings

The holy bishop of Lyon, France, Pothinus was about ninety years old when he was dragged before the tribunal of the heathens. Having refused to adore their idols, he was cruelly treated and thrown into prison scarcely alive, where he expired after two days' confinement, today in 177.

Pimpernel Predictions

Today's flower is the pimpernel (*Anagallis arvensis*). When it was seen on this morning with its little red flowers widely extended there was a distinct danger of fires nearby, but if the petals were closed rain was on the way.

Eclectic Events

1635: The first Italian immigrant arrived in New York City.
1851: Maine became the first state to enforce prohibition.
1835: P.T. Barnum and his circus began their first tour of the U.S.
1874: The cornerstone for the American Museum of Natural History was laid.
1896: Britain gave Marconi a patent for his wireless invention.
1910: A plane flew from Dover to Calais and return non-stop.
1930: Mrs M. Niezel gave birth on a vessel passing through the Panama Canal.
1946: Women voted for the first time in Italy.
1953: Queen Elizabeth II of England was crowned.

Romance Rules

Madelaine de Scuderi was the sister to a famous playwright of seventeenth-century Paris. Her brother George couldn't afford to maintain his sister in idleness, so he would lock Madelaine in a room every day until she had completed a set amount of writing, then publish her romances under his own name. It turned out that the romances were much more popular than his plays, and the word soon got out that they had been composed by his sister. She became immensely wealthy and popular from the sale of her works, and was the centre of literary life in the city. When she died on June 2, 1701 at the age of 94, she had written over forty volumes.

Catholicism Condemned

On June 2, 1780 Lord George Gordon headed a mob of 40,000 people carrying a petition to the British Parliament objecting to the repeal of laws punishing Roman Catholics. Killed were 210 rioters; 248 were wounded; and Lord Gordon was charged with high treason.

3
JUNE

Births

George V (English king) 1865; Tony Curtis (American actor) 1925.

Deaths

Jethro Tull (English inventor) 1740; Georges Bizet (French composer) 1875; Johann Strauss (Austrian composer) 1899; John XXIII (Italian pope) 1963.

Proverb

A dripping June
Set all in Tune

A Hoer is Buried

Jethro Tull, was an inveterate inventor and an indefatigable advocate of hoeing. His greatest innovation was the discovery of drill sowing, which reduced by a third the amount of seed needed to plant a field. He died and was buried on June 3, 1740.

A Day for Jack Jovette

Jack Jovette Day is celebrated in Virginia in memory of this day in 1781 when Jack Jovette rode from the Cuckoo Tavern to Charlottesville to warn Thomas Jefferson of the approach of the British, thus permitting Jefferson to escape.

A New Game in Britain

On June 3, 1876 the game of lacrosse was introduced into Britain by twelve members of the Montreal Club who gave an exhibition of the national game of Canada at Hurlingham.

A Water Tank Bursts

Today in London in 1876 the bursting of a storage tank on the top of St George's Hospital caused serious injury to several patients whose beds were swept away by the flood of 5,000 gallons of water.

A Day for Broken Dolls

A Buddhist ceremony in Japan, where little girls and their mothers bring all broken dolls to be enshrined by a priest, takes place each June 3.

An Empress is Buried

Empress Josephine once had her horoscope read by an old woman named Euphemie. "Your first husband will be born in Martinique, but will pass his life in Europe, with girded sword. He will perish in a tragical manner. Your second husband will fill the world with glory and fame. You will then become an eminent lady, more than a queen. Then after having astonished the world you will die unhappy." All came to pass as foretold with Josephine's first husband, the Comte de Beauharnois. After he was guillotined in 1793, she married Napoleon Bonaparte, then a young general, who filled the world with his fame and made her empress. She died unhappy, some years after their divorce, on May 29, 1814, and was buried with much dignity on June 3.

A Bloody Offering

The Romans dedicated this day to Bellona, daughter of Phorcys and Ceto, and goddess of war who appeared in battled armed with a whip to animate the combatants. The priests of Bellona at Cappadocea used to consecrate themselves to the goddess by cutting great incisions in their thighs and then catching the flowing blood in their cupped hands as an offering.

An Infidel is Divided

The capture of Antioch occurred today in 1097 by the first crusaders. The sword of Godfrey divided a Turk, said an eye witness, from the shoulder to the haunch; and one-half of the infidel fell to the ground, while the other was carried by his horse to the city gates.

4
JUNE

Births

George III (English king) 1738; Rosalind Russell (actress) 1911; Robert Merril (opera singer) 1919.

Deaths

Conrad II (Roman emperor) 1039; William II (last German emperor) 1941; Sonny Tufts (film star) 1976.

Crownings

1133: Lothar II became head of the Holy Roman Empire.
1260: Kublai was made khan of the Mongols.
1365: Charles IV was crowned king of Burgundy.
1508: Louis II became king of Hungary.
1789: Louis XVII became heir to the French crown.
1831: Leopold I was elected king of Belgium.

A Grisly Discovery

Today in 1880 a singular discovery was made, at no. 139 Harley Street in London, the residence of Mr Jacob Q. Henriquez, of the body of a woman unknown. Mr Spendlove, the butler for the last eighteen months, had noticed an uncanny smell about for a time. He decided to move a tub under the cistern and discovered human remains. The decomposed and mutilated body had been stuffed into the tub approximately two years previously and covered with chloride of lime. Remarkable evidence came up concerning the behaviour of Mr Henriquez's menservants of two years earlier, but a verdict of murder by a person unknown was recorded.

An Old King's Birthday Party

Throughout his reign George III's birthday was a day of celebration all over Britain. On June 4, 1819, when George was 81, his birthday was remarkably celebrated by the inhabitants of the town of Bexhill, on the coast of Sussex, who were noted at the time for their longevity. Twenty-five old men whose ages totalled 2025 years, and averaged 81 years, sat down to dinner, and were served by fifteen other men whose ages averaged seventy-one years. The bells were rung by six men who averaged sixty-one years. At the time Bexhill had a population of just over 800.

A Cheese Discovery

A shepherd returned to a cave today in 1070 near Roquefort in France where he had left an uneaten lunch of barley, bread, and goat's milk cheese several weeks earlier. The cheese and bread were heavy with black mould but he ate them regardless. The bread was foul but the cheese surprisingly delicious. He rushed some of it to a nearby monastery where the monks sampled it. Soon after they began curing cheese in the same cave and called it Roquefort cheese.

A Blow for Women's Rights

On June 4, 1913 Emily Wilding Davison, a young English suffragette ran onto the Epsom Downs track directly in the path of the king's prize horse and tried to seize the reins. The horse trampled her, and she died four days later. The daughter of suffragette leader Emmeline Pankhurst later wrote of this deed: "Probably in no other way and at no other time and place could she so effectively have brought the concentrated attention of millions to bear upon the cause."

Women's Rights Approved

On June 4, 1919, the Women's Suffrage Bill was passed by the U.S. Senate.

An Unsuccessful Exhibition

Today in 1888 an Irish exhibition was opened in London. Its closure shortly thereafter was probably due to the notable lack of Irish exhibits.

5
JUNE

Births

Socrates (philosopher) 468 B.C.; Igor Stravinsky (composer) 1882; William Boyd (Hopalong Cassidy) 1898.

Arsenic, 1851

On this day in 1851 the British Parliament passed an act labelling arsenic as having deadly properties and making its use by lay persons illegal. Prior to then, in times of plagues, it had been employed in construction of amulets worn to ward off pestilence.

Justice, 1880

This morning in 1880 a man named John Key, gave himself up to a policeman in Cambridge Road, Bethnel Green, confessing to having murdered his wife with a flat iron. It appeared that Key had been a hard-working, sober, and industrious man, while the deceased woman was a shamefully drunken and debauched creature who had made his life a misery. Recommendation to mercy was returned with a verdict of guilty and a death sentence commuted to penal servitude for life.

Architecture, 1852

On June 5, 1852, members of the Delta Kappa Epsilon fraternity donated $50 and their labour to build the first fraternity house in America—a basic log hut forty feet long by twenty feet wide on land donated by Kenyon College, Ohio.

Politics, 1855

Today in 1855, the *Know Nothing Party,* also known as the American Party held its first national convention in Philadelphia. The Know Nothings were really members of a secret organisation who divided themselves into three degrees with various qualifications. They had a feeble showing in the 1856 election.

Machines, 1874

The new air machine for the better ventilation of the British House of Commons came into operation for the first time today in 1874. This apparatus allowed a constant supply of air, cooled to any required degree, supplied at the rate of from 60,000 to 90,000 "gallons" per minute.

Deaths

Abul Abbas (caliph of Bagdad) 754; Louis x (French king) 1316; Carl Maria von Weber (composer) 1826.

Marriage, 1607

On June 5, 1607, Dr John Hall, a celebrated physician was wed to Susannah Shakespeare, daughter of Mr and Mrs William Shakespeare. The bride was described as being beautiful with a character of universal charity and a strong religious feeling.

Bananas, 1876

Today in 1876 refreshment vendors at the Philadelphia Centennial Exhibition sold a new delicacy—individually wrapped bananas at 10 cents each.

Proverb

A noise like of a hidden brook.
In the leafy month of *June,*
That to the sleeping woods all night
Singeth a quiet tune.
    Samuel Taylor Coleridge (1772-1834)

Dragons, 221 B.C.

Today in China was traditionally set aside at *Dragon Boat Festival Day* to commemorate the attempt by boatmen to rescue the great poet Chu Yuan in the year 222 B.C.

6
JUNE

Births

Diego Velasquez (Spanish painter) 1599; Alexander Pushkin (Russian poet) 1799.

Deaths

Ludovico Ariosto (Italian poet) 1533; Jeremy Bentham (English philosopher) 1832; Carl Jung (Swiss psychologist) 1961; Robert F. Kennedy (U.S. senator) 1968.

Finnish Festival

A festival honouring Finland's most famous composer, Johan Julius (Jean) Sibelius is held on this day in Helsinki each year.

Number 6 People

Those born today have magnetic personalities and are loved and often worshipped by others. They are very determined types—sometimes to the point of obstinacy   except when they themselves become deeply attached and become devoted slaves to those they love.

Henry Wadsworth Longfellow, LLD

Today in 1868 the American poet Longfellow arrived in England to receive an honorary Bachelor of Law degree at Cambridge University.

Action in Factories

On June 6, 1844 the Factory Act of England established an Office of Factory Inspectors who toured factories making rulings as to the health and hours of work of those who laboured therein.

Dapple, Dickey, and Reverend Doctor John

Jeremy Bentham was an English philosopher who wrote that the end of life is happiness and that the highest morality is the pursuit of the greatest happiness by the greatest number. He was also an eccentric recluse who refused to see visitors. Until he died on June 4, 1832, Bentham lived along with his walking stick, named Dapple, his teapot, named Dickey, and his cat, named the Reverend Doctor John Langborne.

Ike Fires up His Troops

Prior to the Allied invasion of Europe Dwight D. Eisenhower gave a speech to his troops on D-Day June 6, 1944: "The eyes of the world are upon you. The hopes and prayers of liberty-loving people everywhere march with you."

Terror in the Streets

On June 6, 1712 four Mohocks were tried at the Old Bailey Court in London for riot, assault, and beating watchmen. (The Mohocks were a group of aristocratic ruffians who infested London streets at that time, getting their pleasure at the expense of innocent pedestrians.) These four had slit two person's noses, cut a woman in the arm with a penknife so as to disable her for life, rolled a woman in a tub down a hill, misused other women in a barbarous manner by setting them on their heads, and overturned several coaches and chairs with people in them by means of short, lead-filled clubs. The judge fined the culprits the sum of three shillings and four pence each.

Drive-in Movies

Today in 1933 the world's first drive-in movie theatre opened in Camden, New Jersey with accommodation for 500 cars and a screen forty by fifty feet.

7
JUNE

Births
Beau Brummel (man of fashion) 1778; Paul Gaugin (artist) 1848.

Deaths
Mohammed (the prophet) 632; E.M. Forster (novelist) 1970.

Battle of the Bees
The *Carlisle Patriot* reported that on June 7, 1827, at the village of Cargo, in Cumberland, in the North of England, there took place a battle between two huge swarms of bees for control of a hive. One swarm had already occupied the hive when the other descended on them from above. Both took to the air again and battled to the death. The air all about was filled with a large humming and the ground beneath the battle was littered with the bodies of the slain insects.

The Dunmow Flitch
Back in the middle ages it was decided, probably as a joke, by the monks of a priory in Dunmow, England, to award a flitch—or side—of bacon to any married couple that could swear under oath that they had lived a whole year together without fighting. Just as the jolly monks foresaw, claims on the award were few and far between, but in every century there were a few. On June 7, 1701 after testifying and swearing the oath before a court of five spinsters, William and Jane Parsely of Easton, County Essex, were awarded the pork for their connubial bliss and were borne aloft in a jubilant procession through the town.

A Royal Wrestling Match
On June 7 in 1520 King Henry VIII of England and King Francis I of France met at a wrestling tournament on the Field of the Cloth of God in France. After having a drink together, Henry said "My brother I must wrestle with you" and endeavoured once or twice to trip up the French king's heels; but the French king, who was a dextrous wrestler, twisted him round and threw him on the earth with a prodigious violence.

The Fleur de Lis
Today's flower is the spurious fleur de lis (*Iris spuria*), which in heraldry represents the royal arms of France. One theory about its origins to this place of prominence suggests that the original coat of arms of the Franks was three toads or frogs, which eventually became a source of scorn. Gradually they were embellished and changed to resemble the flower.

The Human Salamander
On June 7, 1826, Monsieur Chabert, of Paris who billed himself as the Human Salamander gave a remarkable demonstration of his resistance to poison and fire. First he made a hearty meal of phosphorus, washed down with solutions of arsenic and oxalic acid. For dessert he took a few spoonsful of boiling oil, and washed his hands afterward in a bowl of molten lead. Finally, to relax after dinner, Chabert climbed into a hot oven with a rump steak and a leg of lamb. He remained there until the steak was done, climbed out and gave it to the audience to eat, then got back in again until the leg of lamb was quite tender. The audience dined again with the unscathed Human Salamander looking on.

Birth

Joseph Balsamo, alias Count Alessandro di Cagliostro (quack) 1743.

Death

Thomas Paine (political writer, author of *Common Sense* and *The Rights of Man*) 1809.

The Perfect Quack Face

Something about Cagliostro so infuriated Thomas Carlyle that he continued to verbally blast him for many years: "Fittest of visages, worthy to be worn by the quack of quacks! A most portentous face of scoundrelism: a fat, snub, abominable face; dew-lapped, flat-nosed, greasy, full of greediness, sensuality, ox-like obstinacy; a forehead impudent, refusing to be ashamed, and then two eyes turned up seraphically languishing, as if in divine contemplation and adoration; a touch of quizz too; on the whole perhaps the most perfect quack-face produced by the eighteenth century."

An Odorous Activist

Thomas Paine, the English political writer and activist, died on this day in 1809 in Baltimore, Maryland. He was a rigorous advocate of the independence of the American colonies and associated himself with the French revolutionists. He was also extremely absent-minded and often forgot to bathe as Mr Elkanah Watson, a New Englander who travelled with him in France describes: "I often officiated as his interpreter, although humbled and mortified at his filthy appearance, and awkward and unseemly dress . . . at L'Orient he was absolutely offensive and perfumed the whole apartment. He was soon rid of his respectable visitors, who left the room with marks of astonishment and disgust."

Moneywort

Today's flower is the moneywort (*Lysimachia nummularia*), alias the herb twopence, alias creeping Jenny.

The King of Liars

"The quack of quacks, the most perfect scoundrel that in these latter ages has marked the world's history, we have found in the Count Alessandro di Cagliostro . . . unfortunate child of nature; by profession healer of diseases, abolisher of wrinkles, friend of the poor and impotent, grand master of the Egyptian Mason lodge of high-science, spirit summoner, gold-cook, grand cophta, prophet, priest, and thaumaturgic moralist and swindler; really a liar of the first magnitude, thoroughpaced in all provinces of lying, what one may call the king of liars." Thus wrote Thomas Carlyle, of the great imposter Cagliostro, who made himself fabulously wealthy in his lifetime, and travelled and worked in noble circles throughout Europe. He was born Joseph Balsamo, son of a small shopkeeper of Palermo, Sicily on June 8, 1743.

A Cream Machine for Ice

The first commercially made ice cream was offered for sale today in 1786 in New York by Mr Hall of 76 Chatham Street. He made use of a device which had earlier been listed in the expense ledger of George Washington as "a cream machine for ice."

A Wind Machine for Cleaning

On June 8, 1869, Mr Ives W. McGaffey of Chicago, Illinois, received a patent for his invention of a machine that sucked up dirt by means of the whirling force of wind in a container. He called it a vacuum cleaner.

Proverb

A cold and wet June spoils the rest of the year

9
JUNE

Births

John Howard Payne (composer) 1792; Cole Porter (composer) 1893; George Axelrod (playwright) 1922.

Deaths

St Columba (Columkille) 597; William Lilly (astrologer) 1681; Charles Dickens (author) 1870.

Charles Dickens' Will

Charles Dickens died on this day in 1870, in London. In his will he asked that no monument be erected to him and that he wanted only his name and his dates on his tomb. "I rest my claim to the remembrance of my countrymen on my published works."

Home Sweet Home

John Howard Payne, an American playwright/composer born on June 9, 1792, was the creator of the phrase "Home Sweet Home." It was the title of a song in a melodrama of his entitled *Clari, or the Maid of Milan.* The play is forgotten but the song lingers on.

An Anti-Homesickness Saint

The saint who died on this day in 597 was known as St Columba to the Irish and Columkille or Colum Cille to the Scots. He is credited with spreading the Gospel over the north of the British Isles and is believed to have been born at Gartan in Donegal. A stone marking his birthplace was slept on by Irish emigrants who wished to avoid homesickness in their new life abroad. Today in Scotland was the *Day of Colum Cille* remembered in a Highland song:

> Day of Colum Cille the beloved;
> Day the warp should be put to use,
> Day to put the sheep to pasture.

A Pyrotechnic Prophet

William Lilly, who died on June 9, 1681 was the last of the great astrologers of the middle ages. One remarkable prophecy of his made in his *Merlinus Angicus* for 1666 predicted with astonishing accuracy the great fire of London of that year. So good was the prediction that Lilly was arrested on suspicion of having been complicit in starting the blaze. He was, however, later released.

Vestal Virgins

June 9 marked the beginning of the *Vestalia,* the ancient Roman feast to the goddess Vesta. Vesta was a virgin sister of Zeus, and the goddess of the hearth and the home. She was supposed never to be seen by man. In Rome a perpetual fire dedicated to her was cared for by vestals, who were six virgin priestesses, from whom the term vestal virgins originated.

A Cure for Laziness

The weather now is hot, and laziness
Is a disease which many doth possess:
Best thing for this disease, I understand,
Is Oyl of Whip, laid on with a strong hand.
Poor Robin's Almanac, June 1685

The Man-Hater is Consumed

Today in 1887 a fire occurred at the premises of Messrs Pickford in London. A large quantity of merchandise was consumed, but the large stud of draught horses—with one exception, known as "the Man-hater," who refused to allow anyone to approach him—was got out safely, and galloped off in the direction of Hampstead.

10
JUNE

Births

Sessue Hayakawa (actor) 1889; Philip Mountbatten (duke of Edinburgh) 1921; Judy Garland (actress) 1922.

Deaths

Frederick "Barbarosa" (king of Burgundy) 1190; Thomas Hearne (antiquary) 1735; Nicholas Rimsky-Korsakov (composer) 1908.

Fire, 1194

A raging inferno destroyed much of Chartres in France.

Fire, 1248

Bergen in Norway was devastated by fire.

Election, 1376

Wenceslaus was elected king of Germany.

Battle, 1429

Joan of Arc and company defeated the earl of Suffolk and company.

Settlers, 1610

The first Dutch settlers landed on Manhattan Island.

Exploration, 1673

Marquette's party arrived at a tributory of the Mississippi River.

Tornado, 1682

The first recorded tornado in America hit New Haven, Connecticut.

Witchcraft, 1692

Bridget Bishop was hanged for witchcraft in Salem, Massachusetts.

Housing, 1800

The first log house in America was built at Bethany, Pennsylvania.

War, 1801

Tripoli declared war on the United States.

Battle, 1826

Janissaries (Turkish rebels) were wiped out by the sultan's army.

Museum, 1837

The Versailles Palace became a national museum in France.

Madman, 1839

A madman attempted to storm Buckingham Palace and attack Queen Victoria.

Cholera, 1849

Six hundred and seventy-two persons died in Paris in a cholera epidemic.

Exhibition, 1854

Queen Victoria opened the Crystal Palace Exhibition building in London.

Invasion, 1898

The United States Marines invaded Cuba.

Patent, 1902

Thomas Callahan received a patent for an American window envelope.

Alcoholics, 1935

W. Wilson and R. Smith established Alcoholics Anonymous in the U.S.

Panda, 1938

Pandora, a giant panda, arrived at the Bronx Zoo in New York.

War, 1940

Italy declared war on Britain and France.

Births

Sir Kenelm Digby (alchemist) 1603; John Constable (artist) 1776; Richard Strauss (composer) 1864.

A Cure for Warts

Sir Kenelm Digby, a speculative philosopher and alchemist, was born today in 1603, in Goathurst, England. Among his many marvellous discoveries in alchemy was a cure for warts. He recommended that the hands be washed in an empty basin into which the moon shines. He also wrote in 1660 in a paper to the Royal Society: "It may be, some ages hence, voyage to the southern unknown tracts, yea, possibly, to the moon, will not be more strange than one to America."

Deaths

Roger Bacon (philosopher/inventor) 1292; James III (Scottish king) 1488; George I (English king) 1727.

Kamehameha Day

June 11 is celebrated in Hawaii with a festival in memory of King Kamehameha I, who united all the Hawaiian Islands in the 18th century.

Troy Stormed

Today in 1184 B.C., after a ten-year siege, the Greeks finally stormed the gates of Troy and seized the city.

Malta Seized

On June 11, 1798, Napoleon seized Malta, then known as the key of the Mediterranean.

Coronation Chair Plot

On June 11, 1914, women suffragettes attempted to blow up the coronation chair in Westminster Abbey, London.

Endeavour Grounded

Today in 1770 Captain Cook discovered the Great Barrier Reef off the coast of Australia by grounding his ship the *Endeavour* on it.

A Fabulous Inventor

Roger Bacon or Fryer Bacon as he was often called, who died on this day in 1292 at Oxford in England, was a famous scholar and philosopher and sometime inventor of fabulous things. He is given credit for developing gunpowder in Europe and he once designed huge magnifying glasses for the king to use in his war against France. By using the lenses to magnify the suns rays, fires could be set in French towns from a distance and "ere nine of the clocke, Fryer Bacon had burnt the state house of the town, with other houses, only by his mathematical glasses, which made the whole towne in an uproar . . . the king set upon the towne and tooke it away with little or no resistance."

St Barnabas Day

Before the change of calendars the summer solstice fell on June 11, St Barnabas Day (named after an apostle of the 1st century), which was the beginning of the midsummer or nightless days, as they were called. Hence the old saying:

Barnaby Bright, Barnaby Bright,
The longest day and the shortest night.

In Glastonbury, England there used to be an old walnut tree of which it was said it stood bare until St Barnabas Day, when all its leaves and flowers shot out at once.

12
JUNE

Births

Charles Kingsley (novelist) 1810; David Rockefeller (banker) 1915; Anne Frank (diarist) 1929.

Deaths

Maximus (Roman emperor) 455; St Ternan (bishop) 5th century.

An Archery Edict

In a proclamation to the sheriffs of London on June 12, 1349, King Edward III, aware of the importance of the bowman to English military history, and afraid of the demise of the art, ordered that "Every one of the said city, strong in body, at leisure times on holidays, use in their recreation bows and arrows, or pellets and bolts, and learn and exercise the art of shooting, forbidding all and singular on our behalf, that they do not after any manner apply themselves to the throwing of stones, wood or iron, handball, football, bandyball, cambuck or cockfighting, nor such vainlike plays, which have no profit in them."

Proverb

O, my Luve's like a red red rose
That's newly sprung in June:
O, my Luve's like the melodie
That sweetly play'd in tune.
  Robert Burns (1759-1796)

A Magical Trick

On June 12, 1923 in New York, the internationally known magician, Harry Houdini thrilled a large audience by struggling free from a straitjacket, while suspended head downward, forty feet above the ground.

An Unsinkable Stone

Today in Scotland was once celebrated as the day of St Ternan, who died on June 11 in the 5th century. After serving for years as bishop of the Picts he gained sainthood chiefly because of a bell that he owned which had remarkable powers. To go about his good work in the northern islands he used a slab of stone as a means of conveyance over the waters.

Victor Hugo Gaoled

Today in 1851, M. Victor Hugo was sentenced to a fine of 500 francs and six months imprisonment for writing an article in the *Événement* condemnatory of capital punishment.

Charles Dickens' Domestic Bliss

Today in 1858, Charles Dickens published in his periodical, *Household Words,* a solemn declaration in his own name and his wife's that lately whispered rumours touching certain domestic troubles of his were altogether untrue.

Trouble in the Heavens

A great solar eclipse took place today in 1748, as well as great storms of thunder, lightning, and hail of extraordinary size over much of Europe.

Trouble in Paris

Today in Paris in the year 1402, there occurred a massacre of 3,500 souls by the direction of John, duke of Burgundy. The streets and palace yard ran red with the blood of these wretched victims.

Hoopla in Hollywood

Today in Hollywood in 1963 the movie premiere of *Cleopatra* with Elizabeth Taylor, Richard Burton, and Rex Harrison took place. It was the "longest, costliest, and most publicised motion picture ever made," costing $40 million to produce and running for four hours and three minutes.

13

Births

William Butler Yeats (poet) 1865; Basil Rathbone (actor) 1892; Red Grange (football player) 1904.

Deaths
The Virgin Mary (mother of Jesus) 40; St Anthony (orator) 1231; Ludwig II (insane Bavarian king) 1886.

British Devil Dispossession
George Lukins was dispossessed by seven clergymen of the same number of devils, in the Temple Church at Bristol, England in 1788.

British Women Marching
On June 13, 1908, 7,000 women marched from Victoria Embankment to the Albert Hall, London in a women's suffrage demonstration.

American Troops Marching
Today in 1864 General Grant crossed the James River and marched against Petersburg, Virginia, where he was repulsed in two assaults.

American Stowaway Discovery
On June 13, 1929 Armond Lotti, Jean Assolant, and Rene Lefevre flew the monoplane *Yellowbird* from Maine to Comillas, Spain—a non-stop flight of 3,128 miles in twenty-nine hours, fifty-two minutes. They were proceeding to Paris when they discovered the presence of an American stowaway.

American Paper Deluge
Today in 1927, 750,000 pounds of paper showered onto·the aviator Charles Lindberg during a ticker-tape parade in his honour in New York City.

St Anthony's Golden Tongue
St Anthony of Padua, Italy was a protector of animals—he is usually represented with a pig as his page—and was known as a great preacher and patron saint of the illiterate. On one occasion at Rimini, in order to convert a heretic, Anthony caused the fish in the water to lift out their heads and listen to his sermon. On his death today in 1231 his tongue was removed and enshrined in a church dedicated to him in Padua.

French Name Calling
On June 13, 1874, after hot disputes for two days in the French Legislative Assembly, Mr Gambetta called the Bonapartists "misérables." For this he was punched by Comte de Sainte Croux who was fined and jailed.

French Mind Changing
On June 13, 1848, Charles Louis Napoleon Bonaparte (nephew of Napoleon I), who had earlier been sentenced to prison, was elected to the French National Assembly.

French Treason Trial
On June 13, 1887, eight Alsatians, members of the Ligue des Patriotes, were tried for treason because they advocated the reunion of Alsace-Lorraine with France. Four were sent to prison, four were acquitted.

Portuguese Predictions
In Portugal this was considered a good day for young women to find out who their husbands would be. They filled their mouths with water and did not let it out until they heard a man's name. This name was bound to be that of their future mate.

14
JUNE

Births

Harriet Beecher Stowe (author) 1811; John Bartlett (quotation compiler) 1820; Burl Ives (actor/singer) 1909.

Deaths

Duke of Gandia (bastard son of Pope Alexander VI, murdered) 1497; Jean Kleber (French general, assassinated) 1800; Abdul Aziz (Ottoman sultan, assassinated) 1876.

Roman Republic Begins, 510 B.C.

Today in 510 B.C. the Roman Republic was organised and the first consuls were elected.

Cromwell Wins, 1645

Oliver Cromwell won a victory over Rupert and the Royal Cause at Naseby, England in 1645.

Lutherans Can Worship, 1666

On June 14, 1666 Lutherans of New Netherlands were permitted to worship in their homes.

Lutheran Church Begins, 1710

On June 14, 1710 Governor Hunter arrived in New York from England with 3000 Palantines fleeing persecution; a Lutheran church was formed.

First Diving Suit, 1834

On June 14, 1834 Leonard Norcross obtained a U.S. patent for his submarine diving suit. It was made of an airtight rubber with a brass helmet which rested on the shoulders. An airhose connected the helmet to the boat. The feet were weighted down with lead.

A Long Petition, 1839

Today in 1839 a Chartist petition presented to the British House of Commons, signed by 1,280,000 people, in the form of a cylinder of parchment the diameter of a coach wheel, was literally rolled into the House.

U.S. Flag Adopted, 1777

Today in 1777 the Continental Congress, at Philadelphia, adopted a resolution declaring: "That the flag of the thirteen United States shall be of thirteen stripes of alternate red and white, with a union of thirteen stars of white in a blue field, representing the new constellation."

Napoleon Wins, 1800

On June 14, 1800 Napoleon Bonaparte defeated the Austrians at Marengo in Italy.

The U.S. Army Begins, 1775

The United States Army began in 1775 when Congress authorised the recruiting of ten companies of riflemen to serve the colonies for one year.

Chilled-Shot Experiment, 1864

Today in England in 1864 Captain Palliser's chilled shot was experimented with. In every case it went through a four-and-one-half inch armour plate and deep into the backing beyond.

Non-Stop Transatlantic Flight, 1919

On June 14, 1919 the first non-stop transatlantic flight was made by Captain J. Alcock and Arthur Brown from Newfoundland to Clifden, Ireland in sixteen hours and twelve minutes.

15
JUNE

Births

Edward (the Black Prince) 1330; Eduard Grieg (composer) 1843; Saul Steinberg (artist) 1904.

Deaths

St Vitus (martyr) 4th century; Thomas Campbell (poet) 1844; James Polk (11th U.S. president) 1849.

The Black Prince

Edward, son of Edward III, was Prince of Wales, the first duke of Cornwall, and from his black armour popularly known as the Black Prince. His is the name most intimately associated with the memory of English chivalry. When he was only sixteen years old he led the division of the English armies that bore the brunt of the battle in the great victory against the French at the battle of Crecy. The Black Prince was born on June 15, 1330.

The Rising of the Nile

June 15 was considered to be the first day of the annual Nile floods. In ancient Egypt, if the flood was late by so much as one day, sacrifices of beautiful young girls were performed by drowning them in the river to propitiate the gods.

New London Bridge

On June 15, 1825 the first stone of the new London Bridge was laid with great ceremony.

Magna Carta Day

On June 15, 1215 King John of England signed the Magna Carta, considered to be the first document of human freedom. The signing took place at Runnymede on the banks of the Thames.

Farmer's Day

June 15 is the traditional day in Korea to transplant rice seedlings.

Electricity Day ✓

Benjamin Franklin's spectacular experiment while flying a kite in a thunderstorm proved the identity of the electricity in lightning today in 1752.

King George's Dark Day

Today in 1839 a woman, describing herself as Sophia Elizabeth Guelph Sims, made application at the Mansion House in London for advice and assistance to prove herself the lawful child of King George IV and Mrs Fitzherbert.

King Valdemar's Day

On June 15, 1219, King Valdemar and his troops liberated Denmark and raised the Danish flag in Europe which, legend has it, came to Valdemar from heaven as a guarantee of victory.

St Vitus Dance

St Vitus, the patron saint of actors and dancers and the curer of rabies, epilepsy, sleeping sickness, St Vitus Dance, and other shaking diseases was boiled in oil today in the 4th century.

The next is Vitus sodde in oyle, before whose ymage faire
Both men and women bringing Hennes for offring do repair:
The cause wherof I do not know, I thinke, for some disease
Which he is thought to drive away from such as him do please.
Naogeorgus, medieval poet

Charles Goodyear's Happy Day ✓

On June 15, 1844 Charles Goodyear patented a process for vulcanising rubber after experimenting endlessly, searching for a way to prevent it from sticking and melting in hot weather.

Births

Edward I (English king) 1239;
Gustavus V (Swedish king) 1858.

Deaths

John Suckling (English poet) 1641;
Jean Baptiste Gresset (French poet) 1777.

Hundreds of People Blown Away

Iowa State was desolated by a tornado today in 1882, the path of which was estimated to extend over 150 miles with an average breadth of half a mile. Hundreds of people were blown away and entire trains blown off the rails.

Millions of Caterpillars Loose

Today in 1884 immense swarms of caterpillars made their appearance in the mountains districts of East Glamorganshire in Wales. The insects were brown with black longitudinal stripes about an inch and a half in length. Millions were found in peat holes, gutters, and mountain brooks.

Two Thousand Persons Swallowed

An earthquake near Ponnah, in the East Indies, which swallowed up a large district and more than 2,000 persons, occurred today in 1819.

A Lady Martyr Pardoned

Today in 1456 King Charles VII of France annulled a judgment of heresy against Joan of Arc, twenty-five years after she had been burnt at the stake.

A Lady is Launched

Lieutenant Valentina Tereshkova became the world's first woman astronaut, as she was launched into orbit from a Russian base today in 1963.

Proverb

It is the month of June,
The month of leaves and roses,
When pleasant sights salute the eyes
And pleasant scents the noses.
N.P. Willis (1806-1867)

One Man Blown Away

Today in 1885 a balloon containing a French gentleman was picked up in the Channel. M. Glorieux had on the previous day ascended from Lille hoping to descend in the neighbourhood of Paris. The wind however, after keeping him a long time hovering between Calais and Boulogne, finally took him out to sea where he was nearly wrecked.

One Man Wounded

In a duel today in 1838 in London, between Lord Castlereagh and M. de Meky, husband of Madame Grisi, arising out of a declaration of attachment made to Madame by his lordship, Castlereagh was slightly wounded by the first shot, after which the parties separated mutually satisfied.

Two Royal Boys Imprisoned

On June 16, 1483 Edward V, the boy king of England, and his brother, the duke of York, were arrested and confined to the Tower of London by their uncle, Richard, duke of Gloucester. The young princes were declared illegitimate and Gloucester took the throne as Richard III. Skeletons, believed to be those of the princes, were unearthed in the Tower during the reign of Charles II.

Six Thousand Men Killed

On June 16, 1487 the last great battle to take place on English soil was fought, signifying the end of the War of the Roses between the houses of York and Lancaster. Six thousand men were killed at the Battle of Stoke, which secured the English throne for the Tudor monarchs.

17
JUNE

Births

Charles Gounod (composer) 1818; John Hersey (author) 1914; Dean Martin (entertainer) 1917.

Deaths

St Nectan (headless saint) 6th century; fifty-four Parisians (guillotined) 1794; Eugen Weidman (guillotined) 1939.

A Headless Saint

St Nectan was a Welsh hermit who lost his head today in the 6th century to a band of robbers. He then picked up his head and dropped it down a well. Foxglove flowers sprang up wherever his blood splashed on the ground.

The Guillotine Falls

Today in 1794 fifty-four people were guillotined in Paris during France's "Reign of Terror." Today in 1939 the last person to be *publicly* guillotined in France was the murderer Eugen Weidmann, before a large crowd at Versailles at 4:50 a.m.

A Watergate Break-in

The Democratic National Headquarters in the Watergate Hotel were broken into by people in the pay of the Republican Committee to re-elect the president of the United States (1972).

Proverb

A swarm of bees in June
Is worth a lucky spoon

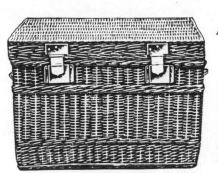

"The Whites of their Eyes"

The battle of Bunker Hill today in 1775, was the first of the American War of Independence. Though nominally a British victory, the American revolutionists took great heart from it in discovering that they could indeed stand up to British armed might. During the battle Israel Putnam, an American revolutionary soldier, is attributed with having said, "Men, you are all marksmen: don't one of you fire until you see the whites of their eyes."

Basket Coffins Proposed

Considerable interest was excited by a suggestion made by Mr Seymour Hadon to the *London Times* that the heavy coffins now used for burial should be superceded by light wicker baskets, arguing that the resolution of human clay into elementary substances is an operation most quickly performed when the dead are allowed to come into immediate contact with the earth (1875).

Smokeless Gunpowder Discovered

H. Maxim and R. Schupphaus got the U.S. patent for their smokeless gunpowder invention. It was adopted by the government, enabling the establishment of a dynamite factory and smokeless powder plant (1890).

The U.S. Attacks Canada

A small force of American colonials, under William Pepperrell, supported by a fleet of merchantmen commanded by Sir Peter Warren, attacked Louisbourg, Nova Scotia, Canada, and forced its surrender (1745).

Old Men Marry Young Lasses

According to *Poor Robin's Almanac* the eclipse of the moon of June 17, 1684, portended "a great hornifying, where old men marry young, buxom lasses."

18

JUNE

Births

Paul McCartney (Beatle) 1942.

Deaths

Marcus and Marcellianus (twin martyrs) 286.

Twin Brothers Martyred

Marcus and Marcellianus were twin brothers of an illustrious family in Rome. Remaining firm in their religion, they were condemned by Fabian to be bound to two pillars, with their feet nailed to the same. In this posture they were stabbed to death with lances today in 286.

Aboard Noah's Ark

Many historians believe that the passengers aboard Noah's Ark first saw the tops of mountains during the receding of the flood on this day in 2349 B.C.

Joan of Arc Defeats the Britsh

On June 18, 1429, the French led by Joan of Arc, defeated the English at Patay with heavy loss. The victory enabled Charles VII to enter Rheims, where he was crowned king.

The British Defeat the French

The Battle of Waterloo took place today in 1815, at which the British force led by the duke of Wellington defeated Napoleon Bonaparte and the French.

The Horned Poppy

The flower for June 18 is the *Chelidinium glaucum* or horned poppy.

A Flaming Irish Whisky Spree

Fire in a bonded warehouse in Dublin today in 1875 destroyed a very large quantity of whisky and led to the serious injury of many people who attempted to satisfy their craving for the burning spirit as it flowed through the streets.

The British Wear Trousers

On June 18, 1823, British soldiers for the first time appeared with trousers as part of their uniform. Prior to that date they had worn breeches and stockings.

Susan B. Anthony Stands Firm

Susan B. Anthony, the American leader of the women's suffrage movement, led a group of women to the polls in Rochester, New York and insisted on voting. She was arrested, tried, convicted, and on this date in 1873 was sentenced to pay a fine of $100—which she refused to do.

A Flight of Scottish Herrings

A remarkable phenomenon occurred today in Scotland in 1875. An island named Inishgowla was literally covered with herrings, much to the astonishment of the islanders who were unable to explain from whence their flight originated.

Across America by Car

On June 18, 1903, Tom Fitch and Marens Kraarup left San Fransisco in a nine-horsepower, one-cylinder Packard, *Old Pacific,* and motored across the continent, arriving in New York 61 days later.

"This Was Their Finest Hour"

"Let us therefore brace ourselves to our duty and so bear ourselves that if the British Commonwealth and Empire last for a thousand years, men will say 'This was their finest hour.' "

    Winston Churchill in a speech on June 18, 1940

19
JUNE

Births

James (Scottish and English king) 1566; Blaise Pascal (genius) 1623; Wallis Simpson (duchess of Windsor) 1896.

Deaths

Julius and Ethel Rosenberg (spies) 1953.

Father's Day Begins

The first Father's Day was held on June 19, 1910 in the U.S., inspired by a YMCA worker, Mrs John Dodd. The rose was the official flower for the day—red for living fathers, white for the dead.

A Speech from a President

In President John Kennedy's message to the U.S. Congress concerning civil rights today in 1963 he said: "There are no 'white' or 'colored' signs on the foxholes or graveyards of battle."

A Letter from a Field Marshal

Gebhard Blücher, the Prussian field marshal, in a letter to his wife today in 1815, commented on the Battle of Waterloo of yesterday. "What I promised I have performed. On the 16th I was forced to fall back a short distance; the 18th—in conjunction with my friend Wellington—completed Napoleon's ruin."

An Infant King

James, the son of Henry Lord Darnley and Mary, queen of Scots was born today in 1566 and placed in an elaborate wooden cradle in the palace at Edinburgh. Thirteen months later he was crowned King James VI of Scotland and in 1603 he became James I of England.

Baseball Begins

The first formal baseball game was played June 19, 1846 between the Knickerbocker Club of New York and the New York Baseball Club at Hoboken, New Jersey. The New York Baseball Club won 23 to 1. At that time, there were no standard rules, though the game was loosely based on the English game of "rounders." The home team provided balls that were of different sizes and weights.

A Boy Genius

Blaise Pascal, born on this day in 1623 was a French mathematical prodigy publishing his first treatise at the age of sixteen. His tutors, deciding that the classics were better for him than mathematics, took away all his books. When he was found working out Euclid's theorems of geometry on the floor in charcoal without the aid of the texts, his tutors surrendered to his genius and returned the books. Pascal gave up mathematics for religion at the age of twenty-five.

Those Born Today

Persons born today are ambitious, creative, inventive, strongly individualistic, definite in their views, determined, and occasionally obstinate. Their lucky days are Sunday and Monday and their colours are yellow, gold, and bronze. Their lucky jewels—topaz, amber, and diamonds—should be worn next to their skin.

Births

John Plantagenet (son of Henry IV) 1389; Lillian Hellman (U.S. playwright) 1905; Errol Flynn (Australian actor) 1909; Audie Murphy (U.S. war hero/actor) 1924; Chet Atkins (U.S. guitarist) 1924.

Deaths

Louis I (Roman emperor) 840; Richard Brandon (English executioner) 1649; Charles Coffin (French poet) 1749; Anna Maria Porter (British novelist) 1832; William IV (English king) 1837; Santa Anna (Mexican revolutionary) 1876; Alfred Harcourt (U.S. publisher) 1954; Bernard Baruch (U.S. financier/ statesman) 1965.

Running Royalty Returned

On June 20, 1791, King Louis XVI and his queen attempted to flee from France to get foreign aid to restore his authority. The running couple were apprehended at Varennes and returned to Paris.

Awesome Obelisk Arrives

On June 20, 1880 the U.S.S. *Dessoug* unloaded in New York an obelisk ninety feet high, weighing 443,000 lbs. It had been built beside the Nile in Egypt in 1565 B.C. and was moved to Alexandria in 22 B.C. William Vanderbilt paid to have it brought to the States.

Royal Relics Removed

June 20th was once celebrated in England as the day of the removal of relics of Edward, king of the West Saxons, from Wareham to Salisbury. Among the treasures were said to have been a feather of the Holy Ghost, the thumb of St Thomas, the face of a seraphin, with only part of the nose, and the snout of a seraphin, thought to have belonged to the preceding.

An Axeman Goeth

On June 20th, 1649, Richard Brandon, the official executioner of the City of London, died peacefully in his sleep at Rosemary Lane. Among the many heads that were removed by his axe was that of Charles I for which he was paid £30. A handkerchief that Brandon removed from the king's torso later brought him ten shillings when he sold it as a souvenir.

A Sea Serpent Seen

A great sea serpent was observed at Plymouth in the U.S. today in 1815. Its extension above the surface of the water was more than 100 feet, and the head appeared to be about six-to-eight feet long.

A Crowned Queen Cries

Today in 1837 saw the accession of Queen Victoria to the British throne. She was awakened at 5 a.m. by the arrival of the archbishop of Canterbury and the lord chamberlain. She did not keep them waiting and appeared in a loose white nightgown and shawl, her nightcap thrown off, and her hair falling upon her shoulders, her feet in slippers, tears in her eyes, but perfectly collected and dignified.

Christopher Columbus Condemned

On June 20, 1499 Queen Isabella of Spain, moved with indignation, condemned Columbus' enslavement of the gentle Indians he discovered in the West Indies and procured their instant liberation.

Rioters in Red Regalia

Today in 1792, thousands of Frenchmen wearing special regalia and red bonnets of liberty marched into Paris and rioted in the streets to make demands for the reform of the king, Louis XVI.

Births

Rockwell Kent (artist) 1882; Jean Paul Sartre (author) 1905; Francois Sagan (author) 1935.

Deaths

Thales (Greek philosopher) 546 B.C.; Captain Backhouse (eccentric) 1800; Daniel Lambert (large man) 1809.

Daniel Lambert's Epitaph

In remembrance of that prodigy
of nature, Daniel Lambert, a native of
    Leicester, who was possessed of an
    excellent mind
and in personal greatness he had no
    competitor.
He measured 3 feet 1 inch round the
    leg;
9 feet 4 inches round the body and
    weighed
52 st. 11 lbs [739 pounds].
He departed this life 21st June, 1809
    aged 39 years.
    On a tombstone in Stanford, England

A Theory Holding Water

Thales, who died on this day in 546 B.C., was the earliest Greek philosopher and the prototype of the absent-minded thinker. He once fell down a well while wandering along in a philosophical reverie. Perhaps it was this experience that gave rise to his bold proposition that everything in the universe was made out of water.

An Eclipse Influences Marriages

Poor Robin's Almanac describes what influence a solar eclipse of today in 1685 will have on marriages. "There will be many pitched battles between married couples for the empire of the breeches and many a young fop that wants nothing but a wife, shall light on a subtle baggage, that shall have beauty enough for him, and some to spare for a friend."

Henry Hudson's Last Voyage

On June 21, in 1611, the English explorer Henry Hudson, discoverer of the Hudson River, the Hudson Straits, and Hudson's Bay, was set adrift with his young son in a small boat in that bay by mutineering seamen from his ship *Discovery*. He was never seen again.

The First Poem in English

June 21 is the first day of summer in the northern hemisphere. The following poem, written about this day, is thought to be the first ever written in English although its date is unknown.

Summer is ycomen in,
Loud sing cuckoo;
Groweth seed,
And bloweth mead,
And springeth the weed new.

The Crab Influences Life

The sun is vertical over the tropic of Cancer today and is entering the crab in the Zodiac. People born under this sign from today until July 23 are described thusly by William Lilly in *Christian Astrology* of 1647.

Manners or Actions when well placed or dignified
She signifieth one of composed Manners, a soft tender creature, a Lover of all honest and ingenuous Sciences, a Searcher of, and Delighter in Novelties, naturally propense to flit and shift his Habitation, unstedfast wholly caring for the present Times, Timorous, Prodigal, and easily Frighted, however loving Peace, and to live free from the cares of this Life; if a Mechannick, the man learnes many Occupations, and frequently will be tampering with many wayes to trade in.

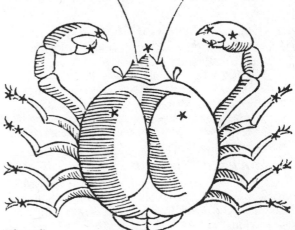

When ill
A meer Vagabond, idle Person, hating Labour, a Drunkard, a Sot, one of no Spirit or Forecast, delighting to live beggarly and carelesly, one content in no condition of Life, either good or ill.

Births

Rider Haggard (author) 1856; John Dillinger (criminal) 1903.

For Whom the Bells Tolled

St Paulinus is reputed to be the inventor of bells and today in the year 431 he died and was buried beneath the bells of St Felix church in Nola, Italy. The moment St Paulinus gave up his soul to God, all who were in his chamber felt a sudden trembling, as if by some shock of an earthquake, and the church bells rang.

The Bloodiest Battle of All

The Battle of Morat, in Switzerland, fought between the Swiss and the forces of Charles the Bold, duke of Burgundy, on June 22, 1746, was famous as possibly the most bloody of all times. "Cruel as at Morat" became a proverb. When the two armies met, each about 30,000 strong, not a single Burgundian and very few of the Swiss survived.

An Admiral's Entry and Exit

On June 22, 1893, the HMS *Victoria* collided with the *Camperdown*. Admiral Sir George Tryon and most of his men died at sea. However at the same time at a party given by his wife in London, 2,000 miles away, many guests saw Sir George open the drawing room door, enter and walk in, and stride across the room to exit by another door. Lady Tryon only heard of his death some days later.

Braddock Out, Louis In

"The Brown Bomber," Joe Louis, became the heavyweight boxing champion of the world after knocking out Jim Braddock in the eighth round at Comiskey Park in Chicago, today in 1937.

Count Zeppelin's Passenger Service

On June 22, 1910 Count Zeppelin started the first airship passenger service between Friedrichshafen and Dusseldorf, a distance of 300 miles. The first airship was called *Deutchland*.

Deaths

St Paulinus (bell inventor/saint) 431; Catherine Philips (poetess) 1664; Judy Garland (entertainer) 1969.

A Duel with Balloons

On June 22, 1808, in Paris, M. de Grandpré and M. le Pique fought a duel from aerial balloons. Each went aloft in his own craft with a blunderbuss, and the idea was not to score a hit on the other man, but on the other man's air bag. Pique fired first, and missed. Grandpré fired, hit his opponent's balloon, and sent it hurtling down. Pique died in the crash. Grandpré continued in a triumphal ascent, and landed about seven leagues outside Paris.

A Case of Reappearing Kegs

Every year at sunrise on June 22nd, a remarkable occurrence is said to take place at Fedan More gorge in Scotland. This was where a man called Macrae ran for safety while being pursued by royalist soldiers. Macrae had undertaken to transport some kegs of gold to Prince Charles who was hiding in Skye. On being ambushed he uttered a spell (fath-fith) which made the kegs, but not himself invisible. Captured in Fedan More and executed he was not able to reclaim the kegs, which become visible once a year on this day.

23
JUNE

Births

Gottfried Leibnitz (mathematician/ philosopher) 1646; Josephine (Napoleon's wife) 1763.

Deaths

St Alban (martyr) 303; William S. Hart (film actor) 1946.

A Pop-Eyed Execution

St Alban was beheaded on this day in the year 303 in Rome. On his way to execution he reached a bridge thronged with spectators blocking the passage. St Alban raised his eyes to Heaven and the waters under the bridge divided. His executioner was immediately converted and begged to die with him. Another executioner was found and, as a signal of divine vengeance, as soon as he delivered the fatal stroke, his eyes popped out of his head.

Midsummer Eve Hijinks

June 23rd was celebrated throughout Europe as midsummer eve. In rural areas during the middle ages the eve was celebrated with huge bonfires around which the people danced and through whose flames they sometimes would jump. In some places a large wheel was packed with straw, set alight, and then rolled down a hill. Anyone who rolled down the hill with the wheel was said to insure his good luck in the coming year. It was also said that anyone in possession of the seeds of the fern on midsummer eve would be turned invisible for the night. Great efforts were sometimes made to obtain the potent seeds.

A Midsummer Eve Prognostication

At eve last Midsummer no sleep I sought,
But to the field a bag of hemp-seed brought:
I scattered round the seed on every side,
And three times, in a trembling accent cried:
"This hemp seed with my virgin hand I sow,
Who shall my true love be, the crop shall mow."
I straight looked back, and, if my eyes speak truth,
With his keen scythe behind me came the youth.
John Gay (1685-1732)

A Learned Cod Fish

On June 23, 1626 a large cod fish cut open at the Cambridge market in England was found to contain a copy of John Frith's book of religious treatises.

Snake Jewellery Luck

Once upon a time, tonight was thought to be the evening when snakes meet up and form a circle with all their heads in the centre. With a lot of hissing and frantic behaviour they were said to create a hard glass bubble where all their heads join. Anyone who found this jewel was deemed to be in for a very lucky life.

Raising the Devil

In medieval England it was believed possible to raise the Devil by running backwards around ancient druid stones. It could only be done at midnight on midsummer eve and then the devil would arrive with a bowl of porridge in exchange for the runner's soul.

Madness, Death, or Poetry

To sleep among an encirclement of druid stones tonight would result in either death, madness, or the power to be a poet.

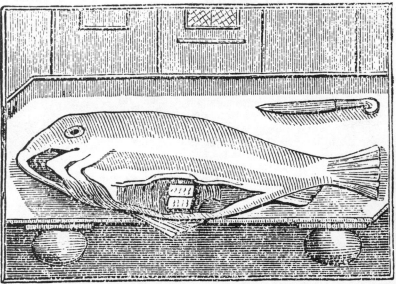

24
JUNE

Births

Jack Dempsey (boxer) 1895; Billy Cooper (golfer) 1931.

Deaths

Vespian (Roman emperor) 79; Lucrezia Borgia (art patron) 1519; Grover Cleveland (24th U.S. president) 1908.

Divorced

King Henry VIII of England divorced Anne of Cleves, his 4th wife, today in 1540.

St John the Baptist

The Christian church usually marked the festivals of saints on the day of their death, but John the Baptist's feast was excepted because he was sanctified in his mother's womb—born free from original sin. He retired into the wilderness and remained there lest the purity of his heart should be sullied if he had any commerce with men. Today is his day.

St John's Wort

Today's flower, St John's wort (*Hypericum perforatum*), was believed to have the power to move about in order not to have its leaves plucked. Hung over doors it could keep out evil.

Midsummer Day Predictions

Cut your thistles before St John
You will have two instead of one.

If it rains the 24th of June
Hazelnuts will not prosper.

Never rued the man
That laid in his fuel before St John.

St John's Day

Then doth the joyful feast of John the Baptist take his turn,
When bonfires great, with lofty flame, in every town do
    burn;
And young men round with maids do dance in every
    street,
With garlands wrought of motherwort, or else with
    vervain sweet,
And many other flowers fair, with violets in their hands,
Whereas they all do fondly think, that whosoever stands
And through the flowers beholds the flame, his eyes shall
    feel no pain.
    Anonymous, medieval England

A Cat Sacrifice

During the middle ages, at Aix-en-Provence, on the festival of St John, a number of cats were put into a basket and burned alive in a fire kindled by the clergy in the public square. Hymns and anthems were sung, and processions were made by the priests and the people in honour of the sacrifice.

A Day to See Fairies

Midsummer Day, on June 24, was reputed to be a good day for spying fairies, especially at midnight and at twilight. People used to kill their babies if they were ugly, thinking them to be changelings left by the fairies who had stolen the real baby.

Midsummer Day Decorating

Each year on midsummer day the citizens of rural English villages lavishly decorated the village well and held music recitals and morris dancing around it.

Births

John Horne Tooke (writer) 1736.

Deaths

Eleanor (widow of Henry III of England) 1291; General Custer (hero) 1876; Stanford White (architect) 1906.

Duke Says He's King, 1483

The duke of Gloucester proclaimed himself King Richard III of England.

Catherine and Henry Wed, 1503

Catherine of Aragon, widow of Arthur, Prince of Wales, was betrothed to his brother, who would become King Henry VIII of England.

The Fork Comes to America, 1630

Governor John Winthrop introduced the table fork to America, bringing it to Massachusetts from England in a leather case.

Cannibalism at Sea, 1727

Survivors of a sunken sailing ship arrived in Newfoundland having drifted for a month at sea and eating their dead companions.

Custer's Last Stand, 1876

Lieutenant Colonel George Armstrong Custer and his force of 208 men were slain in a battle lasting twenty minutes, by the Sioux led by Sitting Bull, at the Little Big Horn River in Montana.

Sarah Bernhardt Sued, 1880

Sarah Bernhardt was condemned to pay costs and damages of £4,000 for breach of engagement with the Comédie Française.

Italian Political Unrest, 1880

A twenty-six-year-old tailor named Cordigliani threw two large stones on the ministerial benches in the Chamber of Deputies in Rome.

Toscanini First Conducts, 1886

Arturo Toscanani, a 19-year-old cellist in the Rio de Janeiro Opera House, conducted *Aida* when the regular conductor failed to appear. He was so successful that he decided to embark on a career as a conductor.

Madison Square Garden Shooting, 1906

Stanford White, American architect, was shot and killed in Madison Square Roof Garden by Harry K. Thaw, because of trouble over Thaw's wife, Evelyn Nesbit Thaw.

A Minimum Wage Act, 1938

President Franklin D. Roosevelt signed the Wage and Hours Act, which provided a minimum hourly wage of twenty cents, rising to forty cents at the end of six years. The work week was limited to forty-four hours for the next year, dropping to forty hours three years after the bill was enacted.

Korean War Begins, 1950

The Korean War began when North Korean forces invaded South Korea.

Colour TV Begins, 1951

The first commercial colour broadcast in television history was presented by the CBS network in the U.S.

26
JUNE

Births

George Morland (artist) 1763; Abner Doubleday (baseball inventor) 1819; Peter Lorre (actor) 1904.

Deaths

Julian (Roman emperor) 363; Francisco Pizzaro (explorer) 1541; George IV (English king) 1830.

Today's Illness

According to numerology people born today are prone to troubles with the liver, bile, intestines, and digestive system. They are also likely to suffer from any or all of the following: headaches, blood poisoning, all blood diseases, and rheumatism. Ideally they should avoid all meats and become vegetarians.

The Pied Piper's Revenge

Today in 1284, the Pied Paper of Hamelin, Germany, who had charmed the rats and mice out of Hamelin and into the river, and who had been refused his fee of 1,000 guilders by the town fathers, had his revenge as he lured 130 of their children to a similar fate.

The Travels of Mr Edison's Voice

Colonel Gourand, in a letter to the *London Times* on June 26, 1888, announced that a perfected phonograph had been received in England from Mr Edison, the eminent American electrician. Mr Edison's voice was heard 3,000 miles from the place where—and exactly ten days after—he had spoken into the instrument.

Transatlantic Cable Laid

Today in 1858, two ships—the *Agamemnon* and *Niagara*—commenced laying the Atlantic telegraph cable. By evening 146 miles of it was on the bottom.

St Lawrence Seaway Opens

On June 26, 1959 the St Lawrence Seaway was officially dedicated, with Queen Elizabeth and President Eisenhower officiating.

American Firsts on June 26

1614: The Virginia Company held the first American lottery, offering a prize of 4,500 crowns. It became a frequently used method of raising money.

1721: Dr Zabdiel Boylston performed America's first vaccinations against smallpox on his six-year-old son and two servants.

1797: Charles Newbold got the patent for the first cast iron plough in the U.S.

1819: William Clarkson was granted a patent for the first bicycle in the U.S.

1870: The first broadwalk in the world was completed at Atlantic City, New Jersey.

1919: *The Illustrated Daily News* was published; it was the first illustrated daily newspaper in America.

1958: The Mackinac Straits Bridge connecting upper and lower Michigan was opened.

Births

Louis XII (French king) 1462; Charles IX (French king) 1550; Charles XII (Swedish king) 1682.

Deaths

Runjeet Singh (maharajah) 1839; Joseph Smith (Mormon founder) 1844; Wanda Gag (author) 1946.

Maharajah Mourned

On June 27, 1839 there died at Lahore, India in his sixtieth year, Maharajah Runjeet Singh, a chief of Lahore. Four princesses—his wives—and seven slave girls were permitted to burn themselves on his funeral pyre.

Mormon Murdered

In 1844, Joseph Smith, a founder of the Mormon church, announced himself as a candidate for the presidency of the United States. This prompted his enemies to act, and he and his brother Hyrum were arrested on charges of treason and conspiracy. They were lodged in the jail at Carthage, Illinois, and there on this date, they were murdered by a mob.

U.S. Army Execution

On June 27, 1776, the first army execution in the U.S. took place in New York. Thomas Hickey, one of George Washington's guards, had plotted with others to capture Washington and turn him over to Sir William Howe.

Mid-air Gas-up

On June 27, 1923, Captain Lowell Smith lowered a forty-foot steel, wire-encased hose from his de Havilland plane and fuelled a plane piloted by Lieutenant Richter over Coronado, California in the first successful mid-air refuelling.

Today's Love Forecast

Persons born on June 27 can find harmonious vibrations from people born on the 3rd, 6th, 9th, 12th, 15th, 18th, 21st, 24th, 27th, or 30th of any month. However today's people will do almost anything for affection and can easily be made fools of when in love.

The Roman Empire Finished

On this day in 1787 the English historian, Edward Gibbon, finished his gigantic work, *The Decline and Fall of the Roman Empire*. He wrote of the occasion: "It was on the day, or rather the night of the 27th of June, between the hours of 11 and 12, that I wrote the last words of the last page in a summer house in the garden. After laying down my pen I took several turns in the covered walk of acacias, which commands a prospect of the county."

Today's Trials and Tribulations

People born on June 27 are associated with the number 9 in numerology which means that they are likely to suffer great danger arising from their own foolishness and impulsiveness. They should be on the lookout for fires and explosions; however they are unlikely to get through life without injury from one or the other. As a general rule they can expect to have several operations on their body and people born on June 27 are often wounded or killed in warfare or in the battle of life.

28
JUNE

Births

Alexander (the Great) 356 B.C.; Henry VIII (English king) 1491; Jean Jacques Rousseau (philosopher) 1712.

Deaths

Archduke Francis Ferdinand and wife (heir to the Austro-Hungarian throne) 1914.

Today's Flower

The blue cornflower or *Centaura cyanus* is the flower accorded June 28 by medieval monks.

Hard Boiled Egg Dispensers

To help Pennsylvania farmers dispose of an egg surplus, slot machines dispensing hard boiled eggs for a nickel a-piece were installed in cafes and taverns throughout the state in 1938.

The Cause of World War One

Today in 1914 Archduke Francis Ferdinand, heir to the throne of Austria-Hungary, and his wife were assassinated by a young Serbian nationalist, Gavrilo Princip at Sarajevo, Bosnia. This act lead to World War I.

Ned Kelly Nabbed

Today in 1880 a famous gang of Australian bushrangers, known as Kelly's Gang, was brought to book by the Melbourne police at a place called Glen Rowan. The gang had "stuck up" Glen Rowan and fortified themselves in the hotel. During the siege all the gang were shot except Ned Kelly, their leader, who had armoured himself with quarter-inch iron plates. However when shot in the legs, which were unprotected, he was brought down "roaring with savage ferocity." During the battle, Kelly's sisters, in elaborate riding habits and feathered hats, were riding about just behind the line of police, interested spectators of the proceedings. Kelly was later hanged.

Charles II Cures the Evil

"Saturday being appointed by his Majesty Charles II to touch such as were troubled with the EVIL, a great company of poor afflicted creatures were met together, many brought in chairs or baskets, and being appointed by his Majesty to repair to the Banqueting House, his Majesty sat in a chair of state, where he stroked all that were brought to him, and then put about each of their necks a white ribbon, with an angel of gold upon it."
The Mercurius Politrius, June 28, 1660

Sheep Suit Spun Swiftly

In 1811, Sir John Throckmorton wagered a thousand pounds that he could sit down to dinner on some particular day in a well-made suit of wool from sheep that were shorn the same morning. At five in the morning of June 28 two sheep were shorn. the wool was washed, carded, stubbed, roved, spun, and woven; the cloth was scoured, fulled, tented, raised, sheared, dyed, and dressed; the tailor made up the finished cloth into garments, and at a quarter to six in the evening Sir John sat down to dinner in his new suit, one thousand pounds richer.

29
JUNE

Births

Peter Paul Reubens (artist) 1577; Nelson Eddy (singer) 1901; Prince Bernhard (husband of the Dutch Queen Juliana) 1911.

Poetic Justice

Elizabeth Barrett Browning, wife and fellow poet of Robert Browning, died today in Florence in 1861. Not everyone appreciated her work. "Thank God, no more *Aurora Leighs!*" thundered Edward Fitzgerald (famous for his *Omar Khayyam*) when he heard of her passing. It was in her poem "Aurora Leigh" that Elizabeth wrote: "Since when was genius found respectable?"

A Travelling Frog

On June 29, 1872 a fine specimen of the horned frog was placed in the reptile house of Regent's Park Zoo. The creature was posted by an Irish lady residing in San Diego, California, on May 28 by book post, registered as a present for her son in London. The package took four weeks in transit during which the frog had no food and was subjected to great changes in temperature.

Deaths

St Peter (apostle) 68; Elizabeth Barrett Browning (poet) 1861; Joseph Hansom (cab inventor) 1882; Ignace Paderewski (Polish pianist/composer) 1941.

The Pope's Name Change

Peter, the apostle of Christ, was crucified on this day in 68. It is out of esteem for him, the first bishop of the church, that the custom developed that pope's change their name when they accede to the office. In 884 Peter di Porca was elected pope. Deeming it presumptuous to be called Peter II he became Sergius, the second pope of that name.

The Yellow Cock's Comb

Today's flower is the *Rhinanthus crista-galli* or yellow cock's comb.

"The yellow floure called Yellow Cock's Combe which floureth now in the fields is a sign of St. Peter's Day, whereon it is always in fine floure, in order to admonish us of the denyal of our Lord by St. Peter, that if even he the Prince of the Apostles did fall through feare, and denied his Lord, so are we fallible creatures the more liable to yield to a similar tentatioun."
Florilegium, 1830

A Dutiful Daughter

On June 29, 1880 a young lady pedestrian accomplished at Stapleton near Bristol, England, the extraordinary feat of walking 1,000 miles in as many consecutive hours. The task was undertaken in order that her father might win a wager of £30.

A Terrible Royal Scandal

On June 29, 1839, *The Morning Post* in London featured a story that the duchess of Montrose and Lady Sarah Ingestre were among those who hissed Her Majesty, Queen Victoria, on the Ascot racecourse. Lady Lichfield was said to be implicated in conveying this report to Her Majesty, but afterwards denied in writing that she had given utterances to such terrible scandal.

A Wayward Husband

On June 29, 1840, Mister Robert Taylor of Durham, England, aged twenty years, was charged with six acts of bigamy.

A Theatre Fire

Today in 1613 the Globe Theatre, London, burned down during a performance of Shakespeare's *King Henry VIII*.

Births

Lena Horne (entertainer) 1917; Susan Hayward (actress) 1919.

Deaths

Lola Montez (actress/adventuress) 1861; Paul Klee (artist) 1940.

The Thames Reeks, 1858

On June 30, 1858 the state of the Thames gave rise to much anxious deliberation. Parliamentary committees could not sit in the rooms overlooking the river; several of the officers became sick and the attendance of members was as brief as possible. The water was of a deep blackish-green tint and gave off noxious odours.

Proverb

A leaky May and a warm June
Bring on the harvest very soon.

Witch-Hunting, 1646

John Gaule, Vicar in Huntingdonshire, England, gave a sermon today in 1646: "Every old woman with a wrinkled face, a furr'd brow, a hairy lip, a gobber tooth, a squint eye, a squeaking voice, or a scolding tongue . . . a dog or cat by her side, is not only suspected but pronounced for a witch."

Pillory Put Away, 1837

An act of British Parliament on June 30, 1837 put an end to the pillory as a means of punishment in the United Kingdom.

Today's Flower

The common rock rose, yellow cistus, and *Helianthemum chamaecistus* are one and the same flower for this day.

A Shower of Frogs, 1892

During the storm that raged with considerable fury in Birmingham, England, a shower of frogs fell in the suburb of Mosely. Almost white in colour, they were found scattered about several gardens.

A Mighty Meteor, 1908

In the morning of this day in 1908 an enormous area of the Tungaska region of Siberia was totally devasted by a gigantic meteor. The blast flattened trees over several miles and effects were felt over 1,500 square miles. It was believed that the meteorite weighed one million tons but broke up before it hit the earth at more than 90,000 mph.

On the Wagon, 1795

"Whereas the subscriber, through the pernicious habit of drinking, has greatly hurt himself in purse and person, and rendered himself odious to all his acquaintance, and finding there is no possibility of breaking off from the said practice, but through the impossibility to find the liquor; he therefore begs and prays that no persons will sell him, for money or on trust, any sort of spiritous liquors, as he will not in future pay it, but will prosecute anyone for an action of damage against the temporal and eternal interests of the public's humble, serious, and sober servant, JAMES CHALMERS"
The Bahama Gazette, June 1795

A Daring Acrobat, 1859

Emile Blondin, a professional acrobat from France, crossed Niagara Falls on a tightrope in just five minutes time today in 1859.

JULY

Then came hot July, boiling like to fire,
That all his garments he had cast away;
Upon a lion raging yet with ire
He boldly rode, and made him to obey;
(It was the beast that whilom did foray
The Nemeaen forest, till Amphitrionide
Him slew, and with his hide did him array:)
Behind his back a scythe, and by his side
Under his belt he bore a sickle circling wide.
   Edmund Spenser

JULY

History

July, until the reforms of Julius Caesar, was the fifth month of the Roman calendar and was named *Quintilis*. In the Alban calendar it had thirty-six days, under Romulus thirty-one, and was reduced to thirty by the order of Numa. The great Caesar was very interested in the month because it was the time of his birth. With his reforms July again attained thirty-one days, and became the seventh month of the year. It was Mark Antony who changed the name to July in honour of Caesar. Says an old chronicler, "This month he selected for such honorary distinction, when the sun was generally most potent, the more effectually to denote that Julius was the emperor of the world, and therefore the appropriate leader of one half of the world."

   The Anglo-Saxons called July *Hey Monath,* because it was usually the month of the hay harvest. They also sometimes called it *Maed Monath,* because it was the month in which the meads were in bloom.

Birthstones

The carnelian or the ruby are the birthstones for the month of July. Carnelians gave a contented mind and, if worn in a silver ring, ensured many friends and preserved the wearer from losses and harm. The ruby had even greater virtues. Like the bloodstone, it gave courage, and it also prevented impure thoughts, preserved chastity, and killed any poisonous reptile that it touched.

Weather

Now comes July, and with his fervid noon
Unsinews labour. The swinkt mower sleeps;
The weary maid rakes feebly; the warm swain
Pitches his load reluctant; the faint steer,
Lashing his sides, draws sulkily along
The slow encumbered wain in Midday heat.
   Medieval poem

Health

Take heed of great thirst, for nothing bringeth the pestilence or diseases sooner than extreme thirst, and fervent heats, and cold taken suddenly upon them, take no Physick, bleed not but upon violent occasion.
   The Fly Almanac, 1679

1

Births

George Sand (author) 1804;
Genevieve Bujold (actress) 1942.

Deaths

Chevalier de la Barre (heretic) 1765;
Dyce Sombre (Indian price) 1851;
Allan Pinkerton (detective) 1884.

A Heretic Dies, 1765

On July, 1765, the nineteen-year-old
Chevalier de la Barre was decapitated
and then burned at Abbeville, France,
for the crime of having defaced a
statue of Christ that stood on a bridge
in that same town.

The Battle of Gettysburg, 1863

The most important and hotly contested battle of the Civil
War began at Gettysburg, Pennsylvania today in 1863. The
defeat of the Confederates under General Lee by the
federal forces under Meade marked the turning point in
the war.

Ass Baiting Abhored, 1783

"I am profess'd Enemy to Persecution of all kinds,
whether against Man or Beast; though I am not so much a
Pythagorean as to extend my philosophy to those
creatures, which are design'd for our food and
nourishment; but we ought to make the manner of their
Deaths as easy to them as possible, and not destroy or
torment them out of Wantoness. Upon this principle I
abhor Cockfighting, and throwing at Cocks, as well as
Bull-baiting, Bear-baiting, and Ass-baiting."
   An English critic of blood sports, 1783

Postage Stamps for Sale, 1847

On July 1, 1847, postage stamps were put on sale in New
York. Two values were available—a 5¢ issue with a
picture of Benjamin Franklin and a 10¢ issue with a
picture of George Washington.

A Mad Escapader Dies, 1851

There died today in 1851 at his apartments in Davis Street,
London, Dyce Sombre, the son of an Indian princess of
great wealth; his mad, freakish escapades had led to
frequent appearances in English law-courts.

Death and Taxes, 1862

On July 1, 1862, the U.S. Congress
enacted the International Revenue
Law, which levied a tax on practically
everything outside of the grave; the
money was needed for the war effort.

Dominion Day in Canada

Today is Dominion Day in Canada,
observing the Canadian
confederation under the British
North America Act of 1867.

Agrimony in Flowers

Agrimonia eupatoria, or agrimony, is
the flower for July 1.

The Battle of the Boyne, 1690

On Tuesday, July 1, 1690, the revolution in England was
completed and Protestant rule confirmed in England by
the defeat of James II at the Battle of the Boyne, on the
banks of the Boyne River about twenty miles north of
Dublin. The deposed James fled to France and the victor
assumed the throne as William III.

A Detective Dies, 1884

Allan Pinkerton, founder of the Pinkerton National
Detective Agency, died today in 1884. He established a
private detective agency that had considerable success in
solving train and express-company robberies in the U.S.
In 1861, he foiled a plot to assassinate Lincoln on his way
to his inauguration, and in the Civil War, organised and
directed an espionage system behind Confederate lines.

2
JULY

Births

Thomas Cranmer (archbishop) 1489; Christopher Willibald von Gluck (composer) 1714.

Deaths

Michel de Nostradamus (prophet) 1556; Samuel Richardson (writer) 1761; Dionysius Diderot (writer) 1784; Emile Coué (psychologist) 1926; Ernest Hemingway (writer) 1961.

Passions Moved by Virtue

Samuel Richardson, who died on this day in 1761, was an eminent English printer and inventor of a new species of moral romance. Dr. Johnson styled him "an author from whom the age has received great favours, who has enlarged the knowledge of human nature and taught the passions to move at the control of virtue."

An Explosion in the Air

On July 2, 1912, the dirigible *Alcron* exploded 2,000 feet over Atlantic City, killing the builder and a crew of four.

The Ultimate Prediction

Among the many accurate predictions of Nostradamus, the French astrologist who was a favourite of Catherine de Medici and personal physician to King Charles IX of France, was his own death on this day in 1556.

Better Every Day

"Every day and in every way I am becoming better and better." So said the French psychologist and thinker Emile Coué whose days ended on this one in 1926.

Lord Nelson's Coat and Vest

Today in 1845 the undress uniform coat and vest that Lord Nelson wore at the battle of Trafalgar was discovered in private hands by Sir Harry Nichols. Prince Albert caused them to be purchased in his name for £150.

President Garfield is Shot

At 9:00 a.m. on July 2, 1881 President Garfield and Mr Blaine, secretary of state, were entering the railway station at Washington when a man named Charles Guiteau, a lawyer in Chicago and a disappointed office-seeker, fired two shots at the president wounding him in the arm and hip. The president fought for his life for two months but died in September.

An Explosion in the Senate

On July 2, 1915 Erich Muenter, alias Frank Holt, a German teacher at Cornell University, planted a bomb that exploded in the U.S. Senate reception room. The next day he shot and wounded J.P. Morgan who was handling the British government's war contracts. Muenter later committed suicide in prison.

Staircase Wit

There died today in 1784, near Paris, Dionysius Diderot, a celebrated French poet and one of the chief writers of the *Dictionnaire Encyclopédique*, a book containing invaluable information in every department of physical science. Among his profundities was *L'esprit de l'escalier* or staircase wit: the good retort thought of after the conversation is finished.

Passion Moved by Patriotism

A speech by Garibaldi while beseiged in Rome with his men, today in 1849: "I offer neither pay, nor quarters, nor food; I offer only hunger, thirst, forced marches, battles and death. Let him who loves his country with his heart, and not merely with his lips, follow me."

A Saying is Born

On the second of July, 1744, a great-great-great-grandson was born, through a long chain of daughters, to an eighty-nine-year-old Mrs Wainright in England. The event is thought to have originated the words of an old saying, "Rise, daughter, go to thy daughter; for thy daughter's daughter has a son."

3
JULY

Births

Louis XI (French king) 1423; George Saunders (actor) 1906; Stavros Niarchos (shipping magnate) 1909.

Deaths

St Phocas (martyr) 303; Dolly Pentreath (Cornish lady) 1778; Mohammed V (Turkish sultan) 1918.

Ungrateful Guests

On July 3 in the year 303 in Rome, executioners were dispatched with an order to kill a man called Phocas on the spot wherever they should find him. Unknown to them, they stopped at Phocas' house for refreshments. Phocas received them with his usual hospitality, and having been told of their mission, he told the executioners that he was the man for whom they were searching. After recovering from their surprise, they struck off his head.

Reduced to Penury

On July 3, 1751, William Dellicot an Englishman, was convicted of the theft of a penny, for which crime he was forced to forfeit his whole fortune of 200 pounds.

A Bleeding Image

On this day in 1518 a drunken soldier came out of a tavern in La Rue aux Ours in Paris. He had just lost his money and his clothes gambling, and being in an offensive mood, struck the image of the Virgin Mary that stood in the street. The tale says that thereupon the image started to bleed profusely. The soldier was seized, tortured, and burned for his sacrilege; the holy image was taken to Rome; and for many years after Parisians celebrated the event by carrying a dummy of the soldier through the street in procession and then setting it afire.

A Dog Day Poem

To Dog-days now warn people to take heed,
To deal with whores, lest the pox they speed,
But some of their reason's with lust so tainted
They neither fear the whole that is poxt nor painted.
*Poor Robin's Almanac,*1683

Today's Flower

The common mallow *(Malva sylvestris)* bears seed pods often eaten by children in olden times. These "cheeses" had an insipid flavour but were not unwholesome.

Fevers, Hysterics, and Frenzies

In Roman times, Sirius, or Canicula, the Dog Star, rose in conjunction with the sun each year beginning on July 3, and continued to do so until August 11. The days in between were under the influence of the star, and were known as the *Dog Days.* They fell during the worst heat of the summer.

According to Hippocrates and Pliny, today when the Dog Star first rises in the morning, the sea boils, wines sour, bile increases, dogs grow mad, other animals grow languid, and men are prey to fevers, hysterics, and frenzies. The Romans annually sacrificed a brown dog to Canicula to appease his rage.

A Death in Mousehole

Today in 1778 in the village of Mousehole in Cornwall, England, Dolly Pentreath aged 102 died. She was the last fluent and native speaker of the Cornish language. Her epitaph reads in part:

Coth Doll Pentreath eans ha dean,
Marow ha kledyz ed Paul pleu.
(Old Doll Pentreath, one hundred aged and two,
Deceased, and buried in Paul parish too).

Today's Quiz

On July 3, 1839 the Academy of Sciences at Paris met to examine a young Sicilian boy, Vito Mangiamele, who was a prodigy of mental arithmetic. The examiners asked what number it was that if its cube was added to five times its square, and then forty-two times the number plus forty subtracted from the result, the answer would be zero. Vito answered correctly as the question was being repeated for clarity. (The number is five.)

Births

Calvin Coolidge (13th U.S. president) 1872; Louis Armstrong (musician) 1900; Meyer Lansky (mobster) 1902; Abigail Van Buren (columnist) 1918.

Deaths

John Adams (2nd U.S. president) 1826; Thomas Jefferson (3rd U.S. president) 1826, James Monroe (5th U.S. president) 1831.

The Declaration of Independence, 1776

"We hold these truths to be self evident, that all men are created equal, that they are endowed by their creator with certain unalterable rights, that among these are life, liberty and the pursuit of happiness. That to secure these rights, Governments are instituted among men, deriving their just powers from the consent of the governed."

From the document signed at the Continental Congress, Philadelphia, 1776, which asserted the independence of the thirteen American colonies, separated them from England, and made them the United States

Independence Day, USA, 1826

July 4, 1826, had a touch of solemnity to it. It was the semicentennial of the Declaration of Independence, but the festivities were marred by the deaths on that day of both Thomas Jefferson and John Adams. Jefferson was the third U.S. president, and the chief author of the declaration; Adams was the second president, and its chief advocate.

America in a Half Hour, 1832

On July 4, 1832 the song "America," written on a scrap of paper in half an hour by Dr Samuel Francis Smith, was first performed by Boston school children in the Park Street Church. This original manuscript is now in the Harvard Library.

U.S. and U.K. Together, 1918

Today in 1918, British and American troops went into action together, fighting side by side against the Germans in World War I.

Knockout at Toledo, 1919

On July 4, 1919, Jack Dempsey won the heavyweight championship of the world by a knockout in his bout with Jess Willard at Toledo, Ohio.

New York Celebrates, 1876

Today in 1876 the centenary of the Declaration of American Independence was observed as a day of thanksgiving throughout the U.S. New York was magnificently decorated; there was a torch-light procession in which upwards of 10,000 people participated; and at midnight a monster concert took place in Union Square, with some hundred thousand spectators present.

The Statue of Liberty, 1884

On July 4, 1884 the Statue of Liberty was presented by France to the United States to commemorate the French and American revolutions. The statue was designed by F.A. Bartholdi in the form of a woman with uplifted arm holding a torch. The colossal lady, 152 feet high, was placed at the entrance to New York City harbour.

Washington Monument, 1848

On July 4, 1848 President Polk laid the cornerstone of the Washington Monument.

Hawaii Joins Up, 1960

Hawaii, today in 1960, was admitted to the United States, thus becoming the fiftieth star on the flag.

5
JULY

Births

John Broughton (pugilist) 1704; Cecil Rhodes (statesman) 1853; Henry Cabot Lodge Jr (statesman) 1902.

A Rebel Routed

On July 5, 1685, the duke of Monmouth's rebel army was defeated soundly by royal forces at Sedgemoor in England. The misguided nobleman was captured sleeping in a ditch while in a drunken stupor.

Deaths

Magdalen (Scottish queen) 1537; Ivan VI (Russian czar) 1764; Porfiro Rubirosa (playboy) 1965.

Anxiety Antidotes

Those born today, or anyone suffering from July jitters can seek solace in carrots, parsnip, kale, oats (in the form of oatmeal or bread), parsley, mushrooms, marjoram, caraway seeds, thyme, and nuts of all kinds.

July Jitters

People born today have a tendency to overwork their nervous system. They are inclined to attempt too much mental effort which results in neuritis, nervous tics, and twitching in the face, eyes, and hands. They can expect nervous prostration, insomnia, and paralysis unless preventive measures are taken, particularly at ages fourteen, twenty-three, forty-one, and fifty.

An Extraordinary Explosion

An extraordinary explosion of gas completely wrecked a great part of Percy St and Charlotte St in London, today in 1880. Some workmen were engaged in cutting out the joint of a main pipe, when is some manner the mixture of gas and atmospheric air exploded, killing two men, one of whom was actually blown some distance down the main pipe. A series of explosions followed bursting up the roadway and pavements, smashing railings and areas, and bombarding the houses with stones and granite cubes.

A Religious Rage

Today in the year 1100, Jerusalem was taken by the crusaders after a siege of nearly five weeks. Impelled by a mixture of military and religious rage, they spared no one—attacking garrisons, men, women, and children with equal ferocity. Up to 10,000 people were butchered in cold blood by those who called themselves Christians.

A Pugilist Poked

John Broughton, who was born on this day in 1704, grew up to be boxing's first recognised champion. He kept a booth for boxing in Tottenham Court Road, London, where he challenged all comers and was the innovator of many of the sport's familiar rules, such as the division of the bout into rounds. Broughton held his title for eighteen years until he was defeated in a grudge match by a butcher who blinded him with a cheap shot to the eyes.

A Royal Romance

In the summer of 1536, James V, the young Scottish monarch, voyaged to France to see the dughter of the Duc de Vendome, with a view to marriage. Instead, he was smitten by Princess Magdalen, the ravishingly beautiful young daughter of King Francis I. According to a Scottish historian of the time, the feeling was mutual: "fra the time she saw him, and spak with him she became so enamoured of him, and loved him so weel, that she would have no man alive to her husband, but he only." Their beautiful love story ended tragically soon, when Magdalen died of fever on this day in 1537.

6
JULY

Births

John Paul Jones (American naval hero) 1747; Maxmilian (Mexican emperor) 1832; Dorothy Kirsten (American opera singer) 1919.

Deaths

Thomas More (English chancellor) 1535; Courvoisier (French statesman) 1840; Andrew Crosse (English experimenter) 1855.

Marriage, 1893

King George V of England to Victoria Mary of Teck.

Crowning, 1483

Richard III and Anne, crowned king and queen of England.

Matters Come to a Head

Sir Thomas More, the chancellor of England, was beheaded on July 6, 1535 by Henry VIII for his refusal to sanction the king's marriage to Anne Boleyn. His head was stuck on a pole on London Bridge, which dismayed his eldest daughter Margaret. One day, as she was passing the bridge in a boat, and looking on the head she began to lament: "That head has lain many a time in my lap, would to God it would fall into my lap as I pass under." Whereupon the head did just that. The skull still remains in her vault in St Dunstan's Church in Canterbury.

A Brief Struggle

The French statesman Courvoisier was hung in Paris on July 6, 1840. His appearance upon the scaffold was the signal for a shout of execration from the thousands assembled below, but he appeared totally unmoved, and stood firmly while the executioner fastened the noose. He died after a brief struggle.

Flies in the Ointment

Andrew Crosse, an amateur electrical experimenter, died on this day in 1855 after having raised storms of controversy with one of his experiments. Each time he passed a current through a solution of potassium silicate tiny little insects would grow in the liquid. As many times as he tried the experiment he got the same results. Unfortunately, in the middle of the nineteenth century biology was not advanced enough to take the results seriously, and Crosse became the butt of scientific derision.

A Needle Versus a Mad Dog

Today in 1885, the French bacteriologist, Louis Pasteur, for the first time inoculated a human being, a boy badly bitten by a mad dog. The boy survived to become superintendent of the Pasteur Institute in Paris.

Dynamite Versus Pinkertons

On July 6, 1892, a labour riot broke out at the Carnegie Steel Works at Homestead, Pennsylvania. Three hundred Pinkerton men, trying to land barges at the works, were met by armed strikers and in the ensuing fight eleven strikers and nine detectives were killed and many were wounded. Cannon and dynamite were used by the strikers, the Pinkertons were forced to surrender, and the barges they came on were looted and burned.

A Religious Reconciliation.

Today in 1439 the pope and the emperor of Constantinople signed a document in Florence which united the Latin and Greek churches after a 600-year difference of opinion.

7

JULY

Births

Marc Chagall (artist) 1887; Andrei Gromyko (Russian statesman) 1909; Ezzard Charles (boxer) 1921.

A Group Execution, 1865

Six suspected conspirators, among them Messrs Payne, Asteroth, and Harrold and Mrs Mary Eugenia Surratt, were hanged in Washington on July 7, 1865, in connection with the assassination of Abraham Lincoln.

A Fiery Exit, 715

Today in 715, *Romulus* the legendary founder of Rome and one of the twin sons of Mars and the vestal Rhea Silvia who were suckled by a she-wolf, disappeared dramatically in a chariot of fire as he reviewed his people in Rome.

A Roman Girl's Feast

The *Caprotina* was a Roman holiday held in honour of Philotis, a servant girl who saved the city from destruction. After the seige of Rome by the Gauls, it was attacked by the Fidenates under Lucius Posthumius. The attackers demanded all the wives and daughters of the city as the price of peace. Philotis suggested that all the slave girls be dressed as matrons and sent out to the beseigers; she herself marched at their lead. After the Fidenates had feasted over their victory and were asleep or drunk, she gave the signal that brought the Roman armies out of the city and down upon the unsuspecting heads of the attackers. At the annual feast held in Philotis' honour, only women officiated.

A Clever Disguise, 1553

In 1553, Mary Tudor was being pursued by the duke of Northumberland who had plans to imprison her. She hid in Sawston Hall, home of the Huddlestone's, on July 7 then fled dressed as a milkmaid just as the duke's men moved in. They burned down the house in spite. The Huddlestone's had their home rebuilt by Mary when she became queen and her portrait was hung in the hall. It is said her ghost still visits the house and garden.

Deaths

Edward I (English king) 1307; Arthur Conan Doyle (creator of Sherlock Holmes) 1930; six americans (conspirators) 1865.

God Save the King, 1607

The British National anthem, "God Save the King," written by Ben Jonson and composed by Dr Bull was first sung in Merchant Taylor's hall in London today in 1607.

Today's Flower

The traveller's joy *(Clematis vitalba)* is the whiteflowered or wild virgin's bower; it derived its name from among the religious orders, who were our first botanists, and who in the sacred retirement of their abbey gardens, cultivated both botany and popular medicine before systematic botanists rendered the former science intricate, and academical physicians had made the latter a trade instead of a perpetual act of charity.

Catholic Annal, 1830

A U.S. Lady Canonised, 1946

On July 7, 1946, Mother Frances Xavier Cabrini was canonised by Pope Pius XII, the first United States citizen to be made a saint.

Births

Jean de la Fontaine (fable writer) 1621; John D. Rockefeller (oil magnate) 1839; Nelson A. Rockefeller (politician) 1908.

Deaths

Peter (the Hermit) 1115; Edward (the Black Prince) 1376; Percy Bysshe Shelley (poet) 1822.

A Crack in the Liberty Bell

The Liberty Bell, first hung in 1753 in Independence Hall, Philadelphia, bore the inscription, "Proclaim Liberty throughout all the Land unto all the inhabitants thereof." It was hidden during the British occupation of Philadelphia in 1777-78 and was later brought back. Today in 1835 a crack appeared in this symbol of U.S. freedom.

A Speedy Cyclist

Today in 1880 the fifty-mile Amateur Bicycling Championship was won at Stamford Bridge, Walham Green, England by Mr H.L. Corits, in two hours fifty-six minutes and eleven seconds.

A Wine-Drinking Elephant

On July 8 in 1629 the king of Spain sent King Charles I of England a gift of an elephant and five camels. Written instructions for the care of the beasts read in part: "The camels are to be daily grazed in the park, but brought back at night, with all possible precautions to screen them from the vulgar gaze." The elephant "from April unto September, he must have a gallon of wine the daye."

A Dearth of Respectable Persons

The adoption of the Declaration of Independence was celebrated by the people of Philadelphia on this day in 1776. A mass meeting was held in Independence Square where the document was read to a great crowd of people. Charles Biddle, in his autobiography, said, "I was in the old State House Yard when the Declaration of Independence was read. There were few respectable persons present." Mrs Deborah Logan, who lived in a house facing the square on the east, wrote that "the first audience of the Declaration was neither very numerous nor composed of the most respectable class of citizens."

A Royal Art Investor

Today in 1643 King Charles I of England sent an agent to a sale of paintings by the artist Bartolomeo della Stone in Venice with instructions to purchase works of art on his behalf.

The First U.S. Passport

On July 8, 1796, Francis Barre, being "a citizen having occasion to pass into foreign countries about his lawful affairs" obtained the first passport issued by the Passport Division of the U.S. State Department.

The First Lady at Yale

On July 8, 1891 Miss Irene Coit, of Norwich, Connecticut, was notified that she would be admitted to Yale—the first time the University granted a Certificate of Admission to a woman.

A Hungry Stomach has no Ears

Jean de la Fontaine, the French poet and writer of fables who was born on July 8, 1621 left several profundities for posterity: "The stronger man's argument is always the best." "This fellow did not see further than his own nose." "Help yourself and heaven will help you." "What God does, He does well." "A hungry stomach has no ears."

9 JULY

Births

Anne Radcliffe (novelist) 1764; Edward Heath (British prime minister) 1916.

Deaths

Vincent de Groof (flying man) 1874; Zachary Taylor (12th U.S. president) 1850.

The Voyage of Vasco de Gama

On July 9, 1497 Vasco de Gama, the famous Portuguese admiral, sailed from Lisbon on his voyage to the East Indies by way of the Cape of Good Hope, to begin the most difficult as well as the longest voyage that had ever been made in the history of navigation. He returned two years, two months, and five days later in 1499. The discovery of a passage to the east by the Cape of Good Hope was one of the most important events in modern history, diverting the tide of eastern commerce from the Italian states to the more northern parts of Europe, bringing about the decline of Venice from her commerical and maritime grandeur.

The Significance of Number 9

Today's number has special significance in numerology. On the 9th day it was the custom of the ancients to bury their dead. It was at the 9th hour that Christ died on the cross. The Romans held a feast in memory of the dead every 9th year. Hebrew writings teach that God has descended nine times to earth and both the first and second temples of the Jews were destroyed on the 9th day of the Jewish month called Ab. In Freemasonry there is an Order of Nine Elected Knights which uses 9 roses, 9 lights, and 9 knocks.

The Fashions of the 17th Century

A dramatic pastoral, entitled *Rhodon and Iris*, opened today in 1631, in Norwich, England. A part of the performance featured the fashions of ladies of that period:

Chains, coronets, pendants, bracelets and earrings;
Pins, girdles, spangles, embroideries and rings;
Shadows, rebatoes, ribbands, ruffs, cuffs, falls,
Scarfs, feathers, fans, masks, muffs, laces, curls,
Thin tiffanies, cobweb lawn and farthingales,
Sweet falls, veils, wimples, glasses, crisping-pins,
Pots of ointment, combs with poking sticks and bodkins,
Coifs, gorgets, fringes, rolls, fillets and hair laces.

The Flying Man Falls

A Belgian, Vincent de Groof, known as the "Flying Man," while attempting to descend by a newly invented parachute from a balloon, fell suddenly to the ground from a height of eighty feet and died within a few seconds of being found. De Groof appeared to have over-balanced himself falling forwards clinging to the ropes; the apparatus, instead of inflating with the pressure of the air, collapsed and fell with great violence to the street below (1874).

The Goat Mother

Today in 1812 the British frigate *Swallow* was engaged in battle with a French vessel near Majorca. One of the sailors named Phelan had his wife and infant son Tommy on board. Both the parents were killed and buried at sea. Little Tommy, only three weeks old, was then placed in the company of a female Maltese goat belonging to the captain. The goat became accustomed to the child and would lie down voluntarily to suckle him. Under the care of his goat mother, Tommy prospered and grew up to become a sailor.

The Flower of the Day

Today's flower is the carnation (*Dianthus carsophyllus*) or clove gilliflower.

The curious choice Clove July flower,
Whose kinds light the Carnation,
For sweetness of most sovereign power
Shall help my wreath to fashion;
Whose sundry colours of one kind,
First from one root derived;
Them in their several suits I'll bind,
My garland so contrived.
Michael Drayton (1563-1631)

Births

James McNeill Whistler (artist) 1834; Marcel Proust (author) 1871; David Brinkley (broadcaster) 1920.

A Falling Down of London Bridge

Today in 1220 a dreadful fire consumed London Bridge and parts of the city at each end of it. The disaster caused the bridge to collapse and 3,000 persons to perish in the flames.

Deaths

Hadrian (Roman emperor) 138; Benedict VII (pope) 938; Benedict VIII (pope) 1024.

Burial

Today in 1958 Robert Earl Hughes was buried in a coffin the size of a piano crate in Benville Cemetery, Illinois. He weighed *1,069 lbs,* according to the *Guinness Book of Records*—the highest undisputed weight for a human remains.

A Secret Beneath a Beard

The death of the emperor Hadrian after a reign of twenty-one years occurred today in 138. He built the fortification known as Hadrian's wall extending from Newcastle to Carlisle, and first adopted an imperial beard to conceal the warts upon his face.

An Alcoholic Seizure

On July 10, 1930 the U.S. Prohibition Bureau reported having arrested 68,186 people and seizing 17,146 stills in the previous 12 months.

A Pot of Paint in the Public's Face

The painter James McNeill Whistler was born today in 1834 in Lowell, Massachusetts but lived most of his life in London where his work was not always appreciated by the art critics. In 1877 John Ruskin made the following disparaging remarks: "I have seen and heard much of the cockney impudence, but never expected to hear a coxcomb ask two hundred guineas for flinging a pot of paint in the public's face." Whistler sued him for damages and obtained a verdict of one farthing which he then wore as a charm on his watch chain.

Life in a Corked Bedroom

Marcel Proust, born on July 10, 1871 was one of the greatest French writers of the twentieth century. On the death of his mother in 1905, he retreated to his cork-lined bedroom, from which he rarely ever ventured again until his death in 1922. During his seclusion he composed his vast semi-autobiographical novel, *La Recherche de Temps Perdu.*

Black Phantom

Whiddon Park Guest House in Chagford, Devon, England was visited by a young woman, dressed in black, who stood at a doorway, smiled, then vanished, on July 10, 1971. It was thought that the phantom, which had been seen before, was Mary Whiddon, who was shot by a jealous lover over 300 years earlier, as she stood at the alter of Chagford Church.

Death Valley Record

On July 10, 1913 in Death Valley, California, the thermometer registered 134 degrees Fahrenheit, the highest temperature ever recorded in the United States.

A Speech in Ireland

In a speech today in 1790, the Irish judge, John Philpot Curran, said: "The condition upon which God hathe given liberty to men is eternal vigilance."

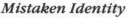

Forgotten Lines

The eighteenth-century comedian Charles Macklin had a remarkable professional longevity. It was in 1790, at the age of one hundred years, that he made his final appearance on the stage, playing for the last time his famous role of Shylock. But on that occasion his memory failed him, and with great grace and solemnity he came forward in the second act and apologised to the audience. He never acted again, but lived another seven years and died on July 11, 1797.

Proverb

Prepare yourselves, Harvest cometh on;
The field's the staff we all rely upon.
For King and People from the field are fed,
And poor folk thence expect their welcome bread.

Violent Politics

On July 11, 1804, U.S. Vice-President Aarón Burr challenged Alexander Hamilton, the secretary of the Treasury, to a duel over Hamilton's supposed interference in Burr's election to the governorship of New York. Hamilton appeared at the duel but refused to fire. Burr deliberately fired and his shot entered Hamilton's side, his pistol going off involuntarily as he fell to the ground. Thus ended the life of a statesman who's political philosophy is still admired. When on a writing spree he would go to bed, regardless of the time of day, sleep for six hours, then arise, drink strong coffee, and write steadily for up to eight hours.

Iron Swimming Pools

A floating structure of iron containing a large covered swimming bath moored in the River Thames just above Charing Cross was opened for use today in 1875, the first of a species of floating baths along the course of the river. The supply of water, obtained from the river and let in by suitable cocks, passed through a filtering apparatus which completely removed all mud and other matter but allowed the water to retain its natural salts and soft refreshing qualities. The charge for admission was one shilling.

Births

John Quincy Adams (6th U.S. president) 1767; Yul Brynner (actor) 1920.

Deaths

Charles Macklin (comedian) 1797; Alexander Hamilton (U.S. statesman) 1804.

Mistaken Identity

On July 11, 1892 the U.S. Patent Office decided that J.W. Swan and not Thomas A. Edison was the inventor of the electric-light carbon for the incandescent lamp.

War and Peace on July 11

1302: The Flemish infantry defeated the French Cavalry in the *Battle of the Spurs*.

1718: The English fleet defeated its Spanish counterpart at Messina.

1814: British troops captured Eastport, Maine from the Americans.

1859: French-Austrian accord over Italy was reached with the signing of the *Treaty of Villafranca*.

1869: "Buffalo Bill" and the U.S. Cavalry surprised the Indians at Summit Spring, Nebraska.

1877: The *Battle of the Clearwater* in the Nez Percé War began.

1915: The German cruiser *Konigsberg* was sunk by the British in the Rufiji River.

1916: The *Second Battle of the Somme* began.

1936: Hitler signed a treaty guaranteeing Austria's frontier.

1942: Allied bombers raided Danzig and Flensburg.

1943: Allied forces took ten towns in the invasion of Sicily.

12
JULY

Births

Julius Caesar (emperor) 100 B.C;
Henry David Thoreau (writer) 1817;
Oscar Hammerstein II (composer)
1895.

Deaths

Desiderius Erasmus (scholar) 1536;
Dolly Madison (wife of the 4th U.S
president) 1849.

Today's Riot

On July 12, 1871 during an
Orangemen's Parade, rioting broke
out between Protestant and Catholic
Irish factions in New York, resulting
in over 100 people being killed and
many wounded.

Lady Pentweazle's Hairdo

On July 12, 1776 Samuel Foote
appeared before the king and queen
at Haymarket theatre in London in
the role of Lady Pentweazle, wearing
a huge head-dress that mocked the
women's style of the day. It was built
up of feathers, hair, and wool, and
measured over a yard wide. The
fashionable head-dresses of the 18th
century were remarkably elaborate. A
lofty pad or cushion was placed on
the lady's head and her hair was
combed up over it. Frequently the
tower was bedizened in an incredible
manner and became a mountain of
wool, hair, powder, muslin, lawn, net,
lace, gauze, flowers, feathers and
wire.

Dolly Madison's Successes

Dolly Madison, wife of James Madison, the 4th president
of the United States, died on this day in 1849. She was
noted for the magnificence of her entertaining, as well as
for her charm, tact, and grace. When President Jefferson
made Madison secretary of state in 1802, she was invited
to act as hostess at White House social affairs, as Jefferson
was a widower. When her husband was inaugurated in
1809, she became mistress of the White House in her own
right, and leader of the social life of the capital. When the
British invaded the city in 1814, she saved many state
papers from the White House, as well as a portrait of
Washington.

Today's Number

The number 12 is symbolic of suffering and anxiety and
often foreshadows one being sacrificed for the plans or
intrigues of others. People born on this day have a
tendency to suffer from an overworked nervous system
and are inclined to have severe attacks of neuritis and
sciatica and assorted skin troubles.

Julius Caesar's Record

Julius Caesar was born today in 100 B.C. The philosopher
Pliny observed that he used his eyes to read, his ears to
listen, his hand to write, and his mind to dictate. When he
wasn't thus engaged Julius Caesar was at war. During his
lifetime he is said to have conquered 300 nations, taken
800 cities, and defeated three million men, one-third of
whom died in battles against him.

Thoreau on Owls

Henry David Thoreau, the celebrated American writer,
philosopher, and nationalist, was born on July 11, 1817.
He once said: "I rejoice that there are owls. Let them do
the idiotic and maniacal hooting for men. It is a sound
admirably suited to swamps and twilit woods which no
day illustrates, suggesting a vast and undeveloped nature
which men have not recognised. They represent the stark
twilight and unsatisfied thoughts which all have."

13
JULY

Births

Clement x (pope) 1590; Ferdinand III (Roman emperor) 1608; Bosley Crowther (critic) 1905.

A French Celebration

The French celebrated the eve of the fall of the Bastille on this day. Singing and rejoicing accompanied a dramatic procession that passed through the darkened streets of Paris. Lanterns, torches, bands, and patriotic songs stirred the hearts as the marchers wended their way to the home of a prominent citizen who would provide drinks for all the torch bearers.

Deaths

Bertrand de Guesclin (French statesman) 1380; Jean-Paul Marat (French revolutionary) 1793; Billy the Kid (American outlaw) 1881.

An English Storm

A terrible thunderstorm broke over Manchester and Salford in England on this afternoon in 1880, and a house in Bridge Street, which was struck by lightning, fell in ruins into the river Irwell. Three persons were killed, Thomas Fildes, a hairdresser, Ebenezer Way, a grocer, and Annie Jones, who assisted her uncle, a tobacconist, whose shop was part of the building that fell.

An American Riot

On July 13, 1863, a large mob attacked and set fire to an orphan asylum in New York that was providing shelter for several hundred orphans. Their action was to protest the draft legislation that would permit drafted men to avoid service on payment of $300. At the end of four days rioting about 1,000 people had been killed.

Go West Young Man

Today in 1865 Horace Greeley, a newspaper editor and founder of the *New York Tribune*, said: "Go West, young man, go West," a phrase he had borrowed from the *Terre Haute Express* in Indiana. Thousands acted on his advice.

The Worst Boy in the World

Bertrand de Guesclin was the flower of French chivalry of the fourteenth century, and rose eventually to become the constable of France. He came of a noble but poor family. "Never was there so bad a boy in the world," said his mother. "He is always wounded, his face disfigured, fighting or being fought; his father and I wish he were peaceably underground." When the young Bertrand was only fourteen, wearing borrowed armour and riding a borrowed horse, he defeated fifteen knights in a row at jousting. He only desisted when it came time to ride against his father. De Guesclin died on July 13, 1380, and was buried at the foot of the king's tomb at St Denis.

A Bathtub Murder

When the French revolution began in 1789 Jean-Paul Marat founded *L'Ami du peuple,* in which he vented his hatred and suspicion of all who were in power. Outlawed, he published his paper from various hiding places. While hiding in the sewers of Paris, he contracted a skin disease that necessitated treatments in a warm bath. On this day in 1793, he was stabbed to death in his bath by Charlotte Corday, who thought he was acting as the evil genius of France. Prior to her execution for the crime her last words were: "Tis guilt makes shame and not the scaffold."

Births

Irving Stone (author) 1903; Ingmar Bergman (film maker) 1918; Arthur Laurents (playwright) 1920.

Deaths

Lady Duff Gordon (writer) 1869; Alfred Krupp (German industrialist) 1887; Adlai Stevenson (U.S. statesman) 1965.

A Storming, 1789

The Bastille of Paris, the great state prison of France, was stormed and destroyed by the populace on July 14, 1789. The Bastille was composed of eight strong stone towers and surrounded by a moat 120 yards wide. Thirteen cannons on its summit were its defence. Its dungeons and cages were infamous, and the fortress had long been a symbol of despotic royal power. Its fall marked the beginning of the French Revolution, and according to some historians, the beginning of the modern era. The diary entry by King Louis XVI for July 14, 1789 consisted of a single word: "Rien" (nothing).

A Horsewhipping, 1837

On July 14, 1837 a horse thief was whipped publicly outside the court house at Providence, Rhode Island. The law authorising whipping was abolished shortly afterwards.

A Coup d'Etat, 1958

In a swift coup d'etat, the Iraqi army seized control of Baghdad and proclaimed a republic, killing King Feisal II and Crown Prince Abdul Illah on this day in 1958.

A Separation, 1531

King Henry VIII of England and his queen, Catherine of Aragon, parted for the last time on July 14, 1531. Henry later divorced her on the grounds that her previous marriage to his brother Arthur, Prince of Wales, made her marriage to him invalid.

An Eclipse, 1748

Today in 1748 at 9:00 a.m. a solar eclipse began, lasting until nine minutes after 12:00. During that time, the planet Venus made a beautiful appearance through telescopes in the form of a crescent or new moon.

A Refusal, 1776

On July 14, 1776 George Washington refused to receive a letter from the British Admiral Lord Howe addressed to "George Washington, Esquire." Another letter addressed to "George Washington, etc., etc., etc.," was similarly refused. Finally he accepted one which was correctly addressed to General George Washington.

A Removal, 1894

On July 14, 1894 the chief of police of Bristol, Connecticut, ordered all nickle-in-the-slot machines be removed from the city's cigar shops.

An Explosion, 1737

Today in 1737, when the courts were sitting in Westminister Hall in London, a large brown paper parcel containing fireworks exploded with a fearful din causing confusion and terror in the Hall. As the crackers rattled and burst they threw out balls of printed criticisms of several unpopular, recently passed acts of Parliament. A reward of £200 was offered for the detection of the author of this "wicked and audacious outrage."

15

JULY

Births

Rembrandt van Rijn (artist) 1606;
Errol Garner (jazz musician) 1921;
Julian Bream (classical guitarist) 1933.

Deaths

Mrs Kirkeen (housewife) 1743; Carlo
Farinelli (male soprano) 1782;
Winthrop Mackworth Praed (comic
poet) 1839.

Marriage

On July 15, 1773, in Blackpool,
Ireland, Mr William Riordan, aged
seventy-four was wed to Miss
Murrough of Mallow, aged fifteen.

Mr Praed's Comic Poems

Winthrop Mackworth Praed, an
English poet who specialised in
light-hearted verse, died on July 15,
1839. In an epic poem, "The Belle of
the Ball," he described a youthful
love affair:

Our love was like most other loves—
A little glow, a little shiver;
A rosebud and a pair of gloves,
And hanky panky by the river;
Some jealousy of someone's heir;
Some hopes of dying broken-hearted;
A miniature; a lock of hair;
The usual rows; and then we parted.

St Swithin's Weather Forecast

In this month is St Swithin's day,
On which, if that it rain, they say,
Full forty days after it will,
Or more or less, some rain distil.
Poor Robins Almanac, 1697

New Orleans' Cuisine

"And if the stomach is the centre and
origin of civilisation as some astute
philosophers maintain, the French
element of progress is still in the
ascendency here."
From *Every Saturday*, a New Orleans
magazine, July 15, 1871

Mrs Kirkeen's Third Passing

On July 15, 1743, Mrs Kirkeen of Dublin finally died in
earnest. Twice before she had been readied for burial
when, much to the apparent disappointment of Mr
Kirkeen, she awoke. When she seemed to pass away for
the third time her loving husband had her nailed in the
coffin and quickly buried to avoid further inconvenience.

Carlo Farinelli's Rich Voice

Carlo Farinelli, Italian male soprano, died on this day in
1782. He won fame in France and Italy and, in 1737,
became official singer to Philip V of Spain, and renounced
his public career. His sole duty was to sing the same four
songs each night to the king, from whom he received an
astronomical fee.

St Swithin's Day

Today is St Swithin's Day for some people. Noted for his
humility, St Swithin, the bishop of Winchester in England
had requested to be buried in the churchyard instead of
within the church. He died in 862, but some years later,
after he was canonised, the monks felt it improper that
the remains should lie out under the sky. They set July 15,
891 for their removal to the church, but on the appointed
day it rained torrentially, and continued to do so for forty
days until the decision was made to leave the remains
where they were and to build a chapel over his grave.

Prittlewell Fair

On July 15, 1826 Jonas Asplin, M.D. wrote a description of
a fair given in his town, Prittlewell in Essex, England.
"Morning very fine. Arranged the stalls in front of my
house. The fair is a very decent one. An exhibition on our
right of a Giant, Giantess, an Albiness, a native of Baffins
Bay, and a Dwarf—very respectable."

16
JULY

Births

Carneades (philosopher) 217 B.C., Sir Joshua Reynolds (painter) 1723; Mary Baker Eddy (religious leader) 1821.

Deaths

Anne Askew (religious martyr) 1546; Czar Nicholas II and family (Russian royalty) 1918.

Today's Epitaph

To the memory of
Emma and Maria Littleboy
The twin children of George and
  Emma Littleboy
of Hornsey who died 16th July 1837
Two Littleboys lie here, yet strange to
  say,
the little boys are girls.
  Found on a stone in Hornsey, England

First Day in Islam

Day one of the Islamic calendar was July 16, 622, the day that Mohammed fled from Mecca to Medina. The anniversary of the day in Islamic reckoning is known as the *Hejira*, from the Arabic word for "flight."

Immolation Day in Greece

In a festival held annually on this day in Rhodes, the ancient Greeks sacrificed a condemned criminal on the alter of Saturn by setting him alight.

Pigeon Defeats Train

Today in 1877 a race was held from Dover to London between the Continental Mail Express train and a carrier pigeon conveying a document of an urgent nature from the French police. The distance, as the pigeon flies, between Dover and London is seventy miles; by rail a little over seventy-six. When the train came into Cannon Street Station the bird had already been at its "home" almost twenty minutes.

A Reglious Lady's Birth

Mary Baker Eddy, the founder of the Christian Science Church, was born on this day in 1821. Her third husband, Asa G. Eddy, was one of her disciples. When he died in 1882 from an organic disease of the heart, as shown by an autopsy, she insisted that he had died from "mesmeric poisoning," administered by one of her pupils. She had already advanced the theory that there was such a thing as "malicious animal magnetism" which could be used to injure men and women.

A Religious Lady's Death

Anne Askew, a Protestant lady, was burnt alive in Smithfield, England today in 1546, in her twenty-sixth year after having been first racked with the most savage cruelty in the Tower of London for renouncing the errors of popery. Her accuser was her husband, her judge the Lord Chancellor and her incendiary, the Lord Mayor of London.

A Royal Family's Death

Today in 1918 the royal family of Russia, the Czar Nicholas II, the Czarina Alexandra, their children, and members of their household staff were murdered by Bolsheviks on orders from the Ural Regional Council during the Russian Revolution.

Kissing Banned

On this day in 1439, an act was passed in England that banned kissing in an attempt to prevent the spread of germs during a dreadful time of pestilence which had scoured England and France for two years. The plague had also caused an intermission in the hostilities between the two nations.

17
JULY

Births
Phyllis Diller (comedienne) 1921.

Deaths
St Alexius (confessor) 5th century.

King Charles Crowned, 1492
On July 17, 1492 Charles the VII of France was crowned at the Cathedral of Rheims by Joan of Arc who wore her suit of armour. The crowning was the culmination of her struggle to wrest the crown away from the English and to drive them out of France.

Gold Rush Fever, 1897
On July 17, 1897 the steamship *Portland* arrived in Washington loaded with the first major gold shipment from the Klondike. With news of this, the Klondike gold rush began.

A Secret Saint, 5th Century
St Alexius is a perfect model of the most extreme contempt for the world. The day before his intended marriage he left Rome in disguise, and resided in a hut, embracing extreme poverty. After some time, being discovered to a stranger of distinction, he returned home as a poor pilgrim, and lived unknown in his father's house, bearing the ill treatment of the servants with the greatest patience. A little before he died today in the 5th century he revealed himself by a letter to his parents.

Today's Firsts
1841: The English humour magazine *Punch* was first published.
1850: The first photograph (daguerreotype) of a star was taken.
1861: The first U.S. paper money was issued.
1898: The first Puerto Rican parliament met.
1917: The British royal family first used the name of Windsor.

Elephant Tusks and Lentils, 1885
In the course of certain building operations going on near the Monte Testaccio in Rome, two of the ancient warehouses or granaries used by the Romans for the storage of imports were discovered. One of these was found to be filled with elephants' tusks and the other with lentils.

Today's Balloon
Today in 1862 Mr Glashier made his first scientific ascent from Wolverhampton, England in a new balloon, sixty-nine feet in height, fifty-four feet in diameter, and with a capacity of 95,000 cubic feet of gas. The leading facts being sought were connected with the decrease of temperature and the distribution of water through the atmosphere.

A Speedy Sinking, 1880
At a quarter-past five in the evening today in 1880, five miles off Dungeness, England in a thick fog, the screw steamer *Centurion* and the ship *Hydaspes* bound for Melbourne came into collision. The *Hydaspes* sank in sixteen fathoms of water eleven minutes after she was struck. The passengers and crew were fortunately saved.

A Large Iceberg, 1586
John Davis, a British explorer and seaman, wrote in his journal on this day in 1586, a description of an iceberg: "The 17th of this month, being in the latitude of 63' 8" we fell upon a most mighty and strange quantity of ice, in one entire mass, so big as that we knew not the limits thereof, and being withal so very high, in form of a land, with bays and capes."

Chess Master, 1880
From Wiesbaden, it was announced today in 1880, that in the Chess Congress, Herr Schwartz of Vienna, Herr Englisch of Vienna, and Mr Blackburn of London, had each won eleven games, and divided the first three prizes equally amongst them.

18
JULY

Births

Rudolph II (holy Roman emperor) 1552; Robert Hooke (scientist) 1635: Gilbert White (naturalist) 1720; William Makepeace Thackeray (novelist) 1811; Horatio Alger (author) 1899; Clifford Odets (playwright) 1906; Hume Cronyn (actor) 1911; Red Skelton (comedian) 1913; John Glenn (astronaut) 1921.

Deaths

Francis Petrarch (philospher) 1374; Lydia Becker (suffragette) 1890; Christie Warden (reluctant bride) 1891.

Proverb

A shower of rain in July
When the corn begins to fill,
Is worth a plough of oxen,
And all belongs theretill

Rome Burns Twice

Rome was sacked and burned by Brennus, a Gaul, today in 390 B.C. Part of the capitol was miraculously saved by the cackling of a flock of geese, which warned the inhabitants of the enemy's arrival. In 63 A.D. the city of Rome burned again while the Emperor Nero fiddled.

Cracow Burns Once

On July 18, 1850, a fire in Cracow, Poland, laid waste a large portion of the city.

Today's Flower

The *Chrysanthemum segetum* or yellow ox-eye is named from the Greek *chrusos:* gold, and *anthos:* flower.

Francis Petrarch, 1374

On July 18, 1374 there died at Arqua, near Padua, in the north of Italy, Francis Petrarch, a very learned writer on poetry, history, and moral philosophy, but particularly celebrated for his elevating sonnets, which first exalted Italian poetry to classical fame.

Lydia Becker, 1890

Today in 1890 at Geneva, Switzerland the death occurred of Mrs Lydia Becker, one of the foremost advocates of woman's suffrage and the promoter of various movements to relieve the disabilities of women.

Christie Warden, 1891

On July 18, 1891, when Miss Christie Warden of Hanover, New Hampshire, refused to marry Frank Almy, he shot and killed her.

A Grand Scientific Soirée, 1872

This evening in 1872 a grand scientific soirée was held in the Albert Hall in London when some interesting telegraphic experiments were made. Messages were interchanged between one of the tables in the arena and Teheran as well as with an Indian state from which came the intelligence: "Locusts swarming in Scinde; Sitlej bridge destroyed by floods."

A Violent Shock, 1880

Today in 1880 a violent shock of earthquake visited Manilla in the Philippines, destroying several government buildings and dwelling houses.

Improper Practices, 1838

Today in 1838 the Rev. Gathercole was convicted at York Assizes of publishing in *The Watchman* a libel imputing improper practices to nuns at Darlington and Stockton in England.

Births

Samuel Colt (pistolmaker) 1814;
Edgar Degas (artist) 1843; A.J. Cronin
(author) 1896.

Deaths

Rebecca Nurse (hung) 1692; Madame
Skobeleff (murdered) 1880.

Proverb

A swarm of bees in July
Is not worth a fly

A Woman Hanged, 1692

On July 19, 1692, in Massachusetts,
Rebecca Nurse, a woman of
blameless life, was taken to church in
chains, publicly excommunicated as a
witch, then hanged.

A Swarm of Bees, 1797

On July 19, 1797, Mr Wright of
Norwich, England was out for a quiet
walk in his garden when a swarm of
bees descended from the sky and
completely covered over his head. He
stood stock still for over two hours
while the bees were removed and
put into a hive. He survived the
incident without a sting.

A Play Panned, 1880

This evening in 1880, at the Gaiety Theatre, in London, Mr
John T. Raymond the American comedian, made his first
appearance in England in an American play known in the
U.S. as *The Gilded Age*, and in England as *Colonel Sellers*.
The play was held to be too idiotic for human—or at all
events English—endurance and it was to all intents and
purposes, a failure.

A Woman Murdered, 1880

On July 19, 1880, Madame Skobeleff, the mother of a
distinguished Russian general was murdered by a Russian
captain, Uzatis, and three Montenegrins. She was
travelling for philanthropic purposes and had with her a
sum of 25,000 roubles. The gang was captured, although
Uzatis shot himself in the head. He had been a protégé of
the poor lady, and had been loaded with benefits both by
her and her son.

Women's Rights, 1848

Today in 1848, the first woman's suffrage convention in
the United States was held in the village of Seneca Falls,
New York. It was called by Lucretia Mott, Martha C.
Wright, Elizabeth Cady Stanton, and Mary McClintock. A
Declaration of Sentiments was drafted and signed by a
hundred men and women asserting that woman was the
equal of man, and was entitled to all the rights and
privileges of citizenship, including the right to hold
property, to control her wages, to have a voice in the
management of her children, as well as the right to vote.

A Monkey and Pony, 1842

Today in 1842 a trotting match took place in the grounds
attached to the Rosemary Branch Travern in Hoxton,
England when a grey pony, twelve hands and a half high,
was ridden by one of Mr Batty's monkeys, dressed in
racing costume, and accomplished the distance of
fourteen miles in fifty-seven minutes.

20
JULY

Births

Francis Petrarch (poet) 1304; Max Liebermann (artist) 1847; Sir Edmund Hillary (mountain climber) 1919.

Deaths

Robert II (French king) 1031; Ferdinand I (Rumanian king) 1927; Guglielmo Marconi (wireless inventor) 1937.

Bomb Troubles

Today in 1944 Adolf Hitler was slightly injured by a bomb planted by a group of German officers seeking to assassinate him and end the war.

Chess Capers

Today in 1872 at a chess tournament at the Crystal Palace in London, a novel feature was introduced into the game. Simultaneous and blindfold games were carried on by Herr Zuckertort, a visitor from Berlin who conducted ten games at once without seeing the board.

Moon Message

Astronaut Neil Armstrong uttered his famous words on the moon today in 1969: "That's one small step for man, one giant leap for mankind."

Bee Troubles

On July 20, 1830, Mr Eulert, a Berlin merchant, was travelling with his wife on the road to Wittenberg in a private carriage. Suddenly a swarm of bees appeared, "numerous beyond reckoning," and fell upon the horses, the coachman, and the Eulerts. The three people managed to wrap cloaks about themselves and were not in the end too badly stung. But before Mr Eulert could run and fetch some burning straw to drive the stinging insects away, both horses had lain down, insensible with pain. They died from their stings within twenty-four hours.

Bridge Troubles

As the monks of Waldimar, near Moscow, today in 1851 were setting out in procession to visit an image of the Virgin at a neighbouring village, a wooden bridge thrown over the moat gave way, and out of 200 monks, 158 were drowned.

Sister Ubryk's Troubles

Acting on an anonymous tip today in 1869 a judge visited the convent of the Barefooted Carmelites in Cracow, Poland and found in a filthy cell, seven paces by six paces wide, a half-naked insane woman, known as Sister Barbara Ubryk, who, at the sight of light and people, folded her hands and implored: "I am hungry; have pity on me, give me meat and I shall be obedient." The bishop liberated the wretched creature, placed her under proper care, and censured the nuns for their cruel neglect.

Bulgarian Bombast

Today is St Elijah's Day in Bulgaria. Elijah's is believed to be the hand that sends storms of snow, rain, hail, and thunder as his chariot wheels rumble across the sky. Today it is important to appease his wrath through household rites. It is held that St Elijah was fed by ravens and reached heaven in a chariot of fire.

Goat Troubles

Frank Defatta of Tallulah, Louisiana wouldn't keep his goats from wandering about the neighbourhood. They were in the habit of sleeping on the gallery of Dr J. Ford Hodge's house. Defatta had ignored the doctor's many protests, and on the night of July 19, 1899 the doctor shot one of the goats—whereon Defatta and four others shot and killed the doctor. They were arrested by the sheriff, but taken from him and hanged by a lynch mob.

21
JULY

Births

Francis Parkinson Keyes (author) 1885; Ernest Hemingway (author) 1899; Isaac Stern (violinist) 1920.

Deaths

Robert Burns (poet) 1796; Daniel Lambert (fat man) 1809.

Belgian Independence

Today is National Independence Day in Belgium, commemorating that country's independence and the crowning of Leopold I. In 1830 the nine Belgian provinces were released from rule by the Netherlands and became a state unto themselves.

The First Day of the World

According to ancient Egyptian priests July 21 was the day of the world's creation. After six thousand years, today would also be the day of its destruction.

Six thousand years the world shall
    then expire,
By water once and then destroyed by
    fire;
The first two thousand void, the next
    the law,
The last two thousand under the
    Messiah's awe!
    The Perennial Calendar, 17th century

A Sailor's Feat

The small boat, the *New Bredford,* which left America for England on June 2, having on board only the master Mr Craps and his wife, arrived safely in Mount's Bay tonight in 1877. The boat was only twenty feet long and the captain's hand was rendered almost useless from continuous steering.

A Teacher's Trial

Today in 1925 John Scopes was found guilty of teaching evolution in a Dayton, Tennessee public school, contrary to the accepted interpretation of the biblical account of man's creation. The trial was a dramatic one, with Clarence Darrow appearing for the defence, and William Jennings Bryan aiding the state prosecutor. Scopes was later released by the state supreme court on a technicality, with a fine of $100 and costs.

A Poet's Tomb

On July 21, 1796, at Dumfries Scotland, there passed away after a lingering illness brought on by excessive drinking, the poet Robert Burns. In his thirty-eighth year he left a widow and five small children with another on the way. He was buried in a mausoleum at Dumfries.

The First U.S. Train Robbery

Today in 1873 the notorious gang of outlaws led by Jesse James and his brother Frank held up a train of the *Rock Island Express* at Adair, Iowa, and escaped with $3,000.

A Fat Man's Interment

Today in 1809 at Stamford in England Daniel Lambert aged thirty, and weighing 739 pounds, passed away. A wall of his home had to be removed to make passage for his coffin. It was built from 112 feet of elm and placed upon two axle-trees and four clog-wheels on which it was rolled to the graveyard by twelve men. After his funeral a wager was laid that five men could be buttoned into his waistcoat. Seven men actually accomplished the feat.

Mausoleum of Burns, Dumfries

22
JULY

Births

Alexander Calder (sculptor) 1898;
Stephen Vincent Benét (writer) 1898.

Deaths

Mary Magdalen (saint) 1st century;
Cassius Clay (U.S. statesman) 1903;
John Dillinger (criminal) 1934;
Chi-Chi (a giant panda in the London
Zoo) 1972.

Mary's Weather Forecast

If it should rain today, a medieval
tradition stated that Mary Magdalen is
washing her handkerchief in
preparation for the festival or fair
held in honour of her cousin St
James on July 25.

Proverb

Ne'er trust a July sky

Mary Magdalen's Day

After the crucification of Jesus, Mary
Magdalen, Mary Salome, and the
Virgin Mary were said to have set sail
in the Mediterranean to flee
persecution by the Jews. Their boat
sprang a leak but they were
miraculously saved and landed in the
south of Gaul. There the party
separated and Mary Magdalene, "out
of whom went seven devils"
according to Luke, the ex-harlot who
was restored to purity by repentance
and faith, retired to St Beaume. There
she spent the remainder of her days
in prayer until July 22 sometime in
the 1st century, when she died.

Proverb

As July, so the next January

Cassius Marcellus Clay

Cassius Marcellus Clay, American politician and diplomat,
died on this day in 1903. Clay was an unsuccessful
candidate for governor of Kentucky on an anti-slavery
ticket in 1844. In 1845, he established the *True American*,
an abolitionist paper, at Lexington, Kentucky.

Public Enemy Number One

Today in 1934, John Dillinger, escaped bank robber, a
man responsible for sixteen killings, and known as
"Public Enemy Number One" was shot to death in a
Chicago street as he was leaving the Biograph Movie
Theater. Melvin H. Purvis led the twenty-seven FBI agents
who gunned him down.

A Speeding Horse Arrest

Today in 1881 a horse race was staged in Seattle,
Washington, between Tom Clancy and Robert Abrams,
with city authorities clearing the site for them. After the
race, the winner Clancy was arrested for exceeding the
legal speed limit of six miles per hour.

Torn with Indecision

The jury in a case at Limerick, Ireland were locked up in
the usual way until midnight today in 1844 when they
intimated they had come to a decision. When asked to
hand down the issue paper, the foreman with much
hesitation presented a handful of small pieces of paper,
explaining: "My Lord, this is the issue paper. The fact is
the jury quarrelled among themselves, and tore it up in
this manner. I did all I could to save it, but without effect."
The verdict was guilty with a recommendation to mercy,
but the judge said he could pay no attention to a
recommendation from a jury that had conducted itself so
disgracefully.

Strung up by the Thumbs

On July 22, 1892 H.C. Frick of the Carnegie Steel works in
Pennsylvania was shot by striking worker, Berkman,
during a violent strike where non-union workers replaced
the strikers and the state militia had to intervene.
Berkman received a twenty-two-year prison term. When
Private T. Iams called for cheers for the man who shot
H.C. Frick, he was strung up by the thumbs and
dishonourably dismissed from the militia.

23
JULY

Births
Godfrey Olearius (German divine) 1672; Coventry Patmore (English poet) 1823; Haile Selassie (Ethiopian emperor) 1892.

Deaths
Richard Gibson (tiny artist) 1690; Christobella (lively old lady) 1789.

A Lively Old Lady
Christobella, the viscountess of Say and Sele, died on July 23, 1789 in England, at the age of ninety-five. When she was ninety years old, and had already survived three husbands, she used to say that she had married the first for love, the second for money, and the third for rank—and that she had recently had thoughts of beginning again in the same order.

The Number 23
On July 23 the sun enters the constellation of Leo, the lion. In numerology the number 23 is called the *Royal Star of the Lion* and promises success, help from superiors, and protection from those in high places. For those born today, it is a most fortunate number, promising success in all plans. However, these people are often very highly strung, live on their nerves, and appear to crave excitement.

A Tiny Artist
Richard Gibson, drawing master to King Charles I and Queen Anne of England, died today in 1690. His speciality, painting miniatures, was most appropriate, as he was just over three feet tall and also functioned as the court dwarf.

The Invention of the Ice-Cream Cone
Today in 1904, Charles E. Menches of St Louis, Missouri called on a young lady, bearing in one hand a bouquet of flowers and in the other an ice-cream sandwich. Unable to locate a vase for the flowers the young lady fashioned one of the layers of the sandwich into a container in which she placed the bouquet. Legend has it that this act suggested to her caller a novel way of serving a dip of ice cream.

A Stool-Throwing in Church
In the early part of the 17th century the English kings attempted to introduce reformation into the churches of Scotland. There being no pews in those days, the congregation brought their own collapsible stools. On July 23, 1637 in St Giles Church in Edinburgh the dean, Mr James Hannay, began to read prayers from a book prescribed by King Charles I. A strenuous lady named Jenny Geddes threw her stool at the dean's head and whole sackfuls of the new prayer books followed. The stool is on view in the Antiquarian Museum in Edinburgh.

24
JULY

Births

Simon Bolivar (Venezuelan patriot) 1783; Alexander Dumas (author) 1802; Francisco Lopez (Paraguayan dictator) 1827.

Deaths

St Lupus (bishop) 478; Robert Cocking (parachutist) 1837; Martin Van Buren (8th U.S. president) 1862.

Brave Bishop Halts Hun

St Lupus, bishop of the city of Troyes in France, died today in 478. Troyes was threatened at one point by Attila the Hun, and Lupus went to meet him and asked him who he was. "I am," said Attila, "the scourge of God." "Let us respect whatever comes from God," replied the bishop; "but if you are the scourge with which heaven chastises us, remember you are to do nothing but what that Almighty hand, which governs and moves you, permits." Attila, struck with these words, spared the city.

Charles Causes Furor

Today in 1967 President Charles de Gaulle of France, on an official visit to Canada, stood on a balcony in Monteal and shouted to the crowd below him, "Vive le Québec, Vive le Québec libre!" Québec separatists were ecstatic; the Government of Canada was furious.

Amorous Augustus Arrested

July 24, 1891, forty-seven-year-old Augustus Lewis was arrested in New York for bigamy; he had no less than eight living wives, ranging in age from twenty-two to fifty years.

Awesome English Adder

On July 24, 1855 an English snake was found dead in the highwoods at Colchester, measuring nine feet five inches in length, and eleven inches in girth at the thickest part. It was of the adder species and weighed between 140 and 150 pounds.

Mormon Mentor Eulogises Utah

Brigham Young, leading a party of Mormon pioneers, reached the present site of Salt Lake City today in 1847. Young, riding in a carriage, was driven from the trail to a height from where he could see the surrounding country. On seeing the splendid panorama of the valley in Utah spread out below he said: "Enough. This is the place. Drive on."

Leo the Lion

In astrology Leo the Lion reigns supreme from July 24 to August 23 with the following general and particular significations.

Manner when well dignified

Very faithfull, keeping their Promises with all punctuality, a kind of itching desire to Rule and Sway where he comes: Prudent, and of incomparable Judgment; of great Majesty and Statelinesse, Industrious to acquire Honour and a large Patrimony, yet as willingly departing therewith againe: the Solar man usually speaks with gravity, but not many words, and those with great confidence and command of his owne affection; full of Thought, Secret, Trusty, speaks deliberately, and notwithstanding his great Heart, yet he is Affable, Tractable, and very humane to all people, one loving Sumptuousnesse and Magnificence, and whatsoever is honorable; no sordid thoughts can enter his heart, &c.

When ill dignified

Then the Solar man is Arrogant and Proud, disdaining all men, cracking of his Pedegree, he is Pur-blind in Sight and Judgment, restlesse, troublesome, domineering, a meer vapour, expensive, foolish, endued with no gravity in words or sobernesse in Actions, a Spend-thrift, wasting his Patrimony and hanging on other mens charity, yet thinks all men are bound to him, because a Gentleman borne.

From *Christian Astrology*, 1647

Painter's Parachute Plummets

Today in 1837 an extraordinary and fatal parachute descent was made by Robert Cocking, painter, from Mr Green's balloon, which rose in Vauxhall Gardens in London about 8 o'clock. At 5,000 feet Mr. Cocking began his descent when the balloon shot up with the velocity of a rocket. The parachute, unable to resist the pressure of the atmosphere, collapsed and fell to the earth. The unfortunate man died almost instantly.

25
JULY

Births

Reverend William Burkit (biblical scholar) 1650; Mrs Elizabeth Hamilton author) 1758.

Deaths

St James (apostle) 44; St Christopher (martyr) 3rd century.

A Glass Bead Factory

On July 25, 1621 the London Company sent Captain William Norton and four Italians to Jamestown, Virginia, to revive the disbanded Jamestown glass factory to produce glass beads for trade with the Indians. (The enterprise lasted till the Indian massacre of 1622.)

Today's Magic Herb

If chicory was gathered at noon or at midnight on St James Day, it had the power of making its possessor invisible and would also open locked boxes or doors. But it had to be cut from fields with gold knives and if the gatherer spoke during the cutting he would die instantly. Another property of the chicory plant is discussed in *Dyett's Dry Dinner*, 1599: "it hath bene and yet is a thing which superstition hath beleeved, that the body anoynted with the juyce of chicory is very availeable to obtaine the favour of great persons."

A Good Luck Picture

Another saint of July 25 is St Christopher who died on this day sometime in the third century. His original occupation was to carry people across a stream, on the banks of which he lived. One evening he was carrying a small child across on his back but the weight became so great it seemed the ferryman would sink. The child said "Wonder not my friend, I am Jesus, and you have the weight of the sins of the whole world on your back!" A typographic engraving of this event dated 1423, has inscribed beneath it an assurance to the reader that on the day he sees this picture he will die no evil death.

John Knill's Strange Will

John Knill left a will which was to be fulfilled every fifth year on this day, at St Ives in Cornwall, England. He was the mayor in 1767 and wanted to be commemorated by a ceremony. Thus he made a request that his tomb on the hill be visited by ten young girls in white and two widows over sixty-five, where his ghost was to join them and dance round his monument while spectators sang the 100th Psalm.

St James, Oysters, and Moors

St James the Great, disciple of Jesus and patron saint of Spain, was beheaded in Jerusalem by Herod Agrippa on July 25 in A.D. In London, by an act of the British Parliament, it was illegal to sell oysters until St James Day. The day became known as *Oyster Day*, and legend had it that whoever ate oysters on this day would never want for money. St James was held in the highest veneration by the Spaniards from the time when he miraculously appeared in 847 to help them fight the Moors. Armed with a sword and mounted on a white horse he slew 60,000 Moorish infidels.

26
JULY

Births

George Bernard Shaw (writer) 1856; Carl Jung (psychologist) 1875; Mick Jagger (singer) 1943.

Deaths

John Wilmont (poet) 1680; Otto (Greek king) 1867; Riza Khan Pahlavi (shah of Iran) 1944.

Satirical Poetry

John Wilmont, the earl of Rochester was a leader of the court surrounding King Charles II and led His Majesty in wild pranks and assorted debaucheries in the streets of London. His wit was greater at the close of each epic drinking bout so his friends and the king saw to it that he was seldom sober. During this time he was writing satirical poems about all and sundry including Charles II on whose bedroom door he once scribbled a mock epitaph:

Here lies our sovereign lord the king,
Whose word no man relies on;
Who never says a foolish thing;
Nor ever does a wise one.

Wilmont's poetry and carousing ended with his death on July 27, 1680.

Natural Disasters

1805: A severe earthquake in Naples caused great devastation and loss of life.
1889: The Yellow River in China burst its banks inundating an enormous tract of country to a depth of twelve feet.
1963: The city of Skopje in Yugoslavia was heavily damaged by an earthquake.

Political Upheaval

1890: A revolution in Buenos Aires, Argentina, overthrew President Juarez Celman and a new government pledged to remedy the nation's disorders.
1953: Fidel Castro led 165 raiders in an attack on the army barracks at Santiago to begin an attempt to depose the dictator Fulgencio Batista.

Political Unrest

1863: The Santee Sioux tribe and the U.S. Cavalry battled at Dead Buffalo Lake in Minnesota.
1865: The Cavalry, on the way to rescue a settlers' wagon train, was attacked by Indians at Platte Bridge. Meanwhile the Indians attacked Fort Casper in Wyoming.

Political Appointments

1753: Benjamin Franklin was appointed the first colonial Postmaster General.
1858: Baron Rothschild became the first Jew to be admitted to the British Parliament.
1952: King Farouk of Egypt abdicated in favour of his infant son, Faud.

Political Decrees

1847: Liberia, the only sovereign Negro democracy in Africa, was declared a republic.
1880: The Canton of Schwytz in Switzerland re-established capital punishment.
1956: President Nasser of Egypt nationalised the internationally owned Suez Canal.

27
JULY

Births

Goerge Biddle Airy (astronomer) 1801; Hilaire Belloc (poet) 1870; Leo Durocher (baseball personality) 1905.

Deaths

Celestin I (pope) 432; Nicholas II (pope) 1061; John Dalton (chemist) 1844.

A Poor Man

The epitaph of "Bare Philip" a poor man who died in Kingsbridge, Devon, July 27, 1793 reads:

Here lie I at the Chancel door,
Here lie I because I'm poor,
The further in the more you'll pay,
Here lie I as warm as they.

A Flying Man

On July 27, 1909, Orville Wright set a world record by staying aloft in an airplane over Fort Myer, Virginia, for one hour, twelve minutes, and forty seconds.

A Swarm of Grasshoppers

Today in 1931 a swarm of grasshoppers descended over the states of Iowa, Nebraska, and South Dakota, destroying thousands of acres of crops.

The Purple Loosestrife

Today's flower, the purple loosestrife, is botanically known as *Lythrum salicaria.*

A Persistent Man

On July 27, 1866, after 12 years of remarkable faith and toil, Cyrus W. Field succeeded in laying a reliable working cable, 1,686 miles long, betweeen the New World in Newfoundland and the old at Valentia on the Irish coast. Four previous attempts had failed.

A Thoughtful Man

John Dalton was a humble mathematics teacher in Cumberland, England, who earned eighteen pence per hour lecturing on his subject. He was a frugal man of regular habits who ate every Sunday dinner at a friend's house for forty years and spent every Thursday afternoon on a bowling green. He would not be remembered if it were not for his spare-time thoughts, which resulted in his atomic theory of matter. He died on July 27, 1844.

Seven Sleeping Men

Seven pious young men of the third-century city of Ephesus in 250 A.D., to escape the religious persecution of the Emperor Decius, fled to Mt Coelius where they hid themselves in a cavern. Decius was enraged at their disappearance, and ordered all the caves on the mountainside to be sealed. Nothing was heard of the seven until July 27 in the year 479 when a person digging a foundation for a stable broke the seal and found the sleepers still living. It was only when they tried to buy provisions with antique coins that the seven finally realised the miracle. Eventually, Maximian, Malchus, Martinian, Dionysius, John, Serapion, and Constantine were canonised, and the date of their reawakening made the festival of the seven sleepers.

A Smoking Man

Today in 1586 Sir Walter Raleigh returned from Virginia bringing with him the first tobacco into England.

28
JULY

Births

Joe E. Brown (comedian) 1892; Rudy Vallee (singer) 1901; Jacqueline Bouvier (Kennedy Onassis) 1929.

Deaths

Jacopo Sannazaro (poet) 1458; Johann Sebastian Bach (composer) 1750; Robespierre (autocrat) 1794.

A Dove and Raven Released

Many historians believe that July 28 was the day on which Noah opened the windows of the Ark and sent forth a dove and a raven.

A Novel Boat

Today in 1883 Mr Terry succeeded in crossing the English Channel from Dover to Calais on a floating tricycle.

Proverb

Bow wow dandy fly
Brew no beer in July

A Guillotine Victim

On July 28, 1794, the infamous Reign of Terror of the French Revolution ended with the death of its chief architect, Robespierre, on the same guillotine to which he had condemned so many.

A High-Priced Poem

Jacopo Sannazaro, an Italian poet, died today in Naples in the year 1458. Among the highest sums ever paid for poetical composition were the 6,000 golden crowns given to him by the citizens of Venice for his six eulogistical lines on their city:

Neptune saw Venus on the Adria
    stand
Firm as a rock, and all the sea
    command,
"Think'st thou, O Jove!" said he,
    "Rome's walls excel?
Or that proud cliff, whence false
    Tarpei fell?
Grant Tiber best, view both; and you
    will say,
That men did those, god these
    foundations lay."

Proverb

In July
Shear rye.

Infernal Machine Victims

On July 28, 1835 an attempt was made on the life of Louis Philippe of France with what came to be known as the infernal machine. The machine was a conglomerate of twenty-five gun barrels that fired various missiles simultaneously, and was designed to blanket the street with fire as the king passed in parade on the Boulevard du Temple. The machine was effective, but missed its main target, killing Marshal Mortier and wounding many bystanders.

Bulls and Horses Sacrificed

On this day the ancient Romans celebrated the festival of *Neptune*, god of the sea, rivers, and fountains; also known as the Earthshaker, for his control of earthquakes; and second only to Jove in the Pantheon. His day was celebrated with the sacrifice of bulls and horses.

A Daring Feat

On this day in 1888 a daring feat was accomplished in London by a man known as Professor Baldwin who dropped from a balloon and alighted safely by means of a parachute, which lessened the velocity of his fall. His performances were given daily at Alexandra Palace.

An Appalling Disaster

On July 28, 1883, an appalling disaster occurred on the little island of Ischia which lies outside the Bay of Naples. Earthquake tremors were felt and continued with great violence until the town of Casamicciola was a mass of ruins. Because of the season the island was thronged with summer visitors. No accurate estimate of the loss of life could be made, but it was estimated at being between 1,000 and 3,000.

Births

Rasputin (the mad monk) 1871; Mussolini (dictator) 1883; Booth Tarkington (author) 1869.

Deaths

St Martha (dragon slayer) 1st century; Andrew Marvell (poet) 1678; Sir Cresswell Cresswell (divorce judge) 1863.

Romantic Poetry

Andrew Marvell, a British poet and politician, died today in 1678. The following poem is from a collection of his entitled "To His Coy Mistress":

Now therefore, while the youthful
  hue
Sits on thy skin like morning dew,
And while thy willing soul transpires
At every pore with instant fires,
Now let us sport us while we may;
And now, like am'rous birds of prey,
Rather at once our time devour,
Than languish in this slow-chapt
  power.
Let us roll all our strength, and all
Our sweetness, up into one ball,
And tear our pleasures with rough
  strife,
Through the iron gates of life.
Thus, though we cannot make our
  sun
Stand still, yet we will make him run.

Coronation

James VI, aged 13 months, son of Mary, queen of Scots and Lord Darnley, was crowned king of Scotland, after the abdication of his mother (1567).

Cholera Reaction

Today in 1885 official bulletins issued at Madrid mention 3,168 fresh cases of cholera and 1,252 deaths throughout Spain. In consequence of a proclamation of the existence of cholera at Tudela in Navarre, a riot took place in the town and a train was wrecked by the mob.

Marriage

Mary, queen of Scots, to Henry Stuart, Lord Darnley (1565).

Dragon-Slaying

Today was celebrated as the *Feast of Martha*, a sister of Lazarus and the patroness of housewives and cooks. She once subdued a dragon that lay concealed in the river Rhone during the day and ravaged the country at night. After rendering the beast powerless by sprinkling holy water on him, she bound him with her girdle and slew him. She died on this day sometime during the 1st century A.D. in France.

Powerful Potion

On July 29, 1771, Secretary of State Addison acted to suppress the importation of Aqua Tufania into Britian. Named after the Greek woman who invented it, Aqua Tufania was an extremely poisonous liqueur which was said to have been responsible for over 600 deaths in Naples alone. Its Italian manufacturers claimed they had moral reasons for its production. They wanted to keep the world at ease and quiet by providing an easy and effective way for husbands to get rid of troublesome wives, fathers of unruly sons, and a man of his enemies.

Cherry Feast

Today in 1432 the Hussites threatened the city of Hamburg with immediate destruction. It was proposed by one citizen that all the children between the ages of seven and fourteen be dressed in mourning clothes and sent as supplicants to the enemy. The Hussite chief was so moved by the spectacle that he regaled the children with cherries and other fruits, and spared the city. For many years after the city's children annually celebrated the feast of cherries on July 29 by parading through the city with cherry boughs.

30
JULY

Births

Giorgio Vasari (Florentine artist) 1511; Emily Bronte (British novelist) 1818; Henry Ford (U.S. inventor) 1863; Casey Stengel (U.S. baseball personality) 1891; Henry Moore (British sculptor) 1898.

Deaths

Marie Therese (French queen) 1683; William Penn (U.S. colonist) 1718; Thomas Gray (English poet) 1771; Meiji Tenno (122nd Japanese emperor) 1912; Joyce Kilmer (American poet) 1918.

An Indian Defeat

A force of Iroquois Indians, faced with firearms for the first time, were defeated by French troops and members of the Huron tribe at Ticonderoga, New York, today in 1609.

A Case of Sabotage

Today in 1916 the munitions ship *Black Tom* was blown to smithereens in a suspected case of sabotage at Jersey City, New Jersey.

A Demonstration in Colour

On July 30, 1928 George Eastman gave a demonstration of the first motion pictures in colour, at Rochester, New York.

A Lodge of Freemasons

On July 30, 1733, the Society of Freemasons opened its first lodge in Boston, Massachusetts.

A Legislative Assembly

On July 30, 1619, the first U.S. Legislative Assembly met at an old church in Jamestown, Virginia. The members decided that an annual general assembly was to be summoned by the governor. Its twenty-two members were to be elected by "every free man."

An Airplane Purchase

On July 30, 1909 the Wright brothers of Ohio delivered a bi-plane to the U.S. government, the first government airplane purchase. The plane cost $31,250 and was powered by a 25 h.p. engine.

An Altitude Record

On July 30, 1919 a new airplane altitude record was set by Roland Rohlfs of 30,700 feet at Mineola, Long Island. He bettered this to 34,500 feet on September 18, 1919.

An Ocean Adventure

Today in 1947 Thor Heyerdahl and his raft, *Kon Tiki*, reached Puka Puka Island in Polynesia to support his thesis that the first settlers of Polynesia were of South American origin. Heyerdahl made the crossing from Peru to the Tuamotu Islands on the primitive raft with five companions.

The Saxophone Makes Gains

Today in 1845, the saxophone, invented five years earlier by a Belgian musical instrument maker, Mr Adolphe Sax, was officially introduced into the military bands of the French army.

The Rigours of the New World

Today in 1880 the Princess Louise and Prince Leopold, the former of whom had not yet recovered from the shock to the system caused by a sledge accident, while her brother was suffering from the effects of a sprain, embarked at Québec on board the *Polynesian* for England.

The Cost of a Stolen Wife

On July 31, 1840, action commenced at the Lewes Assizes in England by Captain Richard Heaviside against Dr Lardner, for compensation for the seduction of his wife. Because he had lost an affectionate wife, and his children were deprived of the instruction and example of a mother, he was granted £8,000 damages.

The Painful Price of Vanity

Before he became a pious ascetic, Ignatius Loyola, the founder of the Jesuits, was a vain and pleasure-loving young courtier in Spain. While helping to defend Pampeluna against the French in 1521, his right leg was shattered by a cannon ball. He soon recovered, but the end of a bone stuck out below his knee. So that he would look better in high boots the young gallant had the bone cut off in a painful operation. He died on July 31, 1556, aged sixty-five.

Births

Maximilian II (holy Roman emperor) 1527; Augusta (princess of Brunswick) 1737.

Deaths

Ignatius Loyola (Jesuit founder) 1556; John Hewitt and Sarah Drew (lovers) 1718.

A Declaration of Peace

On July 31, 1915 the German emperor stated: "Before God and history, my conscience is clear. I did not want war."

The U.S. Mint is Born

On July 31, 1792 Mr David Rittenhouse, director of the Mint, laid a cornerstone of a new building in Philadelphia to house the U.S. Mint. It was the first building of the U.S. government.

The Verbascum Thapsus

Today's flower, the great mullein or *Verbascum thapsus*, a stout, herbaceous plant from two to five feet high with yellow flowers, was often introduced by painters into the foreground of landscapes.

Lightning and Two Lovers

On July 31, 1718, two young English lovers, John Hewitt and Sarah Drew, were struck by lightning and killed together while trying to find shelter from a severe storm that caught them out in the fields. They were due to be married in a week. The poet, Alexander Pope, who often stayed at nearby Stanton-Harcourt, wrote an epitaph for the two:

When eastern lovers feed the funeral fire,
On the same pile the faithful pair expire;
Here pitying heaven, that virtue mutual found,
And blasted both, that it might neither wound.
Hearts so sincere, th'Almighty saw well pleased,
Sent his own lightning, and the victims seized.

UGUST

The eighth was August, being rich arrayed
In garment all of gold, down to the ground:
Yet he rode not, but led a lovely maid
Forth by the lily hand, the which was crowned
With ears of corn, and full her hand was found.
That was the righteous Virgin, which of old
Lived here on earth, and plenty made abound;
But after wrong was loved, and justice sold,
She left th'unrighteous world, and was to heaven extolled.
  Edmund Spenser

AUGUST

History

In the old Roman calendars this month was called *Sextilis,*
as the sixth month in the series, and had twenty-nine days.
Under Julius Caesar's reforms *Sextilis* was given thirty
days, and under Augustus thirty-one. Augustus also named
the month after himself, despite the fact that he was born
in September. He considered August to be his lucky
month. Among the Anglo-Saxons August was called *Arn
Monath.* Arn was their word for harvest.

Weather

Dry August, and warm,
Does harvest no harm.

As August so the next February.

Visitors

I therefore caution all wise men
That August visitors should not be admitted.
  Ch'eng Hsiao (220-164 B.C.)

Birthstone

The August birthstone is the sardonyx, a variety of onyx
with white layers alternating with yellow or orange sand.
To wear it ensures married happiness.

1
AUGUST

Births

Juliet Capulet (Romeo's lover) 1578; Francis Scott Key (poet/attorney) 1779; Herman Melville (author) 1819; Yves St Laurent (couturier) 1936.

Deaths

St Peter (martyr) 67; Trajan (Roman emperor) 117; Anne (English queen) 1714; Kooeskoowe (Cherokee Indian chief) 1866.

Columbus' Mistake

On August 1, 1498, Christopher Columbus on his third voyage first sighted the continent of South America as he sailed into the mouth of the Orinoco River in what is now Venezuela. But he mistook it for just another island.

Suffering Troops

Today in 1898 General Shafter, in charge of the American Army fighting the Spanish in Cuba, reported that 4,255 men in his army were sick, 3,164 of them with yellow fever.

Juliet's Birthday

According to Shakespeare, Romeo's young lover, Juliet Capulet, was born on this evening in about 1578. "On Lammas eve at night shall she be fourteen. That shall she, marry; I remember it well. Tis since the earthquake now eleven years 'an she be weaned." The earthquake referred to took place in 1580. Assuming that Juliet was weaned at two years of age, she must thus have been born about 1578.

Lammas Day

This day was the first day of the harvest for the Celts in early England. It was called Lugnasad. It became known as the *Festival of the First Fruits* to the Christians and was a time when loaves made from the first corn were dedicated to God. The Saxons had another name for today—"hlaf-maesse" (loaf-mass)—which became Lammas Day.

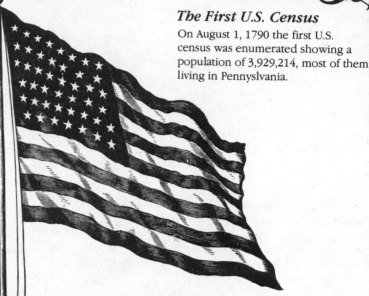

The First U.S. Census

On August 1, 1790 the first U.S. census was enumerated showing a population of 3,929,214, most of them living in Pennyslvania.

The Star Spangled Banner

Francis Scott Key, an American poet and attorney, born on this day in 1779, was held prisoner by the British fleet during the war of 1812. From the deck of a ship he watched the bombardment of Ft McHenry at Baltimore. As it had ceased before daylight, he did not know whether the fort had surrendered, and anxiously waited for the dawn. In the faint light of early morning, he saw through his glasses that the flag was still flying. Then Key, with the back of an old letter as his only paper, wrote a rough draft of the song that became the U.S. National Anthem. The tune was taken from a popular English song, "To Anacreon in Heaven."

St Peter's Escape

Today's saint, Peter, was guarded by sixteen soldiers and fastened to the ground by two chains. In the middle of the night an angel appeared to him, and bade him instantly arise. Following his guide, he passed through the guards. When in the street the angel vanished suddenly. Peter's escape was only temporary. He was executed on this day in the year 67, probably in Rome.

Mark Antony's Setback

On this day in 30 B.C. at Alexandria, the entire fleet of Mark Antony suddenly defected to Octavius Caesar.

2
AUGUST

Births

Constantine I (Greek king) 1868;
James Baldwin (author) 1924.

Deaths

St Stephen (pope, beheaded and
buried in his pontifical chair) 257;
William II (English king, killed in a
hunting accident) 1100; John Palmer
(actor, dropped dead on stage) 1798;
Enrico Caruso (operatic tenor, died
of pleurisy) 1921.

Henry Hudson's Mistake

On August 2, 1610 Henry Hudson
entered the bay in northern Canada
that now bears his name and thought
he had found the Pacific.

San Francisco Invaded

On August 2, 1889 San Francisco was
invaded by millions of crickets.

Today's Battles

216 B.C.:   The Carthaginian general Hannibal, ably
    assisted by his elephants, routed the Romans at Cannae.
47 B.C.:   "I came, I saw, I conquered," said Caesar when
    he defeated Pharnaces, king of Pontus, at Zela.
1704:   The duke of Marlborough and Prince Eugene
    defeated the French and Bavarians at Blenheim, a
    village in Bavaria.
1796:   Napoleon defeated the Austrians at Lontano.
1867:   Three thousand Sioux Indians attacked thirty-two
    U.S. troops but failed to defeat them at the Wagon Box
    Fight.
1914:   Germany invaded France and Poland while Russia
    crossed the frontier into East Prussia.

Fifth Avenue Opens

On this day in 1824 the city fathers of New York formally
opened a new thoroughfare, the fifth in the city, naming it
Fifth Avenue.

Today's Illnesses

Care should be taken of one's stomach today, particularly
by those born on August 2, because numerologists believe
that disorders of the stomach and digestive organs are
likely. Specific ailments to beware of are ptomaine
poisoning, gastric troubles, inflammation of the bowels,
internal growths, and tumours.

A Dramatic Death

John Palmer was a famous London actor of the last half of
the eighteenth century. On August 2, 1798, deeply
depressed over the recent deaths of his wife and his
eldest son, he was acting the role of *The Stranger* in
Kotzebue's play of the same name. In the middle of the
third act he appeared agitated and overcome with
emotion. Just after the lines "Oh God! Oh God! There is
another and a better world!" he went into a swoon and
fell to the floor. The audience wildly applauded the skill
of his acting, but in a few moments discovered that
Palmer's faint had been no act. He had dropped dead
before their eyes.

3

AUGUST

Births

Rupert Brooke (poet) 1887; Ernie Pyle (journalist) 1900; Leon Uris (novelist) 1924.

Deaths

Joseph Gesner (writer) 1761; Eugene Sue (novelist) 1857; Joseph Conrad (novelist) 1924.

The First Sealing Wax

The earliest letter in Europe known to have been closed with sealing wax was written from London, August 3, 1554, to the Rheingrave Philip Francis von Daun in Germany, by his agent in England, Gerrard Herman. The wax was a shiny, dark red colour, and the impression bore the initials G.H.

African Discovery

Today in 1858 Lake Victoria was discovered by Captain John Hannen Speke, an African explorer who first suggested the idea that the Nile had its source in the waters of a great lake.

European Gloom

"The lamps are going out all over Europe; we shall not see them lit again in our lifetime."

> Sir Edward Grey, the British foreign secretary in a speech on this day in 1914

Columbus Sets Sail

On August 3, 1492, Christopher Columbus set sail from Palos in Spain bound for the New World with 119 men in a convoy of three vessels, the *Nina*, the *Pinta*, and the *Santa Maria*.

American Events

1795:   The government signed peace treaties with Indian tribes bordering on the U.S. boundaries, giving the Ohio Territory to the U.S.

1848:   A woman's rights convention at Rochester, New York demanded suffrage, preaching, teaching, and property rights.

1851:   Asbury Park and Ocean Grove, New Jersey, held a baby parade, which was two hours in passing.

1886:   Reverend George Haddock, a prohibitionist, was murdered at Sioux City, Iowa, by a prominent friend of the Brewers' Association.

1958:   The U.S. atomic submarine *Nautilus* crossed the North Pole beneath the Arctic ice.

London Sport

Four thousand persons attended an exhibition of the game of baseball today in 1874 at Lord's Grounds between two teams of Americans.

People Born Today

Number 3 people are very ambitious, and never satisfied by being in subordinate positions. Their aim is to rise in the world and to have control and authority over others. They are excellent in the execution of commands and love order and discipline in all things. They readily obey orders themselves, but they also insist on having their orders obeyed.

London Disease

It was announced in London on August 3, 1858 that 1,053 persons had died of cholera in the past week.

4
AUGUST

Births
Percy Bysshe Shelley (poet) 1792.

Deaths
Hans Christian Andersen (writer) 1875.

Beer and Skittles
On August 4, 1739, a farmer from the town of Croyden after drinking heavily in a pub, bet that he could bowl a skittle-ball from that town to London Bridge, eleven miles away, in less than five hundred rolls. He won with four hundred and forty-five.

Marching Mice
Today in 1882, on the sandy plains of Alsace Lorraine in France, millions of field mice were seen crossing the road in formation.

Black and White Justice
On August 4, 1890, two men, one white and one black, were convicted of equal guilt in robbing a store in Whistler, Alabama; the white man was sentenced to five years in prison, the black man to twenty-five years.

A Snakeful of Worms
"We surprised a large viper which seemed very heavy and bloated as it lay on the grass basking in the sun. When we came to cut it up we found that the abdomen was crowded with young, fifteen in number; the shortest of which measured full seven inches, and were about the size of full grown earthworms."

    From the diary of the naturalist Gilbert White of Selborne, 4 August, 1775

A Wayward Bombardment
An experiment off Portsmouth, England with the new Lancaster gun was conducted today in 1854. The target was one of the Needle rocks. The first and second shots failed. The third, fourth, and fifth took a very high flight, went far above the rocks over the lofty hill on which the lighthouse stood, and damaged that structure on bursting. The terrified inhabitants soon made signals of distress, and the firing was discontinued.

Lightening Strakes Twice
Holinsheds Chronicles reports that in 1577: "on Sundaie the fourth of August, betweene the houres of nine and ten of the clocke in the forenoone, whilest the minister was reading of the second lesson in the parish church of Bliborough, a towne in Suffolke, a strange and terrible tempest of lightening and thunder strake thorough the wall of the same church into the ground almost a yard deepe, draue downe all the people on that side aboue twentie persons, then renting the wall up the veusture, cleft the doore, and returning to the steeple, rent the timber, brake the chimes, and fled towards Bongie, a towne six miles off. The people that were stricken downe were found groueling more than halfe an houre after, whereof one man more than fortie yeares, and a boie of fifteene yeares old were found starke dead: the other were scorched. The same or the like flash of lightening rent the parish church of Bongie, nine miles from Norwich, wroong in sunder the wiers and wheels of the clocke, slue two men which sat in belfreie, when the other were at procession or suffrages, and scorche another which hardlie escaped."

5
AUGUST

Births

Guy de Maupassant (writer) 1850;
John Huston (film maker) 1906;
Robert Taylor (actor) 1911.

Deaths

Xerxes I (Persian king) 465 B.C.;
St Oswald (king and martyr) 642;
Herbert Asquith (writer) 1947.

Nature's Bountiful Harvest

The mealy Plum
Hangs purpling, or displays an amber
   hue;
The luscious Fig, the tempting Pear,
   the Vine,
Perchance, that in the noontide eyes
   of light
Basks glad in rich festoons. The
   downy Peach
Blushing like youthful cheeks; the
   Nectarine full
of lavish juice.
   Catholic Annal, August 5, 1830

Damn the Torpedoes

"Damn the torpedoes! Full speed ahead!" shouted
Admiral Farragut on his way to victory at Mobile, Alabama,
today in 1864.

U.S. Income Tax

On August 5, 1861, the government levied the first income
tax in the U.S. All income over $800 was subject to a tax of
three per cent.

St Oswald's Arm

Oswald was a king of Northumberland in England noted
for his benevolence and good humour. But on August 5,
642, he quarrelled with his neighbour Pender, king of
Mercia. In the ensuing battle Oswald was hacked to pieces
until nothing remained but one of his arms. It was
preserved and put on display in Peterborough Cathedral.

Advertising For Love

"A young lady who was at Vauxhall on Thursday night last,
in company with two gentlemen, could not but observe a
young gentleman in blue and gold-laced hat, who, being
near her by the orchestra during the performance,
especially the last song, gazed upon her with the utmost
attention. He earnestly hopes (if unmarried) she will
favour him with a line directed to A.D. at the bar of the
Temple Exchange Coffee-House, Temple-bar, to inform
him whether fortune, family, and character, may not
entitle him upon a further knowledge, to hope an interest
in her heart. He begs she will pardon the method he has
taken to let her know the situation of his mind, as being a
stranger, he despaired of doing it any other way, or even
of seeing her more. As his views are founded upon the
most honourable principles, he presumes to hope the
occasion will justify it, if she generously breaks through
this trifling formality of the sex, rather than, by a cruel
silence, render unhappy one who must ever expect to
continue so if debarred from a nearer aquaintance with
her, in whose power alone it is to complete his felicity."
   An advertisement in the *London Chronicle,* August 5, 1758

6
AUGUST

Births

Louella Parsons (gossip columnist) 1893; Lucille Ball (comedienne) 1911; Robert Mitchum (actor) 1917.

Deaths

Anne Hathaway (Shakespeare's wife) 1623; Ben Jonson (poet and dramatist) 1637.

Mrs William Shakespeare

"Where there's a Will, Anne hath a way," said the dramatist of his wife. They were married when he was barely nineteen and she twenty-six, but she outlived him to die on the 6th of August, 1623, at the age of sixty-seven. She had been living with their daughters Judith (Mrs Quiney) and Susanna (Mrs Hall), who looked after the funeral arrangements in Stratford-on-Avon.

O Rare Ben Jonson

As a boy Ben Jonson had to leave Cambridge for lack of funds and tried his hand at his father's occupation but "could not endure the occupation of a bricklayer." He drifted for a time, was sent to prison for killing a man in a duel, then went to London where he began to write and patronise the Mermaid Tavern with Keats, Shakespeare, Sir Walter Raleigh, and others. Of William Shakespeare, Jonson wrote: "Reader look not on his picture, but his book." And as an epitaph for a lady: "Underneath this stone doth lie, as much beauty as could die." He died on this day in 1637 and was buried in Poet's Corner at Westminster Abbey (standing up as he had requested, so as to take up less space). His epitaph reads: "O rare Ben Jonson.

Today's Flower

The meadow saffron *(Colchicum autumnaie)* is the flower of August 6.

The Electric Chair

On August 6, 1890 William Kemmeler, alias John Hart, convicted of murdering Matilda Ziegler, became the first man executed by electric chair in America.

A Mercy Mission

On August 6, 1914, the U.S.S. *Tennessee* sailed to Europe with $6 million in gold to help American citizens stranded because of the war.

Gertrude Conquers the Channel

Today in 1926 Miss Gertrude Ederle of New York became the first American woman to swim the English Channel. Seven times during her fourteen hours and thirty-one minutes in the water, she floated on her back and sipped chicken soup served from a trailing tugboat.

Births

Mata Hari (spy) 1876.

Deaths

Leonidas (Spartan hero) 480 B.C.;
Herod Agrippa (persecutor of the
Apostles) 44.

Holidays, Fairs, and Feasts

On August 7, 1871 the first holiday of
the *Bank Holiday Act* was generally
observed throughout England.

Today is a national holiday in
Columbia commemorating the
anniversary of the Battle of Boyaca.

In the Roman Catholic church the
feasts of St Victricius and St Cajetan
are observed.

Today in 1920 the *Third Annual Pea
Harvest Festival* was held at Palmer,
Alaska.

August 7 is the day of the *Southdown
Sheep Fair* at Lewes, Sussex in
England.

A Harmless Duel

On August 7, 1906, in a duel between
the French generals André and de
Négrier, General André fired but
missed and General de Négrier did
not fire.

Today's Epitaph

August 7, 1714
Mary, the wife of Joseph Yates,
of Lizard Common within this parish,
was buried aged 127 years.
She walked to London just after the
    fire in 1666;
was hearty and strong at 120;
and married a third husband at 92.
    On a gravestone in Shropshire, England

A Disgusting and Degrading Exhibition

A certain Dr Tanner, who had undertaken to fast for forty
days, and whose proceedings had occupied a
disproportionate space in the columns of the newspapers,
completed his self-imposed penance today. It was a little
difficult to discover, amidst the cloud of verbiage and
detail with which the repulsive story was enveloped by
the New York reporters, whether the precautions taken to
ensure the bona fides of the transaction were trustworthy
or not. That the exhibition could serve no good purpose,
and was disgusting and degrading, admitted no doubt.
  Dickens Dictionary of Dates, 7 August, 1880

General Putnam's Decisiveness

During the American Revolution, General Putnam caught
a man skulking about his headquarters at Peekskill, on the
Hudson River. Under a flag of truce came a message from
the British leader, Sir Henry Clinton, claiming the
prisoner as a British lieutenant. Putnam sent back this
note:

            Headquarters, 7th August, 1777
Edmund Palmer, an officer in the enemy's service, was
taken as a spy lurking within our lines. He has been tried
as a spy, condemned as a spy, and shall be executed as a
spy; and the flag is ordered to depart immediately.
                            Israel Putnam

P.S. He has, accordingly, been executed.

8
AUGUST

Births

Charles A. Dana (editor of the *New York Sun*) 1819; Arthur Goldberg (U.S. statesman) 1908; Esther Williams (swimmer/actress) 1923.

Deaths

Alexander VI (pope) 1503; George Canning (British statesman)1827; A head waiter (of the George Inn) 1853.

Marriages

King Henry VII of England to Catherine Howard, his fifth wife (1540); King Leopold I of Belgium to Princess Louise of France (1832).

Musical Flies

"Discoursed with Mr Hooke, about the nature of sounds, who told me that he is able to tell how many strokes a fly makes with her wings (those flys that *hum* in their flying), by the note that it answers to in mussick, during their flying. That I suppose is a little *too* much refined."

From the diary of Samuel Pepys, August 8, 1666

The U.S. Dollar Begins

On August 8, 1786 the silver dollar and the decimal system of money was adopted by an act of U.S. Congress: "That the money unit of the United States of America be one dollar—that the several pieces shall increase in decimal ratio—that the smallest coin be a copper, of which 200 shall pay for one dollar."

A Fowling-Piece Accident

Today in 1853 the head waiter of the George Inn in Portsmouth, England, was shot in the lobby of that house by the accidental explosion of a fowling piece that Mr Powell, of Chicester, had taken with him and neglected to discharge or uncap before packing up.

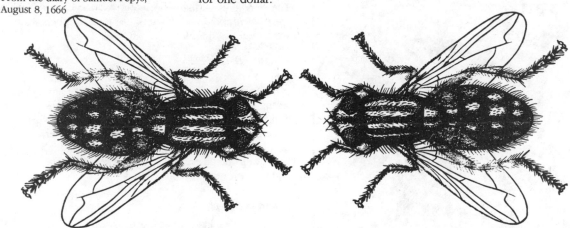

New York Becomes New Orange

On August 8, 1672 in the war between Holland and England, New York was taken by the Dutch without a shot being fired. They renamed it New Orange.

Queen Elizabeth's Heart and Stomach

Queen Elizabeth I of England gave a speech at Tilbury today in 1588 to her troops: "I know I have the body of a weak and feeble woman, but I have the heart and stomach of a king, and a king of England too; and think foul scorn that Parma or Spain, or any prince of Europe, should dare to invade the borders of my realm."

Pearls in the Sugar

Today in 1889, clams containing pearls, some of them valued at $100, were found in the Sugar River in Wisconsin.

Daughters Returned

On August 8, 1851, Calvin Page of Boston, Massachusetts, had returned to him two daughters who had been held prisoner by the Pai Ute Indians of Dakota for twelve years.

9
AUGUST

Births

Isaak Walton (fisherman/writer) 1593; John Dryden (poet) 1631; John Oldham (poet) 1653.

Deaths

Damascus II (pope) 1048; Madame Vestris (singer/actress) 1857; Ruggiero Leoncavallo (composer) 1919.

Today's Flower

The flower for August 9 is *Nicotiana tobacum*, the tobacco plant, a member of the nightshade family (*Solanaceae*). It is a violent poison when received into the stomach, and detrimental to the health of the millions of people who smoke it.

Women's Wrongs

On August 9, 1851, the Brooklyn police captured a lady burglar—the third in two weeks arrested for that crime.

Isaak Walton

Isaak Walton, born today in 1593, is best known for *The Compleat Angler*, in which he said, "No man can lose what he never had; Everybody's business is nobody's business; An excellent angler, and now with God."

John Dryden

In his poem "Absalom and Achitophel," John Dryden, who was born on August 9, 1631, had this to say: "Beware the fury of a patient man" and "None but the brave deserves the fair." He also wrote an epitaph intended for his wife:

Here lies my wife: here let her lie!
Now she's at rest, and so am I.

John Oldham

The poet John Oldham, born today in 1653, wrote *Satires upon the Jesuits* in which he said: "Racks, gibbets, halters, were their arguments."

Three in a Bed

John Orr McGill, Jane Clayton, and two others were tried at the Liverpool Assizes for the abduction of Ann Crellin, a young woman of considerable property. She was decoyed and taken in a state of perpetual intoxication to Gretna Green, where some marriage ceremony was performed between her and McGill, with whom she found herself in bed alongside Jane Clayton. McGill was sentenced to eighteen months, the others to twelve.

Today's Balloon

Today in 1884 a remarkable ascent was made from Meudon near Paris by M. Renard in a cigar shaped balloon. After travelling a short distance with the wind the balloon described a semi-circle returning against the wind. The motive power was stored in accumulations and the steering power was worked by electricity.

Today's Diseases

Number 9 persons, those born today in particular or anyone who believes in numerology, are more or less inclined to fevers of all kinds, measles, smallpox, chicken pox, and scarlet fever. They should avoid rich food and all alcoholic beverages.

10
AUGUST

Births

John (king of Bohemia) 1296; Albert II (king of Germany) 1397; Herbert Hoover (31st U.S. president) 1874.

Deaths

St Lawrence (martyr) 258; Thomas Topham (strong man) 1749.

A Tiny Masterpiece

On the 10th of August, 1575, Peter Bales, an early writing master during the reign of Elizabeth I, presented to the queen, all inscribed within the circle of a penny, the Lord's Prayer, the creed, the decalogue, two short prayers in Latin, his own name and motto, the day of the month, the year of the Lord, and the reign of the queen. (Later he inscribed the whole bible in a book that fit within a walnut shell.)

A Mammoth Creature

On August 10, 1889, the skeleton of a mammoth, with a backbone thirty-six feet long, was found at St James, Nebraska. It had been at least fifteen feet high.

A Giant Swindle

Today in 1851 the president and vice-president of the National Capital Building and Loan Association of North America, with stock of $20 million, were arrested by U.S. Post Office authorities for swindling.

Murder by Chance

Today in 1862 at the Warwick Assizes in England, George Gardner, was found guilty of murdering his fellow servant, Sarah Kirby. He claimed she would never draw him the correct quantity of beer and that vexed him. He had been of two minds as whether to kill her, and solved his doubt by throwing up the "spud" of the plough. If it had fallen flat, he said he would not have killed her, but it came down point foremost, and he had no other choice but to do her in.

Done to a Turn

St Lawrence suffered martyrdom at Rome, under Valerian, by being slowly roasted over a fire on a red-hot gridiron today in the year 258. Valerian's orders were: "Bring out the grate of iron; and when it is red hot, on with him, roast him, broil him, turn him; upon pain of our high displeasure, do every man his office, O ye tormenters." The martyr felt not the torments of his persecutors, and said to them: "Let my body be now turned, one side is broiled enough." When by the prefect's orders this was done, he said, "It is dressed enough, you may eat."

Tough Thomas Topham

Thomas Topham was an English strong man who died on August 10, 1749. During his regular exhibitions he used to roll up a seven-pound pewter dish as if it were a piece of paper, crush a pewter quart between two fingers as if it were an egg shell, lift two hundredweight over his head on his little finger, break a rope that could hold twenty hundred-weight, lift an oak table six feet long with his teeth, smash a coconut against his ear, bend an iron bar into a semi-circle with one blow against his naked arm, and throw his horse over a turnpike gate.

Today in Time

Construction of the world's most famous astronomical observatory, at Greenwich, England, the centre from which the world's time is regulated, commenced today in 1675, on the order of Charles II. At the time its main function was to improve astronomical observations for the purpose of better navigation.

11
AUGUST

Births

Thomas Betterton (celebrated actor) 1635; Dr Richard Mead (distinguished physician) 1673; Joseph Nollekens (notable sculptor) 1737.

Deaths

2,140 persons (in Java) 1772.

Under the Sun

A man hath no better thing under the
  sun
than to eat, drink and to be merry.
  Ecclesiastes, 8:15

The Next Solar Eclipse

The last solar eclipse to occur in the twentieth century will be on August 11, 1999.

Other Aerial Events Today

1877: The first satellite of the planet Mars was discovered.
1918: German aircraft fought with British coastal motor boats in the English Channel.
1927: Herr Rossitten of Germany set a glider duration record, being aloft for fourteen hours and seven minutes.
1940: *The Battle of Britain* flared up again with sixty-two German and twenty-six British aircraft shot down.

A Killer Cloud in Java

On the night of the 11th of August, 1772, on the island of Java, a bright cloud was observed covering a mountain in the district of Cheribou, and several sounds like gunshots were heard. A huge portion of the cloud detached itself from the rest, and boiled like the angry sea while emitting globes of fire so luminous that the night was lit like the day. For twenty miles around houses and plantations were destroyed by the charged cloud; 2,140 died, as well as innumerable livestock.

A Column of Vapour in England

On Sunday evening, August 11th, 1805, a very unusual exhalation was observed coming from an elm tree at Clapton. Between 6 and 7 o'clock in the afternoon, the sky being clear, the weather warm and dry, a column of darkish vapour appeared from the top of an elm. The column was about two to three feet high and after it had continued a few seconds it disappeared, and after a few seconds more, reappeared, and continued in this manner, on and off, for nearly half an hour, when it became too dark to distinguish it any longer.

The Skies of August

"In fine dry summers the sky is often strikingly beautiful at this time, particularly with light easterly breezes. The clouds then exhibit every conceivable variety of whimsical figures, and are richly coloured with the most natural tints by the setting sun."
  Catholic Annal, 1830

12
AUGUST

Birth, 1762

On the twelfth of August, 1762, at twenty-four minutes after seven, an heir apparent to the throne of England was born. The mother, Queen Charlotte (of Mecklinburgh Strelitz in Germany) was attended by several physicians and the archbishop of Canterbury stood by her bedside to give his blessing. The father, King George III, in the company of certain officers of state was in a room adjoining the queen's bedroom, with the door open. When one of the physicians walked through the door to inform the king of the arrival of George IV, he was presented with a five-hundred-pound note.

Cricket, 1874

On August 12, 1874, a match of cricket, played between eleven ladies of the parish of Nash and a similar team of ladies of the parish of Great Harwood, Buckinghamshire, caused unusual curiosity and excitement in England. The Nash ladies scored 115 in one inning against 86 scored by the ladies of the other team in two innings.

Murder, 1893

Today in 1893 Deputy U.S. Marshal Whitmaster of the Indian Territory was killed in the Cherokee Strip by Laura Maundas, a female horse thief.

Death, 1591

There occurred, on August 12, 1591, in Leith, Scotland, the death of Dick, a cat, whose passing was commemorated in verse by his owner, Mr Huddesford. The moment of death of this "premiere cat upon the catalogue" came just after a meal of fish when Dick

Had swallow'd down a score without
    remorse,
And three fat mice slew for a second
    course,
But, while the third his grinders dyed
    with gore,
Sudden those grinders clos'd—to
    grind no more!
And, dire to tell! commission'd by
    Old Nick,
A catalepsy made an end of Dick.

Gold, 1896

On this day in 1896, George Cormack discovered gold in Klondike Creek in the Yukon Territory of Canada.

Revenge, 1843

Today in 1843, Lieutenant Mackay, adjutant of the British Fifth Fusiliers was shot on parade at Parsonstown Barracks by one of the soldiers he was drilling.

Accordion, 1856

On August 12, 1856, Mr Anthony Faas received the first patent issued in America for an accordion.

Holiday, 1970

On this day in 1970, Queen Sirikit's birthday was celebrated as a national holiday in Thailand.

Weather, 1880

On August 12, 1880 a great storm almost entirely destroyed Brownsville, Texas, and wrecked 300 houses at Matamoras, on the Mexico-Texas border, besides doing a vast amount of damage to the surrounding country.

13
AUGUST

Births

Alfred Hitchcock (film maker) 1899; Ben Hogan (golfer) 1910; George Shearing (jazz musician) 1919; Fidel Castro (Cuban leader) 1927.

Australian Exploration, 1844

On August 13, 1844 Dr Leichhardit and party set out on their exploring expedition across that part of the Australian continent lying between Moreton Bay and Port Essington.

Heavenly Discovery, 1847

On this day in 1847, Mr Hind, a Britsh astronomer discovered a new asteroid at 9:30 in the evening. It was proposed that this new visitant be called Iris.

Deaths

St Hippolytus (martyr) 252; St Radegund (queen of the Franks) 587; St Wigbert (abbot) 747; Zwendibold (king of Lorraine) 900.

Mexico Conquered, 1521

The infamous Spanish adventurer, Hernando Cortez re-conquered Mexico today in 1521. He had been driven out earlier, but this time he had more troops.

Manteo Baptised, 1587

Manteo, an American Indian, set a precedent today in 1587 when he became the first of his kind to be converted to protestantism and baptised into the church of England.

English Giraffe, 1827

Today in 1827 a royal present in the form of a giraffe from Mehemed, the pasha of Egypt, arrived at Windsor Castle, the first of its breed to arrive on the island.

Today's Riot, 1840

In a riot today in 1840, at Calne, Wiltshire, arising out of the opposition of the poorer classes in the district to the new constabulary force, one special constable was killed, others injured, and several houses sacked.

Coaching Feat, 1885

A coaching feat of marvellous rapidity was performed today in 1885. The "Old Times" coach driven by James Selby accomplished the journey from London to Brighton and back in less than eight hours.

Rider Replaced, 1888

Today in 1888 Count Molke resigned as chief of the German General Staff and was replaced by Count Waldersee. The step was taken because Count Molke, of an advanced age, was now unable to mount a horse.

Wretched Colonies, 1852

"These wretched Colonies will all be independent in a short time, and are a millstone round our necks." Thus wrote the English politician Benjamin Disraeli on this day in 1852.

Alarming Accident, 1880

On August 13, 1880, in southwest England, an accident of an extraordinary and somewhat alarming nature happened to a party of ladies at the Bridgenorth Floating Bath, causing great perplexity and considerable personal inconvenience. The river Severn had greatly increased in volume due to heavy rain and it soon became apparent, to the dismay of the ladies, that the bath was sinking. They had barely succeeded in seeking safety on the bank when the bath sank to the bottom of the river. Some of the unfortunate ladies, being in an extreme state of undress, found shelter in a cattle shed nearby until blankets were brought and the victims of this curious contretemps managed to reach their respective homes.

Mechanical Device, 1932

On this day in 1932 a coin-operated mechanical device was installed at the London Zoo by which for 6d. a joy horn sounded bringing the sea lions to the fore and a fish was thrown into the water.

14
AUGUST

Births

John Galsworthy (author) 1867; John Ringling North (circus showman) 1903.

Deaths

Pius II (pope) 1464; William Randolph Hearst (newspaper publisher) 1951.

Jerry Murphy's Revenge

Today in 1894, Jerry Murphy, the city jailer at Leavenworth, Kansas, having received a dismissal order from his office, unlocked the prison doors and set free all the prisoners.

A Premature Epitaph

Here lies the body of John Eldred.
At least he will be here when he is
  dead;
But now at this time he is alive
The 14th August, Sixty Five.
    In an Oxfordshire churchyard, 1765

The U.S. Mail Goes to Sea

On August 14, 1919, a United States aeromarine flying boat dropped a bag of mail on the forward deck of the liner *Adriatic,* one-and-a-half hours after it had sailed from New York City. It was the first air mail delivery at sea.

The U.S. Mail is Robbed

On this day in 1962 a mail truck robbery near Plymouth, Massachusetts netted the takers $1,500,000.

A Victorious Byrd

On August 14, 1890, Governor Byrd was re-elected by the Indians of the Indian Territory in America. He guaranteed his victory by surrounding the polls with militia men who did not allow any votes to be cast for his opponents.

A Beard-Puller Jailed

On August 14, 1891, a fifteen-year-old boy, member of a Brooklyn, New York gang of beard-pullers, whose victims were mainly Jewish, was sentenced to twenty-five days in jail for the act.

The First Printed Book

Today in 1457 the first book ever printed was published by Faust, a wandering astrologer who lived in Germany. It was *The Book of Psalms*, part of an edition of the Bible that he had begun in 1450. Faust carried several copies of it to Paris and upon offering them for sale was thrown into prison on the suspicion that he had dealt with the devil, for the French could not otherwise conceive how so many books should so exactly agree in every letter and point unless the devil had lent his assistance. To prove his innocence Faust had to disclose his secret. It is upon this adventure that many ludicrous dialogues between Faust (Dr Faustus) and the devil are based in travelling puppet shows and in dramas by Goethe and Marlowe.

15
AUGUST

Births

Napoleon Bonaparte (French emperor) 1769; Sir Walter Scott (author) 1771; Ethel Barrymore (actress) 1879; Anne (English princess) 1950.

Deaths

Will Rogers (humorist) 1935.

Marriage

On this day in the year 1548, Mary, queen of Scots was married to the Dauphine, heir to the French throne. The bride was six years old.

An Arithmetical Error

On August 15, 1975 the landlord of the Blue Bell Inn at Lichfield in Staffordshire, received a bill for £1,494,000,000. The British Post Office agreed that it had made an arithmetical error.

Will Rogers

The American "Cowboy Philospher," Will Rogers, was killed today in 1935 along with the flyer, Wiley Post, when their plane crashed near Point Barrow in Alaska. Some of his salty comments on the human condition include: "I was born because it was a habit in those days, people didn't know anything else. Communism is like prohibition, it's a good idea but it won't work. You can't say civilization don't advance, for in every war they kill you a new way. Income tax has made more liars out of the American people than golf. Everybody is ignorant, only on different subjects. Everything is funny, as long as it's happening to somebody else."

A Lucky Child

The festival of the Assumption of the Blessed Virgin Mary has been celebrated in the Roman Catholic church on August 15 ever since its institution in the year 813. On this day in the seventeenth century a poor Frenchwoman met a procession in honour of the virgin near Notre-Dame at Paris. As the bishop passed she cried out so earnestly for a blessing for her child that the crowd parted and let her through. She passed the child up to the clergyman, and while he was giving it his blessing, the woman disappeared into the throng. Thus the baby got a new and richer mother—the church—on the day that the Virgin mother was received into heaven.

Steamboat Service

The first European steam passage service was announced on August 15, 1812 in the *Greenock Advertiser* in Scotland. The ship, the *Comet,* would ply the Clyde between Glasgow and Greenock, leaving the former city every Tuesday, Thursday, and Saturday. The best cabins went for 4s. the trip.

A Non-Stop Record

On August 15, 1929 the *Graf Zeppelin* made a world distance record for a non-stop flight from Germany to Tokyo, travelling 6,980 miles in 101 hours and 53 minutes.

16
AUGUST

Births

Nathan Hale (author) 1784; George Meany (labour leader) 1894; Frank Gifford (sportscaster) 1930.

Deaths

St Roch (confessor) 1327.

"Vive Madame de Tilly"

On this day in 1880 Madame de Tilly was brought before the Assizes of Charente Inférieure in France on a charge of having thrown a bottle of vitriol into the face of Marie Marechal, a milliner. The Comte de Tilly had been involved in a blatant affair with Mlle Marechal, and Madame de Tilly claimed she had not wanted to kill the girl or injure her eyesight, but simply impair her beauty. The injuries incurred were severe and horrible, one eye being completely destroyed. Apparently Madame de Tilly showed great concern for her victim, paying her medical expenses and giving her 20,000 francs besides, and this had such an effect on the jury that they acquitted her. Those in attendance cheered, waving their hats and crying "Vive Madame de Tilly."

Today's Food

Persons born today, or anyone interested in taking advantage of the fruits, herbs, and vegetables recommended by numerologists, should eat lettuce, cabbage, chicory, cucumber, colewort, linseed, mushrooms, sorrel, apples, grapes, and all fruit juices.

Sound as a Rock

St Roch, as known as Roche, Ruck, Roque, and Rock, died today at Montpelier, France in the year 1327. At one time during his life he was infected by the plague and retired to a forest to die. But a hound brought him bread each day and an angel squeezed the pestilence from a sore on his thigh and he survived. After that time he cured others of the plague and made them as well as himself or as the saying went, "Sound as a Rock."

Powerful Christian Medicine

On August 16, 1191, Richard I, leader of the crusaders, commanded that 2,500 Saracen hostages be put to the sword beneath the walls of Acre, the seaport on the coast of Israel that he had just captured. Then his Christians removed the gall bladders of the murdered Turks to make medicine from their bile.

An Anti-Christian Pow-Wow

Today in 1894 the chiefs of the Sioux and Onondaga tribes in America held a great council for the preservation of their traditional religion, urging their people to cast aside Christianity and return to the faith of their fathers.

Mr Stanley's Interesting Talk

On August 16, 1872 Mr Stanley, the explorer, detailed to a crowded and enthusiastic meeting at Brighton his travels in search of Dr Livingstone and their happy termination in the discovery at Ujiji of the pale, careworn, grey-headed old man "dressed in a red shirt and crimson jo ho, with a gold band around his cap, an old pair of tweed pants, and his shoes looking worse for wear." (The ex-Emperor Napolean III—Louis Napoleon— was among the audience who applauded Mr Stanley's talk.)

Births

Davy Crockett (U.S. hero) 1786; Mae West (American actress) 1893.

Deaths

Carloman (Frankish king) 754; Frederick II (Prussian king) 1786; William Bennison (poisoner) 1850.

Marriage

Désirée Clary married Bernadotte, Napoleon's appointee as king of Sweden and Norway (1798).

Divorce

On grounds of adultery, the divorce trial of Caroline, estranged wife of King George IV of England, began on August 17, 1820, in the House of Lords. They had been married in 1795 but were separated after one year and the birth of a daughter.

Abdication

Today in 1498, Cesare, the bastard son of Rodrigo Borgia (Pope Alexander VI), who had been appointed Cardinal Borgia by his father, renounced his office to marry a French princess.

Accounting

On August 17, 1891, J.L. Bay, an expert accountant employed to examine the suspected books of ex-treasurer of Arkansas, Mr Woodruff, was himself arrested on a charge of stealing $100,000.

Archaeology

Today in 1883, during the excavations carried on by the French school near Athens on the island of Delos, a private house was discovered near the theatre of Apollo. A court surrounded by pillars and twelve rooms were revealed, the floor of the court of beautiful mosaic containing flowers, fishes, and other ornaments and in the middle of the court, a cistern full of water.

Execution

On August 17, 1850 William Bennison was executed at Edinburgh for poisoning his wife with arsenic. The criminal was greatly celebrated for his "gift" in prayer and when his wife had passed forever from his cruel treatment, he thanked God that she had gone to glory. "I have seen many a death-bed," he said, "but never a pleasanter one than my wife's."

Eureka

Today in 1880 Eureka, a town in the mining districts of Nevada, which had been destroyed by fire the previous year, was again almost entirely burnt down, the loss being estimated at $1,000,000.

Toadflax

Today's flower, *Linaria vulgaris,* is known also as yellow toadflax or great toadflax.

Sleeping

On August 17, 1697 Samuel Clinton, of Tunbury near Bath in England, fell into a deep sleep from which he did not awake (even when bled by a doctor and having pins stuck deep into his arm) until the following nineteenth of November. When he finally bestirred himself again his mother ran to him to ask how he felt. "Very well, thank you," he said. "I'll take some bread and cheese."

Entertainment

On August 17, 1859, Mr Blondin commenced his performances on a rope stretched above and across the falls of Niagara. He ran on the rope, crawled along it like an ape, stood on it, swung from it by one foot, and finally carried a man across it on his shoulders.

18
AUGUST

Cathy Corbett
Lee Atkinson

Births

Virginia Dare (first white child born in America) 1587;
Shelley Winters (actress) 1922; Robert Redford (actor)
1937.

Deaths

Genghis Khan (Mongol leader) 1227; Ole Bull (violinist)
1880.

A Birth in America

On August 18, 1587 the first baby was born in America of
English parents. She was Virgina Dare, of Roanoke Island,
North Carolina, the granddaughter of the governor, John
White.

A Death in Norway

Ole Bull, the violinist, died today in 1880 in his native city
of Bergen, Norway. Ole Bornemann Bull was born in
1810, and had a stormy life, making and losing fortunes
more than once. He was greatly appreciated in the United
States, although not so well known in England.

A Meteor in Europe

On a Monday, August 18, 1783, at about eight in the
evening a bright meteor, which was eventually called the
Great Fiery Meteor, was seen throughout Europe.

A Blue Light in England

On the morning of this day in 1821 the sun shone over
England with a remarkable blue colour which was caused
by the refraction of light through a thin cloud.

An Aerial Bombardment in Texas

Today in 1891 General R. Dyrenforth conducted
experiments for the government near Midland, Texas for
the artificial production of rain by firing explosives into
the upper air. Initial reports of success were later denied.

A Hurricane in Jamaica

On August 18, 1880, a tremendous hurricane at Jamaica
rendered thousands of persons homeless, destroyed
several churches and the barracks at Kingston, and swept
away the crops, fruit-trees, etc., over a large area. Three
wharves were swept away, and eight large and thirty-two
other vessels were wrecked in the harbour.

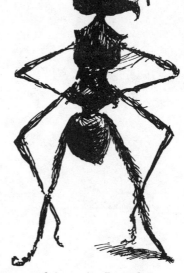

A Plague of Ants in London

There occurred on this day in 1874, in the suburbs of
London, a visitation of vast armies of ants, both winged
and wingless. In some areas they formed dark patches on
the lawns and on the walls of houses.

A Comet in Ireland

Today in 1750 a bright comet appeared in the skies over
Dunleavy in Ireland between the hours of eight and nine
in the evening. Though it was a dark night the brilliance
of the comet made it possible to pick a pin up from the
ground.

A Right to Hiss in England

On August 18, 1880, Julius Henry was attending a music
hall about 11 p.m. and had hissed after a song sung by a
child of about five years, called "Little Queen Flo." He had
done so, he claimed, as much to protest against a child
performing at such a late hour as to express his
disapproval of the act. The manager forcibly removed Mr
Henry who had him summoned for assault. A judge
concluded that anyone at a place of amusement has a
right to express his opinion on the exhibition, but the
defendant was fined 20s.

19 AUGUST

Births

Orville Wright (airplane inventor) 1871; Coco Chanel (couturier) 1883; Willie Shoemaker (jockey) 1931.

Deaths

Octavius Caesar Augustus (1st Roman emperor) 14; Blaise Pascal (author) 1662; Count Rumford (soldier of fortune) 1814.

Whirlwinds in France

Today in 1845 severe whirlwinds at Rouen, in France, destroyed in a few seconds three factories and buried most of the workmen in the ruins. Upwards of 200 people were killed or wounded and the whole valley of Daville, through which the whirlwind took its course, presented a scene of desolation.

Revolutionary Daughters in America

On August 19, 1890 the Daughters of the American Revolution was organised in New York, with the first lady, Mrs Harrison, accepting the presidency of the society.

Celestial Inspiration for Today

Then awake! the heavens look bright, my dear;
'Tis never too late for delight, my dear;
And the best of all ways
To lengthen our days
Is to steal a few hours away from the night, by dear!
Thomas Moore (1779-1852)

Shadows Over the Earth

A great eclipse today in 1868 caused a shadow, such as never before fell on the earth within historic times. It swept at the rate of 200 miles an hour from the Straits of Bab-el-Mandel across the two Indian peninsulas, over Borneo and Celebes, and touched the northern extremity of Australia. It passed out many hundreds of miles upon the Pacific Ocean before leaving the earth.

Potatoes in Germany

Sir Benjamin Thompson, better known as Count Rumford, was born at Rumford in New England in 1752. He was a loyalist during the American Revolution, and was knighted by George III for his services. He then went into the service of the king of Bavaria in the remarkable capacity of general reformer. Perhaps his most curious achievement was the successful introduction of the potato to the German diet. He died on August 19, 1814.

Earwigs in England

On August 19, 1775, a horde of earwigs descended on the town of Stroud in England, destroying flowers, fruits, and even cabbages. The disagreeable intruders infested all of the houses in multitudes so that the populace was forced to flee to the surrounding countryside.

Thunderstorms in England

On this day in 1871 terrible and disastrous thunderstorms raged with violence through the counties of Gloucester, Hereford, Worcester, and Warwick in England. In Derbyshire, Mr Thomas Middleton, a farmer, was seated at table taking tea with his wife when a flash of lightning struck his residence. It descended through a bedroom, broke the bedstead into small pieces and then passed to the room where Mr Middleton was, killing him instantly and injuring his wife in the leg.

20
AUGUST

Births

Robert Herrick (English poet) 1591.

Deaths

St Bernard (French abbot) 1153.

Inspiration from Women

The poet Robert Herrick, who also
wrote his name as Errick, Heyrick,
and Hearick, was born today in 1591.
He lived to be over eighty and,
though he was a celibate, much of his
poetry was for and about women:

Fain would I kiss my Julia's dainty leg,
Which is as white and hairless as an
   egg.
  "On Julia's legs"

Her pretty feet
Like snails did creep
A little out, and then
As if they started at bo-peep
Did soon draw in agen."
  "Upon Her Feet"

Whenas in silks my Julia goes,
Then, one thinks how sweetly flows
That liquefaction of her clothes.
  "Upon Julia's Clothes"

Inspiration from Stones

Such was the eloquence of St
Bernard that mothers hid their sons
and husbands from him lest he
should steal them by convincing
them to become monks. He always
contended that most of what he
learned of the Scriptures he learned
from the woods and fields. "Trust to
one who has had experience," he
said. "You will find something far
greater in the woods than you will
find in books. Stones and trees will
teach you that which you will never
learn from masters." St Bernard died
on August 20, 1153 in France.

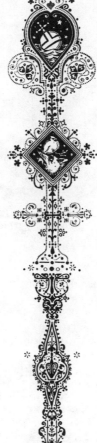

A Slight to the Queen

Today in 1888, at the Irish Exhibition in London, a band
from Cork, engaged to play for a week, refused to
perform "God Save the Queen." It was supposed that they
were afraid of persecution on their return to Ireland. The
bandmaster, however, declared that their refusal was
given because they had not rehearsed the tune.

A Tribute to Spitfires

Referring to the aerial success of the Royal Air Force in
the Battle of Britain, Winston Churchill's words rang out
in a speech given today in 1940: "Never in the history of
human conflict was so much owed by so many to so few."

A Whale's Revenge

There occurred today in 1857 the destruction of the
whaling ship *Ann Alexander,* of Massachusetts, in the
South Pacific, by the repeated attacks of a whale that the
crew had harpooned. Having destroyed two small boats
first, it rushed with great violence against the vessel and
knocked a hole through her bottom about the foremast,
and a little above the keel. The crew took to the
remaining boats and were picked up two days later by the
Nantucket.

Today's Fortunes

People born on August 20 are likely to find kindred spirits
in those born on the 1st, 10th, 19th, or 28th of any month
and to a lesser degree in people born on the 7th, 16th, or
25th of any month. Anyone born today has Sunday,
Monday, and Friday as lucky days.

21
AUGUST

Births

St Francis de Sales (patron of writers) 1567; Count Basie (jazz musician) 1906; Margaret Rose (British princess) 1930.

Deaths

Gregory IX (pope) 1241; Lady Mary Wortley Montague (writer) 1762; Mary Ann Geering (poisoner) 1849.

Guilty of Poisoning

Today in 1849 Mary Ann Geering was executed in front of Lewes gaol, in England, for the series of crimes known as the Guestling Poisonings, the convict in this case having caused the death of her husband and two sons by poison for the purpose of obtaining "burial money" from a society of which they were members.

Not Guilty of Poisoning

Today in 1844 James Cockburn Belaney was tried at the Central Criminal Court in London for murdering his wife by administering prussic acid. The post-mortem examination showed death to have resulted from that poison, and it was established that the prisoner was seen to have a quantity of it in his possession a few minutes before his wife's death. The jury returned a verdict of *not* guilty.

U.S. Women Evaluated

On August 21, 1621 one widow and eleven maids consigned to the colony of Virginia from London were ordered to be sold for tobacco at the rate of 120 pounds of the best leaf for each.

A Prayer for Today

"Oh Lord, thou knowest that I have nine houses in the City of London, and likewise that I have lately purchased an estate in the county of Essex. Lord, I beseech Thee to preserve the two counties of Essex and Middlesex from fires and earthquakes; and as I have a mortgage in Hertfordshire, I beg Thee likewise to have an eye of compassion in that county. And Lord, for the rest of the counties, Thou mayest deal with them as Thou art pleased. And sanctify, O Lord, this night to me, by preserving me from thieves and fire, and make my servant honest and careful, whilst I, Thy servant, lie down in Thee, O Lord. Amen."

Fog's Journal, circa 1775

U.S. Single-Handed Feat

On this day in 1876 Alfred Johnson, a Dane, arrived on British shores after sailing alone in his vessel *The Centennial* from Gloucester, Massachusetts. He had undertaken the voyage in his boat—16-1/2 feet long by 2-1/2 feet deep by 5-1/2 feet wide—to show what Americans were capable of doing.

U.S. Secret Society

On August 21, 1852, several American newspapers announced the formation in Alabama and other southern States of a secret society called the *Order of the Lone Star,* whose object was declared to be the extension of the institutions, the power, the influence, and the commerce of the U.S. over the whole of the western hemisphere and the islands of the Atlantic and Pacific seas.

An Eclipse of the Sun

"The sun remained obscured for no little time, there was darkness greater than that of night, no one could see where they trod and the stars shone brightly in the sky: the birds, moreover, wonderful to say, fell down to the ground in fright at such startling darkness...amid the scream of women who cried that the last day of the world had arrived."

An eye-witness account of a total eclipse observed in Spain and Portugal, August 21, 1560

22
AUGUST

Births

Milan Obrenovic IV (king of Serbia) 1854; Claude Debussy (composer) 1862; Jacques Lipchitz (sculptor) 1891; Ray Bradbury (author) 1920; Carl Yastrzemski (baseball player) 1939.

Deaths

Abu Bakr (Moslem caliph) 634; Nicholas III (pope) 1280; Richard III (English king) 1485; William Whiston (heretic) 1752; John Flower Mirfin (duellist) 1838.

Marriages

Ulysses S. Grant, American general, to Julia Boggs Dent (1848); Leopold II, Belgian king, to Marie Henriette, "the Rose of Brabant" (1853).

Sheppard's Soap

On August 22, 1865 William Sheppard received the U.S. patent for making liquid soap—a mixture of one pound of common soap to one hundred pounds of ammonia.

Dwarf Display

The Widow Bignall placed an advertisement in the *Massachusetts Spy* today in 1770. The notice informed seekers of the bizarre fact that a twenty-two-inch-high dwarf could be seen at her Boston home, admission one shilling. The exhibiton of this fifty-three-year-old man was the first such event in the colonies.

Phleum pratense

Today's flower is the herb Timothy *(Phleum pratense),* a member of the cattail family, named after Timothy Hanson who cultivated it in North America.

Christ's Coat

On this day in 1843 Pope Gregory XVI pronounced the garment preserved at Treves to be the identical coat worn by Christ at the crucifixion. It was exhibited to an immense gathering of Catholic pilgrims.

Yankee Yacht

On August 22, 1851 the yacht *America,* built by a syndicate of members of the New York Yacht Club, sailed against fourteen yachts belonging to the Royal Yacht Squadron in a race around the Isle of Wight. The *America* won the race and the prize, an ornate silver cup valued at £100. This event began the America Cup sailing challenges.

Brave Bather

On August 22, 1886 William J. Kendall swam through the Niagara Rapids wearing a cork vest.

Wordy Writer

William Whiston, an eccentric English writer, died on August 22, 1752. For years, his brain, which teemed with odd theological, literary, and scientific notions, kept the Church of England in a fidget. In 1696 he published his first book entitled: *A New Theory of the Earth from its Original to the Consummation of all Things, wherein the Creation of the World in Six Days, the Universal Deluge, and the General Conflagration as laid down in the Holy Scriptures are shown to be perfectly agreeable to Reason and Philosophy.*

Dead Duellist

On this day in 1838, in a duel on Wimbledon Common in England, between John Flower Mirfin and Francis L. Eliot, the former died from his wounds. The parties had previously quarrelled at Epsom races, and again in town, at a disreputable haunt known as the Saloon.

Births

Louis XVI (French king) 1754; Astley Cooper (surgeon) 1768; Geoffrey Faber (publisher) 1889; Gene Kelly (actor) 1912.

Deaths

Pliny (naturalist) 79; Flavius Stilicho (Roman general) 408; George Villiers (much-titled man) 1628; Rudolph Valentino (actor) 1926.

A Merciless Stepmother

The first recorded eruption of the volcano Vesuvius occurred on Augsut 23, in the year 79 A.D. The Roman naturalist Pliny (the elder) was suffocated while examining it. It was he who said "It is far from easy to determine whether Nature has proved a kind parent to man or a merciless stepmother."

A Much-Titled Man

George Villiers was a favoured member of the court of King James I of England, much given to sartorial splendour. He had twenty-seven suits of clothes made from silk with rich embroidery in lace, silver, gold, and gems and, when he threw parties, often spent £5,000 for an evening's entertainment. He had as many titles as suits, among them: Duke of Buckingham, Gentleman of the Bedchamber, Master of the Horse, and Knight of the Garter. He was assassinated today in 1628.

Today in Rome

On this day the ancient Romans celebrated the *Vulcanalia,* the festival of the god of fire and patron of blacksmiths and metal workers, Vulcan. He was the son of Juno (without benefit of mother) and was tossed out of Olympus by Jove for insolence. He was crippled in the fall and is always represented as lame in one foot. It is said that at the request of Jove, Vulcan created the first woman that ever appeared on earth, Pandora.

Today in the Heavens

Today the sun enters the constellation of Virgo, the sixth sign of the Zodiac lying between Leo and Libra. Virgo, usually represented as a young girl clutching a bunch of corn, is thought to be Ceres, the Roman goddess of growing vegetation. In Egypt Ceres was known as Isis.

Today in Flowers

The flower for August 23 is the common tansy *(Tanacetum valgare),* a bitter and aromatic plant once used as medicine and the principal ingredient in a nauseous dish called tansy pudding.

Trouble in America

On August 23, 1775, King George III proclaimed the existence of open rebellion in the colonies, and called on loyal persons to give information against the disloyal colonists.

Tobacco in America

Statistics released today in 1879 showed that Virginia, Maryland, North Carolina, Missouri, and Tennessee were supplying 300,000,000 pounds of tobacco, or about three-fifths of this total annual American product to the world.

24 AUGUST

Births

Letizia Bonaparte (Napoleon's mother) 1750; Aubrey Beardsley (illustrator) 1872.

Deaths

Henry VII (holy Roman emperor) 1313; Theodore Hook (novelist) 1841.

Hook's Hoax

Theodore Hook, a novelist who died on August 24, 1841, was the instigator of the famous *Berners Street Hoax* in London in 1809. He had worked up a grudge against a woman who lived at 54 Berners Street. He sent out thousands of letters above the woman's name inviting people to her house for various reasons at the same time of the same day. When the day came the street was blocked entirely with the carriages and wagons of coal dealers, painters, upholsterers, piano movers, undertakers, tailors, pastry cooks, chimney sweeps, fishmongers, butchers, grocers, surgeons, lawyers, clergymen, and many, many others. Finally the assemblage was topped by the arrival of the lord mayor of London, the governor of the Bank of England, the chairman of the East India Company, and the duke of Gloucester. Hook gleefully watched the chaos from a window across the street.

St Bartholomew's Day

Though the day of his death is not known, August 24 is celebrated as the festival of the apostle, St Bartholomew. He died by being flayed alive with knives on the order of King Astyages of Armenia, and in memory of the event, until the time of Edward IV, it was customary at Croyland Abbey in England to give away knives on the day of his feast.

St Bartholomew's Day Massacre

St Bartholomew's day, 1572, was the date of the horrible massacre, instigated by the young King Charles IX, of the protestant Huguenots by the French Catholics. The slaughter began in Paris, but spread to the rest of the country quickly, and before it was over more then 30,000 people had been killed.

Waffle-Iron Day

On August 24, 1869 Cornelius Swartwout patented the waffle-iron in the United States.

Virgo, the Virgin

Those born under this sign (August 24 to September 23) are subject to the following fortunes according to *Christian Astrology,* published in 1647.

Manners when well placed
Being well dignified, he represents a man of subtil and politick braine, intellect, and cogitation; an excellent disputant or Logician, arguing with learning and discretion, and using much eloquence in his speech, a searcher into all kinds of Mysteries and Learning, sharp and witty, learning almost any thing without a Teacher; ambitious of being exquisite in every Science, desirous naturally of travell and seeing foraign parts: a man of an unwearied fancie, curious in the search of any occult knowledge; able by his owne Genius to produce wonders; given to Divination and the more secret knowledge; if he turne Merchant no man exceeds him in way of Trade or invention of new ways whereby to obtain wealth.

Manner when ill placed
A troublesome wit, a kinde of Phrenetick man, his tongue and Pen against every man, wholly bent to foole his estate and time in prating and trying nice conclusions to no purpose; a great lyar, boaster, pratler, busybody, false, a tale-carrier, given to wicked Arts, as Necromancy, and such like ungodly knowledges; easie of beleefe, an asse or very ideot, constant in no place or opinion, cheating and theeving every where; a newes-monger, pretending all manner of knowledge, but guilty of no true or solid learning; a trifler; a meere frantick fellow; if he prove a Divine, then a meer verball fellow, frothy, of no judgement, easily perverted, constant in nothing but idle words and bragging.

25 AUGUST

Births

Ivan IV (the Terrible, Russian czar) 1530; Charles Etienne Louis Camus (mathematician) 1699; Louis I (Bavarian king) 1786; Bret Harte (author) 1836; Louis II (Bavarian king) 1845; Van Johnson (actor) 1916; Leonard Bernstein (conductor/composer) 1918; Althea Gibson (tennis player) 1927.

Deaths

Gratianus (Roman emperor) 383; Louis IX (French king) 1270; Margaret (English queen of Henry VI) 1482; Christian V (king of Norway and Denmark) 1699; Thomas Chatterton (poet) 1770; David Hume (philosopher) 1776; James Watt (steam engine inventor) 1819; William Herschel (astronomer) 1822; Michael Farraday (scientist) 1867.

Marriages

1558:   King Francis II of France married Mary, queen of Scots.
1843:   Robert Taylor of Liverpool was sentenced to fourteen years in jail for five acts of bigamy.

Religion

1560:   Protestantism was formally effected in Scotland.

Independence

1825:   Uruguay declared its independence from Brazil.

Oil Discovered

1859:   The first commercially viable oil well in the U.S. was discovered at Titusville, Pennsylvania.

Natural Hazard

1769:   A lightning bolt at a theatre in Venice killed several persons, melted ladies' earrings, and shattered a cello in the orchestra into a thousand pieces without injurying its player.

Honoured Artist

1840:   A statue of the painter Reubens was unveiled in Antwerp, his native city.

Historic Visit

1939:   Sir Neville Chamberlain visited with Adolph Hitler.

Military Happenings

1537:   The Honourable Artillery Company was chartered in England.
1580:   Antonio, pretender to the Portuguese throne, was routed by the Spanish.
1689:   Fifteen hundred Iroquois Indians attacked Montréal, killing all of its 200 inhabitants.
1814:   The British destroyed the U.S. Library of Congress and 3,000 books.
1881:   Forty thousand Scottish volunteers were reviewed by Queen Victoria.
1939:   A pact of mutual assistance was signed by Britain and Poland.
1940:   RAF planes dropped the first bombs on Berlin.

Sports

1886:   England defeated the U.S. twice in the first U.S. International Polo Match. The scores, at Newport, Rhode Island, were 10-4 and 14-2.
1952:   Virgil Trucks pitched a no-hitter as Detroit beat New York 1-0 in a baseball game.

Arrivals and Departures

1718:   Eight hundred French immigrants arrived in Louisiana to found New Orleans.
1927:   Paul Redfern left Georgia in a monoplane for a non-stop flight to Brazil and was never heard from again.

26
AUGUST

Births

Robert Walpole (English statesman) 1676; Prince Albert (Queen Victoria's husband) 1819.

Deaths

Lope Felix de Vega-Carpio (playwright) 1635; Anton van Leeuwenhoek (microscope inventor) 1723.

Sky Sign Controversy

A correspondence on "Sky Signs"—huge erections of swinging letters on the tops of high buildings designed to advertise the merits of various commodities—was begun in the *London Times* today in 1890. The signs were condemned both for their "hideous effect" and for obscuring the already limited view of famous buildings.

Suffrage Success

"The right of citizens of the United States to vote shall not be denied or abridged by the United Sates or by any State on account of sex." Thus read the Nineteenth Amendment to the U.S. Constitution, passed today in 1920, after years of effort by the women's suffrage movement.

Prolific Playwright

Lope Felix de Vega-Carpio, usually known as Lope de Vega, the Spanish dramatist of the sixteenth and seventeenth centuries, was probably the most prolific literary writer that ever lived. Before his death on August 26, 1653, he wrote over 1,800 plays. Most of them were three-act comedies in verse, and it was said of him that he needed only twenty-four hours, when pushed, to complete one. Once, at Toledo, he wrote five plays in two weeks.

Heliotrope Heartaches

Today's flower is the *Petasites pragrams* or winter heliotrope, which according to mythology owes its origins to the death of Clytie, who pined away in hopeless love for Apollo.

She with distracted passion pines away,
Detesteth company; all night, all day,
Disrobed, with her ruffled hair unbound,
And wet with humour, sits upon the ground.
For nine long days all sustenance forbears;
Her hunger cloy'd with dew, her thirst with tears:
Nor rose; but rivets on the god her eyes,
And ever turns her face to him that flies.
At length to earth her stupid body cleaves:
Her wan complexion turns to bloodless leaves,
Yet streak'd with red; her perish'd limbs beget
A flower, resembling the pale Violet;
Which with the Sun, though rooted fast, doth move;
And being changed, changeth not her love.
  Ovid

Crécy Cannons

According to some old chroniclers it was at the *Battle of Crécy,* where the English under Edward III and his son, the Black Prince, defeated a much larger army of Frenchmen under King Phillip, that cannons were first used in warfare. The battle took place on this day in 1346.

Births

Theodore Dreiser (auhtor) 1871; Lyndon Baines Johnson (36th U.S. president) 1908; Tuesday Weld (actress) 1943.

Deaths

Titian (artist) 1576; Sixtus v (pope) 1590; Le Corbusier (architect) 1965.

Julius Caesar Visits England

After embarking from the port now called Boulogne with 8,000 men in 80 ships and a few fast-moving war galleys, Julius Caesar made the first Roman landing on the British Isles at about ten in the morning of Sunday, 27th August, 55 B.C., about eight miles north of Dover.

John Milton's Books Burnt

As well as *Paradise Lost,* John Milton wrote several tracts against the power of the monarchy in England. When Charles II came to power Milton's friends feared for his life, hid him, and staged a mock funeral for him. Charles remarked when he heard of the funeral that he "applauded his policy in escaping the punishment of death by a reasonable show of dying." Nevertheless, the king was still unsatisfied, and on August 27, 1660 had as many copies of Milton's works as he could find publicly burnt by the hangman.

Anti-Rent Insurrection

On August 27, 1845 several "Anti-Renters" of Delaware Country, New York, disguised themselves as Indians to resist the collection of rents and killed the sheriff.

An Opera House Fire

Today in 1892 the Metropolitan Opera House in New York was virtually destroyed by fire, together with a million dollars worth of scenery and costumes.

The Biggest Blast of All Time

Today in 1883 the volcano on the island of Krakatoa, in the Sundra Straits between Java and Sumatra blew up, killing 36,000 people. The eruption was heard 3,000 miles away, and a tidal wave caused by the explosion sank dozens of ships. A rain of thick, black mud drenched Batavia, 100 miles away and a rain of ash was scattered over 3,300 miles. After the explosion, the volcano collapsed, and sank below the sea.

An Eccentric Pope

The son of a poor pig dealer, Sixtus v rose to become one of the greatest popes. During his reign he was known for the severity, and sometimes the eccentricity, of his rule. He made adultery a capital crime, but also extended the same punishment to the husband who did not complain of it. On another occasion he refused to commute the death sentence of a sixteen-year-old on account of his age. "I will give him ten of my own years to make him subject to the law," he said. Sixtus died on August 27, 1590.

28
AUGUST

Births
Leo Tolstoy (author) 1828; Roger Tory Peterson (ornithologist) 1908.

Deaths
St Augustine (confessor) 430; Count Axel Oxenstjerna (Swedish statesman) 1654.

Elopement
The poet Percy Bysshe Shelley, with Harriet Westbrook (1811).

A Cable Message
Today in 1879 the first message conveyed by the newly laid cable between Natal and Mozambique stated that King Cetawayo had been captured in the Ngome Forest by Major Marter of the First Dragoon Guards.

Martin Luther King Speaks
"I have a dream today. I have a dream that one day every valley shall be exalted, every hill and mountain shall be made low, the rough places will be made plains, and the crooked places will be made straight, and the glory of the Lord shall be revealed and all flesh shall see it together... and if America is to be a great nation this must become true."
> From a speech given by Martin Luther King Jr after leading 250,000 people on a freedom march to Washington, August 28, 1963.

The Goldenrod
Today's flower is the goldenrod or *Solidago virgaurea*.

Love and Peace
On August 28, 1891, Alfred Love was elected president of the Universal Peace Union in the United States.

An Aerial Collision
On August 28, 1736, a man crossing the bridge over the Savock, near Preston, Lancashire, saw two large flights of birds collide with such force that over 180 of the creatures fell to the earth, either unconscious or dead. The man gathered them all and sold them at the Preston market on the same day.

Speeding to Jail
The first jail sentence in the United States for speeding in an auto was handed down in Newport, Rhode Island on August 28, 1904.

The Blubberhouse Bag
On this day in 1872 the *Norwich Mercury* published a report that Lord Walsingham, at his shooting moors at Blubberhouse, Yorkshire, had killed with his own gun, the astounding number of 842 head of grouse.

Tom Thumb Performs
On August 28, 1830 the "Tom Thumb," a locomotive designed by Peter Cooper, carried twenty-six passengers for thirteen miles along the Ohio-Baltimore Railroad Company tracks—the first to carry passengers.

Clementine Corson Swims
On August 28, 1926 Mrs Clementine Corson, of New York, swam the English Channel in fifteen hours, twenty-eight minutes.

29
AUGUST

Births

John Locke (philosopher) 1632; Jean Ingres (artist) 1780.

A Three-Wheeled Adventure

Today in 1884 Mr H.J. Webb arrived at John O'Groats at the top of Scotland, having travelled 898 miles from Land's End at the southern tip of England in seven days, eighteen hours, and fifty minutes, via tricycle.

A Costly Wager

On August 29, 1750, the earl of March won his wager of a thousand guineas with Mr Theobald Taafe, by furnishing a carriage to be drawn by four horses that could cover nineteen miles in less than an hour. The earl did it in fifty-three minutes and twenty seconds. (The earl's profit on the escapade amounted to just three hundred guineas as he had spent seven hundred on seven horses and three carriages that had been destroyed in experiments prior to today's event.)

Deaths

St John (the Baptist) 30; Edmund Hoyle (gamester) 1769.

According to Hoyle

The well-known proverb on the rules of games of chance, "according to Hoyle," refers to one Edmund Hoyle, the author of a treatise on *whist* published in 1743. He is said to have given instructions in the game for a guinea per lesson. He died in London on August 29, 1769, at the age of ninety-seven.

John the Baptist Beheaded

On August 29, 30 A.D., while John the Baptist was languishing in a dungeon, Salome was dancing her famous dance before Herod in honour of his birthday. He was so pleased with her performance that he granted her whatever she might wish. She asked for the head of John the Baptist. Herod had been afraid to execute John because he feared the wrath of the people, but sent an executioner to the cells. The man returned with the saint's head on a silver platter. (Salome eventually died a just death when her head was cut off by ice that she had just fallen through.)

Reservations in America

On August 29, 1758 the New Jersey Legislature established the first U.S. Indian Reservation on a tract of 1,600 acres.

A Marine Accident

On August 29, 1782, the great British warship, the 108-gun flagship, *The Royal George,* under the command of Admiral Kempenfeldt, was heeled over her moorings in Portsmouth for repairs to her hull, when she suddenly tipped a little too far and water poured into the portholes. The ship went down in mere moments, and of the 1,100 people on board, 900 lost their lives.

30
AUGUST

Births

Mary Shelley (author of *Frankenstein*) 1797; Raymond Massey (actor) 1896.

Deaths

Cleopatra (Egyptian queen) 30 B.C.; Benjamin Pope (miser) 1794; John Nield (miser) 1852.

Mental Superiority

In numerology the number 30 is one of thoughtful deduction and retrospection. Those born today, or anyone devoting today to thought, can expect to have mental superiority over others, but only if they will it so, the number not being self-motivated.

A Gas and Electric Car

On August 30, 1929 Colonel E.H. Green took delivery of a new type combination gas and electric automobile built by the General Electric Company of Schenectady, New York. It had a sixty horsepower engine and no clutch or gear shift. Two foot pedals on each side of the central brake pedal were used for acceleration.

An Eccentric Miser

John Camden Nield inherited his father's estate of £250,000 and parted with his pennies only with the greatest reluctance. He lived in a large house in London alone with a cat, and slept on a board. Once, when one of the parish churches that he owned in the county developed a leaky roof, he had it covered with calico (because he got it free). He wore the same clothes all his life, refusing to brush them because they would wear out faster. When he died today in 1852 he left all his fortune, now grown to £500,000, to Queen Victoria.

Banned in Boston

On August 30, 1637 Anne Hutchinson was tried in the colony of Massachusetts for "traducing the ministers and the ministry," and sentenced to banishment. Emigrating from England in 1634 and having been accustomed to listening to religious discussion in her home, she began to hold informal meetings of women in Boston at which she talked about the sermon on the previous Sunday. She was accused of advocating a religion that absolved its adherents from observing the moral law, and her views were condemned by a synod of the churches. She and her family emigrated to Rhode Island.

An Obstinate Miser

Mr Benjamin Pope, a Southwark tanner, and possessor of a fortune over £100,000 spent the last twelve years of his life in the King's Bench debtor's prison in London rather than pay a debt of £10,000. Even when the court reduced the debt to £1,000 he refused to pay. It was said of him that he was so stingy that he would make a pint of ale last for two days. He died with his wealth intact on August 30, 1794.

31
AUGUST

Births

Gaius Caligula (Roman emperor) 12; Marcus Antonius (Roman emperor) 161; Yoshihito (123rd Japanese emperor) 1879.

Deaths

St Aiden (bishop) 651; Leofric (Lady Godiva's husband) 1057; John Bunyan (author) 1688.

St Aiden's Power

St Aiden, born in Ireland, was bishop of the island of Lindisfarne. On one occasion while riding his cart and two oxen laden with wood, he fell off a high cliff toward the sea below. During their descent St Aiden made the sign of the cross and all landed safely on the beach without a stick of wood being lost.

A U.S. Earthquake

On August 31, 1886 the first major earthquake recorded in America wrecked the eastern United States, killing forty-one people in Charleston, South Carolina, and causing $5 million property damage.

A British Proclamation

On this day in 1290, a proclamation of King Edward I exiled all Jews from England forever, under penalty of death.

Today's Grasshoppers

1476: All of Poland was covered by a plague of grasshoppers that ravaged the crops and caused widespread famine.

1742: Great damage was done to pastures and crops in Pennsylvania, and in the southwestern counties of England by swarms of grasshoppers.

John Bunyan's Wit

John Bunyan, the Baptist preacher and author of *The Pilgrim's Progress,* was imprisoned in Bedford prison at the Restoration of 1860. He remained there, on and off, for twelve years. One day a Quaker called on Bunyan in jail with what he professed was a message from the Lord. "After searching for thee in half the jails of England, I am glad to have found thee at last," the man said.

"If the Lord sent thee," Bunyan replied, "You would not have needed to take so much trouble to find me out, for He knows that I have been in Bedford jail these past seven years."

He was accused by detractors of not having written *The Pilgrim's Progress* to which he replied in verse:

It came from mine own heart, so to
    my head,
And thence into my fingers trickled;
Then to my pen, from whence
    immediately
On paper I did dribble it daintily.

JOHN · BVNYAN · 1662.

EPTEMBER

Next him September marched eke on foot,
Yet he was hoary, laden with the spoil
Of harvest riches, which he made his boot,
And him enriched with bounty of the soil;
In his one hand, as fit for harvester's toil,
He held a knife-hook; and in th' other hand
A pair of weights, with which he did assoil
Both more and less, where it in doubt did stand,
And equal gave to each as justice duly scanned.
   Edmund Spenser

SEPTEMBER

History

The Roman Senate would have given this month the name *Tiberius* but that emperor opposed it. The Emperor Domitian gave it his own name, *Germanicus.* The Senate under Antonius Pius gave it that of *Antonius.* Commodus gave it his surname, *Herculeus;* and the Emperor Tacitus his own name, *Tacitus.* But these appellations have all gone into disuse and September it is. When the year began in March, September was the seventh of the months and so got its name from the Latin word *Septum,* meaning seven. Julius Caesar gave the month a thirty-first day, which Augustus subsequently took away from it. It has remained with thirty ever since. Among the early Anglo-Saxons September was called *Gerst Monath,* from their word for barley, for this was the month in which the barley was harvested.

Prognostications

Because September was under the dominion of Vulcan, the child of mischief and the demon of the storm, the Romans expected volcanic eruptions, earthquakes, and hurricanes as likely to occur this month. But the English poet Leigh Hunt (1784-1859), was more optimistic: "...September is the month of consummations — the fulfiller of all promises — the fruition of all hopes — the era of all completeness."

Birthstones

Aficionados of gems have a choice of two birthstones for September: the sapphire, one of Jupiter's stones, which was thought to have many magical properties, or the chrysolite, which was an antidote to melancholy.

1
SEPTEMBER

Births

Engelbert Humperdinck (German composer) 1854; Edgar Rice Burroughs (creator of Tarzan) 1875; Rocky Marciano (boxer) 1924.

Deaths

Adrian IV (pope) 1159; Louis XIV (French king) 1715; Patrick O'Bryen (giant) 1806.

An Arrogant Pope

Nicholas Breakespeare, elected to popedom in 1154 as Adrian IV, was the only English man ever to have obtained that position. His arrogance was such that he obliged Frederick I to prostrate himself before him, kiss his foot, hold his stirrup, and lead the white horse on which he rode. He died today in 1159.

A Failed Potion

Louis XIV, the king of France died on September 1, 1715, aged seventy-seven, of gangrene in his leg. His physicians, having abandoned all hope of saving him, allowed him to sip a potion prepared by a quack doctor named Lebrun. "To life or to death," said the king, raising the glass, "whatever pleased God." It didn't work and his last words today were: "My God, come to my aid; haste to succumb."

Creation Day

In the year 220 Julius Africanus, a Roman chronologist, decreed that the world was created on this day 5,508 years, three months, and twenty-five days before Christ.

Chop Suey Day

On this day in 1896, Chop Suey was concocted and served for the first time in the United States. Created by a chef working for the Chinese statesman Li Hung-Chang, who was visiting the U.S., the chef said, "I call it chop suey—that's what we call 'hash' in China."

Juno Day

Mr Hardin of Lilienthal, near Bremen in the north of Germany, on this day in 1804, discovered a new planet to which he proposed to give the name Juno.

Nutt Day

On September 1, 1878 in Boston, Miss Emma Nutt became the first woman telephone operator in America. Until this time, the operators had all been men.

An Irish Giant

Born in Ireland, Mr Patrick O'Bryen was eight feet, five inches in height and exhibited his person for many years in England as a specimen of gigantic phenomenon, by which he realised an independence sufficient to enable him to enjoy the comforts of life in retirement until his death today in 1806 at Bristol, in his forty-sixth year.

Feast Day

In England today in 1860, the Lancashire Volunteers, to the number of 11,000, were reviewed in Knowsley Park, and afterwards entertained by the earl of Derby. The refreshments provided on the occasion included between five and six tons of pies, several thousand rolls, and twenty-five hogsheads of the famous Knowsley ale.

Expulsion Day

On September 1, 1930, William Randolph Hearst was expelled from France because of the publication in his newspapers of secret documents relating to Franco-British naval negotiations in 1928.

Births

Eugene Field (author of "Little Boy Blue") 1850; Cleveland Amory (author) 1917.

Deaths

Thomas Telford (engineer) 1834; Honourable Dame Edith Lyttelton (writer) 1948.

A New Calendar, 1752

On September 2, 1752, Britain, one of the last of the nations to do so, adopted the *Gregorian Calendar,* the one currently in use.

The Indian Love Call, 1924

Today in 1924 in New York City, theatregoers cheered the opening of Rudolf Friml's operetta, *Rose Marie,* and particularly one song in its score, "The Indian Love Call."

The Great Fire of London, 1666

The Great Fire of London began in the house of a baker named Farryner, in Pudding Lane near the Tower, and burned out of control for three days and nights, during which it destroyed fully two-thirds of the city—436 acres that included 89 churches, the city gates, 13,200 houses, and 430 streets. John Evelyn, the diarist, was there on this night in London in the year 1666: "This fatal night about ten, began that deplorable fire near Fish Street in London...oh the miserable and calamitous spectacle, such as happly the whole world had not seen the like since the foundation of it...all the sky were of a fiery aspect, like the top of a burning oven, and the light seen above 40 miles round about for many nights."

A Bridge Collapse in Portugal, 1880

On this day in 1880, as a battalion of Portuguese troops was crossing a wooden bridge over the Ebro, near Lugrono, it gave way, and ninety-six officers and men, including the lieutenant of engineers who had constructed the bridge were drowned. The bridge had only been finished two days when the accident occurred, and at the time the river was greatly swollen in consequence of recent storms and floods.

A Lock-Picking Award, 1851

On September 2, 1851, the arbitrators appointed in the case awarded to Mr Hobbs, an American locksmith, the 200 guineas offered by Messrs Bramah to any one who would pick the famous lock exhibited in their window in Piccadilly in London.

A Notice from Henry Ford, 1922

On this day in 1922, Henry Ford posted notices in his factory in Detroit, warning each employee that he would lose his job if he had "the odour of beer, wine or liquor on his breath, or possessed any intoxicants on his person or in his home." The poster added: "The 18th Amendment is part of the fundamental laws of this country. It was meant to be enforced."

A Massacre in Paris, 1792

Today in 1792 a dreadful massacre took place in Paris. Several different prisons were broken open and all the state prisoners butchered in the most horrible way. The number of prisoners slain on this occasion was estimated at 12,000. Agents of the slaughter were branded with the name Septemberizers.

3
SEPTEMBER

Births

Louis Sullivan (skyscraper architect) 1856.

Deaths

Richard Tarleton (comedian) 1588; Oliver Cromwell (British statesman) 1658; William Cawsey (horse doctor) 1789.

Coronation

Richard I, the "Lionhearted," was crowned king of England today in 1189. In the ceremony he was annointed on the head, breast, and shoulders and invested by the proper officers with cap, tunic, swords, spurs, and mantle.

Skyscraper Sullivan

The man credited with inventing skyscrapers, Louis Henri Sullivan was born today in 1856. He was an American architect, one of the first to suggest that the function of a building should be expressed by its outward form.

Bulgarian Ransom

On September 3, 1901 Ellen N. Stone, missionary, was captured in Bulgaria by Turkish bandits and ransomed for £25,000.

Funny Dick

Dick Tarleton, a tavern-keeper and celebrated comedian in England, died on this day in 1588. He wrote and sang satirical ballards, or *jigs* while playing a pipe and beating a drum, skipping and shuffling round and round before bewitched audiences in London. One of his jigs, "A Horseload of Fools," always brought down the house:

This fool comes of the citizens,
Nay, prithee, do not frown;
I know him as well as you
By his livery gown:
Of a rare horn-mad family . . .

Today's Flower

The flower for September 3 is the harvest bell or hare bell *(Campanula rotundi-folia)* dedicated to St Simeon Stylites, the younger.

O little drooping bells of blue,
Like rosaries of azure hue,
That catch the Palmer's passing view,
As on he's wending
To some saint's shrine.
Catholic Annal, 1830

Lightning Bill

William Cawsey, a farrier (horse doctor) from London, was struck dead by lightning while standing under a tree in a village near Birmingham. To commemorate the event, as well as to warn others from exposing themselves to the same danger by taking shelter in a thunderstorm under trees, a monument was erected on the spot.

Winston's Back

The Board of the Admiralty sent a message to all Royal Navy ships today, 1939, when Churchill had been reappointed its First Lord. It said: "Winston's back."

Colonial Peace

On September 3, 1783, America and Britain signed a peace treaty in Paris, recognising the independence of the United States.

Lost Day

September 3, 1752, never happened in England, nor did the ten days that should have followed it. When the Gregorian calendar was adopted on September 2, 1752, in order to get back in step, eleven days were lost. The decision caused riots at the time because people thought that the government had stolen eleven days of their lives.

4
SEPTEMBER

Births

Pindar (Greek poet: "Mirth is the best physician to labour") 518 B.C.; Chateaubriand (French writer: "An original writer is not one who imitates anyone, but one whom nobody can imitate") 1768.

Deaths

St Cuthbert (English bishop) 688; John Heidegger (Swiss ugly man) 1749; George Gilbert (American miser) 1890.

St Cuthbert's Beads

An old Northumbrian legend states that when the sea is running high the spirit of St Cuthbert rides in the mist and the wind forging beads for the faithful. After every storm the beaches of the island of Lindisfarne, where he died today in 688, and where Cuthbert was bishop, are strewn with what appear to be beads. Later, zoologists identified the objects as fragments of the exoskeletons of crinoids, a variety of submarine animal.

Heidegger's Ugly Face

John James Heidegger, a Swiss who was Master of Revels to King Charles II, and died today in 1794, was known as the ugliest man of his time. He once bet with the earl of Chesterfield that he could not find an uglier person in all of London. After arduous searching through all the city's streets the earl found a woman who seemed to be as ugly as Heidegger, but when he put on the woman's head-dress for a strict comparison it was found that Heidegger was much uglier.

A Mouse-Skin Coat

On September 3, 1938 fashion experts in London revealed that coats made of mouse skins would be popular in the winter of 1939. Full-length coats would require about 400 skins, costing about £100. They added that the cost could be lowered considerably if customers would catch and supply their own mice.

The First U.S. Newsboy

Today in 1833, Barney Flaherty, a ten-year-old New York boy, became the first known newsboy in the United States after he was hired by the publisher of the *New York Sun* to peddle papers.

The First English Glass

On this day in 1567, Queen Elizabeth granted a patent to two Flemish merchants for the making of glass in England, upon condition that they teach Englishmen their art.

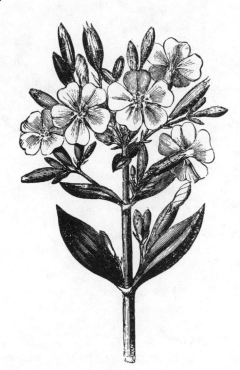

Common Soapwort

Today's flower *Saponaria officinalis,* common soapwort, is named from the Latin *sapo:* soap, because it abounds in a soapy juice.

Gilbert's Cost of Living

On September 4, 1890, George Gilbert, a Youngstown, Ohio, miser died. He had said that he lived the whole year round on three cents a day.

5

SEPTEMBER

Births

Jesse James (American outlaw) 1847; Frank Yerby (American novelist) 1916.

Deaths

St Laurence Justinian (patriarch of Venice) 1455; Suleiman I (Turkish sultan) 1566; Count Barowloski (tiny Pole) 1837; Crazy Horse (Sioux Indian chief) 1877.

Tiny Symmetrical Pole

On this day in 1837 Count Barowloski, the well-known Polish dwarf, died at his cottage near Durham, England, aged ninety-eight. His height was under thirty-six inches, but his body was of the most perfect symmetry and his mind cultivated to an extraordinary degree of travel and study.

Sackcloth and Ashes Saint

As he lay dying on this day in 1455 St Laurence Justinian was offered the comforts of a feathered bed but chose a straw instead, remarking that a Christian ought to die in sackcloth and ashes.

A Cat Hanging

The Tatler for September 5, 1710 gave a jocular account of an *Ecclestiastical Thermometer* which had been invented for testing the degrees of religious zeal in Banbury, Oxfordshire, a place noted for that phenomenon. A poet named Braithwaite, in his "Drunken Barnaby's Four Journeys," also made sport of the town:

To Banbury came I, O profane one!
There I saw a Puritane one
Hanging of his cat on Monday,
For killing of a mouse on Sunday.

The Price of Beef

During the Gold Rush in the Klondike, the first beefsteak to reach Circle City, Alaska was selling on this day in 1896 at $48.00 a pound—the highest known price ever paid for beef.

Marine Sartorial Splendour

On September 5, 1776 the Marine Committee of America standardised naval uniforms. Captains were to wear a blue coat with red lapels, slashed cuffs, standup collar, flat yellow buttons, blue breeches, and a red waistcoat with yellow lace trim.

Women or Abortive Men

On September 5, 1891, Mr Frederick Harrison, president of the English Positivist Society, delivered an address in London on "Women's True Function" contending that "her whole energies and entire life should be devoted to keeping the family, the real social unit, for all moral purposes, more beautiful, more useful than the state—true, refined, affectionate, faithfull, and that she ought not to mix up so sacred a duty with the grosser occupations of politics and trade. Women must choose to be either women or abortive men."

The Ladies' Organ

Today in 1667 a certain Bishop Hachet in England wrote a letter to one of the wealthy ladies in his congregation soliciting funds for his church: "My last proposition is to your noble lady: an organ is bespoken at £600 price, to be called 'The Ladies' Organ,' because none but the honourable and most pious of that sex shall contribute to that sum."

Acute American Embarrassment

The first session of the twenty-fifth Congress of the United States opened with a message from the new president, Martin Van Buren. The document dealt mainly with one subject, the acute financial embarrassment of the country, for the consideration of which Congress had been especially convened three months earlier than usual (1837).

6
SEPTEMBER

Births

Lafayette (French hero of the American Revolution) 1757; Joseph P. Kennedy (American financier) 1888.

Deaths

Michael Tournant (French nobleman) 1734; Stolypin (Russian prime minister, assassinated) 1911.

A Salt-Free Diet

Though he died today in 1734 in Paris, Sieur Michael Tournant aged ninety-eight, had none of the infirmities of old age and resembled a man of thirty-five, supposedly because he had never once eaten salt.

The Mayflower Sails

After two previous false starts, the pilgrim fathers, seventy-four men and twenty-eight women, sailed for America today in 1620 aboard *The Mayflower* in search of religious freedom.

An Amateur Pedestrian Feat

The fastest time for four miles, according to the annals of amateur pedestrianism for 1880, was accomplished by Mr W.G. George, of the Moseley Harriers, in a handicap at the grounds of the London Athletic Club, Fulham. Mr George, who of course started at scratch, won the race easily in nineteen minutes, forty-nine and three-fifths seconds.

A Shorter Tail

On this day in 1709, a very beautiful comet, moving with great swiftness, was seen throughout Europe. Its tail stretched across the heavens like an immense luminous arch, 36,000,000 miles in length, and presented a magnificent spectacle.

Today and Love

Number 6 people, although they are influenced by the planet Venus, tend towards platonic, rather than sensual love. They have romantic ideals, love beautiful things, and are fond of rich colours, paintings, statues, and music. They love to entertain friends but cannot stand discord or jealousy in their relationships.

A Lengthy Tail

On this day in 1858, Donati's comet was visible to the naked eye as a star of the fourth magnitude. Its tail was calculated to measure 80,000,000 miles and the time of its revolution to be 2,495 years.

Fourteen People Whipped

On September 6, 1651 Obadiah Holmes was whipped, receiving thirty stripes for being a Baptist in America. While the blood was flowing he said: "You have struck me with roses." Another thirteen people were similarly punished afterwards for showing him sympathy.

The Foo-Chow-Foo to London Race

Three vessels, the *Serica, Ariel,* and *Taeping,* landed at the London docks today in 1866, to finish the great annual ocean race from Foo-Chow-Foo (in China) to London. The 14,060 mile voyage was accomplished in ninety-nine days with the *Taeping* docking at 9:45 p.m., the *Ariel* at 10:15 p.m., and the *Serica* at 11:30 p.m. The *Taeping* collected the £5,000 premium.

7
SEPTEMBER

Birth

Elizabeth I (Queen Anne Boleyn, wife of Henry VIII, was delivered of a daughter at Greenwich who received the name of Elizabeth. Both mother and daughter were doing well) 1533.

Deaths

St Regina (virgin/martyr) 3rd century; St Evurtius (bishop/confessor) 340; St Cloud (confessor) 560; St Madelberte (virgin) 705; Geoffrey Plantaganet (father of Henry II of England) 1151; Ferdinand IV (king of Castile) 1312; Frederick IV (German emperor) 1493; Ferdinand II (king of Naples) 1496; Catherine Parr (widow of Henry VIII) 1548; Cardinal Guido Bentivoglio (historial writer) 1644; Dr John Armstrong (author) 1799; Leonard Euler (mathematician) 1783; Mrs Hannah Moore (poet) 1833; John Greenleaf Whittier (poet) 1892.

Gloved Gentleman Wins

The first heavyweight title fight, with gloves and three-minute rounds, was held in New Orleans between John L. Sullivan and "Gentleman" Jim Corbett. Corbett won in twenty-one rounds (1892).

Andrew Carnegie Ups Offer

The lord provost of Edinburgh announced at a meeting of the town council that Mr Andrew Carnegie of New York had increased his offer of £25,000 for a free library for Edinburgh to £50,000 (1866).

Number Seven Problems

Though the number 7 is usually considered lucky, people born today and others for whom the number has particular significance, are more easily affected by wrong and annoyance than other people. These difficulties lead to physical disturbances, often in connection with the skin, which is peculiarly delicate. They tend to perspire heavily and their skin is especially sensitive to friction and frequently erupts in disagreeable pimples, boils, and rashes. These problems are most likely to occur at the ages of seven, sixteen, twenty-five, thirty-four, forty-three, fifty-two and sixty-one.

Airborne Horses and Heifers

Mr Simpson of Cremorn Gardens, with M. and Mde Poitevin, appeared at the Westminster Police Court to answer a charge of cruelty to horses, insofar as they had on different occasions attached one to a balloon and permitted it to ascend with a person sitting on its back. The summons was dismissed due to contradictory evidence. Later at the Ilford Petty Sessions the same parties were fined £5 each for permitting a heifer to ascend bearing Madame Poitevin on its back as Europa (1852).

Flower-Bedecked Autos

Socialites held the first automobile parade in the United States at Newport, Rhode Island driving nineteen automobiles all decorated with flowers. First prize was awarded to Mrs Herman Oerlichs whose car was covered with sprays of wisteria; fastened to the radiator was a flock of white doves (1899).

8
SEPTEMBER

Births

Mary (the Virgin) 1st century B.C.; Ludovico Ariosto (poet) 1474; Peter Stuyvesant (New York colonist) 1592; Anton Dvořák (composer) 1841.

Deaths
Charles III (king of Navarre) 1425; Princess Elizabeth Stuart (daughter of Charles I) 1650.

Harvard Opens for Business
Harvard College was formally established on September 8, 1636. It was named after its first patron, the Reverend John Harvard, who left £800 and his library to the College.

New York Captured
On September 8, 1664, a small English fleet took New Amsterdam without a struggle and renamed it New York. Peter Stuyvesant proposed resistance, but was forced by his Dutch council to sign a capitulation. It was an unhappy birthday for Mr Stuyvesant.

A President's Wisdom
Abraham Lincoln made a speech at Clinton, Illinois, today in 1858, in which he said: "You can fool all of the people some of the time; some of. the people all of the time; but not all of the people all of the time."

The Virgin Mary's Birth
Since the year 695 when it was instituted by Pope Servius, the Roman Catholic church has celebrated the *Feast of the Nativity of the Blessed Virgin* on September 8. The pope was inspired by a monk who, each year on this day, heard celestial choirs of heavenly music. The monk asked one of the angels why they were rejoicing and was told it was the anniversary of the birth of Mary, the mother of Jesus.

A Poet's Humble Abode
Ludovico Ariosto, the author of *Orlando Furioso,* was born at the castle of Reggio in Lombardy, Italy today in 1474. In his time he was venerated to the same degree as Shakespeare and became very wealthy. Though his poems frequently described magnificent palaces, he chose to live in a small house in Ferrera. When a visitor asked why this was so, Ariosto pointed to an inscription that ran along the front of his house:

Small is my humble roof, but well
   designed
To suit the temper of the master's
   mind;
Hurtful to none, it boasts a decent
   pride,
That my poor purse the modest cost
   supplied.

An Empress' Madness
On September 8, 1866, the empress of Mexico was reported to have become insane since her arrival in Europe on a mission relating to the disturbed condition of her husband's empire. Her unfortunate condition was first manifested in an interview with the pope, when she declared there had been a conspiracy set afoot to destroy her by poison.

9
SEPTEMBER

Births

William Bligh (Captain of the *Bounty*) 1754; James Hilton (novelist) 1900; a giant panda (the first born in captivity—China) 1963.

Deaths

Henri de Toulouse-Lautrec (artist) 1901; Mao Tse-tung (Chinese leader) 1976.

Baseball

Sandy Koufax pitched a perfect game, and Los Angeles beat Chicago 1-0 (1965).

Trial

Alfred Dreyfus, a French general staff officer, went on trial for the second time, accused of disclosing French government secrets (1899).

Peace

Hostilities between Bulgaria and Russia ceased (1944).

Engines

The first steam engine arrived in the colonies from England to serve as a water pump (1753).

Sports

A fight for the championship of England and a £200 prize, between Caunt and Bendigo of Nottingham was held today in 1845. The fight commenced at Newport Pagnell, moved to Stoney Stratford, back to Wheddon Green, and ultimately to Lutfield Green. The spectators had thus to follow the pugilists between thirty and forty miles. Bendigo won the ninety-three round movable fight (1845).

Unionised

California became the thirty-first state to be admitted to the Union (1850).

Prohibition

An act of Parliment outlawed the sport of bear-baiting (1835).

Licenced

Twenty-seven-year-old Abraham Lincoln received a licence to practise the profession of law (1836).

Re-Named

The Continental Congress decided "that in all continental commissions and other instruments, where heretofore the words United Colonies have been used, the style be altered, for the future, to the *United States*" (1776).

Disaster

The Manhattan Market in New York, was burnt down, damage being done to the amount of 1,000,000 dollars (1880).

Abduction

A party of British volunteers crossed the frontier from Canada to the United States, and carried off Colonel Grogan (1891).

10
SEPTEMBER

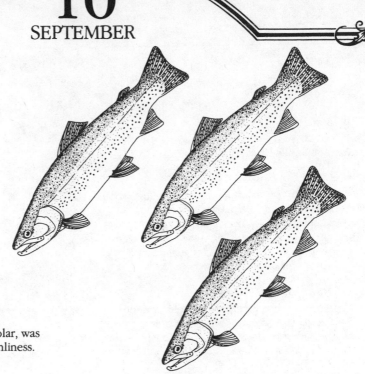

Births

Mungo Park (explorer) 1771; Isaac K. Funk (publisher) 1839; Arnold Palmer (golfer) 1929.

Deaths

William (the Conqueror) 1087; Thomas Sheridan (scholar) 1738; Mary Wollstonecraft (women's rights champion) 1797.

A Shower of Fish

On September 10, 1890, during a shower at Cairo, Illinois, a number of live fish, four inches in length, fell in various parts of the city.

An Abrupt Expiration

Dr Thomas Sheridan, an Irish classical scholar, was equally renowned for his wit and his slovenliness. Jonathan Swift described his house:

A rotten cabin dropping rain;
Chimneys with scorn rejecting smoke;
Stools, tables, chairs, and bedsteads broke.

On the evening of September 10, 1739, while sitting amidst the debris in his home engaged in an after-dinner conversation with a friend concerning the direction of the wind, Sheridan said: "Let the wind blow east, west, north or south, the immortal soul will take its flight to the destined point." At this point Sheridan leaned back in his broken chair and instantly expired.

A Ghastly Explosion

During a battle against Philip I of France, William the Conqueror, the king of England, fell off his horse and ruptured his stomach. Today in 1087 he succumbed to the wound at the age of sixty-one. The king was so obese that he could no longer fit into the masonary coffin that had been previously made for him. The monks who were burying him tried nonetheless to force his body into the casket, with the result that his swollen belly burst open. The stench was so bad that all the mourners were driven from the church at Caen (which he had founded) and poor William was laid to rest very much alone.

A Zippered Hot Dog

On this day in 1927 an American meat-packing firm announced that it had perfected a frankfurter with a zipper. Consumers were advised to boil the "hot dog" in its zippered casing, and then discard it.

The Rebecca Riots

In the year 1880 the Rebecca Riots took place in South Wales as a violent protest against turnpike tolls and gates. The rioters dressed as females and destroyed many of the tollgates. On September 10 an old woman, keeper of a tollgate, was killed; in consquence many persons were tried and punished.

Scape-Goat Day

Today was the day in the Jewish religion when sinners made amends for their misdemeanors by abstaining from eating, drinking, ablutions, anointing, the use of shoes, and the marriage bed. Traditionally two goats were sacrificed. One was killed and the other, "the scape-goat" was let loose in the desert bearing the sins of the people.

Births

O. Henry (writer) 1862; Maria Mercedes Isabella (Spanish princess) 1880.

Deaths

St Protus and St Hyacinthus (eunuchs) 257; Roger Crab (eccentric) 1680; Billy Bishop (war hero) 1956.

A Baby on a Golden Tray

The queen of Spain gave birth to Maria Mercedes Isabella this afternoon in 1880, to the disappointment of the Spaniards, who would have preferred a prince as heir to the throne. The infant was presented to the diplomatic body and other personages of high consideration by the king, who carried his daughter on a golden tray.

Illustrious Eunuch Martyrs

The saints, whose deaths in 257 the Catholic church commemorates on this day, are honoured among the most illustrious martyrs that ennobled Rome with their blood. They are said to have been eunuchs and retainers to that virtuous lady, St Eugenia.

Braver than the Red Baron

William Avery "Billy" Bishop, V.C., died on this day in 1956. Billy Bishop, the World War I Canadian flying ace, shot down seventy-two German aircraft in the course of thirteen months. The American hero, Eddie Rickenbacker, said: "When you speak about men who were absolutely fearless, there were only two—Manfred von Richthofen and Billy Bishop. Of the two, Bishop was the greater. Richthofen was a spider lying in wait for enemies to fly into his net. Bishop was a raider, always flashing into the enemy's territory. Bishop was a man absolutely without fear." Bishop modestly refuted this, saying, "I was often terrified; petrified with fear."

Franklin's War and Peace

"There was never a good war or a bad peace," wrote Benjamin Franklin today in 1773.

$255 for a Swedish Nightingale

On September 11, 1850 Jenny Lind, known as the Swedish Nightingale, appeared in concert in New York. Seven thousand people came to see her and $225 was paid for the first ticket sold.

Ten Years for Stealing

At the Surrey Sessions today in 1839, John Benchey, and Martha Stone were indicted for stealing, with great violence, from the person of Robert Young of Edinburgh, a watch, a pair of spectacles, and a wig. The pair, who had assailed their victim with a cane and an umbrella, were sentenced to ten years in jail.

The Life of Roger Crab

Roger Crab served in Cromwell's army for seven years, had his skull cloven in battle, then was sentenced to death for indiscipline, but survived to set up business as a haberdasher of hats in Buckinghamshire. One day he was seized with religious fervour, gave away his hat shop, and took up residence in a crude hut where he lived the rest of his life on three farthings a week. His food consisted of bran, dock-leaves, mallows, and grass. Several times he was cudgelled and put in the stocks, the wretched sackcloth frock being torn from his back and a merciless whipping applied. He was imprisoned four times for being a wizard but died of old age in his hut today in 1680.

12
SEPTEMBER

Births
Richard Gatling (machine-gun inventor) 1818; Maurice Chevalier (entertainer) 1888; Alfred A. Knopf (publisher) 1892; Ben Shahn (artist) 1898.

Deaths
St Eulogius (patriarch of Alexandria) 608; St Amatus (confessor) 627; another St Amatus (confessor) 690; John Alden (last of the *Mayflower* puritans) 1687.

Marriages
Winston Churchill to Clementine (1908); John F. Kennedy to Jacqueline Bouvier (1953).

The Majority Are Wrong
"When great changes occur in history, when great principles are involved, as a rule the majority are wrong."
  Eugene Debs, pioneer American socialist, 1918

Il Duce Kidnapped
Benito Mussolini, former Italian dictator, was kidnapped by German paratroopers from a hotel in Lake Bracciano, Italy, where he had been held prisoner by the government (1943).

A Pleasure Voyage
Six Liverpool thieves, confined in the prison of Castle Rushin on the Isle of Man, contrived to break out, and seizing the governor's pleasure boat in the bay, sailed off in the direction of Ireland (1843).

The Cedars of Lebanon
The Turkish governor general of Lebanon issued a special ordinance for the protection of the famous cedar forest, which had once covered a large tract of country but had now diminished to a thicket of about 400 trees. A wall was built around the remaining trees and the enclosure placed in charge of a custodian while the practice of cutting down branches as souvenirs was absolutely forbidden (1881).

A Maiden Voyage
The *Lusitania,* the world's largest ship, arrived in New York on her maiden voyage. The five days and fifty-four-minute trip set a new speed record (1907).

A Disastrous Voyage
The German battle cruiser *Hela* was sunk by a British submarine off Heligoland (1914).

Another Disastrous Voyage
The British vessel *Galway Castle* was torpedoed in the North Atlantic by a German U-boat (1918).

A Lengthy Flight
Orville Wright set a new duration record when he stayed in the air one hour, fourteen minutes, and twenty seconds during a forty-five mile flight near Washington (1908).

Women Yes, Alcohol No
A convention was held in Chicago to organise the Prohibition National Society in response to the failure of both major political parties to include prohibition in their platforms. The group members also favoured female suffrage (1869).

13
SEPTEMBER

Births

Laura Secord (heroine) 1775; Clara Schumann (pianist) 1819.

Deaths

Titus (Roman emperor) 81; Michael de Montaigne (essayist) 1592; James Wolfe (general) 1759.

White Sheets in Washington

On September 13, 1926 between 15,000 and 20,000 members of the Ku Klux Klan paraded in Washington in a show of strength.

Obstacles Halt the Terror

Today in 1837 an apologetic letter was received by the Geographical Society from Captain Black of the Royal Navy, describing the iceberg obstacles that prevented his carrying out the mission of discovery on the shores of the Hudson Bay territories, on which he had started in the ship *Terror* in June 1836, and from which he was now returning.

Today's Faulty People

People born on this day, according to numerology, have many faults. In particular they are noted for their rebellious nature and are very highly strung and sensitive, easily wounded in their feelings, inclined to feel lonely and isolated, and are likely to become despondent and melancholy unless they have achieved success. They make few real friends, but to the few they have, they are most devoted and loyal, but are always inclined to take the part of the "underdog" in any argument or any cause they espouse.

Loving the Warts of Paris

Michael de Montaigne, the celebrated French essayist died today in 1592. He knew Latin and Greek by the age of six and had finished all the schooling available in that era by the time he was thirteen. At twenty-one he was appointed a judge in Bordeaux and made his first trip to Paris: "I love it for itself; I love it tenderly, even to its warts and blemishes."

The Future President of America

On September 13, 1872 George Francis Train, adventurer, world traveller, railroader, newspaper publisher, and presidential candidate, spoke of his qualifications for the office: "I am that wonderful, eccentric, independent, extraordinary genius and political reformer of America, who is sweeping off all the politicians before him like a hurricane. I am your modest, diffident, unassuming friend, the future President of America—George Francis Train." (In the November elections, he received no votes.)

Today's Stomach and Liver Precautions

"Patients subject to Cholera and other gastric affections should be particularly cautious to regulate the stomach at this time of year. The prejudice against fruits is a dangerous one for when ripe and taken in moderation fruit is a great preservation against the more formidable forms of disease which in autumn often attacks the stomach and liver."

Catholic Annal, September 13, 1830

A Momentous Victory

"One of the most momentous victories in the annals of mankind" wrote the historian Bancroft of the victory by the British over the French at Québec today in 1759. In the hostilities conducted on the Plains of Abraham behind the citadel of Québec the British general Wolfe was killed and the French general Montcalm was mortally wounded. In one fell swoop Britain added all of Canada to the Empire.

14
SEPTEMBER

Births

Baron von Humboldt (naturalist) 1769; Jan Tschakste (1st president of Latvia) 1859; Margaret Sanger (birth-control advocate) 1883; the Fisher quintuplets (in Aberdeen, South Dakota) 1963.

Deaths

Dante Alighieri (poet) 1321; James Fennimore Cooper (author) 1851; Arthur (duke of Wellington) 1852; William McKinley (25th U.S. president) 1901.

The Messiah is Finished

On this day in 1741, George Frederick Handel, having worked without interruption for twenty-three days, finished his *Messiah*.

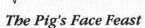

A Sale of Paintings

In England in 1848 at the Stowe sale, the Chandos portrait of Shakespeare was sold to Mr Rodd for 355 guineas. The equally famous Rembrandt, "The Unmerciful Servant," was knocked down to Mr Manson for 2,200 guineas.

The Cool Duke

Arthur, the duke of Wellington, the victor over Napoleon at Waterloo, died on September 14, 1852. In his life he was known for his coolness under fire and at times of stress. On once occasion he was at sea in a foundering ship, and in great danger of being drowned. At bedtime the captain came to him and said, "It will soon be over with us." "Very well," answered the duke, "Then I shall not take off my boots."

The Exaltation of the Holy Cross

The discovery of the cross by his mother, the Empress Helena, led Constantine to build a magnificent church in Jerusalem. The church was opened with a ceremony of Exaltation of The Holy Cross on September 14, 335, and the custom has been honoured annually since.

Holy Rood Day

In medieval English the word *rood* meant the Cross of Christ. School boys were given a day off on Holy Rood Day to go gathering nuts as noted in the lines from an old play:

This day, they say, is called Holy-Rood day,
And all the youth are now anutting gone.

In Scotland on this day it was possible to make a weather prediction:

"If the hart and hind meet dry and part dry on Rood Day fair, for sax weeks, of rain there'll be nai mair."

The Pig's Face Feast

September 14 was the day of the Pig's Face Feast at Avening in Gloucestershire when bell ringers were served with drinks, apple dumplings, and a pig's head. The custom was begun by Matilda, later the wife of William the Conqueror, who had been spurned by her lover Britric who lived at Avening Manor. In a rage she had him dispossessed, imprisoned, and finally executed. Then she repented and held a boar's head feast to celebrate and pray for the beheaded Britric.

The Matador Versus the Wild Bull

On September 14, 1923 Luis Angel Firpo knocked Jack Dempsey out of the ring in the first round of their heavyweight fight. But Dempsey knocked out Firpo in the second round of the thrilling match in the Polo Grounds, New York. "The Manassa Matador dropped the Wild Bull of the Pampas, but not until the matador was gored by the bull, so that he will remember it for many a day," wrote W.O. McGeehan in the *New York Herald*.

15
SEPTEMBER

Births

William Taft (27th U.S. president) 1857; Bruno Walter (conductor) 1876; James Fennimore Cooper (author) 1789.

Deaths

Jumbo (an elephant) 1885.

The Death of Jumbo

Jumbo, a famous elephant who had formerly resided in a zoo, but was travelling on personal appearances in North America, received such severe injuries in a railway collision at St Thomas, Ontario, that he died in a few minutes.

Ludi Circensia

September 15 was the annual date in ancient Rome of the Circensian games, the Roman imitation of the Greek Olympic games. They were held in the Circus at Rome, built by Tarquin. The main event was the Pentathlon, which consisted of five different competitions: leaping, wrestling, throwing the quoit and javelin, foot and chariot racing, and boxing.

A Railway Opening

On the 15th September, 1830 the Liverpool and Manchester Railway was opened with great ceremony. It was the first rail line to depend on steam locomotives for power.

A Successful Balloon Ascent

The first successful balloon ascent in Britain was carried out by Vincent Lunardi, an attaché with the Neapolitan embassy, on September 15, 1784. Lunardi took off from the Artillery Ground in London, and landed near Ware, in Hertfordshire. When Lunardi went up a cabinet council was engaged on very important state deliberations. But King George III said: "My lords, we shall have an opportunity of discussing this question at another time, but we may never again see poor Lunardi; so let us adjourn the council and observe the balloon!"

Regular Mail Service

On September 15, 1858, regular mail service to the Pacific Coast was established by the Overland Mail Coaches. The U.S. government operated the 2,800 mile route at great expense and stipulated the trip between St Louis and San Francisco should be under twenty-five days.

The Nuremberg Laws

Today in 1935 the Nazis enacted the Nuremberg Laws, starting off a program of violent religious and racial persecution. All Jews were deprived of their citizenship, ghettos were revived, and the swastika became the German national flag.

The Battle of Britain

Today in 1940 marked the climax and turning point of the Battle of Britain. On their greatest day, in a running fight with 500 German planes, the RAF, aided by free Polish and Czech pilots, destroyed 185 German aircraft.

Cadiz Plundered

Today in 1596, Cadiz, a large, rich, and handsome town in the province of Andalusia in Spain, was taken and plundered and the ships and harbour destroyed by the earl of Essex, Queen Elizabeth's favourite.

Mexican Booty

Today in 1849 gold dust and Mexican dollars to the value of about £6,000,000 were lodged in the Bank of England. The precious load was conveyed from the London Bridge terminus in fifteen vans escorted by the police.

Births

Tintoretto (Italian painter) 1518; Louis XIV (French king) 1638.

Deaths

St Cyprian (martyr) 258; Mr Yardley (fraudulent debtor) 1735; Gabriel Dante Fahrenheit (German thermometer inventor) 1736.

A Painter's Pseudonym

Tintoretto, the great Venetian painter was born today in 1518. His real name was Jacopo Robusti. His famous name was adopted from his father's trade as a dyer or "tintore."

A Lengthy Reign

Louis XIV, born today in 1638, became king of France in 1643, and reigned for seventy-two of his seventy-seven years. As a child the monarchial reins were held by his mother Anne of Austria but he was still officially the king.

St Cyprian's Sufferings

As bishop of Carthage, Cyprian was continually harassed by pagans, who in derision called him *Coprianus* in allusion to a Greek term for filth. "Cyprian to the lions! Cyprian to the wild beasts!" was their constant cry. They finally had their way on this day in the year 258, although no animals were involved. He was led outside Carthage to an extensive plain planted with trees, which were ascended by numerous spectators, and was there beheaded.

A Debtor and a Fraud

On 16th September, 1735, a Mr Yardley died in the Fleet prison in London, where he had languished for nearly ten years for a debt of £100. Upon his death it was discovered that Yardley had an income of £700 a year, and in his cell he had securities and other effects worth over £5,000.

A Cowboy Becomes President

Today in 1901, aboard the funeral train bearing the body of the late President William McKinley, en route from Buffalo, New York, to Washington, the political boss Mark Hanna bemoaned the fact that Theodore Roosevelt was now the president of the United States. To the editor of the *Chicago Times Herald,* Hanna cried out: "I told William McKinley it was a mistake to nominate that wild man at Philadelphia . . . Now, look! That dammed cowboy is president of the United States!"

Today's Flower

The flower for September 16 is the *Aster tripolium* or sea starwort.

An Affray on the River Eamont

There occurred on this day in 1850 a serious affray between Lord Brougham and a body of watchers on the river Eamont in England. Accompanied by the marquis of Douro, Lady Malet and others, his lordship caused the keepers to cast his nets into the river, when a party of ten watchers from the Eamont Angling Association rushed out and began fighting for their possession. A local constable formally seized the nets and one of Lord Brougham's men was fined £5 for use of an improper net.

£3,000 for Shakespeare's House

Today in 1847, Shakespeare's house at Stratford-on-Avon was sold for £3,000 to the Shakespeare Committee by the trustees appointed under the will of the late owner.

Cherokee Strip Day

Today in 1893 was Cherokee Strip Day in Oklahoma. More than 100,000 homesteaders rushed into the strip, between Oklahoma and Kansas, to claim shares of the six million acres of land opened up by the U.S. government to new settlers.

Births

Marquis de Condorcet (mathematician) 1743; Roddy McDowell (actor) 1928; Stirling Moss (race driver) 1929.

Deaths

James II (English king) 1701; Everett Moore (editor) 1891; Thomas Selfridge (airplane passenger) 1908.

An Editorial Disagreement

On September 17, 1891 E.M. Tate, editor of *The Echo* shot and killed Everett Moore, the editor of *The Alliance Vindicator,* at Dallas, Texas.

A Name Change

On September 17, 1630, the name of a town in Massachusetts—Trimountain—was changed to Boston.

An Airplane Crash

The first airplane fatality occurred on September 17, 1908 when a propellor blade caught in overhead wires, killing Thomas Selfridge and injuring Orville Wright.

A Bank Crash

Today in 1873 the banking firm of Jay Cooke & Co. in New York failed, setting off the panic of 1873.

Betrayed by an Omelet

The Marquis de Condorcet, the French mathematical philosopher who made several breakthroughs in calculus, was born today in Picardy in 1743. During the French Revolution Robespierre accused Condorcet of being a royalist and a price was put on his head. He hid for eight months in a Paris attic but one day he crept out for fresh air. He entered a cabaret and ordered an omelet. "How many eggs," inquired the waiter. "Twelve," responded the famished philosopher, ignorant of the proper dimensions of a working-man's omelet. The waiter became suspicious and called the police, who arrested Condorcet and put him in prison. He escaped the inevitable guillotine by taking poison.

A Constitutional Amendment

Today in 1787 the U.S. Federal Constitution was amended to state that "No religious tests shall ever be required as a qualification to any office or public trust under the United States" (article 7, section 3).

A Hurricane in Miami

On September 17, 1926 Miami was devastated by a hurricane that killed 370 people, left 50,000 homeless, and caused $100,000,000 damage to property.

Curious Burial Instructions

Today in the year 1404, the last will and testament of Sir Lewis Clifford, a wealthy English gentleman who had led a wild life and then found religion, was read: " . . . I recommaund my wretchid and synfule sowle hooly to the grace and mercy of the blessed Trynitie; and my wretchid careyne to be put in the ferthest corner of the chirch-yard, in which my wretchid soule departeth from my body . . . that my stinking careyne be neyther leyd clothe of gold ne of silk, but a black clothe; ne stone ne other thinge, whereby eny man may see where my stinkign careyne lyeth."

18
SEPTEMBER

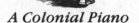

Births

Samuel Johnson (writer) 1709; Greta Garbo (actress) 1905; Peter Sellers (actor) 1925.

Deaths

Domitian (Roman emperor) 96; St Thomas (archbishop) 1555; William Hazlitt (essayist) 1830.

Whistling Shrimp

On the likelihood of Russia rejecting communism: "Those who wait for that must wait until a shrimp learns to whistle."

  Nikita Khrushchev, September 18, 1955

Humorous Tanks

Today in 1916, a reporter for the *London Daily Sketch* described a new instrument of war, the "tank": "When our soldiers first saw these strange creatures lolloping along the roads and over old battlefields, taking trenches on the way, they shouted and cheered wildly, and laughed for a day afterwards."

Johnson's Jottings

Samuel Johnson, a prolific writer born today in 1709, made pithy comments on many topics: "When two Englishmen meet, their first talk is of the weather; Marriage has many pains, but celibacy has no pleasures; When a man is tired of London he is tired of life; I am willing to love all mankind, except an American; A cucumber should be well sliced, and dressed with pepper and vinegar, and thrown out, as good for nothing."

A Colonial Piano

The September 18, 1769 issue of the *Boston Gazette* described the first piano, actually a spinet, built in the colonies. This invention of Mr John Harris had jacks with goose-quill spurts that plucked the strings creating a sound similar to the mandolin.

A Cornerstone Laid

On this day in 1793 President George Washington laid the cornerstone of the United States Capitol building in Washington.

The Price of the Times

Today in 1851 *The New York Times,* founded by George Jones and Henry Raymond, went on sale for one cent a copy.

Fire and Brimstone

St Thomas, the archbishop of Valentia, died today in 1555. He discharged all the duties of a good pastor, and preached with so much zeal and fervour, that the words that came from his mouth seemed so many flashes of lightning or claps of thunder.

Domitian's Demise

The Emperor Domitian, whose reign was known for its incredible cruelty, died on September 18, 96 A.D. by the dagger thrusts of conspirators who included his wife and closest friends. Domitan, whose favourite leisure activity was killing flies slowly, had long been suffering premonitions of his death, and became so fearful that he had all the galleries where he walked lined with highly polished, mirror-like stone, so that he could see around him at all times.

Births

Henry III (French king) 1551; Arthur Rackham (illustrator) 1867; Rachel Field (writer) 1894.

Deaths

James A. Garfield (20th U.S. president) 1861.

Disinterment

On September 19, 1871 President Lincoln's body was removed to its permanent resting place in Springfield, Illinois.

Royal Mourning

After a long and painful struggle President Garfield expired from the wounds of an assassin's bullet at Long Branch this evening in 1881. Her Majesty, Queen Victoria, on hearing the news, telegraphed Mrs Garfield with her deepest symapthies. The court went into mourning for a week, this being the first time that such a mark of respect had been paid by an English sovereign to the president of a republic.

False Teeth

"Whereas many persons are so unfortunate as to lose their foreteeth by accident and other ways, to their great detriment, not only in looks but speaking both in public and in private, this is to inform all such, that they may have them replaced with artificial ones that look as well as natural, and answers the end of speaking to all intents, by Paul Revere, Goldsmith—near the head of Dr Clarke's Wharf, Boston."

An advertisement in the *Boston Gazette,* September 19, 1768

Elopement

Today in 1846 Elizabeth Barrett, accompanied by her faithful maid, Wilson, and her spaniel Flush, fled from 50 Wimpole Street in London and the tyranny of her father, and eloped to Paris with Robert Browning. (The two poets had been married in secret at St Marylebone Parish Church on September 12.)

Today's Epitaph

Here lies the bodies of
Francis Hunnfrodds and Mary his wife
who were both born on the same day
of the week, month and year, Sept. 19th 1600,
marry'd on the day of their birth
and after having had 12 children born to them,
died aged 80 years on the same day
of the year they were born Sept. 19th 1680,
the one not above shown before ye other.

At St Mary's Parish Church, Whitby, England

Mickey Mouse

Today in 1928 Americans were introduced for the first time to Mickey Mouse, when the animated cartoon feature, *Steamboat Willie,* opened at the Colony Theater in New York.

Dixie Sung

The Confederate song "Dixie" was first sung September 19, 1859 by its composer Daniel Decatur Emmett, a blackfaced minstrel singer at Bryant's Minstrel Theatre in New York.

Lord Haw Haw Sentenced

Today in 1945 William Joyce, the notorious "Lord Haw Haw" of the Nazi radio broadcasts during World War II, was convicted of treason and sentenced to hang.

Today's Weather Forecast

According to an old saying in Derbyshire, England, a storm from the south on September 19th foretells a mild winter.

20
SEPTEMBER

Births

Romulus (founder of Rome) 70 B.C.; Sophia Loren (actress) 1934.

Deaths

Lucius Crassus (Roman orator) 91 B.C.; Owen Glendower (Welsh patriot) 1415; Jean Sibelius (composer) 1957.

Military Episodes

331 B.C.: Alexander the Great crossed the Tigris River to attack Persia.
451: The Romans defeated Attila the Hun in France.
1565: The Spanish took Fort Caroline from the French in Florida.
1792: The French defeated the Prussians in France.

Famous Schools

1440: The school at Eton was founded by Henry VI.
1865: Vassar Female College opened in Poughkeepsie, New York.

Religion

1258: Salisbury Cathedral in England was consecrated.
1276: John Peter Juliani was crowned Pope John XXI.
1928: The various sects of methodism were united in England.

Cities and Nations

622: Mohammed changed the name of his city from Yathrib to Medina.
1917: Transcaucasia in Russia became a republic.
1936: Emperor Haile Selassie flew to Geneva to seek aid for Ethiopia.
1966: Guyana joined the United Nations.

American Events

1841: Horace Greeley converted the *New Yorker* into the *Weekly Tribune*.
1870: A U.S. shaving mug with drain holes in the soap compartment was patented.
1873: Bank failures in New York caused the Stock Exchange to close.
1921: Station KDKA in Pittsburgh began radio newscasts.

Historical Oddments

1519: An exploration expedition led by Magellan sailed from Spain.
1808: The Covent Garden Theatre in London burned to the ground.
1839: A fish fell from the sky during a storm in Calcutta.
1883: The first electric tram car ran in Paris.

Today in Numerology

The number 20 is called "The Awakening" or "The Judgment" and is represented visually by a flying, winged angel tooting a trumpet while below a man, woman, and child are shown rising up from a tomb with their hands clasped in prayer. The number 20 is interpreted as the awakening of new purpose and today would seem to be a good day to make new plans. However 20 is not a material number and it is doubtful that any financial gain can be made today.

21
SEPTEMBER

Births

Louis Joliet (explorer) 1645; John McAdam (Scottish inventor of macadamized roads) 1756; H.G. Wells (author) 1866.

A Bee Aficionado

Publius Vergilius Maro—Virgil—died on this day nineteen years before Jesus was born. His chief works were the *Aeneid* an epic poem on the Roman people and *Georgics* an agricultural poem concerning cattle and bees. Selected lines from these include: "Woman is always fickle and changing. Fear lent wings to its feet. And the Britons completely isolated from the whole world. A snake lurks in the grass."

Deaths

Virgil (Roman poet) 19 B.C.; St Mathew (apostle) 1st century; Edward II (English king) 1327; Haakon VII (Norwegian king) 1957.

An Ex-Tax Collector

In the first part of his life St Mathew was a tax collector but he gave that up to become a disciple of Jesus, the first to do so. By the end of his career on September 21, sometime in the 1st century, his writings, now found in the Bible, had become more extensive than any of the gospel chronicles. His efforts including, it is said, using an angel's feather to write the first gospel, are commemorated by various churches today.

St Mathew's Day

According to ancient proverbs St Mathew's Day had varied significance:

On St Mathee
Shut up the bee

On St Mathew
Get candlesticks new

St Mathew
Brings on cold dew

Mathew's Day bright and clear
Brings good wine in the next year

St Matho
Take thy hopper and sow

St Mathie
Sends sap into the tree

Stonehenge is Sold

On September 21, 1915, the mysterious group of stones at Stonehenge on Salisbury Plain in England was auctioned for £6,600 to C.H.E. Chubb, of Salisbury.

A Remarkable Show of Gossamer

"About 9:00 a.m. an appearance very unusual began to demand our attention, a shower of cobwebs falling from very elevated regions, and continuing without any interruption till the close of day. These webs were not single, filmy threads, floating in the air in all directions, but perfect flakes or rags, some near an inch broad, and five or six long. On every side, as the observer turned his eyes, might he behold a continual succession of fresh flakes falling into his sight, and twinkling like stars."
Natural History of Selborne, September 21, 1741, by Gilbert White

The Strength of Conviction

Today in 1881 three bishops of the sect of the Greek church calling themselves "Old Believers" were released from an imprisonment that had lasted since the year 1856. One of these was over 80 years of age and the youngest was about 70. They had been confined all these years in a monastery at Souzdal. Liberty more than once had been offered to them on the condition of their abandoning their episcopal titles, but this they consistently refused to do. They declared that even if they would, they could not divest themselves of the divine office, which came from God and not from them.

22
SEPTEMBER

Witches Pressed and Hanged

On September 22, 1692, two men and seven women were executed at Salem, Massachusetts for witchcraft. One of them was "pressed" to death for standing mute, while the others were hanged.

Mother Not Guilty

On September 22, 1656, the General Provincial Court, meeting at Patuxent, Maryland, ordered the first U.S. jury composed entirely of women to convene in the case of Judith Catchpole, charged with murdering her child. (The jury, made up of seven married women and four single women, brought in a verdict of "not guilty.")

A Heart-Stopping Fight

Today in 1927 almost 105,000 fans crowded into Soldiers' Field, Chicago to see—and millions more followed on radio—the second Dempsey-Tunney fight, an attempt by Dempsey to regain his title. Tunney won in the 10th round by decision. Five radio fans dropped dead of heart failure awaiting the results of the controversial and drawn-out "long count" in the seventh round.

Births

Theodor Edward Hook (novelist) 1788; Alfred Vanderbilt (financier) 1912; Ingemar Johansson (boxer) 1932.

Deaths

St Maurice and 6,600 troops (martyrs) 286; nine witches (executed) 1692; John Bernardi (unconvicted prisoner) 1736; Nathan Hale (American patriot) 1776.

Boston Baked Beans

Today in 1908, in an article on Boston baked beans, the *New York Tribune* commented: "Taking the average height of a Bostonian at 5 feet 6 inches, and the height of a beanpot at 10 inches, one can easily figure that a Bostonian in a year eats more than two and five-sevenths times his own height in baked beans and more than his own weight. Boston pays for baked beans in a year, the price of two of Uncle Sam's modern battleships."

Mass Mute Martyrdom

St Maurice was a general officer of the Thebean legion, which consisted of 6,600 men, who were all well armed; but they had learned to give to God what is God's, and to Caesar what is Caesar's. Maximan having commanded them in vain to sacrifice to the idols, ordered his whole army to surround them today in the year 286. The martyrs suffered themselves to be butchered like innocent lambs, not opening their mouths.

An Unconvicted Prisoner

On September 22, 1736, John Bernardi died in Newgate prison in England after having spent the last forty years of his life there, though he was never convicted of any crime. He had been arrested in 1696 on suspicion of plotting to kill William III, but the crown could never gather the evidence to convict him. By the time he died the authorities could barely remember what he had been imprisoned for in the first place.

Nathan Hale's Last Words

On September 22, 1776 Captain Nathan Hale of the colonial forces was captured while reconnoitering the British on Long Island. He was denied the attendance of a clergyman, and was speedily hanged as a spy by Sir William Howe. All his possessions, including his letters to his mother and friends, were destroyed. His last words on the scaffold were: "I only regret that I have but one life to give to my country."

23
SEPTEMBER

Births

Euripedes (Greek dramatist) 480 B.C.; Octavius Caesar Augustus (1st Roman emperor) 63 B.C.; Mickey Rooney (American actor) 1920.

Deaths

St Thecla (virgin martyr) 1st century; Prosper Mérimée (French writer) 1870; Sigmund Freud (Austrian psychologist) 1939.

A Male Chauvinist Pig?

Euripedes, the tragic dramatist of Athens born today in 480 B.C., seems to have had male chauvinist tendencies: "Woman is woman's natural ally. Man's best possession is a sympathetic wife. A woman should be good for everything at home, but abroad good for nothing."

Wild Beasts at Bay

St Thecla made a vow of perpetual virginity and a Christian life at a very early age. For refusing to break her vows, she was condemned to be torn apart by wild beasts, but they, to the surprise of the bystanders, refused to touch her. Nevertheless she is styled a martyr, though she died peacefully on a September 23 during the 1st century A.D.

An Astronomical Event

On this night in 1846, following the marvellous calculations of Le Verrier of Paris and Adams of Cambridge concerning the celestial phenomenon known as "the perturbations of Uranus," Herr Gaulle of Berlin discovered the existence of a new planet, one of the greatest triumphs of theoretical astronomy. The planet was named Neptune.

Air Mail Pilot Number One

On September 23, 1911, Earl Ovington was sworn in as "air mail pilot number one." His job was to deliver air mail handed to him by the postmaster general at Garden City, Long Island to the postmaster of Mineola six miles away. He flew a Blériot monoplane, the *Dragon Fly,* in this, the first air mail service authorised by the U.S. Post Office.

A Grisly Souvenir

On this day in 1880, the Franklin Search Expedition, under the command of Lieutenant Schwatka, returned to New Bedford, Massachusetts, having discovered relics of Franklin's *Erebus* and *Terror* lost in 1847. The party brought away a portion of the remains of Lieutenant John Irving, third officer of the *Terror,* for what purpose it was not known.

A Fake Scottish Witch

Today in 1843 a witch imposter at Dingwall, Ross-shire, Scotland, was sentenced to three months' imprisonment, for obtaining money under pretence of curing diseases and recovering stolen money.

Excited American Gatherings

British newspapers reported today in 1857 that "Revival meetings, or gatherings of excited people to engage in religious exercises" were becoming common in the United States.

A Wild West Show

September 23, 1897 was the first time *Cheyenne Frontier Day* was celebrated in Wyoming. Since that day the exhibition has grown to a five-day annual festival with rodeos, Indian games and dances, military manoeuvres, and horse races.

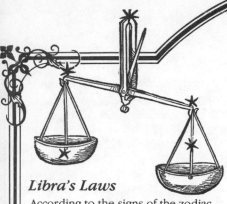

24
SEPTEMBER

Briths

Horace Walpole (English politician) 1717; F. Scott Fitzgerald (American author) 1896.

Deaths

Liberius (Roman pope) 366; Pepin III (French king) 768.

Conspirators Cause Calamity

Today in 1869 was "Black Friday" in New York City. Conspiring speculators had pushed the price of gold up to $164 an ounce, making $11,000,000 in profits for themselves, but causing a great calamity in the business community, which was required to pay duties in gold.

Polygamy Preferred

Today in 1890, President Woodruff of the Mormon church in Salt Lake City, Utah, issued a manifesto in which he advised that the teaching and practice of polygamy should be abandoned by the Mormons. Shortly after it was announced that a large number of Mormons were preparing to found a new colony in North Mexico.

Hip, Hip, Harvest Home

In medieval England it was customary to begin the harvest on or about September 24. In the *Feast of Ungathering* or Harvest Home, as it was sometimes called, crops were brought in on a decorated wagon called the hock cart, while the reapers danced, sang, and shouted, giving vent to the excitement of the day:

Harvest-home, harvest-home,
We have ploughed, we have sowed,
We have reaped, we have mowed,
We have brought home every load,
Hip, hip, hip, harvest-home, hurrah!

Libra's Laws

According to the signs of the zodiac, Libra (the scales) rules from now until October 23, presenting the following fortunes:

Manners and quality when well placed

Shee signifies a quiet man, not given to Law, Quarrel or Wrangling; not Vitious, Pleasant, Neat and Spruce, Loving Mirth in his words and actions, cleanly in Apparel, rather Drinking much then Gluttonous, prone to Venery, oft entangled in love-matters, Zealous in their affections, Musicall, delighting in Baths, and all honest merry Meetings, or Maskes and Stage-playes, easie of Beliefe, and not given to Labour, or take any Pains, a Company keepr, Cheerful, nothing Mistrustful, a right vertuous Man or Woman, oft had in some Jealousie, yet no cause for it.

When ill

Then he is Riotous, Expensive, wholly given to Loosenesse and Lewd companies of Women, nothing regarding his Reputation, coveting unlawful Beds, Incestuous, an Adulterer, Fantastical, a meer Skip-jack, of no Faith, no Repute, no Credit; spending his Meanes in Ale Houses, Taverns, and amongst Scandalous, Loose people; a meer Lazy companion, nothing careful of the things of this Life, or any thing Religious; a meer Atheist and natural man.

Christian Astrology, by William Lilly, 1647

25
SEPTEMBER

Births

Christian Gottlob Heyne (classical editor) 1729; Abraham Gottlieb Werner (geologist) 1750; Felicia Dorothea Hemans (poetess) 1794.

Deaths

Dummy (fortune-teller) 1863; Lord Mountmorres (murdered) 1880; Ring Lardner (author) 1933.

Today with Samuel Pepys

"I did send for a cup of tea (a China drink) of which I never had drank before."

From his diary, 25 September, 1660

French Fortune-Teller's Fate

On this day in 1863 at Castle Hedingham in England there occurred the death of an old Frenchman commonly called "Dummy" who practised fortune-telling to a little extent, and had incurred, in consequence, the evil reputation of being a wizard. Aggrieved by his refusing to heal their imaginary ailments and determined at the same time to rid the parish of a person of such baleful influence, a mob, composed for the most part of small shopkeepers and women, fell upon the old man and besides half suffocating him in a ditch, otherwise maltreated him so severely, that he died.

Mountmorres' Murder

In Ireland, at a place called Rusheen, today in 1880, Lord Mountmorres was brutally murdered. He was found lying in the road with six bullet wounds. The doctor, who was presently in attendance, thought he detected pulsation and directed the dying man removed to the nearest house. The owner, Hugh Flanigan, although he was told that it was possible the man might still be alive, refused to grant him admission, saying if he did so nothing belonging to him would be alive that day twelvemonth.

Today in the Times

On September 24, 1888 a letter appeared in the *Times* of London describing a toad that had been taken out of a bed of clay during the formation of a railway cutting at Greenock. It was alive, though inactive and so limp that it seemed to have no bones. It breathed, but seemed to have lost the use of its eyes. The writer roughly calculated its age at about 30,000 years.

September Celebrations

Come, lads and lasses, pray attend
Unto these lines that's just been penned.
From miles around, both far and near,
They come to see the rigs o' the Fair;
So, Master John, do you beware, and
Don't go kissing the girl's o'Bridgewater Fair.

Today in America

1690:   *Publick Occurences, Both Foreign and Domestic,* the first newspaper in America, published its only issue, being suppressed by royal authority.

1789:   The first session of the first Congress of the United States met in New York and voted ten amendments to the Constitution, which are now popularly known as the Bill of Rights.

Today with Columbus

1492:   An over-zealous watchman in the crow's nest hollered "Land!" aboard Columbus' ship during his first voyage. (The Bahamas weren't sighted until October 12.)

1493:   Columbus sailed on his second voyage, this time with seventeen ships, 1,500 people, animals, and tools to start a colony in the New World.

Today with Balboa

On September 25, 1513, Balboa led an expedition across the Panama Isthmus and discovered the Pacific Ocean. He symbolically took Panama for Spain by wading through the ocean with drawn sword.

26
SEPTEMBER

Births
George Gershwin (composer) 1898.

Deaths
Edgar Degas (artist) 1917.

A Flaming Lance, 1607
A comet like "a flaming lance" that soared through Ursa Major and Serpentis, was visible on this day in 1607.

A Medical Law, 1772
On September 26, 1772, the New Jersey legislature passed a bill forbidding the practice of medicine without a licence. The new law excepted those who pulled teeth, drew blood, or gave free medical advice.

A Band Concert, 1892
On this day in 1892, John Philip Sousa and his band presented their first public concert in America, playing for the first time the bandmaster's "Liberty Bell March."

A Wad of Plunder, 1580
Today in 1580, Sir Francis Drake arrived in England with his ships laden with plunder from Spain.

A Dragon Fight, 1449
On September 26, 1449, at Little Conrad in Suffolk, legend says that two fire-breathing dragons met in mortal combat for an hour, in a clash on the Suffolk-Essex border. The Suffolk dragon was black. The Essex one "red and spotted." Finally the red dragon was victorious and both crawled back to their respective caves. The scene of the battle is called Sharpfight Meadow by the locals.

A Lady in a Chair, 1923
On September 26, 1923 Miss Margaret Bondfield was elected chairman of the General Council of the Trades Union Congress, Britain—the first woman to hold such office.

A Shorthand Conference, 1887
An International Shorthand Conference attended by stenographers from foreign lands was opened in London today in 1887. Discussions on parliamentary reporting, spelling reform, and other subjects were held.

A Tug-Boat Voyage, 1913
On September 26, 1913 a tug boat made a successful passage through the locks of the Panama Canal.

Mecca in America, 1876
On September 26, 1876, *Mecca,* the first temple of the Shriners (Ancient Arabic Order of Nobles of the Mystic Shrine) opened in New York. Only masons were eligible for membership.

The Anti-Masonic Party, 1831
Today in 1831 the Anti-Masonic Party held a national convention at Baltimore to nominate candidates for president and vice-president of the United States. The Anti-Masonic Party was formed following the disappearance from his home in western New York of William Morgan, a Mason, who had been charged with revealing or planning to reveal the secrets of the Masons. The Masons were accused of kidnapping and drowning him in the Niagara River or Lake Erie. What became of him was never satisfactorily explained.

27
SEPTEMBER

Births

Samuel Adams (American patriot) 1722; Augustin de Iturbide (Mexican emperor) 1783; Louis Auchincloss (novelist) 1917.

Deaths

St Vincent de Paul (philanthropist) 1660; Innocent XII (pope) 1700; Milos Obrenovic (Serbian king) 1860.

A Crime in New York

On this day in 1905, crying, "You can't do that on Fifth Avenue," a New York policeman arrested a woman he had observed smoking a cigarette in the rear of an automobile on New York's famous thoroughfare.

A Blast at Birmingham

An enormous explosion took place today in 1859 at Birmingham at the Phillips and Pursall's percussion-cap factory, in which there were stored five million and a half caps, from 3,000 to 4,000 cartridges containing about forty pounds of gunpowder, and a large quantity of other explosive material. The entire building was blown to atoms.

A Lion in Birmingham

Today in 1889 a chase after a lion that had escaped from a travelling menagerie took place in Birmingham. The animal escaped from its cage through a sliding shutter that an elephant had opened with his trunk. As soon as it was perceived, the alarm was raised and pursuit was organised. The frightened animal jumped over a group of children who stood in its path and fled into a large sewer. Into this a lion tamer and a bearhound immediately entered. Over another entrance to the pipe a large cage was placed and the lion, being driven through the sewer, was eventually caught in the trap.

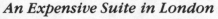

An Expensive Suite in London

Jonathan Swift wrote a complaining letter to a friend from London on September 27, 1710: "I lodge in Bury Street, where I removed a week ago. I have the first floor, a dining-room, and a bed chamber, at eight shillings per week; plaguy deep, but I spend nothing for eating, never go to a tavern, and very seldom in a coach; yet, after all, it will be expensive."

A Fight in New York

Today in 1950, former heavywight boxing champion Joe Louis was defeated by Ezzard Charles at Yankee Stadium, New York in a 15-round decision.

Electric Lights in London

Today in 1880, one of the most important applications of electric lighting that had yet been made in London was inaugurated at the new Royal Albert Dock at Silvertown. The dock was illuminated by twenty-six Siemens lamps, while smaller lamps were placed in the sheds. The results were in all respects satisfactory.

Luck in Today's Number

People born on September 27 in particular, and others to a lesser extent, can insure good luck today by wearing all shades of red or pink. Their lucky stones are the ruby, garnet, and bloodstone which ideally should be worn next to the skin.

28
SEPTEMBER

Births

Georges Clemenceau (French statesman) 1841; Brigitte Bardot (French actress) 1934.

A Horse Kicks His Teacher

Thomas Day was an educator, and a follower of Rousseau's revolutionary educational doctrines. Having resolved that no wife was good enough for him but one trained according to the proper methods, he took two twelve-year-old girls from a foundling hospital in London under his care, in the hope that under his personal tutelage he would create the perfect wife. But he was a better dreamer than a teacher, and in the end was only too happy to give the grown girls away to husbands of their own choice, along with hefty dowries. Frustrated in trying to create the perfect woman, Day turned his talents elsewhere, and on September 28, 1789, was killed by a kick from a horse that he was trying to train by a new method.

Michaelmas Eve Events

Tomorrow being the feast of St Michael, various occurrences took place tonight in medieval England. Michaelmas Eve often saw an odd ceremony of "Crack-nut Sunday" in which all the congregation took to cracking nuts, the reason for which is unknown. In Lincolnshire ballads were sung, bonfires burned, and drinking and story-telling ensued. Master and men were placed on an equal level. The ghost of Sir Walter Raleigh walked the gardens of Sherborne Castle on St Michael's Eve.

God Save the King

Today in 1745 English theatregoers sang "God Save the King" for the first time in history, following the defeat of English forces under Sir John Cope by the Jacobites, led by Bonne Prince Charlie.

An Invasion of Swallows

The general migration of the swallows and sand martins takes place in Europe at this time and they avail themselves of the first northern winds to retire to Africa and other warm countries. On this day in 1781, sand martins, driven back probably from some attempted aerial voyage became prodigiously numerous in and about London, and flew in quantities about the streets. After a few days they disappeared, on the return of a favourable wind.

Deaths

Thomas Day (English educator) 1789; Louis Pasteur (French scientist) 1895.

A Baseball Scandal

Baseball's biggest scandal was disclosed today in 1920. A Grand Jury in Chicago indicted eight players of the Chicago White Sox for "throwing" the 1919 World Series games between their team and the Cincinnati Reds.

The Swallow's Secret Guide

Amusive birds! say where your hid retreat,
When the frost rages, and the tempests beat;
Whence your return, by such nice instinct led,
When Spring, sweet season, lifts her bloomy head?
Such baffled searches mock man's prying pride,
The God of Nature is your secret guide!
Catholic Annal, September 28, 1830

29
SEPTEMBER

Birth

Little Horatio Nelson (later admiral and lord) was born today in 1758, in the parsonage house of Burnham-Thorp in the county of Norfolk of which parish his father was then rector.

Death

On September 29, 1902 Emile Zola, the celebrated French writer, was found suffocated in his bedroom, from a foul chimney. His wife was unconscious but survived.

Michaelmas Day

September 29 is celebrated as the feast of St Michael, the Archangel, and all the holy angels. Michael, the chief of all the angels, was in command of the loyal angels of God that overthrew the rebel angel Lucifer. He is usually represented in military gear with a spear in his hand, and often as standing on the fallen devil.

Michaelmas Goose

Throughout Britain it used to be the custom to dine on goose on Michaelmas, but the origins of the practice are open to speculation. According to some, Queen Elizabeth I was eating a goose on Michaelmas when tidings were brought of the defeat of the Spanish Armada. She was overjoyed, and resolved to eat goose each Michaelmas thereafter; and the rest of the land soon adopted the court custom. According to others, because Michaelmas was one of four quarterly rent days when rural tenants paid their landlords, farmers used to bring a goose to their lord on Michaelmas to buy his leniency, goose being very good in the fall. Thus, for the landlord's table at least, there was always goose on September 29.

Michaelmas Proverbs

At Michaelmas by custom, right divine,
Geese are ordained to bleed at Michael's shrine.

The Michaelmas Daisy among dead weeds
Blooms for St Michael's valourous deeds.

If you eat goose on Michaelmas Day, you will not want for money all year.

On Michaelmas Day the devil puts his foot on the blackberries.

A Michaelmas Caution

Geese now in their prime season are,
Which, if well roasted, are good fare:
Yet, however, friends, take heed
How too much on them you feed,
Lest, when your tongue run loose,
Your discourse do smell of goose.
Poor Robin's Almanac, September 29, 1695

A Michaelmas Tradition

In Shropshire farmhands were hired for a year from Michaelmas Day. If one wished to leave employ it was customary to cut a stick and place it in the chimney corner. If no stick was left it was accepted by all parties that the farmhand would remain without a word being spoken.

Michaelmas Lawlessness

In the town of Kidderminster in Worcestershire it was the custom to hold a "lawless hour" from 3:00 to 4:00 p.m. during which time people could throw cabbage stalks at each other without penalty.

30
SEPTEMBER

Births

Gnaeus Pompeius (Pompey the Great) 106 B.C.; Deborah Kerr (actress) 1921; Truman Capote (writer) 1924.

Deaths

Isabella (queen of Charles VI of France) 1435; Edith (wife of President Theodore Roosevelt) 1948.

Famous Last Words

British Prime Minister Neville Chamberlain gave a speech today on his return from the Munich Conference: "This is the second time in our history that there has come back from Germany to Downing Street Peace with Honour: I believe it is peace for our time" (1938).

A Quiet Monumental Occasion

The foundation-stone of the Nelson Monument was laid in Trafalgar Square. The block with which the ceremony was performed being a piece of Dartmoor granite weighing fourteen tons. The proceedings were conducted in a private manner, owing to the absence from London of most of the gentlemen composing the monument committee (1840).

Women's War Effort

President Wilson in a speech to the U.S. Congress declared the Woman's Suffrage Amendment ought to be adopted "as a vitally necessary war measure" (1918).

An Epitaph on a Skull

Ladies, when you your perfect beauties see,
Think 'em but tenants to Mortality:
I was as you are now, young, fair and cleere,
And you must once be as you see me here.

30 September 1707

An epitaph on the skull of Lady Wilmot at Wantage Church, Berkshire, England

Almost Without a Hitch

The broad-gauge railway line between London and Birmingham opened for passenger traffic. There was a slight collision near Banbury that destroyed one coach, but no lives were lost (1852).

Much Ado About Nothing

French and Spanish troops fought it out on the streets of London over a minute point of protocol concerning the order of precedence of ambassadorial carriages in a procession to welcome the Swedish envoy to the city. The French wanted their carriage to come before the Spanish, and the Spanish vice-versa. Under a promise from the British not to intercede, the Spanish won the battle, but it cost twelve dead and forty wounded just so that they might be first in the line (1661).

A Painless Bicuspid Extraction

Dr William Morton, a dentist of Charleston, Massachusetts, extracted a tooth for the first time with the help of anesthesia (ether). He subsequently recorded the episode, writing, "Toward evening, a man residing in Boston came in, suffering great pain and wishing to have a tooth extracted. He was afraid of the operation and asked if he could be mesmerized. I told him I had something better, and saturated my handkerchief and gave it to him to inhale. He became unconscious almost immediately. It was dark, and Dr Hayden held the lamp while I extracted a firmly rooted bicuspid tooth. He recovered in a minute and knew nothing of what had been done to him" (1846).

Octized October

Then came October full of merry glee;
For yet his noule was totty of the must,
Which he was treading in the wine-fat's see,
And of the joyous oyle, whose gentle gust
Made him so frolic and so full of lust:
Upon a dreadful scorpion he did ride,
The same by which Dianae's doom unjust
Slew great Orion; and eeke by his side
Had his ploughing share and coulter ready tyde.
  Edmund Spenser

OCTOBER

History

October got its name from the Latin word *Octo,* meaning "eight," because it was the eighth month in the older Roman calendars. The Romans dedicated the month to the god Mars and sacrificed a horse named October Equus to him. A race was run between two horses hauling chariots. The winner became the sacrificial victim. The Saxons called the month *Wyn Monath* or wine-month, because it fell in the season of wine making.

Then, for 'October Month,' they put
A rude illuminated cut —
Reaching ripe grapes from off the vine,
Or pressing them, or tunning wine;
Or, something to denote that there
Was vintage at this time of year.

Proverbs

In October dung your field
And your land its wealth shall yield.

Much rain in October
Much wind in December.

There are always twenty-one fine days in October.

When birds are fat in October expect a cold winter.

Birthstone

Though it signified hope, this month's birthstone — the opal — is considered unlucky for everyone except those born in this month. People born in other months who wear opals are leaving themselves open to misfortune.

1
OCTOBER

Births

Vladimir Horowitz (pianist) 1904; Julie Andrews (actress) 1935.

Deaths

Michael the Stammerer (Greek emperor) 829; Paul I (Russian emperor) 1754.

Lewd Cohabitation

Today in 1871 U.S. troops were despatched to Salt Lake City, Utah and Brigham Young was arrested for lewdly cohabiting with sixteen young women.

Ye Pudding Season

The first of October in England celebrated the start of the pudding season. At Ye Olde Cheshire Cheese Inn in London a fifty-to-eighty-pound pudding filled with steak, larks, spices, mushroom, and gravies was cooked for sixteen hours. It was traditional that "It shall come to pass that with ye aid of Old Ale tongues shall be loosened and the Guests will vie with one another as to who has eaten Ye Pudding for ye greatest number of years."

An Ass Race

Today in 1743, an ass race took place in Therberton, Suffolk, at the Lion and Castle Pub.

A Blacksmith Blasphemer

On this day in 1843 a blacksmith named Thomson entered the Secession Church, Glasgow, where St George's Free Congregation was assembled for worship. Ascending to the pulpit, he then composedly filled a glass with whisky and proposed a toast to "The Crown and the Congregation." On attempting to leave the church he was seized by one or two of the astonished onlookers and conveyed to the police. He was fined £10 or 60 days. The outrage, he said, had been committed to gain a bet of five shillings.

Manifest Drunkenness

On October 1, 1917 a French law imposed a fine for the first offence and prison for the second offence for anyone found in a state of "manifest drunkenness."

Faith in Americans

John Wanamaker, a prominent merchant of Philadelphia, said he had complete faith in the American public despite the seriousness of the financial panic of 1873. He inserted an advertisement to this effect in the Philadelphia newspapers, today in that year saying: "Checks taken from buyers. Change given in cash."

Political Manoeuvres

By the secret treaty of San Ildefonso, signed today in 1800, Spain sold Louisiana to France. Napoleon Bonaparte, in turn, promised Tuscany—with the title of king—to the duke of Parma, son-in-law of King Charles IV of Spain.

The Human Ruminant

The *Annual Register* of October 1, 1767, gives an account of one Roger Gill, a shoemaker of Winbourne, in Dorsetshire, who was known as the human ruminant "for chewing his meat or cud twice over, as an ox, sheep or cow." Gill would chew his cud for up to an hour and a half after each meal, and claimed that the regurgitated food was much sweeter than before. The origin of his bovine habits was never ascertained but they were certainly essential to his health, for after he lost the ability to bring his food back up for a working over, he soon sickened and died.

2
OCTOBER

Births

The Chevalier D'Eon (a man or a woman) 1728; Groucho Marx (American comedian) 1895; Mahatma Gandhi (Indian leader) 1869.

Tit for Tat

Today in 1780 Major John Andre, arrested as a British spy in connection with the treason of Benedict Arnold, was convicted and hanged at Tappan, New York, as Nathan Hale had been hanged by the British as an American spy four years earlier.

A Sexual Secret

The Chevalier D'Eon, who was born on this day in 1728, led two lives—the first as a man and the second as a woman. As temporary ambassador of Louis xv of France to George III of England during the peace negotiations between the two countries in 1761, he or she performed the job brilliantly and was decorated for those efforts. After that D'Eon somehow came to be regarded as a woman and went about in woman's clothes and became known as Madame D'Eon. A memoir was published stating that, though born female, she had been raised as a male for the purpose of advancing her station in life. When the Chevalier died in 1810 his or her secret was buried forever.

The Public Be Damned

Today in 1882 William H. Vanderbilt, the U.S. railroad tycoon, commented on whether he operated railroads for the public benefit: "The public be damned! What does the public care for the railroads except to get as much out of them for as little consideration as possible!"

Plenty of Hell

On this day in 1915 a large crowd of Americans turned out for the gospel revival meeting conducted by the Reverend Billy Sunday, a former baseball player whose favourite admonition was: "I'll give you hell enough before you get through with this meeting. I'll give you all the hell in the Bible. The Lord put it there, and if you don't like it, fix it up with the Lord, not with me."

Deaths

Aristotle (Greek philosopher) 322 B.C.; Major John Andre (British spy) 1780; Elizabeth Cody Stanton (American suffragette) 1902.

Marching Geese

In Nottingham, a royal charter was granted today in 1284 for an annual *Goose Fair* when geese were to be brought to market. Because the journeys were often long, the birds were shod by having their feet dipped in tar and then sand to protect them.

Sensible Women Don't Vote

Former U.S. President Grover Cleveland was quoted in the *Ladies Home Journal* of October 2, 1905 on the question of giving women the right to vote: "We all know how much further women go than men in their social rivalries and jealousies. Sensible and responsible women do not want to vote. The relative positions to be assumed by man and woman in the working out of our civilization were assigned long ago by a higher intelligence than ours."

Old Man's Day

Old Man's Day at Broughing, Hertfordshire, takes place today. The custom is to ring the church bells at first as though for a funeral and then as for a joyous occasion. The tradition began when Matthew Wall, a wealthy sixteenth-century farmer died. On his way to burial his coffin was dropped and Wall revived and knocked on the coffin lid to be let out.

Births

Giovanni Baptista Beccaria (Italian philosopher) 1716; Eleanora Duse (Italian actress) 1859; Thomas Wolfe (novelist/playwright) 1900.

Deaths

Several birds (in France) 1468; A horse (in England) 1737; Two horses (in France) 1754.

A King Strangles Several Birds

The crafty and unscrupulous King Louis XI of France had for several years been trying to undermine the powers of Charles the Bold, duke of Burgundy. Charles invited Louis to visit him in the town of Peronne. There he received word of the king's underhanded dealings, arrested him, and made him sign a humiliating treaty. In a rage Louis returned to his palace today in 1468 and ordered a cage of tame jays and magpies, an earlier gift from Charles the Bold, brought before him. Then, the birds, who had been taught to cry the word "Peronne," had their necks wrung by the vengeful king.

Two Exhausted French Horses Die

Today in 1754, Lord Powerscourt wagered with the Duke d'Orleans that he could ride the forty-two miles from Fountainbleau to Paris in two hours. He performed the task in one hour, thirty-seven minutes, and twenty-two seconds along the route, lined with crowds of Parisians. Powerscourt collected his reward of one thousand *louis-d'ors* but the two horses he had ridden died this evening from the severity of the feat.

On an Autumnal Morn

It yet is not day;
The morning hath not lost her virgin
blush,
Nor step but hers soiled the earth's
tinsel robe.
Now full of heaven this solitude
appears,
This healthful comfort of the happy
swain;
Who from his hard but peaceful bed
roused up,
In his morning exercise saluted is
By a full quire of feathered choristers,
Wedding their notes to the
enamoured air.
Catholic Annal, October 3, 1830

Dog Day in Virginia

Fredericksburg, Virginia holds an annual *Dog Mart,* on or about October 3, an event that has been held continuously since the year 1698.

An Old English Horse Dies

On the 3rd of October 1737, a cart gelding belonging to Mr Richard Fendall of the Grange, Southwark, died from an accidental cut on the knee. The death was notable because the horse had been forty-four years in Fendall's possession. It was bought on Michaelmas, 1693 at Uxbridge; was never sick or lame; and within the preceding fifteen years drew a chaise fifty miles in one day.

A Boa-Constrictor's Strange Meal

On October 3, 1851, a boa-constrictor in the Zoological Gardens in London performed the extraordinary feat of swallowing a coarse, thick blanket that had been introduced into its cage for the purpose of affording a little extra heat. (It remained in the creature's stomach until November the 8, when the blanket was disgorged, shorn of its wooly surface and somewhat reduced in size.)

Births

Rutherford B. Hayes (19th U.S. president) 1822; Frederic Remington (U.S. artist) 1861; Buster Keaton (U.S. comedian) 1896; Charlton Heston (U.S. actor) 1924.

Deaths

St Francis of Assissi (Italian friar) 1226; Henry Carey (English composer) 1743; Jacques Offenbach (German/French composer) 1880; Max Planck (German physicist) 1947.

Jacques Offenbach's Opera Efforts

Jacques Offenbach, the well-known composer of *Orphée aux Enfers* died in Paris today in 1880. He was a German Jew, born at Cologne on June 25, 1819, but went to Paris and became a naturalised French citizen. In 1847 he was appointed chef d'orchestre at the Théâtre Français, and in 1855 he opened the Bouffes Parisiens, the burlesque opera.

Max Planck's Distinctions

The renowned German physicist Max Planck, who died today in 1947, was awarded the Nobel Prize in 1918. Among his achievements was the origination of the *Quantum Theory* and *Planck's Constant,* which in physics is the constant in the expression for the quantum of energy, symbolized by *h,* and with the numerical value of 6.61×10^{-27}.

The White House Life-Saving Station

Rutherford B. Hayes, born on this day in 1822, was elected president in 1876. His wife was an ardent advocate of total abstinence from intoxicating liquors, and abandoned the custom of serving wine at state dinners. The White House chef, however, served at the first dinner a sorbet reinforced with liberal quantities of liquor. Mrs Hayes was delighted with the flavour and instructed the chef to serve the sorbet at formal dinners thereafter. It came to be called by foreign diplomats "the life-saving station."

St Francis' Decadent Early Life

St Francis died on this day in 1226. Born in Assisi in 1182 as Giovanni Francesco Bernardone, he was the wayward son of a wealthy merchant who tried to make him tread a straight and narrow path by making him a partner in his business. But Francis wasted his money in wild living, splendid dress, and gluttonous banqueting, making the streets of Assissi ring at night with his songs and frolic.

The Vision of St Francis

The crowning glory of the life of St Francis was a vision in which he saw the crucified Saviour. After the spectacle had departed he found the wounds of nails in his hands and feet. On his right side was a red wound, as if made by the piercing of a lance, which for the rest of his life often oozed blood.

St Francis Sees the Light

At the age of twenty-five, Francis was seized with a violent illness and when he recovered vowed to become religious and never to refuse alms to a poor person. He exchanged his rich garments for those of a filthy beggar, gave away so much money, and mortified himself with such severity that his father thought he was insane. To bring his son to his senses, Mr Bernardone beat him unmercifully, put him in fetters and locked him up. When this failed, Francis was disinherited and kicked out into the streets with nothing but the clothes on his back.

St Francis' Personal Habits

Such was the fervour of his devotions that crowds of people threw away their possessions and followed him into poverty. The *Franciscans* wore long, grey robes and no shoes. Their leader slept on the ground, used a stone for a pillow, never ate cooked food, and sprinkled everything he ate with ashes. He refused to look at women saying: "To converse with women, and not be hurt by it, is as difficult as to take fire into one's bosom and not be burned."

5
OCTOBER

Births

Dionysius Diderot (philospher) 1713; Chester Alan Arthur (21st U.S. president) 1830; Joshua Logan (film maker) 1908.

"A Defeat without a War"

Winston Churchill gave a speech on the Munich Agreement in the House of Commons, today in 1938: "All is over. Silent, mournful, abandoned, broken, Czechoslovakia recedes into the darkness. . . We have sustained a defeat without a war."

Deaths

Henry III (holy Roman emperor) 1056; Augustus III (Polish king) 1763; Tecumseh (Shawnee Indian chief) 1813.

"The Noblenesse of the Asse"

"The Asse refuseth no burden, he goes whither he is sent without any contradiction. He lifts not his foote against anyone; he bytes not; he is no fugitive, nor malicious affected. He doth all things in good sort; and his goodly, sweet and continual brayings—they are for me a melodious and proportionable kinde of musicke."

From a pamplet in England, October 5, 1595

Today in the Water

1767: A catch of pilchards, netted in St Ives Bay in Cornwall, England filled 7,000 hogsheads. Each of these contained 35,000 of the fish for a total catch of 245,000,000.

1817: An immense sea serpent was observed by several persons cavorting in the Sound near New York City.

1869: A U.S. patent was granted to Mr Spofford and Mr Raffington for their invention of a "water velocipede"—a pedal boat.

1880: Mr Laycock, an Australian, and Mr Blackman of London sculled from Putney to Mortlake on the Thames for a wager of £100. Mr Blackman gave up at Chiswick and Laycock completed the distance at his leisure.

Today in the Air

1905: The Wright brothers made a twenty-four mile flight over Dayton, Ohio, staying aloft for thirty-eight minutes.

1930: The British airship *R-101* crashed into a hill near Beauvois in France, burst into flames, and killed forty-eight of the fifty-four passengers.

1931: Clyde Pangborn made the first non-stop, transpacific flight when he flew a single-engine Bellanca monoplane from Japan to Washington. The trip took forty-one hours and thirteen minutes.

1954: Hurricane Hazel began a two week rampage that began in the U.S. Carolinas and extended into Ontario, Canada.

6
OCTOBER

Births

Dr. John Key (founder of Caius College, Cambridge) 1510; Dr Nevil Maskelyne (astronomer) 1732; Madame Campan (biographer of Marie Antionette) 1752; Johann Ebel (author of the first Swiss guidebook) 1764; Louis Philippe I (king of France) 1773; John W. Griffiths (clipper-ship developer) 1809; Jenny Lind Goldschmidt (vocalist) 1820; George Westinghouse (inventor) 1846; Thor Heyerdahl (explorer) 1914.

St Faith's Day

St Faith or Fides, a virgin, and several of her companions were martyred today in the 4th century. St Faith's Day, as celebrated in the north of England, featured a husband-divining ritual carried out by three young girls with a cake made from flour, springwater, sugar, and salt. During the baking process each girl turned the cake three times. When it was baked they each took a third, then the third was cut in nine pieces, each one being passed through a wedding ring three times. (The ring had to belong to a woman married at least seven years.) When this elaborate procedure was complete, each maiden ate her nine pieces and before bed said;

O good St Faith, be kind tonight,
And bring to me my heart's delight;
Let me my future husband view,
And be my vision chaste and true.

St Bruno's Flower

Medieval monks decreed that today's flower, the late-flowering feverfew (*Pyrethum scrotinum),* be dedicated to St Bruno.

Deaths

St Faith (virgin martyr) 4th century; Charles the Bald (king of France), 877; St Bruno (confessor) 1101; William Tyndale (Protestant theologian, burnt at the stake) 1536; Mrs Frances Trollope (novelist) 1863; Henry Timrod ("Poet Laureate of the U.S. Confederacy") 1867; Sir John Young (governor-general of Canada) 1876; Charles Stewart Parnell (Irish patriot) 1891; Alfred, Lord Tennyson (poet) 1892.

Opening Nights

1766:   The Irish actor, John Henry, became the first matinée idol in America following his appearance in Philadelphia this evening in the *The Roman Father*.

1863:   While the public was curious about the first "Turkish baths" to open in America, only one hardy soul ventured to try them out in the establishment operated by Charles H. Shepard in Brooklyn, New York.

St Bruno's Insomnia

St Bruno, the confessor and founder of the Carthusian monks, died today in 1101. He meditated perpetually on eternity and often could not sleep for thinking about the wonderful nature of everlasting duration.

7

OCTOBER

Births

Hans Holbein (German artist) 1543; Heinrich Himmler (German Nazi) 1900.

Deaths

Charles the Simple (French king) 929; Edgar Allan Poe (American poet) 1849.

Bloodcurdling Kurds, 1880

Several thousand Kurdish horsemen, under a son of the Sheik Abdullah, a Turkish Kurd, crossed the Persian frontier and joined the Perisan Kurds under Hamzeh Aga. The latter then assumed command, and the Kurds marched into the interior—ravaging, raping, pillaging, and plundering in all directions.

A Dismal Failure, 1903

An experrmiment by Samuel P. Langley, secretary of the Smithsonian Insitution, to launch an airplane and prove that man could fly, ended in failure on the Potomac River. Langley's plane was launched from a houseboat equipped with a runway. According to observers, the plane merely slid over the edge of the houseboat and sank into the river.

A Staggering Defeat, 1916

The most one-sided intercollegiate football score in American history took place at Atlanta, Georgia, as Georgia Tech trounced Cumberland University, 222-0.

Conjugal Indifference, 1736

On October 7, 1736, a man and his wife at Rushal, in Norfolk, had a dispute after which the man went out and hanged himself. The coroner's inquest called it suicide, and ordered him to be buried in the cross-ways; but his wife sent for a surgeon and sold his body for half a guinea. While the surgeon was feeling about the corpse the wife said, "He is fit for your purpose, he is as fat as butter." The deceased was thereupon put into a sack, with his legs hanging out, thrown onto a cart, and conveyed to the surgeon's laboratories for unspecified experiments.

Forget Me Not

Today's flower is the forget me not *(Myostis alpestris)* of which there are several species.

Small fragile weed, while thus I view
Thy constant tint of constant blue,
I pray, in life whate'er my lot,
May those I love Forget Me Not.

When last I left my native plain,
Perhaps never to return again,
Each tree and shrub on that dear spot
Appear'd to say, Forget me Not.

From this, thou little lonely weed,
My love for thee does all proceed;
To think of thee will bring to thought,
That those I love Forget me Not.
  Catholic Annal, 1830

Aboard a Slave Ship, 1644

The English diarist John Evelyn was invited on board the *Gally Royal,* a slave ship at Marseilles, today in 1644: "The spectacle was to me new and strange, to see so many hundreds of miserably naked persons, their heads being shaved close, and having only high red bonnets, a pair of coarse canvas drawers, their whole backs and legs naked, double chained about their waist and legs, in couples and made fast to their seats, and all commanded in a trice by a cruel and imperious seaman."

8
OCTOBER

Births

John Hay (U.S. historian) 1838; Eddie Rickenbacker (U.S. World War I pilot) 1890.

Deaths

Franklin Pierce (14th U.S. president) 1869; Wendell Willkie (U.S. presidential candidate) 1944.

Fire by Cow

On October 8, 1872, Chicago, then a shambling city built of wood, was almost entirely destroyed by a great fire that legend says was started by Mrs O'Leary's cow, when it knocked over a lantern. Several hundred people were killed, and some $200 million worth of property was destroyed.

Trial by Dog

In the fall of 1361, M. Aubrey de Montidier failed to return from a journey through the forest of Bondy near Paris, but his faithful dog did. Howling and whining, the animal led Montidier's friends to a spot in the woods where he began digging up the ground. The men dug on the spot with spades and soon found the body of their murdered friend. Later when the dog saw the Chevalier Macaire, he immediately lept at his throat. The king of France, hearing the story, ordered that the dog and Macaire fight it out in trial by combat. An open space on the Ile Notre Dame was chosen, and on the 8th of October 1361, the contest was held. Macaire was armed with a club, but it did him no good. The dog avoided all his blows and soon had him on the ground by the throat, at which point, in the presence of the king, Macaire confessed his murder.

Entry by Camel

The Moslem era began today in the year 622, when Mohammed, the prophet of Islam, made his public entry into Medina. He was mounted on a she-camel.

Strike by Students

In England today in 1889 an amusing sequel to the strikes that had been so frequent during the summer and autumn was provided by strikes of school boys in several towns. The truants demanded shorter hours, half holidays on Wednesdays, and "no caning and no homework."

Experiment by Rifle

Today in 1846 Professor Schönbein performed a series of experiments in London with his gun-cotton before the chairman of the East India Company and a number of scientific persons. A rifle charged with fifty-four-and-one-half grains of gunpowder sent a ball through seven boards, each one-half inch in thickness, at a distance of forty yards.

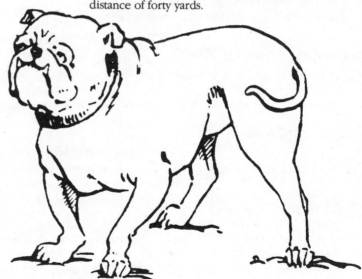

Victory by Panhard

On this day in 1904 the first automobile race for the Vanderbilt Cup started at Hicksville, Long Island, over a thirty-mile course. The winner was George Heath, driving a Panhard.

Movie by Plane

The first movie to be shown in the air was on October 8, 1929 when a plane of Transcontinental Air Transport of America showed a newsreel and two cartoons while 5,000 feet in the air.

9
OCTOBER

Births

Miguel de Cervantes (author of *Don Quixote)* 1547; Aimee Semple McPherson (evangelist) 1890; John Lennon (Beatle) 1940.

Steam Calliope Day

On this day in 1855 Joshua C. Stoddard of Worcester, Massachusetts received a patent for the first calliope in history—a steam organ with an eight-note keyboard that became popular on Mississippi River boats.

Mouldy Cheese Day

On the ninth day at night, in the sky
  you do view,
You may behold the stars, how they
  do burn blew;
This shall cause much wonder, but
  the effects are these,
Much practice of knavery, and much
  mouldy cheese.
    Poor Robin's Almanac, October 9, 1685

From Sword to Pen

Miguel de Cervantes Saavedra was born today in 1547 about twenty miles from Madrid. As a child he wrote verses on the walls of his house and read everything he could find, even scraps of paper lying in the streets. He joined the papal army in Rome in 1571 as a common soldier, was wounded twice by swords (losing the use of his left arm), captured by Algerians and then sold as a slave there in 1576. His last attempts to escape caused him to be sentenced to death four times. The last time this happened the hangman's rope was actually around his neck but he was saved and freed from bondage by the payment of 500 gold ducats to the Algerians by his friends in Spain. He failed in several business ventures, then turned to writing. His best known work, *Don Quixote* was published in Madrid in 1605.

Magic Lantern Day

Today in 1894 an invited audience at the Carbon Studio in New York was delighted with a showing of the first magic lantern feature picture. Entitled *Miss Jerry,* the principal leads were played by Blanche Bayliss and William Courtenay. The work—written, directed, photographed, and produced by Alexander Black—featured five stereoptican slides per second projected against a screen.

Deaths

St Denis (patron saint of France) 272; Sir Wilfred Grenfell (medical missionary) 1940; Pius XII (pope) 1958.

Leif Ericson Day

Today in Norway is celebrated as Leif Ericson Day in honour of that explorer landing at "Vinland" (some historians believe it was New England) on October 9 in the year 1000.

A Headless Saint

St Denis is the patron saint of France, and was the first bishop of Paris. Today in the year 272, after suffering decapitation under the persecution of Valerian, he is said to have picked up his head and walked with it for two miles before he lay down and died. In honour of the event, the spot where he became a martyr was known as *Mons Martyrum,* the mountain of the martyrs, which later became the famous Parisian district of Monmartre.

Births

Benjamin West (artist) 1738; Guiseppe Verdi (composer) 1813; Helen Hayes (actress) 1900.

Deaths

Doctor John Blow (composer) 1708; John McClosky (1st U.S. cardinal) 1885; Carol I (king of Rumania) 1914.

Marriage

Sir Thomas Grosvenor to Mary Davies, 1677. (Mary's dowry was 500 acres of soggy ground to the west of London. Today, those acres are the districts of Belgravia, Mayfair, and Pimlico.)

A Shocking Tuxedo

A tail-less dress coat for men, introduced from England, was worn for the first time in the United States at the Tuxedo Club, New York. The coat was worn by a club member, Griswold Lorillard. Most of the guests at the club that evening were shocked at such informality (1866).

A Booke Review

"There is published a Booke of Eighteen-pence price, called *The Compleat Angler,* or, *The Contemplative Man's Recreation:* being a Discourse of Fish and Fishing, by one Isaak Walton. Not unworthy the perusall."

   In a London newspaper, October 10, 1653

A Stolen Skull

The skull of Guiteau, murderer of President Garfield, was stolen from the Medical Museum, Washington, where it had been exhibited (1882).

A Pugilistic Encounter

Tom King defeated the American champion, Heenan, in a pugilistic encounter near Wadhurst, Sussex. At the twentieth round the ring was broken into by the excited spectators, and for five additional rounds the fight was carried on amid much confusion. Heenan was then unable to respond to the call of his second (1863).

An Independence Day

The Chinese Revolution began today in 1911 with the Wuchang uprising, which overthrew the royal family. It is celebrated as *Chinese Independence Day.*

A Ganging Day

In Bishop's Stortford, England, today was Ganging Day, when young men chose a leader to follow through hedges, ponds, and swamps. If they met anyone, this person was unceremoniously "bumped" by being picked up and swung against an obstacle.

A Dog Day

In Hull, Yorkshire today involved the extraordinary enterprise, followed particularly by little boys, of whipping any dogs found wandering the streets.

A Strange Ceremony

Today (Old Michaelmas Day Eve in England) saw the holding of *Weyhill Fair* in Hampshire. One of the customs during the day was the "Horning-the-Colt" ceremony, which involved a young man being placed on a chair and a cap with two horns set on his head with a cup placed between them. The following song was sung after which the "colt" drank from the cup and then bought a round for all in the inn:

So swift runs the hare and so cunning the fox,
Why shouldn't this young heifer grow up to be an ox,
And drink with his daddy with a pair of large horns.
With a pair of large horns.

A Near Mutiny

"Here the men could bear no more; they complained of the length of the voyage. But Admiral Columbus encouraged them as best he could, holding out high hopes of the gains they could make. He added that it was no use their complaining, because he had reached the Indies and must sail on until with the help of our Lord he discovered land."

   Bartolomé de Las Casas, historian, in *Columbus' Log Book,* October 10, 1492

11
OCTOBER

Births

Bernard Partridge (*Punch* cartoonist) 1681; Eleanor Roosevelt (wife of the U.S. president) 1884; Joseph Alsop Jr (writer) 1910.

Deaths

Ulrich Zwingli (Swiss Protestant reformer) 1531; Harry Rowe (trumpeter) 1800; Anton Bruckner (composer) 1896.

Churchill Corresponds

On October 11, 1889 Winston Churchill sailed to South Africa to cover the Boer War as chief correspondent of the *London Morning Post.*

Trumpeter Extraordinaire

Harry Rowe, of York, England, held the distinguished post of trumpet-major to the high sheriffs of Yorkshire for fifty years. He served as trumpeter in the duke of Kingston's regiment of light horse at the battle of Culloden in 1746, where his virtuosity on his instrument was said to have played no small part in the defeat of the Scottish troops. On his retirement he ran a travelling puppet show in which he manipulated all the characters while providing musical accompaniment on his trumpet. He died in the poorhouse of York today in 1800.

Blackberries Cursed

It was considered unlucky to gather or eat blackberries after this day, *Old Michaelmas Day,* in medieval England. According to tradition, when he was cast out of Heaven on the first Michaelmas Day, Satan fell into a blackberry bush, and placed a curse on the fruit. On each anniversary of his fall, he renews the curse by scorching blackberries with his breath, stamping or spitting on them, throwing his cloak or his club over them, or wiping his tail upon them.

Baltimore Celebrates

The celebration of the 150th anniversary of the foundation of the City of Baltimore in Maryland was begun today in 1880, with great processions being organised, and banquets and opportunities for speech-making without end.

Sea Serpent Debunked

Today in 1848 Captain McQuhae, of the ship *Daedalaus* sent the British Admiralty an official report on the subject of the sea serpent seen by him and his crew on the passage home from the East Indies. From the account and sketch provided, Professor Owen came to the conclusion that the creature seen from the *Daedalaus* was not a cold-blooded reptile of the snake or serpent species, but a large seal floated down on an iceberg, and seeking for shelter. The learned professor was further of the opinion that no such creature existed in nature as the so-called sea serpent.

Invention Rejected

On this day in 1868 Thomas Alva Edison filed papers for his first invention, an electrical vote recorder designed to tabulate floor votes in the U.S. Congress in a matter of minutes. (Congress rejected it.)

12
OCTOBER

Births

Edward VI (English king) 1537; Pedro I (Brazilian emperor) 1798; Ralph Vaughan Williams (English composer) 1872.

Columbus' Mistake

Though he went to his grave in the belief that he had come ashore on some remote part of India, when Christopher Columbus landed on October 12, 1492 and planted a cross in gratitude for his safety through a perilous journey, it was on Watlin's Island, one of the Bahamas group.

Deaths

Elizabeth Fry (philanthropic Quakeress) 1845; Madame Rachel (suffragette) 1880; Edith Cavell (nurse) 1915; Sonja Henie (ice skater) 1969.

Elizabeth Fry

Elizabeth Fry, a Quaker reformer, spent much of her life improving the state of English prisons and the lot of prisoners in them, and of convicts on their voyage to Australia. She died today in 1845, aged sixty-five.

Madame Rachel

"Madame Rachel, that benefactress to her species whose efforts in the great cause of making ladies beautiful for ever and improving their lot was twice rewarded by an ungrateful country with sentences of penal servitude, died today in Woking Prison, in the sixty-first year of her age."

> *Dickens Dictionary of Dates of 1880,* London

Edith Cavell

Edith Cavell, an heroic English nurse, was shot today in 1915 by a German firing squad in Brussels after admitting she had assisted some 200 English, French, and Belgian patriots to gain their freedom from occupied Belgium. Miss Cavell faced the firing squad with a dignity that moved the world. To a British chaplain who administered a final sacrament, she remarked, "Patriotism is not enough. I must have no hatred or bitterness towards anyone."

Public Flagellation

On October 12, 1681, Mrs Celiers, a midwife in London, was publicly flogged for involving herself in politics.

Public Condemnation

On October 12, 1871, President Grant publicly condemned the sinister Ku Klux Klan and ordered the arrest of over 600 citizens of South Carolina involved with its activities. Habeas corpus was suspended in several counties.

Public Demonstration

Today in 1960 the regular decorum of the United Nation's General Assembly was shattered by Premier Nikita Khrushchev as he angrily denounced Assembly President Frederich H. Boland and some delegates for not voting on the Soviet draft declaration against colonialism. After interrupting several speakers, Khrushchev removed one of his shoes and repeatedly pounded his desk with it.

Public Indifference

So engrossed were the inhabitants of Montréal with their constitutional struggle, that when a new theatre was opened this night in 1838 not one person was found in attendance. The doors were quietly closed again.

Publick Hospital

On October 12, 1773 "The Publick Hospital for Persons of Insane and Disordered Minds" was incorporated at Williamsburg, Virginia. Zachariah Mallory was the first patient. This was the first state-supported hospital for ths insane in America.

Births

Ernest Gann (American author) 1910; Yves Montand (French actor) 1921; Margaret Thatcher (English stateswoman) 1925.

Quick Courtship

Today in 1839 James Bryan, a native of Ayrshire and a person of weak intellect, presented himself at Windsor as a suitor for the hand of Her Majesty, Queen Victoria. He was abruptly dismissed.

Sixteen Pallbearers

When Mr Jacob Powell of Stebbing in Essex died on the 13th of October, 1745, he had sixteen men carry him to his grave. That was because Mr Powell measured five yards around the middle, and weighed 560 pounds.

Police Brutality

Mr Cannon, a ferocious London chimney sweep, was sentenced to death today in 1852 for a savage attack on police constable Dwyer, at the Bricklayers Arms. In a savage rage he first rushed against the officer head forwards, and having thrown him upon the ground, commenced trampling upon his prostrate victim. He had been convicted twenty times before for assaults, chiefly on constables, but on this occasion, to his great astonishment, he was not indicted on the ordinary charge, but for inflicting bodily injury with intent to murder.

Medal Trafficking

On October 13, 1887 the French General Cafferel of the War Office was convicted by a military tribunal of dishonourable conduct in trafficking in decorations.

Deaths

Claudius (Roman emperor) 54; Anatole France (French writer) 1924; Jacob Powell (English fat man) 1745.

Quick Turnover

Queenstown in Upper Canada, was taken by U.S. troops today in 1812, but recaptured by British forces the same day.

Theatrical Opening

Today in 1962 drama critics and the audience applauded the opening in New York of the first full-length play by Edward Albee, *Who's Afraid of Virginia Woolf?*

Water Worshipping

Annually on October 13 the ancient Romans celebrated the *Fontinalia,* a feast in honour of the blessing of good water, in which wells and fountains were garlanded and had sacrificial offerings made to them.

Architectural Event

On October 13, 1792 George Washington laid the cornerstone for the Executive Mansion in Washington. Designed by James Hoban, an imitation of the palace of the duke of Leinster, in Dublin Ireland, it won for its architect the $500 prize that had been offered in a competition. It was burned by the British in 1814 and restored in 1818 when the stone was painted white to cover the marks left by the fire. From that restoration, the name White House replaced Executive Mansion.

Births

James II (English king) 1633; William Penn (founder of Pennsylvania) 1644; Dwight D. Eisenhower (34th U.S. president) 1890.

Babies in America

On October 14, 1854 the first Baby Show in America was held in Springfield, Ohio, as a joke rather than a serious contest. One hundred twenty-seven babies were entered, with the winner receiving a silver plate service and salver.

Prediction on Cars

"At present the horseless carriage is a luxury for the wealthy; and although its price will probably fall . . . it will never, of course, come into as common use as the bicycle."

The Literary Digest, New York, October 14, 1899

Balloon on Roof

Today in 1844 Mr Hampden, the aeronaut, in endeavouring to make a descent near Dublin, alighted upon a house where the chimney was on fire. The balloon caught fire and exploded; the unfortunate voyager narrowly escaped by dropping down the side of the house.

Deaths

Harold (English king) 1066.

Statute on Bedding

In England a statute of this day in 1495 decreed that "no person shall sell in the fairs or markets any feather-beds, bolsters, or pillows except they shall be stuffed with one manner of feathers, and not unlawful stuffs, and with no scalded feathers, or fen-down, *but be utterly damned forever!"*

Davis on Greenland

John Davis, an English seaman and explorer, made a diary entry on his voyage to Greenland today in 1586: "The people eat all their meat raw, they live most upon fish, they drink salt water, and eat grass and ice with delight: they are never out of water."

Roosevelt in Pain

Today in 1912 former President Theodore Roosevelt, campaigning for a third term was shot by a would-be assassin in Milwaukee. Though in great pain he refused to have his chest wound treated at a hospital until he spoke at a scheduled political rally, saying, "It may be the last speech I shall deliver, but I am going to deliver this one."

Harold at Hastings

On October 14, 1066, Harold, the last Saxon king of England, was killed instantly by an arrow that penetrated his left eye at the *Battle of Hastings* in England. Harold's Saxon army lost the contest and William, duke of Normandy (later William the Conqueror) became the king. The event was commemorated on the Bayeux Tapestry.

Penn of Pennsylvania

Willam Penn, a Quaker, was born today in 1644 in London. On the same day in 1655 an act was passed in Massachusetts prohibiting the immigration of Quakers, appointing twenty lashes and imprisonment to such as should arrive, and death if they returned after being sent away. By 1682 the law had been forgotten and William Penn founded the colony of Pennsylvania as a refuge for persecuted Quakers.

15
OCTOBER

Births
Virgil (poet) 70 B.C.; C.P. Snow (author) 1905; Mohammed Zahir Shah (king of Afghanistan) 1914.

Laid to Rest in the Rafters
In a will approved on October 15, 1724, Henry Trigg, a grocer from Stevanage in Hertford County, England, requested that instead of being buried his body was to be committed to the "West End of my Hovel" where it was to be laid on a small floor built upon the rafters. Trigg's will was complied with, and many years later the remains could still be seen there.

Bare-Foot Friars Inspire
Today in Rome in 1764, Edward Gibbon first conceived the idea of writing his great work, *The Decline and Fall of the Roman Empire,* while the bare-footed friars were singing vespers in the Temple of Jupiter.

The World's Worst Driver
On October 15, 1966 within a space of twenty minutes, a seventy-five-year-old man in McKinney, Texas, earned himself the title of the World's Worst Driver. He committed four hit-and-run offences, drove on the wrong side of the road four times, and caused six accidents.

Florence Nightingale's Appointment
On this day in 1854 Mr Sidney Herbert solicited on behalf of the British Government, the assistance of Miss Florence Nightingale, to organise and superintend the nursing department of the soldier's hospital iniScutari in the Crimea.

Bread Buttering by Thumb
Today in 1714 King Charles XII of Sweden was seen buttering his bread with the royal thumb. This conformed to the best practices of contemporary etiquette, however, because table knives had not yet been invented.

A Celebration in Cologne
Cologne, Germany, today in 1880, was the scene of a great function, the occasion being the celebration of the completion of the cathedral, which had taken 600 years—on and off—to build. The city was brilliantly decorated and filled with an enormous assemblage of people, who showed the utmost enthusiasm.

Deaths
1917:   Mata Hari (Gertrud Margarete Zelle), the most famous spy of World War I, was executed at Vincennes Barracks outside Paris by a firing squad.

1945:   Pierre Laval, the former French premier, was executed by a firing squad at Fresnes prison for betraying his country to Nazi Germany during World War II. He tried to cheat his executioners by swallowing poison a few hours before he was scheduled to die, but was revived and forced to face his captors.

1946:   Herman Goering, convicted at the Nuremberg Trials as a war criminal, and sentenced to be hanged, committed suicide.

A Hallucination in Georgia
Today in 1856 the *London Times* published an extraordinary narrative concerning "Railways and Revolvers in Georgia," in which an eye-witness described a series of duels said to have taken place among the passengers in the railway cars between Macon and Augusta in Georgia. Five people were said to have been killed, and one boy coolly murdered and thrown out of the train. The story was thought to illustrate the present lawless conditions of the southern states, but in the end it was admitted that the narrator, "John Arrowsmith, Liverpool," must have been labouring under a hallucination.

16 OCTOBER

Births

Noah Webster (dictionary writer) 1758; Oscar Wilde (author) 1856; David Ben-Gurion (Israeli prime minister) 1886; Eugene O'Neill (playwright) 1888.

Deaths

Ridley and Latimer (English bishops, burnt at the stake) 1555; Marie Antoinette (French queen, guillotined) 1793.

Today's Odd Bequests

1769: "First, I give to dear Lord Hinton,
At Tryford school—not at Winton,
One hundred guineas for a ring,
Or some such memorandum thing:
And truly, much I should have blundered,
Had I not giv'n another hundred
To Vere, Earl Poulett's second son,
Who dearly loves a little fun."
Nathaniel Lloyd, Twickenham

1782: "I desire that my body may be kept as long as it may not be offensive; and that one or more of my toes or fingers may be cut off, to secure a certainty of my being dead."
William Blackett, Plymouth

1785: "I give to Elizabeth Parker the sum of £50, whom, through my foolish fondness, I made my wife; and who in return has not spared, most unjustly, to accuse me of every crime regarding human nature, save highway-robbery."
Charles Parker, Middlesex

1788: I do give and bequeath to Mary Davis the sum of five shillings, which is sufficient to enable her to get drunk for the last time at my expense."
David Davis, Clapham

1793: "I leave my right hand, to be cut off after my death, to my son Lord Audley; in hopes that such a sight may remind him of his duty to God, after having so long abandoned the duty he owed to a father who once affectionately loved him."
Philip Thicknesse, London

1794: "I give unto my wife Mary Darley, for picking my pocket of 60 guineas, and taking up money in my name, the sum of one shilling."
William Darley, Ash

1796: "I give and bequeath £5 a year, to be paid weekly by my husband, to take care of my cats and dogs as long as any of them shall live. To my servant boy George Smith, my jackass, to get his living with."
Catherine Williams, Lambeth

1810: "To my only son, who never would follow my advice, and has treated me rudely in many circumstances, I give him nothing."
Richard Crawshay, Glamorgan

1813: "I do give and bequeath to my beloved parrot, the faithful companion of 25 years, an annuity for its life of 200 guineas a year, as long as this beloved parrot lives. And I also will and desire that 20 guineas, directly on my death, be expended on a very high, long, and large cage for the aforesaid parrot."
Elizabeth Orby Hunter, London.

Births

Jean Arthur (actress) 1908; Rita Hayworth (actress) 1918.

Deaths

St Hedwiges (duchess of Poland) 1243; Ninon de Lenclos (courtesan) 1706.

A Saint Fears the End of the World

In spite of her fears, St Hedwiges, the duchess of Poland, died a peaceful death today in 1243. She spent her lifetime in awful anticipation of the end of the world, which she felt was likely to occur at any moment. Whenever it thundered and stormed she prayed continually and was not content to begin each day until she heard all the masses in the church wherever she was.

A Boy Falls in Love with his Mother

Ninon de Lenclos, a famous French courtesan of the seventeenth century, had many lovers, among them King Louis XIV, La Rouchefoucald, Molière, and La Bruyère. Even one of her sons fell under her spell. The identity of his mother had been kept secret from Villiers, the product of a love affair between the courtesan and the Marquis de Gersay. When he was nineteen Villiers met de Lenclos and fell hopelessly in love with her. She tried to discourage him, but to no avail, and finally confessed that she was really his mother. The distraught Villiers committed suicide. Ninon de Lenclos died today in 1706, at the age of ninety.

Four Prunes for Breakfast

Today in 1824 boardinghouse-keepers in New York banded together because of the high cost of living and voted to serve boarders only four prunes a-piece at breakfast.

Wench-Wooing in the Seventeenth Century

"It was a happy age when a man might have wooed his wench with a pair of kid-leather gloves, a silver thimble, or with a tawdry lace; but now a velvet gown, a chain of pearls, or a coach with four horses will scarcely serve the turn."

My Lady's Looking Glass, October 17, 1616.

Twice a Widow, Always a Virgin

St Ethelreda, or St Audry as she was known in parts of Britain, was the daughter of a king of East Anglia. She earned an exalted reputation by her piety and good works, and after she was canonised on October 17, 695 her remains were removed from the common cemetery of the nuns to a splendid marble coffin within the church of Ely. Although she had taken a nun's vows she was twice forced by her father into marriage with young princes, neither of whom survived her, which earned her the epitaph "twice a widow, yet always a virgin."

St Audry's Gaudy Necklace

St Audry, when she was dying of a swelling in her throat, thought herself punished for the gaudy lace necklace (of the sort made on the Isle of Ely) she used to wear as a girl. In time the lace pieces became known as Audry's lace, which became tawdry lace, from which came the word "tawdry," meaning any sort of cheap and glittery finery.

Edgar Allan Poe Booed in Boston

On October 17, 1845, the editor of the *Boston Transcript* reported that the "singularly didactic excordium" of Edgar Allan Poe's reading of "The Raven" the night before at the Lyceum had caused the audience to walk out on him. (Poe answered by saying he was ashamed of having been born in such a city.)

18
OCTOBER

Births

Peter II (Russian czar) 1715; Charles Mudie (English library founder) 1818; Melina Mercouri (Greek actress) 1925.

Deaths

St Luke (apostle) 63; John VII (pope) 707; Gregory XII (pope) 1417; Pius III (pope) 1503; Christopher Brovaway (incest victim) 1730.

A Multi-Talented Saint

St Luke, one of Jesus' apostles, was a doctor, painter, writer, and evangelist. He was trained and practised as a physician, before becoming a disciple of Jesus. As well as writing his gospel he had a talent for painting and is said to have left behind many pictures of Jesus and the Virgin Mary after he was crucified on an olive tree today in the year 63 at Antioch in Syria.

A Look at a Future Lover

St Luke's Day in England offered girls an opportunity for insight into their future love life. Today they could anoint themselves with a preparation of marigolds, marjoram, thyme, and wormwood mixed with virgin honey and vinegar, and repeat three times in bed:

St Luke, St Luke, be kind to me,
In dreams let me my true love see.

A Victim of Incest

Here lyeth the body of
Christopher Brovaway who
Departed this life ye 18th day
of October Anno Domini 1730
Aged 59 years.

And Thir lyes Alice
Who By hir Life
Was my sister, my mistress,
My mother and my wife.
  An epitaph at Marham, Norfolk

(Christopher was the son of an incestuous relationship between a brother and sister and raised as an orphan. Unknown to him, he was apprenticed to his sister Alice, fell in love with her, and they were married. When by accident they discovered the truth of their relationship, Alice went mad and Christopher died of shock today in 1730.)

A Stone in the Face

Today in 1839, in Paris, the queen of France was struck on the face with a stone thrown into the royal carriage near the Tuilleries by a madwoman named Giordet.

A College for Women

On October 18, 1875 Newnham College for women was opened at Cambridge University, England.

An Undesirable Alien

On October 18, 1913 Mrs Emmeline Pankhurst, the British suffragette, was refused admission to the U.S. because she was declared "an undesirable alien."

A Fair for the Confederates

On October 18, 1864, a fair in aid of the Confederate cause was opened in Liverpool, England by ladies of English nobility and secession women from America.

Births

Thomas Browne (philosopher) 1605; Leigh Hunt (poet/writer) 1784; Fannie Hurst (novelist) 1889.

St Peter's Austerity

Today's saint, Peter of Alcantra, took the habit of the austere of St Francis at the age of nineteen. He lived a life of severe penance and mortification, denying himself sleep, food, and other necessities to such a degree that he died today in 1562 of self-denial.

Deaths

John (English king) 1216; St Peter (confessor) 1562; Sir Thomas Browne (philosopher) 1682; Jonathan Swift (writer) 1745.

King John's Excesses

John succeeded his brother Richard the Lionheart as king of England in 1199. He quarrelled with Pope Innocent III, alienated his barons and subjects by bad administration and heavy taxation, and was forced to sign the *Magna Carta*. He died today in 1216 after consuming an excessive number of peaches washed down with too much beer.

Jonathan Swift's Temper

Jonathan Swift, the Irish-born satirist and author of *Gulliver's Travels,* was only fond of humour when it was not at his own expense. He once stomped out of an inn in a rage after having thrown his meal across the room. He had complained about his meal by asking a cookmaid how many maggots she had gotten out of a piece of mutton served to him. "Not so many as are in you head," she replied. He died on October 19, 1745.

Thomas Browne's Philosphy

Thomas Browne, an English philosopher who was born today in 1605 and died today in 1682, had several curious theories. Among them that storks will only live in free states, that elephants have no joints, that men weigh heavier dead than alive, and that "man is the whole world, but woman is only the rib or crooked part of man." In spite of this latter belief he married Mrs Mileham of Norfolk in 1641. They lived happily together for forty years and had ten children.

Abe Lincoln's Beard

To an 11-year old girl, Grace Bedell, who wrote to him saying that she would try to persuade her four brothers to vote for him for president if he grew a beard, Abraham Lincoln wrote today in 1860: "My dear little Miss . . . As to whiskers, having never worn any, do you not think people would call it a piece of silly affectation if I were to begin it now?" (By November, the then-President Lincoln was beginning to sprout a beard.)

The Earl of Sandwich's Etiquette

Today in 1744 the earl of Sandwich, inventor of the sandwich, said in London that sandwiches should be eaten with "a civilised swallow and not a barbarous bolt."

W.O. Jenkin's Deviousness

On October 19, 1919 W.O. Jenkins, the American consul for Mexico was kidnapped by Mexican banditos and held for ransom. Shortly after Jenkins was arrested by Mexican police and charged with colluding with the bandits who kidnapped him.

20
OCTOBER

Births

Christopher Wren (architect) 1632;
Art Buchwald (columnist) 1925;
Mickey Mantle (baseball player) 1931.

Deaths

Charles VI (French king) 1422;
Charles VI (Austrian emperor) 1740;
Grace Darling (heroine) 1842.

Marriages

U.S. President Benjamin Harrison to
Caroline L. Scott (1853); Jacqueline
Bouvier Kennedy to Aristotle Onassis
(1968).

A Young Heroine

Grace Darling was the daughter of
the lighthouse keeper on Longstone,
one of the Farne Islands off the coast
of Northumberland. In September of
1838 the *Forfarshire,* a steamer with
sixty-three persons on board,
foundered in a vicious storm and
went aground on the rocks about a
mile from the Longstone lighthouse.
The waves were running so high that
all the local boatman were afraid to
embark on a rescue mission. But
young Grace persuaded her father to
come with her, and together they
rowed a boat through the maelstrom
and took the nine persons still alive
off the disintigrating wreck. Grace
became an immediate heroine to all
of Britain, and was awarded medals
and given testimonials. Her biography was written and Longstone
lighthouse became a tourist
attraction. She died of consumption
four years after the event on October
20, 1842 at the age of twenty-seven.

Today and the Printed Word

1822: *The Sunday Times,* a British
weekly newspaper, was first issued.

1852: An advertisement in the
Burlington Free Press offered the
first steam-heated factory in
America for sale: "The factory
building and dye houses are
heated by steam conducted
through iron pipes in the most
modern and approved manner."

1873: Handbills in New York
announced the opening of P.T.
Barnum's Hippodrome featuring
the impressario's "Greatest Show
on Earth."

1879: The *Reading Room* of the
British Museum in London was first
lighted by electricity.

1890: A book was published under
the title, *In Darkest England and
the Way Out,* by General Booth of
the Salvation Army. The book set
forward a plan by which the
regeneration of the masses of the
population (which he designated
the "submerged tenth") was to be
brought about. It would have three
branches, the city colony, the farm
colony, and the colony over the
sea. Those who had no money at
all to benefit from the food and
shelter already supplied by the
Salvation Army, could earn them in
the labour yards attached to each
shelter. Various people subscribed
to the scheme.

1927: Major Thompson of Chicago
was so determined to "drive King
George out of Chicago" he
arranged to have all pro-English
books in the Chicago Public Library
burned.

1960: *The New York Times* was
published simultaneously in New
York and Paris.

GRACE DARLING

Births

Katsushuka Hokusai (Japanese painter who signed his work "the old man crazy about drawing") 1760; Samuel Taylor Coleridge (poet and legendary talker) 1772.

Deaths

Samuel Foote (prankster, humorist, and wit) 1777; Horatio, Lord Nelson (killed at Trafalgar) 1805.

A Souvenir of Lord Nelson

On October 21, 1805, the British fleet under Horatio Nelson met the combined fleets of Spain and France at the battle of Trafalgar. Four hours later the British emerged victorious but Nelson was killed by a musket ball that entered his left shoulder. Mr Beattie, the surgeon on board Nelson's ship *Victory,* removed the bullet from the fallen hero and had it mounted in crystal and silver as a locket.

Two Night's Bright Light

Today in 1879 Thomas Alva Edison invented a workable electric incandescent lamp after fourteen months of experimentation at his Menlo Park, New Jersey, laboratory. "The longer it burned, the more fascinated we were... There was no sleep for any of us for forty hours," said Edison.

Poking Fun at Adolph

Today in 1940 Prime Minister Winston Churchill taunted Hitler during a radio broadcast, saying, "We are waiting for the long-promised invasion. So are the fishes."

Noisey Cows and Murdered Tunes

Samuel Foote, who died on this day in 1777, spent his lifetime exercising his talent for humour. While at Oxford he delighted in such pranks as tying a bundle of hay to the rope of the church bell at night so that grazing cattle would wake everyone up. "Why do you hum that air?" he once asked a friend who had been going over the same tune for hours. "It forever haunts me," was the reply. "No wonder," answered Foote, "You are forever murdering it."

Endless Talking, Hither and Yawn

For the poet and critic Samuel Taylor Coleridge, born today in 1722, writing was always difficult, but talking his favourite pastime. Thomas Carlyle wrote of him: "I have heard Coleridge talk, with eager musical energy, two stricken hours, his face radiant and moist, and communicate no meaning whatsoever to any individual of his hearers. Besides, it was talk not flowing anywhither, like a river, but spreading everywhither in inextricable currents and regurgitations like a lake or a sea; terribly deficient in definite goal or aim, nay, often in logical intelligability; *what* you were to believe or do, or any earthly or heavenly thing, obstinately refused to appear from it."

Births

Franz Liszt (Hungarian pianist/composer) 1811; Louis Riel (Canadian rebel) 1844; Miss Britton (illegitimate child) 1919.

Deaths

Hsi and Ho (Chinese astronomers) 2137 B.C.; Sir Cloudesley Shovell (English admiral) 1707; Edward Gurling (English zoo-keeper) 1852.

The Luck of Number 22

People born today can look to Saturday, Sunday, and Monday as their lucky days. Their lucky colours are electric blue or grey and their lucky stone is the sapphire, which they should wear next to the skin if possible. They need all the luck they can get because numerology says that they are argumentative, rebellious, opinionated, and make a great number of enemies who constantly work against them.

Daughter of a President?

On October 22, 1919 a woman named Nan Britton gave birth to a baby girl in Asbury Park, New Jersey, and claimed the infant to be the daughter of Senator (later President) Warren G. Harding of Ohio. This charge was later enlarged, but not conclusively proved in a book that rocked the American nation: *The President's Daughter.*

The Sun and Moon out of Tune

The ancient Chinese classic, the *Shu Ching,* tells of two astronomers who drank too much wine and failed to perform the necessary rites of shooting arrows and beating drums today in 2137 B.C. when "the sun and moon did not meet harmoniously in Fang." Modern astronomers have identified this event as a total eclipse visible in China at that time. (The ancient astronomers Hsi and Ho were executed for their drastic oversight.)

A Child in the Pot

According to Skye's *Local Records,* on October 22, 1735, James and Elizabeth Leesh of County Durham, at the Sign of the Salmon Inn, played a single game of cards with their child as the wager. Against the child Henry and John Trotter, Robert Thomson, and Thomas Ellison put up four shillings. The latter won the hand and the youngster was duly handed over to the winners.

Parachute Fall-Out

Today in 1797 André Jacques Garnerin made the first successful parachute descent from a balloon at Monceau Park in Paris. To gain altitude he hitched his balloon and parachute to a car, rose to 3,000 feet then released his thirty-foot-wide canopy from the balloon. During his descent Garnerin swung back and forth like a pendulum and was violently ill on several spectators gathered on the ground beneath him.

Death from a Nose Bite

Today in 1852 Edward Gurling, a keeper in the Zoological Gardens in London, died after a few hours illness, from the effects of the bite of a cobra snake that he had rashly taken out of its case and placed round his neck. The wounds were small punctures on each side of his nose.

Births

Sarah Bernhardt (actress) 1845; Gore Vidal (writer) 1925; Johnny Carson (TV personality) 1925.

Deaths

Brutus (Roman soldier) 42 B.C.; Anincius Manlius Severinus Boethius (philosopher) 525; W.G. Grace (cricketer) 1915.

Archbishop Usher's Origin of the World

According to Archbishop James Usher of seventeenth-century Ireland, the planet earth and everything on it was created on October 23, 400 B.C. at 9 a.m.

Blanche Scott's Aerial Effort

Today in 1910 the residents of Fort Wayne, Indiana were all agog over the first woman to make a public airplane flight by herself. Blanche S. Scott flew over a local park to a height of twelve feet.

Boris Pastnernak's Nobel Refusal

Today in 1958 Boris Pasternak, the Russian poet and author, won the Nobel Prize for literature for his novel, *Dr. Zhivago.* He was expelled from the Soviet Writers' Union on October 28, and wired his "voluntary refusal" of the prize to the Swedish Academy because ". . .of the meaning given to this honour in the community to which I belong."

William Lilly's Suspected Pyrotechnics

Today in the year 1666, William Lilly (the astrologer whose predictions are quoted in this book) was examined before a committee of the House of Commons concerning the causes of the Great Fire of London which he had predicted in his *Heiroglyphick,* published some months before the fire. (No charges were brought against him.)

Sir Gervase Scroop's Suspended Animation

On October 23, 1642, at the battle of Edgehill, in England, Sir Gervase Scroop fell from the effects of sixteen severe wounds. Three days later, after heavy frosts, his son retrieved the body and was surprised to find it still warm. Fuller, an historian of the time records: "That heat was, with rubbing, within a few minutes, improved into motion; that motion, within some hours, into sense; that sense, within a day into speech; that speech, within certain weeks, into perfect recovery; living more than ten years after, a monument of God's mercy and his son's affections."

Today's Weather

1366: A great meteor shower passed over Europe raining small pieces of meteorites over a wide area.

1874: A severe cyclone in the Bay of Bengal took 2,000 lives at Midnapore.

1878: A hurricane in Philadelphia destroyed many churches, factories, and homes.

1944: A hurricane finally ended in Florida after eleven days of destruction.

Boethius' Beheading Taken Philosophically

Boethius, a Roman philosopher, was beheaded for suspected treason by Theodoric, king of the Goths, in Italy on this day in 525. It is said of him that after the beheading his corpse was scoffingly asked by the executioner, "Who hath put thee to death?" "Wicked men," answered the body, which then took up its own head and walked with it to a nearby church for burial.

24
OCTOBER

Births

Sarah J.B. Hale (author of "Mary Had a Little Lamb") 1788; Moss Hart (playwright) 1904.

Deaths

John Doe (fictious person) 1852; Richard Roe (fictious person) 1852.

John Doe and Richard Roe Die

Both John Doe and Richard Roe were born with the *Magna Carta* in 1215 a provision of which required the production of witnesses before every criminal trial. The two fictitious names were thenceforth commonly inserted as the names of the alleged witnesses, and their use spread to other proceedings. In every process of ejectment, instead of the real parties to the suit being named, John Doe, plaintiff, sued Richard Roe, defendant. They were finally dispensed with by an act passed in England in 1852, which sentenced them to death, to take effect on the 24th of October of that year. Despite their documented demise, their names still crop up occasionally.

A Lady in a Barrel Survives

Today in 1901 in a stunt to raise money to repay a loan due on her Texas ranch, Mrs Anna Edson Taylor went over Niagara Falls in a barrel—the first person to survive such an attempt. She was strapped in her barrel with a leather harness and surrounded by cushions.

The Stock Market Crashes

"A little distress selling on the stock exchange" explained one banker today in 1929, describing the Black Thursday panic selling on the New York Stock Exchange that signalled the beginning of the stock market crash.

King Charles Corresponds

"You will have heard of our taking of New Amsterdam, which lies just by New England. 'Tis a place of great importance to trade. It did belong to England heretofore, but the Dutch by degrees drove our people out and built a very good town, but we have got the better of it, and 'tis now called New York."

A letter from King Charles II of England to his sister Henrietta, October 24, 1664

King Charles Eats Cranberries

On this day in 1667 King Charles II of England tasted his first cranberries and took an immediate fancy to them. Ten barrels of the berries had been presented to the English court by explorers returning from Cape Cod, Massachusetts, in the New World.

Scorpio (the Scorpion) Signifies

William Lilly, the astrologer questioned yesterday in 1666 about the Great Fire of London, interpreted the sign of Scorpio (October 24 to November 22) in his *Christian Astrology:*

Manners when well dignified
In feats of Warre and Courage invincible, scorning any should exceed him, subject to no Reason, Bold Confident immoveable, Contentious, challenging all Honour to themselves, Valiant, lovers of Warre and things pertaining thereunto, hazarding himselfe to all Perils, willingly will obey no body, or submit to any; a large Reporter of his owne Acts, one that slights all things in comparison of Victory, and yet of prudent behaviour in his owne affaires.

When ill placed
Then he is a Pratler without modesty or honesty, a lover of Slaughter and Quarrels, Murder, Theevery, a promoter of Sedition, Frayes and Commotions, an Highway-Theefe, as wavering as the Wind, a Traytor, of turbulent Spirit, Perjured, Obscene, Rash, Inhumane, neither fearing God or caring for man, Unthankful, Trecherous, Oppressors, Ravenous, Cheaters, Furious, Violent.

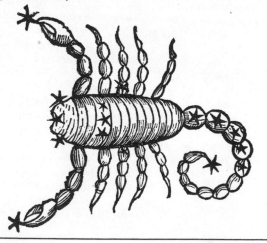

Births

Johann Strauss (composer) 1825; Georges Bizet (composer) 1838; Pablo Picasso (artist) 1881.

Deaths

Demosthenes (orator) 322 B.C.; the Sts Crispin (martyrs) 287; William Hogarth (painter/engraver) 1764.

The Battle of Agincourt

On St Crispin's Day 1415, the English under Henry V, against all odds, defeated a French army under Constable d'Albret, which was better provisioned and more than six times larger in number. The English had only 6,000 men at arms, and about 24,000 foot soldiers, mostly archers, and were matched against over 100,000 of French cavalry alone. Yet with a loss of only 1,600 men they took the lives of 7,000 French knights and 120 great lords.

The Shoemaker Saints

St Crispin and his brother Crispinian were Roman Christians who suffered martyrdom together under the persecution of the emperor Maximian on October 25, 287. They were said to have preached to the people during the day and at night earned their living by making shoes, and thus they became the patron saints of shoemakers and those who would avoid sore feet:

Dear Saint, the saint of those who make good shoes,
Thee for my patron saint I also choose;
Whene'er I walk in highway, trail or street,
Bring thou unblistered home my grateful feet.

The twenty fifth of October
Cursed by the cobbler
That goes to bed sober.

Shoemaker Snubs Charles

Charles V, emperor of the Holy Roman Empire, often walked incognito among his subjects to learn their feelings about his rule. One St Crispin's Day in Brussels, his boot needed immediate repair and he was directed to a shoemaker. But the man was celebrating their saint's day with his friends in the trade. "What friend!" said the fellow to the disguised king, "Do you know no better than to ask one of our craft to work on St Crispin's Day? Was it Charles himself I'd not do a stitch for him now; but if you'll come in and drink St Crispin, do and welcome; we are as merry as the emperor can be." For their hospitality Charles awarded the cobblers a new crest—a boot adorned with his imperial crown.

Hogarth Collects a Debt

Early in his career, William Hogarth who died today in 1764, painted an accurate portrait of a certain very ugly nobleman who had commissioned the work. But his lordship refused to accept and pay for the painting and Hogarth wrote him a note referring to his pressing necessity for money: "If therefore his Lordship does not send for it in three days, it will be disposed of, with the addition of a tail and some other appendages, to *Mr. Hare, the famous wild-beast man;* Mr. Hogarth having given that gentleman a conditional promise on the Lordship's refusal." Hogarth was paid within two days and the painting was given to the ugly lord.

An Enormous Punch Bowl

On the 25th of October, 1694, Admiral Edward Russel, then commanding a Mediterranean fleet, gave a grand entertainment at Allicante in Spain. The tables were laid under the shade of orange trees, in four garden walks meeting at a common centre, at a marble fountain that had been turned into a giant punch bowl for the occasion. Four hogsheads of brandy, one pipe of Malaga wine, twenty gallons of lime juice, twenty-five hundred lemons, thirteen hundredweight of fine white sugar, five pounds of grated nutmeg, three hundred toasted biscuits, and eight hogsheads of water formed the ingredients of the monster punch. An elegant canopy placed over the potent liquor prevented waste by evaporation or dilution by rain; while in a boat specially built for the purpose, a ship-boy rowed around the fountain to assist in filling the cups of the 6,000 persons who drank from it.

26
OCTOBER

Births

Dominic Scarlatti (composer) 1685; Joseph A. Hansom (cab inventor) 1803; Mohammed Reza Pahlavi (shah of Iran) 1919.

Deaths

Abulfeda (Moslem historian) 1331; Elizabeth Stanton (suffragette) 1902; Igor Sikorsky (helicopter inventor) 1972.

Coronations

1760:   George III crowned king of England.
1967:   Mohammed Reza Pahlavi crowned shah of Iran.

Hostilities

1644:   The *Second Battle of Newbury* began in England.
1664:   The Royal Marines were organised in England.
1676:   *Bacon's Rebellion* ended in the colony of Virginia.
1774:   A military force of "Minute Men" was organised in America.
1854:   The Boers killed 900 African tribesmen in South Africa.
1896:   The Italian-Abyssinian war ended.
1914:   The British battleship *Audacious* hit a mine in the North Sea.
1940:   The *Empress of Britain* was torpedoed by a German U-boat.
1942:   The *President Coolidge* hit a mine in the South Pacific.
1942:   The U.S.S. *Hornet* was damaged in the Santa Cruz Islands.
1944:   The U.S. defeated the Japanese navy off the Philippine Islands.
1947:   The British army withdrew from Iraq.
1951:   Rocky Marciano knocked out Joe Louis in New York.

Beginnings

1277:   Walter de Merton founded Merton College at Oxford in England.
1289:   The medical and law schools at Montpelier in France were united into a university.
1369:   Charles V, king of France, known as "Charles the Wise," dedicated a monument to his personal chef, Benkels, who had recently invented a recipe for pickled fish that was particularly favoured by His Majesty.
1751:   The *Society of Antiquarians* was inaugurated in London.
1825:   The Erie Canal was opened in America.
1831:   Asiatic cholera made its first appearance in England.
1868:   The State of Illinois first used its seal.
1887:   Gala performances of Mozart's *Don Giovanni* were given in Paris, Vienna, Prague, and throughout Germany to celebrate the centenary of its first production.
1968:   Flushing Meadow Park Zoo was opened in New York City.

Endings

1529:   The papal legate ended a British visit without granting a divorce to Henry VIII.
1784:   The first U.S. daily newspaper, the *Pennsylvania Evening Post and Daily Advertiser,* ceased publication.
1793:   The *U.S. National Gazette* ceased publication.

Numbers

In the world of numerology persons born today are given to philosophising, tend to believe in the occult, are religiously committed, and have a fatalistic outlook on life. They are often lonely and misunderstood during their lifetime, but occasionally gain recognition after their death.

Births

Catherine (wife of King Henry V of England) 1401; Mrs Hester Chapone (moral writer) 1727; Captain James Cook (explorer) 1728; Dr Andrew Combe (physiologist) 1797; Theodore Roosevelt (16th U.S. president) 1858; Dylan Thomas (poet) 1914; Theresa Wright (actress) 1918.

Deaths

Maxentius (Roman emperor) 312; Eugenius II (pope) 827; Albert II (German king) 1439; Michael Servitus (heretic) 1553; Urban II (pope) 1590; William II (Dutch king) 1650; John Thomson (painter) 1840; Ida Pfeiffer (travel writer) 1858.

Ida Pfeiffer

At the age of forty-five, Ida Pfeiffer, the Viennese mother of two sons became a famous voyager and travel writer, and the first European to visit then unknown parts of many lands. She made voyages to the Holy Land, Scandinavia, and two trips around the world. She financed them by sales of books describing her travels, and by the sale of geologic and zoologic specimens that she brought back. She died on October 27, 1858, in London, from a fever she had contracted on her final voyage to the then *terra incognita,* Madagascar.

Today in Transportation

1829: The first patent for a baby carriage was issued in the U.S.
1904: The first subway in America started its operations in New York, running from the Brooklyn Bridge to midtown Manhattan.
1915: Shackleton's exploration party abandoned their ice-bound ship in the Antarctic.
1925: A train wreck at Victoria, Mississippi, injured several people.
1961: The U.S. super aircraft carrier *Constellation* was commissioned.
1964: Art Arfons set a land speed record of 536.71 miles per hour in his *Green Monster* vehicle.
1970: The Russian lunar spacecraft, *Zonda, 8* returned to earth.

Today and the Law

1871: William Marcy Tweed, better known as "Boss" Tweed, the corrupt political dictator of Tammany Hall in New York City, was arrested on charges of defrauding the city of millions of dollars.
1879: Adolphus Rosenberg, proprietor of *Town and Talk* was sentenced at the Old Bailey in London to eighteen months imprisonment for publishing libels on Mrs Langtry and Mrs Cornwallis West.
1919: Even though President Wilson vetoed the Prohibition Enforcement Bill, the two U.S. houses of government voted over his veto to adopt it.

Today's Natural Phenomena

1602: A great meteor shower occurred in northern Europe.
1780: A solar eclipse darkened the skies of the western hemisphere.
1949: Southeastern India was ravaged by a cyclone.
1959: A severe hurricane hit the east coast of Mexico.
1962: A typhoon in Thailand caused considerable damage.
1969: Northern Yugoslavia was rocked by a strong earthquake.

Today and Royalty

97: The Roman emperor Nerva appointed Trajan as his successor.
1834: Don Carlos, pretender to the Spanish throne, was deprived of his inheritance.
1952: Jigme Dorji Wangchuck became the dragon king of Bhutan.

28
OCTOBER

Births

Henry III (holy Roman emperor) 1017; Desiderius Erasmus (scholar) 1467; Jonas Salk (scientist) 1914.

Deaths

Alfred the Great (English king) 901; John Wallis (mathematician) 1703; John Locke (philosopher) 1704.

Angelo Guiseppe Roncalli Takes Office

On October 28, 1959 Angelo Guiseppe, Cardinal Roncalli, 76, patriarch of Venice, was elected pope, taking the name of John XXIII.

Suffragettes Take the House of Commons

On October 28, 1908 two women suffragettes chained themselves to the grill of the balcony in the gallery of the British House of Commons.

How to Learn the Language of Birds

"Associate with two fellows on the 28th day of October, and goe with dogges as to hunt. Carry home with thee the beast that thou shalt find first. Prepare it with the heart of a foxe, and thus thou shalt understand the voice of birds."

An item of old British folklore

King Alfred Tells the Time

The death of Alfred the Great, king of England, occurred today in 901. This Saxon king was a just ruler, a scholar, an effective leader against the Danish invaders, and a dedicated time-keeper. Alfred adopted a curious way of measuring time so as to observe the canonical hours more punctually—clocks at that time being unknown. He caused waxen candles, marked by notches every inch, to be kept burning in his oratory before the figures of the saints, hence measuring the hours.

Tom Trotter Beats His Wife

In England it was once customary to punish minor offences by subjecting the guilty party to public ridicule, indignation, and humiliation. Punishment included the cucking-stool [sic], the whirligig, the drunkard's cloak, the stocks, the pillory, and *Rough Music.* The latter, sometimes called *Riding the Stang* was conducted by villagers, who gathered in front of the culprit's house with noise-making equipment including cows' horns, frying pans, tea kettles, and pots and pans, shouting out cries of "Shame! Shame!" On October 28, 1862 it happened to Tom Trotter in a small English village.

Ran, tan, tan; ran, tan, tan,
To the sound of this pan;
This is to give notice that Tom Trotter
Has beaten his good woman!
For what and for why?

'Cause she ate when she was hungry,
And drank when she was dry.
Ran, tan, tan, ran, tan:
Hurrah, hurrah! for this good woman.

Miss Liberty Takes a Stand

Today in 1886 Bartholdi's colossal statue of *Liberty Enlightening The World,* presented by France to America, and destined to be used as a lighthouse at the entrance of New York Harbor, was inaugurated by President Cleveland. The statue of bronze measures 151 feet in height and is placed on a pedestal of 154 feet, forming the highest figure monument in the world at that time.

John Eliot Preaches to the Indians

On October 28, 1646 John Eliot, apostle to the Indians, preached the first sermon in their native tongue to Indians assembled in a wigwam at Nonantum in New England.

Births

Edmund Halley (astronomer) 1656; James Boswell (biographer) 1740; John Keats (poet) 1796; Joseph Goebbels (propagandist) 1897.

Deaths

Sir Walter Raleigh (explorer) 1618; Henry Welby (hermit) 1636; Jean d'Alembert (mathematician) 1783; Joseph Pulitzer (publisher) 1911.

The Self-Doubt of a Poet

The poet John Keats, born today in London in 1796, had something in common with Byron and Shelley: a small head. He developed all of his five senses to a high degree and once covered his tongue with cayenne pepper in order that he might better appreciate a cold draught of claret after it. All his life he sorrowed that he had done nothing worthy of abiding fame—once saying "Let my epitaph be: Here lies one whose name was writ on water." His last words when he died in 1821, at the age of twenty-five, were: "Thank God it has come."

The Name of a Horse

On October 29, 1841, Lord Palmerston wrote to Mr Byng regarding the pronunciation of the name of his horse "Iliona" about which bets had been taken up at Newmarket. "There can be no doubt that in point of prosody the 'o' in Iliona is short."

The Trial of a Tiger

Today in 1857 a tiger, in the course of conveyance from the London Docks to the premises of Mr Jamrach, a dealer in animals, burst out of a van and attacked a boy in the streets. One of the attendants overpowered the brute with a crowbar and got it back to the cage. The boy survived, but brought an action against the owner, his counsel pleading in aggravation that the tiger was then being exhibited as the one "that ate the boy in the Minories."

The Confidence of an Admiral

Sir Walter Raleigh, the renowned English admiral and explorer, was decapitated today in 1618 in Old Palace Yard at Westminster, having been charged with treason by King James I. His behaviour on the scaffold was unaffected and cheerful. When asked by the executioner which way he should lay his head, he answered, "So the heart be right, it is no matter which way the head lies."

The Irony of the Sea

Today in 1880 the vessel *Ocean Queen* foundered on the rocks off the shore of Wells in Norfolk, England. A lifeboat sent from shore to aid the distressed ship, tried in vain to get close in the heavy seas and was finally swamped, with the loss of eleven men. At low tide the crew of the *Ocean Queen* walked ashore.

The Diet of a Hermit

On October 29, 1636, Henry Welby, the Grub Street Hermit died. For the last forty-four of his eighty-four years he lived in three rooms of a house on Grub Street in London without seeing anyone at all except, on very rare occasions, a single, aged maidservant. Until his fortieth birthday he was a prosperous country gentleman of Lincolnshire, but a duel fought with his brother so disenchanted him with the world that he resolved to retreat from it entirely. Day in and day out Welby's main food was oatmeal, and on High Days he would sometimes eat the yoke of an egg.

30
OCTOBER

Births

John Adams (2nd U.S. president) 1735; Ezra Pound (poet) 1885; Ted Williams (baseball player) 1918.

Deaths

Edmund Cartwright (power-loom inventor) 1823; John Chubb (safe inventor) 1872; Ernest Feydeau (novelist) 1873.

Meaty Milestones

1485:   When Henry VII was crowned at Westminster today, he instituted the body of royal attendants called yeomen of the guard, who in later times came to be known as the famous Beefeaters.

1581:   The Meat Carvers' Guild of Venice tightened up its working conditions, and announced that hereafter each carver would not perform for more than six guests.

Near Misses

1937:   Astronomers calculated that the earth missed destruction by less than three seconds when a minor planet—Hermes—weighing 500,000 tons passed close to the earth at a speed of 186,000 miles per second. A slight change in its course would have caused it to explode on earth with such force as to obliterate the entire population.

1938:   Orson Wells caused a national panic in the United States that threatened to engulf the entire nation when he broadcast a radio dramatisation of H.G. Wells' *The War of the Worlds* on the CBS network.

Direct Hits

1944:   Allied bombers made concentrated attacks on Cologne and Berlin that severely damaged both cities.

1961:   Against world-wide opposition Russia staged a giant nuclear explosion in Siberia.

1965:   A heavy blast levelled the market place in Cartagena, Columbia.

Napoleon on Slavery

The Emperor Napoleon in a letter addressed to his cousin, the minister of Algeria and the colonies, today in 1858 intimated the withdrawal of his sanction from the attempt to obtain negro labourers on the African coast. "If their enrolment," he writes, "be only the slave trade in disguise, I will have it on no terms." He recommended that an effort be made to obtain Indian coolies as free labourers.

Pepys on Plays

"Tom Killigrew's way of getting to see a play when a boy. He would go to the Red Bull, and when the man cried to the boys: 'Who will go and be a devil, and he shall see the play for nothing?' Then would he go in and be a devil upon the stage."
   From the diary of Samuel Pepys, October 30, 1660

Weather Forecast

"When great abundance of migratory birds arrive early they usually forbode a hard winter. The same prognostic of a severe winter is to be inferred from a preponderance of berries in bushes and hedges."
   Catholic Annal, October, 1830

31
OCTOBER

Births
Jan Vanmeer (artist) 1623; Juliette Gordon Low (founder of the Girl Scouts) 1860.

Deaths
Eric Weiss (Harry Houdini, escape artist) 1926; Ramon Novarro (actor) 1968.

Luther's Last Stand
Today in 1517 Martin Luther nailed his 95 theses against the abuse of the practice of Indulgence to the door of the Castle Church in Wittenberg, Germany. His preface read: "Here I take my stand: I can do no other, so help me God—Amen."

Margaret's Final Decision
On October 31, 1955, Princess Margaret ended three weeks of world-wide suspense and announced that she had decided not to marry Group Captain Peter Townsend.

Stalin's Public Withdrawal
Today in 1961 in Moscow, the body of Joseph Stalin was removed from public display within a mausoleum in Red Square, and buried in a simple grave alongside the Kremlin Wall.

The Origins of Halloween
Today in ancient England the Druids celebrated *Samhain* or "Summer's End" with human sacrifices, augury, and prayers. Spirits were thought to be about as the sun began its downward course, natural laws were suspended, and the harvest was gathered in. Later it became Hallow E'en, still with ghosts, goblins, and divinations, but also much gaiety and hijinks.

Hey-how for Hallow E'en
When all the witches are to be seen,
Some in black and some in green,
Hey-how for Hallow E'en.

Halloween Nuts
Another popular game for girls to play on Halloween was to place hazel nuts along the firegrate, each one assigned the name of a possible husband, and to chant: "If you love me pop and fly; if you hate me burn and die."

Halloween Apples
Apples played a major role in Halloween celebrations with ducking for apples, or apple-bobbing, being the most popular pastime. In one Halloween ceremony it was required that a young woman who wished to see the face of her future husband should eat an apple by candlelight before a mirror. She would then see the face of her spouse-to-be looking at her over the shoulder of her reflection. Another method of husband divination involved peeling an apple:

I pare this apple round and round again;
My sweetheart's name to flourish on the plain:
I fling the unbroken paring o'er my head,
My sweetheart's letter on the ground to reach.

Halloween Snails
It used to be believed that one could learn the initials of the name of a future spouse by setting a snail to crawl through ashes on the hearth on Halloween night. The creature would then obligingly leave the letters written as he trailed through the ash.

Halloween Fires
In Lancashire, near Marton and the Fylde, country people often tried today to help the souls of friends in purgatory. They lit bonfires and a circle of men threw up masses of burning straw with pitchforks which they believed was an effective ceremony to relieve the sufferings in Hell.

November

Next was November; he full grosse and fat
As fed with lard, and that right well might seem;
For he had been a fatting hogs of late,
That yet his brows with sweat did reak and steam,
And yet the season was full sharp and breem;
In planting eeke he took no small delight;
Wheron he rode not easy was to deeme;
For it a dreadful centaiur was in sight,
The seed of Saturn and fair Nais, Chiron hight.
  Edmund Spenser

NOVEMBER

History

Though it is the eleventh month on our calendar,
November came ninth in the old Roman calendar, and is
named from the Latin word *novem,* meaning nine. among
the old Saxons it was known as *Wint Monath,* or wind
month, from the gales that were said to start blowing at
this time of year. It was also known to them as *Blot
Monath,* or blood month, because it was the time of year
that they slaughtered great numbers of cattle to be salted
for winter use. November, the month when winter begins,
used to be known as the month of gloom, blue devils, and
suicides.

Birthstone

This month's birthstone, the topaz—the symbol of
fidelity—also protected the wearer from poison.

No!

No sun — no moon!
No morn — no noon —
No dawn — no dusk — no proper time of day —
No sky — no earthly view —
No distance looking blue —
No road — no street — no "t'other side the way" —
No end to any row —
No indication where the crescents go —
No top to any steeple —
No recognitions of familiar people —
No courtesies for showing 'em —
No knowing 'em!
No travelling at all — no locomotion —
No inkling of the way — no notion —
"No go" — by land or ocean —
No mail — no post —
No news from any foreign coast —
No park — no ring — no afternoon gentility —
No company — no nobility —
No warmth, no cheerfulness, no healthful ease —
No comfortable feel in any member —
No shade, no shine, no butterflies, no bees,
No fruits, no flowers, no leaves, no birds,
November!
  Thomas Hood (1799-1845)

1
NOVEMBER

Births

Benvenuto Cellini (sculptor) 1500; Mathew Hale (judge) 1609; Nicolas Boileau (poet) 1636.

Deaths

Charles II (Spanish king) 1700; Auguste Navarre (gymnast) 1880; Alexander III (Russian czar) 1894.

Punky Night and Mangel-Wurzels

All Saint's Night was Punky Night in Somerset when children put candles into scooped out mangel-wurzels (beets), which were carved into images of faces, houses, and trees. The children marched round the streets singing the Punky Song:

Soul! Soul! for an apple or two!
If you have no apples,
Pears will do.
If you have no pears,
Money will do.
If you have no money,
God bless you.

The Great Lisbon Earthquake

The first of November 1755 was the date of the great earthquake that destroyed the Portuguese city of Lisbon in a rapid series of twenty-two shocks, and killed over 60,000 people. The whole Portuguese coast, as well as those of Spain and Morocco were also hit hard, and the exact death toll is unknown. In Morocco, a whole town of 8,000 people disappeared into a huge crack in the earth's crust. The epicentre of the quake was in the Atlantic, and the tremors were followed by huge tidal waves that destroyed whatever the shaking earth had left undamaged along the coasts.

Stamp Act Reactions

Today in 1765 the American colonies reacted strongly to the duties levied on them by the Stamp Act that Britain had put into effect. Flags were flown at half mast, bells tolled, and business was suspended. In New York ten boxes of stamps were seized and destroyed; in Connecticut the Stamp Officer was threatened with hanging; in Boston houses were destroyed and stamps burnt or thrown to the wind.

All Saint's Day

This festival takes its origin from the conversion in the seventh century of the Pantheon in Rome, built originally by Marcus Agrippa, into a Christian temple, and its dedication by Pope Boniface IV to the Virgin and all the martyrs. The anniversary was first celebrated on May 1, but was subsequently changed to November 1 and then entitled All Saint's Day in general commemoration of all the saints.

On All Saints day the stags are lean,
Yellow are the tops of the birch;
   deserted is the summer dwelling:
Woe to him who for a trifle deserves
   a curse.
   Llywarch Hen (16th-century Welsh poet)

Toasting Judged Wrong

In his will, Mathew Hale, an eminent judge born on this day in 1609, left the following injunction to his grandchildren: "I will not have you begin or pledge any health, for it is become one of the greatest artifices of drinking, and occasions of quarrelling in the kingdom. If you pledge one health, you oblige yourself to pledge another, and a third, and so onwards; and if you pledge as many as will be drank, you must be debauched and drunk."

Balloonist Creates Impression

On this day in 1880 close to Nevilly, at the gates of Paris, a trapeze was attached to a balloon, which was sent up in the afternoon. A professional gymnast named Auguste Navarre volunteered, for fifty francs, to perform several feats on it in mid-air. When the balloon had reached the height of some 700 yards, Navarre let go, and not having fastened himself to the trapeze, as he had been advised to do, came crashing down into a garden, where his body made a hole in the ground two feet deep.

Births

Daniel Boone (U.S. frontiersman) 1734; Marie Antoinette (French queen) 1755; Warren G. Harding (29th U.S. president) 1865.

Deaths

Jenny Lind (Swedish singer) 1887; William Firth (English artist) 1909; George Bernard Shaw (Irish playwright) 1950.

Horse-Headed Hob Horror

Another custom in Cheshire held today was called *Old Hob.* It consisted of a man, covered in a white sheet and carrying the head of a dead horse, moaning and running through the streets to frighten the populace.

The Balfour Declaration

On November 2, 1917, the Balfour Declaration declared that "His Majesty's Government views with favour the establishment of a national home for the Jewish people in Palestine."

Byron on Boone

Daniel Boone, American frontiersman, was born on this day in 1734. Lord Byron wrote of Boone in *Don Juan,* and gave him an international reputation.

Of all men, saving Sylla, the
  man-slayer,
Who passes for in life and death most
  lucky,
Of the great names which in our
  faces stare,
The General Boone, back-woodsman
  of Kentucky,
Was happiest among mortals
  anywhere;
For killing nothing but a bear or
  buck, he
Enjoy'd the lonely, vigorous, harmless
  days
Of his old age in wilds of deepest
  maze.

The Media

1867:   The magazine *Harper's Bazaar* was founded.
1903:   The London *Daily Mirror* began publication.
1936:   The British Broadcasting Corporation began television service from Alexandra Palace with daily two-hour broadcasts.

Decorating the Dead

Today, *All Soul's Day,* was devised by Odilon, abbot of Cluny in the ninth century, as the day on which ceremonies are performed for the souls of the departed faithful. It was established as a general festival throughout the Christian church in 998. At Naples, it was the custom of this day to throw open the charnel houses, which were lighted up with torches and decked with flowers, while crowds thronged through the vaults to visit the bodies of their friends and relatives, the fleshless skeletons of which were dressed up in robes and arranged in niches along the wall.

Antics and Acrobatics

In England on All Soul's Day the Cheshire Soulcakers, a group of mummers, performed *King George and the Dragon* wherein a boastful Turk challenges King George to a fight at the end of which the king would be taken back to Turkey in the form of mince pies. In the ensuing mock battle George does in the Terrible Turk but a Quack Doctor revives him. At this point Hobby Horse or Beelzebub arrives on the scene and the play disintegrates into a series of foolish antics and acrobatics.

3
NOVEMBER

Births

Lucan (poet) 39; William Cullen Bryant (poet) 1794; Karl Baedeker (guidebook publisher) 1801.

Deaths

St Rumald (patron of Brackley) 3rd century; St Wenefride (virgin martyr) 5th century; Henri Matisse (painter) 1954.

A Short-Lived Saint

St Rumald was born at Sutton, in Northamptonshire. Immediately he came into the world he exclaimed: "I am a Christian! I am a Christian! I am a Christian!" He then made a full and explicit confession of his faith; desired to be forthwith baptised; appointed his own godfathers; and chose his own name. He was baptised by Bishop Widerin, and immediately after the ceremony walked to a certain well near Brackley (which now bears his name) and there preached for three successive days, after which he made his will. This done, he instantly expired on this day sometime in the third century.

Immolation Site Inundated

St Wenefride was a holy virgin of exemplary piety, who was burned by the infamous Caradoc, prince of North Wales. At the place where she was immolated, a well of pure water sprang up, the stones at the botton of which were marked with red streaks in memory of her innocent blood, shed on that spot today in the fifth century.

Lyon Torrent

Today in 1840, the French city of Lyon was flooded by the sudden and unlooked-for rising of the river Saône. Many large bridges were carried away, and the torrent rushed with resistless force through some of the busiest and most populous streets of the city.

Illinois Housewives Irate

Today in 1837 Illinois housewives were up in arms over the high cost of living. A pound of butter cost as much as eight cents, a dozen eggs six cents, beef was three cents a pound, and pork two cents. Coffee and sugar were luxuries at twenty cents and ten cents a pound. A good hired girl cost two dollars a week, besides her keep.

Autumn Lady's Tresses

The flower assigned to November 3 by medieval monks is autumn lady's tresses, known botanically as *Spiranthes autumnalis,* from the Greek *speira:* a spiral, and *anthos:* a flower.

Turmoil by Tobacco Toughs

Today in 1854 a tumultuous riot took place at Cambridge between the police and certain belligerant Cambridge undergraduates, who interrupted a lecture being delivered in the Town Hall against the use of tobacco.

Dahomey Doyen's Demands

On this day in 1848 Guezo, king of Dahomey, demanded that Queen Victoria put an end to the slave-trade in all dominions except his own, and solicited the gift of the Tower of London guns and blunderbusses for the purpose of fighting his neighbours.

Drury Lane Disturbance

A hectic disturbance in Drury Lane Theatre occurred on this day in 1848, arising out of the excited enthusiasm exhibited for Mr Julkien's new arrangement of the British National Anthem. Several people were injured, including Mr Julkiens.

Births

Will Rogers (humorist) 1879; Frederick Banting (co-discoverer of insulin) 1891.

Deaths

St Emeric (Hungarian prince) 11th century; John Benbow (admiral) 1702; Felix Mendelssohn (composer) 1847.

Today's Flower

Though it is a beautiful evergreen tree with reddish bark, deep green leaves, and drooping creamy-white flowers, the berry-like fruit of the strawberry-tree is very bitter. This factor originated Pliny's name *Unedo,* "One-I-eat" (as if no one would eat a second—though birds like it), from which its bontaical name of *Arbutus unedo* is derived.

An Uncomfortable Present

In England an extraordinary attempt to poison the family of Mr Samuel Ashdown was made today in 1880. A large quantity of strychnine was placed in and upon a saddle of mutton, which was then wrapped in grey calico, packed in a hamper, and sent off per Great Western Railway in the most matter-of-fact way possible. Fortunately some suspicion was excited and the meat was not touched. No clue to the sender of this very uncomfortable present was ever discovered.

An Admirable Exchange

During the war with France in 1702 John Benbow led a squadron of seven British ships against five French ones under the command of Admiral Ducasse. When he finally caught up with the French, five of the captains under Benbow refused to enter the attack, the other ship joining him was quickly disabled, and the *Breda,* Benbow's own ship undertook the fray alone. After three days battle the French escaped. Later Ducasse sent the English admiral the following letter: "Sir: I had little hope on Monday last but to have supped in your cabin (i.e. to have been your prisoner) but it pleased God to order it otherwise, and I am thankful for it. As for those cowardly captains that deserted you, hang them up; for, by God, they deserved it! Yours—Ducasse." Benbow died of wounds received in the attack on November 4, 1702.

St Emeric and America

St Emeric, a somewhat obscure and pious Hungarian prince who died on this day in the eleventh century, is remembered for more than his saintliness. Through his celebrity in older days, his name became a popular one. Its Italian form was *Amerigo*; and the Americas were named after the Italian Amerigo Vespucci, the Florentine merchant who claimed to have discovered South America in 1497.

An Uncharitable Diatribe

In the issue of November 4, 1905, Edward William Bok, editor of the *Ladies Home Journal,* began his campaign to elevate American taste in furniture and aimed one of his first attacks at the so-called Morris Chair. This chair, Mr Bok charged ". . .cost $31, with gaping carved lion heads for arms, and ball-and-claw feet, heavy to move, carved out of all proportion to size, a hideous piece of furniture."

Marriage

Abraham Lincoln, thirty-three, to Mary Todd, twenty-three, in Springfield, Illinois, 1842. ("The bridegroom," said one guest, looked as "pale and trembling as being driven to slaughter.")

Births

Hans Sachs (poet) 1494; Will Durant (historian) 1885.

Deaths

Casmir III (Polish king) 1370; Kurrach Singh and Nebal Singh (Indian sovereigns) 1840.

Bad Day at Lahore

Kurrach Singh died at Lahore today in 1840. His favourite wife and three female attendants sacrificed themselves on the funeral pyre. On the return of the procession to the palace, a beam from a gateway fell on the new sovereign, Nebal Singh. He died in a few hours.

Guy Fawkes in America

"Saturday last, being the fifth of November, it was observed here in memory of the horrid and treasonable popish gunpowder plot to blow up and destroy King, Lords and commons and the gentlemen of his majesty's council. The Assembly and Corporation and others the principal gentlemen and merchants of this city, waited upon his honor, the Lieutenant Governor at Fort George, where the royal healths were drunk as usual under the discharge of cannon, and at night the city was illuminated."

The *New York Gazette,* November 7, 1737

Guy Fawkes at the Zoo

1844: A California grizzly bear was successfully operated on for cataracts of the eyes on Guy Fawkes Day at the Zoological Gardens.

1872: A hippopotamus born today at the Zoological Gardens was christened "Guy Fawkes."

Guy Fawkes Caught

On November 5, 1605, Guy Fawkes was apprehended at the door of a vault beneath the old House of Lords in London with a darkened lantern, a tinder box, and three matches in his possession. He was making preparations for the lighting (the following day) of the fuse to the thirty-six barrels of gunpowder that had been secretly placed in the vault by himself and his co-conspirators. So came to an end the famous *Gunpowder Plot,* an attempt to take the lives of James I and the assembled Parliament, and replace them with a Catholic monarchy. After Fawkes confessed the plot before the king, all the conspirators were either killed while being apprehended, or tried and executed later.

Guy Fawkes Day

The anniversary of the Gunpowder Plot is celebrated as Guy Fawkes Day in England. Young boys dress up scarecrows as Fawkes and carry them about the city. In the evening the effigies are burnt in bonfires and fireworks are set off. In former times the bonfire held at Lincoln's Inn Fields in London was an especially magnificent ceremony. It used upwards of two hundred cartloads of fuel, and over thirty Guys (as the effigies were called) were burnt around it.

A Guy Fawkes Chant

Remember, remember, the fifth of November,
Gunpowder, treason and plot;
I see no reason why Gunpowder Treason
should ever be forgot.
A stick and a stake
For King James' sake
Holla, boys, Holla, make the town ring;
Holla, boys, Holla, boys, God save the King.

6
NOVEMBER

Births

Noah (of the ark) 2948 B.C.; Julian (Roman emperor) 331; John Philip Sousa (U.S. composer) 1854; Dr James Naismith (Canadian inventor of basketball) 1861.

Deaths

St Leonard (patron of prisoners) 559; Innocent III (pope) 1406; Sir John Falstaff (English knight) 1460; John IV (Portuguese king) 1656; Charlotte (English princess) 1817; Charles X (French king) 1836; Peter Tchaikovsky (Russian composer) 1893.

Patron Saint of Prisoners

St Leonard, a French nobleman who became religious and built a monastery for himself in the forest near Limoges, died on this day in 559. According to legend there was no water within one mile of his monastery "wherefore he did do make a pyt all drye, the which he fylled with water by his prayers—and he shone there by so grete myracles, that who that was in prison, and called his name in ayde, anone his bondes and fetters were broken."

Today in Sport and Theatre

1860: The *New Princess's Theatre* was opened tonight in London with the performance of *Hamlet,* with Mr Edwin Booth as the Prince of Denmark. Although the critics recognised in Mr Booth a scholarly student of Shakespeare and an actor of experience and conscientiousness, the American *Hamlet* had not the elements of a popular success.

1860: The finish in London of a *Go-As-You-Please Six Days' Race* resulted in the victory of Rowell, who had before distinguished himself in competitions of this kind, and who now covered himself and his country in glory for beating the previous "best on record" credited to a coloured gentleman named Hart, who had covered 565 miles in a race in America. Rowell's record was rather more than 566 miles, with some little time to spare.

1869: The first formal intercollegiate football game in America was played at New Brunswick, New Jersey between Princeton and Rutgers with each team made up of twenty-five men. (Final score: Rutgers 6, Princeton 4.)

1882: Lily Langtry, known in England as "The Jersey Lily," made her American debut at Wallack's Theatre in New York, playing in Tom Taylor's play, *An Unequal Match.*

1889: At the Garrick Theatre, New York, the curtain went up for the first time on *Sherlock Holmes,* starring William Gillette, who also dramatised the famous Conan Doyle classic.

1903: Maude Adams launched a stage classic when she opened in New York in Sir James Barrie's *Peter Pan.* (This original run went right through to June 8, 1906.)

Today in Politics

1860: Abraham Lincoln was elected president of the United States.

1936: The Spanish loyalist government left Madrid for Valencia.

1937: Italy joined Germany and Japan in an anti-Comintern pact.

Today's Invention

1923: A U.S. patent was issued to Colonel Jacob Schick for his invention of the electric shaver.

Births

Madame Marie Sklodowska Curie (co-discoveror of radium) 1867.

Deaths

Eleanor (Mrs Franklin D.) Roosevelt (humanitarian) 1962.

Today in Flowers

Today's plant is the field gentian *(Gentiang compestris),* an herb with pale flesh-coloured flowers named after Gentius, an ancient king of Illyria, who is said to have discovered its medicinal value.

Ann Turner's Hat

On the seventh of November 1615, Ann Turner, a physician's widow, appeared before Judge Edward Coke in London on a charge of murder. When the judge asked her to remove her hat she replied that if she could wear it in front of God in church, surely she could wear it before a judge in court. Coke replied ". . .from God no secrets are hid, but it is not so with man whose intellects are weak; and because the countenance is an index to the mind, all covering should be taken away from the face." Mrs. Turner duly removed her hat but promplty replaced it with a kerchief. She was found guilty.

Baroness Borrows Rings

At a London court today in 1848 an inquiry was made into charges made by Sir J. Hoare of Bath, against the Baroness St Mart, of stealing from him two valuable diamond rings. In the course of a visit to Bath, the rings had been shown by Sir John to the baroness. After trying them on her finger she said she returned them to their owner, but he denied having received them. He further denied having at any time made an offer of marriage to her. The baroness was acquitted.

Madame Curie

Marie Sklodowska was born in Poland today in 1867 but lived most of her life in France where she met her husband Pierre Curie. Their teamwork in the laboratory resulted in the discovery of radium in 1898. As a reward Marie and Pierre had the standard unit of radium measurement, the *curie,* named after them. On November 7, 1911—six years after her husband's death—Marie received the Nobel Prize.

Eleanor Roosevelt

Many people eulogised Eleanor Roosevelt after her death today in 1962, but no one surpassed the words of her friend, Adlai E. Stevenson: "She would rather light candles than curse the darkness, and her glow has warmed the world."

Today in the Press

1665: The first gazette in England was published, but at Oxford, not London, because the court was there on account of the plague. When the epidemic subsided, the publication moved back to the capital with the court and became the *London Gazette.* It was published every Saturday. The word "gazette," which originally meant a small, loose-leaved newspaper giving the news of the world, came from the Italian word *"gazetta,"* the name of an old Venetian coin which was once the price of such a sheet.

1837: A pro-slavery mob in Illinois severely beat the Reverend E. Lovejoy, editor of an abolition paper, broke his press and threw it into the river before setting fire to the building where the paper was printed.

1874: *Harper's Weekly* ran the first cartoon depicting an elephant as the symbol of the Republican Party in America.

The Tragedy of Madame Roland

Madam Roland was born Manon Philipon in Paris in 1756. She was deeply sensitive and romantic, weeping passionately at the age of fourteen because she couldn't have been an heroic Roman or Spartan woman in the past. Her husband, M. Roland, minister of the interior, begged her to hide with him in the country when the French Revolution began. She refused and was imprisoned on May 31, 1793. At her trial she appeared dressed carefully in white, with her beautiful black hair descending to her waist. On the scaffold she refused the offer of the executioner to execute her before a man so that she might be spared the agony of the awful sight. Her last words on this day in 1793 were: "O Liberty! how many crimes are committed in thy name."

Births

Margaret Mitchell (author of *Gone with the Wind*) 1900; Katherine Hepburn (actress) 1909; Christian Barnard (doctor) 1922; Alain Delon (actor) 1935.

Deaths

Duns Scotus (scholar) 1308; John Milton (poet) 1674; Madame Roland (brave romantic) 1793.

The Troubles of Captain Boycott

Because he represented those who were intimidating the peasantry, the Englishman Captain Boycott, agent to the earl of Erne in Ireland, was subjected to such persecution that he could get absolutely no one to assist him to gather in his crops. His unfortunate circumstances added the verb "to boycott" to the English language.

Based on *Dickens Dictionary of Dates,* November 8, 1880.

A Big Blaze in Boston

A disastrous fire began in Boston, laying waste a large portion of the city and causing a gigantic loss to those engaged in commerce. All the railways coming into Boston ran fast trains bringing firemen from neighbouring cities. The police, being unable to maintain order, had U.S. troops and marines sent in to assist. There was extensive plundering and 200 thieves, some of them women and children, were arrested. In all it was reported that 776 buildings were destroyed and fourteen persons killed (1872).

Sarah Bernhardt in New York

Sarah Bernhardt, the internationally famous French actress, made her American debut in New York, playing the leading role in *Adrienne Lecouvreur* (1880).

Adolph Hitler in Munich

Adolph Hitler and General Ludendorff led a group that seized the government in Munich, Bavaria. Their plot, hatched in a beer hall, later became known as the Beer Hall Putsch (1923).

A Female Seminary in Massachusetts

Mount Holyoke Female Seminary in South Hadley, Massachusetts, started classes with eighty students, each of whom agreed to pay $64 a year for tuition and board. Mary Lyon was the principal of the school (1837).

A Narrow Victory for Kennedy

John Fitzgerald Kennedy narrowly defeated Richard M. Nixon for the presidency of the United States (1960).

A Landslide Victory for Roosevelt

Franklin Delano Roosevelt won a landslide victory over Herbert Hoover (472 electoral votes to 59), for the presidency of the United States (1932).

9
NOVEMBER

Births

Ivan Turgenev (Russian writer) 1818; Edward VII (English king) 1841; Ed Wynn (U.S. actor) 1886.

Deaths

Robert Blum (Austrian insurrectionist) 1848; Neville Chamberlain (English prime minister) 1940; Charles de Gaulle (French president) 1970.

A Condemned Man's Letter

Robert Blum was executed at Vienna today in 1848 for the part he had taken in the insurrectionary movement there. A few minutes before his execution, he wrote to his wife: "Farewell for the time men call eternity, but which not be so. Bring up our—now only your—children to be honest men, so that they will never disgrace their father's name. All that I feel and would say at this moment escapes me in tears; only once more, then, farewell."

The Significance of Number 9

"Here is wisdom. Let him that hath understanding court the number of the beast, for it is the number of man, and his number is 666" (Revelations, chapter XIII, verse 18). Numerologists have decided that this cryptic passage from the bible may be translated into the number 9 by adding 666 together to arrive at 18, and 1 plus 8 equals 9. "The number of man," 9, represents force, energy, destruction, and war. It denotes energy, ambition, and leadership in anyone born on this day. Number 9 persons are fighters and usually successful because of their grit, strong will, and determination.

The Lord Mayor's Procession

November 9 in London is the day of the annual pageant of the installation of the Lord Mayor of the city. In former times the procession to Westminster, featuring the Chariot of Justice, was an impressive spectacle:

Suppose that you have seen
The new appointed Mayor at
  Queenstairs
Embark his royalty; his own company
With silken streamers, the young
  gazers pleasing,
Painted with different fancies; have
  beheld
Upon the golden galleries music
  playing
And the horns echo, which do take
  the lead
Of other sounds: O do but think
You stand in Temple Gardens and
  behold
London herself, on her proud stream
  afloat;
For so appears this fleet of majestry
Holding due course to Westminster.
  William Shakespeare, *Henry V*

Women's Rights in England

Today in 1848, the Court of Common Pleas in England passed judgment in the case of Miss Becker, which involved the rights of women to exercise suffrage. The judges agreed that there was not sufficient evidence for saying women had a right to vote, while on the other hand there was the uninterrupted practice of centuries to show that they had not so voted. The Lord Chief Justice concluded that the term "men" in the Act did not include women, and even if it did, the women would come within the term "incapacitated."

A Violent Earthquake in Europe

A violent earthquake occurred this morning in 1880 through southern Austria, from Vienna to the Adriatic and the frontiers of Bosnia. It was at its worst at Agram, the capital of Croatia, which was almost destroyed by a succession of shocks, occurring at intervals and accompanied by volcanoes of boiling mud. Severe loss of life was also occasioned.

10
NOVEMBER

Births

Martin Luther (church reformer) 1483; Jacob Epstein (sculptor) 1880; Richard Burton (actor) 1925.

Deaths

Leo the Great (pope) 461; Wladislaus III (Polish king) 1444; Shah Alam (Indian emperor) 1806.

Irresponsible Cooks at Cambridge

There was great agitation among the undergraduates at Cambridge today in 1868 over college dinners. The subject was discussed in the Union, and a resolution carried by 223 to 17, that the present system was execrable, and no permanent improvement possible until irresponsible cooks were made college servants.

A Demonstration at the White House

Today in 1917, forty-one women from fifteen states of the Union were arrested outside the White House in Washington for suffragette demonstrations. Included among those arrested were the wife of a former California congressman, and a seventy-year-old woman. Although they did nothing more than picket the White House with placards and posters demanding the right to vote, they drew sentences ranging from sixty days to six months.

An Uprising in New Zealand

An uprising of Maori tribesmen at Poverty Bay in New Zealand on November 10, 1868, resulted in the massacre of fifty-four white settlers. A British force afterwards despatched to the locality succeeded in slaying 200 of those concerned in the outrage.

A Debut at Steinway Hall

Today in 1888 a thirteen-year-old boy from Vienna named Fritz Kreizler, made his American debut at Steinway Hall in New York.

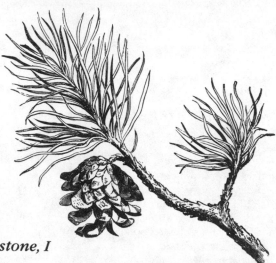

"Dr. Livingstone, I Presume?"

Today in 1872, Henry M. Stanley, a travelling correspondent sent out by the publisher of *The New York Herald,* discovered Dr Livingstone at Ujiji in Zanzibar. As the procession of native guides and assistants entered the town, Stanley observed a group of Arabs in the centre of which was a pale-looking, grey-bearded white man who was clad in a red woollen jacket and wore upon his head a naval cap with a faded silk band. He immediately recognised the European as Dr Livingstone, but a dignified Arab chieftain standing by confirmed Mr Stanley in a resolution to show no symptom of rejoicing or excitement. Slowly he bowed and said: "Dr. Livingstone, I presume?" To which the latter, fully equal to the situation, simply smiled and replied, "Yes, and I feel thankful that I am here to welcome you."

The Tree of the Day

Because flowers are in short supply at this time of year, the medieval monks occasionally had to resort to trees. The *Pinus sylvestrus* or Scots fir, the plant for November 10, is a native of Scotland and grows up to 100 feet high.

Lord Mayor's Day Aftermath

"Languid countenance—a little nervous this morning—fresh demand for soda water and ginger beer—confounded headache—much breakfasting at the coffee houses—scraps of mutton in great request—shall be home early tonight my dear—let me have a little broth—deuce the Lord Mayor—I'll never go again."
  Morning Advertiser, London, November 10, 1824

11

NOVEMBER

Births

Henry IV (holy Roman emperor) 1050; Charles II (Spanish king) 1661; Charles IV (Spanish king) 1748; Victor Emmanuel III (Italian king) 1869; Gustav VI (Swedish king) 1882.

Deaths

St Martin (patron of reformed drunkards) 397.

St Martin's Wine

In Europe the Christian festival in honour of St Martin became identified with a Roman *vinalia,* or wine festival in honour of Bacchus, and today was the day on which the year's new wines were traditionally first tasted. Barnaby Googe's translation from *Neogeorgus,* shows how St Martin's Day was celebrated in fifteenth-century Germany:

To belly cheer, yet once again,
Doth Martin more incline,
Whom all the people worshippeth
With roasted geese and wine.
Both all the day long, and the night,
Now each man open makes
His vessels all, and of the must,
Oft times, the last he takes,
Which holy Martin afterwards
Alloweth to be wine,
Therefore they him, unto the skies,
Extol with praise devine.

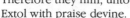

St Martin's Ass

One of the legends about St Martin deals with a pilgrimage on foot to Rome. Satan met him and jeered at him for travelling in a way not suitable to his high office of bishop of Tours. According to the legend, Martin touched Satan, who was instantly changed into an ass. Martin mounted him and continued his journey. Whenever the ass lagged, Martin would spur him on at full speed until at last Satan exclaimed: "Cross thyself; thou plaguest and vexest me without necessity; for owing to my exertions thou will soon reach Rome, the object of thy wishes."

St Martin's Beer

In England St Martin's Day was known as *Martinmas* when much beer was consumed, as shown in a medieval ballad:

It is the day of Martinmas,
Cuppes of ale should freelie passe;
What though Wynter has begunne
To push down the summer sunne,
To oure fire we can betake
And enjoye the crackling brake,
Never heeding Wynter's face
On the day of Martinmas.

St Martin's Weather

If ducks do slide at Martinmas
At Christmas they will swim;
If ducks do swim at Martinmas
At Christmas they will slide.

If the wind is in the southwest at Martinmas, it keeps there till after Candlemas, with a mild wind up to then and no snow to speak of.

St Martin's Cloak

St Martin, bishop of Tours, died on this day in the year 397. The saint once divided his cloak, by cutting it with his sword, with a beggar whom he found perishing with cold at the gate of Amiens. The fragment of the cloak was preserved, and became one of the most holy relics of France; French monarchs carried it to war before their banners. The spot in which the cape was kept comes from the French word "chape" (for cape) and was known as the "chapelle," and its keeper as the "chapelain," from which come the English words "chapel" and "chaplain."

12
NOVEMBER

Births

Elizabeth Cady Stanton (U.S. suffragette) 1815; Auguste Rodin (French sculptor) 1840; Grace Kelly (U.S. actress/Monagesque princess) 1929.

The First Air Raid in America

On November 12, 1926, during a feud between rival beer and liquor factions, the Sheltons and the Birgers of Williamson Country, Illinois, a plane swooped low over Charles Birger's farmhouse and dropped three bombs. Fortunately, because they were poorly made, they didn't explode. This was the first recorded airplane bombing in the U.S. No one was convicted.

Deaths

Boniface III (Italian pope) 606; Canute I (king of Denmark, Norway, and England) 1035; Sir John Hawkins (English navigator) 1595.

Hawkins Hit, Drake Missed

In a battle at San Juan, Puerto Rico, today in 1595, Sir John Hawkins, navigator for Sir Francis Drake, was killed. A few moments later a cannonball shot the stool, on which he was seated, from beneath Sir Francis Drake, leaving him unscathed save for his dignity.

A Theatrical Curfew in Paris

By a police regulation of the city of Paris, dated November 12, 1609, the players at the theatres of the Hotel de Bourgogne and the Marais were ordered to open their doors at one o'clock in the afternoon, and at two o'clock precisely to commence the performance, whether or not there were sufficient spectators, so that the play might be over before half-past four. One writer later remarked "...our ancestors both closed and opened the day much earlier than we do now, and observed much more punctually the old recipe for health and strength, 'to rise with the lark and lie down with the lamb.'"

The Wings of Democracy Clipped

Today in 1837 seven professors of Gottingen, including Ewald, the brothers Grimm, and Gervinus, were deprived of their offices and means of livelihood. They had protested against a recent decree of the king of Hanover who had claimed the constitution was in neither form nor substance binding on him. He wrote: "I have cut the wings of this democracy."

or as it was known in English, the Order of Fools. Their insignia was a fool or jester embroidered on the right side of their mantle, and they met annually at Cleves on the first Sunday after Michaelmas. Though the title of the order sounded foolish, it was in fact a benevolent society, similar to the Odd Fellows or the Foresters.

The Order of Fools

On the 12th of November 1381, Adolphus, count of Cleves, instituted D'Order van't Gecken Gesselschaft,

Births

Edwin Booth (actor) 1833; Robert Louis Stevenson (author) 1850.

A Distinguished American Actor

Edwin Booth, one of the most distinguished American actors, was born on this day in 1833. Booth founded the Players Club in New York, and was its first president. In 1888, he bought a house at 16 Gramercy Park for $75,000 and fitted it up as a club house, reserving for his own use a suite of rooms on one of the upper floors where he died in 1893. When his brother, John Wilkes Booth, shot Abraham Lincoln in 1865, Edwin Booth retired from the stage for a year, but was welcomed heartily by the public when he returned to it.

Deaths

Johann Ludwig Lland (poet) 1779; Gioacchino Rossini (opera composer) 1868.

A Shower of Stars at Niagara

On three successive years, from 1831 to 1833, November 13 was marked by widely observed and very brilliant meteor showers around the world. In 1833, at Niagara Falls, the shower was so intense that many people, remembering the words of Apocalypse—"The stars of heaven fell unto the earth, even as the fig tree casteth her untimely figs, when she is shaken of a mighty wind"—were terror-struck with the fear that the end of the world was nigh.

The Stamford Bull-Run

One November 13th in the time of King John, William, earl of Warren, so enjoyed the sport he got by chasing an accidentally escaped bull through the streets of Stamford, Lincolnshire, that he granted the meadow from which the animal got loose to the town's butchers, on the single condition that they annually provide a bull to be baited and run on the streets. The event was held every year on November 13 until it was discontinued under pressure from the SPCA in 1840. After the animal had been thoroughly teased, baited, and run ragged, the object of the event was to "bridge the bull," that is, trap him on the local bridge that spanned the Welland, and toss him over the rail into the river. At the end of the day the bull was slaughtered and the meat sold in the town very cheaply for everyone's dinner that night.

Come, take him by the tail, boys—
Bridge, bridge him if you can;
Prod him with a stick, boys;
Never let him quiet stand;
Through every street and lane in
    town,
We'll chevy-chase him up and down,
You sturdy bung-straws ten miles
    round,
Come, stump away to Stamford.
  From "The Bullard's Song," a traditional
  poem

The Jeffers Milking Machine

On November 13, 1939 an American named Henry Jeffers demonstrated his invention of the rotolactor, a rotating milking machine that permitted 1680 cows to be milked in seven hours.

Births

Hussein I (king of Jordan) 1935; Charles Philip Arthur George Windsor (English prince and heir to the throne) 1948.

Deaths

Gottfried Wilhelm Leibnitz (German mathematician/philosopher) 1716.

The Birth of an Island, 1963

A volcanic island boiled up through the sea off the coast of Iceland in a vast cloud of steam. A few weeks later, the island, now 567 feet high and over a mile long, was named Surtsey after a legendary Norse giant.

Eddie Rickenbacker's Rescue, 1942

Captain Eddie Rickenbacker, World War I flying ace, engaged in a special mission for the American government, was rescued in the Pacific, along with seven members of the armed forces, after drifting 23 days on a life raft. The men had been missing since October 21, following their flight from Hawaii.

The World's First Street Car, 1832

The first streetcar in the world made its appearance on the streets of New York. New Yorkers were referring to the new conveyance as a "horse car," because the car was drawn by two horses on tracks laid on Fourth Avenue between Prince and 14th streets. A total of thirty persons could be accommodated in the three compartments of each car.

Leibnitz's Only Mistake, 1716

Leibnitz was a full-blown genius who excelled at everything he chose to do. His memory and store of knowledge was such that King George I called him "the living dictionary." He was once caught in a storm off the coast of Italy. The Italian captain of the ship, knowing only that his passenger was German and protestant, and ignorant of the fact that he was also one of the most acclaimed geniuses of his time, began to deliberate with the crew on the propriety of throwing the heretic overboard as a propitiatory sacrifice to the violence of the tempest. Leibnitz knew Italian, and got hold of a rosary and immediately began telling the beads with great fervour. The ruse saved his life. His cleverness failed him only one time. He died in Hanover on November 14, 1716, from the effects of a concoction he had prepared to relieve his rheumatic pains.

Little Georgia Magnet's Powers, 1891

A good deal of interest was aroused in the performance at the Alhambra Theatre in London of a Mrs Abbott, known as "Little Georgia Magnet." The lady claimed to be able by magnetic force to perform feats of strength that seemed to be utterly beyond her physical powers. For example, a man embraced a chair, Mrs Abbott touched it with her fingers and the man staggered back and forth like a drunken man. No one could lift Mrs Abbott by her bare arms, but anyone could lift her upon placing a handkerchief between his hands and her flesh, as a handkerchief was a non-conductor of Mrs Abbott's force.

Nellie Bly's Lack of Nicety, 1889

To prove that she could outdo the record of Jules Verne's hero in "Around the World in Eighty Days," Nellie Bly, a reporter for the *New York World,* set out from Hoboken, New Jersey, on the first stage of her world tour. ("Nellie Bly" was the pen name of Elizabeth Cochrane, credited as the first person to make America conscious of the woman reporter.) Her trip was startling in itself, but to most ladies it was not the journey that seemed unbelievable, but the fact that she was travelling without an umbrella, which was considered "not quite nice."

15
NOVEMBER

Births

Andrew Marvell (poet) 1620; William Cowper (poet) 1731; Irwin Rommel (the Desert Fox) 1891.

Deaths

Albertus Magnus (scholar) 1280; Johann Kepler (astronomer) 1630; Christopher Gluck (composer) 1787.

The Very Olde Man

"Old Parr," Thomas Parr of Alberbury in Shropshire was put to rest in Westminster Abbey today in 1635 at the age of 152. He lived all of his life in the same cottage, married for the first time at eighty and again at 120 after his first wife died. John Taylor, the "Water Poet" wrote about him in a poem "The Olde, Olde, very Olde, Man" wherein some of Old Parr's diet was revealed:

He was of old Pythagoras' opinion,
That green cheese was most wholesome with an onion;
Coarse meslin bread, and for his daily swig,
Milk, buttermilk, and water, whey and whig;
Sometimes metheglin, and by fortune happy,
He sometimes sipped a cup of ale most nappy.

The Mason-Dixon Line

On November 15, 1763, Carles Mason and Jeremiah Dixon began running the Mason and Dixon line, the southern boundary of the free state, Pennsylvania, and the symbol of boundary between slavery and freedom.

A Barrymore Bon Mot

Today in 1904 Ethel Barrymore created a line that was to become her trademark in years to come. At the final curtain of her new play, *Sunday in New York,* the actress responded to the enthusiastic audience applause by saying, "That's all there is; there isn't any more."

Columbus Sees Smoke

On November 15, 1492, Christopher Columbus noted in his journal the use of tobacco among the Indians of the New World, the first recorded reference to tobacco.

Jolson Blackens His Face

On this day in 1909 sitting before a mirror in his dressing room in a Brooklyn N.Y. theatre, Al Jolson started to experiment with grease paint and ended up devising the "blackface" routine that was to become his trademark.

The Colt's-Foot Cures

Today's flower, the sweet colt's-foot or *Tussilago farfara,* is really a pernicious weed and is named from the Latin *tussis,* a cough, to cure which its leaves were boiled and the tea drunk. Asthmatic persons smoked its dried leaves, and the down on the undersurfaces of the leaves were used as tinder by people and as nest lining by goldfinches.

16
NOVEMBER

Births

Tiberius (Roman emperor) 42 B.C.; George S. Kaufman (playwright) 1889; Paul Hindemith (composer) 1895.

Deaths

Henry III (English king) 1272; Gustavus Adolphus (Swedish king) 1632; Frederick William II (Prussian king) 1797.

Viola Dietrick's Sentence

On November 16, 1893, Viola Dietrick, head of a gang of women outlaws in Kokomo, Indiana, was sentenced to one year in jail for various criminal offences.

Siamese Ambassadors' Servility

Today in 1857 three Siamese ambassadors were received at Windsor Castle by the queen. The peculiar mode of approaching Majesty enjoined by Siamese etiquette was adopted on this occasion by the ambassadors. They drew near the Royal Throne in a position between crouching and crawling, and pushed their presents before them as they advanced.

Tiberius' Short-Sightedness

Tiberius, the Roman emperor born today in 42 B.C., was once visited by a craftsman who presented him with a remarkable gift. He showed the ruler a rather ordinary looking goblet he had made, but when he dashed it down on the floor the cup did not break. The man had invented an unbreakable glass. But instead of having the glassmaker rewarded, as he no doubt expected he would be, Tiberius had the man killed because he had invented what the emperor was sure would make gold and silver less precious than dust. The craftsman's secret died with him, and it was 2,000 years before it was discovered again.

Maude Roydan's Unforgivable Sin

Today in 1928 the Woman's Home Missionary Society of Oak Park, Illinois, cancelled a lecture date with Miss Maude Royden, English preacher and Bible teacher, after members of the society learned that Miss Royden smoked cigarettes!

Henry Fournier's Great Speed

Today in 1901 three automobile racers in Brooklyn, New York sped over Ocean Parkway at a rate better than a mile a minute, the first automobile drivers to achieve those records in America. The fastest speed was achieved by Henry Fournier, who drove a mile in fifty-one and four-fifths seconds.

Today at the Hungerford Revels

In olden times the village of Hungerford in Wiltshire was the scene of the Hungerford Revels, a day of fun and games for all. Among the favourite sports was a contest wherein two men stood toe to toe facing each other with one hand tied to their side and a thick, three-foot-long stick in the other. The object of the contest was to strike the opponent over the head, the victor being the one who first made the blood flow one inch from some part of his opponent's head. Other, less serious games, included climbing the greasy pole; old women drinking hot tea (the fastest winning a prize of snuff); grinning through horse collars; racing between thirty old women for a pound of tea; chasing a pig with a soaped tail, and jumping in sacks for a cheese.

17
NOVEMBER

Births

Louis XVIII (French king) 1755; Bernard Montgomery (English field marshal) 1887; Rock Hudson (American actor) 1925.

Deaths

John de Mandeville (English explorer) 1372; "Bloody" Mary Tudor (English queen) 1558; Catherine "the Great" (Russian empress) 1796.

Marriages

Prince Ronald Bonaparte to Mademoiselle Blanc of Monaco (1880); Lyndon Baines Johnson to Claudia A. "Lady Bird" Taylor (1934).

Queen Elizabeth's Day, 1679

Each November 17th it had been customary in London to observe the accession of Queen Elizabeth with great rejoicing, but in 1679 the day was devoted to a turbulent satirical saturnalia against the Catholic church. A report from a pamphlet, *London's Defiance to Rome,* described the procession which featured a mock pope: "giving pardons very plentifully to all those that should murder Protestants, and bedecked with bloody daggers arrayed over a splendid gown of scarlet, on his head a triple crown of gold and around his neck a glorious collar of gold and precious stones, St. Peter's keys, a number of beads and other Catholic trumpery. Attending His Holiness was the pope's doctor with jesuit's powder in one hand and an urinal in the other." The procession ended with great bonfires and symbolic burnings at the stake.

The U.S. Congress Comes Home, 1800

The Congress of the United States had no fixed abode until 1800. It first met at Philadelphia, but for various reasons and at various times, it was compelled to abandon that city and sat at York and Lancaster in Pennsylvania, at Princeton, New Jersey, and at Baltimore and Annapolis in Maryland. It was sitting at New York when Washington was inaugurated in 1789, but not long afterward returned to Philadelphia. That city expected to be the permanent seat of the government, and it built a president's house. But in order to bring about an agreement for paying the war debts of the states, it was arranged to move the national capital south to the banks of the Potomac. Congress held its first session in Washington today in 1880.

The Opening of the Suez Canal, 1869

The Suez Canal in Egypt opened formally with considerable pomp and circumstance. Egypt played host to 6,000 foreign guests, led by Emperor Franz Josef of Austria-Hungary and the Empress Eugénie of France. As the canal was declared officially open to traffic, a display of fireworks was set off on each bank and a squadron of yachts passed through the locks, the first one bearing the Emperor Franz Josef, the Empress Eugénie, and the khedive of Egypt.

The Knight Tilter

At a tournament held on the 17th of November 1559, the first anniversary of the accession of Elizabeth I to the English throne, Sir Henry Lee of Quarendon made a vow of chivalry that he would annually present himself in the tilt yard in honour of the queen, to maintain her beauty, worth, and dignity against all comers, unless prevented by age, infirmity, or other accident. Elizabeth graciously accepted Sir Henry as her knight and champion, and the nobility and gentry of the court formed themselves into the society of Knights Tilters, which annually held a grand tourney on this day. In 1590 Sir Henry resigned, due to age, and with the queen's consent appointed the earl of Cumberland as his successor.

18
NOVEMBER

Births

Eugene Ormandy (conductor) 1899; George Gallup (pollster) 1901.

Deaths

"Boatswain" (Lord Byron's dog) 1808; Chester Arthur (21st U.S. president) 1886.

Today in History

2347 B.C.: Noah is said to have left the Ark, possibly in search of fish as it was a Friday.

1307: William Tell shot the apple off his son's head in Switzerland.

1414: Sigismund was crowned king of Germany.

1518: Cortez embarked from Cuba for Mexico with ten armed vessels.

1626: St Peter's Basilica at the Vatican was consecrated.

1755: The American northeast was rocked by earthquakes.

1783: A meteor shaped like a fiery dragon was seen in Italy.

1805: Thirty women meeting at the home of Mrs Silas Lee in Wiscasset, Maine organised the Female Charitable Society, the first woman's club in America.

1840: The last load of British convicts landed in Australia.

1842: A whale, sixteen feet long, was caught in the Thames River in London.

1852: More than a million people lined the streets of London to view the public funeral of the duke of Wellington, "England's greatest soldier." (The funeral had been held up two months after His Grace's death to await the opening of Parliament.)

1865: "The Celebrated Jumping Frog of Calaveras County," Mark Twain's first fiction, appeared in the *Saturday Press*.

1870: English mail was delivered to France by pigeon.

1872: Susan B. Anthony and twelve suffragettes were arrested for trying to vote.

1880: Umhlonhlo, an African chief, together with 700 Pondos was chased out of his village which was then burned by 230 colonists near Durban.

1883: Standard time went into effect in the United States.

1886: Thomas Stevens arrived in Shanghai, having travelled nearly 12,000 miles by bicycle from San Francisco.

1901: The U.S. and Britain signed a treaty giving the former the right to build, maintain, and control a canal in Panama.

1903: The U.S. signed a treaty with Panama to build a canal across the country in return for $10,000,000 cash and $250,000 to be paid annually.

1913: Lincoln Beachy performed the first loop-the-loop manoeuvre in an airplane over San Diego, California.

1919: New York staged an enthusiastic reception for the Prince of Wales on his first visit to the United States. Ticker tape was used for the first time as the prince's motorcade moved up Broadway, while every type of boat in the harbour saluted him with whistle blasts.

Births

Charles I (English king) 1600; James Abraham Garfield (20th U.S. president) 1831.

Deaths

Anthony Mathioli (the Man in the Iron Mask?) 1703; Franz Schubert (composer) 1828.

Black Patches on Ladies' Faces

"Our ladies have lately entertained a vain custom of spotting their faces, out of an affectation of a mole, to set off their beauty, such as Venus had; and it is well if one black patch will serve to make their faces remarkable, for some fill their visages full of them, varied into all manner of shapes:

Her patches are of every cut,
For pimples and for scars,
Here's all the wandering planets' signs,
And some of the fixed stars.
    Artificial Changeling, November 19, 1653 (London)

Time Keeping by Cock

"The dark time of the year is now approaching, when Cocks are said to crow more than ordinary. That the ancients counted the watches of the night by Cock crowings, we have abundant proof. So in King Lear: 'He begins at Curfew, and walks till the first Cock.' "
    Catholic Annal, November 19, 1830

Abe Lincoln's Message Missed

Today in 1863 President Lincoln, speaking at ceremonies dedicating the battlefield of Gettysburg, Pennsylvania as a national cemetery, surprised his listeners by talking for just two minutes, confining his remarks to a few sentences: ". . .we here highly resolve that these dead shall not have died in vain; that this nation, under God, shall have a new birth of freedom; and that government of the people, by the people, and for the people, shall not perish from the earth." (The president's speech was considered so insignificant that most newspapers the next day carried it on inside pages, in contrast to the two-hour oration delivered by Edward Everett, which was printed all over the country on page one.)

The Man in the Iron Mask?

The famous Man in the Iron Mask is believed to have been Count Anthony Mathioli, an Italian, and secretary of state to Charles III, duke of Mantua. He had been paid a bribe by Louis XIV of France for his aid in helping to establish French influence in Italy, but at the last moment reneged on his promises and French diplomacy was betrayed. For revenge Louis had Mathioli captured and kept in solitary confinement in a barren fortress high on a cliff on the island of St Marguerite, off the coast of Cannes. He was later moved to the Bastille in Paris. In all he was confined for twenty-four years until his death at the age of sixty on November 19, 1703. Louis caused Mathioli to wear the mask—actually made of velvet and whalebone—whenever there was any danger of the identity of the prisoner becoming known, which might have further hurt French prestige.

Carrie Nation Creates a Stir

On this day in 1903, frustrated in her attempt to interview President Theodore Roosevelt at the White House, Carrie Nation, the famous prohibitionist, created a stir in the gallery of the Senate by attempting to make a speech and sell replicas of her celebrated hatchet.

Births

Sir Wilfred Laurier (Canadian prime minister) 1814; Selma Lagerlof (Swedish writer) 1858; Robert Kennedy (U.S. senator) 1925.

Deaths

St Edmund (king and martyr) 870; Roger Payne (bookbinder and drunkard) 1797; Mountstuart Elphinstone (English diplomat) 1859.

A Fallen King Commemorated

St Edmund was king of East Anglia when the Danes landed there in 867. The marauders chased the king and his men around the countryside for three years, ravaging, raping, pillaging, and committing horrible barbarities en route. Finally, today in 870, the Danes caught Edmund, tied him to a tree, and used him as target practice in a contest with bows and arrows. The place where he fell and was later buried is now called Bury St Edmunds in Suffolk.

A Staged Piece of Absurdity

At the Folly Theatre in London tonight in 1880, Mr J.L. Toole produced a piece of absurdity by Mr H.J. Byron which, without any pretensions except to afford an eccentric and amusing part for Mr Toole, entertained the audience, who were made to laugh "consumedly."

A Diamond in the Rough

Roger Payne was the most celebrated bookbinder in England, an artist to whom book lovers flocked to have him provide suitable covers for the great treasures of literature. As one historian said "Roger Payne rose like a star diffusing lustre on all sides, and rejoicing the hearts of all true sons of bibliomania." But, in person, he was a filthy, ragged, ale-sodden creature who lived and worked in a deplorably rancid den that was unapproachable by his patrons. The countess of Spenser's French maid fainted when she saw him. Roger is said to have used ale for meat, drink, and washing and when remonstrated at would sing an old song in praise of his favourite beverage:

All history gathers, from ancient
   forefathers,
That ale's the true liquor of life;
Men lived long in health, and
   preserved their wealth,
Whilst barley-broth was rife.

He passed away on this day in the year 1797, drunk, happy, and with a sizable fortune.

A Negative Response

The Republican-owned *Chicago Times* ran an editorial today in 1863, commenting on Lincoln's Gettysburg address: "The cheek of every American must tingle with shame as he reads the silly, flat and dishwashery utterances of the man who had to be pointed out to intelligent foreigners as the President of the United States."

A Grateful Football Fan

Today in 1953 Hugh Roy Cullen, chairman of the Board of Regents of Houston University in Houston, Texas, gave $2,250,000 to the University because of its football team's recent victory over Baylor University.

Proverb

If there's ice in November to bear a
   duck,
There'll be nothing after but sludge
   and muck.

Maiden Aunt Workers Bemoaned

An article in the woman's magazine, *Pictorial Review,* on November 20, 1923 bemoaned the fact that the maiden aunt, once the mainstay in thousands of American homes, was going out to find a job. The article reported that "8,549,511 women are earning money in the United States."

The Cape of Good Hope Rounded

On the 20th of November 1497, Vasco da Gama, in command of three vessels and 160 men in the service of King Emmanuel of Portugal, rounded the Cape of Good Hope on the southern tip of Africa on his way to India. The Cape had been discovered, almost by accident, some years earlier by Bartholomew Diaz, but da Gama was the first European to round it and complete a voyage to the sub-continent.

21
NOVEMBER

Births

François Marie Arouet de Voltaire (French writer) 1694; René Magritte (Belgian artist) 1898; Stan Musial (American baseball player) 1920.

Deaths

Henry Purcell (English composer) 1695; Schinderhannes (German thief) 1803; Robert Benchley (American humorist) 1945.

John the Scorcher

Schinderhannes, or "John the Scorcher," was the nickname of a Robin Hood-like thief who worked in the Rhine valley in the vicinity of Cologne near the end of the eighteenth century and the early part of the next. Like Robin, John often robbed from the rich to give to the poor, was famous for his audacity—he once gave his carbine to his victims while he went through their pockets—and for his many hairbreadth escapes. However, unlike Robin, he was also very cruel. He got his nickname from his nasty habit of sticking the feet of his victims in the fire if they would not tell him the whereabouts of their valuables. John and nineteen of his band were apprehended in October of 1803, convicted, and on November 21 of the same year, their twenty heads were cut off all within six minutes.

Plants of the Day

The same students of the occult who discovered the influence of numbers over destinies have tabled plants and herbs in the world of nature that are sympathetic to people born on certain days. For people born today the following plants will ward off disease, pain, and illness: beets, borage, bilberries, asparagus, dandelion, endive, ewerwort, longwort, sage, cherries, barberries, strawberries, apples, mulberries, peaches, olives, rhubarb, gooseberries, pomegranates, pineapples, grapes, mint, saffron, nutmegs, cloves, sweet marjoram, St John's Wort, almonds, figs, hazelnuts, and wheat.

Flower of the Day

Although visually attractive, the common wood sorrel (*Oxalis acetosella*), today's flower, is named from the Greek *oxus:* acid, which describes its taste.

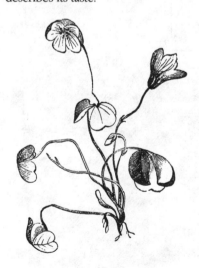

White House Blues

Today in the year 1800 Abigail Adams, wife of the 2nd U.S. president, John Adams, who had arrived in the new city of Washington only five days before, sat down and wrote a letter to her sister back home in Massachusetts, describing life in the executive mansion: ". . .Not one room is finished of the whole. . .It is habitable by fires. . .thirteen of which we are obliged to keep daily, or sleep in wet or damp places. . .We have not the least fenceyard. . .and the great unfinished audience-room I make a drying room of, to hang the clothes in. . ."

Hot-Air Power

On November 21, 1783, Monsieur Philatre de Rozier and his friend the Marquis d'Arlandes, soared aloft to a height of 300 feet at Annonay in France. They landed after a pleasant journey of five miles, thus completing the first unconfirmed manned voyage in a hot-air balloon. The idea for the mode of power had come from a paper manufacturer, Joseph Montgolfier, who had been inspired by watching smoke rise up a chimney in his fireplace. He took one of his paper bags, held it over the flames, and observed it rise gently to the ceiling.

Births

George Eliot (writer) 1819; André Gide (writer) 1869; Benjamin Britten (composer) 1913.

The Patron Saint of Ecclesiastical Melody

Cecilia was a Roman lady of good family who devoted herself to celibacy in order to get to heaven more easily. Although she was wed to a nobleman named Valerian she somehow managed to maintain her vows. She spent much of her life singing hymns while accompanying herself on the piano. On one occasion an angel was so enraptured with her harmonious strains as to quit the abodes of bliss to visit the saint and play for her. There are two accounts of her death on this day in the year 230. Either she was boiled in a cauldron, or half-decapitated and left to die after her executioner was mysteriously unable to finish his work.

Deaths

St Cecilia (virgin martyr) 230; Robin Hood? (outlaw) 1247; Jack London (novelist) 1916.

Our Lady of the Music

Eventually St Cecilia came to be regarded as the patroness of all music and it was customary for musicians and composers to pay tribute to their saint on this day. Purcell's *Te Deum* and *Jubilante* were first performed on St Cecilia's Day in 1694 and Dryden wrote a poem of praise to her in *Alexander's Feast:*

At last divine Cecilia came,
Inventress of the vocal frame;
The sweet enthusiast from her sacred
   store
Enlarged the former narrow bounds,
To harmonious melodious sounds,
With nature's mother's wit, and arts
   unknown before.

A Lytell Geste [History] of Robyn Hood

The most satisfactory and reliable evidence of the life and times of Robin Hood is found in a manuscript, with the above title, written at the end of the fourteenth century and printed by Winken de Word, one of England's earliest printers, in 1495. Robin, born at Locksley in Nottingham in 1160, conducted his predatory operations around Sherwood forest for eighty-seven years. At the end of that time he was induced to enter a convent in Kirklees, Yorkshire, for medical assistance. Here, one of his many enemies opened one of his veins and allowed him to bleed to death, today in the year 1247. As the folk hero was sinking fast, his last words were to his trusty lieutenant, Little John:

Give me my bent bow in my hand
And an arrow I'll let free,
And where the arrow is taken up,
There let my grave digged be.

The arrow fell on a spot near the extreme edge of Kirklees Park, where a monument to Robin Hood can still be found.

Anti-Canine Properties

On November 22 the sun enters the constellation of Sagittarius, the archer. According to an old manuscript of magic from the fourteenth century, an aspect of Sagittarius seems to be some dominion over dogs: "When you wish to enter where there are dogs, that they may not hinder you, make a tin image of a dog, whose head is erected towards his tail, under the first face of Sagitarry, and say over it, 'I bind all dogs by this image, that they do not raise their heads or bark,' and enter where you please."

23
NOVEMBER

Births

Abigail Adams (wife of U.S. president) 1744; Franklin Pierce (14th U.S. president) 1804; Boris Karloff (actor) 1887; Harpo Marx (comedian) 1893.

Deaths

St Clement (patron of hatters) 100; St Amphilochius (bishop) 100; St Daniel (bishop) 545; St Tron (confessor) 693.

Today in Human Nature

Beginning on November 23 and continuing until December 22, Sagittarius (the archer) reigns supreme, resulting in the following behavioural patterns according to *Christian Astrology* of 1647:

Manners & Actions when well placed Then he is Magnanimous, Faithful, Bashfull, Aspiring in an honourable way at high matters, in all his actions a Lover of faire Dealing, desiring to benefit all men, doing Glorious things, Honourable and Religious, of sweet and affable Conversation, wonderfully indulgent to his Wife and Children, reverencing Aged men, a great Reliever of the Poore, full of Charity and Godlinesse, Liberal,

hating all Sordid actions, Just, Wise, Prudent, Thankful, Vertuous: so that when you find 4 the Significator of any man in a Question, or Lord of his Ascendant in a Nativity, and well dignified, you may judge him qualified as abovesaid.

When ill
When 4 is unfortunate, then he wastes his Patrimony, suffers every one to cozen him, is Hypocritically Religious, Tenacious, and stiffe in maintaining false Tenents in Religion; he is Ignorant, Carelesse, nothing Delightfull in the love of his Friends; of a grosse, dull Capacity, Schismaticall, abasing himselfe in all Companies, crooching and stooping where no necessity is.

St Clement Invents Felt

St Clement is the patron saint of hatters for it is believed he was the inventor of felt. The legends claim that while he was on a long pilgrimage he tried to ease his sore feet by putting wool between them and his sandals. The pressure from walking and the moisture from his feet caused the wool to mat until it became felt.

Today in the Tower of London

Edward Arden, a heretic, was stretched on a rack in the Tower of London on this day in 1583. Then he was placed on a circular machine of iron called the Scavenger's Daughter, named after its inventor Mr Scavenger, in order to have his neck, hands, and feet stretched and dislocated.

Today in the United States

1896: Today's issue of the *Home Maker's Magazine* said, "The barbecue is to Georgia what the clambake is to Rhode Island, what a roast beef dinner is to our English cousins, what canvasback duck is to the Marylander, and a pork and beans supper is to the Bostonian."

1903: Enrico Caruso made his American debut in New York, singing the role of the Duke in *Rigoletto,* at the Metropolitan Opera House.

1906: Joseph Smith, president of the Morman Church of Utah, was convicted of polygamy.

1930: Although England was a "wet" country, Henry Ford vowed he would not allow his English workmen to drink, even in their homes. (The American industrialist was an ardent supporter of the prohibition movement.)

24
NOVEMBER

Births

Benedict Spinoza (philosopher) 1632; Laurence Sterne (writer) 1713; William F. Buckley (writer) 1925.

Deaths

John Knox (reformer) 1572; Joseph Brant (Mohawk chief) 1807; Lord Melbourne (statesman) 1848.

Exploration, 1969

The spacecraft *Apollo XII* splashed down in the Pacific on returning from the moon.

Proverb

November take flail
Let ships no more sail

Disaster, 1880

A disastrous collision occurred near Spezzia between the French steamer *Uncle Joseph,* an iron screw of 823 tons, and the Italian steamer *Ortigia* of 1,583 tons. The *Uncle Joseph* sank immediately, and there being no adequate means of rescue at hand, the loss of life was terrible. Of the 305 persons on board, only thirty passengers and twenty-three crew were saved.

Statue, 1875

The colossal statue of the prince consort, forming the central figure of the Albert Memorial, was raised to its place on the pedestal of the structure in London.

Starter, 1903

Clyde Coleman received the U.S. patent for an electric self-starter for an automobile. (The invention was not very practical but it was taken over by General Motors who developed it.)

Gallantry, 1735

Today, near Rumford in Essex, a butcher was approached by a well-dressed lady, seated side-saddle on a horse who, to his astonishment, presented a pistol and demanded his money. In amazement he asked what she meant, and received his answer from a genteel looking man who rode up beside her, said he was a brute to deny the lady's request, and enforced this conviction by telling the butcher that if he did not gratify her desire immediately he would shoot him through the head. The butcher could not resist an invitation to be gallant when supported by such an argument. He placed six guineas and his watch in her hand.

Venus, 1639

The first transit of Venus over the sun's disc ever observed was seen by Jeremiah Horrox at Hool, an obscure village north of Liverpool.

Aviation, 1930

For the first time in history, a woman started out on a transcontinental air flight across the United States. Miss Ruth Nichols set out from Mineola, Long Island, in a Lockheed-Vega plane. (She arrived in California seven days later.)

Proverb

Thunder in November means winter will be late in coming—and going.

Waterproofing, 1830

"Take one pound of drying (boiled linseed) oil, two ounces of yellow wax, two ounces of spirits of turpentine, and one of Burgandy pitch, melted carefully over a slow fire. With this composition new boots and shoes are to be rubbed in the sun, or at a distance from the fire, with a small bit of sponge, as often as they become dry, until they are fully saturated; the leather then is impervious to wet, the shoes and boots last much longer, acquire softness and pliability, and thus prepared, are the most effectual perservatives against cold."
Everyday Book, November 24, 1830

Debut, 1859

Maurice Strakosch, theatrical impresario, presented his seventeen-year-old sister-in-law, Adelina Patti, to music lovers at the Academy of Music in New York. Miss Patti received a tremendous ovation for her performance in the title role of *Lucia di Lammermoor,* her world debut as an opera singer.

25
NOVEMBER

Births

Lopez de Vega (Spanish poet/dramatist) 1562; Andrew Carnegie (Scottish-American industrialist/philanthropist) 1834.

Catherine's Flower

Today's flower, the common butter bur *(Petasites vulgaris)* is dedicated to St Catherine and named from the Greek *petasos*, an umbrella, from the large size of its leaves.

Deaths

St Catherine (virgin/martyr) 4th century; Isaac Watts (preacher/hymn writer) 1748.

Marriages

U.S. President William Henry Harrison to Anna T. Symmes (1795); Miss Jessie Wilson, daughter of President and Mrs Woodrow Wilson, in the East Room of the White House to Francis B. Sayre, before 300 guests (1913).

Catherine's Wheel

St Catherine, patroness of Christian philosophers, was martyred under the persecution of the Emperor Maximinus II who had her burnt at the stake today in the 4th century. Prior to that he had designed a special death for her on an engine of torture made up of four wheels covered with razor-sharp blades. When the machine was set in motion the victim was supposed to be cut to ribbons. When Catherine was being tied to the machine a flash of lightning rent the heavens, the binding cords were broken, and the machine was destroyed.

From the intended instrument of her death, round windows in ecclesiastical architecture are sometimes called Catherine-wheel windows, and in some places the revolving fireworks known as pin-wheels are called Catherine-wheels. From a corrupted pronunciation of the latter term came the sign and name of several English pubs and inns—The Cat and the Wheel.

Catherine's Inspiration

The miraculous story of St Catherine and her escape from the dreaded wheel is said to have inspired the text of the first play written in English. Its author was a learned Norman named Geoffrey who later became Abbot of St Alban's.

Catherine's Prayer

Sweet St. Catherine, send me a
    husband,
A good one, I pray:
But arn a one better than narn a one,
Oh St. Catherine, lend me thine aid,
And grant that I never may,
Die an old maid.
    A prayer of the day for medieval ladies
    as they went "Cather'ning"

Catherine's Jump

St Catherine was also the patron saint of spinsters, lacemakers, and spinners. It was the custom for lacemakers to dress up in men's clothing today and wander around to neighbours for refreshment. The traditional fare consisted of "wiggs," which were oblong buns made from fine flour, and a "hotpot," which was warmed beer, eggs, and rum. Later Catherine wheels were lit and "Catherines" jumped over candlesticks to see if luck was to follow the next year; if the flame was extinguished it augured ill.

Kit be nimble, Kit be quick,
Kit jump over the candlestick.

26
NOVEMBER

Births

Sir James Ware (Irish antiquary) 1594; John Harvard (minister, philanthropist, and founder of Harvard University) 1607; Dr William Derham (English natural philosopher) 1657; William Sidney Mount (American artist) 1807; Lord Armstrong (English inventor) 1810; Marie Feodorovna (Russian empress) 1847; Sir Henry Coward (English composer) 1849; Maud Charlotte Mary Victoria (Norwegian queen) 1869; Charles W. Goddard (author of *The Perils of Pauline*) 1879; Eric Sevareid (American author/newcaster) 1912; Charles M. Schulz (creator of "Peanuts") 1922.

Today's Disregarded Advice

On this day in 1715 Louis XIV, the king of France, lay on his deathbed. He summoned his grandson, five-year-old Louis, before him and said: "You will soon be king of a great Kingdom. . . Try to keep peace with your neighbours. I have loved war too much; do not copy me in that nor in my extravegence. . . Relieve your people as soon as you can, and do what I have been too unlucky to do."

(The grandson reigned as Louis XV from 1715 to 1774. Under his leadership France was engaged in the Seven Years' War and lost India and Canada.)

Today's Successful Vow

On this day in 1689 James II issued an epistle from Dublin to Pope Innocent XI in Rome in which he pronounced his determination to spread the Catholic religion, not only in the three kingdoms of the British Isles, but over all the American colonies as well.

Deaths

St Peter (martyr and bishop of Alexandria) 311; St Siricius (pope) 399; St Conrad (bishop of Constance) 976; St Nicon Metanoite (confessor) 988; Prince William (son of King Henry I of England) 1120; Silvester Gozzolini (Italian saint) 1267; John Spottiswoode (Scottish archbishop of St Andrews) 1639; Philippe Quinault (French dramatist) 1688; Leonard of Porto Maurizio (Italian saint) 1751; John Elwes (noted English miser) 1789; Dr Joseph Black (Scottish chemist) 1799; John Loudan MacAdam (Scottish inventor of road paving) 1836; Lord George Nugent (English poet and writer) 1850; Nicholas Soult (duke of Dalmatia) 1850; Vincenz Preissnitz (German founder of hydropathy) 1851; John M. Browning (American machine-gun inventor) 1926; Sir Charles G.D. Roberts (Canadian poet) 1943.

Alice in Wonderland

Today in 1864 a young mathematics instructor at Oxford University sent an early Christmas gift to twelve-year-old Alice Liddel, daughter of a country clergyman. The gift was his handwritten manuscript of a story he had written for Alice. The instructor was Charles L. Dodgson, and his story, *Alice's Adventures Underground.* The story is now known as *Alice in Wonderland,* and the instructor by his pen name, Lewis Carroll.

27
NOVEMBER

Births

Jimi Hendrix (American rock guitarist) 1942.

Deaths

Horace (Roman poet) 8 B.C.; St James Intercisius (joyous martyr) 421; Lord Lyttleton (English nobleman) 1779; Ada Augusta Byron (countess of Lovelace and only child of Lord and Lady Byron) 1852.

St James' Joyous Death

St James, surnamed Intercisius, was born at Bethlapeta, a royal city of Persia—for rebuking the idolatry of which nation he was cut to pieces by degrees today in 421. At the loss of each limb he rejoiced in the circumstance of his martyrdom.

Lord Lyttleton's Strange Death

Lord Lyttleton of Pitt Place, Epsom, Surrey died today in 1779. Three days previously he had been warned by a ghost of the time of his death and although he had remained healthy until the last hour, he was then taken with a sudden seizure and died. At exactly that moment, a friend of his, Miles Andrews, saw Lord Lyttleton come into his bedroom, where he said, "It's all up with me, Andrews" and walked out.

An Annual Hibernation

"Here we may also speak of the people, Lucumoria, dwelling among the hills, beyond tne river Olbis. These men die every year the 27th November, which day at Rutheas was dedicated to St. Gregorie; and in the next spring following, most commonly at the fourth and twentieth day of April, they rise again like frogs."
  Batman's Doome, a medieval history

A Cure for the Cramp

"I thank God had a better night of rest than I have had the three last Nights. Had no Cramp at all. My Brother recommending me last Night to carry a small Piece of the roll Brimstone sewed up in a piece of very thin Linnen, to bed with me and if I felt any Sympton of the Cramp to hold it in my hand or put near the affected part, which I did, as I apprehended at one time it was coming into one of my legs, and felt no more advances of it. This I thought deserving of notice, even in so trifling a book as this."
  Diary of a Country Parson, November 27, 1789

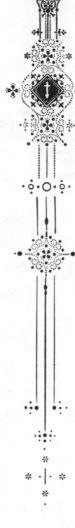

A Protest Against Horse-Tax

On November 27, 1784 a certain farmer by the name of Jonathan Thatcher, in order to protest and defy a new tax on horses imposed a few months previously by the British Chancellor of the Exchequer, William Pitt, rode his cow to and from the market at Stockport.

A Complaint Against Cyclists

Today in 1890 residents of the Boston suburbs sent a complaint to police authorities, charging that it was unsafe to drive their horses and buggies on country lanes, because of "racing bicyclists attired in black tights and long mustaches."

A Solemn Annual Feast

November 27 was the occasion of a solemn annual feast in ancient Rome when two Greeks and two Gauls, one of either sex, were buried alive in the ox-market in order to prevent a Sybilline prophecy that those terrible nations should one day be the masters of the Capitol.

A Big British Wind

Immediately after midnight on November 27, 1703 a violent English windstorm became so powerful that many people took to their cellers for protection, and others were convinced that the end of the world was upon them. Over one million pounds property damage was done in London alone; 1,500 sailors of the navy died as their ships went down at anchor; and the first Eddystone lighthouse, with its builder inside, was completely washed away.

28

NOVEMBER

Births

William Blake (English poet and painter) 1757; Anton
Rubinstein (Russian composer and pianist) 1829.

Deaths

Washington Irving (American writer and diplomat) 1859.

Samuel Pepys' Day

In 1633, Samuel Pepys spent this day on a park bench in
St Paul's Churchyard in London, reading a book called
Hudilnas that he had "borrowed not bought."

Advice for Today

"Bashfulness is more frequently connected with good
sense, than we find assurance; and impudence on the
other hand, is often the effect of downright stupidity."
  *The Anniversary Calendar, Natal Book and Universal
  Mirror,* November 28, 1832

Curtis P. Brady's Permit

Today in 1889 Curtis P. Brady received
the first permit issued by the
Commissioner of Parks in New York
City to drive an automobile through
Central Park. The permit was subject
to Mr Brady's pledge "to exert the
greatest care to avoid frightening
horses" in the park.

J.M. Synge's Bomb

On this day in 1911, theatre-goers
critical of the Irish Players visiting the
United States from Dublin's Abbey
Theatre tried to stop the performance
of J.M. Synge's *Playboy of the Western
World* at the Maxine Elliott Theatre in
New York. The hecklers pelted the
Irish cast with fruit, vegetables, and
eggs; order was restored only after
policemen arrested ten men and
women.

Captain Warner's Failure

Captain Warner, a British military
man had invented a long-range gun.
Today in 1846 he demonstrated his
device before a committee on the
Island of Anglesey. The place was an
eight-mile-long valley, at the extreme
end of which there was a single tree.
This could not be seen, but the exact
bearings were furnished to Captain
Warner and he was asked to fire in
that direction. The first shell fell
short; and none of them reached
three miles. (The Committee deemed
the experiment a failure.)

Proverb

A heavy November snow will last 'till
April.

Washington Irving's Success

Though he began writing at the age
of sixteen, Washington Irving had
difficulty in getting anything
published in America. Sir Walter
Scott, who visited him in 1820 called
him "one of the best and pleasantest
acquaintances I have met in many a
day," and used his influence to
enable Irving's *Sketch-Book* to be
published. He quickly became
famous throughout Europe with
*Bracebridge Hall, Tales of a
Traveller,* and many other books.
Britain gave him honorary medals
and degrees and he was appointed
U.S. minister to the court of Spain. He
returned to America and built his
house "Sunnyside," his own "Sleepy
Hollow," on the banks of the Hudson
River where he died peacefully today
in 1859.

Births

Peter Heylin (historical and theological writer) 1600; Louisa May Alcott (author of *Little Women)* 1832.

Deaths

Horace Greeley (founder and editor of the *New York Tribune)* 1872; Louis A. Godey (publisher of *Godey's Lady's Book)* 1878.

A Newspaper Printed by Steam

The *London Times* edition of November 29, 1814, was the first newspaper to be printed on a steam-powered press. The leading article of the *Times* began as follows: "Our journal of this day presents to the public the practical results of the greatest improvement connected with printing since the discovery of the art itself. The reader of this paragraph now holds in his hands one of the many thousands impressions of the *Times* newspaper which was taken off last night by a mechanical apparatus. A system of machinery, almost organic, has been devised and arranged, which while it relieves the human frame of its most laborious efforts in printing, far exceeds all human powers in rapidity and despatch."

A Paper Published on Ether

Today in 1846 doctors Jackson and Martin of Boston published a paper discussing their discovery of the use of ether in surgery: "It is a mode of rendering patients insensible to the pain of surgical operation by the inhalation of the vapour of the strongest sulphuric ether. They are thrown into a state resembling that of complete intoxication or narcotism. This state continues but a few minutes—5 to 10—but during it the patient is insensible to pain. A thigh has been amputated, a breast extirpated, and teeth drawn without the slightest suffering."

A Letter from the President

On November 29, 1904, President Theodore Roosevelt wrote to his distant cousin, Franklin Delano Roosevelt, telling him he approved of his engagement to the president's niece, Eleanor: "Dear Franklin: We are greatly rejoiced over the good news. I am as fond of Eleanor as if she were my daughter; and I like you, and trust you, and believe in you. . . You and Eleanor are true and brave, and I believe you love each other unselfishly. . . Golden years open before you. . ."

An Elephant Advertisement

A good many people in London were very excited over an announcement in the *Flying Post* today in 1701 stating that "There is lately arrived a large elephant, the biggest that ever was in Europe, and one that performs varieties of exercise for Diversion and Laughter. It is to be seen at the White Horse Inn in Fleet St. from 10 in the morning till 6 at night."

The Power of the Press

Thanksgiving Day was first celebrated on the same day throughout the United States today in 1863. The credit for bringing this about is usually given to Mrs Sarah J. Hale, who began her campaign in 1827 and continued her agitation until September, 1863. As editor of the *Ladies' Magazine* in Boston, and then *Godey's Lady's Book* of Philadelphia, she wrote editorial after editorial in support of her plan to observe a uniform day throughout the country for the expression of thanks for the blessings of the year. Finally, on October 3, 1863, President Lincoln issued the first national Thanksgiving Proclamation, setting the last Thursday in November as the day to be observed.

Written on a Tombstone

On the 29th November
A confounded piece of timber
Came down, bang, slam
And kill'd I, John Lamb
      An epitaph at Huntingdon, England

30
NOVEMBER

Births

Jonathan Swift (satirist) 1667; Mark Leman (editor of *Punch*) 1809; Samuel Langhorne Clemens (Mark Twain) 1835.

Deaths

St Andrew (apostle) 70.

Mark Twain on Café au Lait

Samuel Langhorne Clemens, better known as Mark Twain, was born on this day in 1835. Touring Europe in 1878, he felt nothing but disdain for the food he encountered there. He found the coffee "feeble"; the milk served with it was "what the French call 'Christian' milk—milk which has been baptised."

Mark Twain's Bill of Fare

Twain solved his food problems in Europe in *A Tramp Abroad*:

"It has now been many months, at the present writing, since I have had a nourishing meal, but I shall soon have one, a modest, private affair, all to myself. I have selected a few dishes, and made out a little bill of fare, which will go home in the steamer that precedes me, and be hot when I arrive." (He listed more than eighty dishes, everything from "fried chicken, Southern style" to "Sheep-head and croakers, from New Orleans.")

"Americans intending to spend a year or so in European hotels, will do well to copy this bill and carry it along. They will find it an excellent thing to get up an appetite with, in the dispiriting presence of the squalid table d'hôte."

A Squirrel-Hunt Excuse

It was the custom in Eastling, Kent to have the annual squirrel-hunt today. In actual fact this hunt was merely the assembling of a "lawless rabble" who wandered through the woods with all types of weapons from guns to sticks, ostensibly to hunt squirrels, but in reality to destroy anything they came upon. Thus many hares, peasants, partridges, as well as hedges had a grim day of it. The day finished off at the local pub.

Mark Twain on Foreign Food

"Foreigners cannot enjoy our food, I suppose, any more than we can enjoy theirs. It is not strange; for tastes are made, not born. I might glorify my bill of fare until I was tired; but after all, the Scotchman would shake his head and say, 'Where's your haggis?' and the Fijian would sigh and say, 'Where's your missionary?'"

A Feast of St Andrew

St Andrew was a brother of Peter and apostle of Jesus. After the death of Jesus he travelled as a missionary throughout the middle east. In the year 70 A.D., on November 30, he was first scourged and then crucified on an x-shaped cross, being fastened to it by cords instead of nails to produce a more lingering death. The Feast of St Andrew is celebrated in many parts of the world. One of the earliest St Andrew's societies in the United States was founded in Philadelphia in 1749. At the annual dinner today in 1788, forty-five gentlemen consumed in addition to food: "Thirty-eight bottles of Madeira, twenty-seven bottles of Claret, eight bottles of Port wine, twenty-six bottles of porter, two bottles of cider and two bowls of punch."

Proverb

As November so the following March.

ECEMBER

And after him came next the chill December;
Yet he through merry feasting which he made,
And great bonfires, did not the cold remember;
His Saviour's birth his mind so much did glad.
Upon a shaggy-bearded goat he rode,
The same wherewith Dan Jove on tender yeares,
They say, was nourisht by th' Idaean mayd;
And in his hand a broad deepe bowle he beares,
Of which he freely drinks an health to all his peeres.
  Edmund Spenser

DECEMBER

History

December received its name from the Latin word *decem,*
meaning ten, because it was the tenth and last month of
the old Roman calendars. Under the reign of Romulus the
month had thirty days; Numa reduced it to twenty-nine;
and Julius Caesar gave it thirty-one days. Marcus Valerius
Martialis (Martia), the Roman satiric poet, applied the
epithet *fumosus* (smoky) to the month in reference to the
lighting of fires for warmth, and *canus* (hoary) from the
snows that fall during December. Among the Saxons the
month was called simply *Winter Monath,* but after their
conversion to Christianity they redesignated the month
Heligh Monath, or holy-month.

Birthstone

People born in the month of December are entitled to
wear the turquoise as their birthstone, which it was once
believed would ensure prosperity. The stone also
performed as an indicator of chance, changing colour
when danger, illness, or any misadventure threatened. As
a bonus it prevented quarrels between married people.

Question

What shall we speak of
When we are as old as you?
When we shall hear the rain
And wind beat dark December?
  William Shakespeare

Answer

While I have a home, and can do as I will,
December may rage over ocean and hill,
And batter my door — as he does once a year —
I laugh at his storming, and drink his good cheer.
  Old English song

1

DECEMBER

Births

Princess Anna Commena (Turkish historian) 1083; Alexandra (Danish queen of Edward VII of England) 1844; Mary Martin (American actress) 1914.

Deaths

St Eligius (French bishop and patron saint of goldsmiths, metalworkers, blacksmiths, wheelwrights, veterinarians, saddlers, miners, locksmiths, clockmakers, carriage makers, toolmakers, cab drivers, farmers, labourers, and jockeys) 659.

A Letter

General Washington addressed a diplomatic letter from New York to his great and magnanimous friend Sidi Mohammed, the emperor of Morocco, enclosing a copy of the new American Consitution (1789).

A Mutiny

Midshipman Philip Spencer, Boatswain Samuel Cromwell, and Seaman Elisha Small were hanged from the yard-arm of the U.S.S. *Semers* having been found guilty at a court martial of conspiring a mutiny (1842).

A Statement

In a statement to his children on the eve of his execution, John Brown, the American slave abolitionist claimed: "I am as content to die for God's eternal truth on the scaffold as in any other way" (1859).

A Statue

A colossal bronze statue of Oliver Cromwell, the gift of Mrs Abel Heywood, was unveiled at Manchester (1875).

An Event

One of the greatest events in the history of the American theatre took place at the Fifth Avenue Theatre in New York as Arthur Sullivan stepped into the pit to conduct the score of *HMS Pinafore,* the operetta he had composed in collaboration with William S. Gilbert. The other half of the famous team was portraying a sailor's role in the chorus (1879).

A Telephone

The first telephone was installed in the White House at Washington (1878).

A Blast

An attempt was made on the life of the czar of Russia at Moscow by exploding a mine constructed under the railway. The Czar was returning from Livadia to St Petersburg and had arranged to stay at Moscow on his way through. By accident or design, the train carrying his luggage followed, instead of preceded, the imperial train. An enormous explosion occurred as the second train crossed the lines, the major part of it being thrown off them, but no lives were lost (1879).

An Opening

The world's first drive-in gas station opened for business in Pittsburgh, Pennsylvania (1913).

A Founding

With a fund of less than $100, Father Edward Flanagan founded Boys Town, the "City of Little Men," some 11 miles west of Omaha, Nebraska (1917).

A Woman

For the first time in Britain's history, a woman took her seat in Parliament when Lady Astor was sworn into the House of Commons (1919).

An Arrest

Mrs Rosa Parks, a black seamstress in Montgomery, Alabama, was arrested when she refused to give up her front-section bus seat so that a white man might be seated (1955).

2
DECEMBER

Births

Francis Xavier Quadrio (Jesuit historian) 1695; Georges Seurat (painter) 1859; Dr George Minot (discoverer of anaemia cure) 1885; Sir John Barbirolli (conductor) 1899.

Deaths

Hernando Cortez (conqueror of Mexico) 1547; St Francis Xavier (Jesuit founder) 1552; Gerard Mercator (geographer) 1594; John Brown (revolutionary) 1859.

Inauguration

Napoleon Bonaparte, accompanied by Josephine, was inaugurated as Emperor Napoleon I by Pope Pius VII in the cathedral of Notre Dame in Paris in the year 1804. He placed the crown on his head with his own hands.

President Monroe's Doctrine

On December 2, 1823 President James Monroe said in his message to Congress: "We owe it, therefore, to candor and to the amicable relations existing between the United States and those powers to declare that we should consider any attempt on their part to extend their system to any portion of this hemisphere as dangerous to our peace and safety."

John Brown's Calmness

Convicted of treason, conspiracy, and murder in the first degree, John Brown was hanged in the public square at Charlestown, Virginia today in 1859. The old man remained completely calm before and during his ordeal. As he was driven to the gallows, he looked about the countryside and said to his captors: "This *is* a beautiful country."

Henry Ford's Car

On this day in 1927 Henry Ford unveiled his Model A Ford, successor to his famous Model T. There was so much interest in the new model that one million people—so the *New York Herald-Tribune* estimated—tried to crowd into Ford headquarters in New York to catch a glimpse of it. The price of the roadster had climbed to $385.

Disappearance

Today in 1919, Ambrose Small of Toronto increased his already considerable fortune by selling his cross-Canada chain of theatres. He left his office at 7:00 in the evening, purchased a newspaper, and was never seen again. The mystery of his disappearance has never been resolved.

William Jones' Sentence

A youth named Willam Jones gained access to Buckingham Palace, and continued secreted there several days. His presence was first detected by Mrs Lilley, the nurse of the Princess Royal, who summoned some attendants and had the intruder drawn from his hiding-place under the sofa. He was sentenced to three months' imprisonment as a rogue and a vagabond today in 1840.

December 2 Firsts

1697:   The new St Paul's Cathedral in London was dedicated.

1863:   Ground was broken for the Union Pacific Railroad at Omaha, Nebraska.

1873:   The Reformed Episcopal Church was organised in the U.S.

1942:   A squash court at the University of Chicago was the scene of the first performance of a sustained atomic chain reaction.

1972:   The *Festival of Whirling Dervishes* began at Konya in Turkey.

Births

Nicolo Amati (violin maker) 1596; Gilbert Stuart (painter) 1755; Joseph Conrad (writer) 1857; Andy Williams (singer) 1928.

Deaths

John Hardouin (scholar) 1729; Giovanni Belzoni (entertainer) 1823; Robert Louis Stevenson (author) 1894; John Bartlett (compiler of *Familiar Quotations*) 1905.

A Painter's Single Subject

Gilbert Stuart, born today in 1755, spent his lifetime painting one subject. In 1796 the marquis of Lansdowne commissioned him to do a full-length portrait of George Washington. There was such a demand for these portraits that Stuart painted his original subject over and over again and grew wealthy from the sales.

A Scholar's Unorthodox Theory

John Hardouin was an eminent Jesuit scholar who died on the 3rd of December 1729 at Paris. He was celebrated for his unorthodox theory that held that all the Greek and Latin history, philosophy, science, and divinity from before the middle of the fourteenth century had been forged in the abbeys of Germany, France, and Italy by the monks who were resident there, and planted in the monastic libraries to be "discovered" by their successors.

An Entertainer's Varied Repertoire

Giovanni Battista Belzoni was a celebrated strong man and illusionist who toured Europe for many years. His displays of strength included carrying ten men standing on a series of platforms on his back. A handbill of 1812 advertised his *"Astonishing Feats of Legerdemain:* After a number of Startling Entertainments he will: CUT *A Man's Head Off!!* And put it on Again!! ALSO THE GRAND CASCADE."
  Belzoni the Great died of dysentery in Timbuctoo today in 1823

A College's Open-Door Policy

On December 3, 1833, Oberlin College in Ohio opened as the first fully co-educational college in America with twenty-nine men and fifteen women students. (It also was the first school to advocate abolition of slavery and to accept blacks and women on equal terms with white men.)

A Plant's Deadly Powers

Today's plant the wood spurge *(Euphorbia amygdaloides)* belongs to an order that consists of some 3,000 species around the world. The juice from its root was once used to stupefy fish in Ireland. A South American variety, which can cause blindness when burnt, was used by Indians to poison their arrows. A middle-eastern version instantly kills camels who eat it.

A Composer's Jazz Concerto

Tonight in 1925 George Gershwin, the young American composer, appeared as soloist at a concert in Carnegie Hall, New York, playing his Concerto in F, the first jazz concerto for piano in musical history.

An Attorney-General's Contention

In England, on December 3, 1880, the arguments in the important case of the Attorney-General versus the Edison Telephone Company were concluded. The contention of the Attorney-General was that a message sent through a telephone was in fact a message transmitted along a wire by electricity, and that the use of the telephone was consequently an infringement of the monopoly that had been granted to the government by the act under which telegraphs had been bought up by the Post Office. Their lordships gave judgment in favour of the Attorney-General.

A City's Disastrous Fog

Today in 1962 a heavy fog, one of the worst in years, enveloped the City of London, paralysing almost all transportation. When it lifted four days later, the fog had caused 106 deaths in the city, most of them due to the abnormally high content of sulphur dioxide in the air.

4
DECEMBER

George Washington Weeps

Today in 1783 George Washington bid farewell to the officers of his revolutionary army prior to leaving for Annapolis where Congress was sitting. It was an emotional scene in Frances' Tavern at the corner of Broad and Pearl Streets in New York. Washington kissed each of the officers on the forehead, and he and they were moved to tears by the parting. On his way to the ferry boat he passed between two lines of infantry with tears streaming down his face.

Births

Thomas Carlyle (Scottish literary critic, historian, and writer on social and political problems) 1795.

Deaths

John Gay (English poet and playwright, author of *The Beggar's Opera*) 1732.

Ford's Failed Peace

Today in 1915, in an attempt to end the war in Europe and "get the boys out of the trenches by Christmas," a private peace expedition, headed by Henry Ford, sailed from Hoboken, New Jersey, aboard the chartered liner *Oscar II*. (The group broke up in dissension soon after arriving in Europe.)

Woodrow Wilson's Departure

When Woodrow Wilson sailed for Brest, France on December 4, 1918, he became the first American president to visit a foreign country.

William's Weather Observance

"1664, December 4th: On this day appeared first the comet, which was the forerunner of the blasting of the cocoa trees, after which time they generally failed in America."
From Sir Willam Beeston's Journal

Quotes from Carlyle

You might prove anything with figures.

All reform except a moral one will prove unavailing.

History is the essence of innumerable biographies.

A well-written life is almost as rare as a well-lived one.

Poetry and religion are a product of the smaller intestines.

Silence is as deep as Eternity; speech is as shallow as Time.

The three great elements of modern civilisation are Gunpowder, Printing, and Protestant Religion.

Happy the people whose annals are blank in history books.

Gems From Gay

If with me you'll fondly stray
Over the hills and far away.

Fill every glass, for wine inspires us,
And fires us
With courage love and joy
Women and wine should life employ
Is there aught else on earth desirous?

If the heart of a man is depressed with cares
The mist is dispelled when a woman appears.

Those who in quarrels interpose
Must often wipe a bloody nose.

Life is a jest and all things show it,
I thought so once, and now I know it.

5

DECEMBER

Births

Martin Van Buren (8th American president) 1782; Christina Rossetti (English poet) 1830; Joseph Pilsudski (Polish statesman) 1867; Walt Disney (American cartoonist) 1901.

Deaths

St Sabas (apple abstainer) 532; Macbeth (Scottish king) 1057; Wolfgang Mozart (Austrian composer) 1791; Claude Monet (French painter) 1926.

An American Velocipede School

On December 5, 1868 a velocipede riding school was opened in New York by the Pearshall brothers to teach the art of riding bicycles—known then as velocipedes or curricles.

Roosevelt's Money Refusal

President Theodore Roosevelt wrote to his son Kermit today in 1906, explaining why he couldn't accept the money that went with the Nobel Prize for Peace he had just been awarded: "...It appears that there is a large sum of money—they say about $40,000—that goes with it. Now, I hate to do anything foolish...But Mother and I talked it over and came to the conclusion that...I could not accept any money given to me for making peace between two nations, especially when I was able to make peace simply because I was President..."

A Scottish Football Match

On Tuesday, December 5, 1815, a great football match took place at Carterhaugh, in Ettrick Forest, Scotland between the Ettrick men and the men of Yarrow. The Ettrick side was captained by the earl of Home and the Yarrow team by the poet Sir Walter Scott. The latter wrote two songs for the occasion to inspire his team, one of which began:

Then strip lads, and to it, though
  sharp be the weather,
And if by mischance, you should
  happen to fall,
There are worse things in life than a
  tumble in the heather,
And life is itself but a game of
  foot-ball!

Mozart's Requiem Mass

Mozart was thirty-six years old and living in Vienna when he one day received a visit from a tall, dark, dignified stranger. The man solemnly told the composer that he had come, at the behest of a person who wished to remain anonymous, to request the composition of a mass as a requiem for a friend recently lost. Mozart accepted the commission for a fee of one hundred ducats and promised the work within the month. But as he set to work the task set him to brooding and began to occupy all of his time and imagination; he became convinced that he was writing his own funeral mass. At the turn of the month the stranger returned, but the work was not finished. Mozart asked for another month to finish, during which time all his efforts to find out the stranger's identity were frustrated. The composer now became convinced that the man had really been a visitation from the other world to warn him of his own doom; he rushed on fervidly to finish the work. At the end of the second month the stranger returned once more. This time the now famous *Requiem Mass* was completed, but the composer was no more. Exhausted by the work, he had died on December 5, 1791.

St Sabas' Apple Vow

St Sabas was particularly humble, mortified, and fervent. One day, whilst at work in the garden, he gathered a beautiful apple with an intention to eat it. But reflecting that this was a temptation of the devil, he threw the apple on the ground and trod upon it. He made a vow from that time never to eat any apples as long as he lived, which was until this day in 532.

6
DECEMBER

Births

Baldassarre Castilglione (diplomat) 1475; Joseph Louis Gay-Lussac (chemist) 1778.

Deaths

St Nicholas (archbishop/confessor) 342; Anthony Trollope (novelist) 1882.

Reassembly by St Nicholas

St Nicholas, an archbishop of Myrna, who died today in the year 342, is the patron saint of Russia, mariners, youth, and virgins. An Asian gentleman, sending his two sons to be educated at Athens, desired that they stop at Myrna to receive the benediction of Nicholas. The two boys arrived late at night and put up at the inn of an unscrupulous landlord who, desiring their baggage, murdered the two, cut up their bodies, and put the pieces into barrels of salt pork. But Nicholas, warned in a vision of these horrid murders, went immediately to the inn-yard, and confronted the landlord with his crime. The man confessed immediately and begged the saint's prayers of forgiveness; Nicholas complied, and on the conclusion of the prayer, when he made the sign of the cross over the remains of the youths, the mangled remains reassembled themselves into the two living boys.

A Seizure by the British

On December 6, 1776, Rhode Island was seized from the Americans by the British. At that time the island was a noted resort for invalids, the southern climate being pleasant and healthy. It was also celebrated for its fine women, travellers sometimes calling it "The Eden of America."

A Speech by Lincoln

On December 6, 1863 President Lincoln addressed Congress recommending the adoption of the 13th Amendment by the house: "Fondly do we hope, fervently do we pray, that this mighty scourge of war may speedily pass away. Yet if God wills that it continue, until all the wealth piled by the bondsmen's 250 years of unrequited toil shall be sunk, and until every drop of blood drawn with the lash shall be repaid with another drawn by the sword. . .it must be said the Judgements of the Lord are true and righteous altogether. . .If the people should. . .make it an executive duty to re-enslave such persons, another, not I, must be their instrument to perform it."

Today's Epitaph

Inscription upon the momument of Henry Jenkins in the Bolton, England, churchyard: "Blush not, Marble! To rescue from oblivion the memory of Henry Jenkins; a person obscure in birth, but of a life truly memorable: For, he was enriched with the goods of Nature if not of Fortune; and happy in the duration if not variety of his enjoyments; And, tho' the partial world despised and disregarded his low and humble state, the equal eye of providence beheld and blessed it with a patriarch's health and wealth of days: To teach mistaken man these blessings were intailed on temperance, a life of labour, and a mind of ease. He lived to the amazing age of 169, was interred here December 6th, 1670."

A Slogan for Englishmen by Churchill

Today in 1939 Winston Churchill told the House of Commons what he thought the slogan of every Englishman should be in the war against Germany: "For each and for all, as for the Royal Navy, the watchword should be, 'Carry on, and dread nought.' "

Births

Mary (queen of Scots) 1532; Giovanni Bernini (sculptor) 1598; Rudolf Friml (composer) 1879.

Deaths

Cicero (Roman orator, assassinated) 43 B.C.; Algernon Sydney (English republican, beheaded) 1683; Madame du Barry (mistress of French King Louis xv, guillotined) 1793.

"Uncommon Natural Curiosities"

According to *Gentleman's Magazine,* December 7, 1751, the following "Uncommon Natural Curiosities" were on display in London:

"1. *A Dwarf,* in his 15th year, two feet six inches high, weighing only twelve pounds, yet very proportionable.

2. *Joan Coan,* a Norfolk dwarf, aged twenty three, weighed with all his clothes, but thirty four pounds, of good complexion, and sprightly temper, sung tolerably and mimicked a cock's crowing very exactly.

3. *A Female Rhinocerus,* or true Unicorn, a beast of upwards of eight thousand pounds in weight, in a natural coat of mail or armour, having a large horn on her nose, three hoofs on each foot, and a hide stuck thick with scales pistol proof, and so surprisingly folded as not to hinder its motion.

4. *A Crocodile Alive,* taken on the banks of the Nile in Egypt, a creature *never seen before alive in England."*

Today in Religion

1539: After a bad illness, and despite the fact that he was already married and had children by Princess Catherine of Saxony, Philip, landgrave of Hesse, and one of Martin Luther's chief protectors, in a fit of Christian scruple and conscience, decided that he must regularise his relation with his mistress, Marguerite de Staal. He wanted to be married to both women. To this end he addressed an appeal to Luther to grant him such a dispensation, buried in which, among apt quotations from the Old Testament, were suggestions as to what might happen if he did not comply. In the end pragmatics won out over the laws of Moses, and on December 7, Luther and seven other divines issued a warrant of approval for Philip's second marriage.

1930: Services at the Cathedral of St John the Divine in New York were thrown into an uproar when Judge Ben Lindsey of Denver rose from his seat and shouted at Bishop William T. Manning in the pulpit, "Bishop Manning, you have lied to me!" (Judge Lindsey was famous as an advocate of "companionate marriage" and resented Bishop Manning's demand that the New York Churchmen's Association cancel its invitation to Lindsey to lecture on this controversial subject.)

1965: The Roman and Orthodox churches were reconciled, cancelling their excommunications of each other in 1054.

1969: Buddhists celebrated Bodhi (Enlightenment) Day

8
DECEMBER

Births

Horace (poet) 65 B.C.; Eli Whitney (cotton-gin inventor) 1765; Jean Sibelius (composer) 1865; Sammy Davis Jr (entertainer) 1925.

Deaths

Scaramouche (celebrated zany) 1694; Barthélemi d'Herbelot (orientalist) 1695; Vitus Bering (discoverer of Alaska) 1741; Thomas de Quincey (opium addict/writer) 1859.

Sun Seekers

"To climates warmed by other suns in vain the wretched exile runs; Flies from his country's native skies, but never from himself he flies."

Anniversary Calendar, December 8, 1832

Samuel P. Langley

Today in 1903 Professor Samuel P. Langley, aviation enthusiast and secretary of the Smithsonian Institution, failed in his attempt to fly for the second time, when a power-driven airplane built by himself at a cost of $70,000 plunged into the Potomac River.

Henry Laurens

"I, Henry Laurens, solemnly enjoin it upon my son, as an indispensable duty that, as soon as he conveniently can after my decease, he cause my body to be wrapped in twelve yards of tow cloth, and burned until it is entirely consumed, and then, collecting my ashes, deposit them wherever he may see proper."

From the last will and testament of Henry Laurens of Charleston, South Carolina—the first person to be cremated in America—today in 1792

Quintus Horatius Flactus

Quintus Horatius Flactus (Horace), the Latin poet born today sixty-five years before the year one, wrote *Satires, Odes, Epodes, Epistles* and *Ars Poetica,* all liberally sprinkled with words of wisdom: "It is when I struggle to be brief that I become obscure; Grammarians dispute and the case is still before the courts; Seize today, and put as little trust as you can in the morrow."

Thomas de Quincey

In his book *The Confessions of An Opium Eater,* de Quincey acknowledged his addiction to the substance that kept him in a dazed stupor for much of his life. In his lucid moments, prior to his death today in 1859, he wrote such things as: "If a man indulges himself in murder, very soon he comes to think little of robbing; and from robbing he comes next to drinking and sabbath-breaking, and from that to incivility and procrastination."

Today's Flowers in 1818

In England the winter of 1818 was extraordinarily mild. On the 8th of December the gardens in the neighbourhood of Plymouth showed the following flowers in full bloom: jonquils, narcissus, hyacinths, anaemonies, pinks, stocks, African and French marigolds, the passion flowers, roses, and in great perfection, ripe strawberries and raspberries. In the field and hedges were the sweet-scented violets, heart's-ease, purple vetch, red robin, wild strawberry blossom, and many others. The oak and elm retained much of their foliage and the birds were sometimes heard as in spring.

9
DECEMBER

Births

John Milton (poet) 1608; Joel Chandler Harris (author of *Uncle Remus)* 1848; Elisabeth Schwarzkopf (singer) 1915.

Deaths

Mutawakkil (caliph of Baghdad) 861; Sigismund (king of Hungary, Bohemia, Germany, and Lombardy; also emperor of Rome) 1437.

Friendly Newspaper

Noah Webster established *The America Minerva,* New York's first daily newspaper. Webster said that his paper would be "The Friend of Government, of Freedom, of Virtue, and every Species of Improvement" (1793).

Sinful Settler

The settler Hugh Bewitt was banished from the Massachusetts Colony for declaring himself free of original sin (1640).

Final Founding

The Second Everlasting League was founded in Switzerland (1315).

Travel Problems

Mr Noel, an Englishman domiciled at Negropont, and sixty Greek shepherds were committed for trial at Athens on the charge of complicity in the massacre of English travellers at Marathon (1870).

Merry Christmas

The first Christmas card was created in England (1842).

Italian Women

Women were given the right to witness documents in Italy (1877).

Dutied Fish

Great excitement was caused in Newfoundland by the fact that Canada had imposed duties upon Newfoundland fish (1891).

French Pawnshops

A charter was drafted whereby the Government of France would operate pawnshops (1777).

Venus Fever

The astronomical event known as the "Transit of Venus," looked forward to with interest by scientific men and prepared for by several expeditions sent out by various nations of Europe and the U.S. to those parts of the globe from which it could best be observed, took place today (1874).

Democratic Election

Thirty Indians were killed in a contest to decide whether Short Bull or Two Strikes would be chief of the Pine Ridge Agency (1890).

Theatrical Misfortune

The first regular theatre in the City of London, the Fortune Theatre, was destroyed by fire (1621).

Diverting Play

The time-honoured "Westminster Play" was given this evening before the usual fashionable London audience, who seemed to be diverted as circumstances would permit. It was obvious that a good many of them had but a vague idea as to what it was all about and had to make-believe a good deal. The play this year was the *Andrea* of Terence (1880).

Cloud Claim

The Rocking F Ranch in Nevada formally laid claim to all water in any clouds that passed over it (1947).

Mormon Troubles

In his message to Congress, President Buchanan recommended that an imposing military force be despatched to Utah for the purpose of compelling the Mormons to submit to the authority of the federal government (1857).

The Dynamite-Inventor's Will

Alfred Bernhard Nobel was a Swedish chemist and engineer who invented dynamite and other high explosives from which he became extremely wealthy. When he died today in 1896 his will stated that five *Nobel Prizes* be awarded annually for the most significant achievements in the fields of physics, chemistry, medicine, literature, and service to the cause of peace.

The Prince of Wales Goes to London

On December 10, 1282, Llewellyn, the last native Welshman to be the Prince of Wales, was killed in an ambush by the forces of King Edward I of England. Adam Francton, one of the king's loyal soldiers removed Llewellyn's head and presented it to Edward who received it with great joy. He brought it to London and caused it to be set upon one of the highest turrets of the Tower of London where it remained for some time.

The Price of Peace

On December 10, 1898 the U.S. and Spain signed a peace treaty whereby Spain gave the U.S. Cuba, Puerto Rico and other West Indian islands, Guam, and the Philippines.

Some Prizes Awarded Today

1901: The distribution of the Nobel Prizes was begun for the first time, on the anniversary of the death of Alfred Nobel.

1906: President Theodore Roosevelt received a Nobel Peace Prize for bringing about peace between Russia and Japan.

1955: The largest prize to date in the annals of American radio and TV "Give-away" programs—$100,000—was one by Mrs Ethel Park Richardson, 72, of Los Angeles, after she correctly answered a six-point question about folk songs on the NBC TV program, "The Big Surprise."

1964: The Rev. Martin Luther King, Jr was awarded the Nobel Prize for Peace in ceremonies at Oslo, Norway.

Births

César Franck (Belgian composer) 1822; Emily Dickinson (American poet) 1830.

Deaths

Llewellyn (Prince of Wales) 1282; Alfred Nobel (Swedish chemist/philanthropist) 1896.

Assorted Fires of Today

1520: In a public bonfire behind the walls of Wittemberg, Martin Luther destroyed the *Bull* against himself along with other works of anti-reformers.

1856: The English cathedral at Montréal, Québec was completely destroyed by a fire of unknown origin.

1882: A fire broke out in the buildings occupied by the minister of war in Madrid, destroying the library and archives and injuring twenty-four people.

Today's Arrivals and Departures

1856: Dr Livingstone, the distinguished African missionary and traveller, arrived at London after an absence of sixteen years. After giving a detailed account of the countries through which he had passed, he was presented with the Gold Medal of the Royal Geographical Society.

1881: Mr W. Powell, M.P. for Malmsbury, ascended from Bath on a balloon accompanied by Captain Templer and Mr Gardner. The balloon was brought close to earth near Bridport and the occupants were thrown from the car, Mr Gardner sustaining a fracture of the leg. The balloon again ascended with Mr Powell, of whom nothing was ever heard of again.

A King's Abdication

On December 11, 1936, King Edward VIII abdicated the throne of Great Britain with these words: "I have found it impossible to carry the heavy burden of responsibility and to discharge my duties as King. . .without the help and support of the woman I love. . ."

A Waffle Recipe

Today in 1700 the matrons of Flatbush, New York, famous for their waffles served daily at tea time, told visiting New Englanders how to prepare them: "1 lb butter, 1 lb flour, 1 lb sugar, 10 eggs. Bake in window-pane waffle irons, and when slightly cool, sprinkle with powdered sugar."

A Child's Harpsichord

When he was little more than a year old, Charles Wesley (born today in 1757) was tied to a chair before the family harpsichord by his mother where he would amuse himself for hours by picking his way through the notes. At the age of two years and nine months he surprised his parents by playing a complex tune in correct time. He soon became an excellent child harpsichordist and was often called to amuse George III with renditions of Handel. But his exceptional talents did not outlast his childhood. He finished life as a very average performer and composer, reaching only to an appointment as organist in fashionable St George's Church in Hanover Square in London.

A Halcyon Day

According to the Roman calendar the *Alcyonii Dies,* or halcyon days, begin today and continue for two weeks during which the Mediterranean is supposed to remain unusually calm. Alcyon was the daughter of Aeolus, god of the winds, and was married to Ceyx, who died by drowning. When she discovered her husband's body she threw herself into the sea in distress. The gods turned them both into halcyon birds, who build their nests on the waves and keep them for two weeks during which time the waters stay calm.

Births

Charles Wesley (musician) 1757; Hector Berlioz (composer) 1803;

Deaths

Roger L'Estrange (classics scholar) 1704; Theodore Neuhoff (Corsican king) 1756.

A Strange Epigram

Late in life, Roger L'Estrange, a scholar and translator of the classics ran into an old friend named Lee who had been so changed by time as to be hardly recognisable. Lee wrote the following epigram on the renewal of their friendhsip:

Faces may alter, but names cannot change,
I am *strange Lee* altered, you are still *Lee strange.*

L'Estrange died on Deceember 11, 1704.

A King's Ranson

Theodore Neuhoff, a German rambler and gambler, spent his lifetime in and out of debtor's prisons in Europe. In 1736 he was persuaded by Corsican insurgents to help them get rid of the Italian rulers in return for the kingship of Corsica. The Bey of Tunis gave him arms and men to achieve this end, in exchange for exclusive trade with Corsica. Neuhoff achieved his aims and ruled as king of Corsica for several months but soon fell into disfavour and was forced to flee. Just before his death in 1756 he bought his way out of the King's Bench Prison in London by signing over to his creditors the Kingdom of Corsica.

12
DECEMBER

Births

Edward G. Robinson (actor) 1893;
Frank Sinatra (singer) 1915.

Deaths

Robert Browning (poet) 1889;
Douglas Fairbanks Sr (actor) 1939.

Today in the Arts

1792:   Ludwig van Beethoven, aged
twenty-two, paid the equivalent of
nineteen cents for his first music
lesson from Franz Joseph Haydn in
Vienna.

1850:   Susan Warner's highly
emotional novel, *The Wide, Wide
World* was published, quickly
becoming a best-seller in America.

1882:   With the help of an Edison
generating plant, the Bijou, in
Boston, became the first American
theatre lighted by electricity. Over
300 lamps were used to light the
stage area.

1890:   At a meeting of friends of
Robert Browning held at a house
in London (this being the
anniversary of the poet's death) his
voice was heard reciting the poem
"How they brought the good news
from Ghent to Aix" by means of
Edison's phonograph, the first time
that this instrument had been used
to transmit the voice of the dead.

1937:   The U.S. Federal
Communications Commission
reprimanded the NBC network for
permitting Mae West to "sex-up" a
skit based on the biblical story of
Adam and Eve.

Today's Advertisement

"A Young Man having yesterday left
his master's service in Smithfield, on
a presumption of his pocket being
picked of one hundred pounds, his
master's property, when he was in
liquor; this is to inform him, that he
left it in the shop of his master, who
has found it; and if he will return to
his master's service he will be kindly
received."

Lloyd's Evening Post, December 12,
1781

Today's Royal Proclamation

A Royal Proclamation in Britain,
issued today in 1838, warned justices
that "great numbers of evil-disposed
and disorderly persons have lately
assembled themselves together after
sunset, by torch-light, in large bodies,
and in a tumultuous manner, with
banners, flags and other ensigns, and
have continued so assembled until a
late hour of the night, and during the
time they were so assembled have by
loud shouts and noises and by the
discharge of fire-arms and the display
of weapons of offence, greatly
alarmed the inhabitants of the
surrounding neighbourhoods."

Today's Revolution

On this day in 1880, a revolution
occurred in the small mountainous
Republic of Andorra in consequence
of an attempt first, to set up a foreign
casino and gambling table, and
second to construct a railway
connecting the republic with the
outer world. Order was subsequently
established through the mediation of
the French agent.

Today in Communications

1883:   A terrific gale, which swept
over England and Scotland, caused
much destruction and a complete
stoppage of all telegraph work.
when many wires were laid low.

1901:   The Atlantic Ocean was
bridged today by the miracle of
wireless. Marconi, seated in an
improvised receiving station near
St John's, Newfoundland,
intercepted the letter "S," sent in
Morse Code by an operator at
Poldhu in the British Isles.

13
DECEMBER

Births

William Drummond (poet) 1585; Henrich Heine (poet) 1797; Philip Brookes ("O Little Town of Bethlehem") 1835.

Deaths

St Lucy (virgin and martyr) 304; St Kenelm (king and martyr) 820; Wassily Kandinsky (abstract artist) 1944.

Lucy's Eyes

St Lucy, a native of Syracuse, was martyred today in 304 under the persecution of Emperor Dioclesian. She was eagerly sought in marriage by a young nobleman but persistently refused him in favour of a life of religious devotion. When her young lover desperately complained to Lucy that he was haunted day and night by the beauty of her eyes, which is supposed to have been very great, she cut them out of her head, sent them to him on a plate, and begged him to henceforth leave her unmolested. Lucy is the saint invoked against eye diseases, haemorrhages, and dysentery.

Kenelm's Head

St Kenelm of Mercia was the son of Kenulph, of royal blood, descended from Wibba, father of King Penda. He was murdered very young, today in 820, but being a pious child the place of his murder was discovered by a ray of light over the corpse.

In Clent Cowpasture, under a thorn,
Of head bereft, lies Kenelm
  Kingborn.

Menuhin's Preference

On December 13, 1927, Yehudi Menuhin, a ten-year-old child violinist, made his New York debut at a concert in Carnegie Hall. (When it was all over, the audience wanted nothing more than to flock backstage and congratulate the little boy. The little boy wanted nothing more than a big dish of ice cream.)

Christian Spirits

On December 14, 1873 the women of Fredonia, New York, formed a society to "visit saloons, in a Christian spirit," under the leadership of Mrs Judge Barker. (From this group the Women's Christian Temperance Union was formed.)

Today's Health

"Be virtuous; govern your passions; restrain your appetitites. Avoid salted meats: those who eat them have pale complexions, slow pulse and are full of corrupted humours. Immediately after you awake, rub your breast where you heart lies. Avoid a stream of wind as you would an arrow. It is unwholesome to fan yourself during perspiration. Wash your mouth with lukewarm tea, before you go to rest. When you lie down, banish all thought.

The Everyday Book and Everlasting Calendar of Popular Amusements, 1830

Ockeld's Temper

Today in England in 1862, at the Worcester Assizes, William Ockeld, aged seventy years, was sentenced to be executed for murdering his wife, quite as old as himself, by beating her to death with a mop, the only provocation alleged in defence being that the old woman disturbed the prisoner at night by moaning in bed.

14
DECEMBER

Births

Michael de Nostradamus (prophet) 1503; Tycho Brahe (astronomer) 1546; Henry IV (French king) 1553; Paul I (Greek king) 1901.

Deaths

Sir John Oldcastle (prototype of Shakespeare's Falstaff, burnt as a Lollard) 1417; James V (Scottish king in the thirty-first year of his age and thirtieth of his reign, heart attack) 1542; George Washington (first president of the United States, after telling his doctors, "I thank you for your attention. You had better not take any more trouble about me, but let me go off quietly") 1799; Prince Albert (husband of Queen Victoria, of typhoid fever. The queen was inconsolable, and refused to see anyone except her children) 1861.

Trial

In France, the trial of Madame W. Jeufosse, her three sons, and a gamekeeper began today. They were charged with shooting Monsieur Guillot, a neighbour who was encouraged about the chateau so long as he confined his attention to the governess, but excited the most bitter hostility when it was known that he wished to ingratiate himself in the affections of Jeufosse's daughter. The jury returned a verdict of not guilty (1857).

Philosophy

"What a bustle we make about passing our time, when all our space is, but a point! What aims and ambitions are crowded into this little instant of our life! Our whole extent of being is no more in the eye of Him who gave it than a scarce perceptible moment of duration."

Alexander Pope, December 14, 1713

Travels

1836: The first railway in London, from that city to Greenwich, opened for business.

1885: The unparalleled feat of travelling from San Fancisco to London in fourteen days was accomplished today by several passengers who reached Liverpool in the Cunard ship *Umbria*.

1911: Roald Amundsen, the Norweigan explorer, and four men reached the South Pole via dog team.

Women

1911: The first woman surgeon was admitted to the Royal College of Surgeons.

1914: The first woman was elected to the British Parliament but did not take her seat.

1918: Women first voted in a British General Election.

1934: Women were given the right to vote in Turkey.

Nations

1939: Russia was expelled from the League of Nations.

1955: Albania, Austria, Bulgaria, Cambodia, Ceylon, Finland, Hungary, Ireland, Italy, Jordan, Laos, Libya, Nepal, Portugal, Rumania, and Spain joined the United Nations.

1967: Southern Yemen, formerly Aden, joined the United Nations.

15
DECEMBER

Births

Nero (Roman emperor) 37 A.D.; Jerome Bonaparte (Napoleon's younger brother) 1784; Antoine Henri Becquerel (scientist) 1852; Maxwell Anderson (playwright) 1888; J. Paul Getty (millionaire) 1892.

War and Peace

1745:   The Prussians routed the Saxons at Kesseldorf.
1914:   The Russians drove the Austrians out of Belgrade in Yugoslavia.
1917:   An Allied War Council was established at Versailles.
1917:   An armistice was signed between Russia and Germany.
1940:   Laval was dismissed from the Vichy government in France.
1942:   Rommel retreated from Mersa Brega.
1944:   U.S. Forces landed on the island of Mindoro.

Legalities

1791:   What is regarded as the first law school in the United States was established when the trustees of the University of Pennsylvania, at Philadelphia, elected James Wilson as professor of law.
1791:   The United States Bill of Rights, the term applied to the first ten amendments to the Constitution, went into effect.
1871:   The Alabama Claims Commission began its sitting.
1922:   The British Broadcasting Corporation was legally incorporated.
1944:   The U.S. Congress created the post of Admiral of the Fleet.
1948:   A Federal Grand Jury in New York indicted Alger Hiss, former State Department official, on two perjury counts.

Deaths

Jan Vermeer (artist) 1675; Isaak Walton (fisherman/writer) 1683; James Murrell (witch doctor) 1860; Sitting Bull (Sioux Indian chief) 1890; Gergory Rasputin (the Mad Monk) 1916.

Marriages

King George IV of England to his mistress Maria Fitzherbert (1785); King Badouin of Belgium to Dona Fabiola de Mora y Aragon of Spain (1960).

A Seventh Son

James Murrell, who lived in Hadleigh, Essex, was born the seventh son of the seventh son and made his living as a white magician and witch doctor. Some of the equipment of "Cunning Murrell" consisted of a telescope that could see through walls, a magic mirror for finding lost property, and a copper charm to determine the honesty of clients. Murrell's strange habits included always travelling at night, and carrying an umbrella at all times. He accurately predicted the time of his death to the minute: December 15, 1860.

Numerologicalities

In the complicated mathematical calculations of numerology, people born today are subject to the rules of the number 6. This decrees that they can make friends easily, especially with all persons born under the vibration of the numbers 3, 6, or 9. Persons born on December 15 can look to blue and pink as their lucky colours, but they should avoid black and purple at all costs, especially in underwear. Their lucky stone is the turquoise, which should be worn next to the skin.

16.
DECEMBER

Births

Ludwig van Beethoven (German composer) 1770; Jane Austen (English novelist) 1775; Noel Coward (English actor/playwright) 1899; Margaret Mead (American anthropologist/author) 1901.

A Grimm Fairy Tale

The German brothers Grimm, Wilhelm and Jacob, were inseparable in their life and labours of collecting fairy tales. They lived in the same house, worked in adjoining rooms, and refused honours and appointments unless both were included in the distinction. When they were both middle aged an old aunt took pity on the two bachelors and convinced them that they ought to marry. After much deliberation the brothers decided that really only one of them need marry, and the one wife could look after the finances and linen of both. Their aunt then selected a suitable young lady. The elder, Jacob, was convinced that it was his duty to take the leap. Unfortunately he had no idea of how to go about courting the young woman, so Wilhelm offered his services in effecting an introduction. At this point the young girl of twenty-two still had no idea of her suitors' intentions. Wilhelm made his overtures for his brother, but within a week was helplessly in love with the future Mrs Grimm, and the feeling was mutual. Jacob, relieved of his onerous responsibility, was delighted, and declared the tidings to be the most joyous he ever heard. So Wilhelm was married, and during the honeymoon Jacob celebrated with a vacation of his own. The three lived happily together until the death of Wilhelm on December 16, 1859.

Deaths

Wilhelm Grimm (fairy tale collector) 1859.

A Spiritual Flight

Today in 1868 Daniel Douglas Home, an American spiritualist and medium, levitated out one window and into another seventy feet above the ground. Home was born in Scotland and brought to the United States as a small child. At thirteen he claimed to have discovered his gifts for dealing with spirits and began a triumphant career as a medium. He always retained his amateur status, but grew well-to-do from gifts showered on him. In his drawing-room seances, furniture moved with no apparent cause, ghostly hands appeared, and furniture and Home himself would rise in the air. Although numerous efforts were made to expose him, none was successful.

In Livingstone's Footsteps

Today in 1875, Lieutenant Cameron, who had not been heard of since quitting Ujiji in May 1874, arrived at Loanda on the West Coast with fifty-seven followers, having successfully accomplished the journey from sea to sea across the African Continent. Dr Livingstone had up to this time been the only traveller who succeeded in this feat.

The Boston Tea Party

On December 16, 1773, seven thousand people assembled at a town meeting in Boston. As the evening came on about fifty men, dressed as Indians, and yelling blood-curdling war-cries, led the crowd to the wharves where 342 chests of tea, on which the English tax had been imposed, were dumped into Boston harbour.

17
DECEMBER

Births

John Greenleaf Whittier (poet) 1807; Arthur Fiedler (conductor) 1894.

Deaths

Simon Bolivar (revolutionary) 1830; Kaspar Hauser (foundling) 1833;

416 Disorderly Students

Today in 1880, 416 students at the University of Moscow, having had a difference of opinion with the rector, held a meeting of a somewhat disorderly sort in the courtyard of the university and, refusing to disperse when ordered to do so by the superintendent of police, were all arrested after a severe conflict, and marched off to the House of Detention.

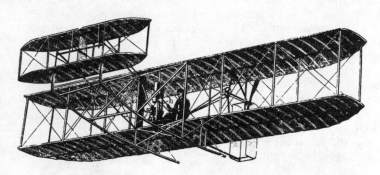

Twelve Seconds Above Kitty Hawk

On December 17, 1903, at Kill Devil Hill, North Carolina, near the village of Kitty Hawk, the Wright Brothers proved that controlled, heavier-than-air flight was possible. The first flight of *The Flyer,* with Orville Wright aboard, covered 120 feet, reached an altitude of ten feet, and lasted twelve seconds. (Later with Wilbur aboard, *The Flyer* stayed aloft for fifty-nine seconds.)

4,000 Gallons of Moonshine

On December 17, 1892, U.S. Revenue authorities in North Carolina captured ten illicit stills in Wilkes County and three in Catawba County. In total, they captured 4,000 gallons of moonshine and one moonshiner.

The Number Seventeen is Immortal

Today's number is a highly spiritual one and represents, in those born under it, triumph in adversity and a fortunate number in relation to future events. It is considered a number of immortality and the name of a person born today is quite likely to live on after him.

Identity Unknown

The life of Kaspar Hauser is a puzzle that has never been solved. On the afternoon of May 26, 1828, a young man about sixteen years old was found standing helplessly in the marketplace of Nuremberg in Germany. He could speak only a few phrases, was obviously ignorant, dressed like a peasant, and carried a letter addressed to the captain of the Sixth Regiment f Horse stationed in the town. For the captain he wrote his name on a piece of paper: Kaspar Hauser. The letter, written from some place in Bavaria in 1828, stated that the writer was a poor labourer, father of ten children, and that Kaspar had one day been left on his doorstep. He brought up the boy secretly and stated that he had taught him reading, writing, and Christian doctrine. The letter concluded by saying that the boy's father had served in the Sixth Regiment.

Later, when Kaspar was able to speak, he related that he had been brought up in a dark place underground, had been fed on bread and water only, and had never encountered another person, having his food brought and being cleaned while he was asleep. Eventually he was handed over to a Professor Daumer, who kept him and tried to educate him. His progress was small. Without the mystery of his origin ever having been solved Kasper Hauser left the world as curiously as he appeared in it. A messenger appeared one day and engaged for a rendevous at which Kaspar was supposed to learn the secret of his birth. He kept the meeting, but all he got for his trouble was a stab wound in the chest. The wound proved mortal, and Kaspar Hauser died of it on December 17, 1833.

18
DECEMBER

Births

Prince Rupert (duke of Bavaria and military commander) 1619.

Elizabeth (Russian empress, daughter of Czar Peter the Great, born before her parents were married) 1709.

Joseph Grimaldi (famous English clown) 1779.

Leopold I (German-born king of Belgium) 1790.

Isaac Hecker (founder of the *Paulist Fathers)* 1819.

Edward MacDowell (American composer) 1861.

Sir J.J. Thompson (English physicist and author) 1856.

Francis II (archduke of Austria) 1863.

Ty Cobb (American baseball star) 1886.

Christopher Fry (English playwright) 1907.

Abe Burrows (American playwright/author) 1910.

Willie Brandt (German statesman) 1913.

Betty Grable (American actress and "pin-up" girl) 1916.

Keith Richard (British songwriter and Rolling Stone) 1943.

Marriage

President Woodrow Wilson, a widower for a little over a year, to Mrs Edith Bolling Galt, widow of a Washington jeweller (1915).

Today's Major Events

1914: Egypt was proclaimed a British protectorate.

1918: U.S. President Woodrow Wilson was awarded a gold medal in Paris.

1935: In her debut at the Metropolitan Opera in New York, Australian soprano Marjorie Lawrence, singing the role of Brunnhilde in *Die Gotterdammerung* sent her horse through a ring of real flames burning on the stage, the first time this had ever been attempted by an opera singer.

1936: The first giant panda to be imported into the United States arrived at San Francisco from China.

1939: The German vessel *Admiral Graf Spee* was scuttled at Montevideo, Uruguay.

1948: Dutch troops invaded Indonesia.

Deaths

Saints Rufus and Zozimus (martyrs) 116.

St Gatian (first bishop of Tours and confessor) 300.

St Winebald (abbot and confessor) 760.

Robert Nanteuil (celebrated French engraver) 1678.

Heneage Finch (Earl of Nottingham) 1682.

Veit Ludwig von Seckendorf (political and theological writer) 1692.

Antonio Stradivarius (violin maker) 1737.

Soame Jenyns (religious and general writer) 1878.

Pierre Louis de Préville (celebrated French comedian) 1799.

Johann Gottfried Von Herder (theologian and philosopher) 1803.

Dr Alexander Adam (Scottish classical scholar and teacher) 1809.

Thomas Dunham Whittaker (antiquarian writer) 1821.

John Baptiste Lamarck (naturalist) 1829.

General Lord Lynedoch (military hero) 1943.

Marie Louise (Napoleon's second wife) 1847.

Samuel Rogers (English poet) 1855.

William Sheldon (organiser of the London Omnibus Service) 1883.

19
DECEMBER

Peacetime Events

1606: Colonists from England sailed to Jamestown, Virginia.

1722: The Ostend Company of the Dutch East Indies traders was chartered.

1732: Benjamin Franklin began to publish his *Poor Richard's Almanac.*

1776: "The American Crisis," essays on the Revolutionary War, appeared in *The Pennsylvania Journal.*

1787: New Jersey ratified the U.S. Constitution.

1871: Birmingham, Alabama became a city.

1887: Jake Kilrain (American) and Jem Smith (English) boxed to a draw at Rouen, France.

1903: Williamsburg Bridge was opened in New York City.

1906: The U.S. aircraft carrier *Constellation* burned in the Brooklyn Navy Yard.

1960: Maryland's State House became a U.S. national landmark.

1963: America launched the nineteenth *Explorer* satellite.

Births

William Parry (English explorer) 1790; Mary Aston Livermore (U.S. suffragette) 1821.

Deaths

Emily Bronte (English novelist) 1848; William Turner (English artist) 1851.

Royal Events

960: Reconstruction of the Japanese Imperial Palace began at Kyoto after a fire.

1155: Henry II and Eleanor of Aquitaine were crowned king and queen of England.

1406: Angelo Coraorrio became Pope Gregory XII.

1923: King George III of Greece and his family left that country.

Wartime Events

1675: The Narragansett Indians made their last stand against the English in King Philip's War.

1777: American troops camped at Valley Forge, Pennsylvania.

1813: British troops captured Fort Niagara in the War of 1812.

1915: Allied forces began the evacuation of Gallipoli on the Dardanelles.

1916: Allied forces captured Monastir from the Germans.

1931: Germany launched her first post-treaty battleship.

1934: Ethiopia and Somaliland began a border dispute.

1939: The German liner *Columbus* was scuttled.

1943: Four war crinimals were hung at Kharkov in Russia.

1944: The U.S. Army advanced into Germany, pushing back German troops.

1944: The Omura aircraft factory was bombed.

1946: French and Communist forces began fighting in Vietnam.

20
DECEMBER

Births

John Wilson Croker (writer) 1780; Harvey Samuel Firestone (rubber manufacturer) 1868.

Deaths

Moss Hart (playwright) 1961; John Steinbeck (writer) 1968.

A Marvellous Flying Machine

In the December 20, 1709 edition of the *London Evening Post* there was a description and illustration of a flying ship said to have been recently invented by a Brazilian priest and brought to the notice of the Portuguese king. "Father Bartholomew Laurent says that he has found out an Invention, by the Help of which one may more speedily travel through the Air than any other Way either by Sea or Land, so that it may go 200 Miles in 24 Hours; send Orders and Conclusion of Councils to Generals, in a manner, as soon as they are determined in private Cabinets; which will be so much more the Advantageous to your Majesty, as your Dominions lie far remote from one another. . ."

A Bath in Metal and Mahogany

On December 20, 1842 Adam Thompson of Virginia had a party at his house, which was the first in America to have a bathtub. During the party, he invited his guests to try out the seven-foot-long, four-foot-wide structure, made of sheet metal, and encased in mahogany. (When news of this was reported in the newspapers the next day, politicians and doctors were angry and Virginia placed a $30 tax on bathtubs and increased the water rates.)

An Onion Stuck with Pins

On this night of the calendar year in old England, young girls would stick nine pins into a large peeled onion and sing, "Good St. Thomas, do me right; Send me my true love this night."

Games Yes, Women No

"For women, as far forth as ye may, avoid their company. Yet if the French King command you, you may sometimes dance, so measure be your mean. Else apply yourself to riding, shooting or tennis, with such honest games."
A letter from King Edward VI of England (fourteen years old) to a friend in the French court, December 20, 1551

Actors Stripped and Imprisoned

"Some stage players in St. John Street were apprehended by troopers, their clothes taken away, and themselves carried to prison" (*Whitelocke's Memorials,* December 20, 1649).

When civil war broke out in England, one of the first acts of Parliament, in September 1642, was the outlawing of all stage plays. Instead, Parliament recommended to the people "the profitable and seasonable consideration of repentence, reconciliation, and peace with God, which probably will produce outward peace and prosperity, and bring again times of joy and gladness to these nations."

Bachelors Taxed in Missouri

Today in 1820 the State of Missouri levied a tax against bachelors. The statute ordered unmarried men between the ages of twenty-one and fifty to pay a tax of $1.00 a year.

Lady Chatterley Banned in Boston

On December 20, 1929 Boston bookseller James De Lacey was sentenced to one month in jail and fined $500 for selling D.H. Lawrence's *Lady Chatterley's Lover.*

21
DECEMBER

Births

Jean Baptiste Racine (French playwright) 1639; Benjamin Disraeli (British statesman) 1804; Josef Stalin (Russian premier) 1879.

Deaths

St Thomas (apostle) 1st century.

St Thomas Settles Disputes

In his fourteenth-century book of travel tales Sir John Mandeville writes: "Men of Assyria carried the body of St Thomas into Mesopotamia, into the city of Odessa. And the arm and the hand that he put to our Lord's side after his resurrection is yet lying in a vessel without the tomb. When there is any dissention between two parties, both parties write their causes on two bills and put them in the hand of St Thomas; and anon, the hand casts away the bill of the wrong cause and holds still the bill with the right cause."

St Thomas Martyred

After Jesus was crucified St Thomas travelled to spread the gospel throughout the middle east and then to India. By effecting numerous conversions in this latter country he raised the ire of the Brahmins who threw stones and darts at him for some time and finally ended his life today, sometime during the 1st century, by running a lance through his body at the city of Melapoor.

A Variety of Miracles

Marco Polo, who passed through India in the thirteenth century, reported on the annual pilgrimage today by Christians to the spot where St Thomas had been martyred: "The Christians collect the earth, which is of a red colour, and reverentially carry it away with them, employing it afterwards in a variety of miracles and giving it with water to the sick, by which many disorders are cured."

St Thomas and the Winter Solstice

December 21, being the winter solstice in the northern hemisphere, is the day of the year there with the least hours of sunlight. It is also the feast day in the English church of St Thomas, who is the patron of builders and architects. The coincidence of the two is expressed in the following old couplet:

St Thomas gray, St Thomas gray,
The longest night and the shortest day.

Believing in St Thomas

If scanty be my hand and praise,
And witless folk should call me a lion
For that my book contains strange lays,
I will not storm or burst with ire.
Let him who credits not my tales,
Travel as far as I have been,
Then may he tell if truth prevails,
In what I say that I have seen
> Sir John Mandeville in a poem addressed to unbelievers of his story about St Thomas

Gooding, Doleing, Corning, and Mumping

"Going a Gooding" on St Thomas' Day used lo prevail in England. Women begged money, and in return presented the donors with sprigs of palm and branches of primroses. In some places the custom was called Doleing and in others Mumping (begging). In Warwickshire poor people engaged in "Going a Corning," carrying a bag in which they received contributions of corn from farmers.

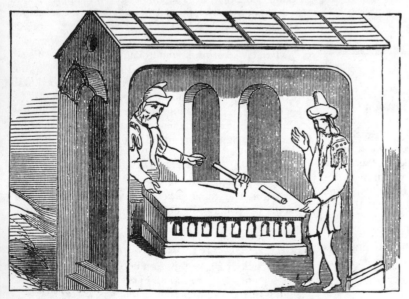

Births

James Edward Oglethorpe (philanthropoist and founder of Georgia) 1696; François de la Vérendrye (explorer) 1715; Giacomo Puccini (composer) 1858.

Deaths

Giles de Laval (the original Bluebeard) 1440; Richard Plantagenet (a king's son?) 1550; Mrs Mapps (bone-setter) 1737; George Eliot (novelist) 1880.

Richard Plantagenet: King's Son?

When Sir Thomas Moyle was having his mansion built in Eastwell, Kent, in 1545 he noticed his bricklayer foreman was reading in Latin. The man claimed he was Richard III's illegimate son and was disguised to avoid the Tudors. Sir Thomas took him in and on his death on December 22, 1150 he was registered as "Richard Plantagenet," the name adopted by Richard, duke of York as a surname for the English royal family. Thus the last member of the House of York lived and died virtually unnoticed.

George Eliot: Novelist

George Eliot sprang into fame in 1859 as the author of *Adam Bede*. The next book was *The Mill on the Floss,* and then came what is sometimes called one of the most perfect short stories in the English language, "Silas Marner." George Eliot was the pen-name of Mrs Cross, formerly Miss Mary Ann Evans and Mrs Lewes. She died suddenly this evening in 1880 at her house in Cheyne Walk in London at the age of sixty.

Mrs Mapps: Bone-Setter

Mrs Mapps practised her profession of bone-setting from Epsom in England, having learned it from her father. She once straightened the body of a man whose back had stuck out two inches for nine years. A gentleman who went into her office with one shoe-heel six inches high, came out again cured of a lameness of twenty years' standing, and with both legs equal. She grew rich from her miraculous re-alignments and travelled about in a splendid carriage, waving the crutches of her patients as trophies of honour. She often worked in company with Taylor the occultist and Ward the worm-doctor. Mrs Mapps passed away on December 22, 1737.

General Sherman's Gift to Lincoln

On December 22, 1864 a message was received by President Lincoln at the White House from General William T. Sherman in Georgia which read, "I beg to present you as a Christmas gift the city of Savannah."

Giles de Laval: Bluebeard

Giles de Laval, the marshal de Retz, was a captain under Jean d'Arc, and through a series of inheritances became the richest man in all of France. Though ostensibly a religious man, he was also an incredible profligate and libertine, and had to sell off one estate after another to pay for his extravagances and pleasures. Laval's deepest tastes were depraved and criminal. In 1440 he confessed to the assault, torture, and murder of scores of children from the countryside about his various estates. In most cases he burned the bodies completely, but the remains of at least 126 victims were found. For his crimes the monster was sentenced to be strangled to death, and the sentence was carried out on December 22, 1440. Laval was the model for Perrault's fairy-tale tyrant and murderer, Bluebeard.

23
DECEMBER

Births

Alexander I (Russian emperor) 1777; José Greco (Spanish dancer) 1918.

Deaths

Henri de Lorraine (French duke) 1588; Mère de Youville (French nun) 1771.

Sentenced, 1894

Captain Alfred Dreyfus, who had been convicted after a closed-door trial, of delivering documents connected with French defence to a foreign power, was sentenced to perpetual imprisonment in a fortress.

Retirement, 1783

George Washington resigned his army commission, and retired to his estate of Mount Vernon.

Obituary, 1925

William Allen White, editor of the *Emporia* (Kansas) *Gazette,* reported the death of the celebrated publisher, Frank Munsey in an outspoken and hard-hitting obituary notice: "Frank Munsey, the great publisher, is dead. Frank Munsey contributed to the journalism of his day the great talent of a meat packer, the morals of a money changer, and the manners of an undertaker. He and his kind have succeeded in transforming a once noble profession into an eight per cent security. May he rest in trust!"

Fools

"It was formerly the custom for every great house in England to keep a fool dressed in petticoats that the heir of the family might have an opportunity of joking upon him and diverting himself with absurdities."
The Anniversary Calendar, December 23, 1832

Escapes

1688: James II, the king of England with Catholic sympathies, fled to France to escape his outraged Protestant subjects.

1815: The French general Lavallette made a daring exit from his place of imprisonment in Paris by dressing in his wife's clothes, while she dressed in his.

Knitting

On the island of Guernsey tonight was called *La Longue Vielle,* when people sat up late feasting on biscuits and cheese as well as on mulled wine. However it was not a purely frivolous activity, for the time was also spent preparing goods such as knitting for the marketplace.

Capricorn

Capricorn (the goat) dictates the fortunes of those born between today and January 20. Seventeenth-century astrologers believed that—except for Leo and Cancer—each of the signs of the zodiac had a twin. Thus, according to *Christian Astrology* (1647) by William Lilly, Capricorn characters are identical to Aquarians.

Manners & Actions, when well dignified
Then he is profound in Imagination, in his Acts severe, in his words reserved, in speaking and giving very spare, in labour patient, in arguing or disputing grave, in obtaining the goods of this life studious and solicitous, in all manners of actions austere.

When ill
Then he is envious, covetous, jealous and mistrustfull, timorus, sordid, outwardly dissembling, sluggish, suspitious, stubborne, a contemner of women, a close lyar, malicious, murmuring, never contented, ever repining.

24
DECEMBER

Births

Kit Carson (American frontiersman) 1809; Howard Hughes (American millionaire) 1905; Ava Gardner (American actress) 1922.

Deaths

George of Cappadocia (Arian bishop) 361; Vasco da Gama (Portuguese navigator) 1524; William Makepeace Thackeray (English novelist) 1863.

Sweet Fanny Adams

In Alton, Hampshire in 1867, the event took place on December 24 which gave rise to the expression "Sweet Fanny Adams." A young girl out playing in the fields with friends failed to return home and after a search was found dismembered in a nearby field. At the same time as this, the British Royal Navy had their salt tack rations replaced by low-grade tinned meat and the sailor's labelled it "Sweet Fanny Adams," which moved into the language to signify worthlessness.

Christmas Cocks, Oxen, Asses, and Bees

It is said that on Christmas Eve the cock crows all night, and by his vigilance keeps away all evil spirits for the night. The belief was alluded to by Shakespeare in *Hamlet:*

It faded on the crowing of the cock.
Some say, that ever 'gainst that season comes
Wherein our Saviour's birth is celebrated,
The bird of dawning singeth all night long:
And then, they say, no spirit can walk abroad;
The nights are wholesome; then no planets strike,
No fairy takes, nor witch hath power to charm;
So hallow'd and so gracious is the time.

In many parts of Europe it was believed that on Christmas Eve, in honour of their fellows who were present at the nativity and said in legend to have kept the infant Christ warm with their breath, the oxen and asses kneel down and face east in their stalls. "The ox knoweth his owner, and the ass his master's crib" (Isaiah i. 3). While the quadrupeds were kneeling, the bees were said to be singing in their hives.

Some Christmas Eve Customs

Christmas Eve and Day customs are an amalgam of the practices of many lands and ages. From old Scandinavia comes the burning of a log on the lord's hearth each Christmas, the main convivial event of the season. The custom arose from the ancient rite of the winter solstice when huge bonfires were built to honour the god *Thor*. The custom of decorating a tree for the season comes from medieval Germany. The hanging of mistletoe comes from the Druids in England, who at their own solstitial festival used to cut it from their most sacred tree, the oak, in belief of its great curative powers. Christmas mummery and pageants had their origins in the Roman Saturnalian festivals, where men and women wore the clothes of the opposite sex, and masks of all sorts.

THE YULE LOG.

25
DECEMBER

Births

Jesus Christ (source of the Christian religion) 0; Isaac Newton (discoveror of gravity) 1642.

Deaths

Persius (poet) 62; Samuel de Champlain (explorer) 1635.

Christmas and the Law

1541:   England's Unlawful Games Act proclaimed that, from this day forward, only archery could be played on Christmas.

1644:   There was a time during the Puritan ascendancy in England when the observance of Christmas was forbidden. A law was passed in 1644 making December 25 a market day and ordering that the shops should be kept open. The making of plum puddings and mince pies was forbidden as a heathen custom. This law was repealed after the Restoration, but the Dissenters ridiculed the celebration of Christmas by calling it "Fool-tide" in burlesque of Yuletide.

1659:   The General Court of Massachusetts passed a law in 1659 making the observance of Christmas a penal offence. (This law was later repealed as the English law had been, but it was many years before there were any general Christmas celebrations in New England.)

A Christmas Carol

On this day in 1818 "Stille Nacht, Heilige Nacht" (Silent Night, Holy Night), composed the day before by Franz Gruber, a schoolmaster, was sung for the first time in the village church of Oberndorff, Austria.

Christmas Dinner

Now thrice welcome Christmas,
    which brings us good Cheer,
Minced Pies and Plum Porridge, good
    Ale and strong Beer;
With Pig, Goose and Capon, the best
    that may be,
So well doth the Weather and our
    Stomachs agree.
    Poor Robin's Almanac, 1695

Christmas dinner at Mount Vernon (George Washington's home) was customarily served at three o'clock in the afternoon, an hour about which the general was altogether precise. He was likely to tell late guests, "Gentlemen. . .I have a cook who never asks whether the company has come, but whether the hour has come."

The Christmas Flower

The flower for December 25 is the holly or *Ilex aquifolium*. The word holly is a corruption of "holy" from the use of its boughs as decoration in churches at Christmas.

The First Christmas

The date of Christmas was not set until the time of Julius I, who presided as bishop of Rome from 337 to 352. In earlier times different communities of Christians celebrated the birth of Jesus at varying points in the year; some on the 1st or 6th of January, some on the 29th of March, about the time of the Jewish Passover, and some on the 29th of September, about the time of the Feast of Tabernacles. Towards the fourth century more and more communities came to celebrate the nativity about the time of the winter solstice. Then Julius, on the solicitation of St Cyril of Jerusalem, made strict enquiries into the matter, and according to what seemed to be the most sound traditions, chose the 25th of December as the date.

26
DECEMBER

Births

Thomas Gray (poet) 1716; Henry Miller (author) 1891; Mao Tse-tung (revolutionary) 1893.

Deaths

St Stephen (the first martyr) 33; Antoine de la Motte (dramatist) 1731; Stephen Girard (millionaire) 1831.

Gray's Elegy

The poet Thomas Gray was born today in 1716 in Cornhill, London. He is best known for his "Elegy Written in a Country Churchyard" in which he wrote:

Far from the madding crowd's
  ignoble strife,
Their sober wishes never learned to
  stray;
Along the cool sequestered vale of
  life
They kept the noiseless tenor of their
  way.

The curfew tolls the knell of the
  parting day,
The lowing herd winds slowly o'er
  the lea,
The ploughman homeward plods his
  weary way,
And leaves the world to darkness and
  to me.

Boxing Day

Boxing Day in England began as the day when the young apprentices of trades people exacted gratuities, in the form of Christmas boxes, from their masters' customers. An anonymous poem written sometime in the eighteenth century records some of the gifts:

Now Christmas is come, and now
  Pappy's come home,
With a Pegtop for Tommie; a Hussit
  for Sue;
A new bag o' Marbles for Dick; and
  for Joan
A Workbox; for Phoebe a Bow for her
  shoe;
For Cecily, singing, a Humming top
  comes;
For dull drowsie Marie a Sleepingtop
  meet;
For Ben, Ned and Harry, a Fife and
  two Drums;
For Jessie a box of nice Sugarplumbs
  sweet.

St Stephen's Day

St Stephen, the Christian church's first martyr, died by being stoned to death today in 33 A.D. as recorded in the *Acts of the Apostles*. The Feast of St Stephen used to be considered the best day of the year for sweating and bleeding horses:

Then followeth Saint Stephen's day,
  whereon doth every man,
His horses jaunt and course abroad,
  as swiftly as he can,
Until they doe extremely sweate,
  and then they let them blood,
For this being done upon this day,
  they say doth do them good,
And keepes them from all maladies,
  and sickness through the year,
As if that Stephen any time,
  took charge of horses heare.
    Naogeorgus, translated by Barnaby
    Googe (circa 1563)

Nason's Percolator

On December 26, 1865 James Nason of Franklin, Massachusetts, was awarded a patent for his invention of a coffee percolator, the first such device in the United States.

Washington's Eulogy

On December 26, 1799 Henry Lee of Virginia delivered a eulogy to George Washington before both houses of Congress, describing Washington as:

"First in war, first in peace and first in the hearts of his country-men."

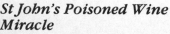

St John's Poisoned Wine Miracle

Despite much persecution during his lifetime, St John, the last surviving apostle, was the only one of them who was not martyred, and is said to have died peacefully at Ephesus in 100 A.D. According to legend a priestess of Diana once challenged John to drink a cup of poisoned wine to test the power of his God. The saint did so unharmed after having made the sign of the cross over the cup. From this legend came the custom of drinking a cup of hallowed wine on St John's Day, which was supposed to protect the drinker from the effects of poison throughout the following year.

Joanna Southcott's Abdominal Growth

Joanna Southcott was a self-appointed prophetess who declared herself to be the foretold woman to whom, by miraculous birth, the Messiah would be born. When she was well over sixty she suddenly appeared to be pregnant, and the numbers and faith of her followers increased dramatically. An elaborate cradle was constructed and over 100,000 converts around London awaited the birth. Instead of bearing the Messiah the poor woman died on December 27, 1814. Her swollen abdomen was caused by a tumour found at an autopsy. Still, numbers of her followers refused to believe she was dead, and took vows not to cut their hair or beards until the child was born.

Births

Johann Kepler (astronomer) 1571; Louis Pasteur (scientist) 1822.

Deaths

St John (apostle) 100; Joanna Southcott (prophetess) 1814.

Carrie Nation's Bottle-Breaking Binge

Today in 1900, Carrie Nation, violently opposed to alcoholic beverages, staged her first big "raid" as she marched on the saloon in the basement of the Carey Hotel in Wichita, Kansas, and smashed all the liquor bottles within reach.

Brenda Frazier's Coming-Out Party

Brenda Diana Duff Frazier, the highly publicised debutante of the season, made her bow to society at a coming-out party in New York's Ritz-Carlton Hotel tonight in 1938. The party, staged at a cost of $50,000, was attended by 1,500 guests.

P.G. Wodehouse's American Swindlers

Propaganda from Germany received today in 1940 stated that P.G. Wodehouse, the noted British writer and humorist, held by the Nazis in an East German internment camp, was writing a novel about American swindlers.

Tripp's Goose Ownership Riot

On December 27, 1888, six men belonging to American and Russian Mennonite groups were injured in a riot over the ownership of a goose, at Tripp in the Dakotas.

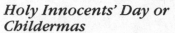

28
DECEMBER

Births

Woodrow Wilson (28th U.S. president) 1856.

Deaths

Theodore Dreiser (author) 1945; Paul Hindemith (composer) 1963.

The Birth of the Cinema

Louis and Auguste Lumière, two French photographers, invented a portable camera and a machine to project Kinetoscope (an earlier Edison invention) onto a large screen. On this night in 1895, they rented a basement at 14 Boulevard des Capucines, in Paris, installed a hundred chairs and gave the first showing of their invention to a paying audience.

The Invention of Chewing Gum

On December 28, 1869 William Semple of Mount Vernon, Ohio obtained the patent for "the combination of rubber with other articles in any proportions adapted to the formation of an *acceptable chewing gum.*"

The Warnings of the Number 28

In occult symbolism the number 28 is portrayed as a rayed moon from which drops of blood are falling; a wolf and a hungry dog are seen below catching the falling drops of blood in their opened mouths, while still lower a crab is seen hastening to join them. In numerology today's number means bitter quarrels, wars, social upheavals, and revolutions. There is a distinct danger of storms, fires, and explosions. This day should be lived with a great deal of care, caution, and circumspection.

Holy Innocents' Day or Childermas

Childermas has been observed from very early times in commemoration of the slaughter of children in Bethlehem (the Holy Innocents) ordered by Herod in his attempt to kill the infant Saviour. Holy Innocents' Day is traditionally considered to be the unluckiest day of the year—not a day for marriages, or for any new business to be entered upon; it was bad luck to wear new clothes today, to cut fingernails, or to scrub, wash, or scour. It was once customary to give all children a smart whipping on this day, so that the memory of Herod's cruelty should stick in their minds all the better.

A Narrow Escape from a Snow-Drift

There occured today in 1849 the narrow escape of Madame Sontage and other musical celebrities from perishing in a snow-storm on the railway near Lavencekirk, Aberdeenshire in Scotland. The engine became imbedded in a snow-drift and the party took refuge in the house of a hospitable farmer in the neighbourhood.

A Gigantic Flour Fraud

Today in 1891 a gigantic fraud was announced to have been discovered in connection with the measures taken for the relief of the famine sufferers in Russia. A large consignment of barley flour purchased by a committee at St Petersburg from merchants at Liban was found to be adulterated with many non-farinaceous and unwholesome substances. It mostly consisted of dust.

29
DECEMBER

Births

Marquise de Pompadour (mistress of Louis XV of France) 1721; William Macintosh (raincoat inventor) 1776; Andrew Johnson (17th U.S. president) 1808.

Deaths

St Thomas Becket (archbishop of Canterbury) 1170; Christina Rossetti (poet) 1894; Paul Whiteman (band leader) 1967.

Today in Flowers

The flower for December 29, as decreed by medieval monks, is the genista heath *(Erica genistopha),* dedicated to St Thomas Becket.

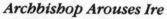

Today in the Press

1788:   The *New York Daily Gazette* was founded.

1865:   The last number of the *Liberator,* an American abolitionist newspaper, appeared.

1871:   George Cruikshank, who had illustrated Charles Dickens' novel *Oliver Twist,* wrote to *The Times* claiming to have originated that work and been the author of most of the characters.

1918:   The *Sunday Express,* an English weekly, was first issued.

Today on the Stage

1755:   Sarah Siddons made her debut on the London stage at Drury Lane Theatre

1845:   The two Misses Cushman appeared at the Haymarket Theatre in London as Romeo and Juliet.

1850:   Lola Montez, the dancer, first appeared in the U.S. at the Broadway Theatre in New York.

Philadelphia Pepper Pot

Thanks to the ingenuity of an army chef, George Washington's troops at Valley Forge were saved from mutiny today in 1777. Faced with starvation, with little equipment and few clothes, the general begged his camp chef to concoct a warming dish to raise his men's morale against the bitter cold. The chef managed to secure a large quantity of tripe, some pepper corns, and a few vegetables, and invented what he called "Philadelphia Pepper Pot," thereby both nourishing the weary soldiers and preventing an incipient revolt within the ranks.

Archbishop Arouses Ire

"No one shall set the sea between me and my Church. I did not come here to run away: anyone who wants me may find me." So spoke Thomas Becket to Reginald Fitzurse, Hugh de Morville, William de Tracy, and Richard le Breton who had come looking for him today in the year 1170. (The four confronted Becket in the cloisters of the cathedral at Canterbury, having been sent by King Henry II to demand satisfaction from the archbishop with whom Henry had been feuding for many years.) Becket's lack of humility enraged the four courtiers and they proceeded to harrass him. After much invective on both sides Fitzurse struck Becket on the head with his sword and knocked his hat off. Tracy followed with a more deadly stroke and Thomas Becket became a saint.

Births

Rudyard Kipling (poet/writer) 1865; Stephen Leacock (humorist) 1869.

Deaths

Robert Goodale (murderer) 1885; Amelia Jenks Bloomer (feminist) 1894.

Kipling on England

Though he is best known for his poems and stories on India where he was born today in 1865, Rudyard Kipling had much to say about England of which he was a citizen:

It was not preached to the crowd
It was not taught by the State
No man spoke it aloud,
When the English began to hate.

He laughed one of those thick, big-ended British laughs that don't lead anywhere.

He spoke and wrote trade-English—a toothsome amalgam of Americanisms and epigrams.

Leacock on Life

Stephen Leacock was born in the small Canadian town of Orillia, Ontario, today in 1869. After an early career in banking he turned to writing:

I detest life-insurance agents; they always argue that I shall someday die, which is not so.

It takes a good deal of physical courage to ride a horse. This, however, I have. I get it at about forty cents a flask, and take it as required.

The great man walks across his century and leaves the marks of his feet all over it, ripping out the dates on his galoshes as he passes by.

Fun on Ice

"Sitting on the jawbones of horses or cows the children take in their hands poles shod with iron, which at times they strike against the ice; they are carried along with as great rapidity as a bird flying, or a bolt discharged from a cross-bow."

History of London, December 30, 12th century

Miracle at Sea

On the 15th of May, 1834 the *Resolute,* one of the British ships searching for the missing Sir John Franklin was abandoned in the treacherous ice in the Northwest Passage. Captain Buddington of the American whaler *George Henry* found the *Resolute* 474 days later adrift in the Davis Strait about forty miles from Cape Mercy. Miraculously she had made the 1,000-mile voyage from Melville Island, near which she had been deserted, through the Barrow Straits, Lancaster Sound, and Baffin Bay. By a resolution passed by the U.S. Congress, the ship was to be given back to England. After extensive restoration work done by the Americans, the Union Jack was once again hoisted on the *Resolute* on December 30, 1856.

Horror on Scaffold

Robert Goodale was executed within Norwich Gaol today in 1885 for the murder of his wife. As the clock struck, the bolt of the scaffold was withdrawn and the culprit disappeared, but to the horror of those present, the rope immediately recoiled, the head having become completely separated from the body by the drop, which was the usual one of six feet.

Churchill on Chickens

Winston Churchill gave a speech to the Canadian Parliament today in 1941: "When I warned them [the French Government] that Britain would fight on alone whatever they did, their Generals told their P.M. and his divided Cabinet: 'In three weeks England will have her neck wrung like a chicken.' Some chicken! Some neck!"

31
DECEMBER

Births

Jacques Cartier (explorer) 1491; Hermann Boerhave (physician) 1668; Dr Johann Caspar Spurzheim (phrenologist) 1776.

Deaths

Commodus (Roman emperor) 192; John Wycliffe (reformer) 1384; Giovanni Alfonso Borelli (anatomist) 1679.

Year-End Fight

On December 31, 1891, in a prize fight contest at Indianapolis, a woman defeated a man of some local reputation as a pugilist, winning the $500 prize.

Year-End Queen

Today in 1842, Miss Newell attended the Guildhall Police Court for the purpose of urging her claim to the sovereignty of England. She had obtained, she said, a divine revelation to that effect. Shaking hands with the presiding magistrate, Sir Chapman Marshall, she remarked: "Pardon me, if I take leave of you in the words of the good old song, 'Adieu, thou dreary pile'."

Year-End Thought

On the thirty second day of the thirteenth month of the
   eighth day of the week,
On the twenty fifth hour and the sixty first minute, we'll
   find all things that we seek.
     Sam Walter Foss (1885-1911)

New Year's Eve

Ring out wild bells to the wild sky,
The flying cloud, the frosty light:
The Year is dying in the night;
Ring out, wild bells, and let him die.

Ring out the old, ring in the new,
Ring, happy bells, across the snow:
The Year is going, let him go;
Ring out the false, ring in the true.

Ring out the grief that saps the mind,
For those that here we see no more;
Ring out the feud of rich and poor,
Ring in redress to all mankind.

Ring out a slowly dying cause,
And ancient forms of party strife;
Ring in the nobler modes of life,
With sweeter manners, purer laws.

Ring out the want, the care, the sin,
The faithless coldness of the times;
Ring out, ring my mournful rhymes,
But ring the fuller minstrel in.

Ring out false pride in place and
   blood,
The civic slander and the spite;
Ring in the love of truth and right,
Ring in the common love of good.

Ring out old shapes of foul disease;
Ring out the narrowing lust of gold;
Ring out the thousand wars of old;
Ring in the thousand years of peace.
    Alfred, Lord Tennyson (1809-1892)